EPHESIANS

Society of Biblical Literature

Studies in Biblical Literature

Number 13

Ephesians
Empowerment to Walk in Love
for the Unity of All in Christ

John Paul Heil

EPHESIANS

*Empowerment to Walk in Love
for the Unity of All in Christ*

John Paul Heil

Society of Biblical Literature
Atlanta

EPHESIANS
Empowerment to Walk in Love
for the Unity of All in Christ

Library of Congress Cataloging-in-Publication Data

Heil, John Paul.
    Ephesians : empowerment to walk in love for the unity of all in Christ
/ by John Paul Heil.
        p.   cm. — (Society of Biblical Literature studies in biblical
literature ; 13)
    ISBN 978-1-58983-267-1 (paper binding : alk. paper)
    1. Bible. N.T. Ephesians—Criticism, interpretation, etc. I. Title.

BS2695.52.H45 2007
227'.5066—dc22   2007016197

14 13 12 11 10 09 08 07   5 4 3 2 1

Printed in the United States of America on acid-free, recycled paper
conforming to ANSI/NISO Z39.48-1992 (R1997) and ISO 9706:1994
standards for paper permanence.

Contents

Abbreviations

AB	Anchor Bible
AGJU	Arbeiten zur Geschichte des antiken Judentums und des Urchristentums
AnBib	Analecta biblica
ANTC	Abingdon New Testament Commentaries
AT	*Annales theologici*
AUSS	*Andrews University Seminary Studies*
BBR	*Bulletin for Biblical Research*
BDAG	Bauer, W., F. W. Danker, W. F. Arndt, and F. W. Gingrich. *Greek-English Lexicon of the New Testament and Other Early Christian Literature*. 3d ed. Chicago, 1999
BDF	Blass, F., A. Debrunner, and R. W. Funk. *A Greek Grammar of the New Testament and Other Early Christian Literature*. Chicago, 1961
Bib	*Biblica*
BibInt	*Biblical Interpretation*
BIS	Biblical Interpretation Series
BJRL	*Bulletin of the John Rylands University Library of Manchester*
BK	*Bibel und Kirche*
BNTC	Black's New Testament Commentaries
BSac	*Bibliotheca sacra*
BT	*The Bible Translator*
BTB	*Biblical Theology Bulletin*
BZNW	Beihefte zur Zeitschrift für die neutestamentliche Wissenschaft
CBQ	*Catholic Biblical Quarterly*
CBQMS	Catholic Biblical Quarterly Monograph Series
CNT	Commentaire du Nouveau Testament
ConBNT	Coniectanea biblica: New Testament Series
CTR	*Criswell Theological Review*
DDD	Dictionary of Deities and Demons in the Bible. Edited by K. van der Toorn, B. Becking, and P. W. van der Horst. Leiden, 1995
DPL	*Dictionary of Paul and His Letters*. Edited by G. F. Hawthorne and R. P. Martin. Downers Grove, 1993

EBib	Etudes bibliques
EDNT	*Exegetical Dictionary of the New Testament*. Edited by H. Balz, G. Schneider. ET. Grand Rapids, 1990-1993
ETR	*Etudes théologiques et religieuses*
EvQ	*Evangelical Quarterly*
ExpTim	*Expository Times*
FB	Forschung zur Bibel
FRLANT	Forschungen zur Religion und Literatur des Alten und Neuen Testaments
HTKNT	Herders theologischer Kommentar zum Neuen Testament
HTS	Harvard Theological Studies
HvTSt	*Hervormde teologiese studies*
IBS	*Irish Biblical Studies*
ICC	International Critical Commentary
JBL	*Journal of Biblical Literature*
JETS	*Journal of the Evangelical Theological Society*
JOTT	*Journal of Translation and Textlinguistics*
JSNT	*Journal for the Study of the New Testament*
JSNTSup	Journal for the Study of the New Testament: Supplement Series
JTS	*Journal of Theological Studies*
JTSA	*Journal of Theology for Southern Africa*
MTZ	*Münchener theologische Zeitschrift*
Neot	*Neotestamentica*
New Docs	*New Documents Illustrating Early Christianity*. Edited by G. H. R. Horsley and S. Llewelyn. North Ryde, N. S. W., 1981-
NIGTC	New International Greek Testament Commentary
NIV	New International Version
NovT	*Novum Testamentum*
NovTSup	Supplements to Novum Testamentum
NRSV	New Revised Standard Version
NRTh	*La nouvelle revue théologique*
NTOA	Novum Testamentum et Orbis Antiquus
NTS	*New Testament Studies*
PRSt	*Perspectives in Religious Studies*
RB	*Revue biblique*
ResQ	*Restoration Quarterly*
RevExp	*Review and Expositor*
RivB	*Rivista biblica italiana*
RRef	*La revue réformée*
SANT	Studien zum Alten und Neuen Testaments
SBLAbib	Society of Biblical Literature Academia Biblica
SBLDS	Society of Biblical Literature Dissertation Series
SBLMS	Society of Biblical Literature Monograph Series
SBLSCS	Society of Biblical Literature Septuagint and Cognate Studies
SBLSP	*Society of Biblical Literature Seminar Papers*

SNTSMS	Society for New Testament Studies Monograph Series
SP	Sacra pagina
ST	*Studia theologica*
TBei	*Theologische Beiträge*
TDNT	*Theological Dictionary of the New Testament.* Edited by G. Kittel and G. Friedrich. Translated by G. W. Bromiley. 10 vols. Grand Rapids, 1964-1976
TGl	*Theologie und Glaube*
TJ	*Trinity Journal*
TLNT	*Theological Lexicon of the New Testament.* C. Spicq. Translated and edited by J. D. Ernest. 3 vols. Peabody, Mass., 1994
TTZ	*Trierer theologische Zeitschrift*
TU	Texte und Untersuchungen
TynBul	*Tyndale Bulletin*
USQR	*Union Seminary Quarterly Review*
WBC	Word Biblical Commentary
WMANT	Wissenschaftliche Monographien zum Alten und Neuen Testament
WTJ	*Westminster Theological Journal*
WUNT	Wissenschaftliche Untersuchungen zum Neuen Testament
ZNW	*Zeitschrift für die neutestamentliche Wissenschaft und die Kunde der älteren Kirche*

CHAPTER 1

Introduction

A. Ephesians:
Empowerment to Walk in Love for the Unity of All in Christ

An explanation of the carefully chosen words of the title of this book, "Ephesians: Empowerment To Walk in Love for the Unity of All in Christ," will serve to introduce it. The first word, "Ephesians," indicates that this book is concerned in a comprehensive way with the whole of the New Testament document that is commonly referred to as Paul's Letter to the Ephesians. It will present an entirely new chiastic structure embracing all of the fifteen units comprising the Letter. In addition, it will show that within this overall macro-chiastic structure all of the Letter's fifteen units likewise contain their own individual chiastic structures. These macro- and micro-chiastic patterns serve as a key to understanding what and how Paul, the implied author of the Letter to the Ephesians, is communicating to his implied audience.

The next word in this book's title, "Empowerment," indicates its aim to demonstrate that Ephesians not only employs many and various expressions for "power," but actually communicates or imparts power to its audience.[1] Central to appreciating Ephesians as a communication of power is the real-

---

1. Clinton E. Arnold, *Ephesians: Power and Magic: The Concept of Power in Ephesians in Light of Its Historical Setting* (SNTSMS 63; Cambridge: Cambridge University, 1989). On the communicative and transformative power of Ephesians, see Mary Breeze, "Hortatory Discourse in Ephesians," *JOTT* 5 (1992): 313–47; Elna Mouton, "The Communicative Power of the Epistle to the Ephesians," in *Rhetoric, Scripture, and Theology: Essays from the 1994 Pretoria Conference* (ed. Stanley E. Porter and Thomas H. Olbricht; JSNTSup 131; Sheffield: Sheffield Academic Press, 1996), 280–307; idem, *Reading a New Testament Document Ethically* (SBLAbib 1; Atlanta: Society of Biblical Literature, 2002); Roy R. Jeal, *Integrating Theology and Ethics in Ephesians: The Ethos of Communication* (Studies in Bible and Early Christianity 43; Lewiston, NY: Mellen, 2000).

1

ization that it was written to be read publicly (probably by Tychicus; cf. Eph 6:21–22) as an oral performance delivered to a communal assembly, most likely in a liturgical setting.[2] Through this public reading of the Letter Paul intends to share with his audience his insight into the mystery of the Christ (3:4), centered on the great power God effected in raising the Christ from the dead, a power available to the audience of believers (1:19–20) as a gift of God's grace through Paul (3:2, 7). The very experience of listening to the Letter's elaborate and ornate language of power and grace communicated by way of the oral patterns of its chiastically arranged units not only persuades but empowers the audience to the conduct envisioned for it by Paul.[3]

The words "To Walk in Love" in the title indicate the conduct to which the Letter to the Ephesians empowers its implied audience. In both Greek (περιπατέω) and English the verb "to walk" can designate "sphere of activity," "comportment," "mode of living," "habit of conduct," or "behavior."[4] "To walk" was chosen for the title because the Greek verb περιπατέω occurs at structurally significant places throughout the Letter (2:2, 10; 4:1, 17; 5:2, 8, 15), as we will see later, and it occurs as a key command within what we hope to demonstrate is the Letter's central theme of love: "Walk in love, as also the Christ loved us" (5:2a).

The phrase "in Love" was selected for the title because the book will feature love as the theme central to the overall purpose of the Letter to the Ephesians. Throughout the Letter the noun "love" (ἀγάπη) occurs ten times (1:4, 15; 2:4; 3:17, 19; 4:2, 15, 16; 5:2; 6:23), the verb "love" (ἀγαπάω) also occurs ten times (1:6; 2:4; 5:2, 25 [2x]; 28 [3x], 33; 6:24), and the adjective "beloved" (ἀγαπητός) occurs once (6:21). Within the ten occurrences of the noun "love," of special significance are the six instances of the poignant prepositional phrase "in love" (ἐν ἀγάπῃ; 1:4; 3:17; 4:2, 15, 16; 5:2) to designate the dynamic domain or sphere of love constituted by the complex

---

2. For treatments of the oral performance of NT documents, see: Whitney Taylor Shiner, *Proclaiming the Gospel: First Century Performance of Mark* (Harrisburg, PA: Trinity Press International, 2003); William David Shiell, *Reading Acts: The Lector and the Early Christian Audience* (BIS 70; Boston: Brill, 2004), 209 : "Paul's letters also give examples of the kinds of documents that need to be discussed in light of delivery. How were they performed, and what vocal inflection would have been used?" On the public performance of Paul's letters, see Pieter J. J. Botha, "The Verbal Art of the Pauline Letters: Rhetoric, Performance, and Presence," in *Rhetoric and the New Testament: Essays from the 1992 Heidelberg Conference* (ed. Stanley E. Porter and Thomas H. Olbricht; JSNTSup 90; Sheffield: JSOT, 1993), 409–28; Luther M. Stirewalt, *Paul: The Letter Writer* (Grand Rapids: Eerdmans, 2003), 13–18; E. Randolph Richards, *Paul and First-Century Letter Writing: Secretaries, Composition, and Collection* (Downers Grove, IL: InterVarsity, 2004), 202.

3. On oral patterns in Paul's letters, but which unfortunately does not include a discussion of Ephesians, see John D. Harvey, *Listening to the Text: Oral Patterning in Paul's Letters* (Grand Rapids: Baker, 1998).

4. BDAG, 803; Roland Bergmeier, "περιπατέω," *EDNT* 3.75–76.

interaction of God's love for us in Christ empowering both our love for God/Christ and for one another.

That the closing verses of the Letter to the Ephesians contain, in contrast to the similarly worded opening verses (1:1–2), notable appearances of both the noun and verb for "love" offers a further clue that love is its central theme:

> 1:1–2: Paul, apostle of *Christ Jesus* through the will of *God*, to the holy ones in Ephesus, the *believers* who are in *Christ Jesus*. *Grace* to you and *peace* from *God* our *Father* and the *Lord Jesus Christ*.

> 6:23–24: *Peace* to the brothers and LOVE (ἀγάπη) with *faith* from *God* the *Father* and the *Lord Jesus Christ*. *Grace* be with all who LOVE (ἀγαπώντων) the *Lord Jesus Christ* in immortality.[5]

Our treatment of the key theme of love in Ephesians will include, however, not only the twenty-one occurrences of the Greek terms for love but also the many other related expressions within the love word field, such as "blessed," "chosen," "grace," "give", "gift," and so on.[6]

The final phrase of the title, "for the Unity of All in Christ," indicates the ultimate outcome envisioned for and empowered by the conduct of walking in love. The cosmic unity of everything in Christ is the first and most comprehensive expression of the "mystery" in Ephesians: "Having made known to us the mystery (μυστήριον) . . . as a plan for the fullness of times, to unite under one head all the things in the Christ, the things in the heavens and the things on earth in him" (1:9–10).[7] In the climactic conclusion of what will be seen as the central unit in the macro-chiasm of the Letter (4:1–16), which contains the only two references in the NT to the Greek word for "unity" (ἑνότης; 4:3, 13), the key role of love for this cosmic unity is expressed: "Being truthful in love (ἐν ἀγάπῃ) let us make all things grow into him, who is the head, Christ, from whom the whole body, joined and held together with every ligament of support according to the working in measure of each

---

5. On the ending of a Pauline letter as significant for understanding the whole letter, but unfortunately without consideration of Ephesians, see Jeffrey A. D. Weima, *Neglected Endings: The Significance of the Pauline Letter Closings* (JSNTSup 101; Sheffield: JSOT, 1994); Markus Müller, *Vom Schluß zum Ganzen: Zur Bedeutung des paulinischen Briefkorpusabschlusses* (FRLANT 172; Göttingen: Vandenhoeck & Ruprecht, 1997).

6. Arnold, *Power and Magic*, 99: "Love holds an exceedingly prominent place in the entire epistle." Harold W. Hoehner, *Ephesians: An Exegetical Commentary* (Grand Rapids: Baker, 2002), 104–5: "The theme of 'love' is dominant in Ephesians. . . . This frequent use of love seems to furnish the key to the purpose of the book." See also François S. Malan, "Unity of Love in the Body of Christ: Identity, Ethics, and Ethos in Ephesians," in *Identity, Ethics, and Ethos in the New Testament* (ed. Jan G. van der Watt; BZNW 141; Berlin: De Gruyter, 2006), 257–302.

7. Chrys C. Caragounis, *The Ephesian Mysterion: Meaning and Content* (ConBNT 8; Lund: Gleerup, 1977), 143.

individual part, brings about the growth of the body for the upbuilding of
itself in love (ἐν ἀγάπῃ)" (4:15–16).[8]

B. Authorship

Although in all of the textual traditions of Ephesians the name "Paul"
(1:1; 3:1) designates the sender of the Letter, many scholars in modern times
have questioned and/or denied that the historical apostle Paul could have
written Ephesians because in their estimation it differs too greatly from the
so-called main or undisputed letters of Paul.[9] For them "Paul" is a pseud-
onym and Ephesians was written by someone other than the historical
Paul. Recent studies in the role of coauthors, coworkers, and secretaries in
the composition of Pauline letters, however, have indicated the complexity
involved in the question of their authorship. This could account for differences among the Pauline letters.[10] Furthermore, the appeal to pseudonymity
involves problematical assumptions and whether there are any pseudonymous writings in the NT is debatable.[11]

We follow those scholars who have recently studied the issue of the
authorship of Ephesians most thoroughly and arrived at the conclusion that
the historical apostle Paul, the Paul who is the main author of the "undis-

---

8. Hoehner, *Ephesians*, 105: "Love in action within the community of believers fosters
unity. . . . Unity without love is possible, but love without unity is not. Love is the central
ingredient for true unity, laying the foundation for internal and external unity."

9. For a recent discussion of how Ephesians differs from the undisputed Pauline letters,
see Mark Harding, "Disputed and Undisputed Letters of Paul," in *The Pauline Canon* (ed.
Stanley E. Porter; Pauline Studies 1; Leiden: Brill, 2004), 156–58. But for a recent demonstration that the ecclesiology of Ephesians does not deviate from that of the undisputed
letters but is compatible with it, see Jean-Noël Aletti, "Les difficultés ecclésiologiques de la
lettre aux Éphésiens: De quelques suggestions," *Bib* 85 (2004): 457–74.

10. Stirewalt, *Paul*; E. Randolph Richards, *The Secretary in the Letters of Paul*
(WUNT 42; Tübingen: Mohr Siebeck, 1991); idem, *Paul*. For the suggestion that Paul's
imprisonment during the composition of Ephesians (3:1; 4:1; 6:20) "would have necessitated
more assistance from a secretary, or amanuensis, than the letters written in freedom," see
Michael J. Gorman, *Apostle of the Crucified Lord: A Theological Introduction to Paul and
His Letters* (Grand Rapids: Eerdmans, 2004), 502.

11. Terry L. Wilder, *Pseudonymity, the New Testament, and Deception: An Inquiry
into Intention and Reception* (Lanham, MD: University Press of America, 2004), 265 n. 52:
"Though the case against the traditional authorship of some of the disputed Pauline letters
is sometimes strong, several scholars today believe that no pseudonymous works exist in the
NT. Scholars hold this view with good reason because (*a*) the greatest weakness of pseudepi-
graphic theories is the number of assumptions upon which they rest, and (*b*) they have been
encouraged by recent studies which focus on Paul's use of a secretary, a co-author, and tradition when writing his letters. A resort to pseudonymity is not necessary." Ben Witherington,
Letters and Homilies for Hellenized Christians, vol. 1: *A Socio-Rhetorical Commentary on
Titus, 1–2 Timothy, and 1–3 John* (Downers Grove, IL: InterVarsity, 2006), 38: "[A]lthough
there may be pseudepigrapha within the New Testament, the burden of proof falls squarely
on the shoulders of those who make that claim."

puted" letters of Paul, is indeed also the main author of the Letter to the Ephesians.[12] Nevertheless, even those who maintain that the historical Paul is not the author of Ephesians must admit that a figure named "Paul" is the textual or implied author of the Letter. And it is with this implied author "Paul" that we are concerned in this investigation of the theme of love in the Letter to the Ephesians.

This implied author "Paul" sent the Letter while in prison (3:1; 4:1; 6:20), so that Ephesians is one of the Pauline "captivity" letters, in addition to Philemon, Colossians, Philippians, and 2 Timothy. Rome, Ephesus, or Caesarea have been suggested as possible locations for Paul's imprisonment while composing Ephesians. It seems intriguingly plausible to link the sending of Ephesians from Caesarea with both Philemon and Colossians, with which it appears to be very closely related.[13] At any rate, that the implied

---

12. Peter Thomas O'Brien, *The Letter to the Ephesians* (Grand Rapids: Eerdmans, 1999), 4–47, esp. 37: "[W]e examined a range of arguments raised by contemporary scholars against the Pauline authorship of Ephesians. In spite of the perceived difficulties with the traditional view, we contended that the case against it is anything but proven. In fact, the denial that Paul wrote the letter raises more problems than it solves." Hoehner, *Ephesians*, 2–61, esp. 60–61: "The Pauline authorship of Ephesians not only has the earliest attestation of any book of the NT but this attestation continued until the last two centuries. The early attestation is highly significant. The early church was not only closer to the situation but also they were very astute in their judgment of genuine and fraudulent compositions. This overwhelming support for the Pauline authorship of Ephesians should not be easily dismissed. . . . Although Ephesians differs from other Pauline literature, the differences do not sufficiently argue for the rejection of Pauline authorship of this letter. Variations can be accounted for due to differences in content and differences in the character and needs of the recipients of the letter. Furthermore, it must be accepted that a genius such as Paul is not sterile in his expressions; allowances must be made for development in his own thinking." See also Nigel Turner, *A Grammar of New Testament Greek* (Edinburgh: Clark, 1976), 84–85; Gordon D. Fee, *God's Empowering Presence: The Holy Spirit in the Letters of Paul* (Peabody, MA: Hendrickson, 1994), 659–60; Klyne R. Snodgrass, *Ephesians: The NIV Application Commentary* (Grand Rapids: Zondervan, 1996), 23–29; F. Beisser, "Wann und von wem könnte der Epheserbrief verfasst worden sein?" *KD* 52 (2006): 151–64.

13. Bo Reicke, *Re-examining Paul's Letters: The History of the Pauline Correspondence* (Harrisburg, PA: Trinity Press International, 2001), 83: "[I]t seems impossible not to regard Paul as the authority behind Ephesians and his captivity in Caesarea as the backdrop of the letter. Stylistic peculiarities may indicate the assistance of a collaborator; but there is no reference to any such person in the text, and it does not seem impossible that Paul was able to address neophytes in Asia Minor with the solemn rhetorical diction found in Ephesians. Chronologically, Ephesians may have been written somewhat later than Philemon and Colossians since Timothy is not mentioned. But A.D. 59 must still be the year of composition, because Tychicus was expected to take all three letters with him, delivering the letters to Philemon and to the Colossians in Colossae, before continuing on with Ephesians (cf. Col. 4:7—Tychicus with Philemon's servant Onesimus in 4:9, who was returned to Colossae—and Eph. 6:21, where Tychicus is still mentioned but not Onesimus)." See also E. Earle Ellis, *History and Interpretation in New Testament Perspective* (Biblical Interpretation Series 54; Atlanta: Society of Biblical Literature, 2001), 86.

author "Paul" was in prison somewhere for its composition and sending is significant for the interpretation of Ephesians.[14]

C. Audience

Paul, the implied author, addresses the Letter "to the holy ones who are in Ephesus, the believers who are in Christ Jesus" (1:1), as the authorial or implied audience. Although the words, "in Ephesus," are lacking in some important early manuscripts, the preponderance of text-critical evidence, both external and internal, favors their retention as the original reading.[15]

The absence of the words "in Ephesus" from some manuscripts as well as what some consider to be an impersonal tone of the Letter, which is not addressed to a single church and lacks personal greetings to individuals at Ephesus, has led to the theory that Ephesians may be a circular or encyclical letter. It should be noted, however, that Paul does not send extended personal greetings to churches he knew well in such undisputed letters as 1 and 2 Corinthians, Galatians, and Philippians. And while Ephesians may be considered "impersonal" in that it only mentions two persons by name— Paul (1:1; 3:1) and Tychicus (6:21), Paul is very personally concerned to share with his audience the mystery with which he has been gifted by God for them (3:1–4). He earnestly prays for them (1:15–23; 3:14–21), exhorts them (4:1ff.), requests their prayers for him (6:18–20), and sends Tychicus to them, "so that you also may know the things concerning me, what I am doing" (6:21).[16]

---

14. On the significance of Paul being in prison for the interpretation of Ephesians but arguing for a Roman imprisonment, see Richard J. Cassidy, *Paul in Chains: Roman Imprisonment and the Letters of St. Paul* (New York: Crossroad, 2001), 94–104.

15. Bruce Manning Metzger, *A Textual Commentary on the Greek New Testament: Second Edition* (Stuttgart: Deutsche Bibelgesellschaft, 1994), 532; Clinton E. Arnold, "Ephesians, Letter to the," *DPL*, 244–45; Markus Barth, *Ephesians: Introduction, Translation, and Commentary on Chapters 1–3* (AB 34; New York: Doubleday, 1974), 67: "Four arguments are used in favor of considering these words [in Ephesus] authentic: (a) the mention of a place in the openings of genuine Pauline letters; (b) the presence of the words 'who are,' which in other addresses prepare the reader for the name of a place; (c) the prescript, 'To the Ephesians,' which is found in all MSS since the end of the second century and may, though certainly not written by the author, contain the result of careful research; and (d) the mission of Tychicus (6:21–22) which according to II Tim 4:12 directed him to Ephesus." Hoehner, *Ephesians*, 78–79, 144–48, and 140: "The inclusion of 'in Ephesus' is supported as the best reading. Externally, it has excellent support in the date and character, geographical distribution, and genealogical relationships of the manuscripts. Internally, the inclusion of 'in Ephesus' has good support in both the transcriptional and intrinsic probabilities." For possible reasons for the omission of the words "in Ephesus" from certain early manuscripts, see John Muddiman, *A Commentary on the Epistle to the Ephesians* (BNTC; London: Continuum, 2001), 62.

16. O'Brien, *Ephesians*, 48: "[T]hat he [Paul] prays for his readers (1:16) and asks them to intercede for him so that he may proclaim the mystery of the gospel boldly and clearly

It should also be noted that although Tychicus carries and presumably reads to their respective audiences both Colossians and Ephesians (cf. Col 4:7–8; Eph 6:21–22), Ephesians, unlike Colossians (see Col 4:16), lacks an explicit directive for it to be read elsewhere. In addition, there are no examples in antiquity of leaving a blank space in the prescript of letters so that they could be used as encyclical letters.[17] Although it appears to be relevant for and may well have been read to congregations outside of Ephesus, the primary destination and implied audience of the Letter are all of the various local churches within the great Asia Minor metropolis of Ephesus—"the holy ones who are in Ephesus" (1:1).[18]

Although addressed primarily to an implied audience of believers living in the large city of Ephesus, the Letter to the Ephesians, while presupposing the general influence of the social and historical environment of the metropolis of Ephesus upon the audience, makes little explicit or specific mention of its Ephesian locale.[19] This can be taken as another indication

---

(6:19–20) suggests that the letter is not wholly impersonal." See also Hoehner, *Ephesians*, 21–24.

17. Hoehner, *Ephesians*, 78: "Some suggest that this letter was encyclical and possibly the city name was omitted so that Tychicus or anyone who read the letter could fill in the city's name. However, there is no lacuna in any manuscript, even those which omit 'in Ephesus,' and no such lacunae exist in examples of letters in the ancient world." See also Rainer Schwindt, *Das Weltbild des Epheserbriefes: Eine religionsgeschichtlich-exegetische Studie* (WUNT 148; Tübingen: Mohr Siebeck, 2002), 62; Snodgrass, *Ephesians*, 21.

18. Arnold, *Power*, 6: "One needs to be cautious not to assume that there was only one local congregation in Ephesus. By the time Ephesians was written there may have been a network of new churches established within the city. This consideration is made all the more plausible by recognizing that the lower estimates for the population of Ephesus in the first century begin at a quarter of a million. It is also possible that churches existed in villages in the immediate vicinity of Ephesus, e.g. throughout the Cayster valley. These considerations greatly expand the potential 'Ephesian' readership." Hoehner, *Ephesians*, 141: "Paul may have intended this as a circular letter even though he did not specifically state it. Accepting the ἐν Ἐφέσῳ as genuine and yet considering it circular is not a contradiction. There is no real doubt about the destination of the Colossian letter and yet Paul in Col 4:16 tells them to have it read to the church in Laodecia and that, in turn, they were to read the letter he had sent to the Laodecians. Also, since Ephesus was the center of his western Asia Minor ministry and it is probable that the other churches of that area were established by him or his disciples during his long stay at Ephesus, it is reasonable to think that a letter to the Ephesian church would go to the satellite churches in that area." For the view that Ephesians is a "catholic" letter pseudonymously addressed to a universal audience, see Gerhard Sellin, "Adresse und Intention des Epheserbriefes," in *Paulus, Apostel Jesu Christi: Festschrift für Günter Klein zum 70 Geburtstag* (ed. Michael Trowitzsch; Tübingen: Mohr Siebeck, 1998), 171–86. For a view of Ephesians as a pseudonymous testament to Pauline theology for the post-apostolic times, see Michael Gese, *Das Vermächtnis des Apostels: Die Rezeption der paulinischen Theologie im Epheserbrief* (WUNT 99; Tübingen: Mohr Siebeck, 1997).

19. For information on the ancient city of Ephesus, see Richard E. Oster, "Holy Days in Honour of Artemis," *NewDocs* 4 (1987): 74–82; Steven J. Friesen, *Twice Neokoros: Ephesus, Asia, and the Cult of the Flavian Imperial Family* (Religions in the Graeco-Roman

that Ephesians may be an encyclical letter intended for a more general audience living both in the metropolis of Ephesus and its environs. That wives, husbands, children, parents, slaves, and masters are directly addressed in the "household code" of Ephesians (5:21–6:9) indicates that the various households in which believers gathered for worship would have been the normal setting for the public reading of the Letter.[20]

As we will see, a major concern of Paul in Ephesians is to assure the implied audience, characterized as "you" who came to believe (1:13) after "we," Paul and all those who first hoped in the Christ (1:12), came to believe, that they are nevertheless united to and incorporated within those who first believed as part of the cosmic unity that is a major theme of the Letter.[21] Although the "we" are generally identified as Jewish Christians and the "you" as Gentile Christians, more specificity and nuance are in order here. It is not a matter of Gentile Christians ("you") being united with Jewish Christians ("we") in general, but of those originating from a Gentile cultural environment and coming to faith more recently, be they Gentiles or Jews, being united with those originating from a Jewish cultural environment and coming to faith earlier, be they Jews or Gentiles.

World 116; Leiden: Brill, 1993); Helmut Koester, ed., *Ephesos: Metropolis of Asia. An Interdisciplinary Approach to Its Archaeololgy, Religion, and Culture* (HTS 41; Valley Forge, PA: Trinity Press International, 1995); Rick Strelan, *Paul, Artemis, and the Jews in Ephesus* (BZNW 80; Berlin: De Gruyter, 1996), 24–125; Arnold, *Power*, 13–28; Eckhard J. Schnabel, "Die ersten Christen in Ephesus: Neuerscheinungen zur frühchristlichen Missionsgeschichte," *NovT* 41 (1999): 349–82; Schwindt, *Weltbild*, 63–134; Hoehner, *Ephesians*, 78–89. But note the sober realism in the comments by O'Brien (*Ephesians*, 49) that "a specific knowledge of the ancient city of Ephesus, in spite of the increasing amount of information available to us, especially through the inscriptions, does not assist us a great deal in interpreting the letter" and by Snodgrass (*Ephesians*, 21) that "specific knowledge of Ephesus—as amazing as this ancient city was—does not help us much in interpreting the letter."

20. Peter Balla, *The Child-Parent Relationship in the New Testament and Its Environment* (WUNT 155; Tübingen: Mohr Siebeck, 2003), 174: "The very fact that all the members of a household are addressed in the Codes implies that the early Christian congregations gathered in houses. The richer members of the congregations received the congregations into their homes for services of worship. This is supported by archaeological evidence which shows that until the third century there were probably no separate buildings built as 'temples' by Christians."

21. Arnold (*Power*, 167–68) rightly draws attention to the importance of cosmic "powers" in Ephesians. He suggests that Ephesians was written especially to converts of the Artemis cult to comfort their fears of these powers. On the Artemis cult, see Gerard Mussies, "Artemis," *DDD*, 91–97. See also Thorsten Moritz, " 'Summing Up All Things': Religious Pluralism and Universalism in Ephesians," in *One God, One Lord: Christianity in a World of Religious Pluralism* (ed. Andrew D. Clarke and Bruce W. Winter; Grand Rapids: Baker, 1992), 89–92; Chris Forbes, "Paul's Principalities and Powers: Demythologizing Apocalyptic?" *JSNT* 82 (2001): 61–88; idem, "Pauline Demonology and/or Cosmology? Principalities, Powers, and the Elements of the World in their Hellenistic Context," *JSNT* 85 (2002): 51–73.

Although the "we" would be predominantly Christians of a Jewish origin, including Paul, they could include some Gentiles as well, e.g. those like Titus, an early Greek believer who accompanied Paul yet did not become Jewish by being circumcised (Gal 2:1–3). And although the "you" may be predominantly recent Christians of a Gentile origin, they could include those of a Jewish origin who lived in the Diaspora in a Gentile environment without being circumcised, so that they would have been considered "Gentiles" by circumcised Jews (cf. Timothy in Acts 16:1–3, a Christian disciple who was an uncircumcised Jew with a Jewish mother and Greek father, before being circumcised and joining Paul). The "you," then, could include Gentile pagan converts, former Gentile proselytes and "God-fearers," who frequented Jewish synagogues, as well as Diaspora Jews.[22] At any rate, the "you," those who came to believe more recently, are the Ephesian implied audience addressed by Paul as representative of the "we," those who came to believe earlier (Eph 1:12–13; 2:11–22).[23]

D. Literary-Rhetorical, Audience-Oriented Method

We will approach Ephesians as having the literary genre of an actual "letter," written to be publicly read as an oral performance substituting for the personal presence of the imprisoned Paul.[24] We will employ a literary-

22. Francis Watson, *Paul and the Hermeneutics of Faith* (London: Clark, 2004), 530–31: "The Pauline Gentiles are indeed Gentiles; and yet they have been brought into Israel's ancestral heritage, as mediated through the earliest Jewish Christian or Christian Jewish community, to which Paul belongs and to which he remains to some degree accountable ... the Pauline 'Gentile' communities appropriate not only Jewish scripture but also the characteristic Jewish orientation towards Jerusalem as the spiritual centre of their developing worldwide community." Strelan (*Ephesus*, 291–93) points out "that in Ephesus there was a 'church' of both Jews and gentiles, and that the number of Jews was significant, even if they were not the majority. There is little doubt about that point. What is not considered in scholarship is the *possibility* that the issues traditionally understood to be between Jew and gentile in Ephesians can also be understood to be between Jew and Jew (p. 291; his emphasis). . . . Is it possible that the expression τὰ ἔθνη ἐν σαρκί (2:11) refers to Jews who in the flesh are like the gentiles, that is, they are uncircumcised? Such Jews were considered outside the covenant in some circles, but in the circle of Christ they can claim to be 'fellow-citizens and saints and members of the household of God' (2:19). I admit to speculation at this point, but the point remains that the Jewish element in the community addressed in *Ephesians* cannot be ignored" (p. 293; his emphasis). On the Jewish element within the Ephesian audience, see also Thorsten Moritz, "Reasons for Ephesians," *Evangel* 14 (1996): 8–14; Margaret Y. MacDonald, "The Politics of Identity in Ephesians," *JSNT* 26 (2004): 419–44. On Jewish attitudes towards Gentiles in Ephesians, see Tet-Lim N. Yee, *Jews, Gentiles and Ethnic Reconciliation: Paul's Jewish Identity and Ephesians* (SNTSMS 130; Cambridge: Cambridge University Press, 2005).
23. Kôshi Usami, *Somatic Comprehension of Unity: The Church in Ephesus* (AnBib 101; Rome: Biblical Institute, 1983), 20–70.
24. On the literary genre of Ephesians, see Holland Hendrix, "On the Form and Ethos of Ephesians," *USQR* 42 (1988): 3–15; O'Brien, *Ephesians*, 68–73; Hoehner, *Ephesians*,

rhetorical method that treats Ephesians as a letter with a rhetorical strategy
of persuading the implied audience to the viewpoint of Paul, the implied
author. We use the term "rhetorical" in its broadest and most general sense.
Rather than applying the categories of either ancient Greco-Roman rhetoric
or the modern "new rhetoric" to Ephesians, our rhetorical method is entirely
text-centered. We will determine Paul's rhetorical or persuasive strategy by
carefully and closely listening to the chiastic structures of the text of the
Letter.[25]

Our method is "audience-oriented" in that it is concerned to determine
how the implied audience is meant to respond to Paul's rhetorical strategy
as it unfolds in the progression of the chiastically arranged text of the Letter.
Paul as the implied author of Ephesians presupposes a certain competency
on the part of his implied audience. Within the rhetorical strategy of the
Letter Paul utilizes a number of various traditions—Jewish, Christian, and
Gentile, assuming his audience is familiar with them.[26] This would accord
with an implied audience composed of recent converts of both Gentile and
Jewish origins living within the cosmopolitan society of the first-century
metropolis of Ephesus and its environs. Our focus, then, is upon how the
"you," the implied audience of recent believers that is united to and incorporated within the "we" of the entire body of believers, are empowered to
play their role in the pragmatics of the central theme of love that pervades
the Letter to the Ephesians.[27]

E. Summary

1. This book will propose and demonstrate new chiastic structures for
the entire Letter to the Ephesians as a key to experiencing it as a means
of communicating the power involved in God's love for us and our love

---

69–77, esp. 77: "It seems best to conclude that Ephesians is an actual letter with a mixture
of genre and styles, such as other Hellenistic and Pauline letters."

25. For a text-centered approach to the rhetoric of another Pauline letter, see D. Francois Tolmie, *Persuading the Galatians: A Text-Centered Rhetorical Analysis of a Pauline Letter* (WUNT 190; Tübingen: Mohr Siebeck, 2005). On Ephesians and rhetoric, see
O'Brien, *Ephesians*, 73–82.

26. Markus Barth, "Traditions in Ephesians," *NTS* 30 (1984): 3–25; Thorsten Moritz,
A Profound Mystery: The Use of the Old Testament in Ephesians (NovTSup 85; Leiden:
Brill, 1996).

27. On the audience-oriented method, see Warren Carter and John Paul Heil, *Matthew's
Parables: Audience-Oriented Perspectives* (CBQMS 30; Washington: Catholic Biblical Association, 1998), 8–17; John Paul Heil, *The Meal Scenes in Luke-Acts: An Audience-Oriented
Approach* (SBLMS 52; Atlanta: Society of Biblical Literature, 1999), 2–4; idem, *The Transfiguration of Jesus: Narrative Meaning and Function of Mark 9:2–8, Matt 17:1–8, and Luke
9:28–36* (AnBib 144; Rome: Biblical Institute, 2000), 22–24; idem, *The Rhetorical Role
of Scripture in 1 Corinthians* (Studies in Biblical Literature 15; Atlanta: Society of Biblical
Literature, 2005), 5–10.

for God/Christ and one another that contributes to the cosmic unity of all things in Christ.

2. Although it is debated whether the historical apostle Paul composed Ephesians, this investigation follows those who argue that he did. At any rate, according to the text of Ephesians, Paul, imprisoned somewhere, is the implied author who sent Tychicus to carry the Letter to its destination.

3. Although the words "in Ephesus" are lacking in some early manuscripts of Epehsians, this investigation follows those who argue that they are the original reading, so that the Letter's implied audience are "the holy ones in Ephesus, the believers who are in Christ Jesus" (1:1). This implied audience of the holy ones in Ephesus are the "you" (1:13), those (most likely including believers of both Gentile and Jewish origin) who became believers more recently than the "we" (1:12), but are nevertheless united to and incorporated within the "we" that comprise the entire body of holy ones who believe in Christ.

4. This investigation will employ a text-centered literary-rhetorical and audience-oriented method concerned with demonstrating how the implied audience are persuaded and empowered by the progression of the Letter's chiastic structures to play their role in the pragmatics of the central theme of love that pervades Ephesians and that effects the cosmic unity of all things in Christ.

CHAPTER 2

The Chiastic Structures of Ephesians

A. The Fifteen Micro-chiastic Units of the Letter

To be absolutely convincing the determination of an extended chiastic structure should be based upon a methodology with very rigorous criteria. It must be clear that the chiasm has not been subjectively imposed upon the text but actually subsists and operates objectively within the text. Our investigation will be guided by the following list of nine criteria for detecting an extended chiasm:

1. There must be a problem in perceiving the structure of the text in question, which more conventional outlines fail to resolve.

2. There must be clear examples of parallelism between the two "halves" of the hypothesized chiasm, to which commentators call attention even when they propose quite different outlines for the text overall.

3. Verbal (or grammatical) parallelism as well as conceptual (or structural) parallelism should characterize most if not all of the corresponding pairs of subdivisions.

4. The verbal parallelism should involve central or dominant imagery or terminology, not peripheral or trivial language.

5. Both verbal and conceptual parallelism should involve words and ideas not regularly found elsewhere within the proposed chiasm.

6. Multiple sets of correspondences between passages opposite each

other in the chiasm as well as multiple members of the chiasm itself are desirable.

7. The outline should divide the text at natural breaks which would be agreed upon even by those proposing very different structures to account for the whole.

8. The center of the chiasm, which forms its pivot, should be a passage worthy of that position in light of its theological or ethical significance.

9. Ruptures in the outline should be avoided if at all possible.[1]

More explanation regarding the criteria and characteristics of the chiastic structures, both the macro- and micro-chiasms, in this particular investigation of Paul's Letter to the Ephesians is in order. One of the main features of this investigation is that all of the proposed chiasms are based on precise verbal parallels found objectively in the text, rather than on thematic or conceptual parallels, which can often be subjective. Indeed, the main criterion for the establishment of chiasms in this investigation is the demonstration of these verbal parallels. We will seek to determine how the subsequent occurrence(s) of a paralleled word or phrase develops the first occurrence after a central unparalleled element or central parallel elements serve as a pivot from the first to the second half of the chiasm.

This has consequences for some of the characteristics of the proposed chiasms. Since they are based strictly on verbal parallels, they may or may not exhibit a balance in the length of the various parallel elements or units—one parallel element or unit may be much longer or much shorter than its corresponding parallel. This may seem odd to a modern audience, but an ancient audience would presumably be attuned to the key verbal parallels that are heard rather than the balance of length between the elements or units of a given chiasm. The main presupposition of this investigation is that if there are demonstrable verbal parallels with a pivotal section between them, then a chiasm is operative regardless of a certain lack of balance between various elements or units. This is especially important to keep in mind for

1. For a more detailed version of this list and an example of an extended biblical chiasm, see Craig L. Blomberg, "The Structure of 2 Corinthians 1–7," *CTR* 4 (1989): 4–8. And for more discussion of criteria and more biblical examples of extended chiasms, see Wayne Brouwer, *The Literary Development of John 13–17: A Chiastic Reading* (SBLDS 182; Atlanta: Society of Biblical Literature, 2000). See also John W. Welch, "Chiasmus in the New Testament," in *Chiasmus in Antiquity: Structures, Analyses, Exegesis* (ed. John W. Welch; Hildesheim, Germany: Gerstenberg, 1981), 211–49; idem, "Criteria for Identifying and Evaluating the Presence of Chiasmus," in *Chiasmus Bibliography* (ed. John W. Welch and Daniel B. McKinlay; Provo, UT: Research, 1999), 157–74; Ian H. Thomson, *Chiasmus in the Pauline Letters* (JSNTSup 111; Sheffield: Sheffield Academic Press, 1995), 13–45.

the proposed D′ unit (5:15–6:9) within the macro-chiastic structure, which contains several micro-chiastic sub-units, but nevertheless as a whole exhibits objectively within the text strict and precise verbal parallels with the D unit (2:1–10).

Additionally, some of the verbal parallels involve what might be considered by a modern audience as rather ordinary or trivial words, such as pronouns like "you" or "we." While these may not seem to be significant enough words to establish chiastic parallels, it should be kept in mind that, as we will see, there is a very important dynamism within the Letter to the Ephesians between the "we"—earlier believers—and the "you"—later believers. What may seem to be insignificant words or phrases on the surface to a modern audience may have been very significant indeed to the original audience.

Not all of the proposed chiasms have the same number of elements or units. And while the extended macro-chiastic structure of the Letter contains a single unparalleled central H unit (4:1–16), which serves as the central pivot of the entire macro-chiasm, some of the micro-chiasms may exhibit a single unparalleled central element, for example, A-B-C-B′-A′, while others may exhibit dual, parallel central or pivotal elements, for example, A-B-C-C′-B′-A′. Nevertheless, both of these types operate as chiasms in the ears of the implied audience, since they both involve a pivot from the first to the second half of the chiasm. In one type a central unparalleled element serves as the pivot, whereas in the other type two parallel elements together serve as the pivot to the second half of parallel elements. In addition, while the central unparalleled H unit of the macro-chiastic structure may be considered to be the climactic point of the Letter as a whole, in the micro-chiastic units this need not be the case. In the micro-chiasms, then, it may often be more accurate to speak of the central element or elements as the pivotal point of the chiasm and the final A′ element as the climax.

Chiastic patterns serve to organize the content to be heard and not only aid the memory of the one delivering or performing a document, but also make it easier for the implied audience to follow and remember the content. A chiasm works by leading its audience through introductory elements to a central, pivotal point or points, and then reaching its conclusion by recalling and developing, via the chiastic parallels, aspects of the initial elements that led to the central, pivotal point or points. Since chiasms were apparently very common in ancient oral-auricular and rhetorical cultures,[2] the original ancient audience may and need not necessarily have been consciously identifying or reflecting upon any of these chiastic structures in themselves as they heard them. They merely experienced the chiastic phenomenon, which had

---

2. For some of the evidence of this see Brouwer, *Literary Development*, 23–27.

an unconscious effect on how they perceived the content.[3] But a discovery, delineation, and bringing to consciousness of the chiastic structures of ancient documents can greatly aid the modern audience to a more proper and precise interpretation of them.

In what follows, then, we will first demonstrate how the text of Paul's Letter to the Ephesians naturally divides itself into fifteen distinct literary units based upon their micro-chiastic structures as determined by precise verbal parallels found objectively in the text. Where applicable we will point out how other linguistic and grammatical features often confirm the integrity of these units. Secondly, we will demonstrate how these fifteen units form a macro-chiastic pattern based upon precise verbal parallels found objectively in the text between the chiastically paired units. Thirdly, we will illustrate where the central theme of love occurs and how it functions within the micro- and macro-chiastic structures of the Letter.[4]

1. Opening Address and Greeting of Grace and Peace (1:1–2)

A: [1a] Paul, apostle of *Christ* (Χριστοῦ) Jesus
B: [1b] through the will of God (θεοῦ),

---

3. On chiasms as an aid to both listener and performer, see Joanna Dewey, "Mark as Aural Narrative: Structures as Clues to Understanding," *Sewanee Theological Review* 36 (1992): 50–52. See also Holly E. Hearon, "The Implications of Orality for Studies of the Biblical Text," in *Performing the Gospel: Orality, Memory, and Mark. Essays Dedicated to Werner Kelber* (ed. Richard A. Horsley et al.; Minneapolis: Fortress, 2006), 3–20. Whitney Taylor Shiner, "Memory Technology and the Composition of Mark," in *Performing the Gospel: Orality, Memory, and Mark. Essays Dedicated to Werner Kelber* (ed. Richard A. Horsley et al.; Minneapolis: Fortress, 2006), 164: "It is not clear that the audiences always followed these chiastic structures. It is more likely that the chiastic structures are there because they provide a convenient way to organize material in one's mind and are an easy way to remember material for dictation or performance."

4. On the interpretive significance of chiastic structures, see Ronald E. Man, "The Value of Chiasm for New Testament Interpretation," *BSac* 141 (1984): 146–57; Augustine Stock, "Chiastic Awareness and Education in Antiquity," *BTB* 14 (1984): 23–27; John Breck, "Biblical Chiasmus: Exploring Structure for Meaning," *BTB* 17 (1987): 70–74. For a discussion of chiasm in relation to chain-link interlock, see Bruce W. Longenecker, *Rhetoric at the Boundaries: The Art and Theology of the New Testament Chain-Link Transitions* (Waco, TX: Baylor University Press, 2005), 16–17, 22–23. For examples of chiastic structures of other Pauline letters, see A. Boyd Luter and Michelle V. Lee, "Philippians as Chiasmus: Key to the Structure, Unity and Theme Questions," *NTS* 41 (1995): 89–101; Stanley E. Porter and Jeffrey T. Reed, "Philippians as a Macro-Chiasm and Its Exegetical Significance," *NTS* 44 (1998): 213–31; John Paul Heil, "The Chiastic Structure and Meaning of Paul's Letter to Philemon," *Bib* 82 (2001): 178–206; Murray J. Harris, *The Second Epistle to the Corinthians: A Commentary on the Greek Text* (NIGTC; Grand Rapids: Eerdmans, 2005), 110–14. For a recent proposal of a comprehensive chiastic structure for the Letter to the Hebrews, see Gabriella Gelardini, *"Verhärtet eure Herzen nicht": Der Hebräer, eine Synagogenhomilie zu Tischa be-Aw* (BIS 83; Leiden: Brill, 2007).

C: ¹ᶜ to the holy ones who are *in* (ἐν) Ephesus,⁵
C′:   ¹ᵈ the believers who are *in* (ἐν) Christ Jesus,⁶
B′:   ²ᵃ grace to you and peace from *God* (θεοῦ) our Father
A′:   ²ᵇ and the Lord Jesus *Christ* (Χριστοῦ).⁷

Directed to "the holy ones," the "believers who are in Christ Jesus,"
and "you," the opening address and greeting of "grace and peace *from* God
our Father and the Lord Jesus Christ" in Eph 1:1–2 is grammatically set off
from the eulogy that begins in 1:3, which is directed *to* the God and Father
of our Lord Jesus Christ.⁸ The integrity of this first unit is further secured by
its A-B-C-C′-B′-A′ chiastic structure. The double occurrence of the genitive
singular of "Christ" (Χριστοῦ) establishes the parallelism of the A (1:1a)
and A′ (1:2b) elements of the chiasm.⁹ The double occurrence of the genitive singular of "God" (θεοῦ) establishes the parallelism of the B (1:1b) and
B′ (1:2a) elements and further distinguishes this first unit from the second
unit (1:3–14), whose only occurrence of "God" is in the nominative singular
(θεός in 1:3). And prepositional phrases with "in"—"in (ἐν) Ephesus" in
1:1c and "in (ἐν) Christ Jesus" in 1:1d—determine the parallelism between
the central C (1:1c) and C′ (1:1d) elements of this first unit.

Although no explicit terms for "love" appear in this first unit, the "grace"
and "peace" that come from God (1:2), as we will see later (cf. 6:23–24), are
part of the theme of love in Ephesians.

2. To the Praise of His Glory in Love (1:3–14)

A: ³ Blessed is the God and Father of *our* (ἡμῶν) Lord Jesus Christ,
who has blessed us in every *Spiritual* (πνευματικῇ) blessing in the
heavenly places in Christ, ⁴ as he chose us in him before the foundation of the world that we might be *holy* (ἁγίους) and blameless

5. For the acceptance of the words "in Ephesus" as the original reading despite their
absence in some early manuscripts, see ch. 1.
6. We understand the καί before πιστοῖς ("faithful") in 1:1 as epexegetical, so that only
one rather than two groups are addressed; the holy ones who are in Ephesus are the faithful
in Christ Jesus. Hoehner, *Ephesians*, 142: "[I]n the present context it is better to see καί used
as epexegetical or explicative, indicating that both adjectives refer to the same group and is
to be translated 'that is' or 'namely' or omitted in the translation." See also Barth, *Ephesians
1–3*, 68; Muddiman, *Ephesians*, 59.
7. All translations of Ephesians are my own and strive to be as literal and true to the
Greek text as possible.
8. Although "holy ones" (ἅγιοι) occurs throughout Ephesians to refer to believers in
general (1:15, 18; 2:19; 3:8, 18; 4:12; 5:3; 6:18), this is the only time it refers specifically to
the implied audience of the Letter. Likewise, this is the only time the audience are referred
to as the "faithful" (πιστοῖς), though the singular (πιστός) describes Tychicus, the probable
carrier of the Letter, as "faithful" in 6:21.
9. "Christ" also occurs in the C′ element (1:1d) of the chiasm, but in the dative
singular.

before him in love, ⁵ having predestined us to sonship through
Jesus Christ to himself, according to the pleasure of his will, ⁶ *to
the praise of the glory* (εἰς ἔπαινον δόξης) of *his* (αὐτοῦ) grace
with which he graced us in the Beloved,

B: ⁷ *in whom* (ἐν ᾧ) we have redemption through his blood,
the forgiveness of transgressions, according to the wealth of
his grace ⁸ which he lavished on us, in all wisdom and insight, ⁹ having made known to us the mystery *of his will* (τοῦ
θελήματος αὐτοῦ), according to his pleasure which he *purposed* (προέθετο) in him,

    C: ¹⁰ as a plan for the fullness of the times, to unite under
one head all *the* (τὰ) things *in* (ἐν) the Christ,

    C′:   *the* (τὰ) things in the heavens and *the* (τὰ) things on
earth *in* (ἐν) him,

B′:   ¹¹ *in whom* (ἐν ᾧ) also we have obtained an inheritance having been predestined according to the *purpose* (πρόθεσιν) of
the one who is working in all things according to the counsel
of his will (τοῦ θελήματος αὐτοῦ) ¹² in order that we might be
to the praise of his glory, who first hoped in the Christ,

A′:   ¹³ in whom also you, having heard the word of the truth, the gospel of your salvation, in whom also having believed, you were
sealed with the *Holy* (ἁγίῳ) *Spirit* (πνεύματι) of the promise,
¹⁴ who is the first installment of *our* (ἡμῶν) inheritance, for redemption of the possession, *to the praise of his glory* (εἰς ἔπαινον
δόξης αὐτοῦ).

Grammatically the integrity of the second unit in 1:3–14 is established
by the fact that it is composed of a single complex and poetic sentence. Each
of the six sub-units or elements comprising this second unit ends on a rather
rhythmic note. The first five elements all end with the preposition "in" (ἐν)
and a word referring to Jesus Christ—"in the Beloved" (1:6), "in him" (1:9),
"in the Christ" (1:10b), "in him" (1:10c), and "in the Christ" (1:12). The
sixth element ends with a final, climactic occurrence of the refrain, "to the
praise of his glory" (1:14; cf. 1:6, 12).

An A-B-C-C′-B′-A′ chiastic pattern further secures this unit's unity and
distinctness. The only two occurrences in the unit of the genitive of the
first-person plural pronoun "our"—"of our (ἡμῶν) Lord Jesus Christ" in
1:3 and "of our (ἡμῶν) inheritance" in 1:14, which form a literary inclusion
framing the unit, the only two occurrences in the unit of terms referring to
the "Spirit"—"in every Spiritual (πνευματικῇ) blessing" in 1:3 and "with the
Holy Spirit (πνεύματι)" in 1:13, as well as the only two occurrences in the
unit of the term "holy"—"that we might be holy (ἁγίους)" in 1:4 and "with
the Holy (ἁγίῳ) Spirit" in 1:13, contribute to the parallelism of the A (1:3–6)

and A´ (1:13–14) elements, which is further confirmed by the first and last occurrences in the unit of the refrain "to the praise of his glory" (εἰς ἔπαινον δόξης αὐτοῦ in 1:6, 14; cf. 1:12), referring to God's glory.

The B (1:7–9) and B´ (1:11–12) elements each begin with the prepositional phrase "in whom" (ἐν ᾧ in 1:7, 11) referring to Jesus Christ. That these occurrences of the phrase are followed by first-person plural verbs ("we have" in 1:7; "we have obtained an inheritance" in 1:11) distinguishes them from the occurrences of the same phrase in 1:13, which are followed by references in the second-person plural ("you" and "having believed"). The verb "purposed" (προέθετο) in 1:9 of the B element parallels the noun "purpose" (πρόθεσιν) in 1:11 of the B´ element. The last two occurrences in the unit of the phrase "of his will" (τοῦ θελήματος αὐτοῦ in 1:9, 11; cf. 1:5), referring to God's will, further confirm the parallelism of the B and B´ elements.

Occurrences of the accusative neuter plural article "the"—"all the (τὰ) things" in 1:10b—and "the (τὰ) things in the heavens and the (τὰ) things on the earth" in 1:10c—as well as occurrences of the preposition "in"—"in (ἐν) the Christ" in 1:10b—and "in (ἐν) him" in 1:10c—indicate the parallelism between the central C (1:10ab) and C´ (1:10c) elements of the chiasm.[10]

Key terms for "love" in Ephesians make their first two appearances—both in dynamic prepositional phrases—in the opening A (1:3–6) element of this second unit. In 1:4 Paul states that God "chose us in him before the foundation of the world that we might be holy and blameless before him in love (ἐν ἀγάπῃ)." And the unit concludes in 1:6 with the words, "to the praise of the glory of his grace with which he graced us in the Beloved (ἐν τῷ ἠγαπημένῳ)."

3. The Gift of Christ in Love as Head Over All to the Church (1:15–23)

A: [15] For this reason, I, also, having heard of the faith regarding you in the Lord Jesus and of the love for all (πάντας) the holy ones, [16]

---

10. For a succinct overview of various past proposals for a different structure of Eph 1:3–14, see Hoehner, *Ephesians*, 160–61. See also Charles J. Robbins, "The Composition of Eph 1:3–14," *JBL* 105 (1986): 677–87; H. Richard Lemmer, "Reciprocity between Eschatology and Pneuma in Ephesians 1:3–14," *Neot* 21 (1987): 159–82; Jan Harm Barkhuizen, "The Strophic Structure of the Eulogy of Ephesians 1:3–14," *HvTSt* 46 (1990): 390–413; Johannes P. Louw, "A Discourse Reading of Ephesians 1.3–14," in *Discourse Analysis and the New Testament: Approaches and Results* (ed. Stanley E. Porter and Jeffrey T. Reed; JSNTSup 170; Sheffield: Sheffield Academic Press, 1999), 308–15; Claudio Basevi, "La Benedizione de Ef 1, 3–14: Il disegno di salvezza di Dio Padre," *AT* 14 (2000): 305–42; Stefano Romanello, "Ef 1,3–14: Una pericope discussa," *RivB* 50 (2002): 31–62. Thomson (*Chiasmus*, 46–83) proposes an unconvincing chiastic structure for 1:3–10 only.

do not cease giving thanks for you, making mention of you[11] in my prayers, [17] that the God of our Lord Jesus Christ, the Father of glory, may *give* (δώῃ) you the Spirit of wisdom and revelation in knowledge of him, [18] the eyes of your heart having been enlightened so that you may know what is the hope of his calling, what is the wealth of the glory of his inheritance in the holy ones,

B: [19] and what is the *surpassing* (ὑπερβάλλον) greatness of his *power* (δυνάμεως) for us who believe according to the working of the might of his strength,

    C: [20] which he worked *in* (ἐν) the Christ, raising him from the dead

    C′:   and seating him *at* (ἐν) his right hand *in* (ἐν) the heavenly places,

B′:   [21] *far above* (ὑπεράνω) every ruler and authority and *power* (δυνάμεως) and dominion and every name that is named, not only in this age but also in the one to come.

A′:[22] And *all things* (πάντα) he subjected under his feet and *gave* (ἔδωκεν) him as head over *all things* (πάντα) to the church, [23] which indeed is his body,[12] the fullness of the one who is filling *all the things* (τὰ πάντα) *in all ways* (ἐν πᾶσιν).

There is a grammatical transition from the second unit (1:3–14) in which Paul spoke in the first-person plural throughout to the third unit (1:15–23) in which Paul begins to speak in the first-person singular—"Therefore, I also" (1:15). An A-B-C-C′-B′-A′ chiastic structure establishes the integrity of the third unit. The only occurrences in this unit of the plural adjective "all" (πᾶς)—"all (πάντας) the holy ones" in 1:15, "all things" (πάντα) twice in 1:22, and "all the things in all ways" (τὰ πάντα ἐν πᾶσιν) in 1:23, as well as the only occurrences of the verb "to give" with God as the subject—"may give" (δώῃ) in 1:17 and "gave" (ἔδωκεν) in 1:22, determine the parallelism between the A (1:15–18) and A′ (1:22–23) elements of this unit's chiastic pattern.[13]

The only two occurrences in the third unit of "the holy ones"—"for all the holy ones (τοὺς ἁγίους)" in 1:15 and "among the holy ones (τοῖς

---

11. For the inclusion of ὑμῶν at this point in the Greek text, see Hoehner, *Ephesians*, 253 n. 1.

12. Hoehner, *Ephesians*, 290: "Although there is debate regarding the distinction between the relative and the indefinite relative pronouns, it seems that the indefinite relative pronoun does carry a qualitative force so that it could be rendered 'which, in fact, is,' or 'which indeed is.' " See also Thomas Kingsmill Abbott, *A Critical and Exegetical Commentary on the Epistles to the Ephesians and to the Colossians* (ICC; Edinburgh: Clark, 1897), 34; BDAG, 729–30.

13. The adjective πᾶς also occurs twice in 1:21 but in the singular rather than the plural as in the A and A′ elements of the chiasm.

ἀγίοις)" in 1:18—form a literary inclusion framing and securing the unity of the A element in 1:15–18. And the only four occurrences in the third unit of the adjective "all" or "everything" (πᾶς) in the neuter plural—"everything" (πάντα) twice in 1:22 and "all things in all things" (τὰ πάντα ἐν πᾶσιν) in 1:23—secure the unity of the A´ element in 1:22–23.

The only uses in the third unit of words beginning with ὑπερ—"surpassing" (ὑπερβάλλον) in 1:19 and "far above" (ὑπεράνω) in 1:21, as well as the only occurrences of the genitive singular of the word for "power" (δύναμις)—"of his power (δυνάμεως)" in 1:19 and "far above every . . . power (δυνάμεως)" in 1:21, determine the parallelism between the B (1:19) and B´ (1:21) elements of the chiasm in the third unit. And the occurrences of the preposition "in" or "at"—"in (ἐν) the Christ" in 1:20a and "at (ἐν) his right hand in (ἐν) in the heavenly places" in 1:20b—indicate the parallelism between the central C (1:20a) and C´ (1:20b) elements of the chiasm in the third unit.

Another of the key terms for "love" in Ephesians appears at the beginning of this third unit. In 1:15 Paul declares to his implied audience, "Therefore, I also, having heard of your faith in the Lord Jesus and of your love (ἀγάπην) for all the holy ones."

4. Walking by the Great Love with Which He Loved Us (2:1–10)

A: ¹ And you (ὑμᾶς) being dead in your (ὑμῶν) transgressions and sins, ² in which you once walked (περιεπατήσατε) according to the age of this world, according to the ruler of the authority of the air, of the spirit that is now working in the sons of disobedience,

B: ³ among whom also we (ἡμεῖς) all once lived in the desires of our (ἡμῶν) flesh doing the wishes of the flesh and of the thoughts, and we were by nature children of wrath as also the rest.

C: ⁴ But God being rich in mercy, because of his great love (ἀγάπην)

C´: with which he loved (ἠγάπησεν) us,

B´: ⁵ even being dead as we (ἡμᾶς) were in transgressions, made us alive with the Christ—by grace you have been saved!— ⁶ and raised us up with him and seated us with him in the heavenly places in Christ Jesus, ⁷ that he might show in the ages to come the surpassing wealth of his grace in kindness upon us (ἡμᾶς) in Christ Jesus.

A´: ⁸ For by the grace you have been saved through faith, and this is not from you (ὑμῶν), of God is the gift; ⁹ it is not from works, so no one may boast. ¹⁰ For his work are we, created in Christ Jesus for good works which God prepared beforehand, that we might walk (περιπατήσωμεν) in them.

An A-B-C-C´-B´-A´ chiastic pattern establishes the integrity of the fourth unit in 2:1–10. The only occurrences in the fourth unit of the second-person plural pronoun "you"—"And you (ὑμᾶς) being dead in your (ὑμῶν) transgressions" in 2:1 and "this is not from you (ὑμῶν)" in 2:8, as well as the only occurrences in this unit of the verb "walk"—"in which you once walked (περιεπατήσατε)" in 2:2 and "that we might walk (περιπατήσωμεν) in them" in 2:10, determine the parallelism of the A (2:1–2) and A´ (2:8–10) elements of the chiasm.

Double occurrences of the first-person plural pronoun "we" in both the B (2:3)—"in which also we (ἡμεῖς) all once lived in the desires of our (ἡμῶν) flesh"—and B´ (2:5–7)—"even when we (ἡμᾶς) were dead in transgressions" in 2:5 and "the surpassing wealth of his grace in kindness upon us (ἡμᾶς)" in 2:7—elements establish their parallelism within the chiasm.[14]

Occurrences in this unit of terms for "love"—"because of his great love (ἀγάπην)" in 2:4a and "with which he loved (ἠγάπησεν) us" in 2:4b indicate the parallelism between the central C (2:4a) and C´ (2:4b) elements of the chiasm. Thus, both the noun and verb for "love" appear explicitly at the center of the chiasm in the fourth unit.

5. The Peace That Establishes Unity as a Gift of Love (2:11–22)

> A: ¹¹ Therefore remember that once *you* (ὑμεῖς), the Gentiles *in the flesh* (ἐν σαρκί), those called "uncircumcision" by what is called "circumcision" *in the flesh* (ἐν σαρκὶ) done by hands, ¹² that you were at that time without Christ alienated from the community of Israel and *strangers* (ξένοι) of the covenants of the promise, not having hope and *Godless* (ἄθεοι) in the world.
>
> B: ¹³ But now in Christ Jesus *you* (ὑμεῖς) who once were *far away* (μακράν) have become *near* (ἐγγύς) in the blood of the Christ. ¹⁴ For he is *our* (ἡμῶν) peace, who made the both one, that is, he destroyed the dividing wall of partition, the hostility, in his flesh, ¹⁵ abolishing the law of the commandments in decrees,
>
> C: that the two he might create *in himself* (ἐν αὐτῷ)
>
> D: into *one* (ἕνα) new person, making peace,
>
> D´: ¹⁶ and that he might reconcile the both in *one* (ἑνὶ) body to God through the cross,
>
> C´: killing the hostility *in himself* (ἐν αὐτῷ).
>
> B´: ¹⁷ And coming he preached peace to *you* (ὑμῖν) who are *far away* (μακράν) and peace to those who are *near* (ἐγγύς), ¹⁸

---

14. The first-person plural pronoun occurs only once in the C´ element of the chiasm in 2:4b.

so that through him *we* both *have* (ἔχομεν) the access in one Spirit before the Father.

A´:   [19] So then you are no longer *strangers* (ξένοι) and aliens, but you are fellow citizens with the holy ones and members of the household of *God* (θεοῦ), [20] built upon the foundation of the apostles and prophets, Christ Jesus himself being the capstone, [21] in whom the whole building being fitted together is growing into a temple holy in the Lord, [22] in whom *you* (ὑμεῖς) also are being built together into a dwelling place of *God* (θεοῦ) *in the Spirit* (ἐν πνεύματι).

An A-B-C-D-D´-C´-B´-A´ chiastic structure establishes the integrity of the fifth unit in 2:11–22. The antithetical correlation between the audience's situation in the "flesh" and in the "Spirit"—"you (ὑμεῖς), the Gentiles in the flesh (ἐν σαρκί), those called the 'uncircumcision' by what is called 'circumcision in the flesh (ἐν σαρκὶ)" in 2:11 and "you (ὑμεῖς) also are being built into a dwelling place of God in the Spirit (ἐν πνεύματι)" in 2:22, the occurrences of words referring to God—"Godless" (ἄθεοι) in 2:12 and "of God" (θεοῦ) in 2:19 and 2:22, and the only two occurrences not only in the fifth unit but in the entire Letter of the word "stranger"—"you were strangers (ξένοι) of the covenants of the promise" in 2:12 and "you are no longer strangers (ξένοι)" in 2:19, determine the parallelism of the A (2:11–12) and A´ (2:19–22) elements of the chiasm in the fifth unit.

The only two occurrences of the pair, "far away" and "near," in relation to the "you" of the implied audience not only in this unit but in the entire Letter—"you (ὑμεῖς) who once were far away (μακράν) have become near (ἐγγύς)" in 2:13 and "peace to you (ὑμῖν) who were far away (μακράν) and peace to those who were near (ἐγγύς)" in 2:17—and the only references in this chiasm to "we"—"our (ἡμῶν) peace" in 2:14 and "we have" (ἔχομεν) in 2:18—establish the parallelism of the B (2:13–15a) and B´ (2:17–18) elements.

The only two occurrences in this unit of the prepositional phrase "in himself"— "that he might create in himself (ἐν αὐτῷ)" in 2:15b and "killing the hostility in himself (ἐν αὐτῷ)" in 2:16b—determine the parallelism of the C (2:15b) and C´ (2:16b) elements of the chiasm.

Occurrences of terms for "one"—"one (ἕνα) new person" in 2:15c and "one (ἑνὶ) body" in 2:16a—indicate the parallelism between the D (2:15c) and D´ (2:16a) elements at the center of the chiasm in the fifth unit.[15]

Although no explicit term for "love" appears in this fifth unit, the refer-

---

15. For proposals of different, much more complex chiastic structures of 2:11–22, but lacking in strict linguistic parallels, see Giovanni Giavini, "La structure litteraire d'Eph 2:11–22," *NTS* 16 (1970): 209–11; John C. Kirby, *Ephesians, Baptism, and Pentecost: An Inquiry into the Structure and Purpose of the Epistle to the Ephesians* (Montreal: McGill University Press, 1968), 156–57; Kenneth E. Bailey, *Poet and Peasant: A Literary-Cultural*

ences to Christ's gift of peace (2:14, 15, 17), as we will see in more detail later, are part of the pervading theme of love in Ephesians.

6. Paul's Gift to Make Known the Mystery of Christ in Love (3:1–13)

A: ¹ Because of this, I, Paul, am the prisoner of the Christ Jesus *on behalf of you* (ὑπὲρ ὑμῶν) Gentiles.

    B: ² As indeed you have heard of the *plan* (οἰκονομίαν) *of the grace of God that was given to me* (τῆς χάριτος τοῦ θεοῦ τῆς δοθείσης μοι) for you, ³ that according to revelation *was made known* (ἐγνωρίσθη) to me the *mystery* (μυστήριον), as I wrote before in brief, ⁴ whereby when reading it you are able to perceive my insight into the *mystery* (μυστηρίῳ) of the Christ, ⁵ which in other generations *was* not *made known* (ἐγνωρίσθη) to human beings as *now* (νῦν) it has been revealed to his holy apostles and prophets in the Spirit,

        C: ⁶ that the Gentiles are *fellow heirs* and *fellow members of the body* and *fellow sharers* of the *promise* in Christ Jesus through the *gospel,*

    B′:   ⁷ of which I became a minister according to the gift *of the grace of God that was given to me* (τῆς χάριτος τοῦ θεοῦ τῆς δοθείσης μοι) according to the working of his power. ⁸ To me, the very least of all holy ones, was given this grace, to preach to the Gentiles the unfathomable wealth of the Christ ⁹ and to enlighten for all what is the *plan* (οἰκονομία) of the *mystery* (μυστηρίου) which had been hidden from the ages in God who created all things, ¹⁰ that *may be made known* (γνωρισθῇ) *now* (νῦν) to the rulers and to the authorities in the heavenly places through the church the manifold wisdom of God, ¹¹ according to the purpose of the ages which he accomplished in Christ Jesus our Lord, ¹² in whom we have the boldness and access in confidence through faith in him.

A′:   ¹³ Therefore I ask you not to lose heart in my tribulations *on behalf of you* (ὑπὲρ ὑμῶν), which is your glory.

An A-B-C-B′-A′ chiastic structure establishes the integrity of the sixth unit in 3:1–13. The only two occurrences in this unit of the phrase "on behalf of you"—"I, Paul, the prisoner of the Christ Jesus on behalf of you (ὑπὲρ ὑμῶν) Gentiles" in 3:1 and "I ask you not to lose heart in my tribulations on behalf of you (ὑπὲρ ὑμῶν)" in 3:13—determine the parallelism of the A (3:1) and A′ (3:13) elements of the chiasm in the sixth unit.

Approach to the Parables in Luke (Grand Rapids: Eerdmans, 1976), 63; Thomson, *Chiasmus,* 84–115; Hoehner, *Ephesians,* 351–52 n. 1.

The only occurrences in this unit of "plan"—"if indeed you have heard of the plan (οἰκονομίαν)" in 3:2 and "to enlighten for all what is the plan (οἰκονομία)" in 3:9, of the phrase "of the grace of God that was given to me"—"if indeed you have heard of the plan of the grace of God that was given to me (τῆς χάριτος τοῦ θεοῦ τῆς δοθείσης μοι)" in 3:2 and "I became a minister according to the gift of the grace of God that was given to me (τῆς χάριτος τοῦ θεοῦ τῆς δοθείσης μοι)" in 3:7, of the verb "made known"— "that according to revelation was made known (ἐγνωρίσθη)" in 3:3, as well as "which in other generations was not made known (ἐγνωρίσθη)" in 3:5, and "that may be made known (γνωρισθῇ)" in 3:10, of "now"—"as now (νῦν) it has been revealed" in 3:5 and "that may be made known now (νῦν)" in 3:10, and of "mystery"—"was made known to me the mystery (μυστήριον)" in 3:3, as well as "my insight into the mystery (μυστηρίῳ)" in 3:4, and "the plan of the mystery (μυστηρίου)" in 3:9, establish the parallelism of the B (3:2–5) and B´ (3:7–12) elements of the chiasm.

The unique occurrences in this unit of "fellow heirs," fellow members of the body," "fellow sharers," "promise," and "gospel" distinguish the unparalleled C (3:6) element at the center of the chiasm in this sixth unit.

Although no explicit term for "love" appears in this sixth unit, the references to God's "grace" and "giving" (3:2, 7, 8), as we will see in more detail later, are part of the pervading theme of love in Ephesians.

7. To Know the Love of Christ that Surpasses Knowledge (3:14–21)

A: [14] Because of this I bow my knees before the Father [15] from whom *every* (πᾶσα) family in heaven and on earth is named,
  B: [16] that he may give you according to the wealth of his glory to be strengthened with *power* (δυνάμει) through his Spirit in the inner person,
    C: [17] that the *Christ* (Χριστόν) may dwell through faith in your hearts, *in love* (ἐν ἀγάπῃ) rooted and grounded,
      D: [18] that *you might have the strength to comprehend* with all the holy ones *what is the breadth and length and height and depth*,
    C´:   [19] and so to know the *love* (ἀγάπην) of the *Christ* (Χριστοῦ) that surpasses knowledge, that you might be filled to all the fullness of God.
  B´:   [20] Now to him who has the *power* (δυναμένῳ) to do far more beyond all that we ask or imagine according to the *power* (δύναμιν) that is working in us,
A´:   [21] to him be glory in the church and in Christ Jesus to *all* (πάσας) the generations, for ever and ever. Amen.

An A-B-C-D-C´-B´-A´ chiastic pattern establishes the integrity of the seventh unit in 3:14–21. The occurrences of "every" or "all" modifying closely related nouns—"every (πᾶσα) family" in 3:15 and "all (πάσας) generations" in 3:21—determine the parallelism of the A (3:14–15) and A´ (3:21) elements of the chiasm in the seventh unit. The only occurrences in this unit of "power"—"to be strengthened with power (δυνάμει)" in 3:16 and "to him who has the power (δυναμένῳ)" as well as "according to the power (δύναμιν) that works in us" in 3:20—demonstrate the parallelism of the B (3:16) and B´ (3:20) elements of the chiasm. The only two occurrences in this unit of "Christ" and "love"—"the Christ (Χριστόν) may dwell through faith in your hearts, in love (ἐν ἀγάπῃ)" in 3:17 and "to know the love (ἀγάπην) of the Christ (Χριστοῦ)" in 3:19 secure the parallelism of the C (3:17) and C´ (3:19) elements of the chiasm. The unique occurrences of "you might have the strength to comprehend" and "what is the breadth and length and height and depth" distinguish the unparalleled D (3:18) element at the center of the chiasm.

Terms for "love" appear in both the C—"that the Christ may dwell through faith in your hearts, in love (ἐν ἀγάπῃ) rooted and grounded" (3:17)—and C´—"to know the love (ἀγάπην) of the Christ that surpasses knowledge" (3:19)—elements of the chiasm in this seventh unit.

8. To Walk toward the Unity of All in Love (4:1–16)

A: [1] I, then, exhort you, I, the prisoner in the Lord, to walk worthy of the calling with which you were called, [2] with all humility and gentleness, with patience, forbearing one another *in love* (ἐν ἀγάπῃ),

B: [3] striving to preserve the *unity* (ἑνότητα) of the Spirit in the bond of peace: [4] one body and one Spirit, as also you were called in one hope of your calling; [5] one Lord, one *faith* (πίστις), one baptism, [6] one God and Father of all, who is over all and through all and in all. [7] But to each one of us grace was given according to the *measure* (μέτρον) of the gift of the Christ.

C: [8] Therefore it says, "Having *ascended* (ἀναβάς) on high he captured the captives, he gave gifts to people." [9] Now this "he *ascended* (ἀνέβη)," what is it, if not that also he *descended* (κατέβη) to the lower parts of the earth?

C´:   [10] The same one who *descended* (καταβάς) is also the one who *ascended* (ἀναβάς) far above all the heavens, that he might fill all things.

B´:   [11] And he gave some as apostles, others as prophets, others as evangelists, others as pastors and teachers, [12] for the equipping of the holy ones for the work of ministry for building up the body of the Christ, [13] until we all attain to the *unity* (ἑνότητα) of the *faith* (πίστεως) and of the knowledge of the Son of God, to a mature person, to the *measure* (μέτρον) of the stature of the fullness of the Christ, [14] that we might no longer be infants, tossed by waves and carried about by every wind of teaching in the craftiness of people in deceitfulness toward the scheming of error,

A′:   [15] but rather being truthful *in love* (ἐν ἀγάπῃ), we might cause all things to grow to him, who is the head, the Christ, [16] from whom the whole body, fitted together and held together through every supporting connection according to the working in measure of each individual part, brings about the growth of the body for the building up of itself *in love* (ἐν ἀγάπῃ).

An A-B-C-C′-B′-A′ chiastic pattern establishes the integrity of the eighth unit in 4:1–16. The only occurrences in this unit of the prepositional phrase "in love"—"forbearing one another in love (ἐν ἀγάπῃ)" in 4:2 and "being truthful in love (ἐν ἀγάπῃ)" in 4:15, as well as "the building up of itself in love (ἐν ἀγάπῃ)" in 4:16—determine the parallelism of the A (4:1–2) and A′ (4:15–16) elements of the chiasm in the eighth unit.

The only two occurrences not only in this unit but in the entire Letter of "unity"—"the unity (ἑνότητα) of the Spirit" in 4:3 and "the unity (ἑνότητα) of the faith" in 4:13, the only two occurrences in this unit of "faith"—"one faith (πίστις)" in 4:5 and "the unity of the faith (πίστεως)" in 4:13, and the only two occurrences in this unit of "measure" in the accusative case (it occurs in the dative in 4:16)—"the measure (μέτρον) of the gift" in 4:7 and "the measure (μέτρον) of the maturity" in 4:13, determine the parallelism of the B (4:3–7) and B′ (4:11–14) elements of the chiasm.

The only occurrences not only in this unit but in the entire Letter of the verbs "ascend" and "descend"—"having ascended (ἀναβάς)" in 4:8, as well as "he ascended (ἀνέβη)" and "he descended (κατέβη)" in 4:9, and "he who descended (καταβάς is himself also he who ascended ἀναβάς)" in 4:10—determine the parallelism of the central C (4:8–9) and C′ (4:10) elements of the chiastic unit.

Three of the Letter's six occurrences of the dynamic prepositional phrase "in love" appear in the A—"forbearing one another in love (ἐν ἀγάπῃ)" (4:2)—and A′—"being truthful in love (ἐν ἀγάπῃ) ... brings about the growth of the body to the building up of itself in love (ἐν ἀγάπῃ)" (4:14–16)—elements of the chiasm in the eighth unit.

9. Walk as the New Person in the Truth of Christ's Love (4:17–32)

A: [17] This then I say and testify in the Lord, that you no longer walk, just as also the Gentiles walk in the futility of their mind, [18] being

darkened in understanding, alienated from the life of *God* (θεοῦ)
because of the ignorance that is in them because of the hardness
of their heart, [19] who, having become callous, have given themselves over to indecency for the practice of *every* (πάσης) kind of
impurity in greediness.

B: [20] But you have not so learned the Christ, [21] inasmuch as
about him you *heard* (ἠκούσατε) and in him you were taught,
as there is *truth* (ἀλήθεια) in Jesus,

   C: [22] that you have *put off* (ἀποθέσθαι) *according to* (κατά)
the former lifestyle the *old person* (παλαιὸν ἄνθρωπον)
who is being corrupted *according to* (κατά) the desires
of deceit,

   C′:   [23] but you are being renewed in the spirit of your mind
[24] and have *put on* (ἐνδύσασθαι) the *new person* (καινὸν
ἄνθρωπον) created *according to* (κατά) God in righteousness and holiness of truth.

B′:   [25] Therefore having put off falsehood, speak *truth* (ἀλήθειαν),
each one with his neighbor, for we are members of one another. [26] Be angry but do not sin; let not the sun set on your
anger, [27] and do not give room to the devil. [28] Let the stealer
no longer steal, but rather let him labor working with his
own hands that which is good, that he might have something
to share with one who has need. [29] Let no harmful word come
out of your mouth, but only such as is good for the building
up of what is needed, that it might give grace to *those who
hear* (ἀκούουσιν).

A′:   [30] And do not grieve the Holy Spirit of *God* (θεοῦ), in whom you
were sealed for the day of redemption. [31] Let *all* (πᾶσα) bitterness and fury and wrath and shouting and reviling be put away
from you along with *all* (πάσῃ) malice. [32] But become kind to one
another, compassionate, being gracious to each other, just as also
God (θεός) in Christ was gracious to us.[16]

An A-B-C-C′-B′-A′ chiastic structure establishes the integrity of the
ninth unit in 4:17–32. Occurrences of the word "God"—"alienated from
the life of God (θεοῦ)" in 4:18 and "the Holy Spirit of God (θεοῦ)" in 4:30,
as well as "just as also God (θεός) in Christ was gracious to us" in 4:32,
together with occurrences of "all" or "every"—"for the practice of every
(πάσης) kind of impurity" in 4:19 and "all (πᾶσα) bitterness" in 4:31, as well

---

16. For the text critical preference of "us" (ἡμῖν) rather than "you" (ὑμῖν) here, see
Hoehner, *Ephesians*, 640 n. 2.

as "along with all (πάσῃ) malice" in 4:31, determine the parallelism of the A (4:17–19) and A´ (4:30–32) elements of the chiasm.

The only two occurrences in this unit of the verb "hear"—"inasmuch as you heard (ἠκούσατε)" in 4:21 and "that it might give grace to those who hear (ἀκούουσιν)" in 4:29, together with occurrences of "truth"—"as truth (ἀλήθεια) is in Jesus" in 4:21 and "speak truth (ἀλήθειαν)" in 4:25, determine the parallelism of the B (4:20–21) and B´ (4:25–29) elements of the chiasm.

The antithesis between the aorist middle infinitives "put off" and "put on," together with the antithesis between "old person" and "new person"—"you have put off (ἀποθέσθαι) according to the former lifestyle the old person (παλαιὸν ἄνθρωπον)" in 4:22 and "you have put on (ἐνδύσασθαι) the new person (καινὸν ἄνθρωπον)" in 4:24, as well as the only occurrences within this chiasm of the preposition "according to"—"according to (κατά) the former lifestyle" and "according to (κατά) the desires of deceit" in 4:22 and "created according to (κατά) God" in 4:24—determine the antithetical parallelism of the central C (4:22) and C´ (4:23–24) elements of the chiasm in the ninth unit.

Although no explicit term for "love" appears in this ninth unit, "that it might give grace" in 4:29 and "being gracious to each other, just as also God in Christ was gracious to us" in 4:32, as we will see in more detail later, are part of the word field of the major theme of love in Ephesians.

10. Walk in Love as Christ Loved Us (5:1–6)

A: ¹ Become then imitators of God (τοῦ θεοῦ) as beloved children (τέκνα ἀγαπητὰ) ² and walk in love just as also the Christ loved us and handed himself over for us as an offering and sacrifice to God for a fragrant aroma.

B: ³ But do not let sexual immorality (πορνεία) and any impurity (ἀκαθαρσία) or greed (πλεονεξία) even be named among you, as is fitting for holy ones,

C: ⁴ no shamefulness or foolish talk or sarcastic ridicule, which are inappropriate, but rather thanksgiving.

B´: ⁵ For this know assuredly, that no sexually immoral (πόρνος) or impure (ἀκάθαρτος) or greedy (πλεονέκτης) one, who is an idolater, has an inheritance in the kingdom of the Christ and God.

A´: ⁶ Let no one deceive you with empty words; for because of these things the wrath of God (τοῦ θεοῦ) is coming upon the sons of disobedience (υἱοὺς τῆς ἀπειθείας).

An A-B-C-B´-A´ chiastic structure establishes the integrity of the tenth unit in 5:1–6. The only two occurrences in this unit of the word "God" in the genitive singular—"imitators of God (τοῦ θεοῦ)" in 5:1 and "the wrath of God (τοῦ θεοῦ)" in 5:6, together with the antithetical correspondence between "beloved children" (τέκνα ἀγαπητὰ) in 5:1 and "sons of disobedience" (υἱοὺς τῆς ἀπειθείας) in 5:6 determine the parallelism between the A (5:1–2) and A´ (5:6) elements of the chiasm.

The only occurrences in this unit of words referring to "sexual immorality," "impurity," and "greed"—"do not let sexual immorality (πορνεία) and any impurity (ἀκαθαρσία) or greed (πλεονεξία) even be named among you" in 5:3 and "no sexually immoral (πόρνος) or impure (ἀκάθαρτος) or greedy (πλεονέκτης) one" in 5:5—determine the parallelism of the B (5:3) and B´ (5:5) elements of the chiasm. And the unique occurrences not only in this unit but in the entire Letter of "shamefulness," "foolish talk," "sarcastic ridicule" and "thanksgiving" distinguish the central C (5:4) unit of the chiasm in this tenth unit.

Explicit words for "love" appear in this tenth unit in 5:1—"as beloved (ἀγαπητά) children"—and 5:2—"walk in love (ἐν ἀγάπῃ) just as also the Christ loved (ἠγάπησεν) us."

11. Walk as Children of Light in Love (5:7–14)

A: ⁷ Do not then become fellow sharers with them; ⁸ for you were once darkness, but now you are *light* (φῶς) in the Lord; walk as children of *light* (φωτός)—

B: ⁹ for the *fruit* (καρπός) of *the light* (τοῦ φωτός) consists in all goodness and righteousness and truth—

C: ¹⁰ *approving* what is *pleasing* to the Lord,

B´:   ¹¹ and do not be connected with the *unfruitful* (ἀκάρποις) works of the darkness, but rather expose them. ¹² For the things done in secret by them are shameful even to mention, ¹³ but all the things exposed by *the light* (τοῦ φωτός) become visible,

A´:   ¹⁴ for everything that becomes visible is *light* (φῶς). Therefore it says, "Awake, O sleeper, and arise from the dead, and the Christ will shine on you."

An A-B-C-B´-A´ chiastic structure establishes the integrity of the eleventh unit in 5:7–14. Occurrences of the word for "light"—"you are light (φῶς) in the Lord; walk as children of light (φωτός)" in 5:8 and "everything that becomes visible is light (φῶς)" in 5:14—determine the parallelism of the A (5:7–8) and A´ (5:14) elements of the chiasm.

Occurrences of words referring to "fruit" together with the only occurrences in this unit of the word "light" with the article "the"—"the fruit (καρπός) of *the* light (τοῦ φωτός)" in 5:9 and "the unfruitful (ἀκάρποις) works of the darkness" in 5:11, as well as "all the things exposed by *the* light (τοῦ φωτός)" in 5:13—determine the parallelism of the B (5:9) and B′ (5:11–13) elements of the chiasm. And the unique occurrences not only in this unit but in the entire Letter of "approving" and "pleasing" distinguish the unparalleled C (5:10) element at the center of the chiasm in this eleventh unit.

Although no explicit terms for "love" appear in this unit, "approving what is pleasing to the Lord," as we will demonstrate later, is a conceptual part of the major theme of love pervading Ephesians.

12. Walk in Love as Those Who Are Wise (5:15–6:9)

The twelfth main unit in 5:15–6:9 consists of four sub-units: 5:15–20, 5:21–33, 6:1–4, and 6:5–9, each of which exhibits its own chiastic structure. The appearances in this twelfth unit of eleven of the twenty-six occurrences of the word "Lord" in Ephesians, with at least one appearance in each of the four sub-units, confirm the integrity of the twelfth unit. Furthermore, this twelfth unit takes its place as the fifth in the series of units in the second or "paranetic" half of the Letter beginning in 4:1 that each begin with a combination of the conjunction "then" (οὖν) and the verb "walk" (περιπατέω).[17] The beginning of the thirteenth unit in 6:10 with "finally" (τοῦ λοιποῦ) indicates a new unit so that the twelfth unit ends with 6:9.[18]

a. Always Thanking God in Love (5:15–20)

A: [15] Watch then how carefully you walk,[19] not as unwise but as wise, [16] making the most of the time, for the days are evil. [17] Therefore do not become foolish, but understand what the will of the *Lord*

---

17. The first unit (4:1–16) of the paranetic part of Ephesians, and thus the eighth unit overall in the Letter, begins: "I, then (οὖν), the prisoner in the Lord, exhort you to walk (περιπατῆσαι) worthy of the calling with which you were called" (4:1); the ninth unit (4:17–32) begins: "This then (οὖν) I say and testify in the Lord, that you no longer walk (περιπατεῖν) . . ." (4:17); the tenth unit (5:1–6) begins: "Become then (οὖν) imitators of God as beloved children and walk (περιπατεῖτε) in love" (5:1–2); the eleventh unit (5:7–14) begins: "Do not then (οὖν) become fellow sharers with them; for you were once darkness, but now you are light in the Lord; walk (περιπατεῖτε) as children of light" (5:7–8); and the twelfth unit (5:15–6:9) begins: "Watch then (οὖν) how carefully you walk (περιπατεῖτε)" (5:15).

18. Hoehner, *Ephesians*, 62.

19. For the choice of the reading "watch then how carefully" (βλέπετε οὖν πῶς ἀκριβῶς) rather than "watch carefully then how" (βλέπετε οὖν ἀκριβῶς πῶς) in 5:15a, see Hoehner, *Ephesians*, 690 n. 1. As Hoehner (ibid., 691) goes on to point out, "the better order textually is for the adverb ἀκριβῶς to modify περιπατέω, 'to walk' . . . This is not only a better textual reading, but it also makes more sense contextually. . . . The point is not how carefully one is to observe but how carefully one is to walk." We might add that while the imperative βλέπετε ("watch") is never modified by an adverb in the NT, as noted by Hoehner (ibid., 690 n. 1), there is a precedent for περιπατέω to be modified by an adverb in Eph 4:1: "to walk worthy" (ἀξίως περιπατῆσαι).

(κυρίου) is. [18] And do not get drunk with wine, in which there is dissipation, but be filled in the Spirit,

B: [19] speaking to each other in *psalms* (ψαλμοῖς) and hymns and Spiritual *songs* (ᾠδαῖς),

B′: *singing songs* (ᾄδοντες) and *singing psalms* (ψάλλοντες) in your hearts to the Lord,[20]

A′:   [20] giving thanks always and for all things in the name of our *Lord* (κυρίου) Jesus Christ to God the Father,

An A-B-B′-A′ chiastic pattern secures the integrity of this first sub-unit in 5:15–20 that begins the twelfth unit of the Letter in 5:15–6:9. The only occurrences in this sub-unit of the word "Lord" in the genitive singular (it appears in the dative singular in 5:19b)—"the will of the Lord (κυρίου)" in 5:17 and "in the name of our Lord (κυρίου)" in 5:20—determine the parallelism of the A (5:15–18) and A′ (5:20) elements of the chiasm. And the only occurrences not only in this sub-unit but in the entire Letter of words referring to "songs" and "psalms"—"speaking to each other in psalms (ψαλμοῖς) and hymns and Spiritual songs (ᾠδαῖς)" in 5:19a and "singing songs (ᾄδοντες) and singing psalms (ψάλλοντες)" in 5:19b—indicate the parallelism of the central B (15:19a) and B′ (5:19b) elements of the chiasm.

Although no explicit term for "love" appears in this sub-unit, "be filled in the Spirit" in 5:18b refers to being filled by Christ with gifts of love within the realm of being in union with the Spirit, and "giving thanks always for all things in the name of our Lord Jesus Christ to God the Father" in 5:20, as we will demonstrate later, is a conceptual part of the theme of love running through the entire Letter to the Ephesians.

b. Husbands and Wives Love One Another (5:21–33)

A: [21] Submitting to one another in *respect* (φόβῳ) for Christ, [22] the wives to their own husbands as to the Lord,[21]

B: [23] for the *husband* (ἀνήρ) is head of the *wife* (γυναικός) as also the *Christ* (Χριστός) is head of the *church* (ἐκκλησίας),

C: he himself is savior of the *body* (σώματος).

---

20. For the text-critical reasons to take the plural "hearts" rather than the singular "heart" as the original reading, see Hoehner, *Ephesians*, 712 n. 4.

21. For text-critical discussions of Eph 5:22 for which there are variant readings that include a form of the verb "submit," see Metzger, *Textual Commentary*, 541; Hoehner, *Ephesians*, 730–31 n. 2.

D: ²⁴ But as the *church* (ἐκκλησία) submits to the *Christ* (Χριστῷ), so also the wives to their husbands in everything. ²⁵ Husbands, love your wives, *just as* (καθώς) also the *Christ* (Χριστός) loved the *church* (ἐκκλησίαν) and handed himself over for her, ²⁶ that he might sanctify her, cleansing her by the washing of the water in the word, ²⁷ that he might present to himself the *church* (ἐκκλησίαν) glorious, not having a blemish or wrinkle or any of such things, but that she might be holy and blameless.

    E: ²⁸ So ought also husbands to *love* (ἀγαπᾶν) their *own wives* (ἑαυτῶν γυναῖκας) as their *own* (ἑαυτῶν) bodies.

    E':   He who *loves* (ἀγαπῶν) his *own wife* (ἑαυτοῦ γυναῖκα) *loves* (ἀγαπᾷ) *himself* (ἑαυτόν).

D': ²⁹ For no one ever hates his own flesh but nurtures and cares for it, *just as* (καθώς) also the *Christ* (Χριστός) (nurtures and cares for) the *church* (ἐκκλησίαν),

    C':   ³⁰ for we are members of his *body* (σώματος).[22]

B': ³¹ "For this reason a *man* (ἄνθρωπος) shall leave his father and mother and shall cleave to his *wife* (γυναῖκα), and the two shall become one flesh." ³² This mystery is great, but I speak with reference to *Christ* (Χριστόν) and the *church* (ἐκκλησίαν).

A': ³³ In any case, also you, each one of you, should so love his own wife as himself, and the wife should *respect* (φοβῆται) her husband.

An A-B-C-D-E-E'-D'-C'-B'-A' chiastic structure secures the integrity of this second sub-unit in 5:21–33 within the twelfth unit of the Letter in 5:15–6:9. The only occurrences in this sub-unit of words referring to "respect"—"submitting to one another in respect (φόβῳ) for Christ" in 5:21 and "the wife should respect (φοβῆται) her husband" in 5:33—determine the parallelism of the A (5:21–22) and A' (5:33) elements of the chiasm.

---

22. There is a variant longer reading of Eph 5:30 that adds: "out of his flesh and out of his bones" (ἐκ τῆς σαρκὸς αὐτοῦ καὶ ἐκ τῶν ὀστέων αὐτοῦ). For an argument that this longer reading is original, see Peter R. Rodgers, "The Allusion to Genesis 2:23 at Ephesians 5:30," *JTS* 41 (1990): 92–94. Hoehner (*Ephesians*, 769) accepts it cautiously: "The longer reading is accepted with great hesitation." According to Metzger (*Textual Commentary*, 541), it is "probable that the longer readings reflect various scribal expansions derived from Gn 2.23 (where, however, the sequence is 'bone . . . flesh'), anticipatory to the quotation of Gn 2.24 in ver. 31."

References to a husband's relation to his wife as compared to Christ's relation to the church determine the parallelism of the B (5:23a) and B´ (5:31–32) elements of the chiasm. In 5:23a "the husband (ἀνήρ) is head of the wife (γυναικός) as also the Christ (Χριστός) is head of the church (ἐκκλησίας)" and in 5:31–32 "for this reason a man (ἄνθρωπος) shall leave his father and mother and shall cleave to his wife (γυναῖκα) . . . but I speak with reference to Christ (Χριστόν) and the church (ἐκκλησίαν).

The only occurrences in this sub-unit of the word for "body" in the genitive singular with reference to the church as the "body" of Christ (it appears in the accusative plural referring to the bodies of husbands in 5:28)—"he himself is savior of the body (σώματος)" in 5:23b and "we are members of his body (σώματος)" in 5:30—determine the parallelism of the C (5:23b) and C´ (5:30) elements of the chiasm.

The correspondence between "just as (καθώς) also the Christ (Χριστός) loved the church (ἐκκλησίαν)" in 5:25 and "just as (καθώς) also the Christ (Χριστός) does the church (ἐκκλησίαν)" in 5:29 indicates the parallelism between the D (5:24–27) and D´ (5:29) elements of the chiasm. In addition, the three references to "church" at the beginning (5:24), middle (5:25) and end (5:27), as well as the double reference to "Christ" (5:24, 25), secures the integrity of the D element.

Occurrences of terms for "love" and the words "his own wife/wives" and "himself"—"So ought also husbands to *love* (ἀγαπᾶν) their *own wives* (ἑαυτῶν γυναῖκας)" in 5:28a and "He who *loves* (ἀγαπῶν) his *own wife* (ἑαυτοῦ γυναῖκα) *loves* (ἀγαπᾷ) *himself* (ἑαυτόν)" in 5:28b—indicate the parallelism between the E (5:28a) and E´ (5:28b) elements at the center of the chiasm in this sub-unit.

Explicit terms for "love" in this sub-unit appear in 5:25: "husbands, love (ἀγαπᾶτε) your wives, as also the Christ loved (ἠγάπησεν) the church," in 5:28: "so ought also husbands to love (ἀγαπᾶν) their own wives as their own bodies. He who loves (ἀγαπῶν) his own wife loves (ἀγαπᾷ) himself," and in 5:33: "each one of you should thus love (ἀγαπάτω) his own wife as himself."

c. Children and Parents Respect One Another in Love (6:1–4)

A: [1] *Children* (τὰ τέκνα), obey your parents in the *Lord* (κυρίῳ), for this is right.

B: [2] "Honor *your* (σου) father and mother,"

C: which is *the first commandment with a promise,*

B´:   [3] "that it may be well with *you* (σοι) and you may live long on the earth."

A´:   [4] And the fathers, do not anger your *children* (τὰ τέκνα), but bring them up in the training and instruction of the *Lord* (κυρίου).

An A-B-C-B'-A' chiastic pattern establishes the integrity of this third sub-unit in 6:1–4 within the twelfth unit in 5:15–6:9. The only occurrences in this sub-unit of "children" and "Lord"—"children (τὰ τέκνα), obey your parents in the Lord (κυρίῳ)" in 6:1 and "do not anger your children (τὰ τέκνα), but bring them up in the training and instruction of the Lord (κυρίου)" in 6:4—determine the parallelism of the A (6:1) and A' (6:4) elements of the chiasm.

The only occurrences in this sub-unit of the second-person singular pronoun "you"—"Honor your (σου) father and mother" in 6:2a and "that it may be well with you (σοι)" in 6:3—determine the parallelism of the B (6:2a) and B' (6:3) elements of the chiasm. The unique appearance in this sub-unit of "the first commandment with a promise" singles out the unparalleled C (6:2b) element at the center of the chiasm.

Although no explicit terms for "love" appear in this sub-unit, "obey" (6:1), "honor" (6:2), and "do not anger" (6:4), as we will see later, can be considered a conceptual part of the central theme of love in Ephesians.

d. Slaves and Masters Respect One Another in Love (6:5–9)

A: 5 Slaves, obey the earthly *masters* (κυρίοις) with respect and trembling in the sincerity of *your* (ὑμῶν) heart as to the Christ,
B: 6 not according to eye-service as people-pleasers but as *slaves* (δοῦλοι) of Christ *doing* (ποιοῦντες) the will of God wholeheartedly,
C: 7 with *good will rendering service* as to the Lord and not to people,
B':   8 knowing that whatever good each *does* (ποιήσῃ), this he will receive back from the Lord, whether *slave* (δοῦλος) or free.
A':   9 And the *masters* (κύριοι), do the same things to them, stopping the threatening, knowing that both their Master and *yours* (ὑμῶν) is in heaven and there is no partiality with him.

An A-B-C-B'-A' chiastic structure establishes the integrity of this fourth and final sub-unit in 6:5–9 within the twelfth unit of the Letter in 5:15–6:9. The only occurrences not only in this sub-unit but in the Letter of the word for "master" in the plural together with the only occurrences in this sub-unit of the genitive plural pronoun "your"—"obey the earthly masters (κυρίοις) . . . in the sincerity of *your* (ὑμῶν) heart" in 6:5 and "the masters (κύριοι), do the same things to them . . . knowing that both their Master and *yours* (ὑμῶν) is in heaven" in 6:9—determines the parallelism of the A (6:5) and A' (6:9) elements of the chiasm.

Occurrences of the term for "slave" as the subject of the verb "do"— "as slaves (δοῦλοι) of Christ doing (ποιοῦντες) the will of God" in 6:6 and "whatever good each does (ποιήσῃ), this he will receive back from the Lord, whether slave (δοῦλος) or free" in 6:8—determine the parallelism of the B (6:6) and B´ (6:8) elements of the chiasm. The unique appearance not only in this sub-unit but in the entire Letter of "with good will rendering service" singles out the unparalleled C (6:7) element at the center of this chiasm.

Although no explicit terms for "love" appear in this sub-unit, "obey with respect and trembling in the sincerity of your heart" (6:5) and "do the same things to them, stopping the threatening" (6:9), as we will see later, can be considered a conceptual part of the dominant theme of love in Ephesians.

13. Be Empowered in Love to Withstand Evil (6:10–13)

> A: ¹⁰ Finally, be empowered in the Lord, that is, in the might of his strength. ¹¹ Put on the *full armor of God* (πανοπλίαν τοῦ θεοῦ) so that you may *have the power* (δύνασθαι) *to stand* (στῆναι) against the schemes of the devil;
> B: ¹² for our struggle is not *against* (πρός) blood and flesh but *against* (πρός) the rulers,
> B´: *against* (πρός) authorities, *against* (πρός) the cosmic powers of this darkness, *against* (πρός) the spiritual beings of evil in the heavenly places.
> A´: ¹³ Therefore, take up the *full armor of God* (πανοπλίαν τοῦ θεοῦ), that you may *have the power* (δυνηθῆτε) *to withstand* (ἀντιστῆναι) on the evil day and having done everything, *to stand* (στῆναι).

An A-B-B´-A´ chiastic pattern establishes the integrity of the thirteenth unit in 6:10–13. The only occurrences not only in this unit but in the entire Letter of "full armor of God" as well as the only occurrences in this unit of the verbs "have the power" and "to stand"—"put on the full armor of God (πανοπλίαν τοῦ θεοῦ) so that you may have the power (δύνασθαι) to stand (στῆναι)" in 6:11 and "take up the full armor of God (πανοπλίαν τοῦ θεοῦ), that you may have the power (δυνηθῆτε) . . . to withstand (ἀντιστῆναι) . . . and . . . to stand (στῆναι)" in 6:13—determine the parallelism of the A (6:10–11) and A´ (6:13) elements of the chiasm.

The triplet of occurrences of the preposition "against"—"against (πρός) authorities, against (πρός) the cosmic powers of this darkness, against (πρός) the spiritual beings of evil in the heavenly places" in 6:12b, which stand in explanatory apposition to the double occurrence of the preposition "against" in 6:12a—"our struggle is not against (πρός) flesh and blood but *against* (πρός) the rulers," distinguishes the parallelism of the B (6:12a) and B´ (6:12b) elements at the center of the chiasm in this thirteenth unit.

Although no explicit terms for "love" appear in this unit, "be empowered" (6:10) and "have the power" (6:11, 13), as we will see later, are part of the key theme of love in Ephesians.

14. Beloved Tychicus Will Encourage Your Hearts in Love (6:14–22)

A: [14] Stand then having girded *your* (ὑμῶν) waists in truth and having put on the breastplate of righteousness,

B: [15] and having shod the feet in preparedness from the *gospel* (εὐαγγελίου) of peace, [16] in all things having taken up the shield of faith, in which you have the power to extinguish all the flaming arrows of the evil one;

C: [17] and *receive* the *helmet* of salvation and the *sword* of the Spirit, which is the *word of God.*

B′: [18] Through every prayer and petition praying at every opportunity in the Spirit, and for this purpose being alert in all persistence and petition for all the holy ones, [19] especially for me, that speech may be given to me in opening my mouth, in boldness to make known the mystery of the *gospel* (εὐαγγελίου), [20] for which I am an ambassador in chain, that in it I might speak boldly as it is necessary for me to speak.

A′: [21] That *you* (ὑμεῖς) also may know the things about me, what I am doing, Tychicus, the beloved brother and faithful minister in the Lord, will make everything known to *you* (ὑμῖν), [22] whom I am sending to *you* (ὑμᾶς) for this very purpose, that you may know the things concerning us and that he may encourage *your* (ὑμῶν) hearts.

As in 4:1, 17; 5:1, 7, 15, the inferential conjunction "then" (οὖν) in 6:14 introduces a new unit in 6:14–22. After the inclusion formed by the occurrences of the aorist active infinitive "to stand" (στῆναι) in 6:11 and 6:13, indicating the integrity of 6:10–13 as a distinct unit, "stand then" (στῆτε οὖν) begins to express the result or inference from what has just been stated about "standing."[23]

An A-B-C-B′-A′ chiastic structure confirms the integrity of the fourteenth unit in 6:14–22. The only occurrences in this unit of the second-person plural pronoun "you"—"stand then having girded your (ὑμῶν) waists" in 6:14 and "that you (ὑμεῖς) may also know about me . . . Tychicus . . . will make everything known to *you* (ὑμῖν)" in 6:21 as well as "whom I am sending to *you* (ὑμᾶς) . . . that he may encourage *your* (ὑμῶν) hearts" in 6:22—determines the parallelism between the A (6:14) and A′ (6:21–22) elements of the chiasm.

Thus, this parallelism between 6:14 and 6:21–22 based on the pronoun "you" indicates that 6:21–22 belongs with 6:14–20, and not, as many scholars present it, with 6:23–24, where the pronoun "you" does not

---

23. Hoehner, *Ephesians,* 837.

occur. Furthermore, the occurrence of the first-person singular pronoun in 6:21—"that you may also know about me (ἐμέ)—confirms the connection of 6:21–22 with the preceding verses, which also contain references to this pronoun—"for me (ἐμοῦ), that speech may be given to me (μοι) in opening my (μου) mouth . . . that about it I might speak boldly as it is necessary for me (με) to speak" in 6:19–20. The first-person singular pronoun, however, does not appear in 6:23–24.

The only occurrences in this unit of the genitive singular "gospel"—"in preparedness from the gospel (εὐαγγελίου) of peace" in 6:15 and "to make known the mystery of the gospel (εὐαγγελίου)" in 6:19—determine the parallelism between the B (6:15–16) and B′ (6:18–20) elements of the chiasm. The unique appearances not only in this unit but in the entire Letter of "receive," "helmet," "sword," and "word of God" distinguish the unparalleled C (6:17) element at the center of the chiasm in this fourteenth unit.

An explicit term for "love" appears in 6:21: "Tychicus, the beloved (ἀγαπητός) brother" will make known everything to you and encourage your hearts, as a gift of love. In addition, "having the power" in 6:16 and praying for all the holy ones and for Paul in 6:18–19, as we will see later, are closely related components of the prominent theme of love in Ephesians.

15. Peace, Love, and Grace (6:23–24)

> A: [23] Peace to the brothers and *love* (ἀγάπη) with faith from God the
>   Father and the *Lord Jesus Christ* (κυρίου Ἰησοῦ Χριστοῦ).
>   B: [24] *Grace* be with *all*
> A′: who *love* (ἀγαπώντων) *our Lord Jesus Christ* (κύριον ἡμῶν Ἰησοῦν
>   Χριστόν) in immortality.

A simple A-B-A′ chiastic pattern establishes the integrity of the fifteenth and final unit in 6:23–24. The only occurrences in this unit of terms for "love" (ἀγάπη in 6:23 and ἀγαπώντων in 6:24) and the "Lord Jesus Christ" (κυρίου Ἰησοῦ Χριστοῦ in 6:23 and κύριον ἡμῶν Ἰησοῦν Χριστόν in 6:24) determine the parallelism of the A (6:23) and A′ (6:24b) elements of the chiasm. The unique appearances of "grace" and "all" distinguish the unparalleled B (6:24a) element at the center of the chiasm in this fifteenth unit.

The final two explicit terms for "love" appear in this final unit: "Peace to the brothers and love (ἀγάπη)" in 6:23 and "grace be with all who love (ἀγαπώντων)" in 6:24. These occurrences of both the noun and verb for "love" thus climax the preeminent theme of love in the Letter to the Ephesians.

B. The Macro-chiastic Structure of the Letter

Having illustrated the various micro-chiastic structures operative in the fifteen distinct units of the Letter to the Ephesians, we will now demonstrate how these fifteen main units form an A-B-C-D-E-F-G-H-G′-F′-E′-D′-C′-B′-A′ macro-chiastic structure embracing the entire Letter.[24]

A: Grace and Peace (1:1–2)
A′:   Peace, Love, and Grace (6:23–24)

Repetitions of significant words indicate the parallelism between the opening and first A unit (1:1–2) and the closing final and fifteenth A′ unit (6:23–24) within the macro-chiastic structure of the Letter to the Ephesians. The opening greeting of "grace (χάρις) to you" in 1:2 of the A unit parallels the final greeting of "grace (χάρις) be with all" in 6:24 of the A′ unit. And the opening greeting of "peace from God our Father and the Lord Jesus Christ (εἰρήνη ἀπὸ θεοῦ πατρὸς ἡμῶν καὶ κυρίου Ἰησοῦ Χριστοῦ)" in 1:2 of the A unit parallels the final greeting of "peace (εἰρήνη) to the brothers and love with faith from God the Father and the Lord Jesus Christ (ἀπὸ θεοῦ πατρὸς καὶ κυρίου Ἰησοῦ Χριστοῦ) in 6:23 of the A′ unit.

B: To the Praise of His Glory in Love (1:3–14)
B′:   Beloved Tychicus Will Encourage Your Hearts in Love (6:14–22)

"That we might be holy (ἁγίους)" in 1:4 and "with the Holy (ἁγίῳ) Spirit" in 1:13 of the B unit parallel "for all the holy ones (ἁγίων)" in 6:18 of the B′ unit. The only adjectival uses of a term for "love" in Ephesians occur in the B and B′ units. "In love (ἀγάπη)" in 1:4 and "in the Beloved (ἠγαπημένῳ)" with reference to Christ in 1:6 of the B unit provide parallels to "the beloved (ἀγαπητὸς) brother" with reference to Tychicus in 6:21 of the B′ unit. "Having made known (γνωρίσας) to us the mystery (τὸ μυστήριον)" in 1:9 of the B unit parallels "to make known (γνωρίσαι) the mystery (τὸ μυστήριον)" in 6:19 of the B′ unit.

The word of "truth" (ἀληθείας) in 1:13 of the B unit parallels in "truth" (ἀληθείας) in 6:14 of the B′ unit. "The gospel (εὐαγγέλιον) of your salvation" in 1:13 of the B unit parallels "the gospel (εὐαγγελίου) of peace" in 6:15 and "the mystery of the gospel (εὐαγγελίου)" in 6:19 of the B′ unit. "The gospel of your salvation (σωτηρίας)" in 1:13 of the B unit parallels "helmet of salvation (σωτηρίου)" in 6:17 of the B′ unit. And "with the Holy Spirit (πνεύματι) of the promise" in 1:13 of the B unit parallels "the sword of the Spirit (πνεύματος)" in 6:17 and "in the Spirit (πνεύματι)" in 6:18 of the B′ unit.

---

24. For some recent alternative structures of the entire Letter, see Peter Scott Cameron, "The Structure of Ephesians," *Filologia Neotestamentaria* 3 (1990): 3–17; Cynthia Briggs Kittredge, *Community and Authority: The Rhetoric of Obedience in the Pauline Tradition* (HTS 45; Harrisburg, PA: Trinity Press International, 1998), 119–45; Hoehner, *Ephesians*, 61–69; George K. Barr, *Scalometry and the Pauline Epistles* (JSNTSup 261; London: Clark, 2004), 66–74; Friedrich Gustav Lang, "Ebenmass im Epheserbrief: Stichometrische Kompositionsanalyse," *NovT* 46 (2004): 143–63.

C: The Gift of Christ in Love as Head Over All to the Church (1:15–23)
C′: To Be Empowered in Love to Withstand Evil (6:10–13)

The only two occurrences in Ephesians of the phrase "the might of his strength"—"according to the working of the might of his strength (τοῦ κράτους τῆς ἰσχύος αὐτοῦ)" in 1:19 and "in the might of his strength (τῷ κράτει τῆς ἰσχύος αὐτοῦ)" in 6:10—appear in the C and C′ units. "In the heavenly places" (ἐν τοῖς ἐπουρανίοις) occurs in 1:20 of the C unit and in 6:12 of the C′ unit. And "every ruler (ἀρχῆς) and authority (ἐξουσίας)" in 1:21 of the C unit parallels "against the rulers (ἀρχάς), against the authorities (ἐξουσίας)" in 6:12 of the C′ unit.

D: Walking by the Great Love with Which He Loved Us (2:1–10)
D′: Walk in Love as Those Who Are Wise (5:15–6:9)

The two occurrences of the verb "walk" that form a literary inclusion framing the D unit—"in which you once walked (περιεπατήσατε)" in 2:2 and "that we might walk (περιπατήσωμεν) in them" in 2:10—parallel the occurrence of "walk" that opens the D′ unit in 5:15—"Watch then how carefully you are walking (περιπατεῖτε)." "Doing the wishes (ποιοῦντες τὰ θελήματα) of the flesh" in 2:3 of the D unit antithetically parallels "doing the will (ποιοῦντες τὸ θέλημα) of God" in 6:6 of the D′ unit. And "because of his great love (ἀγάπην) with which he loved (ἠγάπησεν) us" in 2:4 of the D unit parallels "husbands, love (ἀγαπᾶτε) your wives, as also the Christ loved (ἠγάπησεν) the church" in 5:25 and "so ought also husbands to love (ἀγαπᾶν) their own wives ... he who loves (ἀγαπῶν) his own wife loves (ἀγαπᾷ) himself" in 5:28 of the D′ unit.

E: The One New Person as the Gift of Peace in Love (2:11–22)
E′: Walk as Children of Light in Love (5:7–14)

"Remember that once (ποτε) you, the Gentiles in the flesh ... were (ἦτε) at that time without Christ ... but now (νυνί) in Christ Jesus you who once (ποτε) were far away have become near" in 2:11–13 of the E unit parallels "you were (ἦτε) once (ποτε) darkness, but now (νῦν) you are light in the Lord" in 5:8 of the E′ unit.[25] The temple holy "in the Lord" (ἐν κυρίῳ) that includes the audience in 2:21–22 of the E unit parallels the audience's now being light "in the Lord" (ἐν κυρίῳ) in 5:8 of the E′ unit.[26] And "you are fellow

25. That the only two occurrences in Ephesians of the second-person plural indicative imperfect active verb "you were" (ἦτε) are in 2:12 and 5:8 enhances this chiastic connection.
26. These are the only occurrences of being "in the Lord" (ἐν κυρίῳ) with reference to the audience at this point in Ephesians. The intervening occurrences in 4:1, 17 refer to Paul. There are subsequent occurrences in 6:1, 10, 21.

citizens (συμπολῖται) with the holy ones" in 2:19 together with "in whom you also are being built together (συνοικοδομεῖσθε) into a dwelling place of God" in 2:22 of the E unit antithetically parallel "do not become fellow sharers (συμμέτοχοι)" in 5:7 and "do not be connected with (συγκοινωνεῖτε) the unfruitful works of the darkness" in 5:11 of the E´ unit.

> F: Paul's Gift to Make Known the Mystery of Christ in Love (3:1–13)
> F´: Walk in Love as Christ Loved Us (5:1–6)

There are five references to Christ in the F unit—"prisoner of the Christ (Χριστοῦ)" in 3:1, "mystery of the Christ (Χριστοῦ)" in 3:4, "in Christ (Χριστῷ) Jesus" in 3:6, "wealth of the Christ (Χριστοῦ)" in 3:8, and "in Christ (Χριστῷ) Jesus our Lord" in 3:11, as well as two references to Christ in the F´ unit—"Christ (Χριστός) loved us" in 5:2 and "in the kingdom of Christ (Χριστοῦ)" in 5:5. In addition, there are four references to God in both the F—"grace of God (τοῦ θεοῦ)" in 3:2, 7, "in God (τῷ θεῷ) who created all things" in 3:9, "wisdom of God (τοῦ θεοῦ)" in 3:10—and F´ units—"imitators of God (τοῦ θεοῦ)" in 5:1, "sacrifice to God (τῷ θεῷ)" in 5:2, "kingdom of the Christ and God (θεοῦ)" in 5:5, and "wrath of God (τοῦ θεοῦ)" in 5:6. Finally, "fellow heirs" (συγκληρονόμα) in 3:6 of the F unit parallels "inheritance" (κληρονομίαν) in 5:5 of the F´ unit.

> G: To Know the Love of Christ That Surpasses Knowledge (3:14–21)
> G´: Walk as the New Person in the Truth of Christ's Love (4:17–32)

"To be strengthened with power through his Spirit (πνεύματος)" in 3:16 of the G unit parallels "do not grieve the Holy Spirit (πνεῦμα) of God" in 4:30 of the G´ unit. "In the inner person (ἔσω ἄνθρωπον)" in 3:16 of the G unit parallels the "old person" (παλαιὸν ἄνθρωπον) in 4:22 and the "new person" (καινὸν ἄνθρωπον) in 4:24 of the G´ unit. "That the Christ (Χριστόν) may dwell through faith in your hearts" in 3:17, so that "you may know the love of Christ (Χριστοῦ) that surpasses knowledge" in 3:19 of the G unit parallels "but you have not so learned the Christ (Χριστόν)" in 4:20 of the G´ unit. And "to him be glory in the church and in Christ (ἐν Χριστῷ) Jesus" in 3:21 of the G unit parallels "just as also God in Christ (ἐν Χριστῷ) was gracious to us" in 4:32 of the G´ unit.

> H: Walk toward the Unity of All in Love (4:1–16)

The unique occurrences not only in this H unit in 4:1–16 but in the entire Letter of the key terms "unity"—"to preserve the unity (ἑνότητα) of the Spirit" in 4:3 and "until we all attain to the unity (ἑνότητα) of the faith" in 4:13, "measure"—"according to the measure (μέτρον) of the gift of the Christ" in 4:7, "to the measure (μέτρον) of the maturity of the fullness of the Christ" in 4:13, and "according to the working in measure (μέτρῳ) of each individual part" in 4:16, and "ascend-descend"—"having ascended (ἀναβάς) on high" in 4:8, "what is the meaning 'he ascended (ἀνέβη),' except that he also descended (κατέβη)" in 4:9, and "he who descended (καταβάς) is himself also he who ascended (ἀναβάς)" in 4:10—distinguish this H unit as the unparalleled and pivotal unit at the center of the macro-chiastic structure of Ephesians.

In addition, this is the only unit in the Letter that contains three of the six occurrences of the dynamic prepositional phrase "in love" (ἐν ἀγάπῃ) in 4:2, 15, 16), which, as we will see, is a key component of the major theme of love in the Letter to the Ephesians.

C. Overview of the Parallels and Pivot of the Macro-chiasm in Ephesians

A 1:1–2: grace (χάρις, v. 2)—peace from God our Father and the Lord Jesus Christ (εἰρήνη ἀπὸ θεοῦ πατρὸς ἡμῶν καὶ κυρίου Ἰησοῦ Χριστοῦ, v. 2)
A′ 6:23–24: Peace (Εἰρήνη, v. 23)—from God the Father and the Lord Jesus Christ (ἀπὸ θεοῦ πατρὸς καὶ κυρίου Ἰησοῦ Χριστοῦ, v. 23)—grace (χάρις, v. 24)

B 1:3–14: Spiritual (πνευματικῇ, v. 3)—holy (ἁγίους, v. 4)—Beloved (ἠγαπημένῳ, v. 6)—having made known . . . the mystery (γνωρίσας . . . τὸ μυστήριον, v. 9)—truth (ἀληθείας, v. 13)—gospel (εὐαγγέλιον, v. 13)—salvation (σωτηρίας, v. 13)—Spirit (πνεύματι, v. 13)—Holy (ἁγίῳ, v. 13)
B′ 6:14–22: Spirit (πνεύματος, v. 17)—Spirit (πνεύματι, v. 18)—holy ones (ἁγίων, v. 18)—beloved (ἀγαπητός, v. 21)—to make known the mystery (γνωρίσαι τὸ μυστήριον, v. 19)—truth (ἀληθείᾳ, v. 14)—gospel (εὐαγγελίου, v. 15)—gospel (εὐαγγελίου, v. 19)—salvation (σωτηρίου, v. 17)

C 1:15–23: the might of his strength (τοῦ κράτους τῆς ἰσχύος αὐτοῦ, v. 19)—in the heavenly places (ἐν τοῖς ἐπουρανίοις, v. 20)—ruler . . . authority (ἀρχῆς . . . ἐξουσίας, v. 21)
C′ 6:10–13: the might of his strength (τῷ κράτει τῆς ἰσχύος αὐτοῦ, v. 10)—in the heavenly places (ἐν τοῖς ἐπουρανίοις, v. 12)—rulers . . . authorities (ἀρχάς . . . ἐξουσίας, v. 12)

D 2:1–10: you walked (περιεπατήσατε, v. 2)—we might walk (περιπατήσωμεν, v. 10)—doing the wishes (ποιοῦντες τὰ θελήματα, v. 3)—love . . . he loved (ἀγάπην . . . ἠγάπησεν, v. 4)
D′ 5:15–6:9: you are walking (περιπατεῖτε, v. 15)—doing the will (ποιοῦντες τὸ θέλημα, v. 6)—love . . . he loved (ἀγαπᾶτε . . . ἠγάπησεν, v. 25)—to love . . . loves . . . loves (ἀγαπᾶν . . . ἀγαπῶν . . . ἀγαπᾷ, v. 28)

E 2:11–22: once (ποτε, v. 11) . . . you were (ἦτε, v. 12)—now . . . once (νυνὶ . . . ποτε, v. 13)—fellow citizens (συμπολῖται, v. 19)—in the Lord (ἐν κυρίῳ, v. 21)—you are being built together (συνοικοδομεῖσθε, v. 22)
E´ 5:7–14: you were . . . once . . . now (ἦτε . . . ποτε . . . νῦν, v. 8)—in the Lord (ἐν κυρίῳ, v. 8)—fellow sharers (συμμέτοχοι, v. 7)—be connected with (συγκοινωνεῖτε, v. 11)

F 3:1–13: of Christ (Χριστοῦ, v. 1)—of God (τοῦ θεοῦ, v. 2)—of Christ (Χριστοῦ, v. 4)—fellow heirs (συγκληρονόμα, v. 6)—in Christ (Χριστῷ, v. 6)—of God (τοῦ θεοῦ, v. 7)—of Christ (Χριστοῦ, v. 8)—in God (τῷ θεῷ, v. 9)—of God (τοῦ θεοῦ, v. 10)—in Christ (Χριστῷ, v. 11)
F´ 5:1–6: of God (τοῦ θεοῦ, v. 1)—Christ (Χριστός, v. 2)—to God (τῷ θεῷ, v. 2)—inheritance (κληρονομίαν, v. 5)—of Christ (Χριστοῦ, v. 5)—of God (θεοῦ, v. 5)—of God (τοῦ θεοῦ, v. 6)

G 3:14–21: Spirit (πνεύματος, v. 16)—inner person (ἔσω ἄνθρωπον, v. 16)—Christ (Χριστόν, v. 17)—of Christ (Χριστοῦ, v. 19)—in Christ (ἐν Χριστῷ, v. 21)
G´ 4:17–32: Christ (Χριστόν, v. 20)—old person (παλαιὸν ἄνθρωπον, v. 22)—new person (καινὸν ἄνθρωπον, v. 24)—Spirit (πνεῦμα, v. 30)—in Christ (ἐν Χριστῷ, v. 32)

H 4:1–16: in love (ἐν ἀγάπῃ, vv. 2, 15, 16)—unity (ἑνότητα, vv. 3, 13)—measure (μέτρον, vv. 7, 13)—in measure (μέτρῳ, v. 16)—ascended (ἀναβάς, vv. 8, 10)—ascended (ἀνέβη, v. 9)—descended (κατέβη, v. 9)—descended (καταβάς, v. 10)

D. Outline of the Macro-chiastic Structure of Ephesians

A: 1:1–2: Grace and Peace
B: 1:3–14: To the Praise of His Glory in Love
C: 1:15–23: The Gift of Christ in Love as Head Over All to the Church
D: 2:1–10: Walking by the Great Love with Which He Loved Us
E: 2:11–22: The Peace That Establishes Unity as a Gift of Love
F: 3:1–13: Paul's Gift to Make Known the Mystery of Christ in Love
G: 3:14–21: To Know the Love of Christ That Surpasses Knowledge
H: 4:1–16: Walk toward the Unity of All in Love
G´: 4:17–32: Walk as the New Person in the Truth of Christ's Love
F´: 5:1–6: Walk in Love as Christ Loved Us
E´: 5:7–14: Walk as Children of Light in Love
D´: 5:15–6:9: Walk in Love as Those Who Are Wise
    (1) 5:15–20: Always Thanking God in Love
    (2) 5:21–33: Husbands and Wives Love One Another

(3) 6:1–4: Children and Parents Respect One Another in Love
(4) 6:5–9: Slaves and Masters Respect One Another in Love
C′: 6:10–13: Be Empowered in Love to Withstand Evil
B′: 6:14–22: Beloved Tychicus Will Encourage Your Hearts in Love
A′: 6:23–24: Peace, Love, and Grace

E. Overview of the Theme of Love
in the Fifteen Chiastic Units of Ephesians

(1) A 1:1–2: Grace and peace as gifts of love from God and Christ.

(2) B 1:3–14: "that we might be holy and blameless before him in love (ἐν ἀγάπῃ, 1:4)" and "he graced us in the Beloved (ἠγαπημένῳ, 1:6)"

(3) C 1:15–23: "your love (ἀγάπην, 1:15) for all the holy ones"

(4) D 2:1–10: "because of his great love (ἀγάπην) with which he loved (ἠγάπησεν) us" (2:4)

(5) E 2:11–22: Christ's gift of peace (2:14, 15, 17) is a gift of love.

(6) F 3:1–13: The references to God's "grace" and "giving" (3:2, 7, 8) refer to God's love.

(7) G 3:14–21: "in love (ἐν ἀγάπῃ) rooted and grounded" (3:17) and "to know the love (ἀγάπην) of the Christ that surpasses knowledge" (3:19)

(8) H 4:1–16: "forbearing one another in love (ἐν ἀγάπῃ)" (4:2)

"being truthful in love (ἐν ἀγάπῃ)" (4:15)

"the building up of itself in love (ἐν ἀγάπῃ)" (4:16)

(9) G′ 4:17–32: The references to "give grace" (4:29) and "being gracious . . . as also God in Christ was gracious to us" (4:32) refer to God's love.

(10) F′ 5:1–6: "beloved (ἀγαπητά) children" (5:1) and "walk in love (ἐν ἀγάπῃ) just as also the Christ loved (ἠγάπησεν) us" (5:2)

(11) E′ 5:7–14: That you are "light" (5:8) is a gift of God's love and the

reference to "approving what is pleasing to the Lord" (5:10) is part of the love theme.

(12) D´ 5:15–6:9: "love (ἀγαπᾶτε) your wives as also the Christ loved (ἠγάπησεν) the church" (5:25); "so ought also husbands to love (ἀγαπᾶν) their own wives . . . he who loves (ἀγαπῶν) his own wife loves (ἀγαπᾷ) himself" (5:28); "each one of you should thus love (ἀγαπάτω) his own wife as himself" (5:33)

(13) C´ 6:10–13: The references to "be empowered" (6:10) and "have the power" (6:11, 13) are gifts of God's love.

(14) B´ 6:14–22: "Tychicus the beloved (ἀγαπητός) brother" (6:21)

(15) A´ 6:23–24: "Peace to the brothers and love (ἀγάπη)" (6:23) and "grace be with all who love (ἀγαπώντων) the Lord Jesus Christ in immortality" (6:24)

F. Summary

1. There are fifteen distinct units in the Letter to the Ephesians with each exhibiting its own micro-chiastic structure(s).

2. The fifteen units comprising Ephesians form a macro-chiastic structure with seven pairs of parallel units and an unparalleled pivotal unit (4:1–16) at the center of the chiasm.

3. Explicit terms for "love" appear in nine of the fifteen units of the Letter. Most notably, three of the six occurrences of the dynamic prepositional phrase "in love" appear in the pivotal unit (4:1–16) at the center of the chiasm in 4:2, 15, 16. The other six units contain important references to the major theme of love that pervades the Letter to the Ephesians.

CHAPTER 3

Ephesians 1:1–2: Grace and Peace (A)

A: ¹ᵃ Paul, apostle of *Christ* Jesus
   B: ¹ᵇ through the will of *God,*
      C: ¹ᶜ to the holy ones who are *in* Ephesus,
      C′:   ¹ᵈ the believers who are *in* Christ Jesus,
   B′:   ²ᵃ grace to you and peace from *God* our Father
A′:²ᵇ and the Lord Jesus *Christ.*¹

A. Audience Response to Ephesians 1:1–2

1. Eph 1:1a (A): Paul, Apostle of Christ Jesus

In the opening A (1:1a) element of the chiasm that commences the Letter the audience are addressed by an author-sender who identifies himself as "Paul, apostle of Christ Jesus."² That Paul is an "apostle" (ἀπόστολος) means that he has been "sent out" or authorized to be a delegate or representative to deliver a message on behalf of the one who sent him.³ That Paul is an apostle "of Christ Jesus" tells the audience not only that Paul has been sent by and speaks with the authority of Christ Jesus, but that he is in

---

1. For the establishment of Eph 1:1–2 as a chiasm, see ch. 2.
2. For the preference of the variant reading "Jesus Christ," see Hoehner, *Ephesians*, 133–34 n. 2.
3. Abbott, *Ephesians*, 1. Paul K. Moser ("Apostle," *Eerdmans Dictionary of the Bible* [ed. David Noel Freedman; Grand Rapids: Eerdmans, 2000], 78) defines "apostle" as " 'One sent out,' generally to proclaim a message. NT use is continuous with the OT idea of a special messenger from God." Jan-Adolf Bühner, "ἀπόστολος," *EDNT* 1.143: "Paul employs the concept ἀπόστολος in the service of an emphatically dignified and authoritative self-introduction . . . With this word he describes his task of proclaiming the gospel: he is authorized, as a messenger and representative of the crucified and risen Lord, to bring the gospel to the churches of the Gentile Christians."

service or allegiance to Christ Jesus to whom he belongs as an apostle.[4] This introductory phrase, then, attunes the audience to hear what Christ Jesus himself is going to communicate to them through his devoted apostle Paul in the Letter to follow.

2. Eph 1:1b (B): Through the Will of God

In the B (1:1b) element of the chiasm the audience hear that it is "through the will of God" that Paul is an apostle of Christ Jesus. This communicates three things to the audience: First, Paul is an apostle of Christ Jesus not because of his own initiative, merit, or accomplishment but because he has been chosen, appointed, and thus graced by God.[5] Second, as an apostle Paul speaks with an authority that comes not only from Christ Jesus but through the very "will" (θελήματος)—the salvific purpose or plan—of God himself.[6] And third, as an apostle of Christ Jesus Paul is playing an important role in accord with God's salvific "will" or "decision" that demands his obedience

---

4. Bühner, "ἀπόστολος," 143–44: "The meaning of ἀπόστολος is tied to the peculiar character the word has attained as a result of popular-juridical usage which has drawn on its Hebrew equivalent, šālîaḥ. Already according to pre-NT legal practice, which the rabbinic sources merely fix in written form, the šālîaḥ is the direct representative of the one who sends him and can in that person's place act in a way that is authoritative and legally binding. He is obligated to strict obedience and to act in all matters in the best interests of the one who sends him. The linking of the term 'apostle' with legal titles which point to the perpetual bond to the one who sends and the task given by him to the Church corresponds to the custom of masters who appointed deputies as their representatives in charge of the household. One must add, finally, the countless observations which testify that not only Paul's calling but also his understanding of his mission as a whole is to be understood from the perspective of the OT prophets: in post-biblical Judaism the prophet was also called a šālîaḥ of God." See also Francis H. Agnew, "The Origin of the NT Apostle-Concept: A Review of Research," *JBL* 105 (1986): 75–96; Paul W. Barnett, "Apostle," *DPL*, 45–51. Hoehner, *Ephesians*, 135–36: "In the present context Paul has the office of apostle in mind, declaring that he is an official delegate possessed by Jesus Christ for the purpose of propagating his message. . . . Paul envisions that he is not only owned by Christ but is a fully authorized ambassador sent by him." O'Brien, *Ephesians*, 84: "To speak of himself as an apostle of Christ Jesus not only signifies that he belongs to Christ, but also that he is a messenger who is fully authorized and sent by him. As an apostle he has the authority to proclaim the gospel in both oral and written form, as well as to establish and build up churches."

5. Hoehner, *Ephesians*, 136: "It was not by personal drive or presumptuous human ambition but by God's will and initiative that Paul was made an apostle." On Paul's calling to be an apostle, O'Brien (*Ephesians*, 84) states: "He had not appointed himself to this position; God chose him. Hence the words by the will of God have overtones of God's unmerited grace, and emphasize that there was no personal merit on Paul's part either in becoming an apostle or continuing as one."

6. Margaret Y. MacDonald, *Colossians and Ephesians* (SP 17; Collegeville, MN: Liturgical Press, 2000), 191: "To state that Paul is an apostle 'by the will of God' is to stress Paul's apostolic authority."

and the audience's attention.[7] The audience are thus poised to hear what Christ Jesus has sent Paul to communicate to them that is in accord with the authority of the decisive will of God.

3. Eph 1:1c (C): To the Holy Ones Who Are in Ephesus

Paul addresses the Letter "to the holy ones who are in Ephesus" in the C (1:1c) element of the chiasm.[8] Paul thus makes his audience aware that God has set them, like his chosen people of Israel of old, apart from other peoples as "holy ones" (ἁγίοις), consecrated for service to God.[9] That Paul acknowledges the location of his audience in the Asia Minor metropolis of Ephesus reminds them that God has separated them from the rest of the people of this large city and region, who are living in a Roman pagan environment, to live in this same social, political, and religious environment as God's "holy ones." By addressing his audience as those graced by God to be "holy ones," Paul draws them to himself, similarly graced to be an authoritative apostle of Christ Jesus.[10] An audience graciously established and empowered to be holy by God are thus ready to hear from Paul graciously established and empowered to be an apostle by God.

4. Eph 1:1d (C'): The Believers Who Are in Christ Jesus

The C' element, "the believers who are in Christ Jesus" (1:1d), parallels the C element, "to the holy ones who are in Ephesus" (1:1c), as the central and pivotal elements of the chiasm. The audience of the holy ones, who are geographically and physically located "in" (ἐν) Ephesus, Paul further

---

7. Barth (Ephesians 1–3, 65) explains that " 'God's decision' describes an action and manifestation of the One who is living, personal, wise and powerful. An event in God himself is now revealed. This event is creating history and requiring obedience."

8. On the acceptance of the words "in Ephesus" as the original reading, see ch. 1.

9. O'Brien, Ephesians, 87: "The identification of the readers as 'saints' (lit. 'holy ones') is Paul's regular description of Christians. The antecedents of the term are to be found in the Old Testament. Israel was God's holy people (Exod. 19:6), chosen by him and appointed to his service. Since the one who had brought them into a covenant relationship was holy, Israel herself was to be a holy nation (Lev. 11:44; 19:2, etc.). Christians are 'saints', not in the sense that they are very pious people, but because of the new relationship they have been brought into by God. It is not because of their own doing or good works but on account of what Christ has done. They are set apart for him and his service; as the people of his own possession they are the elect community of the end time whose lives are to be characterized by godly behaviour." See also Stanley E. Porter, "Holiness, Sanctification," DPL, 397–98. For an unconvincing attempt to translate ἁγίοις here as an adjective rather than a noun, see Thomas B. Slater, "Translating ἅγιος in Col 1,2 and Eph 1,1," Bib 87 (2006): 52–54.

10. According to Snodgrass (Ephesians, 38) Paul's primary concern here "was to emphasize that just as he had been appointed by God to be an apostle, they too had been separated to God (separation is the key idea in the word 'holy'). Paul's addressees were holy because God had set them apart to be his people. The focus is entirely on God's action and the reference is to God's saving work."

describes as "believers" (πιστοῖς), who are theologically and spiritually located "in" (ἐν) Christ Jesus.[11] That they are "believers" means not just that they believe in Christ Jesus, but that as believers they are "*in* Christ Jesus," that is, they have been incorporated to live in union with Christ Jesus within a new sphere, realm, or domain of existence determined by what God has done in raising Christ Jesus from the dead and exalting him to the heavenly regions.[12] The audience thus live in two quite different locations simultaneously—"in" Ephesus and "in" Christ Jesus. They are to realize that they are able to live as holy ones separate from yet "in" Ephesus because they are believers who are "in" Christ Jesus.[13]

In this C' element Paul further draws his audience to himself. As Paul is an apostle "of Christ Jesus" (1:1a), his audience are believers who are "in Christ Jesus" (1:1d). This further grabs the attention of the audience. What does the Paul who is sent with the authority of Christ Jesus have to say to the believers who are living in union with Christ Jesus?

---

11. Gerhard Barth, "πιστός," *EDNT* 3.98: "[U]sed absolutely πιστοί simply means believers = Christians." O'Brien, *Ephesians*, 87: "Paul describes his readers first in terms of their being marked out by God to be his holy people, but also in terms of their believing response to the gospel, a response which is ultimately due to God's gracious initiative as well."

12. Snodgrass, *Ephesians*, 38: "With the expression 'in Christ Jesus' we encounter one of the most significant and difficult points in Paul's writings. Paul is not merely saying these people believed in Christ; rather, they were in Christ positionally. This concept of being in Christ is one of—if not the—most important parts of Paul's theology, for this is the center from which he understood and explained salvation." Winfried Elliger, "ἐν," *EDNT* 1.448: "Ἐν Χριστῷ thus refers not to mystical life in Christ; it serves rather, like the related formula ἐν πίστει, 'in faith,' as a characterization of one's realm of existence, which is often set in contrast to the worldly realm (ἐν σαρκί, 'in the flesh')." Andrew T. Lincoln, *Ephesians* (WBC 42; Dallas: Word Books, 1990), 6: "[T]he phrase 'in Christ Jesus' refers to the relationship of union with Christ which results from having been incorporated into him." See also Friedrich Büchsel, " 'In Christus' bei Paulus," *ZNW* 42 (1949): 141–58; Fritz Neugebauer, "Das Paulinische 'In Christo,' " *NTS* 4 (1957–58): 124–38; John A. Allan, "The 'In Christ' Formula in Ephesians," *NTS* 5 (1958–59): 54–62; Michel Bouttier, *En Christ: Étude d'exégèse et de théologie pauliniennes* (Paris: Presses Universitaires, 1962); A. J. M. Wedderburn, "Some Observations on Paul's Use of the Phrases 'in Christ' and 'with Christ,' " *JSNT* 25 (1985): 83–97; Celia E. T. Kourie, "In Christ and Related Expressions in Paul," *Theologia Evangelica* 20 (1987): 33–43; James D. G. Dunn, *The Theology of Paul the Apostle* (Grand Rapids: Eerdmans, 1998), 396–401; Mehrdad Fatehi, *The Spirit's Relation to the Risen Lord in Paul: An Examination of Its Christological Implications* (WUNT 128; Tübingen: Mohr Siebeck, 2000), 269–74; Mark A. Seifrid, "In Christ," *DPL*, 433–36; Hoehner, *Ephesians*, 143.

13. Snodgrass, *Ephesians*, 40: "In Paul's mind, just as these Christians live literally in the region near Ephesus, they also live in Christ. The terrain, climate, values, and history in which people grow up and live helps to define who they are. As really as this region near Ephesus defines who they are, Christ defines who believers really are. He is the 'sphere of influence' or 'power field' in which they live and from which they benefit and are transformed."

5. *Eph 1:2a (B′): Grace to You and Peace from God Our Father*

With its mention of "God" the B′ element of the chiasm—"Grace to you and peace from *God* our Father" (1:2a)—parallels the B element— "through the will of *God*" (1:1b). Paul's greeting of God's "grace" to "you," his audience, expresses his prayer wish that God, who has already graced the audience in making them the holy ones and believers in Christ Jesus, will grant them yet further "grace" (χάρις)—God's gracious, generous, and freely given favor.[14] This concept of the "grace" or "favor" of God is thus not only a gift of God's gracious love but carries with it a connotation of divine empowerment or enablement.[15] God's grace has empowered the audience to become the holy ones and will empower them to live as the holy ones who are in Ephesus (1:1c); it has empowered them to become believers and will empower them to live as believers who are in Christ Jesus (1:1d).[16]

Coupled with God's grace that Paul prays to be given to his audience is "peace" (εἰρήνη)—an overall well-being or harmony.[17] Paul prays that with the grace of God his audience may live in peace with God, with one another

---

14. Lincoln, *Ephesians*, 6: "Paul replaced the standard Hellenistic greeting χαίρειν ['rejoice'] with the similar-sounding but theologically more profound term χάρις, 'grace.'" A. Boyd Luter, "Grace," *DPL*, 374: "[T]he Pauline letters all begin and end by sounding a note of grace. It is not unlikely that the apostle intended all of his writings to be viewed within the all-encompassing framework of divine grace, from beginning to end." No verb is expressed in 1:2; Hoehner (*Ephesians*, 149) suggests that "it is probably best to assume that the present optative verb 'to be' (εἴη) was intended, which expresses a wish 'may grace be to you.' Paul desires the Ephesians to appreciate, accept, and appropriate God's undeserved favor." It is likely that in 1:2 "χάρις is used to refer to all the benefits collectively given through Christ to the elect," according to Jason Whitlark, "Enabling Χάρις: Transformation of the Convention of Reciprocity by Philo and in Ephesians," *PRSt* 30 (2003): 347.

15. Hoehner, *Ephesians*, 149: "χάρις characteristically denotes in the NT God's un-merited or undeserved favor in providing salvation for sinners through Christ's sacrificial death and enablement for the believer." James R. Harrison, *Paul's Language of Grace in Its Graeco-Roman Context* (WUNT 172; Tübingen: Mohr Siebeck, 2003), 243: "It is worth remembering that Paul links χάρις with the language of glory, wealth, mystery, and power— themes that appear throughout Ephesians." See also John Nolland, "Grace as Power," *NovT* 28 (1986): 26–31.

16. According to Harrison (*Grace*, 243), "It is therefore possible that Paul's theology of grace, as formulated in Ephesians, is directed against the influence that magic and the Artemis cult wielded in Ephesus and throughout the province of Asia."

17. Hoehner, *Ephesians*, 149–50: "The second term εἰρήνη, 'peace,' appears in the LXX 290 times and almost always translates שָׁלוֹם, which was the common greeting of the Semitic world. The Hebrew term had the idea of 'well-being' in the very broadest sense. The Greek term is also broad and must be determined by its context. . . . In Ephesians it is used with differences of meaning in the various contexts, but predominantly it has the idea of the sinners' peace with God and the believers' peace with one another." See also Ceslas Spicq, "εἰρενεύω," *TLNT* 1.424–38.

as believers who are in Christ Jesus (1:1d), and with non-believers as the holy ones who are in Ephesus (1:1c).[18]

In a progressive development of the B element of the chiasm, which mentions simply the unadorned term "God" (1:1b), Paul's prays in the B′ element for the bestowal on his audience of the grace and peace that come from "God our Father" (1:2a). The God who decisively willed and thus graced Paul, as a gift of God's love, to be an apostle of Christ Jesus (1:1ab) is the God who is the source of grace and peace for the audience as well. By referring to God as "our *Father*," Paul alerts his audience to their sharing not only with Paul but with all the holy ones and believers in a communal, familial, and personal relationship to God as "Father" (πατήρ).[19] Paul has thus made his audience aware that as the "you" (ὑμῖν), who have been divinely graced, as a gift of God's love, to be holy ones and believers (1:1cd), they are part of the "we," all the holy ones and believers who live under the fatherhood of God "*our* (ἡμῶν) Father" (1:2a).

6. Eph 1:2b (A′): And the Lord Jesus Christ

References to "Christ" in the genitive singular (Χριστοῦ) establish the parallelism between the A—"Paul, an apostle of *Christ* Jesus" (1:1a)—and A′ elements—"and the Lord Jesus *Christ*" (1:2b)—of the chiasm. In a progressive development of the A element, which mentions only "Christ Jesus," the A′ element refers to the "*Lord* (κύριος) Jesus Christ." This enhances Paul's authoritative relationship to his audience; he is an apostle authorized not only by Christ Jesus but by the Jesus Christ who is sovereign "Lord." It also means that the audience, the believers who are in Christ Jesus (1:1d), live in union with as well as under the sovereign lordship of the "Lord" Jesus Christ. The source of the grace and peace, as gifts of God's love, that Paul prays to be granted to his audience, then, is not only God our Father (1:2a) but the "Lord" Jesus Christ (1:2b).[20]

Through the chiasm in 1:1–2, then, Paul informs his audience that not

---

18. Hoehner, *Ephesians*, 150: "Therefore, grace (χάρις) expresses the cause, God's gracious work, and peace (εἰρήνη), the effect of God's work. The grace of God that brings salvation to sinners effects peace between them and God, and that same grace enables believers to live peaceably with one another." See also Judith M. Lieu, " 'Grace to You and Peace': The Apostolic Greeting," *BJRL* 68 (1985): 161–78.

19. Hoehner, *Ephesians*, 150: "Paul in his greetings can state that grace and peace come from God who is not only called Father but 'our' Father. This denotes personal relationship." On the background of the concept of God as Father, see Otto Michel, "πατήρ," *EDNT* 3.53–57.

20. Lincoln, *Ephesians*, 6: "Paul gave the benefits of grace and peace a distinctly Christian framework by specifying God our Father and Lord Jesus Christ as their origin and made his salutation serve as a form of prayer-wish. Here also the writer desires for his readers the experience of the undeserved favor and deep well-being which flow from Christ and from the God who through Christ is known as Father." On the background for the concept of Jesus

only has he himself been graced, as a gift of love from God, to be an authoritative apostle of Christ Jesus (A and B elements), but that they also have been graced, as a gift from God, to be the holy ones who are in Ephesus and at the same time the believers who are in Christ Jesus (C and C′ elements). With his authority as an apostle of Christ Jesus through the gracious will of God, Paul prays that his audience be granted yet further grace as well as the peace that come as gifts of love from both God our Father and the Lord Jesus Christ (B′ and A′ elements). This introductory chiasm has prepared the audience for further experiencing and receiving, through their hearing of Paul's Ephesian Letter itself, the divine grace and peace that will, as gifts of love, empower them to be both the holy ones who are in Ephesus and the believers who are in Christ Jesus.[21]

B. Love Theme in Ephesians 1:1–2

Although Paul has not employed an explicit term for "love" in Eph 1:1–2, he has nevertheless initiated his audience into the dynamics of the theme of love that will be more fully developed throughout the remainder of the Letter. That Paul has been chosen and favored to be an authoritative apostle of Christ Jesus (1:1a) through the gracious will of God (1:1b) means that he has been a recipient of God's love. This powerful will of God also empowers Paul to respond to the love that God has bestowed upon him by obediently and devotedly exercising his authoritative apostleship for the benefit of his Ephesian audience in the Letter that he writes to them. Responding to his God-given apostleship by sending this Letter to represent him, Paul himself is thus demonstrating the dynamics of receiving and responding to the gracious love of God.

As the author of the Letter, the apostle Paul makes his epistolary audience aware that they too have been recipients of God's love, since it was God who graciously consecrated them to be "the holy ones who are in Ephesus" (1:1c) and graciously granted them the faith to be "the believers who are in Christ Jesus" (1:1d). These gracious gifts of God also empower the audience to respond to this love of God by living as both the holy ones and believers God has designated them to be. The audience too, then, are already involved in the dynamics of receiving and responding to the love of God.

Christ as "Lord," see Ceslas Spicq, "κύριος," *TLNT* 2.341–52; Joseph A. Fitzmyer, "κύριος," *EDNT* 2.328–31; Hoehner, *Ephesians*, 150–52.

21. Muddiman, *Ephesians*, 59: "The good wishes, then, are not just from Paul to his addressees; they have a deeper source, as by implication does the rest of the letter." O'Brien, *Ephesians*, 88: "Paul's readers have already experienced, in some measure, God's grace and peace in the Lord Jesus Christ. The apostle recognizes this, and in his salutation he expresses his desire that these twin blessings may be understood and experienced in greater measure, especially through the letter itself, for these two major themes are taken up again and again throughout Ephesians."

Although as holy ones and believers the audience have already received God's love, Paul prays that they continue to be favored with God's love in the form of the gifts of grace and peace that come from both God our Father and the Lord Jesus Christ (1:2). As gifts of God's love both "grace" and "peace" can be considered part of the general theme of love to be developed in the remainder of the Letter. The word "grace" (χάρις) especially connotes the bestowal of God's gracious love.[22]

C. Summary on Ephesians 1:1–2

1. In the opening elements of the chiasm in 1:1–2 Paul indicates that he has not only received God's love in being designated an authoritative apostle of Christ Jesus through the gracious will of God (1:1ab), but responds to God's love by exercising his apostleship in writing this Letter to the Ephesians.

2. As the audience hear the central paralleled elements of the chiasm in 1:1–2, they realize that they too have received God's love and the empowerment to respond to it as both "the holy ones who are in Ephesus" (1:1c) and "the believers who are in Christ Jesus" (1:1d).

3. Paul's introductory prayer wish in the concluding elements of the chiasm in 1:1–2 that continued grace as well as peace be granted to his audience from God our Father and the Lord Jesus Christ (1:2) prepares the audience to further receive and experience, by their listening to what Christ Jesus himself is going to communicate to them in this Letter from his authorized apostle, the empowerment that comes from the grace and peace that are gifts of love from God and Christ.

---

22. Ceslas Spicq, "χάρις," *TLNT* 3.501–3; Klaus Berger, "χάρις," *EDNT* 3.458: "Grace is the opening of access to God in the larger sense precisely by God himself. In Jewish writings God's grace and love are the basis of election." According to Barth (*Ephesians 1–3*, 74) "grace" (χάρις) in the LXX "describes God's love and the steadfastness with which he keeps the covenant." Dunn, *Theology of Paul*, 319–20: "It is important to grasp that for Paul, behind the whole salvation process always lay the initiative of God. No other word expresses his theology so clearly on this point as 'grace' (χάρις). For it summed up not only the epochal event of Christ itself but also the grace which made the vital breakthrough in individual human experience. And it defined not only the past act of God initiating into a life of faith, but also present continuing experience of divine enabling, as well as particular enablings and commissionings. In short, χάρις joins ἀγάπη ('love') at the very centre of Paul's gospel. More than any other, these two words, 'grace' and 'love,' together sum up and most clearly characterise his whole theology." See also Hendrikus Boers, "Ἀγάπη and Χάρις in Paul's Thought," *CBQ* 59 (1997): 693–713.

CHAPTER 4

Ephesians 1:3–14:
To the Praise of His Glory in Love (B)

A: ³ Blessed is the God and Father of *our* Lord Jesus Christ, who has blessed us in every Spiritual blessing in the heavenly places in Christ, ⁴ as he chose us in him before the foundation of the world that we might be holy and blameless before him in love, ⁵ having predestined us to sonship through Jesus Christ to himself, according to the pleasure of his will, ⁶ *to the praise of the glory* of *his* grace with which he graced us in the Beloved,

    B: ⁷ *in whom* we have redemption through his blood, the forgiveness of transgressions, according to the wealth of his grace ⁸ which he lavished on us, in all wisdom and insight, ⁹ having made known to us the mystery *of his will*, according to his pleasure which he *purposed* in him,

        C: ¹⁰ as a plan for the fullness of the times, to unite under one head all *the* things *in* the Christ,

        C′:   *the* things in the heavens and *the* things on earth *in* him,

    B′:   ¹¹ *in whom* also we have obtained an inheritance having been predestined according to the *purpose* of the one who is working in all things according to the counsel *of his will* ¹² in order that we might be to the praise of his glory, who first hoped in the Christ,

A′:   ¹³ in whom also you, having heard the word of the truth, the gospel of your salvation, in whom also having believed, you were sealed with the Holy Spirit of the promise, ¹⁴ who is the first installment of *our* inheritance, for redemption of the possession, *to the praise of his glory.*[1]

A. Audience Response to Ephesians 1:3–14

1. Eph 1:3–6 (A): We Are Blessed in Christ to Live in Love in *the* Beloved

In Eph 1:3–6 the audience hear the A element of this complex, one-sentence chiasm in 1:3–14 as a mini-chiasm in itself, artfully composed of three poetic and rhythmic sub-elements:

> (a) Blessed is the God and Father of our Lord *Jesus Christ*, who has blessed us in every Spiritual blessing in the heavenly places *in Christ* (1:3),
>
> > (b) as he chose us in him before the foundation of the world that we might be holy and blameless before him *in love* (1:4),
>
> (a´) having predestined us to sonship through *Jesus Christ* to himself, according to the pleasure of his will, to the praise of the glory of his grace with which he graced us *in the Beloved* (1:5–6).

The only three occurrences in Ephesians of terms for "bless"—"blessed (εὐλογητός) is the God," "who has blessed (εὐλογήσας) us," and "with every Spiritual blessing (εὐλογίᾳ)"—as well as the concluding triplet of "in" (ἐν) prepositional phrases—"in (ἐν) every Spiritual blessing in (ἐν) the heavenly places in (ἐν) Christ"—establish the unity of the first "a" sub-element in 1:3. The "in" prepositional phrases—"in him" (ἐν αὐτῷ) near the beginning of the verse and "in love" (ἐν ἀγάπῃ) at the end—form a literary inclusion indicating the unity of the second and central "b" sub-element in 1:4. And the three occurrences of the third-person singular pronoun referring to God— "to himself (αὐτόν)" near the beginning of the verse, "of his (αὐτοῦ) will" in the middle, and "of his (αὐτοῦ) grace" near the end—secure the unity of the third "a´" sub-element in 1:5–6.

While there is a rhythmic relationship among all three of these sub-elements in 1:3–6, with the ending of each punctuated by a climactic "in" prepositional phrase, the "a" and "a´" sub-elements are parallel in this regard with phrases in which references to Christ are the object—"in (ἐν) Christ" in 1:3 and "in (ἐν) the Beloved" in 1:6. Indeed, each of the remaining elements of the chiasm in 1:3–14 ends with a punctuating refrain, a rhythmic and climactic "in" prepositional phrase with a reference to Christ as the object, except the final A´ element in 1:13–14, which is the only element in the chiasm that is introduced with two "in" prepositional phrases with a reference to Christ as the object. Thus, the chiasm's B element in 1:7–9 ends

---

1. For the establishment of Eph 1:3–14 as a chiasm, see ch. 2.

with "in him" (ἐν αὐτῷ), the C element in 1:10b with "in the Christ" (ἐν τῷ Χριστῷ), the C′ element in 1:10c with "in him" (ἐν αὐτῷ), and the B′ element in 1:11–12 with "in the Christ" (ἐν τῷ Χριστῷ). The A′ element in 1:13–14 is introduced by "in whom" (ἐν ᾧ) in both 1:13a and 1:13b.[2]

The "b" (1:4) sub-element, then, is the only rhythmic refrain not only within the A element but within the entire chiasm in 1:3–14 to end with a climactic "in" prepositional phrase in which "love" rather than a reference to Christ is the object—"in love" (ἐν ἀγάπῃ).[3] The only two occurrences within the chiasm in 1:3–14 of the name "Jesus Christ"—"of our Lord Jesus Christ" in 1:3 and "through Jesus Christ" in 1:5—further point to the parallelism between the "a" (1:3) and "a′" (1:5–6) sub-elements.[4] While each of the three sub-elements contains instances of the first-person plural accusative pronoun "us" (ἡμᾶς) as the object of God's action—"who has blessed *us*" in 1:3b, "as he chose *us*" in 1:4a, "having predestined *us*" in 1:5a, and "he graced *us*" in 1:6, the b (1:4) sub-element contains the only instance within the A element in which this form of the pronoun functions as the grammatical subject—"that *we* (ἡμᾶς) might be holy and blameless" in 1:4b, further distinguishing the central "b" (1:4) sub-element within the mini-chiasm in 1:3–6.

a. Eph 1:3 (a): We bless the God who blessed us in Christ

After his prayer wish that his audience further experience the grace and peace that come "from God our Father and the Lord Jesus Christ" (1:2), Paul immediately exclaims, "Blessed is the God and Father of our Lord Jesus Christ" (1:3a).[5] In blessing or praising God, Paul is speaking not only for

---

2. O'Brien, *Ephesians*, 89–90: "[T]he thoroughly Christian dimension of this eulogy is evident in the constant repetition of the phrase 'in Christ' (or 'in him', 'in whom')."

3. Its place within the rhythmic refrain of "in" prepositional phrases punctuating the end of every element or sub-element within the chiasm in 1:3–14, except the last, indicates that the phrase "in love" in 1:4 should be taken as the conclusion of that verse rather than as the introduction to the next verse, as some scholars construe it. See, for example, Muddiman, *Ephesians*, 68; Snodgrass, *Ephesians*, 50; Nils Alstrup Dahl, *Studies in Ephesians: Introductory Questions, Text- and Edition-Critical Issues, Interpretation of Texts and Themes* (ed. David Hellholm et al.; WUNT 131; Tübingen: Mohr Siebeck, 2000), 320; Ernest Best, *Ephesians* (ICC; London: Clark, 1998), 122–23; Rudolf Schnackenburg, *Ephesians: A Commentary* (Edinburgh: Clark, 1991), 54; Joachim Gnilka, *Der Epheserbrief* (HTKNT 10/2; Freiburg, Germany: Herder, 1971), 72; Heinrich Schlier, *Der Brief an die Epheser: Ein Kommentar* (Düsseldorf: Patmos, 1968), 52–53.

4. Note also that the a and a′ sub-elements contain similar alliterative uses of cognate verb and noun pairs—"who blessed (εὐλογήσας) us with every Spiritual blessing (εὐλογίᾳ)" in 1:3b and "of his grace (χάριτος) with which he graced (ἐχαρίτωσεν) us" in 1:6.

5. Hoehner, *Ephesians*, 162: "The concept of blessing with reference to God is not expressing a wish, 'blessed be God,' but rather a declaration, 'blessed is God.'" O'Brien, *Ephesians*, 94: "[H]ere Paul *actually ascribes* praise to God (his emphasis)." See also Barth, *Ephesians 1–3*, 76–78; Snodgrass, *Ephesians*, 46. That Eph 1:3a should be understood as

himself but for "us"—his audience and all believers. He thus draws his audience into sharing his exuberant blessing of the God who is not only "our" (ἡμῶν) Father (1:2) but the Father of "our" (ἡμῶν) Lord Jesus Christ (1:3a). This prepares the audience for what the Lord Jesus Christ's relationship to God as his Father means for the audience's relationship not only to God as "our" Father but to Jesus Christ as "our" Lord.

That Paul and his audience declare God "blessed" (εὐλογητός) most appropriately responds to God's having "blessed (εὐλογήσας) us (Paul, his audience, and all believers) with every Spiritual blessing (εὐλογίᾳ) in the heavenly places in Christ" (1:3b).[6] That God has blessed us with "every" (πάσῃ) blessing of a "Spiritual" (πνευματικῇ) nature means that God has showered upon us the full and complete array of blessings available from the divine Spirit of God.[7] These Spiritual blessings have their origin and location "in the heavenly places" and "in Christ."[8] The audience, the believers who are in Christ Jesus (1:1d), are able to experience all the Spiritual blessings of God available in the transcendent heavenly realms because of their union with Christ.[9] This blessing of the God who has blessed us with every

a liturgical refrain to be recited between the six strophes in 1:3–14 is speculatively and unconvincingly proposed by Pierre Grelot, "La structure d'Éphésiens 1,3–14," RB 96 (1989): 193–209.

6. Snodgrass, Ephesians, 46: "To use the same word for our worship of God and of God's showering us with spiritual gifts is foreign to us, but this double meaning of the word bless is common in both the Old and New Testament." Muddiman, Ephesians, 66: "The generosity of God is prior: it arises from God's own nature as 'one who blesses', to which human beings are bound to respond by blessing him in worship."

7. Fee, God's Empowering Presence, 666–67: "As elsewhere, πνευματικός is an adjective for the Spirit, that is, 'pertaining to or belonging to the Spirit'; thus 'πνευματικός blessings' mean 'Spirit blessings, blessings that pertain to the Spirit.' The use of this adjective rather than the genitive of the word 'Spirit' indicates that the emphasis is on the nature of the blessings, rather than their source. But having said that, that the blessings are those that properly pertain to the life of the Spirit, one is not very far away from describing their source as well. What is not helpful is the translation 'spiritual' to describe the nature of these blessings, since that word is almost always understood over against an antonym of some kind, in a way that 'Spirit' is not."

8. Caragounis, Ephesian Mysterion, 152: "τὰ ἐπουράνια (the heavenly places) although overlapping with οὐρανός (heaven) is not completely identical with it. Οὐρανός stretches from the air space where the birds fly and the clouds pour down their rain all the way up to God's very throne, while the ἐπουράνια constitute only the higher layers of this space, from God's throne down to the sphere where the cosmic powers dwell and work. Τὰ ἐπουράνια is thus bound up with the salvation events, and has, in contradistinction to οὐρανός, a heilsgeschichtlich import." In Ephesians when earth and heaven are referred to in a bipolar relationship οὐρανός is the preferred term, while ἐπουράνιος is employed for the place of the risen, ascended, and exalted Christ, according to W. Hall Harris, " 'The Heavenlies' Reconsidered: Οὐρανός and Ἐπουράνιος in Ephesians," BSac 148 (1991): 72–89. And note that in 3:10 the evil "rulers and authorities" are also located "in the heavenly places."

9. Lincoln, Ephesians, 21: "Here in 1:3, against a background of cosmological concerns on the part of the letter's recipients, there is the indication that the blessings of salva-

Spiritual blessing in the heavenly places in 1:3 thus prepares the audience for a further elaboration of what all these Spiritual blessings entail for us who are "in Christ."[10]

b. Eph 1:4 (b): In Christ we may be holy and blameless before God in love

The first blessing to be elaborated is God's gracious election of us—"As he chose us in him before the foundation of the world" (1:4a). "As" (καθώς) expresses both the manner and cause of God's blessing.[11] Because God has blessed us to the extent of choosing us, we respond to this blessing by declaring God blessed (1:3a). Not as a random impersonal choice but with great personal interest God freely "chose" (ἐξελέξατο, in the middle voice) "us," all believers, not for any merit on our part but solely because we are "in him" (ἐν αὐτῷ), that is, united with and incorporated into the person of Christ and into the realm established by Christ.[12] The believers who are "in

---

tion they have received from God link the recipients to the heavenly realm. The blessings can be said to be in the heavenly realms, yet they are not viewed as treasure stored up for future appropriation, but as benefits belonging to believers now.... In Ephesians, through what God has done in Christ, the benefits of the age to come have become a present heavenly reality for believers, and for this reason can also be closely linked with the Spirit of that age." Fee, *God's Empowering Presence*, 668 n. 33: "Paul's point is that our *experience* of these blessings takes place as we ourselves are 'in Christ' in the heavenly realm" (his emphasis). Snodgrass, *Ephesians*, 47–48: " '[I]n Christ' has a 'local' sense and points to incorporation into Christ. That is, Christ is the 'place' where believers reside, the source in which they find God's salvation and blessings, and the framework in which they live and work.... without losing any sense of Christ as person. Christ is the source of all spiritual blessings, and because believers reside in him they can enjoy those blessings. Just as Christ's personhood is not lost, neither is the believer's individuality lost."

10. Hoehner, *Ephesians*, 162: "This verse marks not only the introduction but also the main sentence of the eulogy. It is in essence a summary of the whole eulogy." Rainer Schwindt, "Die Bitte um Gottes Gaben als Mitte christlicher Existenz: Zur Theologie des Epheserbriefes," *TTZ* 111 (2002): 44: "Diese Segensformel kann als programmatische Überschrift über die Eulogie, ja den ganzen Brief gelesen werden." See also Fee, *God's Empowering Presence*, 666.

11. Lincoln, *Ephesians*, 22: "The writer asserts that God has blessed believers both because and to the extent that he elected them." See also Hoehner, *Ephesians*, 175; O'Brien, *Ephesians*, 98.

12. Daniel B. Wallace, *Greek Grammar beyond the Basics: An Exegetical Syntax of the New Testament* (Grand Rapids: Zondervan, 1996), 421: "God chose us for himself, by himself, or for his own interests." Carey C. Newman, "Election and Predestination in Ephesians 1:4–6a: An Exegetical-Theological Study of the Historical, Christological Realization of God's Purpose," *RevExp* 93 (1996): 239: "God chose 'us' (ἡμᾶς), a people. Ἡμᾶς, a first-person, plural, personal pronoun, falls within 'the language of belonging' and refers to the Christian church, to those who are 'in Christ.'... believers, because of their union with Christ, are elected." Snodgrass, *Ephesians*, 49: "Individuals are not elected and then put in Christ. They are in Christ and therefore elect." Lincoln, *Ephesians*, 23: "The notion of being chosen in Christ here in Ephesians is likely then to include the idea of incorporation into Christ as the representative on whom God's gracious decision was focused." We main-

Christ Jesus" (1:1d) and have been blessed "in Christ" (1:3b) are also chosen "in him" (1:4a). That God chose us in Christ "before the foundation of the world" indicates that by their union with Christ believers have been blessed with God's sovereign grace to play a definite role in God's eternal plan.[13]

The role that believers are to play in God's eternal plan is "that we might be holy and blameless before him in love" (1:4b). That God chose us that we might be "holy" (ἁγίους) reinforces for the audience that it is God's gracious blessing that enables not only them to live as the "holy ones" (ἁγίοις) who are in Ephesus (1:1c), but all believers to be holy, that is, set apart from the world and consecrated to God. Coupled with "holy" is "blameless" to form an alliterative pair (ἁγίους καὶ ἀμώμους) with an originally cultic background that now (as already in the OT) refers to moral conduct.[14] God chose believers to be holy and blameless "before him," that is, before God himself.[15] By living morally holy and blameless lives before God in the present assures the audience of being holy and blameless before God at the last judgment.[16]

---

tain that "in him" is a comprehensive prepositional phrase that includes both of the views mentioned by Hoehner, *Ephesians*, 177: "One view is that it could be regarded as a dative of sphere, which connotes the idea that we are chosen in Christ as the head and representative of the spiritual community just as Adam is the head and representative of the natural community. The other view is that it could be relational or instrumental in the sense that God chose believers in connection with or through Christ's work of redemption."

13. Lincoln, *Ephesians*, 23: "To say that election in Christ took place before the foundation of the world is to underline that it was provoked not by historical contingency or human merit, but solely by God's sovereign grace." See also Otfried Hofius, " 'Erwählt vor Grundlegung der Welt' (Eph. 1.4)," *ZNW* 62 (1971): 123–28.

14. Takamitsu Muraoka, *A Greek-English Lexicon of the Septuagint: Chiefly of the Pentateuch and the Twelve Prophets* (Louvain: Peeters, 2002), 24. On the increasingly moralizing interpretation of OT cultic practices, see Stephen Finlan, *The Background and Content of Paul's Cultic Atonement Metaphors* (SBLAbib 19; Atlanta: Society of Biblical Literature, 2004), 48–49. O'Brien, *Ephesians*, 100–101: "The two adjectives holy and blameless were used to describe the unblemished animals set apart for God as Old Testament sacrifices (Exod. 29:37–38; cf. Heb. 9:14; 1 Pet. 1:19). But already within the Old Testament this language was employed to describe ethical purity (e.g., Pss. 15[LXX 14]:2; 18:23 [17:24]). Both terms have lost any cultic overtones in Colossians 1:22 and Ephesians 1:4 (cf. Eph. 5:27; Phil. 2:15; Jude 24), referring instead to ethical holiness and freedom from moral blemish." Hoehner, *Ephesians*, 179: "As those in the Aaronic line could not have any physical defects if they were to serve as priests (Lev 21:16–24), so the believer in Christ will not have any moral defects before God."

15. Hoehner, *Ephesians*, 179: "The 'him' refers to God and not Christ because Christ is not the object but the instrument through whose redemption God can bring the chosen into the presence of himself. This enhances the middle voice of ἐξελέξατο, which substantiates that God chose the believers for his benefit, namely, to be holy and blameless before him." Lincoln (*Ephesians*, 25) interprets living "before him" as being "conscious that God's presence and God's approval are one's ultimate environment."

16. Hoehner, *Ephesians*, 179: "[T]here is a necessary correlation between what God is going to do in the future for the believers and what he is presently doing for them. Since he

The prepositional phrase "in love" (ἐν ἀγάπῃ) that punctuates this central b (1:4) sub-element indicates that the audience and all believers are to be holy and blameless before God within the sphere, realm, or domain of love. Much like "in Christ," "in love" is a very dynamic and comprehensive phrase. As a realm in which believers live, "in love" embraces all of the dimensions and relationships established by God's gracious love. It includes a causal or instrumental dimension—it is by or because of the love God extended to believers in choosing them that God empowers them to be holy and blameless before him. This love of God establishes a dynamic set of relationships within the realm characterized as "in love." This realm includes not only God's love for believers, as indicated by his blessing and choosing them (1:3b–4a), but believers' love for God, as expressed both by their blessing of God (1:3a) and living holy and blameless before God (1:4b).[17] And since "holy and blameless" refers to moral conduct, "in love" implies believers loving one another.[18]

*c. Eph 1:5–6 (a′): As adopted sons we praise God for loving us in **the** Beloved*

"Having predestined us for sonship through Jesus Christ to himself" (1:5a) in the "a′" (1:5–6) sub-element continues the elaboration of "every

---

is preparing believers to go into his presence holy and without blame, certainly that is what he desires for them now."

17. For the close connection between God's choosing and loving in the OT, see LXX Deut 4:27: "Because he [God] loved (ἀγαπῆσαι) your fathers, he also chose (ἐξελέξατο) their seed" (see also 10:15); LXX Deut 7:7–8: "And the Lord chose (ἐξελέξατο) you, for you are the smallest among all the nations; it was because the Lord loved (ἀγαπᾶν) you;" LXX Ps 77:68: "God chose (ἐξελέξατο) the tribe of Judah, Mount Sion which he loved (ἠγάπησεν)" (see also LXX Ps 46:5). On LXX Deut 7:7–8 see John William Wevers, *Notes on the Greek Text of Deuteronomy* (SBLSCS 39; Atlanta: Scholars Press, 1995), 132: "The notion that God loved people already occurred at 4:37 . . . but here his love for Israel is determinative for the people's election as his people, a theme which became central in the NT."

18. Barth, *Ephesians 1–3*, 79–80: "In 1:4 either God's act of election, or the holy and blameless appearance of those chosen by God, or both are qualified by 'in love.' If the phrase were connected with vs. 5, 'love' would determine God's act only, rather than also its effect upon man. Some parallel statements in Deuteronomy on election, also Eph 2:4 and 5:1, suggest that God's love is meant. But other OT passages from the same context, as well as the dominant place of love in the ethical exhortation of Eph 4:22ff., lend equal weight to the assumption that man's love of God or of his fellow man are both focused upon in this passage. It is not necessary to choose between the alternatives, for in the OT the right covenant relationship between God and man is described by the terms 'love,' 'steadfast love,' 'righteousness,' 'faithfulness.' As pointed out earlier these terms denote the reciprocal attitude of both covenant partners and also of human partners toward one another." Newman, "Election," 240: "[H]oliness and blamelessness must be understood comprehensively in terms of character (what a person is), behavior (what a person does), and status (what legal standing a person has before God). Since these blessings are *already* being mediated to us in Christ, *election inaugurates the progressive transformation of the total person*" (Newman's emphasis).

Spiritual blessing" (1:3b) that God has bestowed upon all believers in the "a" (1:3) sub-element, as the aorist active participial phrase "having predestined (προορίσας) us" further specifies and develops the aorist active participial phrase "has blessed (εὐλογήσας) us" (1:3b). And that God "destined" all believers "pre-" or "beforehand" (προορίσας) in the "a'" (1:5–6) sub-element reinforces God's election of all believers in Christ "before" (πρό) the foundation of the world to play a role in God's eternal plan in the "b" (1:4) sub-element.[19]

That within his eternal plan God predestined all believers "to sonship (υἱοθεσίαν) through Jesus Christ" (1:5a) means that God has adopted them into his family to share an intimate and loving father-son relationship to God together with Jesus Christ, that is, our Lord Jesus Christ whose God and Father (1:3a) is also our God and Father (1:2a). This assures the audience that as God's adopted "sons" through Jesus Christ they are heirs of God their Father.[20] It is God's love in predestining us believers to sonship through Jesus Christ "to himself" (εἰς αὐτόν, 1:5a) that empowers us believers to be holy and blameless "before him" (κατενώπιον αὐτοῦ) within the realm of being "in love" (1:4b).[21]

---

19. Walter A. Elwell, "Election and Predestination," *DPL*, 227–28: "Paul uses the verb προορίζω five times (Rom 8:29, 30; 1 Cor 2:7; Eph 1:5, 11) with the basic meaning of 'determine beforehand' or 'predetermine.' . . . In a related way Paul speaks of God's predestining persons to be conformed to the image of Christ (Rom 8:29) and adopted into the family of God (Eph 1:5). . . . In Ephesians 1:4 Paul parallels this divine ordination with election and defines it as being 'before the foundation of the world.' " Hoehner, *Ephesians*, 193: "[B]oth the choosing and predetermining are governed by πρό, 'before.' " See also Best, *Ephesians*, 123. For a suggested background in Psalm 2, see Leslie C. Allen, "The Old Testament Background of (προ)ὁρίζειν in the New Testament," *NTS* 17 (1970–71): 104–8.

20. Lincoln, *Ephesians*, 25: "υἱοθεσία, 'adoption as sons,' . . . is a term taken from Greco-Roman law where it referred to the adoption as sons of those who were not so by birth. . . . In Paul this is applied to the privileged new relationship believers have with God, but must also be seen against the OT background of Israel's relationship with God. . . . Ephesians emphasizes that by God's free predestining choice he adopts believers, taking them into his family and intimate fellowship, establishing them as his children and heirs." See also O'Brien, *Ephesians*, 102–3; James M. Scott, *Adoption as Sons of God: An Exegetical Investigation Into the Background of ΥΙΟΘΕΣΙΑ in the Pauline Corpus* (WUNT 48; Tübingen: Mohr, 1992); idem, "Adoption, Sonship," *DPL*, 15–18; David J. Williams, *Paul's Metaphors: Their Context and Character* (Peabody, MA: Hendrickson, 1999), 64–66; Richard H. Bell, *The Irrevocable Call of God: An Inquiry Into Paul's Theology of Israel* (WUNT 184; Tübingen: Mohr Siebeck, 2005), 202–3.

21. Hoehner, *Ephesians*, 198: "The preposition εἰς denotes direction and relationship, and thus is translated 'to' and 'into,' connoting the coming to and into God's family. Therefore, God predestined us to be adopted as his sons (and daughters), this adoption came through Christ, and this finally brings us to God in order to have fellowship with him as our father." Best, *Ephesians*, 124–25: "Foreordination and election are to be distinguished from the impersonality of Greek concepts of fate because a personal and loving God operates them. Without the knowledge that foreordination is the result of God's love foreordination

"According to the pleasure (εὐδοκίαν) of his will" (1:5b) underlines the free and sovereign decision of the love God extended to us believers whom he predestined to sonship through Jesus Christ to himself.[22] As it was through the resolute "will" (θελήματος) of God that Paul was designated an apostle of Christ Jesus (1:1), so it is in accord with God's resolute "will" (θελήματος) that he predestined us believers to a loving father-son relationship to himself through Jesus Christ (1:5).

The love God manifested toward us believers in blessing (1:3), choosing (1:4), and predestining (1:5) us appropriately leads us "to the praise of the glory of his grace with which he graced us in the Beloved" (1:6). As we are to respond to the love of the God who "blessed" us with every Spiritual "blessing" by declaring God "blessed" in the "a" sub-element (1:3), so we are to respond to the love of the God who "graced" us with his "grace" by praising the "glory" (δόξης), that is, the magnificent splendor, power, and radiance, of that divine grace in the "a´" sub-element (1:6).[23] That God has already "graced" (ἐχαρίτωσεν) us believers with his "grace" (χάριτος) reinforces Paul's prayer wish that God grant even more of his divine "grace" (χάρις) to the audience (1:2) as a gift of God's love.

That God has graced us "in the Beloved" climaxes the rhythm of dynamic "in" (ἐν) prepositional phrases that conclude each of the sub-elements in this A element (1:3–6) of the chiasm in 1:3–14—"in Christ" (ἐν Χριστῷ, 1:3), "in love" (ἐν ἀγάπῃ, 1:4), and "in the Beloved" (ἐν τῷ ἠγαπημένῳ, 1:6). As it is in our situation of being "in Christ" that God has blessed us with every Spiritual blessing in the heavenly places in the "a" sub-element

---

would be wholly inexplicable. . . . The father who adopted a son did so out of his own need, wishing either to continue his family or to provide himself with an heir; he is concerned with his own interests. God however does not adopt in that way for he already has a son and heir; he adopts because he loves those he adopts." Chantal Reynier, "La bénédiction en Éphésiens 1,3–14: Élection, filiation, rédemption," NRTh 118 (1996): 190: "Notre élection est la définition de l'amour qui est en Dieu. . . . Dieu décide (προορίζειν) en toute liberté et souveraineté, il agit sans contrainte et sans condition préalable à son amour." On "to himself" in 1:5a as referring to God rather than to Christ and on its relation to "before him" in 1:4b, see Best, Ephesians, 126; Hoehner, Ephesians, 197–98.

22. On "pleasure" (εὐδοκίαν) in 1:5b Spicq ("εὐδοκέω, εὐδοκία," TLNT 2.106) remarks: "The emphasis is not so much on love—although that is the supreme explanation—as on the absolute freedom of the divine decision." In Phil 1:15–16 those who preach Christ from "good will" (εὐδοκίαν) act out of "love" (ἀγάπης); see Robert Mahoney, "εὐδοκία," EDNT 2.75.

23. Hoehner, Ephesians, 200: "Basically, δόξα has the idea of the reflection of the essence of one's being, the summation of all of one's attributes, whether it refers to God or a human being. The essence of one's being makes an impact, whether good or bad, on others; this impact of one's essential being is that of one's reputation or glory. Because of how God has revealed himself, one thinks of his reputation in categories of splendor, power, and radiance. That reputation is a result of his essential being. Therefore, a human being is to glorify (in the sense of magnify or praise) God because of his glory, reflecting his essential being."

(1:3b), so it is our situation of being "in the Beloved," that is, in Christ as the recipient of God's love, that God has graced us with his grace in the "a´" sub-element (1:6). God's grace of predestining us to be his adopted sons through Jesus Christ (1:5a) means that we too are recipients of the love of the God who is the Father of both Jesus Christ and us believers (1:2, 3) in our situation of being "in the Beloved."[24] Being loved by God in our union with the Beloved thus develops what it means for us to be chosen by God in Christ, the Beloved, that we might be holy and blameless before God "in love" in the "b" (1:4) sub-element.

Our being loved by God in our situation of being "in the Beloved" not only inspires us to respond to God's love by praising the God who graced us with his grace in the "a´" (1:5–6) sub-element and by blessing the God who blessed us with every Spiritual blessing in the "a" (1:3) sub-element, but empowers us to respond to God's love by being holy and blameless before God "in love" in the central "b" (1:4) sub-element.[25] That we have been graced with God's love "in the Beloved" (1:6), then, develops what it means for us to be holy and blameless before God "in love" (1:4b), that is, within the dynamic realm established by the love of God for us that empowers us to live "in love"—loving God and one another in response to God's love for us in Christ, *the* Beloved.

2. Eph 1:7–9 (B): In *the* Beloved God Lavished *the* Wealth *of His* Grace upon Us

In the B element (1:7–9) of the chiasm Paul further informs his audience on how they and all believers are the recipients of God's gracious love.

---

24. Hoehner, *Ephesians*, 204: "Since believers are in Christ, they are also the object of God's love." Lincoln, *Ephesians*, 27: "Being highly favored with grace means, for the believing community, participation in that divine love with which the Father favored the Son, though the community's participation in this relationship is through adoption." On Paul's use of the participle ἠγαπημένος with the article rather than the closely related adjective ἀγαπητός for "the Beloved" in 1:6, see Jean-Noël Aletti, *Saint Paul: Épître aux Éphésiens. Introduction, traduction et commentaire* (EBib 42; Paris: Gabalda, 2001), 64: "Si le participe est utilisé par l'eulogie, c'est pour signifier que les chrétiens ont été l'objet du bon vouloir de Dieu en celui qui est LE bien-aimé, car l'article souligne ici une relation unique. Et ce n'est pas un hasard si cette relation est soulignée au moment même où est rappelée notre adoption filiale." According to Best (*Ephesians*, 129) the use of the participle in the prepositional phrase, "in the Beloved" (ἐν τῷ ἠγαπημένῳ), in 1:6 "may also have been influenced by the ἐν ἀγάπῃ of v. 4; that and the cognate participle form an inclusio indicating a unit of thought."

25. Best, *Ephesians*, 127: "God's foreordination began in his love; it results in the praise of his grace. The initiating love is now depicted as undeserved . . . God's foreordination has not been forced on him by anything in those whom he elects. Realising this they will praise him. Blessed by him, they bless him (v. 3). God has acted so that he may be praised. AE [Author of Ephesians] wishes to show here the proper response to God's foreordaining love."

"In him" (ἐν ᾧ, 1:7, that is, "in the beloved" (ἐν τῷ ἠγαπημένῳ, 1:6), in our union with Christ as the recipient of God's love, which as adopted sons of God we have also received within our situation of being "in love" (1:4b), we presently have "the redemption," the deliverance or liberation, "through his blood," an allusion to the sacrificial death of Christ (1:7a). This redemption is further described as "the forgiveness of transgressions" (1:7b). That these gifts of God's love are "according to the wealth of his grace which he lavished upon us" (1:7c–8a) in the B element intensifies "his grace with which he graced us in the Beloved" (1:6) in the A element. The intensifying words, "wealth" (πλοῦτος) and "lavished" (ἐπερίσσευσεν), give the audience the impression that God has overwhelmed us in an inexhaustible way with his gracious love.[26]

In addition to the redemption and forgiveness we have "in the Beloved" God has lavished the wealth of his grace upon us "in all wisdom and insight" (1:8b).[27] As God blessed us "in every blessing" (ἐν πάσῃ εὐλογίᾳ, 1:3b), so God lavished the wealth of his grace upon us "in all wisdom and insight" (ἐν πάσῃ σοφίᾳ καὶ φρονήσει).[28] God lovingly lavished us in all wisdom and insight in "making known" or revealing to us "the mystery," the hidden secret, of his will, according to God's loving pleasure which he purposed "in him" (1:9), that is, in the Beloved.[29] Whereas God predestined us to sonship "according to the pleasure of his will" (κατὰ τὴν εὐδοκίαν τοῦ θελήματος αὐτοῦ, 1:5), God made known to us the mystery "of his will, according to his pleasure" (τοῦ θελήματος αὐτοῦ, κατὰ τὴν εὐδοκίαν αὐτοῦ) which he "purposed" or intended beforehand in Christ (1:9). As recipients of God's love, of the "pleasure" God already intended in Christ, the Beloved, we are able to understand the profound mystery of God with regard to Christ.

3. Eph 1:10ab (C): To Unite under One Head All Things in the Christ

The content of the mystery God has made known to us believers in accord with his loving pleasure for us established in the Beloved is expressed

---

26. Lincoln, *Ephesians*, 29: "The terms τὸ πλοῦτος and ἐπερίσσευσεν with their connotations of abundance and extravagance help to make this notion of grace emphatic, while at the same time leaving the impression that words fail in attempting to describe the inexhaustible resources of God's giving."

27. On "all wisdom and insight" in 1:8 as gifts of God's grace rather than as attributes of God, see Lincoln, *Ephesians*, 17; O'Brien, *Ephesians*, 107–8; Hoehner, *Ephesians*, 212–13.

28. Lincoln, *Ephesians*, 29–30: "Here in Ephesians we have noted that it is characteristic of the writer's style to use two or more words of similar meaning when one would do, and so it is likely that 'wisdom and insight' constitute a hendiadys. . . . rather than having to be achieved through human effort, mystical technique, or ascetic rigor, such wisdom and insight are available simply through the generosity of God's grace."

29. On why "in him" in 1:9 refers to Christ rather than to God, see Hoehner, *Ephesians*, 215–16.

in the pivotal C (1:10ab) and C′ elements (1:10c) of the chiasm in 1:3–14.[30] This profound mystery will attain its goal "as a plan (οἰκονομίαν) for the fullness of the times" (1:10a)," that is, when God has brought all time to its fulfillment within his eternal plan.[31] At that time God will "unite under one head" (ἀνακεφαλαιώσασθαι) "all the things"—the entirety of creation—"in the Christ" (1:10b).[32] Thus, God has graciously and lovingly given us believers all the wisdom and insight we need to know the mystery (1:8–9) that when time has been finally fulfilled everything in the cosmos will be joined together with us believers in our incorporation into *the* (τῷ) Christ (1:10b), *the* (τῷ) Beloved (1:6), with whom we are united in our situation of being "in love" (1:4b). That God will "unite under one *head* all the things in the Christ" implies that Christ is the "head" under which we and the rest of creation will ultimately be united.[33]

---

30. Moritz, "Summing Up All Things," 96: "The pivotal statement within this opening eulogy is 1:10."

31. Horst Kuhli, "οἰκονομία," *EDNT* 2.500: "[I]t designates the activity of arranging or executing, and therefore also in Eph 1:10 should be understood as an ordering, arranging, or implementing. Therefore, since it is related to the implementation of the decision made by God, it approaches the meaning seen in the common second-century uses as a t.t. [technical term] for 'the plan of salvation,' but is not yet identical with it."

32. Patrick J. Hartin, "ἀνακεφαλαιώσασθαι τὰ πάντα ἐν τῷ Χριστῷ (Eph 1:10)," in *A South African Perspective on the New Testament: Essays by South African New Testament Scholars Presented to Bruce Manning Metzger during His Visit to South Africa in 1985* (ed. J. H. Petzer and Patrick J. Hartin; Leiden: Brill, 1986), 232: "Although the word ἀνακεφαλαιώσασθαι is not to be derived from the word κεφαλή [head], nevertheless from the context of the letter this ἀνακεφαλαιώσασθαι does exercise a relationship to the function which Christ performs as Head. It was probably this connection which suggested this word to Paul in the first place." After countering the objections that ἀνακεφαλαιώσασθαι derives from κεφάλαιον ("main point, summary") rather than from κεφαλή ("head"), Hoehner (*Ephesians*, 221) concludes: "God's purpose in Christ is to unite all things for himself (middle voice) under one head. Consequently, the translation 'to unite under one head' appears to capture the idea." See also Gregory W. Dawes, *The Body in Question: Metaphor and Meaning in the Interpretation of Ephesians 5:21–33* (BIS 30; Leiden: Brill, 1998), 143. Helmut Merklein, "ἀνακεφαλαιόω," *EDNT* 1.83: "Eph 1:10b, c, then, describes the act of God which establishes in Christ the eschatological goal for the sake of which the entire creation was brought into being so that it encompasses the universe in its spatio-temporal dimensions." See also Peter Thomas O'Brien, "The Summing Up of All Things (Ephesians 1:10)," in *The New Testament in Its First Century Setting: Essays on Context and Background in Honour of B. W. Winter on His Sixty-fifth Birthday* (ed. P. J. Williams et al.; Grand Rapids: Eerdmans, 2004), 206–19.

33. Lincoln, *Ephesians*, 34: "Earlier, 'in Christ' has functioned to indicate Christ's being the elect representative in whom believers are included, but now it can be seen that God's comprehensive purpose goes beyond simply humanity to embrace the whole created order. This part of the berakah [1:3–14] helps believers to recognize that to be incorporated into God's gracious decision about Christ is also to be caught up in God's gracious purpose for a universe centered and reunited in Christ." On the cosmic christology of Ephesians, see George H. van Kooten, *Cosmic Christology in Paul and the Pauline School: Colossians and*

4. *Eph 1:10c (C´): The Things in Heaven and the Things on Earth in Christ*

With these central C (1:10ab) and C´ (1:10c) elements we have reached the pivotal point in the chiasm of 1:3–14, the point that begins to lead the audience to the conclusion of the chiasm by recalling and developing aspects of the elements that led to these central points. The expression, "the (τά) things in heaven and the (τά) things on earth," in the C´ element (1:10c) not only rhetorically reinforces the parallel expression, "all the (τά) things," in the C element (1:10b) of the chiasm, but further delineates it. All the things that God will unite under one head include both all the spiritual, invisible powers and entities in the heavenly realm and all the physical, visible powers and entities on the earth.[34]

The prepositional phrase "in him" at the end of the C´ element (1:10c) continues the chiasm's rhythmic pattern of pointedly punctuating the end of an element or sub-element (except the final A´ element in 1:14) with an "in" (ἐν) prepositional phrase. "In him" (ἐν αὐτῷ) at the end of the C´ element (1:10c) not only rhetorically reinforces "in the Christ" (ἐν τῷ Χριστῷ) as the one under whom God will unite all created things at the end of the C element (1:10b), but echoes the "in him" (ἐν αὐτῷ) in whom God has intended his loving pleasure at the end of the B element (1:9), which in turn echoes "in the Beloved" (ἐν τῷ ἠγαπημένῳ) as the Christ in union with whom God has graced us believers at the end of the A element (1:6). And "in the Beloved" at the end of the "a´" sub-element within the A element echoes "in love" (ἐν ἀγάπῃ) at the end of the "b" sub-element (1:4), the situation in which we have been loved by God who blessed us with every Spiritual blessing "in Christ" (ἐν Χριστῷ) at the end of the "a" (1:3) sub-element.

5. *Eph 1:11–12 (B´): We Who First Hoped in the Christ*

Introduced by the prepositional phrase "in whom" (ἐν ᾧ), referring to the Christ in whom God will unite under one head all the things in heaven and on earth (1:10), the B´ element of the chiasm (1:11–12) recalls and develops for the audience the parallel B element (1:7–9), introduced by the same prepositional phrase "in whom" (ἐν ᾧ), referring to "in the Beloved"

Ephesians in the Context of Graeco-Roman Cosmology, with a New Synopsis of the Greek Texts (WUNT 2/171; Tübingen: Mohr Siebeck, 2003), 147–203.

34. Lincoln, *Ephesians*, 34: "The elaboration τὰ ἐπὶ τοῖς οὐρανοῖς καὶ τὰ ἐπὶ τῆς γῆς indicates that we are right to take τὰ πάντα in its widest sense of all things and all beings, that is, the cosmos as a whole and not just humanity. This twofold division of the universe was common in Jewish thought where created reality was seen as having two major parts and where heaven as the upper part of the cosmos was regarded as concealing a presently invisible created spiritual order. . . . The 'things in heaven' include the spiritual forces, both good and evil, which compete for the allegiance of humanity." On the cosmology of the first century, see Timothy B. Cargal, "Seated in the Heavenlies: Cosmic Mediators in the Mysteries of Mithras and the Letter to the Ephesians," *SBLSP* 33 (1994): 804–21.

(1:6). Not only do we believers have the redemption and forgiveness of transgressions as gracious gifts of God's love in our union with the Beloved in the B element (1:7), but it is in our union with Christ, the Beloved, that "also we have been made heirs having been predestined (by God; divine passives) according to the purpose of the one working in all things according to the counsel of his will" in the B′ element (1:11).

That we believers also have been made heirs "having been predestined" (προορισθέντες) for it in the B′ element (1:11) makes explicit what was implicit in God's "having predestined" (προορίσας) us to sonship in the A element (1:5)—as adopted sons of God we have become heirs of God our Father, who has made us God's own inheritance.[35]

That we also have been predestined to be God's heirs or inheritance "according (κατὰ) to the purpose (πρόθεσιν) of the one who is working in all things according (κατὰ) to the counsel of his will (τοῦ θελήματος αὐτοῦ)" in the B′ element (1:11) recalls and develops for the audience God's "having made known to us the mystery of his will (τοῦ θελήματος αὐτοῦ), according (κατὰ) to his pleasure which he purposed (προέθετο) in him" in the parallel B element (1:9).[36] We have been predestined to be God's inheritance, then, in accord with the definitively determined "purpose" of the God who is working in "all things" (τὰ πάντα, in 1:10, 11) to unite them under one head in the Christ (1:10), in whom God decidedly "purposed" or intended to extend his loving pleasure to us believers.[37]

That it is in accord with the counsel of God's "will" in the B′ element (1:11) reinforces the decisiveness and certainty of God's purpose to extend the gracious "pleasure" of his love to us, as it recalls not only that the making known of the mystery of God's "will" is in accord with God's gracious "pleasure" in the B element (1:9), but also that our sonship was in accord

---

35. On the meaning of the passive ἐκληρώθημεν as "we have been made into an inheritance" (by God), see Hoehner, *Ephesians*, 226–27.

36. Hoehner, *Ephesians*, 228: "[I]n this context the idea of 'purpose' fits well since it has been expressed already in the verb form in verse 9 where God made known the mystery of his will according to the good pleasure of his will which he 'purposed' or 'resolved' in Christ. In the immediate context it has the idea that the predestined inheritance as God's possession was according to the purpose, resolve, or decision of the one who is working all things."

37. On 1:11 Hoehner (*Ephesians*, 225–26) points out: "The καί is not qualifying an unexpressed pronoun but, rather, the action of the verb (ἐκληρώθημεν), thus expressing the believers' acquisition of that which God has purposed in Christ in verse 9. The subject of the entire doxology is God, but the emphasis has changed from what God has done, expressed in the active voice, to what believers receive from God, expressed in the passive voice. . . . This context demonstrates that God not only purposed to unite all things in the one head, Christ, in the future 'fullness of the time,' but that the believers of this present age would 'also' be God's inheritance." See also Lincoln, *Ephesians*, 35–36.

with the gracious "pleasure of his will" in the A element of the chiasm (1:5):[38]

1:5: according (κατά) to the pleasure (εὐδοκίαν) of his will (τοῦ θελήματος αὐτοῦ)

1:9: the mystery of his will (τοῦ θελήματος αὐτοῦ), according (κατά) to his pleasure (εὐδοκίαν) which he purposed (προέθετο)

1:11: according (κατά) to the purpose (πρόθεσιν) ... according (κατά) to the counsel of his will (τοῦ θελήματος αὐτοῦ)

After having further impressed the audience in 1:11 with the love we believers have graciously received from God in our union with the Beloved (1:6) within the dynamic realm of our situation of being "in love" (1:4), Paul moves to our response of grateful praise for the love that we have received from God in 1:12 of the B′ element of the chiasm. The audience hear the words "in order that we might be to the praise of his glory" (1:12a) as an abbreviated echo of the words "to the praise of the glory of his grace with which he graced us in the Beloved" at the conclusion of the A element (1:6). Our loving response as believers who have been gifted with the love of God is to praise the glory that God has manifested in loving us who have been incorporated into Christ, *the* Beloved.[39]

After implying all along that "we" who have been loved by God "in the Beloved" include all believers, Paul suddenly delineates the "we" as those "who first hoped in the Christ (ἐν τῷ Χριστῷ)" (1:12b), that is, "in the Christ" (ἐν τῷ Χριστῷ) in whom God will unite under one head all things (1:10). The prepositional phrase "in the Christ" that concludes the B′ element in 1:12 thus continues the rhythmic pattern of "in" prepositional phrases that have punctuated the conclusion of each of the previous elements and sub-elements of the chiasm in 1:3–14—"in Christ" (1:3), "in love" (1:4), "in the Beloved" (1:6), "in him" (1:9), "in the Christ" (1:10b), and "in him" (1:10c). But the words "who first hoped in the Christ" raise for the audience the question of whether there is a distinction between the "we,"

---

38. On the meaning of "counsel" (βουλή) in 1:11 Hoehner (*Ephesians*, 230) states that "the term gives a sense of deliberation: therefore, decisions and plans are not based on a whim but on careful thought and interaction. . . . βουλή describes the intelligent deliberation of God and θέλημα expresses the will of God which proceeds from the deliberation." See also Hans-Joachim Ritz, "βουλή," *EDNT* 1.224.

39. Lincoln, *Ephesians*, 36: "As in v. 4 the purpose of God's choice is that believers be holy and blameless before him in love, and as in vv 5, 6 the purpose of his predestination is that believers be in relationship with himself and to the praise of the glory of his grace, so in vv 11, 12 the purpose of his appointing is that they be to the praise of his glory."

as those "who first hoped (προηλπικότας) in the Christ," that may exclude
from the "we" those believers who hoped in the Christ at a later time.[40]

6. Eph 1:13–14 (A´): To the Praise of His Glory

The implication of a distinction between "we" who first hoped in the
Christ (1:12) and later, more recent believers is made explicit as Paul again
addresses a plural "you" at the beginning of the A´ element in 1:13, resuming the address of his audience as "you" in the opening of the letter (1:2).
But Paul quickly dispels from the minds of his audience any notion that
these later believers, the "you," are in any way excluded from the dynamics
of being "in love" (1:4) "in the Beloved" (1:6).[41] After an introductory "in
whom" (ἐν ᾧ) phrase, recalling for the audience the identical "in whom"
(ἐν ᾧ) phrases that introduced both the B and B´ elements in 1:7 and 1:11
respectively, and which introduced expressions of how the "we" have been
loved by God in order to love God in return by praising his glory, Paul emphatically includes his audience—"also you" (καὶ ὑμεῖς)—in the dynamic
realm of being "in love" (1:4) "in the Beloved" (1:6) as he reaches the conclusion of the chiasm in the A´ element (1:13–14) .[42]

Paul describes the "you" not only as those "having heard the word of

---

40. Lincoln, *Ephesians*, 37: "προελπίζειν is a hapax legomenon in the NT. In compound
verbs the pro- prefix usually stresses the notion of 'ahead of time' or 'beforehand.' " See also
O'Brien, *Ephesians*, 118 n. 119. Muddiman, *Ephesians*, 77: "Since hope inevitably precedes
its realization, the prefix [pro] cannot simply mean that 'we hoped before we experienced'
but must mean 'we hoped before others did'."

41. Many scholars identify the "we" who first hoped in the Christ (1:12) as Jewish
Christians and the "you" who came to faith (and thus hope) later as Gentile Christians. But
that is an oversimplification not supported by the text. The issue is not simply Jewish Christians versus Gentile Christians, but those who first hoped in the Christ, be they Jewish or
Gentile (some of the first believers included Gentiles, e.g. Titus), versus those who came to
faith at a later time, be they Gentile or Jewish. On the presence of Jewish Christians at Ephesus, see ch. 1. Lincoln, *Ephesians*, 38: "The proposed distinction between 'we' as Jewish
Christians and 'you' as Gentile Christians is one that simply does not hold for the rest of the
letter." What is said of "us" in Ephesians refers to all believers and what is said of "you" to
newer believers according to R. A. Wilson, " 'We' and 'You' in the Epistle to the Ephesians,"
in *Papers Presented to the Second International Congress on New Testament Studies Held
at Christ Church Oxford, 1961* (ed. Frank Leslie Cross; TU 87; Berlin: Akademie, 1964),
676–80. See also Donald Jayne, " 'We' and 'You' in Ephesians 1,3–14," *ExpTim* 85 (1974):
151–52.

42. Lincoln, *Ephesians*, 38: "[T]he 'you' in v 13 marks the point at which the letter's
recipients are addressed and explicitly drawn into the blessing offered by believers in general
as they are reminded of their reception of the gospel. The writer makes a distinction between
believers in general and his present audience, and yet is saying that the same blessings have
come upon both groups."

the truth, the gospel of *your* salvation" (1:13a),[43] but as those, again "in whom" (ἐν ᾧ), that is, in their union with Christ, *the* Beloved (1:6, 10, 12), "also have believed" (cf. 1:1) so that "you have been sealed with the Holy Spirit of the promise" (1:13b).[44] That the audience of "you" believers have been sealed (by God, divine passive) with the Holy "Spirit" (πνεύματι) of the promise in the A′ element (1:13b) recalls and develops for the audience how God has blessed "us," the "we" believers, "with every Spiritual (πνευματικῇ) blessing in the heavenly places in Christ" in the parallel A element (1:3b) of the chiasm. That the "you" believers have been sealed as a gift of God's love with the Holy "Spirit"—a specific and the premier example of every "Spiritual" blessing—thus includes the "you" believers within the circle of "we" believers, that is, all believers, who are "in love" (1:4) "in the Beloved" (1:6).[45]

That the "you" believers have been sealed by God with the Spirit that is "holy" (ἁγίῳ) in the A′ element (1:13b) recalls and develops for the audience how the "we," that is, all, believers might be "holy" (ἁγίους) and blameless before God within the dynamic realm of being "in love" in the parallel A element (1:4b). The implication for the audience is that not only they, the "you," but all believers, the "we," have been sealed with the Holy Spirit as a gift of God's love within the realm of being "in love," a Spirit that, being "holy," can in turn empower believers to respond to God's love by living "holy" and blameless lives before God "in love," that is, within the dynamic realm of existence in which believers are both recipients of and respondents to the love God has extended to them by their incorporation into and union with Christ, *the* Beloved (1:6).[46]

That the Holy Spirit given to the "you" believers is the "down payment," "first installment," or "guarantee" (ἀρραβών) of "*our* (ἡμῶν) inheritance" in the A′ element (1:14a) confirms for the audience that the "you" believers

---

43. O'Brien, *Ephesians*, 119: "The appositional expression, *the gospel of your salvation*, with its emphatic personal pronoun *your* reminds the readers of their conversion, and draws attention to what this powerful message has accomplished for them."

44. Hoehner, *Ephesians*, 238: "In this context the sealing refers to ownership. This fits well with the previous verses because the believers are God's heritage (v. 11) and thus belong to him." On the "Holy Spirit of the promise" Fee (*God's Empowering Presence*, 671) notes that "the genitive is to be understood as adjectival (qualitative) and refers to 'the promised Holy Spirit.' " See also Gerhard Sellin, "Über einige ungewöhnliche Genitive im Epheserbrief," *ZNW* 83 (1992): 88–90.

45. Lincoln, *Ephesians*, 40: "Being sealed by the Spirit is a specific blessing for which God is to be blessed, yet at the same time, as v 3 has indicated, there is a sense in which all the blessings of the eulogy can be attributed to the Spirit, since they are 'spiritual' blessings."

46. Fee, *God's Empowering Presence*, 670 n. 40: "The unusual wording and order, τῷ πνεύματι τῆς ἐπαγγελίας τῷ ἁγίῳ (= the Spirit of the promise, the Holy) . . . places emphasis on both the 'promise' and the adjective 'holy.' " Hoehner, *Ephesians*, 240: "The τῷ ἁγίῳ is placed at the end to emphasize the personal righteous character of the Spirit."

are included within the "we" believers.[47] This recalls and develops how the God and Father of "our" (ἡμῶν) Lord Jesus Christ has blessed "us," all believers, with every Spiritual blessing in the parallel A element (1:3) of the chiasm.[48] And that the Holy Spirit is the first installment of *our* "inheritance" (κληρονομίας) in the A´ element (1:14a) further assures the audience that the "you" believers are part of the "we" believers, as it recalls that "*we* have been made an inheritance" (ἐκληρώθημεν) in the B´ element (1:11) of the chiasm.

The goal of all believers, both the "we" believers who first hoped in the Christ (1:12) and the "you" believers who came to this hope later (1:13), being sealed with the Holy Spirit who is the first installment of *our* inheritance is "for the redemption (ἀπολύτρωσιν) of the possession,"[49] that is, the "redemption" (ἀπολύτρωσιν) that we have through the blood of Jesus Christ (1:7), to be God's possession (1:14b; cf. Mal 3:17) "to the praise of his glory" (1:14c).[50] Having received the Holy Spirit as recipients of God's overwhelming love for us in our union with the Beloved (1:6) within the realm of being "in love" (1:4), we believers are empowered to respond to that gracious love of God by praising the glory of God (1:14).

That the gift of the Holy Spirit, the first installment of *our*, that is, all believers', inheritance, empowers all believers who have been loved by God "in the Beloved" (1:6) "to the praise of his glory" in the A´ element (1:14c) corrects for the audience any possible implication of a limiting of this praising to the first believers in the statement that "we might be to the praise

---

47. Alexander Sand, "ἀρραβών," *EDNT* 1.158: "An ἀρραβών is the earnest on the basis of which one obligates oneself to the fulfillment of a promise." See also BDAG, 134. Lincoln, *Ephesians*, 40: "In a down payment, that which is given is part of a greater whole, is of the same kind as that whole, and functions as a guarantee that the whole payment will be forthcoming. The Spirit then is the first installment and guarantee of the salvation of the age to come with its mode of existence totally determined by the Spirit." Fee, *God's Empowering Presence*, 671: "[T]he Spirit as 'down payment' means present possession of what has been promised. On the other hand, as 'down payment' the Spirit also guarantees the future consummation of what is now realized only in part."

48. That the first-person plural pronoun "our" (ἡμῶν) occurs only in 1:3 and 1:14 within the eulogy of 1:3–14, thus serving as a literary inclusion framing it, enhances the parallelism between the A and A´ elements within the chiasm.

49. O'Brien, *Ephesians*, 122: "The whole phrase 'for the redemption of the possession' does not have a purely temporal sense; instead, it indicates the goal of the action described in the main verb, 'you were sealed'." See also Sellin, "Genitive im Epheserbrief," 91–92.

50. On "possession" (περιποιήσεως) in 1:14b Hoehner (*Ephesians*, 244) states: "It is used much in the same way as 1 Pet 2:9 which may go back to Mal 3:17 or possibly Isa 43:21 where it refers to an OT concept that the redeemed people of God are God's possession. In the present context the believers are considered God's possession by the very fact that he has chosen, redeemed, and adopted them." On the future dimension of "the redemption of the possession," see Thomas Witulski, "Gegenwart und Zukunft in den eschatologischen Konzeptionen des Kolosser- und Epheserbriefes," *ZNW* 96 (2005): 228–29.

of his glory, who first hoped in the Christ" in the B´ element (1:12) of the chiasm. Indeed, "to the praise of his glory" in the A´ element (1:14c) serves as the final and climactic abbreviated echo of the words "to the praise of the glory of his grace with which he graced us"—all believers—"in the Beloved" at the conclusion of the parallel A element (1:6) of the chiasm:

> 1:6: to the praise of the glory (εἰς ἔπαινον δόξης) of his (αὐτοῦ) grace with which he graced us in the Beloved

> 1:12: that we might be to the praise of his glory (εἰς ἔπαινον τῆς δόξης αὐτοῦ), who first hoped in the Christ

> 1:14: to the praise of his glory (εἰς ἔπαινον τῆς δόξης αὐτοῦ)

As the final phrase of the chiastic eulogy in 1:3–14, "to the praise of his glory" (1:14c) climactically breaks the rhythmic pattern of punctuating the end of every element and sub-element of the chiasm with an "in" prepositional phrase. This leaves the audience with the lasting impression that the point of we believers being extremely blessed with the love of God "in Christ" (1:3), within the realm of our being "in love" (1:4b), in which God has graced us "in the Beloved" (1:6), having made known to us the mystery, according to his pleasure that he purposed "in him" (1:9), to unite under one head all things "in the Christ" (1:10b), the things in heaven and the things on earth "in him" (1:10c), "in the Christ" (1:12) in whom the first believers hoped, is that we might respond to this extravagant divine love by exuberantly praising God's glory—that we might be "to the praise of his glory!" (1:6, 12, 14):

> 1:3: in Christ (ἐν Χριστῷ)

> 1:4: in love (ἐν ἀγάπῃ)

> 1:6: in the Beloved (ἐν τῷ ἠγαπημένῳ)

> 1:9: in him (ἐν αὐτῷ)

> 1:10b: in the Christ (ἐν τῷ Χριστῷ)

> 1:10c: in him (ἐν αὐτῷ)

> 1:12: in the Christ (ἐν τῷ Χριστῷ)

> 1:14: to the praise of his glory! (εἰς ἔπαινον τῆς δόξης αὐτοῦ)[51]

---

51. O'Brien, *Ephesians*, 123: "The eulogy of vv. 3–14 began with an outburst of praise as Paul blessed God for all the blessings he had showered on his people in the Lord Jesus Christ. The note of praise has been sustained throughout by means of the recurring refrain

The eulogy (1:3–14) that began by declaring God blessed (1:3a) as an anticipatory response for all the blessings believers have been granted as recipients of God's love thus concludes with the climactic third occurrence of the reverberating refrain that continues that response to the gracious love with which God graced us in our situation of being "in love" (1:4b) "in *the* Beloved" (1:6)—"to the praise of his glory!" (1:14c; cf. 1:6, 12).

B. Summary on Ephesians 1:3–14

1. The dynamic and comprehensive phrase "in love" (1:4b) embraces all of the dimensions and relationships established by God's gracious love "in Christ" (1:3b). It is by or because of the love God extended to believers in choosing them that God empowers them to be holy and blameless before him. This love of God establishes a dynamic set of relationships within the realm characterized as "in love." This realm includes not only God's love for believers, as indicated by his blessing and choosing them (1:3b-4a), but believers' love for God, as expressed both by their blessing of God (1:3a) and living holy and blameless before God (1:4b). And since "holy and blameless" refers to moral conduct, "in love" implies believers loving one another.

2. God's grace of predestining us to be his adopted sons through Jesus Christ (1:5a) means that we too are recipients of the love of the God who is the Father of both Jesus Christ and us believers (1:2, 3) in our situation of being "in the Beloved" (1:6). Our being loved by God as we are "in the Beloved" not only inspires us to respond to God's love by praising the God who graced us with his grace (1:6) and by blessing the God who blessed us with every Spiritual blessing (1:3), but empowers us to respond to God's love by being holy and blameless before God "in love" (1:4b).

3. In his extravagantly generous love for us God has graciously given us believers all the wisdom and insight we need to know the mystery (1:8–9) that when time has been finally fulfilled (1:10a) everything in the cosmos will be joined together with us believers under one head in our incorporation into *the* Christ (1:10b), *the* Beloved (1:6), with whom we are united in our situation of being "in love" (1:4b).

4. The final phrase of the chiastic eulogy in 1:3–14, "to the praise of his glory" (1:14c), climactically breaks the reverberating rhythmic pattern of punctuating the end of every element and sub-element of the chiasm with an "in" prepositional phrase. This leaves the audience with the lasting im-

---

'to the praise of his glory' (vv. 6, 12, 14). The recipients of these wide-ranging blessings of salvation, along with Paul, have been stimulated by this recital of God's mighty acts in his Son to express their gratitude and praise."

pression that the point of we believers being extremely blessed with the love of God *in Christ* (1:3), within the realm of our being *in love* (1:4b), in which God has graced us *in the Beloved* (1:6), having made known to us the mystery, according to his pleasure that he purposed *in him* (1:9), to unite under one head all things *in the Christ* (1:10b), the things in heaven and the things on earth *in him* (1:10c), *in the Christ* (1:12) in whom the first believers hoped, is that we, all believers—both those who first hoped in the Christ (1:12) and "you," the audience, who arrived at this faith and hope later (1:13)—might respond to this extravagantly gracious divine love by exuberantly praising God's glory—that we might be "to the praise of his glory!" (1:6, 12, 14).

CHAPTER 5

Ephesians 1:15–23: Gift of Christ in Love as Head Over All to the Church (C)

A: [15] For this reason, I also, having heard of the faith regarding you in the Lord Jesus and of the love for *all* the holy ones, [16] do not cease giving thanks for you, making mention of you in my prayers, [17] that the God of our Lord Jesus Christ, the Father of glory, may *give* you the Spirit of wisdom and revelation in knowledge of him, [18] the eyes of your heart having been enlightened so that you may know what is the hope of his calling, what is the wealth of the glory of his inheritance in the holy ones,

    B: [19] and what is the *surpassing* greatness of his *power* for us who believe according to the working of the might of his strength,

        C: [20] which he worked *in* the Christ, raising him from the dead

        C′:   and seating him *at* his right hand *in* the heavenly places,

    B′:   [21] *far above* every ruler and authority and *power* and dominion and every name that is named, not only in this age but also in the one to come.

A′:   [22] And *all things* he subjected under his feet and *gave* him as head over *all things* to the church, [23] which is indeed his body, the fullness of the one who is filling *all the things in all ways*.[1]

---

1. For the establishment of Eph 1:15–23 as a chiasm, see ch. 2.

A. Audience Response to Ephesians 1:15–23

1. Eph 1:15–18 (A): Among the Holy Ones Whom You Love

In Eph 1:15–18 the audience hear the A element of this complex, one-sentence chiasm in 1:15–23 as a mini-chiasm in itself (cf. 1:3–6 in ch. 4), composed of six sub-elements:

> (a) For this reason, I also, having heard of the faith regarding you *in* the Lord Jesus and of the love for all the *holy ones*, do not cease giving thanks for you, making mention of you in my prayers (1:15–16),
>> (b) that the God of our Lord Jesus Christ, the Father of *glory* (1:17a),
>>> (c) may give you the Spirit of wisdom and revelation in *knowledge* of *him* (1:17b),
>>> (c´) the eyes of your heart having been enlightened so that you may *know* what is the hope of *his* calling (1:18a),
>> (b´) what is the wealth of the *glory* of his inheritance (1:18b)
> (a´) *in* the *holy ones* (1:18c),

The only occurrences in the chiasm of the first-person singular pronoun—"I also" (κἀγώ) at the beginning (1:15) and "my" (μου) prayers at the end (1:16)—form a literary inclusion securing the unity of the "a" (1:15–16) sub-element. The only occurrences in the chiasm of "the holy ones"—"for all the holy ones (τοὺς ἁγίους)" in 1:15 and "in the holy ones (τοῖς ἁγίοις)" in 1:18—as well as the "in" prepositional phrases—"in (ἐν) the Lord Jesus" in 1:15 and "in (ἐν) the holy ones" in 1:18c—establish the parallelism between the "a" (1:15–16) and "a´" (1:18c) sub-elements. The only occurrences in the chiasm of the word "glory"—"the Father of glory (δόξης)" in 1:17a and "the wealth of the glory (δόξης)" in 1:18b—establish the parallelism of the "b" (1:17a) and "b´" (1:18b) sub-elements. And references to "knowledge" of "him" with the third-person singular pronoun referring to God—"in knowledge (ἐπιγνώσει) of him (αὐτοῦ)" in 1:17b and "that you may know (εἰδέναι) what is the hope of his (αὐτοῦ) calling" in 1:18a—indicate the parallelism of the central "c" (1:17b) and "c´" (1:18a) sub-elements of the chiasm in 1:15–18.

a. Eph 1:15–16 (a): Having heard of your love for all the holy ones

The introductory "for this reason" (διὰ τοῦτο) in 1:15a points the audience back to 1:3–14, especially 1:13–14, in which Paul assures his audience of "you" believers that they belong among the "we" believers.[2] Emphatically

---

2. Peter Thomas O'Brien, "Ephesians 1: An Unusual Introduction to a New Testament Letter," *NTS* 25 (1978): 513.

singling Paul out from the "we" believers, the first-person singular pronoun with conjunction, "I also" (κἀγώ), resumes the address of Paul as authoritative apostle to his audience (cf. 1:1).[3]

In addition to "you" (ὑμεῖς), Paul's audience, "having heard (ἀκούσαντες) the word of the truth" and "having believed" (πιστεύσαντες) (1:13) is Paul's ("I also") "having heard (ἀκούσας) of the faith (πίστιν) regarding you (ὑμᾶς) in the Lord Jesus" (1:15a). While "regarding you" (καθ᾽ ὑμᾶς) is grammatically equivalent to "your" (ὑμῶν),[4] rhetorically it places a particular focus on the faith of the "you" believers in relation to the "we" believers.[5] That the faith "regarding you" is "in (ἐν) the Lord Jesus," that is, that the Lord Jesus is not only the object of their faith but the realm in which they continue their life of faith in union with the Lord Jesus, further joins Paul's audience of "you" believers to the "we" believers who "first hoped (and thus believed) in (ἐν) the Christ" (1:12).

That Paul has also heard of his audience's "love for all the holy ones" (1:15b) develops the dynamics of the Letter's theme of love.[6] Their "love" (ἀγάπην) for all the holy ones serves as an explicit example of what was implicit in God's choosing believers in Christ that they might be "holy and blameless before him in love (ἐν ἀγάπῃ)" (1:4b), as it indicates that the dynamic realm of relationships involved in believers being "in love" includes not only God's love for believers in Christ and their love for God but also believers' love for one another. That Paul's audience of "you" believers, those he addressed as the "holy ones" (ἁγίοις) who are in Ephesus" (1:1c), have love for all of their fellow "holy ones" (ἁγίους) (1:15b) is part of what it means for believers to be "holy" (ἁγίους) and blameless before God in their situation of being "in love" (1:4b) "in the Beloved" (1:6b). The "you" believers' love for *all* the holy ones thus further unites them to the "we" believers who are included within *all* the holy ones.[7]

---

3. Hoehner (*Ephesians*, 248) states that the "I also" in 1:15 "specifically points to Paul in contrast to the 'we/us' in verses 3–12, 14 and also sets him as the author apart from the recipients designated by 'you' in verse 13."

4. Maximilian Zerwick, *Biblical Greek* (Rome: Biblical Institute, 1963), 43–44; BDF, §224.

5. On "regarding you" (καθ᾽ ὑμᾶς) in 1:15 Hoehner (*Ephesians*, 249) remarks that "it seems better to think of this unique form as not only indicating simple possession but indicating an active faith in Christ (cf. πιστοῖς, v. 1) that is a peculiar possession of theirs. . . . They had placed their faith in the Lord Jesus. This is not only the initial act of faith mentioned in verse 13, but a continuing faith in the Lord Jesus."

6. For the text-critical reasons for accepting the longer reader that includes the word "love" rather than the shorter reading that omits it, see Metzger, *Textual Commentary*, 533; Hoehner, *Ephesians*, 249 n. 5.

7. Hoehner (*Ephesians*, 250) notes that "this love that seeks the highest good in the one loved is directed toward all the saints, not toward some who may be more lovable." Lincoln, *Ephesians*, 55: "The recipients of this letter have an attitude of solidarity with, and concern for, the welfare of other believers." According to O'Brien (*Ephesians*, 128), "here the read-

That Paul does "not cease giving thanks for you" (1:16a) continues to develop the dynamics of the love theme.[8] Implicitly directed to God, Paul's thanks serves as his response to the way that the love God extended to believers in choosing them to be "in love" (1:4b) "in the Beloved" (1:6b) has inspired the "you" believers to love their fellow believers.[9] And Paul's "giving thanks for *you*, making mention of *you* in my prayers" (1:16) serves as a personal act of love on Paul's part for his fellow "you" believers, reinforcing his prayer wish that his audience be granted even more grace and peace from God our Father and the Lord Jesus Christ (1:2).

b. Eph 1:17a (b): Our Lord Jesus Christ and the Father of glory

Continuing the thrust to make his audience of "you" believers aware that they are included among the "we" believers, Paul addresses his prayers for "you" (ὑμῶν) to the God not just of "your" but of "our" (ἡμῶν) Lord Jesus Christ, the Father of glory (cf. 1:3), in the "b" (1:17a) sub-element. That Paul directs his prayers to God as the Father of "glory" (δόξης) reminds his audience of the reverberating rhythmic refrain inviting believers to respond to God's love by praising God for the glory manifested in God the Father's love for them in the Beloved—"to the praise of his glory (δόξης)!" (1:6, 12, 14).[10]

c. Eph 1:17b (c): Knowledge of God

In the "c" (1:17b) sub-element at the center of this mini-chiasm Paul's prayer that God "may *give* (δώη) to you" is a prayer for a further gift of God's gracious love to Paul's audience of "you" believers. For the "you" believers, who have already been sealed with the Holy Spirit (πνεύματι) of the promise (1:13), Paul prays for a further manifestation or realization of

---

ers' practical expression of care and concern has been directed to all God's holy people, which signifies Christians generally."

8. Hoehner, *Ephesians*, 250: "'Never ceasing to give thanks' may be hyperbolic, for this was the common style of ancient letters and it simply means that Paul did not forget the believers at his regular time of prayer."

9. In the NT "giving thanks" (εὐχαριστῶν) "designates (with few exceptions: Luke 17:16; Rom 16:4) thanks rendered to God, who is explicitly named as a dat. obj. or is to be inferred from the context," according to Hermann Patsch, "εὐχαριστέω," *EDNT* 2.87. Lincoln, *Ephesians*, 55: "His [Paul's] gratitude to God for those whose faith and love are known to him and of whom his previous description in vv 13, 14 is true is based ultimately on God's own work in Christ."

10. On "Father of glory" Hoehner (*Ephesians*, 255) suggests labelling "the genitive as characteristic quality, that is, the Father is characterized by his glory. He is not only a glorious Father but the Father to whom all glory belongs or of whom glory is the characteristic feature." See also Sellin, "Genitive im Epheserbrief," 93–96. Best, *Ephesians*, 161: "Normally 'father of' would be followed by the name of a person, however a metaphorical use of father is found in Jas 1.17; 2 Cor 1.3 (cf Heb 12.9) with the sense 'source of'; thus here he is the source of glory to those who are his children."

the gift of the Spirit—that God "may give you the Spirit (πνεῦμα) of wisdom and revelation in knowledge of him" (1:17b).[11]

In praying that God "may give you the Spirit of wisdom (σοφίας) and revelation in knowledge (ἐπιγνώσει) of him" (1:17b), Paul is further uniting the "you" believers to the "we" believers, as he is praying that God may give the "you" believers a further and more particular experience of the gracious love God has lavished on the "we" believers—"according to the wealth of his grace which he lavished upon us, in all wisdom (σοφία) and insight, having made known (γνωρίσας) to us the mystery of his will" (1:7b–9a). Paul is thus praying that the Spirit the "you" believers have already received may give them the wisdom and revelation they need for a particular and intimate knowledge of God, a further insight into the mystery of God's will that God has made known to the "we", that is, "all," believers.[12]

d. Eph 1:18a (c′): To know the hope of God's calling

Paul's prayer that the audience's gift of the Spirit may result in their "knowledge" (ἐπιγνώσει) of "him" (αὐτοῦ), that is, of God, in the "c" (1:17b) sub-element receives further elaboration and specification in the parallel "c′" (1:18a) sub-element at the center of the mini-chiasm —"the eyes of your heart having been enlightened so that you may know (εἰδέναι) the hope of his (αὐτοῦ) calling".[13] That the "eyes of your heart," that is your thinking and understanding, have been enlightened by God (divine passive) serves as another expression of God's gracious love for the "you" believers.[14]

---

11. According to Fee (God's Empowering Presence, 676 n. 55), "the prayer is not for some further Spirit reception, but for the indwelling Spirit whom they have already received to give them further wisdom and revelation. The emphasis, therefore, is not in receiving the Spirit as such, but on receiving (or perhaps realizing?) the resident Spirit's gifts." For the reasons for interpreting the anarthrous πνεῦμα in 1:17b as the Holy Spirit rather than the human spirit, see Hoehner, Ephesians, 257–58.

12. O'Brien, Ephesians, 132: "Here in the intercession of vv. 17–19, the apostle's prayer to God is that the Spirit, who had been given to the readers at their conversion (cf. v. 13), might impart wisdom and revelation to them so that they might understand more fully God's saving plan and live in the light of it. The mystery had already been made known in Christ (vv. 9–10), but the readers needed to grasp its full significance, not least of all their own part within it. And as the Spirit worked in their midst, giving them insights and revealing God's purposes in Christ, so they would grow in the knowledge of God."

13. Hoehner, Ephesians, 262: "πεφωτισμένους τοὺς ὀφθαλμούς looks back to ὑμῖν in verse 17 and forward to ὑμᾶς in the latter part of verse 18. Thus it could be translated, 'that God may give you the Spirit of insight and revelation in the knowledge of him, [you] having had the eyes of your heart enlightened, in order that you might know. . . .' "

14. Hoehner, Ephesians, 260–61: "The eye is metaphorically the avenue through which the light flows to the heart or mind. . . . καρδία, 'heart,' refers to the physical organ but more frequently it is used figuratively to refer to the seat of the moral and intellectual life. . . . Hence, the 'eyes of the heart' denotes enlightenment of thought and understanding. The word 'heart' is in the singular, denoting that it belongs to each person of the group."

With this enlightenment the "you" believers will be able to deepen their knowledge of God by knowing and thus experiencing the hope of God's calling of them.

Paul's prayer that the "you" believers may know the "hope" (ἐλπίς) of God's calling further aligns them with the "we" believers who "first hoped" (προηλπικότας) in the Christ (1:12b).[15] For the "you" believers to know the hope of God's "calling" (κλήσεως) means for them to presently experience the attitude of the absolutely assured hope to which God has "chosen" (ἐξελέξατο) all believers, namely, "that we might be holy and blameless before him in love" (1:4). And with this hope to which God has chosen and called them to live before him in the realm characterized as "in love," they may thus experience the hope that they will play a role in the mystery of God to unite under one head all things in the Christ (1:10). The goal of this mystery is the ultimate object of the hope of God's calling of them.[16]

e. Eph 1:18b (b´): To know the wealth of the glory of God's inheritance

Paul's reference to God as the Father of "glory" (δόξης) in the "b" (1:17a) sub-element progresses to his prayer that the "you" believers may know what is the wealth of the "glory" (δόξης) of the inheritance of God as the Father of glory in the parallel "b´" (1:18b) sub-element of the mini-chiasm. Paul's prayer that the "you" believers may know what is the "wealth" (πλοῦτος) of the glory of God's inheritance underscores the extravagant, generous, and lavish extent to which God has loved us believers, as it recalls for the audience the "wealth" (πλοῦτος) of God's grace "which he lavished upon us" (1:7b–8a), that is, the grace of God with which he graced us in our union with the Beloved (1:6) in our situation of being "in love" (1:4b).

For the "you" believers to know what is the wealth of the glory of God's "inheritance" (κληρονομίας, 1:18b), which is also "our" inheritance (κληρονομίας, 1:14), means for them to realize and experience that, like the

---

Alexander Sand, "καρδία," *EDNT* 2.250: "Καρδία refers thus to the inner person, the seat of understanding, knowledge, and will."

15. Hoehner, *Ephesians*, 264–65: "Hope in the present context is not the objective hope, that hope which is laid up for the believer (Col 1:5; Rom 8:24) but the subjective hope of all believers. One needs to realize that subjective hope is based on objective hope, a hope that looks back to God's work of redemption in 1:3–14, especially in 1:9–10 where Paul relates that all things are going to be headed up in Christ. Nevertheless, in this verse Paul is referring to the subjective hope. Hope for believers is not the world's wishful thinking, but the absolute certainty that God will make true what he has promised."

16. Lincoln, *Ephesians*, 59: "The language of 'calling' brings to mind that of 'choice,' 'predestination,' and 'appointment' in the eulogy (1:4, 5, 11)." Hoehner, *Ephesians*, 265: "The genitive that follows (κλήσεως, 'calling') could be a genitive of source, 'hope has its origin in his call' or more likely a subjective genitive 'hope produced by his calling' (cf. 4:4). The noun κλῆσις . . . is closely linked with election, for inherent in the verb form is the idea of God's foreknowledge and predestination."

"we" (all) believers, they have been predestined to be adopted sons of God through Jesus Christ (1:5), the one in whom, that is, in our situation of being loved by God as adopted sons in union with "the Beloved" (1:6) Son, "we have obtained an inheritance" (ἐκληρώθημεν, 1:11) from God as the Father of glory.[17]

f. Eph 1:18c (a´): Among the holy ones

It is "in" or "among" (ἐν), that is, in their union with the "holy ones" (ἁγίοις) in the "a´" (1:18c) sub-element, with whom they have been united through their love for all the "holy ones" (ἁγίους) in the parallel "a" (1:15–16) sub-element, that the audience of "you" believers may know what is the wealth of the glory of God's inheritance for all believers. The "you" believers, then, are not only "in" (ἐν) union with the Lord Jesus as those who have faith in the Lord Jesus (1:15), but also, as the holy ones who are in Ephesus (1:1c), the "you" believers are "in" (ἐν) union with the rest of the holy ones (1:18c), since the "you" believers have love for all the holy ones (1:15).

2. Eph 1:19 (B): The Greatness of God's Power for Us Who Believe

After praying that his audience of "you" believers may know "what" (τίς) is the hope of God's calling, "what" (τίς) is the wealth of the glory of his inheritance in the holy ones at the conclusion of the A element (1:18), Paul climactically completes the triplet by praying that they may know "also what (τί) is the surpassing greatness of his power for us who believe according to the working of the might of his strength" in the B element (1:19) of the chiasm in 1:15–23. Continuing to make his audience of "you" believers aware that they are part of the "we" (all) believers, the Paul who has heard of the faith regarding the "you" (ὑμᾶς) believers (1:15) now prays that "you" (ὑμᾶς) may have a knowledge (1:18) and thus an experience of the surpassing greatness of God's power that is for all of "us" (ἡμᾶς) who believe (1:19). As the "you" believers have a love that is "for" (εἰς) all the holy ones (1:15), so the surpassing greatness of God's power—a gift of God's love—is "for" (εἰς) all of us who believe (1:19).[18]

Paul's prayer that God may give—as a further gift of love—to his audience of "you" believers the Spirit of wisdom and revelation resulting in knowledge of "him" (αὐτοῦ), that is, of God (1:17), received further elaboration in terms of their knowing the hope of "his" (αὐτοῦ) calling, the wealth

---

17. O'Brien, *Ephesians*, 136: "Paul prays that his readers might appreciate the extraordinary value which God places on them. He views them as in his beloved Son and estimates them accordingly. And this is true of all who are 'in Christ'."

18. O'Brien, *Ephesians*, 137: "This petition contains a significant change from the second person to the first: the mighty power of God is exercised 'for *us* who believe' rather than simply 'for *you*', the readers. By using the first person Paul includes himself and other Christians. God's might is effective for *all* who believe" (O'Brien's emphasis).

of the glory of "his" (αὐτοῦ) inheritance (1:18), in the A element. And now in the B element of the chiasm Paul's prayer for his audience's intimate knowledge of God progresses to their knowing the surpassing greatness of "his" (αὐτοῦ) power that is in accord with the working of the might of "his" (αὐτοῦ) strength (1:19).[19] Paul's prayer that his audience may enjoy a present experiential knowledge of "the surpassing greatness" of God's power, intensified by the fourfold accumulation of synonymous terms—"power," "working," "might," and "strength"—for us who believe continues to underscore the extravagant, generous, and lavish extent of God's love for all believers.[20]

3. Eph 1:20a (C): The Power God Worked in Raising the Christ from the Dead

Paul's prayer that his audience of "you" believers may know the surpassing greatness of God's power that is in accord with the working of the might of his strength in the B element (1:19) progresses to a specific manifestation of that divine power by continuing the thought of the noun "working" (ἐνέργειαν) with the use of its cognate verb in the C element at the center of the chiasm (1:20a): "which he worked (ἐνήργησεν) in the Christ, raising him from the dead."[21] The "working" of the power of God which he "worked" in the Christ (ἐν τῷ Χριστῷ) in raising him from the dead reminds the audience of the previous description of God as the one who "works in" (ἐνεργοῦντος) all things (τὰ πάντα) according to the counsel of his will (1:11), that is, in

---

19. On "according to the working of the might of his strength" in 1:19 Hoehner (*Ephesians*, 269) points out: "This prepositional phrase does not modify 'toward us who believe' but modifies 'the surpassing greatness of his power.' "

20. The Greek word for "greatness" (μέγεθος), a hapax legomenon in the NT, was found in an inscription probably dating from before the late second century A.D. in the square in front of the theater in Ephesus; see A. L. Connolly, "Standing on Sacred Ground," *New Docs* 4 (1987): 106–7. On the interrelation of the four terms—"power" (δύναμις), "working" (ἐνέργεια), "might" (κράτος), and "strength" (ἰσχύς)—in 1:19 Hoehner (Ephesians, 271) states: "First, ἰσχύς speaks of the inherent strength or of power possessed. Second, κράτος is close to ἰσχύς but denotes even more emphatically the presence and significance of the strength or force of power, or the ability to overcome resistance, or more at the visible aspect of strength, perhaps its supremacy. Third, ἐνέργεια stresses the activity of power, namely, it is power in action. Fourth, δύναμις, found earlier in this verse, denotes capacity in view of its ability or potential power. . . . It seems that δύναμις is the more general term and that the other terms support it, as is the case in this passage. Again these words overlap and the point of using all of these words is not so much to emphasize their distinctiveness but to enforce the idea of God's abundant power available to all believers." For more on the background of these terms for power in 1:19, see Arnold, *Power*, 72–75. Best, *Ephesians*, 170: "For AE [Author of Ephesians] the power of God is closely related to his grace and love (love was related to his electing power in 1.4f)."

21. For the text-critical reasons to prefer the aorist rather than perfect tense of the verb "worked" as the original reading in 1:20, see Hoehner, *Ephesians*, 273 n. 2.

all the things (τὰ πάντα) that God will unite under one head in the Christ (ἐν τῷ Χριστῷ) (1:10)—the content of the mystery of his will that he made known to us who believe as a gracious gift of his love in accord with the good pleasure that he purposed in Christ (1:9), the Beloved (1:6).

4. Eph 1:20b (C'): Christ Seated at God's Right Hand in the Heavenly Places

The power that God worked "in" (ἐν) the Christ in raising him from the dead (1:20a) progresses to God's seating Christ "at" (ἐν) his right hand, a divinely authoritative position (cf. Ps 110:1), "in" (ἐν) the heavenly places (1:20b) to complete the central C and C' elements of the chiasm in 1:15–23.[22] God's having seated Christ "in the heavenly places" (ἐν τοῖς ἐπουρανίοις), by the exercise of his power that is for us believers (1:19), reminds the audience of God's having blessed us believers with every Spiritual blessing "in the heavenly places" (ἐν τοῖς ἐπουρανίοις) in our union with Christ (1:3), as part of the love God granted us so that we might be holy and blameless before him "in love" (1:4).

5. Eph 1:21 (B'): Christ Far Above Every Other Power

The focus on the "surpassing" (ὑπερβάλλον) greatness of God's "power" (δυνάμεως) for us believers in the B element (1:19) progresses to the focus on the Christ risen and exalted by that divine power, so that he is "far above (ὑπεράνω) every ruler and authority and power (δυνάμεως) and dominion and every name that is named, not only in this age but also in the one to come" in the parallel B' element (1:21) of the chiasm.[23] This makes the au-

---

22. Lincoln, *Ephesians*, 61–62: "The language of exaltation used here is that of the common early Christian tradition of Christ's session at the right hand of God, which takes up Ps 110:1 . . . Its terminology of a session at the right hand had parallels in the ancient Near Eastern world where the king was often represented as seated next to the tutelary deity of a particular city or nation. Occupying a place on the god's right hand meant that the ruler exercised power on behalf of the god and held a position of supreme honor. . . . Here the writer continues this tradition in order to evoke Christ's position of supreme favor and honor, his place of victory and power associated with his exaltation to heaven." See also David M. Hay, *Glory at the Right Hand: Psalm 110 in Early Christianity* (SBLMS 18; Nashville: Abingdon, 1973); W. R. G. Loader, "Christ at the Right Hand—Ps. CX.1 in the New Testament," *NTS* 24 (1978): 199–217; Moritz, *Profound Mystery*, 9–22.

23. The context of ὑπεράνω in which it is paralleled by ὑπερβάλλον ("surpassing") in 1:19 and preceded by God's having seated the Christ at his right hand in the heavenly places in 1:21 justifies translating it "far above" rather than simply "above" contra Hoehner, *Ephesians*, 276. O'Brien, *Ephesians*, 141 n. 201: "ὑπεράνω ('high above'; cf. Eph. 4:10) may be intended here to contrast Christ's position with that of the powers, which in the magical papyri were thought to dwell 'above'." Ernst R. Wendland, "Contextualising the Potentates, Principalities and Powers in the Epistle to the Ephesians," *Neot* 33 (1999): 211: "The semi-religious practice of 'name-calling' (ὀνόματος ὀνομαζομένου) was an indispensable aspect of most magical and exorcistic rites of that time." Arnold, *Power*, 54: "Supernatural 'powers'

dience aware that any and every kind of angelic, spiritual power that can be known or imagined to exist in the cosmos, whether present or future, is vastly inferior to the power of God that is for us believers, the power that God worked in raising and seating the Christ at his right hand.[24]

6. Eph 1:22–23 (A'): God Gave Christ as Head Over All to the Church

The love of the "you" believers for "all" (πάντας) the holy ones in the A element (1:15) progresses to the love that God extended to the church—all believers—in subjecting "all things" (πάντα) under the feet of the Christ

---

were called upon by name through these means by one who desired access to their power and assistance." Hoehner, *Ephesians*, 280–81: "God is the namer, as seen in the OT where he gave a new name to Abram (Gen 17:5) and to Jacob (Gen 32:28), and even determined the number of stars and gave all of them their names (Ps 147:4). Thus in the present context after naming specific authorities (v. 21a) over which Christ has authority, Paul indicates that every name that God cites is under Christ's authority (v. 21b). It is a comprehensive statement specifying that regardless of designation or title a ruling power may have whether in heaven or on earth, it is inferior to Christ who is at the right hand of God." See also Thomas G. Allen, "God the Namer: A Note on Ephesians 1.21b," *NTS* 32 (1986): 470–75.

24. Hoehner, *Ephesians*, 279: "There is debate as to whether these terms refer to human or angelic authorities or whether they are good or evil powers. . . . in the context of the book it seems that these rulers are angelic and also evil in character. In the present context, Christ is seated at the right hand of the Father and this may be an allusion to Ps 110 where God will make the enemies of Christ his footstool" (cf. Eph 1:21). O'Brien, *Ephesians*, 142: "Consistent with the use of Psalm 110 elsewhere in the New Testament, Paul identifies the 'enemies' of the Psalm with the invisible 'powers' which have been subjected to Christ." See also Moritz, *Profound Mystery*, 13. This allusion to the "enemies" in Ps 110 is overlooked by Pheme Perkins, *Ephesians* (ANTC; Nashville: Abingdon, 1997), 50. David E. Aune, "Archai," *DDD*, 79: "There can be little doubt that the powers mentioned in Eph 1:21 and 6:12, and specifically the *archai* must be understood as evil supernatural powers." The powers in 1:21 are wrongly interpreted as not demonic or evil by Wesley A. Carr, *Angels and Principalities: The Background, Meaning, and Development of the Pauline Phrase Hai Archai Kai Hai Exousiai* (SNTSMS 42; Cambridge: Cambridge University Press, 1981). They are wrongly interpreted as solely earthly powers by John Paul Lotz, "The Homonoia Coins of Asia Minor and Ephesians 1:21," *TynBul* 50 (1999): 185–88. And they are wrongly viewed as the essence of earthly institutions by Walter Wink, *Naming the Powers: The Language of Power in the New Testament* (Philadelphia: Fortress, 1984), 104–5. It is dubious that "dominion" (κυριότητος) in 1:21 is "an obvious reference to Caesar," as alleged by Ross Saunders, "Paul and the Imperial Cult," in *Paul and His Opponents* (ed. Stanley E. Porter; Pauline Studies 2; Leiden: Brill, 2005), 234. Lincoln, *Ephesians*, 64: "There is also discussion as to whether the powers, which we have claimed to be supernatural beings, might in fact be human rulers or political structures. The popular demythologizing of these powers in current theology, whereby they represent the structures of human society which oppress people, may well be a valid reinterpretation of a NT concept but it is a reinterpretation. The writer himself believes the powers to be spiritual agencies in the heavenly realm standing behind any earthly or human institutions." See also Peter Thomas O'Brien, "Principalities and Powers: Opponents of the Church," in *Biblical Interpretation and the Church: Text and Context* (ed. Donald A. Carson; Exeter, England: Paternoster, 1984), 110–50; Arnold, *Power*, 41–56; Schwindt, *Weltbild*, 362–66.

(cf. Ps 8:7; 110:1),[25] making him head over "all things" (πάντα), so that he is filling "all the things" (τὰ πάντα) "in all ways" (πᾶσιν) in the parallel A′ element (1:22–23).[26] And Paul's prayer that God may "give" (δώη)—as a further gift of his love—to his audience of "you" believers the Spirit of wisdom and revelation in knowledge of him in the A element (1:17) progresses to the love that God has already granted to all believers when he "gave" (ἔδωκεν) Christ as head over all things to the church in the A′ element (1:22) of the chiasm in 1:15–23.[27]

That God gave Christ as "head" (κεφαλήν) over "all things" (πάντα) to the church (1:22) further explicates the mystery that God is going "to unite under one head" (ἀνακεφαλαιώσασθαι) "all things" (τὰ πάντα) in the Christ (1:10).[28] It makes the audience realize that as members of the church, which has been given—as a gift of God's love—the Christ who is head over all things, they have a significant role to play in the mystery in which God is eventually going to unite all things in the universe under this Christ who is already head over all things.

That the church is indeed the "body" (σῶμα) of Christ (1:23a) implies that Christ is not only "head" over all things (1:22) but is also in an intimate head-body relationship with the church of all believers. This develops the close union believers have with Christ within the dynamic realm of their being "in" Christ (1:3, 6, 7, 11, 13, 15). Not only are believers "in" Christ, but as the church they are Christ's "body," organically and intimately linked to him as their "head." As "head" over all things and the church, Christ

---

25. On the fusion of Ps 8:7 and Ps 110:1 in Eph 1:20–22, see Aquila H. I. Lee, *From Messiah to Preexistent Son: Jesus' Self-Consciousness and Early Christian Exegesis of Messianic Psalms* (WUNT 2/192; Tübingen: Mohr Siebeck, 2005), 219–20. Hoehner, *Ephesians*, 283: "The metaphorical language 'under his feet' has the idea of victory over enemies. It is used of the winner of a duel who places his foot on the neck of his enemy who has been thrown to the ground." See also BDAG, 858.

26. Lincoln, *Ephesians*, 66: "πάντα, which in the original psalm [Ps 8:7 alluded to in Eph 1:22] referred to that part of the creation below humanity in the hierarchy, now has the same scope as τὰ πάντα in 1:10, 23 so that the whole universe, heaven and earth, cosmic powers and human beings, is seen as subordinated to the exalted Christ."

27. Lincoln, *Ephesians*, 66: "ἔδωκεν has been translated in line with its normal meaning as 'gave' . . . The indirect object here in v 22b is τῇ ἐκκλησίᾳ, and the use of the verb in its more usual sense brings out the characteristic emphasis of Ephesians on God's grace [and thus love] toward the Church." See also Hanna Roose, "Die Hierarchisierung der Leib-Metapher im Kolosser- und Epheserbrief als 'Paulinisierung': Ein Beitrag zur Rezeption paulinischer Tradition in Pseudo-Paulinischen Briefen," *NovT* 47 (2005): 139.

28. Dawes, *Body*, 143: "[I]t remains possible that the author of Ephesians has chosen ἀνακεφαλαιώσασθαι because it does contain a certain echo of the word κεφαλή. For the thought expressed by this verse is certainly similar to that which we have found in Eph 1:22, that of the cosmic authority of Christ."

not only authoritatively rules over all things and the church, but also is the source of divine power and love for all things and the church.[29]

But as "head" Christ has a different relationship to all things than he does to the church as his "body." Indeed, as the "body" of Christ the church is "the fullness of the one who is filling all things in all ways" (1:23b).[30] That the church is the "fullness" (πλήρωμα)[31] of the Christ who is "filling" (πληρουμένου)[32] all things in all ways means that, together with God's gift of Christ as head over all things to the church (1:22), the church has received the "fullness," that is, the full array of Spiritual blessings, grace, and power as gifts of God's love that Paul has so eloquently made his audience realize that they possess in their union with Christ, their "head."[33] Indeed, God has blessed the audience of believers with *every* (πάσῃ) Spiritual blessing in their

29. Clinton E. Arnold, "Jesus Christ: 'Head' of the Church (Colossians and Ephesians)," in *Jesus of Nazareth: Lord and Christ. Essays on the Historical Jesus and New Testament Christology* (ed. Joel B. Green and Max Turner; Grand Rapids: Eerdmans, 1994), 365: "Christ is given in his exalted status to the church. He has defeated the powers on the cross and now possesses full authority over them. The head of the church is a victorious Lord. For this reason Christ can impart all of the empowering resources the church needs." See also Roose, "Hierarchisierung," 132–41.

30. For a summary of the problems involved in the interpretation of 1:23, see Roy Yates, "A Re-examination of Ephesians 1:23," *ExpTim* 83 (1972): 146–51. See also George Howard, "The Head/Body Metaphors of Ephesians," *NTS* 20 (1974): 350–56; Andrew C. Perriman, " 'His body, which is the church . . .' Coming to Terms with Metaphor," *EvQ* 62 (1990): 123–42; Gert M. M. Pelser, "Once More the Body of Christ in Paul," *Neot* 32 (1998): 525–45. For a discussion of the Hellenistic-Jewish background of the church as "body" and as "fullness," see Rudolf Hoppe, "Theo-logie und Ekklesio-logie im Epheserbrief," *MTZ* 46 (1995): 234–40. On the "body" metaphor in Eph 1:22–23, see Annemarie C. Mayer, *Sprache der Einheit im Epheserbrief und in der Ökumene* (WUNT 2/150; Tübingen: Mohr Siebeck, 2002), 129–30.

31. We understand the noun "fullness" (πλήρωμα) in 1:23 to have a "passive" rather than "active" sense. For an unconvincing attempt to give it an active sense, see D. P. Leyrer, "Ephesians 1:23—The 'Fullness' of Ascension Comfort," *Wisconsin Lutheran Quarterly* 99 (2002): 135–37. For questionable views that it is deliberately ambiguous, see Josef Ernst, *Pleroma und Pleroma Christi: Geschichte und Deutung eines Begriffs der paulinischen Antilegomena* (Biblische Untersuchungen 5; Regensburg, Germany: Pustet, 1970), 114–20; Dawes, *Body*, 248.

32. Roy R. Jeal, "A Strange Style of Expression: Ephesians 1:23," *Filología Neotestamentaria* 10 (1997): 136–37: "If the active form πληροῦντος had been used, the rhetorical symmetry of Ephesians 1:23 would have been destroyed. The author has, consequently, chosen the middle/passive form as part of the stylistic interplay of words, so that a rhythmic, rhyming effect could be maintained [between αὐτοῦ and πληρουμένου]. This understanding is very important because it supports the view that the participle τοῦ πληρουμένου should be understood as active in meaning despite being of middle or passive morphology." See also BDAG, 828; Schwindt, *Weltbild*, 437–38. For different but unconvincing construals of this participle, see Ignace de la Potterie, "Le Christ, Plérôme de l'Église (Ep 1,22–23)," *Bib* 58 (1977): 500–524; Georg Korting, "Das Partizip in Eph 1,23," *TGl* 87 (1997): 260–65.

33. Hoehner, *Ephesians*, 300: "[I]t is the character, essence, and power of God that is filling the church." Lincoln, *Ephesians*, 80: "Christ is filling all things in terms of his sover-

union with Christ in the heavenly places (1:3) where Christ is seated at the right hand of God (1:20) as "head" over all things (1:22) and of his "body," the church (1:23a).

As "head" over all things, Christ not only rules with divine authority over all things that God has subjected under his feet (1:22), but is filling all things in all ways (1:23b). This develops the audience's insight into the mystery of God ultimately uniting all things in Christ (1:9–10). Whereas God is the one "who is working in all things" (τοῦ τὰ πάντα ἐνεργοῦντος, 1:11), Christ, as the "head" seated at the right hand of God (1:20), is the one "who is filling all things in all ways" (τοῦ τὰ πάντα ἐν πᾶσιν πληρουμένου, 1:23b), so that God may ultimately unite under one head all things in the Christ (1:10).

That Christ, as the "head" over all things (1:22), is "filling all things in all ways" (1:23b) means that he is providing everything necessary for all things in the cosmos to be ultimately united under one head in the Christ (1:10). This assures the audience that, in addition to their having already been filled with the "fullness" of God's Spiritual blessings, grace, and power as members of the church that is the "body" of Christ (1:23a), they will continue to be filled with everything that they, as part of all things, need from the Christ whom God has given them as head over all things (1:22) to play their role in the mystery of God ultimately uniting all things under one head in Christ (1:10). Paul has assured his audience, then, that they have been filled and will continue to be filled by God's gracious gifts of love that he gave them in Christ as head over all things, so that they may be holy and blameless before God "in love" (1:4), that is, in their union with the Beloved (1:6), the Christ who is head of the church as his body (1:22–23).

B. Summary on Ephesians 1:15–23

1. That Paul has heard of his audience's "love for all the holy ones" (1:15b) develops the dynamics of the Letter's theme of love. Their "love" for all the holy ones serves as an explicit example of what was implicit in God's choosing believers in Christ that they might be "holy and blameless before him *in love*" (1:4b), as it indicates that the dynamic realm of relationships involved in believers being "in love" includes not only God's love for believers in Christ and their love for God but also believers' love for one another. That Paul's audience of "you" believers, those he addressed as the "holy ones" who are in Ephesus" (1:1c), have love for all of their fellow "holy ones" (1:15b) is part of what it means for believers to be "holy" and blameless before God in their situation of being "in love" (1:4b) "in the Beloved" (1:6b).

---

eign rule, but he fills the Church in a special sense with his Spirit, grace, and gifts (cf. 4:7–11), so that only the Church *is* his fullness" (Lincoln's emphasis).

2. Paul's "giving thanks for *you*, making mention of *you* in my prayers" (1:16) serves as a personal act of love on Paul's part for his audience of fellow believers, reinforcing his prayer wish that they be granted even more grace and peace from God our Father and the Lord Jesus Christ (1:2).

3. That Paul directs his prayers to God as the Father of "glory" (1:17a) reminds his audience of the reverberating rhythmic refrain inviting believers to respond to God's love by praising God for the glory manifested in God the Father's love for them in the Beloved—"to the praise of his glory!" (1:6, 12, 14).

4. In praying that God "may give you the Spirit of *wisdom* and revelation in *knowledge* of him" (1:17b), Paul is further uniting the "you" believers to the "we" believers, as he is praying that God may give the "you" believers a further and more particular experience of the gracious love God has lavished on the "we" believers—"according to the wealth of his grace which he lavished upon us, in all *wisdom* and insight, having made *known* to us the mystery of his will" (1:7b-9a).

5. That the "eyes of your heart" (1:18a), that is your thinking and understanding, have been enlightened by God (divine passive) serves as another expression of God's gracious love for the "you" believers.

6. For the "you" believers to know the hope of God's "calling" (1:18a) means for them to presently experience the attitude of the absolutely assured hope to which God has "chosen" all believers, namely, "that we might be holy and blameless before him in love" (1:4).

7. Paul's prayer that the "you" believers may know what is the "wealth" of the glory of God's inheritance (1:18b) underscores the extravagant, generous, and lavish extent to which God has loved us believers, as it recalls for the audience the "wealth" of God's grace "which he lavished upon us" (1:7b–8a), that is, the grace of God with which he graced us in our union with the Beloved (1:6) in our situation of being "in love" (1:4b).

8. It is "in" or "among," that is, in their union with the "holy ones" (1:18c), with whom they have been united through their love for all the "holy ones" (1:15), that the audience of "you" believers may know what is the wealth of the glory of God's inheritance for all believers.

9. As the "you" believers have a love that is "for" all the holy ones (1:15), so the surpassing greatness of God's power—a gift of God's love—is "for" all of us who believe (1:19).

10. Paul's prayer that his audience may enjoy a present experiential knowledge of "the surpassing greatness" of God's power, intensified by the fourfold accumulation of synonymous terms—"power," "working," "might," and "strength"—for us who believe (1:19) continues to underscore the extravagant, generous, and lavish extent of God's love for all believers.

11. God's having seated Christ "in the heavenly places" (1:20b), by the exercise of his power that is for us believers (1:19), reminds the audience of God's having blessed us believers with every Spiritual blessing "in the heavenly places" in our union with Christ (1:3), as part of the love God granted us so that we might be holy and blameless before him "in love" (1:4).

12. Paul has assured his audience that they, as the "fullness" of Christ, have been filled and will continue to be filled, by the Christ "who is filling all things in all ways," with God's gracious gifts of love that he gave them in Christ as head over all things, so that they may be holy and blameless before God "in love" (1:4), that is, in their union with the Beloved (1:6), the Christ who is head of the church which his body (1:22–23).

CHAPTER 6

Ephesians 2:1–10: Walking by the Great Love with Which He Loved Us (D)

A: ¹ And *you* being dead in *your* transgressions and sins, ² in which you once *walked* according to the age of this world, according to the ruler of the authority of the air, of the spirit that is now working in the sons of disobedience,

   B: ³ among whom also *we* all once lived in the desires of *our* flesh doing the wishes of the flesh and of the thoughts, and we were by nature children of wrath as also the rest.

      C: ⁴ But God being rich in mercy, because of his great *love*

      C´: with which he *loved* us,

   B´: ⁵ even being dead as *we* were in transgressions, made us alive with the Christ—by grace you have been saved!— ⁶ and raised us up with him and seated us with him in the heavenly places in Christ Jesus, ⁷ that he might show in the ages to come the surpassing wealth of his grace in kindness upon *us* in Christ Jesus.

A´: ⁸ For by the grace you have been saved through faith, and this is not from *you*, of God is the gift; ⁹ it is not from works, so no one may boast. ¹⁰ For his work are we, created in Christ Jesus for good works which God prepared beforehand, that we might *walk* in them.[1]

---

1. For the establishment of Eph 2:1–10 as a chiasm, see ch. 2.

A. Audience Response to Ephesians 2:1–10

1. Eph 2:1–2 (A): You Once Walked among the Sons of Disobedience

After having prayed that his audience of "you" (ὑμᾶς) believers might experience what is the surpassing greatness of God's power for "us" (ἡμᾶς) who believe (1:18–19), continuing to alert his audience that they belong to all of us who believe (cf. 1:12–13), Paul again directly addresses his audience of "you" believers—"and you (ὑμᾶς) being dead in your (ὑμῶν) transgressions and sins" (2:1).[2] This reminds the audience that although God raised Christ from the realm of those who were physically "dead" (ἐκ νεκρῶν, 1:20), "you" were metaphorically or spiritually "dead" (νεκρούς).[3] They were "dead" not only because of "your" transgressions and sins, but they were "dead" even while living in the realm or sphere of their willful transgressions and sins against God.[4]

---

2. Hoehner, *Ephesians*, 307: "The 'you' makes it emphatic and very personal even though it is plural. Paul is addressing the readers directly." O'Brien, *Ephesians*, 157 n. 12: "The ὑμῶν ('your [transgressions and sins]') at the end of the clause balances the ὑμᾶς ('you [were dead]') at the beginning." Lincoln, *Ephesians*, 88: "Particularly in regard to vv 1–3, a number of commentators hold that 'you' refers exclusively to Gentile Christians, while 'we' has in view Jewish Christians. Such a distinction is more plausible here, where it is closer to the explicit discussion of Jews and Gentiles in the second half of the chapter, than it was back in 1:11–13, but it is still unconvincing. It is true that the writer thinks of his readers as predominantly Gentile Christians (cf. 2:11). . . . But the distinction between 'you' and 'we' is not intended to be one between Gentile and Jew so much as one between the readers in particular and Christians in general, including the writer." The "we" and "you" dynamics in Ephesians involve a distinction between the "we" who first hoped in the Christ (1:12), predominantly Jews but including Gentiles, and the "you" (1:13) who came to this faith and hope later at Ephesus, predominantly Gentiles but including Jews. The "we" and the "you," then, are more nuanced than recognized by O'Brien, *Ephesians*, 156 n. 7. On the "Jewish perspective" in Eph 2:1–10, see Yee, *Jews, Gentiles*, 45–70.
3. With regard to the καί ("and") at the beginning of 2:1, Lincoln (*Ephesians*, 92) states that "it functions as a connective with the whole of the preceding pericope rather than with 1:23 specifically. As the rest of the passage will show, the same power that was at work in raising and exalting Christ from physical death has raised and exalted believers from spiritual death."
4. Ernest Best, *Essays on Ephesians* (Edinburgh: Clark, 1997), 75: "Attempts have been made in varying ways to distinguish 'sins' and 'transgressions' in Eph. 2.1, mostly along the lines of a division into sins of omission and commission, but within the context it is better to regard them as together intended to indicate the fullness and variety of sins." Lincoln, *Ephesians*, 93: "The use of the two synonymns here provides another example of the redundancy of style of Ephesians and helps to convey an impression of the immensity and variety of the sinfulness of the readers' past. 'Trespasses and sins' is in the dative and has been translated 'through your trespasses and sins.' This dative should be seen as expressing both the cause and the manifestation of death. Trespasses and sins both bring about the condition of death and characterize the existence of those who are spiritually dead." See also Hoehner, *Ephesians*, 308.

The audience thus recall their situation before they were in the realm of God's love. They were "dead" in their "transgressions" (παραπτώμασιν) before they, as among the "we" believers, received the forgiveness of their "transgressions" (παραπτωμάτων), "according to the wealth of his grace" (1:7), that is, "his grace with which he graced us in the Beloved" (1:6). It is "in the Beloved," that is, in their union "in Christ" (1:3) loved by God that God chose them to be "holy and blameless before him in love" (1:4). But when they were "dead" in the realm of their transgressions and sins, they were not yet holy and blameless before God in the realm of God's love "in the Beloved."

In the realm of their transgressions and sins the audience of "you" believers once "walked" (περιεπατήσατε), that is, conducted themselves, behaved, or lived, "according to the age (αἰῶνα) of this world,"[5] which is further explained as "according to the ruler (ἄρχοντα) of the authority (ἐξουσίας)"—the realm or domain—"of the air" (2:2a). This reminds the audience that they once "walked" according to the evil cosmic powers now subjected to Christ, as it recalls that God raised Christ from the dead and seated him "at his right hand in the heavenly places, far above every ruler (ἀρχῆς) and authority (ἐξουσίας) and power and dominion and every name that is named, not only in this age (αἰῶνι) but in the one to come" (1:20–21).[6]

The audience of "you" believers once "walked" according to the evil ruler not only of the cosmic realm of the air, but of the human sphere—"of the spirit," that is, the spiritual force or influence, "that is now working in

---

5. With regard to the prepositional phrase "in which" (ἐν αἷς) at the beginning of 2:2, Hoehner (*Ephesians*, 309) states: "The preposition ἐν emphasizes the sphere of the walk and the relative pronoun αἷς takes the gender of the nearer noun, although it refers to both nouns." Jeal, *Ethics in Ephesians*, 134 n. 303: "The verb περιπατέω is used eight times in Eph. (2:2, 10; 4:1, 17 [twice]; 5:2, 8, 15) as a metaphor for behaviour. It is a Hebraism used frequently in the LXX. Rabbinic exposition dealing with behaviour was denoted as *halacha*, a way to walk or path to follow." On the interpretation of "age" (αἰῶνα) as a period of time rather than a Hellenistic personal deity, see Arnold, *Ephesians*, 59; O'Brien, *Ephesians*, 158–59; Hoehner, *Ephesians*, 310; Lincoln, *Ephesians*, 95: "Instead of being oriented to the life of the age to come and the heavenly realm, the past lives of the readers had been dominated by this present evil age and this world. Their sinful activities were simply in line with the norms and values of a spatio-temporal complex wholly hostile to God."

6. Lincoln, *Ephesians*, 95: "Supernatural powers hostile to human welfare and to God's redemptive purposes have already figured in 1:21.... In Ephesians, however, not only do such principalities and powers appear, but equally prominent is an ultimate personal power of evil behind them, designated here as the ruler of the realm of the air.... ἐχουσία is used in this verse for the realm or the sphere of the ruler's authority rather than for that authority itself." With regard to "air" (ἀέρος) in 2:2a, Hoehner (*Ephesians*, 312) states: "In the present context it is the place or sphere of the activity of the devil. It denotes both universality and locality." Arnold, *Ephesians*, 60: "The air was regarded as the dwelling place of evil spirits in antiquity."

the sons of disobedience" (2:2b).[7] But the audience have already heard that the power of this "spirit" that is now "working" (ἐνεργοῦντος) in the sons of disobedience has already been countered by the "working" (ἐνέργειαν) of the power of God that he "worked" (ἐνήργησεν) in the Christ when he raised him from the dead (1:19–20), as well as by the purpose of the God who is "working" (ἐνεργοῦντος) in all things to unite under one head all the things in the Christ (1:10–11).[8]

This reminder that the audience of "you" believers once "walked" in a hostile and rebellious rather than loving relationship to God among the "sons" (υἱοῖς) of disobedience (2:2b) deepens their appreciation for the "sonship" (υἱοθεσίαν) for which God has predestined all of us believers through Jesus Christ (1:5).[9] That God has adopted us believers into his family to share an intimate and loving father-son relationship to him together with Jesus Christ is part of "the grace with which he graced us in the Beloved" (1:6). As adopted "sons" who are loved by God in our union with the Beloved Son, rather than "sons" who are disobedient to God in their transgressions and sins against God, we are empowered to be holy and blameless before God within the dynamic realm of being "in love" (1:4b).

---

7. On taking "of the spirit" (τοῦ πνεύματος) as parallel to "of the authority (domain, realm)" (τῆς ἐξουσίας) in 2:2, see Lincoln, *Ephesians*, 96; Hoehner, *Ephesians*, 314–15. On the meaning of "spirit" here Lincoln (*Ephesians*, 96–97) notes: "In references to the Spirit of God πνεῦμα often hovers between personal and impersonal connotations. Here also spirit may be more a reference to a spiritual force or influence than to a personal power. . . . Paul, in 1 Cor 2:12, had recognized that there is a spirit at work in the world which is in antithesis to the Spirit of God. Here in Ephesians, that spiritual force is said to be under the rule of the same evil being who rules the air. The writer makes clear that this ruler's evil influence has both a cosmic and a human sphere. His spiritual influence is now at work in those who are disobedient." Wallace, *Greek Grammar*, 104: "The idea of this text, then, is that the devil controls non-believers both externally (the environment or domain of the air) and internally (attitudes or spirit)."

8. According to O'Brien (*Ephesians*, 160–61) this evil spiritual force's "manner of operation is described by means of a dynamic power term which, together with its cognate noun, always denotes supernatural power in the New Testament. It has already been used in Ephesians of God, who mightily works out everything according to his will (1:11) and who has exerted his mighty strength in Jesus' resurrection and exaltation (1:20)."

9. "Sons of" is a form of expression that "is due to the more vivid imagination of the oriental, who viewed any very intimate relationship—whether of connection, origin or dependence—as a relation of sonship, even in the spiritual sense," according to G. Adolf Deissmann, *Bible Studies: Contribution from Papyri and Inscriptions to the History of the Language, the Literature, and the Religion of Hellenistic Judaism and Primitive Christianity* (2d ed.; Edinburgh: Clark, 1903), 161. Lincoln, *Ephesians*, 97: "The expression 'sons of disobedience' . . . is a Hebraism denoting men and women whose lives are characterized by disobedience. The rebellion against God's will which this term implies includes rejection of the Christian gospel, since the writer states that it is occurring in the present. But the disobedience is not to be limited to this and involves general disregard for God's will." See also Peter Bläser, "ἀπειθέω," *EDNT* 1.118–19.

2. Eph 2:3 (B): We Also Once Lived as Children of Wrath

But all of the "we" believers were in a similar situation as the audience of "you" believers before they came to faith: "among whom also we (ἡμεῖς) all once lived in the desires of our (ἡμῶν) flesh doing the wishes of the flesh and of the thoughts, and we were by nature children of wrath as also the rest" (2:3).[10] As Paul earlier aligned the "you" believers to the "we" believers who first hoped in the Christ with the expression, "in whom also you" (ἐν ᾧ καὶ ὑμεῖς, 1:13), so he now similarly aligns the "we" believers to the "you" believers who "walked" among the sons of disobedience with the expression, "among whom also we" (ἐν οἷς καὶ ἡμεῖς, 2:3). The audience are to realize that they share with Paul and all believers not only the faith but the situation from which they came to faith.

That the "we" believers, like the "you" believers of the audience, once lived among the sons of disobedience in the desires of their own flesh doing the wishes (θελήματα) of their flesh and their thoughts (2:3a) means that they were not yet living in accord with the will (θελήματος) of God,[11] who predestined them to adopted sonship through Jesus Christ to himself (1:5) that they might be holy and blameless before God "in love" (1:4), that is, in their situation of being graced with the grace of God in their union with God's Beloved Son (1:6). Living among the sons of disobedience, the "we" believers, like the "you" believers, were not yet sons who loved the God who loved them in his Beloved Son.

Indeed, not yet being sons "in love" (1:4b), loved by and loving God in their union with the Beloved (1:6b), the "we" believers were "by nature children of wrath as also the rest" (2:3b). They were "children" destined to be punished by God's eschatological "wrath" in the last judgment along with all the rest of the disobedient and unbelieving "sons," who once also included the audience (2:2). They were not yet adopted sons who have obtained an inheritance (1:11) predestined for them from God in their situation of being "in love" in their union with God's Beloved Son (1:4–6).[12]

---

10. Lincoln, *Ephesians*, 97: "In this depiction of the past style of life ποτέ ['once'] is repeated from v 2, and ἀναστρέφειν, 'to live,' is used this time as a synonym for περιπατεῖν to denote ethical conduct." See also Hoehner, *Ephesians*, 318.

11. Doing the wishes of the "flesh" (σαρκός) reinforces living in the desires of our "flesh" (σαρκός) in 2:2. According to Lincoln (*Ephesians*, 98) "flesh" here "stands not simply for a person's physical existence, but for the sphere of humanity in its sinfulness and opposition to God. It is the sphere in which a person not only displeases God but is also in fact incapable of pleasing God (cf. Rom 8:8). It is the sphere in which life is lived in pursuit of one's own ends and in independence of God." Hoehner, *Ephesians*, 321: "[W]e were not only living in the sphere of the desires of the flesh, but we were doing the wishes or dictates of the flesh. Thus, our life in the flesh was not accidental or forced but desirable and natural."

12. "Children of wrath," according to Lincoln (*Ephesians*, 98–99), "is a Hebraism, like 'sons of disobedience' in v 2, which means they were deserving of and liable to wrath. . . .

3. Eph 2:4a (C): The Great Love of the God Who Is Rich in Mercy

Paul's audience of "you" believers, having been reminded that they once "walked" among those who are disobedient to God in their transgressions and sins against God (2:1–2), and having been assured that the "we" believers who preceded them in coming to faith also once lived among the disobedient, so that both the "you" and the "we" believers were destined to be recipients of God's wrath (2:3), now begin to hear of God's response to that situation: "But God being rich in mercy, because of his great love" (2:4a).[13]

As a response to those who were "dead" in their transgressions (παραπτώμασιν) and sins against God (2:1), that God is rich (πλούσιος) in mercy (2:4a) reminds the audience that all of us believers have the forgiveness of transgressions (παραπτωμάτων), according to the wealth (πλοῦτος) of God's grace, which he lavished on us (1:7b–8a). The audience realize, then, that all of us believers are no longer destined to be recipients of God's wrath (2:3), because we have instead already received forgiveness in accord with the wealth of God's grace and mercy.

Alliteratively reinforcing God's being "rich" (πλούσιος) in mercy, the prepositional phrase, "because of his great (πολλήν) love," indicates to the audience the motivation for this mercy (2:4a).[14] It is because of God's great love that God is rich in the mercy and grace of forgiving us believers. "Because of his great love (ἀγάπην)" also reminds the audience of "you" believers of the motivation for the love (ἀγάπην) they have for all the holy ones (1:15b). They have been empowered to love their fellow believers be-

---

The children of wrath, then, are those who are doomed to God's wrath because through their condition of sinful rebellion, they deserve his righteous judgment." Hoehner, *Ephesians*, 322: "The term τέκνα, 'children,' is similar to υἱοῖς, 'sons,' mentioned in verse 2, but it denotes a closer relationship to the parent. . . . Thus to be a son of disobedience is one who by his own choice disobeyed God. To be a child of wrath is one who by his relationship to his parent or ancestor comes under God's wrath." O'Brien, *Ephesians*, 163: "The 'wrath' in view is God's holy anger against sin and the judgment that results."

13. Lincoln, *Ephesians*, 100: "[T]he explanation for the overall mood of the first part of the letter being one of praise and thanksgiving to God rather than despair is summed up by the eloquent little phrase at the start of v 4, ὁ δὲ θεός . . . , 'but God . . . .' The adversative δέ introduces a contrasting situation brought about because of who God is and what he has done. . . . There is now in existence a whole new situation because of God's initiative."

14. It is noteworthy that the only occurrence of the adjective πολλή ("great") in Ephesians describes God's love. Lincoln, *Ephesians*, 100: "In the LXX ἔλεος, 'mercy,' normally represents the term חסד, *ḥesed*, which frequently denotes Yahweh's steadfast covenant loyalty and love . . . Just as the richness of God's mercy has been stressed, so here is the greatness of his love." O'Brien, *Ephesians*, 165: "In the Old Testament his [God's] mercy is often spontaneous. It is shown to a recipient in a desperate, helpless situation, and it is regularly associated with his love, grace, and compassion (note especially Exod. 20:5–6; 34:6–7; Num. 14:18–19; Deut. 7:9–10), features which are explicitly found in the context of Ephesians 2."

cause of God's love for all believers in their dynamic union "in the Beloved (ἠγαπημένῳ, 1:6)," so that all of us believers may be holy and blameless before God within the sphere of being "in love (ἀγάπῃ, 1:4)"—in God's great love for us and our love for all God's holy ones.

4. Eph 2:4b (C′): With Which God Loved Us

The pivot to the parallels of the chiasm in 2:1–10 begins as the audience hear the relative clause, "with which he loved us" in 2:4b. The verb "loved" (ἠγάπησεν) in this C′ element (2:4b) of the chiasm parallels the noun "love" (ἀγάπην) in the C element (2:4a) to function as the center of the chiasm, which contains the only two explicit terms for "love" in 2:1–10 and the Letter's first coupling of the noun and cognate verb for "love." After the aligning of the "you" believers in the A element (2:1–2) of the chiasm with the "we" believers in the B element (2:3), the "us" (ἡμᾶς) in the C′ element (2:4b) includes both the "you" and the "we" believers—God has loved all of us believers with his great love.

The use of both the noun "love" with its cognate verb at the center of the chiasm (2:4) emphatically reinforces the theme of God's love that has been developing in the Letter.[15] It reminds the audience of a similar and closely related expression employing not only the noun "grace" with its cognate verb but also a verbal form of "love" in 1:6:

1:6: τῆς χάριτος αὐτοῦ ἧς ἐχαρίτωσεν ἡμᾶς ἐν τῷ ἠγαπημένῳ

of his grace with which he graced us in the Beloved

2:4: διὰ τὴν πολλὴν ἀγάπην αὐτοῦ ἣν ἠγάπησεν ἡμᾶς

because of his great love with which he loved us

This recall makes the audience realize that the great love with which God loved us believers is the love we have received as the grace with which God graced us in our union with Christ as the Beloved. It is in the Beloved, Jesus Christ as the one whom God preeminently loved, that God has graciously loved us with his great love, so that we may be holy and blameless before God "in love" (1:4b).

---

15. O'Brien, *Ephesians*, 166: "[L]ove is emphatically underscored by the adjective great and the cognate expression 'the great love with which he loved us.'" Hoehner, *Ephesians*, 327: "Paul uses the cognate accusative (cf. 1:3, 6, 20) to give an intensity of meaning. The intensity of love is further expressed by the adjective πολλήν, 'great,' and by the possessive pronoun αὐτοῦ 'his' thus showing that it is 'his great' love."

5. Eph 2:5–7 (B′): God Loved Us in Aligning Us with the Risen Christ Jesus

The aligning of the past sinful situation of Paul's audience of "you" believers with all of "us" believers that began in the B element with the expression, "among whom (the sons of disobedience, cf. 2:2b) also *we* (ἡμεῖς) all once lived in the desires of *our* (ἡμῶν) flesh" (2:3a), continues in the B′ element with the expression, "even when we (ἡμᾶς) were dead in transgressions" (2:5a). But the audience hear a subtle yet pointed development in emphasis from the similar expression at the beginning of the A element:

2:1a: Καὶ ὑμᾶς ὄντας νεκροὺς τοῖς παραπτώμασιν καὶ ταῖς ἁμαρτίαις ὑμῶν

And *you* being dead in *your* transgressions and sins

2:5a: καὶ ὄντας ἡμᾶς νεκροὺς τοῖς παραπτώμασιν

even *being dead* as we were in transgressions

The pronoun "you" (ὑμᾶς) following the conjunction "and" (καί) and reinforced by the pronoun "your" (ὑμῶν) places the emphasis on Paul's audience of "you" believers in the A element (2:1a)—"*you* being dead in *your* transgressions." But the participle "being" (ὄντας) following the conjunction "even" (καί) and reinforced by its predicate adjective "dead" (νεκρούς) places the emphasis on the situation of all of us believers "being dead" spiritually before God in the B′ element (2:5a)—"even *being dead* as we were in transgressions."[16]

With its use of the present participle of the verb "to be," the notice of God's "being" (ὤν) rich in mercy in the C element of the chiasm (2:4a) began to counter the "being dead" situation of the audience of "you" believers expressed with the present participle of the verb "to be" in the A element (2:1a)—"and you being (ὄντας) dead in your transgressions." Whereas "you" were "being" dead in your transgressions, God was "being" rich in mercy. And now God's "being" rich in mercy, because of the great love with which he loved "us" (ἡμᾶς) in the central C and C′ elements (2:4) provides the audience with the motivation—God's great love—for God's "being" rich

---

16. On the καί at the beginning of 2:5 Lincoln (*Ephesians*, 101) remarks that "the καί might well have the force of intensifying the participial clause which it introduces in the light of what has preceded it: 'even when we were dead through trespasses'." Hoehner (*Ephesians*, 329) adds: "Preferably this conjunctive has an ascensive idea ('even') qualifying the participle, thus intensifying the greatness of God's mercy."

in mercy that counters the situation of "us" (ἡμᾶς) "being" (ὄντας) "dead" in transgressions in the B′ element (2:5a).[17]

Because of the great love with which he loved all of "us" (ἡμᾶς) believers, the God "being" rich in mercy (2:4) made all of "us" (ἡμᾶς) believers, when we were "being" dead in transgressions, alive with the Christ (2:5ab). This develops the love theme in Ephesians as it further specifies for the audience how God graced all of "us" (ἡμᾶς) believers with his grace in the Beloved (1:6). The great love with which God loved the Beloved, the Christ whom God loved in making him alive by raising him from his situation of being physically dead (1:20), is the great love with which God graciously loved all of us believers in our situation of being spiritually dead in transgressions by making us spiritually alive with the Christ, thus gracing us with his gracious love in our union with the Christ as God's Beloved.[18]

With its emphasis upon the word "grace," the sudden exclamatory interjection directly addressing the audience, "by *grace* you have been saved!" (2:5c),[19] while reinforcing for the audience of "you" believers that they are part of all of "us" believers who were once "dead" in transgressions but whom God has now made alive with the Christ (2:5ab), primarily and emphatically underlines that it is solely by "grace"—the freely given and wholly unmerited gift of God motivated by the great love with which the God who is rich in mercy loved us (2:4)—that "you," and thus all of "us" believers, have been and still are "saved" (σεσῳσμένοι, perfect passive participle) by God (divine passive) from being spiritually "dead" even while physically living in the realm of our transgressions and sins.[20]

---

17. O'Brien, *Ephesians*, 166 n. 50: "The ὄντας stresses the condition of sinners as 'being' that of death." Hoehner, *Ephesians*, 329: "With the present tense of the participle, Paul shows that we being dead in transgressions was concurrent with God being rich in mercy. Hence, one is a state of deadness and the other is the action of mercy."

18. Thomas G. Allen, "Exaltation and Solidarity with Christ: Ephesians 1.20 and 2.6," *JSNT* 28 (1986): 109: "[L]ove describes not only the motivation of God's action, but the act itself. It is the great love with which he loved us, pointing to God's offering of Christ. Thus, the solidarity between Christ and believers could be said to lie in God's love as manifested in his eternal election of believers in Christ." Hoehner, *Ephesians*, 330: "This phrase 'making alive together with Christ' has reference to spiritual life and not the physical resurrection of the believer. Christ died physically, we were dead spiritually. Christ was raised physically (1:20), we were raised together with Christ spiritually. We were dead spiritually and now he made us alive spiritually."

19. Hoehner, *Ephesians*, 332: "Certainly, its place at the beginning of this parenthetical expression gives emphasis to grace."

20. Hoehner, *Ephesians*, 331: "God's response to the sinners' plight is one of mercy, the motive for his compassion is his love for them, and the basis for his action is his grace." Lincoln, *Ephesians*, 104–5: "'To save' here is an inclusive term characterizing God's acts of making alive, raising up, and seating with Christ as a deliverance from the plight of the old situation to all the benefits of the new. The perfect tense draws attention to the continuing effects of that rescue act for the present." For a recent discussion of salvation in Ephesians,

Reminding the audience of the wealth of God's "grace" (χάριτος) according to which all of us believers have forgiveness of transgressions (παραπτωμάτων) (1:7), as well as of God's "grace" (χάριτος) with which he "graced" (ἐχαρίτωσεν) us in the Beloved (1:6), that "you," and thus all of "us" believers, have been saved by "grace" (χάριτί, 2:5c) further confirms for the audience that the grace with which God graced us in our dynamic union with the Beloved is not only motivated by but a further specification of the great love with which God loved us in making us who were once spiritually "dead" in transgressions (παραπτώμασιν) alive with the Christ (2:5ab). At this point the audience realize that God's great love includes not only God's "mercy" (2:4a), emphasizing the compassion of God's love, but also God's "grace" (1:2, 6, 7; 2:5), emphasizing that God's love is a freely given gift. "Mercy" and "grace" are thus part of the "love" word field which further explain and enrich the love theme pervading Ephesians.

As a dramatically powerful act of the great love with which God loved us (2:4), God not only made us spiritually alive with the Christ but spiritually raised and seated us with him in the heavenly places in our dynamic union in Christ Jesus (2:6).[21] Whereas we all once physically lived "in" (ἐν) the realm of the desires of our flesh in the B element of the chiasm (2:3a), so that we were spiritually "dead" in transgressions (2:5a), God has now made us spiritually alive by both raising and seating us "in" (ἐν) the realm of the heavenly places "in" (ἐν) our union with Christ Jesus in the B′ element (2:6).

Recalling for the audience the great power that God worked in the Christ in raising (ἐγείρας) him from the realm of the physically dead (νεκρῶν) and seating (καθίσας) him at his right hand in the heavenly places (ἐν τοῖς ἐπουρανίοις) (1:20), that God "co-raised" (συνήγειρεν) and "co-seated" (συνεκάθισεν) us, who were spiritually dead (νεκρούς), with Christ in the heavenly places (ἐν τοῖς ἐπουρανίοις) (2:5–6) further develops the love theme in Ephesians. It makes the audience realize that it is as recipients of the great love with which God loved us (2:4) that we are recipients of the

see Petrus J. Gräbe, "Salvation in Colossians and Ephesians," in *Salvation in the New Testament: Perspectives on Soteriology* (ed. Jan G. van der Watt; NovTSup 121; Leiden: Brill, 2005), 294–303.

21. Lincoln, *Ephesians*, 105: "Since 'with Christ,' which is the force of the συν- prefix, and 'in Christ Jesus' both suggest a relationship of solidarity, the combination of the two in v 6 is again characteristic of Ephesians' redundancy of style for the sake of emphasis." But there is no redundancy according to Hoehner, *Ephesians*, 334–35: "This last prepositional phrase [in Christ Jesus] is not connected to the previous prepositional phrase 'in the heavenly realms' but is joined to the verb 'to be seated together with him.' This is not redundant, for it underscores the reason we are seated in the heavenlies with Christ, namely, because we are in him. It is our union with Christ that gives us the right to be in the heavenly places. Although we are in the heavenlies positionally, we remain on the earth to live a resurrected life in connection with the resurrected Christ."

same great power by which God raised and exalted the Christ. The great love with which God loved us is a powerful love—an act of the great power that God worked for us in making us alive, raising, and exalting us with the Christ.

The great love with which God loved us in our union in the Beloved (1:6) includes our being placed in an exalted position of power and authority in the heavenly places in our union in Christ Jesus (2:6). Our position "in the heavenly places" means that together with Christ Jesus we are "far above every ruler (ἀρχῆς) and authority (ἐξουσίας) and power and dominion and every name that is named, not only in this age (αἰῶνι) but also in the one to come" (1:21). The great love with which God loved us (2:4) has thus placed the audience in a position of superior power over the age (αἰῶνα) of this world and the ruler (ἄρχοντα) of the authority (ἐξουσίας) of the air that rendered them spiritually dead in their transgressions and sins (2:1–2).[22]

That God raised and seated us with Christ in the heavenly places (2:6) "that he might show in the ages to come the surpassing wealth of his grace in kindness upon us in Christ Jesus" (2:7) further magnifies for the audience the greatness of the love with which God loved us (2:4). Recalling "the surpassing (ὑπερβάλλον) greatness of his power for us (ἡμᾶς) who believe" (1:19a), "the surpassing (ὑπερβάλλον) wealth of his grace in kindness upon us (ἡμᾶς) in Christ Jesus" further assimilates for the audience the greatness of the power God worked in raising and exalting Christ (1:20–21) with the great love with which he loved us in raising and exalting us with Christ (2:6).[23] Just as the greatness of God's power has a "surpassing" dimension for us, so the wealth of God's grace—an expression of God's great love—has a "surpassing" dimension for us.[24]

Alliteratively linked with God's "grace" (χάριτος), the word "kindness"

---

22. Lincoln, *Ephesians*, 109: "Both the parallel with 1:20 and the depiction of the past in 2:2 as being under the control of the ruler of the realm of the air make clear that this picture of the present involves sharing Christ's victory over such powers." Hoehner, *Ephesians*, 334: "Hence, the position of being seated with Christ in the heavenlies gives the believer a heavenly status with heavenly power to overcome the power of sin and death." See also Eberhard Faust, *Pax Christi et pax Caesaris: religionsgeschichtliche, traditionsgeschichtliche und sozialgeschichtliche Studien zum Epheserbrief* (NTOA 24; Göttingen: Vandenhoeck & Ruprecht, 1993), 58–59; O'Brien, *Ephesians*, 171; Whitlark, "*Enabling* Χάρις," 353.

23. Lincoln, *Ephesians*, 110: "[I]f the raising of Christ from death to sit in the heavenly realms was the supreme demonstration of God's surpassing power, then the raising of believers from spiritual death to sit with Christ in the heavenly realms is the supreme demonstration of God's surpassing grace." See also O'Brien, *Ephesians*, 172.

24. That the present active accusative singular participle for "surpassing" (ὑπερβάλλον) occurs only in these two places in Ephesians enhances this assimilation between God's great gracious love and the greatness of his power.

(χρηστότητι) in 2:7 extends the "love" word field in Ephesians.[25] Because of the great love with which God loved us, not only is God rich (πλούσιος) in mercy (2:4), but the wealth (πλοῦτος) of God's grace is surpassing in kindness upon us. God's great love includes his rich mercy, the wealth of his grace, and his surpassing kindness for us in Christ Jesus. So great is the merciful love with which God loved us (2:4), the surpassing wealth of God's grace in kindness upon us (2:7b), that God's manifestation of it is not yet fully realized in the present time of the audience but will be fully shown for what it is only in the ages to come (2:7a).[26]

6. Eph 2:8–10 (A'): To Walk in the Good Works God Prepared for Us

With an explanatory amplification of his exclamatory interjection, "by grace you have been saved!" (2:5b), in the B' element of the chiasm, Paul again directly addresses his audience of "you" believers at the beginning of the A' element—"For by the grace you have been saved through faith" (2:8a). The addition of the article "the" (τῇ) to the word "grace" (χάριτί) underlines for the audience that it is by "the" grace, that is, the grace of surpassing wealth (2:7) which God granted to all of us believers in making us alive, raising, and seating us with Christ in the heavenly places (2:5–6), "the" grace motivated by the great love with which God loved us (2:4), that they have been saved from spiritual death.[27] By the additional prepositional phrase, "through faith," the audience realize that they have appropriated this salvation through the faith that Paul has affirmed they have in the Lord Jesus (1:15), the faith by which they accepted the grace of what God did for them in raising Jesus from the dead and by which they are in the dynamic realm of being "the faithful in Christ Jesus" (1:1d; cf. 2:6, 7).[28]

---

25. Josef Zmijewski, "χρηστότης," *EDNT* 3.475: "Eph 2:7 directly associates χρηστότης with God's χάρις. Ἐν χρηστότητι can be understood causally, i.e., as one of the 'motivating causes' affecting the divine χάρις, or (probably more appropriately) in a modal sense, indicating the concrete 'way' in which χάρις as God's redemptive action consummates itself in Jesus Christ."

26. Hoehner, *Ephesians*, 339: "Hence, the action of God's love was in conjunction with Christ to make us alive, to raise us, and to seat us in the heavenlies in Christ Jesus for the purpose of demonstrating in the successive ages the surpassing wealth of his grace in the sphere of his appropriate kindness directed toward us who are located in Christ Jesus."

27. Jeal, *Ephesians*, 142: "The definite article has been added to χάρις, identifying it as the grace of God already mentioned in verses 5 and 7." See also O'Brien, *Ephesians*, 174 n. 83; Hoehner, *Ephesians*, 340; Lincoln, *Ephesians*, 111.

28. O'Brien, *Ephesians*, 174: " 'Faith' is usually understood here to denote the human response by which God's salvation is received. If God's grace is the ground of salvation, then faith is the means by which it is appropriated. . . . it is the response which receives what has already been done for us in Christ." Lincoln, *Ephesians*, 111: "Faith is a human activity but a specific kind of activity, a response which allows salvation to become operative, which receives what has already been accomplished by God in Christ." See also Hoehner, *Ephesians*, 341–42; Gerhard Barth, "πίστις," *EDNT* 3.95.

With a concerted emphasis upon "you," the A element of the chiasm reminded Paul's audience of "you" believers of their responsibility for their situation of being spiritually dead—"and you (ὑμᾶς) being dead in your (ὑμῶν) transgressions and sins" (2:1). But now in the A´ element that "this" (τοῦτο), that is, that this salvation by grace through faith (2:8a), "is not from you (ὑμῶν)" (2:8b) underlines for the audience that they are in no way responsible for their new situation of salvation that has made them spiritually alive.[29] Indeed, as Paul emphatically underscores, "of God" (θεοῦ), recalling "God" (θεός) being rich in mercy because of the great love with which he loved us in the central C and C´ elements (2:4), "is the gift" (2:8c).[30] That it is a "gift" (δῶρον) of God reinforces that salvation is by God's freely given "grace," as a specific expression of God's great love for us.[31]

That this salvation is "not from works, so no one may boast" (2:9) reinforces that it is "not from you" (2:8), it is not the result of any works that the group of "you" believers may have accomplished.[32] With its use of the singular pronoun and verb form, the clause, "so no one may boast," persuades each individual in the audience away from a "boasting," that is, a proud reliance before God, on any personal achievement for this salvation and thus instills in each individual an appreciation for this salvation as a

---

29. Lincoln, *Ephesians*, 112: "τοῦτο is probably best taken, therefore, as referring to the preceding clause as a whole, and thus to the whole process of salvation it describes, which of course includes faith as its means." O'Brien, *Ephesians*, 177: "Indeed, in the light of what has already been said about the desperate plight of men and women outside of Christ, dead in trespasses and sins, subject to wrath, and living in terrible bondage (Eph. 2:1–3), it was impossible for the readers to turn to their previous behaviour as the basis for achieving salvation. Their former life and works had caused the very predicament from which they needed to be delivered."

30. Jeal, *Ephesians*, 143: "The word order of the phrase θεοῦ τὸ δῶρον makes an emphatic contrast to the immediately preceding ὑμῶν; God, not humans, is the provider of salvation." O'Brien, *Ephesians*, 176 n. 93: "Literally the clause reads 'God's is the gift'." Hoehner, *Ephesians*, 344: "[L]iterally 'and this is not of yourselves, of God is the gift."

31. Gerhard Schneider, "δῶρον," *EDNT* 1.365: "[O]nly in Eph 2:8 does it [δῶρον] designate a gift of God." Jeal, *Ephesians*, 143: "The noun δῶρον, in its only occurrence in the Pauline letters, may simply agree with the neuter τοῦτο so as to emphasize that salvation in general is a gift by grace through faith, or it may be intended to effect *homoeteleuton* in the final -ν sounds of οὐκ ἐξ ὑμῶν, θεοῦ τὸ δῶρον, and οὐκ ἐξ ἔργων." Hoehner, *Ephesians*, 343: "[S]alvation does not have its origin or source (ἐκ) with humans. Rather, as expressed in the first part of the verse, its basis is grace and, as shown in verses 4–5, its origin is in God and his love."

32. Hoehner, *Ephesians*, 344–45: " 'Works' is a broad term referring to human effort, which is the same as 'works of the law' in a Jewish context. . . . From God's vantage point it is his grace not a human being's works that is the basis of salvation. From a human's vantage point, it is faith and not works that is the means to salvation."

pure gift of God's grace motivated by the great love with which God loved us (2:4).[33]

The progression from the explanation, "for by the grace you are (ἐστε) saved" (2:8a), to the explanation, "for his work are we (ἐσμεν)" (2:10a), continues Paul's assimilation of his audience of "you" believers to all of "us" believers. Indeed, the accusation that "you" once "walked" (περιεπατήσατε) "in" (ἐν) your transgressions and sins by which you were "dead" (2:1–2) in the A element of the chiasm progresses to the exhortation that "we"—the "you" along with all of us believers—should now "walk" (περιπατήσωμεν) "in" (ἐν) the good works which God prepared beforehand for us who have been created in Christ Jesus in the A' element (2:10).[34]

The divine origin of the gift of the salvation that is by grace and through faith—"of God (θεοῦ) in emphatic position is the gift" (2:8)—progresses to the divine origin of all of us believers—"for his (αὐτοῦ in emphatic position in reference to θεοῦ in 2:8) work are we" (2:10a).[35] That we have been "created" (by God, divine passive) in our situation of being "in" Christ Jesus for the good works which God prepared beforehand (προητοίμασεν), that we might "walk" in them (2:10b) reminds the audience that God chose us in our situation of being "in" Christ before (πρό) the foundation of the world that we might be holy and blameless before God within the dynamic realm of being "in love" (1:4).[36] This suggests to the audience that our "walking" in the good works (yet to be specified) which God has prepared beforehand for us, who have been chosen and created in Christ Jesus, is a way that we

---

33. On the concept of "boasting," see Josef Zmijewski, "καυχάομαι," EDNT 2.276–79. O'Brien, Ephesians, 178: "Here in Ephesians the apostle makes it plain that salvation by grace destroys all human boasting. Men and women have nothing which they can bring as their own to the living God."

34. Lincoln, Ephesians, 116: "An inclusion on περιπατεῖν rounds off the contrast which the pericope contains. In contrast to the walking in trespasses and sins of vv 1, 2, the new situation brings a walking in good works. God's saving power reaches its intended goal when there is a changed lifestyle." See also Beat Weber, " 'Setzen'-'Wandeln'-'Stehen' im Epheserbrief," NTS 41 (1995): 478.

35. On the word "work" (ποίημα) here Lincoln (Ephesians, 114) notes that "the reference is to believers as God's new creation. In Paul's letters believers are regarded as God's work (cf. Rom 14:20 and Phil 1:6). In Ephesians the writer has been talking of God's power at work for believers (1:19). He can now say that his readers not only benefit from that work but as new creatures are themselves the product of that work. The stress in the Greek is on the first word in the clause, αὐτοῦ, 'his.' "

36. O'Brien, Ephesians, 178–79: "The prepositional phrase in Christ Jesus may be taken simply as instrumental, signifying 'through God's activity in Christ'; but it may also indicate 'in our union with Christ Jesus', and in the light of the surrounding context (esp. vv. 6, 7) the latter nuance is probably correct. Christ Jesus is the 'sphere' of God's new creation, just as divine election (1:4) is in him." Lincoln, Ephesians, 114: "So good works are not the source but the goal of the new relationship between humanity and God. Salvation is not 'by works' but 'for works.' "

might be holy and blameless before God "in love"—a way to respond to the great love with which God loved us (2:4).[37]

The emphatic focus upon God as the origin of us, our salvation, and good works in the A′ element—"*of God* is the gift" (2:8c), "for *his* work are we" (2:10a), and "for the good works which *God* prepared beforehand" (2:10b)—points the audience back to the emphatic focus upon God as the origin of the great love we have received—"but *God* being rich in mercy, because of the great love with which he loved us" (2:4)—in the central C and C′ elements of the chiasm. God expressed this great love for us by making us alive, raising, and seating us with Christ in a position of great power in the heavenly places (2:5–6), thus empowering us to "walk" in the good works God prepared beforehand for us (2:10) rather than in our transgressions and sins (2:1–3).[38] The great love with which God loved us empowers us to "walk" in these good works as a way that we might be holy and blameless before God "in love" (1:4), that is, within the dynamic realm in which we have received God's great love that has empowered us to have the love for all the holy ones (1:15) that makes us truly holy and blameless before God.[39]

B. Summary on Ephesians 2:1–10

1. The coupling of the noun "love" with its cognate verb at the center of the chiasm (2:4) emphatically reinforces the theme of God's love that has been developing in the Letter. It reminds the audience that the great love with which God loved us believers is the love we have received as the grace with which God graced us in our union with Christ as the Beloved (1:6). It is

37. Lincoln, *Ephesians*, 115–16: "The formulation is an emphatic way of underlining the ethical dimension already present in the assertion of 1:4 that God chose believers before the foundation of the world, in order that they might be holy and blameless before him in love." O'Brien, *Ephesians*, 180: "In Ephesians 2:10 good works is a general and comprehensive expression for godly behaviour. It is not further defined, but its implication will be taken up and amplified in the exhortatory sections of the letter (in 4:17–6:20)." Hoehner, *Ephesians*, 348: "The attributive adjective ἀγαθοῖς, which describes the works as good, normally has a moral as well as a beneficial connotation. In other words, we are created in Christ Jesus for works that are morally and beneficially good for us, for those around us, and for God."

38. O'Brien, *Ephesians*, 181: "Believers are God's work, and the good deeds which he has purposed for us to walk in, which are achieved only through his enabling power, can be thought of as already prepared in his mind and counsel from before eternity." Hoehner, *Ephesians*, 349: "God has prepared beforehand good works for believers that he will perform in the through them as they walk by faith in his power. It is not doing a work for God but God doing a work in and through the believer."

39. For the relation between Eph 2:8–10 and the Pauline theme of justification by faith, see Stephen Westerholm, *Perspectives Old and New on Paul: The "Lutheran" Paul and His Critics* (Grand Rapids: Eerdmans, 2004), 404–5. See also Andrew T. Lincoln, "Ephesians 2:8–10: A Summary of Paul's Gospel?" *CBQ* 45 (1983): 617–30.

in the Beloved, Jesus Christ as the one whom God preeminently loved, that God has graciously loved us with his great love, so that we may be holy and blameless before God "in love" (1:4b).

2. The great love with which God loved the Beloved, the Christ whom God loved in making him alive by raising him from his situation of being physically dead (1:20), is the great love with which God graciously loved all of us believers (2:4) in our situation of being spiritually dead in transgressions (2:1–3) by making us spiritually alive with the Christ (2:5ab), thus gracing us with his gracious love in our union with the Christ as God's Beloved.

3. With its stress upon the word "grace," the sudden exclamatory interjection directly addressing the audience, "by *grace* you have been saved!" (2:5c), emphatically underlines that it is solely by "grace"—the freely given and wholly unmerited gift of God motivated by the great love with which the God who is rich in mercy loved us (2:4)—that "you," and thus all of "us" believers, are now in a situation of being "saved" by God from being spiritually "dead" even while physically living in the realm of our transgressions and sins (2:1–3, 5a).

4. God's great love includes not only God's "mercy" (2:4a), emphasizing the compassion of God's love, but also God's "grace" (1:2, 6, 7; 2:5, 7), emphasizing that God's love is a freely given gift. "Mercy" and "grace" are thus part of the "love" word field which further explain and enrich the love theme pervading Ephesians.

5. The great love with which God loved us (2:4) is a powerful love—an act of the great power that God worked for us in making us alive, raising, and exalting us with the Christ (2:5–6). It has placed us in a position of superior power over the age of this world and the ruler of the authority of the air that rendered us spiritually dead in our transgressions and sins (2:1–3).

6. The great love with which God loved us (2:4) empowers us to "walk" in the good works God has prepared beforehand for us (2:10) as a way that we might be holy and blameless before God "in love" (1:4), that is, within the dynamic realm in which we have received God's great love that has empowered us to have the love for all the holy ones (1:15) that makes us truly holy and blameless before God.

CHAPTER 7

Ephesians 2:11–22: The Peace That Establishes Unity as a Gift of Love (E)

A: ¹¹ Therefore remember that once *you*, the Gentiles *in the flesh*, those called "uncircumcision" by what is called "circumcision" *in the flesh* done by hands, ¹² that you were at that time without Christ alienated from the community of Israel and *strangers* of the covenants of the promise, not having hope and *Godless* in the world.

   B: ¹³ But now in Christ Jesus *you* who once were *far away* have become *near* in the blood of the Christ. ¹⁴ For he is *our* peace, who made the both one, that is, he destroyed the dividing wall of partition, the hostility, in his flesh, ¹⁵ abolishing the law of the commandments in decrees,

   C: that the two he might create *in himself*

   D: into *one* new person, making peace,

   D′: ¹⁶ and that he might reconcile the both in *one* body to God through the cross,

   C′: killing the hostility *in himself*.

   B′: ¹⁷ And coming he preached peace to *you* who are *far away* and peace to those who are *near*, ¹⁸ so that through him *we* both have the access in one Spirit before the Father.

A′: ¹⁹ So then you are no longer *strangers* and aliens, but you are fellow citizens with the holy ones and members of the household of God, ²⁰ built upon the foundation of the apostles and prophets, Christ Jesus himself being the capstone, ²¹ in whom the whole building being fitted together is growing into a temple holy in the

Lord, [22] in whom *you* also are being built together into a dwelling place of *God in the Spirit*.[1]

A. Audience Response to Ephesians 2:11–22

1. Eph 2:11–12 (A): You Were Once Without God and God's People

After having repeatedly assimilated the "you" believers to the "we" believers, most recently in 2:8–10 where "you" who have been saved by grace through faith (2:8a) are part of the "we" who, as a work created by God, may walk in the good works God prepared beforehand (2:10), Paul again directly and emphatically addresses his audience of "you" believers at the beginning of the A element of the chiasm in 2:11–22—"Therefore remember that once *you* (ὑμεῖς)" (2:11a).[2] What the "you" are to "remember" is their pre-Christian situation "in the flesh," that is, in the earthly and physical realm, from a Jewish point of view: "Therefore remember that once you, the Gentiles in the flesh, those called 'uncircumcision' by what is called 'circumcision' done by hands" (2:11).[3]

This Jewish characterization of the "you" forms a mini-chiasm in 2:11 that underscores for the audience their disadvantage and inferiority as the "you" who are "Gentiles" in relation to those who are Jews on the level of being "in the flesh":

    a: the Gentiles in the flesh (ἐν σαρκί)
       b: those called (λεγόμενοι) uncircumcision
       b´: by what is called (λεγομένης) circumcision
    a´: in the flesh (ἐν σαρκὶ) done by hands

In the "a" sub-element, from the Jewish perspective, the "you" are

---

1. For the establishment of Eph 2:11–22 as a chiasm, see ch. 2.

2. Hoehner, *Ephesians*, 353: "The pronoun ὑμεῖς is in the first part of the sentence for emphasis."

3. O'Brien, *Ephesians*, 185: The exhortation to remember, which stands like a rubric over vv. 11, 12, does not mean that they have actually forgotten what they were, only that Paul wants to call these matters to their attention so that they will have a greater understanding and appreciation of the past and the mighty reversal Christ has effected on their behalf." Yee, *Jews, Gentiles*, 124–25: "[T]he intention of the author in bidding his Gentile recipients to 'remember' (μνημονεύετε) is not so much to resuscitate injurious memories of the past. Nor was his intention to preserve from decay the remembrance of how humankind has fostered division within itself. Rather, his modest aim is to evoke in his Gentile recipients the awareness that the estrangement which they experienced before they had any positive connections with Christ was an ethnic one. This in turn enables him to explain why ethnic reconciliation, the removing of that which stands in the way of a right relationship between Jews and Gentiles, is necessary. Perhaps the author would also wish to put on record what could possibly return to haunt the community-body 'in Christ' in the present or future—and if that were the case, the 'memory' invoked is for the sake of prevention."

characterized pejoratively as "Gentiles" (ἔθνη), that is, non-Jews, as is physically evident "in the flesh."[4] As those who are "in the flesh," the Gentiles are called "uncircumcision," literally, "foreskin" (ἀκροβυστία), in the "b" sub-element because they do not remove the flesh of the foreskin from their males. As the chiasm pivots to the "b´" sub-element, the Gentiles are "called" (λεγόμενοι) "uncircumcision" by what is "called" (λεγομένης) "circumcision" (περιτομῆς), a designation for the Jews who remove the flesh of their foreskins as a sign of the covenant that establishes them as God's chosen people.[5] The chiasm climaxes in the "a´" sub-element with a contrastive parallel to the "a" sub-element. Whereas the uncircumcised Gentiles are simply "in the flesh" without further ado ("a"), the Jews are also "in the flesh" but with their distinguishing mark of circumcision that is "done by hands" as God directed them to do ("a´"). Hence, on the level of the "flesh" the Gentiles are inferior to the Jews.[6]

Paul then specifies what his audience, addressed as "Gentiles in the flesh" and "uncircumcision," are to "remember" and thus realize about their

---

4. O'Brien, *Ephesians*, 186: "This description arises from a Jewish standpoint since neither Romans nor Greeks would call themselves 'Gentiles'." Hoehner, *Ephesians*, 354: "Paul is stating that the Jews considered the Gentiles inferior just by what can be observed in the flesh." See also Best, *Essays*, 87–101.

5. O'Brien, *Ephesians*, 186 n. 129: "ἀκροβυστία ('uncircumcision') and περιτομή ('circumcision') are abstract nouns used as collective nouns." Hoehner, *Ephesians*, 354: "The term ἀκροβυστία, 'uncircumcision,' is anarthrous and thus is given the qualitative force of contempt in this context."

6. The chiasm in 2:11 is suggested by Horacio E. Lona, *Die Eschatologie im Kolosser- und Epheserbrief* (FB 48; Würzburg, Germany: Echter, 1984), 258. Jeal (*Ephesians*, 150 n. 391) claims that "full chiastic order is not consistent especially because τὰ ἔθνη and χειροποιήτου are not equivalents." But "in the flesh" is what establishes the parallelism between the "a" and "a´" sub-elements, and the whole point of the chiasm is the contrast between "the Gentiles" (τὰ ἔθνη), who do nothing with their hands to remove the foreskin, and what is "done by hands" (χειροποιήτου) by the Jews who practice circumcision. Although "done by hands" often has a negative connotation (what is only material or human and not spiritual or divine), it is fully positive in this context with its Jewish perspective (contra Theo K. Heckel, "Juden und Heiden im Epheserbrief," in *Kirche und Volk Gottes: Festschrift für Jürgen Roloff zum 70. Geburtstag* [ed. Martin Karrer et al.; Neukirchen-Vluyn: Neukirchener Verlag, 2000], 186). For the argument, see Yee, *Jews, Gentiles*, 83–87, who concludes: "The well-calculated expression of our author is therefore to represent the importance of 'circumcision made by hands' to Jews who wished to display their ethnic solidarity and their unswerving allegiance to the law and the covenant made between God and Israel. From the perspective of the Jews circumcision 'made by hands' was entirely agreeable in God's eyes (e.g., Gen. 17.9–14; Lev. 12.3, etc.). The Jews have responded faithfully to the divine promise given to their ancestors and their allegiance to the ancestral custom based on the Torah is not to be questioned. That is the kind of mood which the author of Ephesians wishes to transmit." Accordingly, rather than being translated by a pejorative "so-called," λεγομένης in 2:11 should be translated simply as "called."

pre-Christian situation from a Jewish viewpoint.[7] At that time in which they were without Christ they were "alienated from the community of Israel" (2:12a).[8] In other words, as Gentiles who did not practice circumcision, the rite of initiation into the Jewish community, they were not members of, and from the Jewish viewpoint, were "alienated" (ἀπηλλοτριωμένοι) from God's chosen people of Israel.[9] They thus did not have any of the advantages and privileges of being in a covenantal relationship with God or God's people.

That the audience of "the Gentiles in the flesh," the "uncircumcision," are to "remember" that they were at the time that they were without Christ also "strangers of the covenants of the promise" (2:12b) causes them to re-

---

7. Yee, Jews, Gentiles, 97: "[T]he author has made a substantial break halfway through his argument in v. 11c (οἱ λεγόμενοι ἀκροβυστία . . . χειροποιήτου) in order to particularise what is truly meant for his recipients to be categorised as 'Gentiles in the flesh', and therefore finds it necessary to resume as well as to elaborate his argument in v. 12 by introducing another statement about the Gentiles which is closely associated with the Jews. The two ὅτι-clauses in vv. 11b and 12a are inextricably bound with each other, constituting the content of memory: that is, the Gentiles' unJewishness."

8. Ephesians 2:12a is usually construed with a comma after "Christ" to form a clause in which "without Christ" is the predicate : "you were at that time without Christ, alienated from the community of Israel." But for an alternative periphrastic construal without the comma that better fits the context—"you were at that time that you were without Christ alienated from the community of Israel," see Stanley E. Porter, Verbal Aspect in the Greek of the New Testament, with Reference to Tense and Mood (Studies in Biblical Greek 1; New York: Lang, 1993), 470; Yee, Jews, Gentiles, 98–99: "Different from the non-periphrastic rendering is that the phrase 'at that time without/apart from Christ' completes or modifies the perfect participle ἀπηλλοτριωμένοι rather than the auxiliary verb, and serves as a temporal-marker indicating when estrangement has actually taken place. The periphrastic rendering thus provides a sense which a simple verb does not usually possess and changes inevitably the semantic landscape of vv. 12a, b: it helps to lay bare what had happened when the Gentiles had no positive connections with Christ. . . . In favour of this rendering, it is no longer necessary for us to emphasise, as most commentators have done, the parallelism between the Gentiles' being 'apart from Christ' (or Israel's Messiah) and their being 'alienated from the body politic of Israel' or other God-given blessings." On the πολιτεία of Israel, which we have translated as "community," Yee (Jews, Gentiles, 96) states: "In our present context, the expression ἡ πολιτεία τοῦ Ἰσραήλ can be best understood as Israel in which the 'circumcision'/Jews have coalesced to develop into a kind of 'league' or 'alliance' on the basis of an ethnos. This is a body politic which goes beyond any community in a specific locality (such as the Jewish synagogue). Indeed, it will be quite impossible to speak of the body politic of Israel or the community of God's choice in any parochial sense."

9. Yee, Jews, Gentiles, 99–100: "Used in its active sense the term ἀπηλλοτριόω normally carries overtones of dislike, denoting a hostile attitude, 'to cause to feel an aversion', to cause to become estranged', or 'to abandon or to dispose of'. The negative overtones of the term should be retained in the passive form of the verb. The perfect tense of the verb may well suggest the continuing effect of estrangement that had been inflicted on the Gentiles. Given the fact that ἀπηλλοτριωμένοι is also collocated with λεγόμενοι of v. 11b (both verbs in passive voice), we have good reason to suppose that the connection between these verbs is very close and that each has reference to the 'circumcision', i.e., the Jews who nicknamed the Gentiles the 'uncircumcision' were also the agent of estrangement (vv. 11b, 12a)."

alize that they had no share in the promise that God made to the people of Israel in the various covenants made with the patriarchs.[10] That they were strangers of the covenants of "the promise" (τῆς ἐπαγγελίας) deepens the audience's appreciation that they now, as believers, have been sealed with the Holy Spirit of "the promise" (τῆς ἐπαγγελίας) (1:13).

Since the audience did not have the promise of future salvation contained in the covenants God made with the Jewish people, they were in a situation of "not having hope" (2:12c). They had absolutely no hope whatsoever, no future to look forward to.[11] The "remembering" of their pre-Christian situation of not having "hope" (ἐλπίδα) thus deepens the audience's appreciation for Paul's prayer that they know what is the "hope" (ἐλπίς) of God's calling (1:18), which includes God's having chosen them so that they have the hope of looking forward to being holy and blameless before him in love (1:4). And that the audience formerly were "Godless in the world" (2:12d) causes them to realize that, although they may have believed in and worshipped various gods, from the Jewish viewpoint they not only did not believe in the one and only true God, but they had been abandoned by this God, rendering them absolutely "Godless."[12]

With regard to the love theme in Ephesians, this A element (2:11–12) of the chiasm in 2:11–22 reminds the audience that before they became believers "in Christ," they were not part of the people who were loved by and loved God and one another within a covenantal relationship. They were

---

10. O'Brien, *Ephesians*, 189: "Here the plural covenants suggests a series of covenants with Abraham (Gen. 15:7–21; 17:1–21), Isaac (Gen. 26:2–5), Jacob (Gen. 28:13–15), Israel (Exod. 24:1–8), and David (2 Sam. 7), while the genitive 'of the promise' probably refers to the foundation promise made by God to Abraham. The Gentiles' exclusion from the community of God's people meant that they had no share in the covenants which promised the messianic salvation." Yee, *Jews, Gentiles*, 104–5: "[T]he author has used vigorous language to emphasise that the Gentiles who lay outside the orbit of the body politic of Israel were 'outsiders' to the various 'covenants' which God had promised the Jewish patriarchs. . . . Gentiles as 'aliens', and their ineligibility and unsuitability in the covenants, had become a significant part in the theological thinking of the Jews. What could hardly be expressed more clearly is the fact that, instead of being seen as inclusive, able to embrace non-Jews, the 'covenants of the promise' have become a boundary marker, distinguishing the Jews who lay within their orbit from the Gentiles."

11. Yee, *Jews, Gentiles*, 105 n. 120: "The position of the noun ἐλπίς ["hope"] is emphatic."

12. O'Brien, *Ephesians*, 190: "Finally, their being without God in the world signifies that they had no relationship with the true God, the God of Israel. Like many other Gentiles they may have had a pantheon of deities to whom they were devoted, but Paul's comment is not a description of those who did not believe in a deity or deities . . . it is an evaluation, this time of those who, in contrast to Israel, which had a relationship with the true God, were God-forsaken." Yee, *Jews, Gentiles*, 110: "The identification of Gentiles as 'having no hope and godless in the world' carries heavily charged ethno-religious overtones. In the religious milieu of the Jewish world the Gentiles who 'have not' these blessings contrasted sharply with the privileged position of the Jews, indicating both their impiety and strangeness."

not recipients of the love with which God loved Israel by giving them the circumcision in the flesh, making them the community of Israel with covenants that gave them a promise to hope in and a relationship with the one and only God. By directing them to remember this situation in which they were not in a loving relationship with God and with the people of God, Paul deepens his audience's appreciation and gratitude for the great love with which God has now loved us (2:4) in the Christ event as well as the motivation of their love for all the holy ones (1:15), which unites them with their fellow believers as those who are "in Christ," in union with one another and with God's Beloved (1:6).[13]

2. Eph 2:13–15a (B): You Who Were Far Are Now Near in Christ Our Peace

After the audience of "you" believers were reminded of the unfortunate situation that they, as well as the "we" believers, were in prior to their experience of the love God extended to them in the Christ event (2:1–3), they heard of God's dramatic reversal of that situation: "But God being rich in mercy, because of his great love with which he loved us" (2:4). Similarly, after the audience of "you" believers were reminded of their situation of being alienated from the people of Israel who were loved by and loved God and one another in the A element (2:11–12), they hear again how God has loved them in the Christ event in the B element: "But now in Christ Jesus *you* who once were far off have become near in the blood of the Christ" (2:13).[14]

That "you" (ὑμεῖς in emphatic position) are now in the dynamic realm of being "in" (ἐν) Christ Jesus (2:13a; cf. 2:7, 10) transforms the situation in which "you" (ὑμεῖς in emphatic position) from the Jewish viewpoint were Gentiles "in" (ἐν) the realm of the flesh (2:11) at the time of their being "without Christ" (2:12).[15] That "you" have "become" or "been brought" (ἐγενήθητε) near by God (divine passive) is an expression of God's love for

---

13. Hoehner, *Ephesians*, 351: "[T]he dominate theme of this epistle is love, and certainly no union can be truly successful unless love is its basis and mode of operation."

14. Lincoln, *Ephesians*, 138: "νυνὶ δὲ ἐν Χριστῷ Ἰησοῦ, 'but now in Christ Jesus,' has a similar effect to ὁ δὲ θεός, 'but God,' in 2:4, in announcing the dramatic change in the Gentiles' situation." O'Brien, *Ephesians*, 190: "This mighty change parallels the divine reversal of vv. 1–10 (also described by means of the 'once-now' schema: But . . . God, v. 4), where God out of his great love and mercy made those who were dead in their trespasses and sins alive in Christ Jesus."

15. Hoehner, *Ephesians*, 362: "The pronoun ὑμεῖς, 'you,' which refers back to 'you, the Gentiles in the flesh' in verse 11, is emphatic by its mere mention as well as its repetition in the context."

them in their union with Christ Jesus (2:13b).[16] And the means by which "you" became near—"in the blood (αἵματι) of the Christ" (2:13c)[17]—recalls for the audience that we believers "have redemption through his blood (αἵματος), the forgiveness of transgressions, according to the wealth of his grace" (1:7), that is, "his grace with which he graced us in the Beloved" (1:6).[18] In Christ Jesus, in their dynamic union with the Beloved, the audience of "you" believers who were "far off" have been graced with the love of God by being brought "near."[19]

Paul then explains to his audience the significance of God having brought the "you" believers "near" in the blood of the Christ: "For *he* is our

---

16. Hoehner, *Ephesians*, 362–63: "The verb ἐγενήθητε, 'have been brought,' is a passive which indicates that the Gentiles were recipients of God's action rather than a result of self-effort." See also Yee, *Jews, Gentiles*, 115.

17. Hoehner, *Ephesians*, 363: "Here again, as frequently in Ephesians, the article precedes the noun 'Christ' emphasizing that by the blood of Israel's promised Messiah, reconciliation was accomplished." Yee, *Jews, Gentiles*, 120: "The use of the phrase 'the blood of the Christ' is also an acknowledgement that there is no way out for the human family in estrangement except through the sacrificial death of the Messiah Jesus. . . . The arthrous 'Christ' in v. 13b may be understood as 'the previously referred to Christ [Jesus]' (v. 13a)" (n. 181).

18. Hoehner, *Ephesians*, 363: "The preposition ἐν shows the instrumental means or cause of bringing the Gentiles near. This preposition has much the same import as διά in verse 7 [1:7]. . . . the significance of the 'blood of Christ,' discussed in 1:7, speaks of the sacrificial death of Christ." Yee, *Jews, Gentiles*, 119–20: "In our present context, the expression 'the blood of Christ' refers to Jesus's death which has the effect of making the Gentiles 'near' (1.7). . . . Here the 'blood' language is probably drawn from the understanding of Jesus's death in terms of cultic sacrifice, that is, as a (sin)-offering which represents the divided human family."

19. Contra Barth, *Ephesians*, 278; Peter Stuhlmacher, " 'He Is Our Peace' (Eph. 2:14): On the Exegesis and Significance of Eph. 2:14–18," in *Reconciliation, Law, and Righteousness* (Philadelphia: Fortress, 1986), 187, and Moritz, *Profound Mystery*, 48, "the use of the language of 'near' and 'far' here does not constitute a quotation of Isa 57:19, or even necessarily an allusion to it," according to Lincoln, *Ephesians*, 138; idem, "The Church and Israel in Ephesians 2," *CBQ* 49 (1987): 610. Hoehner, *Ephesians*, 362: "[T]he terms 'far' and 'near' were used in the OT to describe the Gentile nations as 'far off' (Deut 28:49; 29:22; 1 Kgs 8:41; Isa 5:26; Jer 5:15) while describing Israel as 'near' (Ps 148:14)." See also Lincoln, *Ephesians*, 138–39; O'Brien, *Ephesians*, 191 n. 143. Yee, *Jews, Gentiles*, 120–21: "[I]t is not necessary for us to sidetrack at this point into debates about the possible candidates to whom the Gentiles are brought near, since the author's aim is primarily to construct a new space for the Gentiles who were marginalised by the Jews who practised ethnocentricity. . . . Only when we take into account the Gentiles' otherness from the perspective of the Jews can we appreciate the full force of the author's argument in v. 13. While v. 13a sums up the estranged condition of the human family, with its different sections kept apart from one another, v. 13b is meant to obliterate the social distance between Jews and Gentiles. This is achieved by constructing a new space for the Gentiles who were at the periphery of the Jewish 'world'."

peace" (2:14a). That "*he*" (αὐτός in emphatic position),[20] Christ, in his very person is the embodiment of our "peace" (εἰρήνη) develops for the audience the Letter's theme of peace as a gift of God's love. In 1:2 Paul uttered a prayer-wish for his audience—"Grace to you and peace (εἰρήνη) from God our Father and the Lord Jesus Christ." Here peace was coupled with grace as gifts motivated by and further specifications of the gracious love that comes from both God and Jesus Christ. But now the person of Christ Jesus himself *is* our peace as the gift of God's love.[21]

While "peace" in the biblical tradition generally refers to an overall state of well-being and harmony both in relationship to God and fellow human beings, in this context the emphasis is on the peace that Christ himself is for the alienation between Jews and Gentiles.[22] Indeed, that Christ is "our" (ἡμῶν) peace means that he is peace for all of us believers—both the "you" believers, predominantly Gentiles who came to believe at a later time, and the "we" believers, predominantly Jews who were the first to hope in the Christ (cf. 1:12–13). That Christ is "our" peace thus continues Paul's assimilation of his audience of "you" believers with the "we" believers into all of us believers as recipients of the gift of God's love that is Christ our peace.[23]

With regard to the theme of love in Ephesians, that Christ is our peace introduces the audience to a new dimension in the expressions of God's love for us. Previously believers were coupled with Christ as recipients of God's love. In other words, in their dynamic union with Christ believers shared in the love Christ received from God as the Beloved (1:6; 2:4–10). But now Christ becomes not only one who is loved by God but one who extends God's love to believers. He is not only the object but the acting subject of God's love, as confirmed by the next clause, "who made the both one" (2:14b).[24]

---

20. Hoehner, *Ephesians*, 366: "The personal pronoun αὐτός, 'he,' is at the beginning for the sake of emphasis." See also Yee, *Jews, Gentiles*, 141 n. 54. O'Brien, *Ephesians*, 193 n. 149: "All of the references to the intensive personal pronoun αὐτός ('he') in Ephesians focus emphatically on Christ: 2:14; 4:10, 11; 5:23, 27."

21. Hoehner, *Ephesians*, 366–67: "Peace is an abstract idea that is personified in Christ. . . . Thus, it means 'he in his own person' is peace."

22. Hoehner, *Ephesians*, 367: "Paul will, within this section, show that the peace is primarily between the Jewish and Gentile believers and secondarily between human beings and God."

23. O'Brien, *Ephesians*, 193: "The term 'peace' in both the Old and New Testaments came to denote well-being in the widest sense, including salvation, the source and giver of which is God alone."

24. O'Brien, *Ephesians*, 192: "From the opening words he himself (v. 14) it is clear that Christ rather than God who has been the major actor in the preceding paragraphs (1:3–14, 15–23; 2:1–10), is the central figure. The emphasis is now placed on Christ's reconciling work, and this stress continues throughout vv. 14–18. He is the subject of the finite verbs and participles which focus on reconciliation and the removal of alienation." See also Lincoln, *Ephesians*, 140.

That Christ made the both one begins to explain for the audience, in positive terms, what it means that Christ is our peace as an extension of God's love for us. That Christ "made" (ποιήσας) the both one continues God's creative activity toward us, according to which we are God's "work" or "making" (ποίημα), created in Christ Jesus (2:10), as a further expression of the great love with which God loved us (2:4). That Christ made "the both" (τὰ ἀμφότερα, neuter plural) one refers to the Gentiles (τὰ ἔθνη, neuter plural) in the flesh, those called the "uncircumcision," as well as to those called the "circumcision" in the flesh, the Jews (2:11).[25] As our peace Christ made both the Jews and the Gentiles, formerly alienated from one another into two distinct groups, into one single entity, thus transforming a situation of alienation into a situation of peaceful unity.[26] This "making" of the both into one (2:14b), this creative activity of Christ as our peace, continues the creative activity of God toward us as yet a further expression of the great love with which God loved us (2:4) in the Christ event.[27]

With an epexegetical or explicative (rather than coordinating) conjunction καί, "that is,"[28] Paul begins to further elucidate for his audience, in negative terms which complement the positive terms that Christ "made the both one" (2:14b), how Christ in himself, in his very person, is our peace (2:14a): "that is, he destroyed the dividing wall of partition, the hostility, in his flesh, abolishing (in his flesh) the law of the commandments in decrees" (2:14c–15a).[29]

---

25. Yee, *Jews, Gentiles*, 142: "Since there is nothing in the previous verses (vv. 11–13) that corresponds with the ideas of 'both' (τὰ ἀμφότερα) other than the obvious polarisation (and alienation) of the 'circumcision' and the 'uncircumcision'—a point missed by most commentators (vv. 11b and 11c), the neuter formulation here reflects most probably Jews and Gentiles who were estranged from one another by the act of (un)circumcision. To be sure, the formulation echoes the Jewish perspective that humanity can be divided into 'two' and that only one of the two is entitled to God's grace." See also O'Brien, *Ephesians*, 194.

26. Best, *Ephesians*, 253: "The two groups are not strictly Jews and Gentiles; it is Christians from both these groups who are made into the new group. Jews and Gentiles as such still exist as independent groups." Yee, *Jews, Gentiles*, 142–43: "[T]he author amplifies the reconciling activity of Christ in making/creating the non-Jews, who were situated at the extremity of the Jewish world (v. 13a), and the Jews, who had turned Israel's privileges into ethnic and national assets, into one harmonious whole (cf. v. 10). He assumes that the two parts of humanity are kept apart because of Jewish ethnocentricity, and that Christ, the embodiment of 'peace', has come to bridge the gap between the two ethnic groups."

27. On the verb "making" as denoting creative activity, see Yee, *Jews, Gentiles*, 142 n. 60.

28. Zerwick, *Biblical Greek*, 154, #455 ζ; BDF, 228–29, §442 (9); BDAG, 495; Schlier, *Epheser*, 124.

29. For various ways in which the grammatical construction can be construed here, see Hoehner, *Ephesians*, 371–73. We have opted for a construal in which "the hostility" (τὴν ἔχθραν) is the second object of the participle "destroyed" (λύσας) in 2:14c rather than the first object of the participle "abolishing" (καταργήσας) in 2:15a. To the objection that it is awkward to have the objects of "destroyed" on either side of it, as "it is more natural

"The dividing wall of partition" (2:14c), a metaphor of emphatically pronounced separation (as a genitive of apposition, "of partition" [τοῦ φραγμοῦ] reinforces and intensifies "the dividing wall" [τὸ μεσότοιχον]),[30] refers to the alienation that separates Jews from Gentiles, as expressed in 2:11–13.[31] The specification of this metaphor as "the hostility" or "the enmity" (τὴν ἔχθραν, 2:14d) underscores how the alienation that separates Jews and Gentiles is not merely neutral but involves mutual animosity. With regard to the love theme, then, this dividing "wall" of hostility reminds the audience of the mutual hatred that separated rather than mutual love that can unite Jews and Gentiles, now that Christ has made the both one (2:14b).

That Christ destroyed the dividing wall of partition, the hostility, between Jews and Gentiles "*in his (αὐτοῦ) flesh*" (in emphatic position, 2:14e) accentuates, intensifies, and further elucidates for the audience how "he" (αὐτός), Christ, in himself, in his very person, is our peace (2:14a) as God's gift of love to us. That it was "*in his flesh*" that Christ destroyed the hostility between Jews and Gentiles parallels and complements that it was "in the blood of the Christ" that God brought the audience of "you" believers "near" (2:13), as a reference to the sacrificial death of Christ on the cross.[33]

---

for phrases which are in apposition to follow one another than to be interrupted by the participle" (Lincoln, *Ephesians*, 124; cf. O'Brien, *Ephesians*, 196 n. 164), we would argue that this awkward interruption is intentional on the part of Paul in order to facilitate an accentuation that the hostility is destroyed "in his flesh" and, by thus placing the prepositional phrase, "in his flesh," in an emphatic and ambivalent position between "the hostility" and "the law of the commandments in decrees," to allow it to be governed by both participles. In other words, it is "in his flesh" that Christ destroyed the hostility and it is "in his flesh" that Christ abolished the law of the commandments in decrees.

30. Hoehner, *Ephesians*, 368–69: "The noun μεσότοιχον is rarely used in classical literature, not used in the LXX, and occurs only here in the NT. It is from τοῖχος, 'wall,' and μέσος, 'middle,' hence, the middle or dividing wall. The following word φραγμός is used to denote 'fencing in, blocking up,' 'railing' of a bridge, or 'fortification.' . . . The genitive appears to function appositionally, thus the middle wall which consists of a partition. A wall stands between two parties to separate them."

31. Yee, *Jews, Gentiles*, 151: "Jewish ethnocentrism and the attitude to exclude—rather than a particular locus, be it the balustrade of the temple or the law per se—best explains the 'wall' that stands between Jew and Gentile, preventing one ethnic group from advancing to the 'other'."

32. Lincoln, *Ephesians*, 142: "The objective situation of hostility because of the law's exclusiveness engendered personal and social antagonisms. The laws which forbade eating or intermarrying with Gentiles often led Jews to have a contempt for Gentiles which could regard Gentiles as less than human. In response, Gentiles would often regard Jews with great suspicion, considering them inhospitable and hateful to non-Jews, and indulge in anti-Jewish prejudice."

33. Hoehner, *Ephesians*, 374: "This prepositional phrase [in his flesh] refers to the crucified Christ and is parallel with the phrase, 'by the blood of Christ' in verse 13 and 'through the cross' in verse 16."

With the emphatic prepositional phrase, "*in his flesh*" (ἐν τῇ σαρκὶ αὐτοῦ), the audience experience the profound irony that it was in the sacrificial death of his own "flesh," in his own body, that Christ destroyed the hostility between the Gentiles "in the flesh" (ἐν σαρκί) and the "circumcision" (Jews) "in the flesh" (ἐν σαρκί) (2:11).

The implication for the audience is that "in his flesh" (2:14e) is also the location for Christ's "abolishing the law of the commandments in decrees" (2:15a). With its threefold description of the various dimensions of the Jewish legal and social system to accentuate its oppressive nature, "the law of the commandments in decrees" climaxes the audience's experience of the progression from the metaphor of the dividing wall of partition between Jews and Gentiles (2:14c) to its specification as "the hostility" (2:14c) to the precise cause of this divisive hostility in the Jews' (ab)use of their laws, commandments, and decrees to separate themselves from the Gentiles.[35] The audience realize that by abolishing the law, its commandments, and its decrees and destroying "*in his flesh*" the hostility they caused, Christ made both the Jews and Gentiles one (2:14b), so that in himself he is the embodiment of our peace (2:14a) as God's gift of love to us.[36]

---

34. Yee (*Jews, Gentiles*, 153–54) points out this word-play on "flesh," "which is closely associated with the source of enmity between Jew and Gentile: the 'flesh' (cf. 'Gentiles in the *flesh*', v. 11a; the 'foreskin', v. 11b; the 'circumcision in the *flesh*', v. 11c; cf. Gal. 6:12–13), which served as one of the most explicit boundary markers, marking off the Jews from the Gentiles, and the symbol of alienation between the two human groups, is now destroyed by Christ in his own 'flesh' (= body) on the cross. One cannot rule out the possibility that here the 'flesh' on the cross also makes a *contemptuous* pun with the 'flesh' that excludes" (Yee's emphasis).

35. It is not the abrogation of the Law as a whole but only some of its rules that are in view according to J. Joosten, "Christ a-t-il aboli la loi pour réconcilier juifs et païens?" *ETR* 80 (2005): 95–102. Joosten offers the following translation of Eph 2:15: "He made the two peoples into one, breaking down the wall that divided them. He canceled the law of the commandments concerning some ordinances." But according to Lincoln (*Ephesians*, 142), "This lengthy formulation—literally, 'the law consisting of commandments which are expressed in regulations'—is characteristic of the style of Ephesians and, at the same time, conveys a sense of the oppressiveness of all the law's commandments. But it is clearly the law itself and all its regulations, not just some of them, which are in view."

36. Yee, *Jews, Gentiles*, 160–61: "In short, the author has spoken critically of the law, but this by no means amounts to a personal attack on the law. Rather, he is speaking from an insider's perspective on the law which Jews had deemed significant but used as an instrument of division in order to reinforce their distinctive identity and the 'body politic' as based on a particular *ethnos*. This, the enmity between Jew and Gentile, lies not with the Torah *per se* but with the human attitude that perverted the gifts of God into signs of separation and exclusiveness." For a structure of Eph 2:13–18 that places 2:15a and the abolition of the law in a central position, see Sigurd Grindheim, "What the OT Prophets Did Not Know: The Mystery of the Church in Eph 3,2–13," *Bib* 84 (2003): 544–45. But in our view the unity of Jews and Gentiles as expressed in 2:15c and 2:16a is at the center of 2:11–22 in accord with its chiastic structure.

3. Eph 2:15b (C): That the Two He Might Create in Himself

After the description of the destructive activity of Christ as our peace (2:14a) in the B element (2:14c–15a), with the C element of the chiasm in 2:11–22 the audience begin to hear the purpose for this destructive activity in the return to the description of Christ's constructive activity: "that the two he might create in himself" (2:15b). With the masculine plural accusative "the two" (τοὺς δύο) the audience experience a progression from the neuter plural accusative "the both" (τὰ ἀμφότερα, 2:14b) as references to the division between Jews and Gentiles. Whereas the neuter "both" referred to Jews and Gentiles as two systems or classes (the Gentiles [τὰ ἔθνη, neuter plural] uncircumcised in the flesh vs. the Jews circumcised in the flesh in 2:11), the masculine "two" refers to them more concretely as persons.[37]

That Christ might "create" (κτίσῃ) the two (2:15b) makes explicit the creative activity connoted by his having "made" (ποιήσας) the both one (2:14b). In addition, that Christ might "create" (κτίσῃ) the two reminds the audience that we believers have been "created" (κτισθέντες) by God "in Christ Jesus" (2:10), God's Beloved (1:6), as a further expression of the great love with which God loved us (2:4). The audience are to realize that Christ's creative activity on our behalf continues God's creative activity on our behalf as a gift of God's love for us.[38]

That "in himself" (ἐν αὐτῷ) Christ might create the two (2:15b) continues Paul's concerted emphasis upon the very person of Christ as the locus of our peace with a pointed use of the third-person singular personal pronoun in reference to Christ:[39]

2:14a: For *he* (αὐτός) is our peace

---

37. Hoehner, *Ephesians*, 378: "Whereas the neuter form of the substantival adjective τὰ ἀμφότερα was used in verse 14 because it referred to two parties, systems, or classes under which Jews and Gentiles were grouped, here they are conceived concretely as persons, and thus the masculine τοὺς δύο is used. Also, the masculine is used in view of the following ἄνθρωπον. The two persons become one new person."

38. O'Brien, *Ephesians*, 199–200: "Once the divisive law by which Jews and Gentiles had been alienated from one another was set aside, there was nothing to keep the two elements of humanity apart. Christ brought them together in a sovereign act that was nothing less than a new creation. Paul has already spoken of God's salvation in terms of a new creation (2:10). Believers are his workmanship who have already been created in Christ Jesus for good works, and these are part of God's intention for that new creation. Here in v. 15 the same creation language is employed for this new creation, but now the focus of attention is on Christ's mighty work: he is the creator of a new humanity through his death." See also Lincoln, *Ephesians*, 143.

39. Hoehner (*Ephesians*, 377 n. 2) prefers the variant reading ἑαυτῷ rather than αὐτῷ for "himself." But αὐτῷ has the same reflexive sense as ἑαυτῷ here (see Zerwick, *Biblical Greek*, 66–67; BDF, 147–48, §283) and is to be preferred as the original reading since it better facilitates the progression from αὐτός in 2:14a to αὐτοῦ in 2:14e to αὐτῷ in 2:15b and in 2:16b. See also Dawes, *Body*, 171 n. 5.

2:14e: in *his* (αὐτοῦ) flesh
2:15b: in *himself* (αὐτῷ)

The audience thus realize that Christ in himself is the embodiment of our peace (2:14a) because the destructive activity that he accomplished "in his flesh" (2:14e) by his death on the cross makes possible the constructive activity—"that the two he might create"—that he accomplished "in himself" (2:15b). With regard to the love theme, then, this develops how in our union with the Beloved (1:6) we are loved not only by God but by Christ himself because of what Christ accomplished for us "in himself."

4. Eph 2:15cd (D): Into One New Person, Making Peace

With the first of the central elements of the chiasm in 2:11–22, the D element, the audience hear the goal of the constructive activity that follows upon the destructive activity of Christ as our peace, namely, that the two—Jews and Gentiles—he might create in himself "into one new person, making peace" (2:15cd). This further explains and specifies for the audience the unity between Jews and Gentiles that Christ as our peace brought about in himself.[40] That Christ made the both "one" (ἕν, 2:14b) progresses to his creation in himself of "one" (ἕνα) new corporate person (2:15c) in contrast to the "two"—the Jews and Gentiles conceived of as two distinct corporate persons. Out of two separated and hostile corporate persons Christ has created in himself one entirely "new" (καινόν) corporate person or humanity.[41]

The result of Christ's creation of the two in himself into one new person was his creative activity of "making peace" (2:15d). That Christ, in his divine creative activity, "made (ποιήσας) the both one" (2:14b), that is, destroyed the hostility (2:14cd), the opposite of peace, was for the purpose of "making (ποιῶν) peace" between Jews and Gentiles. Christ "in himself," in his body and person, is our "peace" (εἰρήνη) (2:14a) because he not only destroyed the hostility "in his flesh" (2:14cde) but created the two "in him-

---

40. Schnackenburg, *Ephesians*, 115: "Christ . . . builds this new entity in his own person, it is he himself in a new dimension."

41. Hoehner, *Ephesians*, 378–79: "The word 'one' (ἕνα) makes a definite contrast to the 'two' (δύο) hostile groups, which they once were when outside of Christ. . . . In the present context καινός is used to show that Christ has created a whole new person entirely different from the two former persons, namely, Jews and Gentiles. It is not that Gentiles become Jews as Gentile proselytes did in pre-NT times nor that Jews become Gentiles, but both become 'one new person' or 'one new humanity,' a third entity." Yee, *Jews, Gentiles*, 166–67: "[T]he vivid imagery of the 'one new man' is not of Christian Jews and Christian Gentiles who had constituted the new humanity in the sense that the church had replaced Israel as the people of God. Indeed, it would be difficult to conceive of the 'one new man' without a close connection to Israel: the author does not conceive of the 'one new man' without a connection to the 'circumcision' or the 'body politic of Israel', but argues that the new humanity no longer defined itself on the basis of an ethnos and by separation of the 'circumcision'/Jew from the 'uncircumcision'/Gentile, but embraced both 'in Christ'."

self" (2:15b) into one new corporate person, thus making "peace" (εἰρήνην). Christ in himself is our peace because he made and created in himself peace for separated Jews and Gentiles.[42] The audience now better realize how, as God's gift of love for us, "peace" (εἰρήνη) comes not only from God our Father but also from the Lord Jesus Christ (1:2). Indeed, Christ in himself *is* our peace (2:14a) as God's gift of love for us.

5. Eph 2:16a (D´): Christ Reconciled Both in One Body to God

With the second of the central elements of the chiasm in 2:11–22, the D´ element, the audience experience the pivot, centering around the chiasm's main point of the unity of Jews and Gentiles, to the parallels that comprise the second half of the chiasm: "and that he might reconcile the both in one body to God through the cross" (2:16a). The "one" (ἕνα) new human being into which Christ created in himself the two—Jews and Gentiles—making peace and thus reconciling them with one another (2:15bc) progresses to the "one" (ἑνὶ) body in which "the both," that is, "the two"—the believing Jews and Gentiles who have been reconciled to one another, are also reconciled to God by Christ through the cross, that is, "in the blood of Christ" (2:13) and "in his flesh" (2:14).[43]

That Christ might reconcile both Jews and Gentiles in one "body" (σώματι) to God in 2:16a reminds the audience that God gave Christ as "head" over all things to the church, which is indeed his "body" (σῶμα) in 1:22b–23a. The one "body" in which the Jews and Gentiles that Christ created and reconciled in himself into one new human person he also reconciled to God is the church. The audience realize that it is as "head" over all things that Christ, the gift (cf. "God gave [ἔδωκεν]" in 1:22b) of God's love to the church, extends that love in himself by reconciling believing Jews and Gentiles in the one body that is the church to God.[44]

---

42. Hoehner, *Ephesians*, 380–81: "The text does not suggest that Christ's death brought about a universal redemption so that all Jews and Gentiles are reconciled. Most Jews and Gentiles would not concede that they are reconciled to each other. Nor does the text propound that Gentiles have been accepted into the people of God, namely, Israel . . . On the contrary, the present context assumes that only believing Jews and believing Gentiles make up this new entity."

43. Hoehner, *Ephesians*, 382–83: "It must be understood that the reconciliation spoken of here is not between Jews and Gentiles 'into' one body . . . That particular reconciliation of Jews and Gentiles has already been discussed at verse 15. Rather, it is speaking of those believing Jews and Gentiles, who are in one body, as reconciled 'to God.' " For an unconvincing attempt to interpret the "one body" in 2:16 as the physical body of Christ offered up on the cross, see D. P. Leyrer, "Exegetical Brief: Ephesians 2:16—To What Does 'One Body' Refer?" *Wisconsin Lutheran Quarterly* 100 (2003): 203–5.

44. Contra Dawes (*Body*, 159) and others, the "one body" in 2:16a does not include "a secondary reference to Christ himself." As indicated in 1:22–23 Christ as head over all things is distinct from and given as a gift of God to the church, which is his body. Dawes

6. Eph 2:16b (C´): Killing the Hostility in Himself

With the C´ element of the chiasm in 2:11–22 the audience hear a progressive parallel to the C element regarding the prepositional phrase, "in himself," in reference to Christ.[45] The constructive activity of Christ in himself, "that the two he might create in himself (ἐν αὐτῷ)" in the C element (2:15b) is contrasted by the destructive activity of Christ in himself, "killing the hostility (ἔχθραν) in himself (ἐν αὐτῷ)" in the C´ element (2:16b), which reinforces and develops his having destroyed the hostility (ἔχθραν) in (ἐν) his (αὐτοῦ) flesh (2:14) as the means by which he created the Jews and Gentiles into one new human person and reconciled them in one body to God through the cross (D and D´ elements in 2:15b–16a).[46] Christ's killing the "hostility" in himself in the C´ element (2:16b) now includes not only the "hostility" that existed between Jews and Gentiles (2:14) but also the "hostility" that existed between both Jews and Gentiles on the one hand and God (2:16a) on the other.[47]

Christ's killing the hostility "in himself" (ἐν αὐτῷ) continues to develop for the audience Paul's repeated accentuation upon the very person of Christ as the embodiment of our peace with a concerted use of the third-person singular personal pronoun in reference to Christ:

> 2:14a: For *he* (αὐτός) is our peace

(*Body*, 173 n. 14) himself acknowledges this: "for we have seen that the imagery of head and body can be used to distinguish the Church from Christ." Indeed, to say that the "one body" in 2:16a includes a reference to Christ would be to say that Christ is reconciling not only Jews and Gentiles but himself to God. Rather, Christ, as "head" over all things, is acting here in his capacity as God's gift of love to the church in reconciling to God believing Jews and Gentiles whom he has reconciled to one another and united in the "one body" which is the church.

45. Lincoln, *Ephesians*, 146: "Some take ἐν αὐτῷ in its present context [in 2:16b] as a reference to the cross as the most immediate antecedent. But in the light of the force of αὐτός in its various forms throughout vv 14–16 it is better to take this use as a reference to Christ himself, though it will be his death which is particularly in view." See also O'Brien, *Ephesians*, 204. Taking ἐν αὐτῷ in 2:16b as a reference to Christ himself, then, includes, indeed presupposes, Christ's killing the hostility through his death on the cross.

46. Hoehner, *Ephesians*, 384: "[T]he participle [ἀποκτείνας, "killing"] shows the means of the reconciliation of the one body of Jews and Gentiles to God, namely, by the destruction of the hostility between God and human beings."

47. O'Brien, *Ephesians*, 202–3: "The reconciliation of both with God introduces a new element, and the presupposition is that not only Gentiles but also Israel were alienated from God because of sin. . . . Vv. 1–3 refer first to Paul's Gentile readers being dead in trespasses and sins before coming to faith (vv. 1, 2), and then to Jewish believers (including the apostle himself) being in a similar desperate plight prior to their conversion (v. 3), so that they, too, were by nature objects of wrath and therefore like the rest of humanity. . . . Jews and Gentiles alike, for all their differences, were at enmity with one another and alienated from God; hence the desperate need for this twofold reconciliation, which Paul triumphantly affirms has been effected through the death of Christ." See also Jeal, *Ephesians*, 156–57.

2:14e: in *his* (αὐτοῦ) flesh
2:15b: in *himself* (αὐτῷ)
2:16b: in *himself* (αὐτῷ)[48]

Christ "in himself," that is, in the sacrificial death of his blood (2:13) and flesh (2:14e) on the cross (2:16) not only destroyed the hostility "in himself" (2:14e, 16b) but also created "in himself" the Jews and Gentiles into one new human person and reconciled them both in one body to God (2:15b–16a). That is why "he himself" (αὐτός) *is* our peace (2:14a).

With regard to the love theme the audience have been made aware that Gentiles along with the Jews have been created into one new human person because Christ himself, as "our peace" (2:14a), made "peace" (2:15c) as God's gift of love to us. Acting as the "head" over all things that God "gave" as a gift of love to the church, which is his body (1:22–23), Christ actualized that love by reconciling both Jews and Gentiles to God through the cross in the one body, the church, which includes the audience.[49]

7. Eph 2:17–18 (B′): We Have Access in One Spirit to the Father

With regard to the "far" and "near" motif as well as to the assimilation of the "you" believers to the "we" believers, the audience experience a progressive parallelism from the B to the B′ elements of the chiasm in 2:11–22. In the B element "you" (ὑμεῖς) who once were "far away" (μακράν) have been brought—by God as a gift of God's love—"near" (ἐγγύς) in the blood of Christ, for he himself is "our" (ἡμῶν), including "you" and all believers', peace (2:13–14a), as a gift of God's love. But in the B′ element the Christ who is our peace (2:14a) and made peace in himself (2:15bc) came[50] and preached the good news of peace, thus actualizing peace as God's gift of love, to "you" (ὑμῖν) who are "far away" (μακράν, Gentiles) and to those who are "near" (ἐγγύς, Jews), so that through him "we," including "you" and all believers, both—Jews and Gentiles together—"have" (ἔχομεν), as a gift of the love actualized as peace, the access and thus are brought "near" in one Spirit before the Father (2:17–18).[51]

---

48. See also Schnackenburg, *Ephesians*, 106.
49. On 2:13–16, see B. L. Melbourne, "Ephesians 2:13–16: Are the Barriers Still Broken Down?" *JRT* 57 (2005): 107–19.
50. Lincoln, *Ephesians*, 148–49: "But it [ἐλθών, "coming"] can now be seen a little more specifically as a retrospective reference to vv 14–16, i.e., to that coming of Christ which climaxed in his reconciling death. It is the effect of that accomplishment on the cross (v 16) which can be identified as a preaching of the good news of peace to the far off, the Gentiles, and a preaching of that same good news to the near, the Jews."
51. Fee, *God's Empowering Presence*, 683: "Given the distinct allusions in v. 17 to Isa 52:7 and 57:19, where in the former the Messiah is the proclaimer of peace and in the latter the peace is for 'those who are far and near,' it is altogether likely that Paul is here reflecting once again his understanding of the 'promised Holy Spirit' as fulfilling the eschatological promise that includes the Gentiles." On the Isaianic background here, see Moritz, *Profound*

In the B′ element the audience experience a development in the unity between believing Jews and Gentiles that results from Christ actualizing peace as God's gift of love for us. The Christ who is our peace made the both—Jews and Gentiles—"one" (ἕν, 2:14b) that the two—Jews and Gentiles—he might create in himself into "one" (ἕνα) new person, making peace (2:15bc), and that he might reconcile the both—Jews and Gentiles— in "one" (ἑνί) body to God through the cross (2:16a). Consequently, now we both—Jews and Gentiles—have the access in "one" (ἑνί) Spirit before the Father (2:18).[52] The "you" believers who were sealed with the Holy Spirit (πνεύματι) of promise (1:13) are united with the "we" believers—Jews and Gentiles—in the one Spirit (πνεύματι, 2:18). And Gentiles, considered to be "Godless" by Jews (2:12), are now united with Jews so that both together have access before God as "Father" (2:18).

The audience thus realize that the unity in which both Jews and Gentiles together now have access before God the Father in one Spirit they "have" through "him" (αὐτοῦ, 2:18),[53] "he himself" (αὐτός, 2:14a), the Christ who is our peace and who brought us peace "in himself" (ἐν αὐτῷ, 2:15b, 16b) by reconciling both Jews and Gentiles in one body, the church (1:22–23), to God through the cross (2:16a), preaching peace (2:17) as an actualization of the great love with which God loved us (2:4).[54]

Mystery, 23–55. Lincoln, *Ephesians*, 149: "Here in Eph 2, where v 13 contains sacrificial imagery and vv 20–22 contain temple imagery, the cultic associations of προσαγωγή as unhindered access to the sanctuary as the place of God's presence must be just as strong as, if not stronger than, the political." Udo Borse, "προσαγωγή," *EDNT* 3.161: "Προσαγωγή occurs in the NT only in Rom 5:2; Eph 2:18; 3:12. Although trans[itive] usage is possible, the meaning in these circumstances is probably intrans[itive]: access, approach. The point of departure recalls cultic circumstances: access to the temple, to the holy of holies (cf. Heb 10:19–22), and thence 'to God' (cf. 1 Pet 3:18), 'to the Father' (Eph 2:18) . . . The three occurrences of the word agree that Christians (both Jewish and Gentile, in one Spirit, Eph 2:18) are those who have received this access, which is opened to us by Christ."

52. Hoehner, *Ephesians*, 389: "The numeral ἑνί, 'one,' fortifies the idea of unity. The use of the preposition with the numeral emphasizes both being reconciled ἐν ἑνὶ σώματι τῷ θεῷ, 'in one body to God' (v. 16), and both having access ἐν ἑνὶ πνεύματι πρὸς τὸν πατέρα, 'in one Spirit to the Father.' " O'Brien, *Ephesians*, 210: " 'In one Spirit' corresponds to 'in one body' (v. 16—the two are brought together in 4:4), and again stresses the oneness of Jew and Gentile in the church. The one Spirit lives and works in the one body." Contra Yee (*Jews, Gentiles*, 185) who interprets "in one Spirit" in 2:18 as merely "in a common spirit."

53. Hoehner, *Ephesians*, 388: "The prepositional phrase δι᾽ αὐτοῦ, 'through him,' is placed immediately after the ὅτι for the sake of emphasis. It is only through Christ that we have the privilege which Paul is about to discuss." See also Yee, *Jews, Gentiles*, 184 n. 214.

54. This "great love" of Christ is expressed as his "magnanimity" by Yee, *Jews, Gentiles*, 182: "Christ assumed a laudable role in reconciling estranged humanity to God; he has come disinterestedly between Jew and Gentile, and his inclusivistic approach is a sign of his magnanimity."

8. Eph 2:19–22 (A'): You Are a Dwelling Place of God in the Spirit

With regard to the "you" believers as the Gentiles "in the flesh," who were considered "strangers" and "Godless" by the Jews, the audience experience a progressive parallelism from the A to the A' element of the chiasm in 2:11–22. In the A element an emphatic "you" (ὑμεῖς), those considered Gentiles "in the flesh" (ἐν σαρκί) by the circumcision (Jews) "in the flesh" (ἐν σαρκί) (2:11), were considered "strangers" (ξένοι) of the covenants of the promise and "Godless" (ἄθεοι) in the world (2:12). But now in the A' element "you" are no longer "strangers" (ξένοι) but members of the household of "God" (θεοῦ) (2:19), and in complementary and emphatic contrast to being "in the flesh" (2:11), "you" (ὑμεῖς) are being built together into a dwelling place of "God" (θεοῦ) "in the Spirit" (ἐν πνεύματι) (2:22).[55]

That the Gentile "you" believers of Paul's audience are no longer strangers, alienated from the "community" or "citizenship" (πολιτείας) of Israel (2:12), but are now, together with Jewish believers, "fellow citizens" (συμπολῖται) with the "holy ones" (ἁγίων), that is, with all believers (2:19), transcends citizenship within the community of Israel.[56] It also reinforces and develops the love that they have for all the "holy ones" (ἁγίους) (1:15). As fellow citizens with the holy ones (cf. 1:18), they are now made aware that the love they have for "all" the holy ones includes their love for Jewish believers and places them, who are "holy ones" themselves (1:1c), in a position to receive love from all the holy ones, including especially from those Jewish believers from whom they were previously alienated (2:11–12).

That the Gentile "you" believers of Paul's audience are no longer "aliens," or literally, "those beside a house" (πάροικοι), but are now, together with Jewish believers, "members of the household" (οἰκεῖοι) of God (θεοῦ) (2:19) means that they are no longer Godless (ἄθεοι) in the world, as they were considered to be from a Jewish perspective (2:12).[57] That they are

---

55. Jeal, *Ephesians*, 162: "Finally, the contrast between pre-Christian and Christian existence is ended with the ἐν πνεύματι of 2:22 standing against the ἐν σαρκί of 2:11." Lincoln, *Ephesians*, 159: "[T]he reference to the Spirit should be seen as completing the pericope by a contrast to the emphasis on the flesh at its beginning in v 11, and as emphasizing that for the Gentile readers in their new situation in the Spirit previous distinctions based on physical and ethnic categories—'in the flesh'—no longer count."

56. Jeal, *Ephesians*, 159 n. 439: "Although the word ἅγιος in this clause has been thought to refer to Jews, to Jewish Christians, or to angels, the context of Eph. (cf. 1:1, 15, 18; 3:8, 18; 4:12; 5:3; 6:18) demands that the reference be to all Christians. The recipients of Eph. are now fellow citizens with all other Christians." See also O'Brien, *Ephesians*, 211; Lincoln, *Ephesians*, 150–51; Hoehner, *Ephesians*, 392–94; Benjamin H. Dunning, "Strangers and Aliens No Longer: Negotiating Identity and Difference in Ephesians 2," *HTR* 99 (2006): 1–16.

57. Hoehner, *Ephesians*, 394: "Believers are considered members of the family of God and hence the translation 'members of God's household.' Whereas, ξένος is the opposite of συμπολίτης, so is πάροικος, 'a resident alien,' opposite of οἰκεῖος, 'family members of a

members of the household of "God" (θεοῦ) further develops for the audience how they are recipients of the great love with which "God" (θεός) loved us believers (2:4) in our union with Christ Jesus, who reconciled both believing Jews and Gentiles in one body to "God" (θεῷ) (2:16a). And that they are members of the very "household" or "family" of God further describes for the audience not only the access that both believing Jews and Gentiles together have in one Spirit to God as "Father" (2:18), but also the "sonship" to which God predestined us believers through Jesus Christ to himself as part of the grace with which he graced us in our union with Christ as the Beloved of God (1:5–6).[58]

The aorist passive participle, "built upon," continues the play on words related to "house" or "building," as it portrays the unity of believing Jews and Gentiles as part of a house or building that is built upon the "foundation" of the apostles and prophets (2:20a). As a divine passive, "built upon," confirms for the audience that they are no longer strangers but fellow citizens with the holy ones and no longer "those without a house" (πάροικοι) but "members of the household" (οἰκεῖοι) of God (2:19), because they have been "built upon" (ἐποικοδομηθέντες) the foundation of the apostles and prophets by God himself as a gift of the great love with which God loved us (2:4).[59]

Continuing the "building" imagery, the participial clause, "Christ Jesus himself being the capstone" (2:20b), that is, the crowning, top, or "head" stone of the edifice, reinforces for the audience the elevated role that Christ Jesus himself has in the great love with which God loved us (2:4).[60] That

---

household.' " See also David G. Horrell, "From ἀδελφοί to οἶκος θεοῦ: Social Transformation in Pauline Christianity," *JBL* 120 (2001): 305. Lincoln, *Ephesians*, 152: "There is a move here from the politcal imagery of the state of commonwealth to the more intimate picture of a family. οἰκεῖος appears elsewhere in the NT in Gal 6:10 and 1 Tim 5:8. Here its use can be seen as part of a double contrast—both with v 12, where Gentiles were said to be without God, God-forsaken, while here they are depicted as in the bosom of his family, and with the term used earlier in this verse, which also has associations with οἶκος, namely πάροικοι, 'those who are away from home,' while now Gentiles are to see themselves as at home in God's household." See also Jeal, *Ephesians*, 160.

58. O'Brien, *Ephesians*, 211–12: "In Christ Gentiles are not only fellow-citizens with Jewish believers under God's rule; they are also children together in God's own family. The apostle has just written of the new and glorious access to the Father which Gentiles along with Jews enjoy through Christ (v. 18). He has already drawn attention to the blessings of both being adopted into God's family as sons and daughters (1:5)."

59. Hoehner, *Ephesians*, 397: "The aorist passive participle ἐποικοδομηθέντες . . . may denote cause, namely, the reason we are fellow citizens with the saints and members of God's household is because we have been built on the foundation of the apostles and prophets. The passive emphasizes that we who are in one body are recipients of the action. God is the subject of the building."

60. The word "capstone" (ἀκρογωνιαίου) here is often understood as "cornerstone" and thus part of the "foundation" of the building in accord with the way it is used in its only

Christ Jesus "himself" (αὐτοῦ) is the head or capstone of the building fur-
thers the emphatic uses of the third-person singular pronoun for Christ as
the agent of God's love for us: He "himself" (αὐτός) is our peace (2:14a),
who created Jews and Gentiles in "himself" (αὐτῷ) into one new person
(2:15bc), killing the hostility in "himself" (αὐτῷ) (2:16b), so that through
"him" (αὐτοῦ) believing Jews and Gentiles together have access in one Spirit
to the Father (2:18). As "head" over all things that God gave as a gift of
love to the church, which is Christ's body (1:22–23), the one body in which
Christ reconciled both Jews and Gentiles to God (2:16a), Christ is also the
capstone or "head" stone of the building in which believing Jews and Gentiles are united.

"In whom" (ἐν ᾧ), that is, in union with Christ Jesus as the "head"
or "capstone" (2:20b), "the whole building"—believing Jews and Gentiles
united together upon the foundation of the apostles and prophets (2:20a)
"being fitted together" (2:21a) by God (divine passive) continues to impress
upon the audience that the unity of believing Jews and Gentiles with one
another and with Christ is a gift of God's gracious love manifested in the
Christ event.

---

occurrence in the OT in LXX Isa 28:16. But, as Lincoln (*Ephesians*, 155–56) points out: "The
use of ἀκρογωνιαῖος here is probably not a direct allusion to Isa 28:16 . . . In particular, Ps
118:22, 'The stone which the builders rejected has become the head of the corner,'—had
been seen as an appropriate expression of what God had done in exalting the crucified Jesus
to be Lord of all. The rejected stone had become the keystone of the whole structure (cf.
Mark 12:10; Acts 4:11). In Rom 9:32, 33 Paul employs a conflation of Isa 28:16 (which omits
any reference to the cornerstone) and Isa 8:14, and elsewhere this conflation of Isaiah texts is
combined with Ps 118:22 (cf. Luke 20:17, 18), and all three texts are linked in 1 Pet 2:6–8. Isa
28:16 had already, then, been combined with Ps 118:22 and thus with the notion of Christ's
elevation to the crowning stone of the building. It would not be surprising . . . if ἀκρογωνιαῖος
has similar force to κεφαλὴ γωνίας from Ps 118:22. . . . once 'foundation' terminology is applied to the apostles and prophets instead of Christ, it would be natural . . . to give Christ the
exalted position . . . The writer's view of Christ as heavenly Lord and of the Church as growing toward him elsewhere in Ephesians should, therefore, be judged determinative for the use
to which he has put traditional material here in 2:20." See also Michel Bouttier, *L'Épître de
Saint Paul aux Éphésiens* (CNT IXb; Geneva: Labor et Fides, 1991), 129–30.
    61. On "in whom" as equivalent to "in Christ" with its organic overtones of being in
union with, see R. J. McKelvey, *The New Temple: The Church in the New Testament* (Oxford: Oxford University Press, 1969), 115. On πᾶσα οἰκοδομή as "the whole building" rather
than "every building," see William J. Johnston, *The Use of Πᾶς in the New Testament* (Studies in Biblical Greek 11; New York: Lang, 2004), 165–73. And on "being fitted together"
(συναρμολογουμένη), Hoehner (*Ephesians*, 409) states: "Today the process of fitting stones
together is rather simple because mortar is used. In that day with no use of mortar, there
was an elaborate process of cutting and smoothing the stones so that they fit exactly next to
each other. The prepositional prefix συν-, which is common in Ephesians only, intensifies the
fitting together. It speaks of the inner unity or harmony among believers who, before their
conversion, were at enmity with one another. The present passive participle describes the
manner of their growth. Specifically, as recipients of God's grace, they grow by being care-

That the whole building being fitted together by God "is growing into a temple holy in the Lord" (2:21b) further develops for the audience the unity of believing Jews and Gentiles within the dynamic realm of being "in love"—God's love for believers and believers' love for one another. As fellow citizens of the "holy ones" (ἁγίων, 2:19), that is, all of the "holy ones" (ἁγίους) for whom they have love (1:15), the Gentile "you" believers, who are being fitted together with Jewish believers by the gift of God's love (2:21a), form the whole building that is growing into a temple "holy" (ἅγιον) in the Lord. The image of the "building" thus organically progresses to that of a "holy temple," that is, a temple comprised of "holy ones," believers, who are united by the love of God for them and their love for one another. That the whole building is growing into a temple of "holy ones" who are "holy" in the Lord further specifies for the audience how believers have been chosen by a gift of God's love to be "holy" (ἁγίους) and blameless before God within the realm of being "in love" (1:4) in their union with God's Beloved (1:6).

That the whole building of believers is growing into a temple holy "in the Lord" (ἐν κυρίῳ, 2:21b), which reinforces their union "in him" (2:21a) as a reference to Christ Jesus, who is the "head" or capstone of the building (2:20b), reminds the audience of the only previous occurrence in the Letter of the prepositional phrase "in the Lord" in 1:15. There Paul affirmed not only the faith but the love for all the holy ones that the "you" believers have in their union with the Lord Jesus (ἐν τῷ κυρίῳ Ἰησοῦ). And here it is in their union with the Lord by their faith that the whole building of believers united together by a gift of God's love is growing into a holy temple, a temple of holy ones who have love for one another.[62]

By way of a parallel development of 2:21, "in whom the whole building being fitted together is growing into a temple holy in the Lord," Paul emphatically and climactically reassures his audience of Gentile "you" believers of their role in the unity of Jewish and Gentile believers within the realm of being "in love" in 2:22: "in whom *you* also are being built together into a dwelling place of God in the Spirit."[63] "In whom the whole building

---

fully fitted together rather than growing apart individually from one another. Notice that it is not self-initiative that causes the growth but the gracious action of God."

62. Lincoln, *Ephesians*, 155: "For the writer of Ephesians, the notion of a finished structure with Christ as its head is not at all incompatible with the dynamic imagery of growth. He views the Church as already Christ's fullness (1:23) and yet at the same time as having to attain that fullness (4:13; cf. also 3:19). In 4:15, 16, the passage which repeats a number of expressions found here in 2:20–22, the imagery is precisely that of a body growing up into Christ as the head. So here, on the one hand, the Church is pictured as a finished structure with Christ as the top stone, and yet, on the other hand, it must grow into a temple in him."

63. For an outline of the parallelism between 2:21 and 2:22, see Yee, *Jews, Gentiles*, 208.

is being fitted together (συναρμολογουμένη)" (2:21a) by God (divine passive)
as a gift of God's love progresses to "in whom *you* also are being built together (συνοικοδομεῖσθε)" (2:22a), that is, together with all other believers in
the whole building, by God (divine passive) as a gift of God's love.

"Is growing into a holy temple" (2:21b) progresses to "into a dwelling
place of God" (2:22b).[64] The whole building of believers united together by
God's love is growing into a holy temple, a temple of holy ones, believers,
who love one another, which is also the very dwelling place of "God" (θεοῦ)
himself, the place where God dwells with believers and believers dwell with
God, the place where believers receive and respond to God's love.[65] This
is the "God" (θεοῦ) in whose household the Gentile "you" believers are
members (2:19) rather than being "Godless" (ἄθεοι) in the world (2:12), the
"God" (θεῷ) to whom Christ reconciled both believing Jews and Gentiles in
one body (2:16a) as an extension of the great love with which "God" (θεός)
loved us (2:4).

"In the Lord" (2:21c) progresses to "in the Spirit" (2:22c). That the
whole building grows into a holy temple, a temple of holy ones, as a result of
their union "in the Lord," that is, in the Lord Jesus Christ, who is the "head"
or capstone of the building (2:20b), the "head" God gave to the church,
Christ's body, as a gift of love (1:22–23), progresses to the "you" believers
being built together with all believers into a dwelling place of God as a result
of their union "in the Spirit (πνεύματι)" as a gift of God's love. As the audience recall, it is in their union with this one "Spirit" (πνεύματι) that both
believing Jews and Gentiles have access to God the Father "through him"
(2:18), that is, through the Christ who reconciled the both in one body to
God (2:16a) as a gift of God's love. This is the "Spirit" (πνεῦμα) that comes
from the God of our "Lord" Jesus Christ (1:17) and the "Spirit" (πνεύματι)
with whom the "you" believers were sealed as a gift of God's love.

In the A element of the chiasm in 2:11–22, with an emphatic "you"
(ὑμεῖς), Paul addressed his audience as the Gentiles *in the flesh*, those called
"uncircumcision" by what is called "circumcision" (Jews) *in the flesh* (2:11).
But now in the A′ element, again with an emphatic "you" (ὑμεῖς), Paul assures his audience that now, as a gift of God's love, they are being built
together with all believers, including Jews from whom they had been sepa-

---

64. With "dwelling place" we have reached the climax of the play on words referring
to "house" or "building" in 2:19–22. It progressed from "those beside a house" (πάροικοι,
2:19a) to "members of the household" (οἰκεῖοι, 2:19b) to "built upon" (ἐποικοδομηθέντες,
2:20a) to "building" (οἰκοδομή, 2:21) to "built together" (συνοικοδομεῖσθε, 2:22a) to "dwelling place" (κατοικητήριον, 2:22b).

65. Hoehner, *Ephesians*, 413–14: "[T]his place of settled dwelling is God's in reference
to the body of believers. It is not only a dwelling place but a deep or settled dwelling place.
It has the idea of a dwelling place that is firmly rooted. It signifies the endurance and permanence of God's inhabitance in the body of believers."

rated "in the flesh," into a holy temple (2:21b), into a dwelling place of God *in the Spirit* (2:22) that transcends their status "in the flesh."[66]

In 2:19–22, then, the audience realize that the unity of all believers, especially Gentile believers with Jewish believers, as expressed with a series of words prefixed with σύν—"fellow citizens" (συμπολῖται, 2:19), "fitted together" (συναρμολογουμένη, 2:21), and "built together" (συνοικοδομεῖσθε, 2:22), is a gift of God's love within the realm of being "in love" resulting from their union with the Lord Jesus Christ as the "head" or capstone (2:20b) of the whole building of believers (2:21a), who, as "head" over all things, God gave as a gift of love to the church as Christ's body (1:22–23). In their union with the Lord all believers grow into a "holy temple" (2:21b), a temple of "holy ones" who are loved by God and love one another. And all believers are being built together into the very dwelling place of God as a result of their union with the Spirit (2:22) that is a gift of God's love.[67]

B. Summary on Ephesians 2:11–22

1. By directing them to remember the situation in which they were not in a loving relationship with God and with the people of God (2:11–12), Paul deepens his audience's appreciation and gratitude for the great love with which God has now loved us (2:4) in the Christ event as well as the motivation of their love for all the holy ones (1:15), which unites them with their fellow believers as those who are "in Christ," in union with one another and with God's Beloved (1:6).

2. That Christ is our peace (2:14a) introduces a new dimension in the expressions of God's love for us. Previously believers were coupled with Christ as recipients of God's love. In other words, in their dynamic union with Christ believers shared in the love Christ received from God as the Be-

---

66. Yee, *Jews, Gentiles*, 210–11: "[T]he traditional Jewish meaning of the 'holy' temple is 'transcoded' and given a new twist as the non-Jews are also allotted a proper place in the temple, that is, 'by the Spirit' (ἐν πνεύματι). . . . the 'Spirit' language here is meant to lay bare the inclusiveness of the new Temple in which Gentiles are integral components. In short, the usefulness of temple symbolism is that it enables the author to transpose the Gentiles from the periphery to the centre of the Jewish symbolic world while sustaining the traditional notion that the 'temple' is still the holy space of God's presence."

67. For a discussion of the relation between Eph 2:19–22 and Qumran texts, see Derwood C. Smith, "Cultic Language in Ephesians 2:19–22: A Test Case," *ResQ* 31 (1989): 207–17. For a social scientific approach, see Carmen Bernabé Ubieta, "Neither *Xenoi* Nor *Paroikoi, Sympolitai* and *Oikeioi Tou Theou* (Eph 2:19) Pauline Christian Communities: Defining a New Territoriality," in *Social Scientific Models for Interpreting the Bible: Essays by the Context Group in Honor of Bruce J. Malina* (ed. John J. Pilch; BIS 53; Leiden: Brill, 2001), 260–80. For a possible background of the narrative pattern in Eph 1:20–2:22, see Timothy G. Gombis, "Ephesians 2 as a Narrative of Divine Warfare," *JSNT* 26 (2004): 403–18.

loved (1:6; 2:4–10). But now Christ becomes not only one who is loved by God but one who extends God's love to believers. He is not only the object but the acting subject of God's love (2:14b).

3. Gentiles along with the Jews have been created into one new human person because Christ himself, as "our peace" (2:14a), made "peace" (2:15c) as God's gift of love to us. Acting as the "head" over all things that God "gave" as a gift of love to the church, which is his body (1:22–23), Christ actualized that love by reconciling both Jews and Gentiles to God through the cross in the one body (2:16a), the church, that includes the audience.

4. The unity in which both Jews and Gentiles together now have access to God the Father in one Spirit they "have" through "him" (2:18), "he himself" (2:14a), the Christ who is our peace and who brought us peace "in himself" (2:15b, 16b) by reconciling both Jews and Gentiles in one body, the church (1:22–23), to God through the cross (2:16a), preaching peace (2:17) as an actualization of the great love with which God loved us (2:4).

5. As fellow citizens with the holy ones (2:19; cf. 1:18), the Gentile "you" believers of Paul's audience realize that the love they have for "all" the holy ones includes their love for Jewish believers and places them, who are "holy ones" themselves (1:1c), in a position to receive love from all the holy ones, including especially from those Jewish believers from whom they were previously alienated (2:11–12).

6. The unity of all believers, especially Gentile believers with Jewish believers, is a gift of God's love within the realm of being "in love" resulting from their union with the Lord Jesus Christ as the "head" or capstone (2:20b) of the whole building of believers (2:21a), who, as "head" over all things, God gave as a gift of love to the church as Christ's body (1:22–23). In their union with the Lord all believers are growing into a "holy temple" (2:21b), a temple of "holy ones"—those who are loved by God and love one another. And all believers are being built together into the very dwelling place of God as a result of their union with the Spirit (2:22) which is a gift of God's love.

CHAPTER 8

Ephesians 3:1–13: Paul to Make Known the Mystery of Christ in Love (F)

A: ¹ Because of this, I, Paul, am the prisoner of the Christ Jesus *on behalf of you* Gentiles.

   B: ² As indeed you have heard of the *plan of the grace of God that was given to me* for you, ³ that according to revelation *was made known* to me the *mystery*, as I wrote before in brief, ⁴ whereby when reading it you are able to perceive my insight into the *mystery* of the Christ, ⁵ which in other generations *was* not *made known* to human beings as *now* it has been revealed to his holy apostles and prophets in the Spirit,

      C: ⁶ that the Gentiles are *fellow heirs* and *fellow members of the body* and *fellow sharers* of the *promise* in Christ Jesus through the *gospel*,

   B′: ⁷ of which I became a minister according to the gift *of the grace of God that was given to me* according to the working of his power. ⁸ To me, the very least of all holy ones, was given this grace, to preach to the Gentiles the unfathomable wealth of the Christ ⁹ and to enlighten for all what is the *plan* of the *mystery* which had been hidden from the ages in God who created all things, ¹⁰ that *may be made known now* to the rulers and to the authorities in the heavenly places through the church the manifold wisdom of God, ¹¹ according to the purpose of the ages which he accomplished in Christ Jesus our Lord, ¹² in whom we have the boldness and access in confidence through faith in him.

A´:   [13] Therefore I ask you not to lose heart in my tribulations *on be-half of you*, which is your glory.[1]

A. Audience Response to Ephesians 3:1–13

1. Eph 3:1 (A): Paul Is the Prisoner of the Christ Jesus on Behalf of Gentiles

"Because of this" (τούτου χάριν, 3:1a) refers back to all that Paul has been stating in the Letter to this point, especially the unity of Gentile believers with Jewish believers in 2:11–22.[2] An emphatic "I, Paul" accentuates Paul's status—"*I, Paul,* am *the* prisoner of the Christ Jesus on behalf of you Gentiles" (3:1b).[3] Paul has already told his audience of Gentile "you"

---

1. For the establishment of Eph 3:1–13 as a chiasm, see ch. 2.

2. Jeal, *Ephesians*, 111: "These words, meaning 'because of this,' have rhetorical force in at least two ways. First, they recall to mind the content of what has already been stated. Consequently, those things already discussed, along with their own persuasive power, are kept fresh and retain a prominent place in the minds of the audience members. Second, τούτου χάριν indicates that the foundation for the thoughts that follow in the author's requests for the audience lie in the facts that are recalled. Thus, by recall the memory is stirred, and the bases for the following thoughts are found in the things that are recalled." Although "because of this" (τούτου χάριν) occurs again in 3:14 at the beginning of a prayer by Paul for his audience, there is no indication in 3:1 that Paul is interrupting that prayer, despite the view of most interpreters, who then treat 3:2–13 as a digression or parenthesis. That 3:2–13 is not a digression or parenthesis is indicated by Greg Fay, "Paul the Empowered Prisoner: Eph 3:1–13 in the Epistolary and Rhetorical Structure of Ephesians" (Ph.D. diss., University of Marquette, 1994), 532–61, 667–83. According to Hoehner (*Ephesians*, 417 n. 1), Fay "suggests that Ephesians is a deliberate document for the maintenance of peace between Jews and Gentiles and that 3:1–13 is a strategically synthesized composition on reconciliation to support the main argument for unity in the church." See also Timothy G. Gombis, "Ephesians 3:2–13: Pointless Digression, or Epitome of the Triumph of God in Christ?" *WTJ* 66 (2004): 313–23.

3. Along with NRSV, but not in accord with most interpreters, we take 3:1 to be a complete sentence with "I am" (εἰμί) as the implied main verb. Each of the objections against this offered by Abbott (*Ephesians*, 76–77) and Hoehner (*Ephesians*, 418–19) can be countered: To the objection that it gives too much emphasis to Paul's imprisonment by making it the main rather than an incidental point, it should be noted that while Paul does place emphasis on himself as the prisoner of Christ Jesus, the emphasis is not just on his imprisonment *per se* but on his imprisonment "*on behalf of you Gentiles.*" The objection that it would be inappropriate to have the article if ὁ δέσμιος were the predicate fails to appreciate that the article is employed for added emphasis. According to Cassidy (*Paul in Chains*, 96), "the article might have been used in this way to differentiate Paul from other prisoners . . . Paul is *the* prisoner for Christ. It is also possible that the article underscores the great shift in Paul's own circumstances. He is now Paul, *the* prisoner. The use of the first person pronoun further intensifies the meaning. The author thus pens *four* emphatic words: 'I, Paul, the prisoner.' " It should also be noted that it is for the sake of this emphasis that the main verb "I am" (εἰμί) remains implicit; it allows for the immediate juxtaposition of "Paul" and "*the* prisoner." To the objection that the phrases "because of this" and "on behalf of you Gentiles" would then

believers that he does not cease giving thanks "for you (ὑπὲρ ὑμῶν), making mention of you in my prayers" (1:16), which serves as a personal act of love on Paul's part for his audience, whose love for all the holy ones Paul has just affirmed (1:15b). Now Paul develops that personal love for his audience, as he indicates that his physical imprisonment as a consequence of his spiritual captivity as one who is bound to the Christ Jesus is "on behalf of you (ὑπὲρ ὑμῶν) Gentiles."[4] The audience are to realize that Paul accepts his imprisonment as "the" prisoner of the Christ Jesus for the sake of the unity of Gentile and Jewish believers as part of his love for them as Gentile "you" believers.[5]

2. Eph 3:2–5 (B): Paul Shares His Insight into the Mystery of Christ

That Paul is *the* prisoner of the Christ Jesus as an expression of his love "on behalf of you" (ὑπὲρ ὑμῶν) Gentiles (3:1) is reinforced in 3:2: "As indeed you have heard of the plan of the grace of God that was given to me "for you" (εἰς ὑμᾶς). Indeed, with regard to the dynamics of the love theme in Ephesians, this develops how Paul, as both an apostle (1:1) and the prisoner of Christ Jesus (3:1), mediates to his audience the particular love he has received from God in those roles, intensively expressed as "the grace of God that was given (by God; divine passive) to *me* for *you*."[6]

In 1:10 the audience heard about God's "plan" (οἰκονομίαν) "for the fullness of the times, to unite under one head all the things in the Christ." Thus, Paul can now tell his audience that already "you have heard about the plan (οἰκονομίαν)" (3:2). But now that "plan" of God is described in terms

---

be redundant, it should be noted that "because of this" refers back to the Gentiles' unity with Jews, whereas "on behalf of you Gentiles" refers only to the Gentiles. There is thus no redundancy in these phrases. Finally, to the objection that ὁ δέσμιος should be considered in apposition to ἐγὼ Παῦλος as in 4:1, it should be noted that the usage in 4:1 is not parallel to 3:1. In 4:1 there is already a main verb and only ἐγώ but not Παῦλος occurs.

4. Cassidy, *Paul in Chains*, 95–96: "[T]he fundamental meaning of words in the δεσμ-word group is that of 'binding.' When δέσμιος is translated as 'prisoner,' the root meaning is thus that of 'one who is bound.' " Hoehner, *Ephesians*, 420: "The genitives (τοῦ Χριστοῦ Ἰησοῦ, 'of Christ Jesus') denote not only possession, depicting Paul as Christ's prisoner, but also denote cause, for it was the cause of Christ that made him a prisoner." Lincoln, *Ephesians*, 173: "He can use the term 'prisoner' in both a literal and metaphorical sense at the same time, so that his physical imprisonment can be seen as simply the consequence of his spiritual captivity to Christ."

5. Jeal, *Ephesians*, 111–12: "Paul is made intensely personal to the Gentile audience as one who has personally become a 'prisoner' for their benefit."

6. Lincoln, *Ephesians*, 174: "As in v 1, the readers are explicitly related to Paul's apostleship. That apostleship mediates grace. The grace was given to Paul, but it was for the ultimate benefit of these Gentile Christians—'for you.' " Best, *Ephesians*, 298: "Grace in Pauline writing normally denotes the amazing, redeeming love of God, manifest above all in the inclusion of the Gentiles in the church. . . . the idea is that God gave Paul grace in relation to the Gentiles; they are the ultimate beneficiaries of the grace as εἰς ὑμᾶς indicates."

of Paul's role in it as the mediator to his audience of the love Paul has been graciously given by God "for you."[7] It is "God's plan in respect of the grace given me for you."[8] The implication for Paul's audience of Gentile "you" believers is that their being united to Jewish believers in the one body of the church through the mediation of the love given Paul by God as God's apostle (1:1) and the prisoner of Christ Jesus (3:1) is part of God's plan to unite under one head all the things in the Christ.[9]

The love of God for Paul that he mediates to his audience, expressed as "the grace of God that was given to me for you" (3:2b) is further developed as Paul explains "that according to revelation was made known to me the mystery" (3:3a). That the mystery "was made known" (ἐγνωρίσθη) to Paul by God (divine passive), which is preceded by the phrase, "according to revelation" (κατὰ ἀποκάλυψιν), placed in an emphatic position at the beginning of the clause and implying that the revelation is from God, underscores that the knowledge of the mystery is God's gift of love to Paul.[10]

In addition to the reference to God's "plan" (οἰκονομίαν, 3:2), the words "was made known" (ἐγνωρίσθη) and "mystery" (μυστήριον), as well as Paul's

---

7. Kuhli, "οἰκονομία," 500: "As in Col 1:25, the majority of interpreters assume for οἰκονομία in Eph 3:2 the meaning 'office,' 'administration.' This does not, however, give adequate consideration to the fact that, unlike Col 1:25, the part[iciple] δοθεῖσα modifies not οἰκονομία but χάρις. Consequently, the author is concerned less with Paul's office of apostle than with 'God's plan of salvation . . . and the position of the office of apostle within the divine plan' (Helmut Merklein, *Das kirchliche Amt nach dem Epheserbrief* [SANT 33; Munich: Kösel, 1973], 174). Formal identification of οἰκονομία with God's plan of salvation, however, is not yet complete here. Instead, as in Eph 3:9, only the connection of the term with the ordering and implementation of this plan of salvation, conceived as mystery, is here established."

8. As translated by Best, *Ephesians*, 291.

9. Best, *Ephesians*, 298–99: "Yet in both Eph 1.10 and 3.9 God is the subject [of οἰκονομία] and, since the word is used consciously, there is much to be said for a consistent usage. Moreover this section of the passage stresses God's use of Paul in the conversion of the Gentiles rather than his mission as his own activity. Paul's place is conveyed through χάριτος. . . . It is better then to take God as the subject of οἰκονομία . . . If God administers or arranges to do something he can be expected to do it according to a plan. That God works to a plan is closely linked to the idea of foreordination (cf. 1.4, 5, 9). . . . The salvation of the Gentiles (εἰς ὑμᾶς picks up ὑπὲρ ὑμῶν from v. 1) cannot be understood apart from Paul, and that does not mean apart from what he tells us about it but apart from his place within God's plan of salvation. This also means that the Gentiles, and in particular the readers (εἰς ὑμᾶς), have their place within God's plan."

10. Hoehner, *Ephesians*, 426: "The word ἀποκάλυψις . . . has the meaning of unveiling or disclosing something that had been previously hidden. In the NT it has the theological significance of the unveiling of that which was previously hidden in God and unknown to humans." O'Brien, *Ephesians*, 229: "The divine initiative is signalled here by means of the passive 'was made known', while the phrase 'according to revelation', which is placed first in the clause for emphasis, provides a standard for evaluation and refers to the ground or basis on which Paul became acquainted with the 'mystery'." See also Lincoln, *Ephesians*, 175.

comment, "as I wrote before in brief" (3:3), confirm that Paul is recalling for his audience what he wrote earlier in 1:9–10, namely, that God "made known (γνωρίσας) to us the mystery (μυστήριον) of his will, according to his pleasure which he purposed in him, as a plan (οἰκονομίαν) for the fullness of the times, to unite under one head all the things in the Christ, the things in the heavens and the things on earth in him." Whereas in 1:9–10 God made known the broader cosmic mystery of the unity of all things in Christ "to us" (ἡμῖν), that is, to all of us believers, in 3:2–3 God has made known a more specific aspect of that cosmic mystery, namely, the unity of believing Jews and Gentiles (2:11–22)—as part of "the things on earth" (1:10), "to me" (μοι), that is, to Paul as a gift of God's love that Paul is to mediate to his audience of Gentile "you" believers.[11]

The audience then learn that the Letter itself is the means by which Paul mediates to them the particular gift of love that Paul received from God. Listening to what Paul has written in the Letter when it is being read publicly in the assembly empowers the audience to share Paul's understanding of that part of "the mystery of Christ" (the unity of all things in Christ) that includes the unity of believing Jews and Gentiles: "Whereby when reading it you are able to perceive my insight into the mystery of Christ" (3:4).[12] This adds another key element to the dynamics of the love theme in Ephesians—the Letter to the Ephesians in itself is a gift of Paul's personal love to his audience, who, in receiving this love by listening to it as it is read, are empowered to share in the love God gave especially to Paul as *the* imprisoned apostle of Christ Jesus.

Previously in other generations this mystery of the unity of believing Jews and Gentiles was not "made known" (ἐγνωρίσθη) by God (divine passive)—in contrast to its having been "made known" (ἐγνωρίσθη) to Paul as a gift of God's love (3:3)—to human beings (literally, "the sons of men") as now it "has been revealed" (ἀπεκαλύφθη) by God (divine passive), as a gift

---

11. On the clause "as I wrote before in brief" (3:3b), Lincoln (*Ephesians*, 175) states that "as the majority of commentators propose, the clause is best taken as a reference back to the earlier chapters of the present letter and, more specifically, 1:9, 10 and 2:11–22 with their discussions of the disclosure of the mystery and the inclusion of the Gentiles." See also O'Brien, *Ephesians*, 229.

12. Jeal, *Ephesians*, 168 n. 486: "The verb ἀναγινώσκω and the noun ἀνάγωσις refer not only to reading, but to public, vocal reading, and therefore to hearing by an audience. Consequently, the use of the participle ἀναγινώσκοντες in 3:4 does not detract from the contention that Eph. was 'heard' by many of its first recipients as a 'sermon,' rather than only being read." Lincoln, *Ephesians*, 176: "The recipients of the letter are to make their judgment when they read, and in all probability it is the situation of the public reading of the letter in the assembly which is in view." Best, *Ephesians*, 303: "ἀναγινώσκοντες (the participle has almost an imperatival tone) simply means 'read' and not 'read again', as if implying that they should go back and read again the first part of the letter. The reading would be aloud, as was normal in the ancient world, and would probably have been in the course of worship."

of God's love, to his (God's) holy apostles and prophets in the Spirit (3:5).
The audience realize that, as a gift of God's love, knowledge of the mystery
has been given not only to Paul as the preeminent apostle (1:1), who is *the*
prisoner of Christ Jesus (3:1), but also to the rest of the holy apostles and
prophets as the foundation upon which they have been built by God as a gift
of God's love (2:20a). By God's love they have been built upon a foundation
of apostles and prophets who have received the same special gift of God's
love bestowed preeminently upon Paul.[13]

That the apostles and prophets are described as "holy" closely assimilates them with all believers, as the "holy ones" (1:1, 15, 18; 2:19), built
upon them.[14] Apostles, prophets, and all believers are "holy," that is, consecrated and set apart for God by the gift of God's love (1:4).

And that the mystery of the unity of believing Jews and Gentiles has
now been revealed to God's holy apostles and prophets "in the Spirit" (ἐν
πνεύματι, 3:5), that is, within the dynamic sphere of being in union with the
Spirit, further assimilates the apostles and prophets to all believers. It recalls for the audience that "you" believing Gentiles have been built together
with believing Jews, as a gift of God's love, upon the foundation of the
apostles and prophets (2:20a) into a dwelling place of God "in the Spirit"
(ἐν πνεύματι, 2:22). Apostles, prophets, and all believers are united together
"in the Spirit," that is, "in the one Spirit" (ἐν ἑνὶ πνεύματι) in which both
believing Jews and Gentiles have, as a gift of God's love, access to God the
Father (2:18).

With regard to the theme of love in 3:2–5, the audience realize that
listening to the Letter Paul wrote to them as a gift of his personal love
empowers them to perceive Paul's insight into the mystery of the unity of
believing Jews and Gentiles that God made known as a special gift of God's
love not only to Paul, the preeminent apostle and prisoner of Christ Jesus,
but also to the holy apostles and prophets, the foundation of all the believing holy ones who are united in the Spirit. Listening to the Letter thus
empowers the audience to likewise receive the love God gave especially to
Paul and the holy apostles and prophets to know the mystery. Not only the
mystery of Gentiles being united with Jews but also knowledge of that mystery is a gift of God's love.

---

13. Lincoln, *Ephesians*, 179: "By the amount of space devoted to each, the writer makes
clear that although he is concerned about the apostles and prophets as norms of revelation in
the Church, he regards the revelation to Paul as having primacy (cf. vv 3, 4, 7, 8)."

14. On the adjective "holy" (ἁγίοις) as most likely modifying both apostles and prophets here, see Hoehner, *Ephesians*, 442.

3. Eph 3:6 (C): Gentiles are Fellow Heirs, Members, and Sharers with Jews

With the central C element of the chiasm in 3:1–13 the audience hear not only the content of the mystery made known to Paul and the holy apostles and prophets (3:2–5) of the church by the gift of God's love but also the pivot to a focus on how that mystery is now made known to others through the proclamation of the gospel: "that the Gentiles are fellow heirs and fellow members of the body and fellow sharers of the promise in Christ Jesus through the gospel" (3:6).

That not only "you" Gentile believers (3:1) but "the" Gentile believers in general are, together with Jewish believers, fellow heirs and fellow members of the body and fellow sharers of the promise in their dynamic union with Christ—"in Christ Jesus" (ἐν Χριστῷ ᾿Ιησοῦ, 3:6)[15]—reminds the audience that it was "in Christ Jesus" (ἐν Χριστῷ ᾿Ιησοῦ) that Gentile "you" believers who once were far away have become near as a gift of God's love (divine passive) in the blood of the Christ (2:13). And this was a further description of the great love with which God loved us (2:4) when God raised us up with Christ and seated us with him in the heavenly places "according to our union with and in Christ Jesus (ἐν Χριστῷ ᾿Ιησοῦ)" (2:6).

The audience realize that not only are Jewish and Gentile believers united with the risen Christ as a gift of God's love but that Gentile believers are united with Jewish believers likewise as a gift of God's love. The audience hear the three terms—"fellow heirs" and "fellow members of the body" and "fellow sharers"—as an emphatic rhetorical triplet of closely related concepts, alliterated by their συν- (translated as "fellow") prefixes, echoing a similar triplet of terms with συν- prefixes in 2:19–22.[16] Just as the Gentile "you" believers are "fellow citizens" (συμπολῖται) with the holy ones (2:19), forming a building "being fitted together" (συναρμολογουμένη, divine passive) into a temple holy in the Lord (2:21), in whom the Gentile "you" believers are "being built together" (συνοικοδομεῖσθε, divine passive) with Jewish believers into a dwelling place of God in the Spirit (2:22) as a gift of God's love, so also the Gentile believers are "fellow heirs" (συγκληρονόμα) and "fellow members of the body" (σύσσωμα) and "fellow sharers" (συμμέτοχα) with Jewish believers (3:6) as a gift of God's love.

---

15. O'Brien, *Ephesians*, 236: "Each of these marvellous blessings in which Gentiles participate is said to be in Christ Jesus and through the gospel (v. 6). The former phrase qualifies all three nouns ('fellow-heirs', 'members together', and 'joint partakers'), not simply the last. It is not to be understood instrumentally as 'through Christ'; rather, it signifies that Christ Jesus is the sphere in which this incorporation of Gentiles occurs." See also Lincoln, *Ephesians*, 181; Hoehner, *Ephesians*, 448.

16. As Hoehner (*Ephesians*, 445) points out, all three of these terms "have a συν- prefix to emphasize the union between Jews and Gentiles in the body of Christ. This is a common stylistic feature of Paul. Therefore, the word 'fellow' before each English translated word is used not only to bring continuity in the Greek, but also to reinforce the idea of union."

Although the triplet of terms with συν- prefixes in 3:6 are closely related, the audience hear slightly different nuances and allusions in each with regard to the love theme in Ephesians. That the Gentile believers are "fellow heirs" (συγκληρονόμα) with Jewish believers reminds the audience of Paul's prayer that God enable them to know what is the wealth of the glory of his inheritance (κληρονομίας) in the holy ones (1:18), which is also our inheritance (κληρονομίας) of which the Holy Spirit is the first installment (1:13–14). In our union with Christ we have obtained an inheritance (ἐκληρώθημεν) to which we have been predestined by God (1:11). The inheritance to which believing Jews and Gentiles as "fellow heirs" have been predestined is sonship through Jesus Christ (1:5), in union with whom, as God's Beloved (Son) (1:6), God chose us believers before the foundation of the world that we might be holy and blameless before him within the dynamic realm of being "in love" (1:4).

That the Gentile believers are "fellow members of the body" (σύσσωμα, 3:6) with Jewish believers reminds the audience that in their union with Christ Jesus, and as a further elaboration of the great love with which God loved us (2:4), Christ reconciled both Jewish and Gentile believers in one body (σώματι) to God through the cross (2:16).[17] This one body is Christ's body (σῶμα) which is the church to whom God gave Christ as head over all things as a gift of God's love (1:22–23).

That the Gentile believers are "fellow sharers (συμμέτοχα) of the promise (ἐπαγγελίας)" (3:6) together with Jewish believers recalls for the audience that as Gentiles in the realm of the flesh they were alienated from the community of Israel and strangers of the covenants of the promise (ἐπαγγελίας) (2:12). But that promise has now been transcended by the Holy Spirit of the promise (ἐπαγγελίας) with which both believing Gentiles and Jews have been sealed by God (divine passive), and thus placed in the realm of being "in the Spirit" (2:18, 22; 3:5), as a gift of God's love (1:13).[18]

In sum, the unity of Gentile believers with Jewish believers as fellow

---

17. Dawes, *Body*, 162: "The use of the term σύσσωμα in Eph 3:6 therefore parallels the (metaphorical) use of the term σῶμα in 2:16, for in both places σῶμα (or a closely related term) is used to highlight the unity of Jew and Gentile."

18. O'Brien, *Ephesians*, 235: "The term 'promise' harks back to two earlier passages in Ephesians which speak of 'the covenants of promise' from which Gentiles had been excluded before being brought near to God through the death of Christ (2:12), and (lit.) 'the Holy Spirit of promise' by whom they were sealed when they believed. Accordingly, it has been claimed that this privilege of Gentiles being 'joint partakers of the promise' is not a duplication of the first blessing 'joint heirs', but a reference to the substance of the promise, that is, the Holy Spirit himself (cf. 1:13)." Contra Stephen L. Lortz, "The Literal Interpretation of Ephesians 3:6 and Related Scriptures," *Journal from the Radical Reformation* 8 (1999): 5–12, this does not mean that believing Gentiles are now a part of Israel. As Hoehner (*Ephesians*, 447) remarks: "The church is not the new Israel but a distinct body of believers made up of believing Jews and Gentiles."

heirs and fellow members of the body and fellow sharers of the promise as well as the unity of all believers with and in Christ Jesus (2:6) are gifts of the great love with which God loved us (2:4) and which is the mystery of Christ made known through listening to the reading of the Letter (3:3–4) and through the preaching of the "gospel" (εὐαγγελίου) (3:6), the "gospel" (εὐαγγέλιον) of salvation in Christ Jesus (1:13).[19]

4. Eph 3:7–12 (Bʹ): Paul Became a Minister of the Gospel by God's Love

Paul as "*the* prisoner" of Christ Jesus on behalf of you Gentiles in the A element (3:1) progresses to Paul as a "minister" of the gospel that proclaims the unity of believing Gentiles with believing Jews (3:6) in the Bʹ element (3:7) of the chiasm in 3:1–13. In the B element Paul reminded his audience that they have heard of the plan "of the grace of God that was given to me" (τῆς χάριτος τοῦ θεοῦ τῆς δοθείσης μοι, 3:2) for you Gentiles, that according to revelation was made known to Paul the mystery (3:2–3a). And now, by way of a progressive chiastic parallelism in the Bʹ element, Paul informs his audience that he became a minister through whom that mystery of the unity of believing Gentiles with believing Jews (3:6) is proclaimed in the gospel according to the gift "of the grace of God that was given to me" (τῆς χάριτος τοῦ θεοῦ τῆς δοθείσης μοι) according to the working of God's power (3:7).[20]

With regard to the love theme, that Paul "became" (ἐγενήθην, divine passive) a minister of the gospel as a gift of God's love is emphatically underlined by a threefold expression of words for gift/grace—according to the "gift" of the "grace" of God that was "given" to Paul (3:7a). And that this gift of the grace of God was given to Paul according to the "working" (ἐνέργειαν) of God's "power" (δυνάμεως) (3:7b)[21] reminds the audience of Paul's prayer that they know what is the surpassing greatness of God's "power" (δυνάμεως)

---

19. The mystery of Christ is "the complete union of Jews and Gentiles with each other through the union of both with Christ. It is this double union, with Christ and with each other, which is the substance of the 'mystery'," according to John R. W. Stott, *The Message of Ephesians: God's New Society* (Leicester, England: InterVarsity, 1979), 117. Hoehner, *Ephesians*, 448: "[T]he term 'gospel' is used four times in Ephesians (1:13; 3:6; 6:15, 19) and basically connotes 'good news,' not only the good news of Christ's death that provides salvation for Gentiles but also the good news that they are one in Christ Jesus with believing Jews."

20. O'Brien, *Ephesians*, 238: "Having spoken of the revelation of the mystery to him, the apostle now turns his attention to the preaching of the mystery through him. The saving purposes of God involved not only a revealing of the gospel mystery to Paul, but also the pressing of him into the service of that gospel."

21. Hoehner, *Ephesians*, 451: "[T]his prepositional phrase is connected to the immediately preceding τῆς δοθείσης μοι ['that was given to me'], which would indicate that the gift of grace or enabling power which was given to Paul corresponded to the activity (or working) of power produced by God's own dynamic ability."

for us who believe according to the "working" (ἐνέργειαν) of the might of God's strength, which God "worked" (ἐνήργησεν) in the Christ, raising him from the dead and seating him at God's right hand in the heavenly places (1:19–20). The audience are to realize, then, that this particular gift of God's love to Paul accords with the power that God worked not only in Christ but in us believers in raising us up with and seating us with Christ in the heavenly places (2:6) as a manifestation of the great love with which God loved us (2:4).

The emphatic use of the first-person singular pronoun to single Paul out in the A element—"I (ἐγώ), Paul, am the prisoner of Christ Jesus on behalf of you Gentiles" (3:1)—progresses to the emphatic use of the same pronoun to single Paul out in the B′ element—"To me (ἐμοί) the very least of all the holy ones was given this grace" (3:8a).[22] This accentuates Paul's humiliation. The audience are to realize that Paul is humiliated not only as *the* "prisoner" of Christ Jesus but as the "very least" not only of the "holy" (ἁγίοις) apostles and prophets to whom the mystery of the Christ has been made known as a gift of God's love (3:4–5) but of *all* "holy ones" (ἁγίων)—all believers.[23] Nevertheless, ironically, paradoxically, and amazingly, to the humiliated Paul "has been given" (ἐδόθη), as a gift of God's love (divine passive), this grace to preach not only to the "you" Gentiles of Paul's audience but to "the" Gentiles in general (cf. 3:6) the unfathomable wealth of the Christ (3:8).[24]

Whereas Christ "preached" (εὐηγγελίσατο) the good news of peace to "you" (Gentiles) who are far away and peace to those (Jews) who are near (2:17), God gave Paul the grace to "preach" (εὐαγγελίσασθαι) to the Gentiles the good news of the unfathomable wealth of the Christ (3:8). The unity of believing Gentiles with believing Jews that is expressed as "the mystery of the Christ (τοῦ Χριστοῦ)" in 3:4 of the B element progresses to its expression as "the unfathomable wealth of the Christ (τοῦ Χριστοῦ)" in the B′ element of the chiasm. The audience are to appreciate that although God has made

---

22. Hoehner, *Ephesians*, 452: "The personal pronoun ἐμοί, 'to me,' is emphatic, not only because it is expressed but also because it is placed first."

23. On the adjective, "very least" (ἐλαχιστοτέρῳ), O'Brien (*Ephesians*, 240) declares that "Paul creates a new form of this Greek adjective, that is, a comparative of a superlative ('leaster', 'less than the least')." Gombis, "Ephesians 3:2–13," 322: "Seen in terms of the present age, he [Paul] could not be in a weaker, more shameful, or more vulnerable position."

24. On the rhetorical figure involved here, Jeal (*Ephesians*, 170) states: "Here in 3:8 the figure is employed to enhance the view that all personal merit of Paul is disclaimed; his ministry and the content of his proclamation were wholly a gift of God. The bestowing of grace by God is accented. At the same time, however, this rhetoric tends to place Paul in a favourable light as one who is humbled and awed by the stewardship entrusted to him."

this mystery known to human beings, there is still a humanly "unfathomable" or "unsearchable" wealth involved with it.[25]

Echoing for the audience previous occurrences of the word "wealth" (πλοῦτος) to describe God's grace (1:7; 2:7) and the glory of God's inheritance (1:18), the description of the mystery as the unfathomable "wealth" (πλοῦτος) of the Christ (3:8) underlines the lavishness of God's gracious love in uniting believing Gentiles with believing Jews in union with Christ Jesus (3:6). With regard to the love theme, the audience are to appreciate that it is as a gracious gift of God's love that Paul has been given the grace to preach the good news of the lavish gift of the great love that God granted to believing Gentiles in uniting them with believing Jews in Christ Jesus.[26]

The "plan" (οἰκονομίαν, 3:2) and "mystery" (μυστήριον, 3:3; μυστηρίῳ, 3:4) that was given and made known as a gift of God's love to Paul and the holy apostles and prophets in the B element (3:2–5) progresses, in accord with the chiastic parallelism, to the gift of gracious love that God gave Paul (3:7–8) to enlighten, not just for the Gentiles (3:3–4, 6, 8), but for *all* peoples the "plan" (οἰκονομία) of the "mystery" (μυστηρίου) which had been hidden from the ages in God who created all things in 3:9 of the B′ element (3:7–12) of the chiasm.[27]

That the "plan" (οἰκονομία) of the mystery to unite believing Gentiles with believing Jews as a gift of God's love in Christ Jesus (3:6) had been hidden from the ages in God who created "all things" (τὰ πάντα) (3:9) reminds the audience of God's "plan" (οἰκονομίαν) for the fullness of the times to unite under one head "all things" (τὰ πάντα) in the Christ (1:10). That this is the plan of God who "created" (κτίσαντι) all things (3:9) further indicates to the audience that the unity of believers "created" (κτισθέντες) by the gift of God's love (divine passive) in Christ Jesus (2:10), who made both believing Gentiles and believing Jews one (2:14) that the two he might "create"

---

25. On ἀνεξιχνίαστον here Hoehner (*Ephesians*, 454) points out: "In the NT this word is used only here and in Rom 11:33 and has the idea of that which is 'not to be traced out,' 'indetectable,' 'uninvestigable, unsearchable,' 'inscrutable, incomprehensible, fathomless.' . . . In other words, it is beyond man's ability to investigate; thus it is translated 'unfathomable.'" See also Ioannes Mehlmann, "Ἀνεξιχνίαστος = Investigabilis (Rom 11,33; Eph 3,8)," *Bib* 40 (1959): 902–14.

26. Lincoln, *Ephesians*, 184: "Christ himself constitutes the content of the riches of the gospel, and the wealth of the salvation to be found in him in unfathomable. Yet, for all the glory attributed to Christ by this formulation, in the context its thought is subordinated to the ministry of the apostle. It is to Paul that grace has been given to make these glorious riches of Christ available to the Gentiles."

27. For the retention of "all" (πάντας) as the original reading in 3:9, see Metzger, *A Textual Commentary*, 534; Lincoln, *Ephesians*, 167; O'Brien, *Ephesians*, 243 n. 87; Hoehner, *Ephesians*, 455 n. 1.

(κτίση) in himself into one new person (2:15), is included within God's plan to unite all things under one head in the Christ.[28]

The mystery that has "now" (νῦν, 3:5) been "made known" (ἐγνωρίσθη, 3:3, 5) as a gift of God's love (divine passive) not only to Paul but to the holy apostles and prophets in the B element (3:2–5) progresses, by way of the chiastic parallelism, to the manifold wisdom of God (cf. 1:8, 17) that might "now" (νῦν) be "made known" (γνωρισθῇ), as a gift of God's love (divine passive), to all (3:9), including to the rulers and to the authorities in the heavenly places through the church in 3:10 of the B′ element (3:7–12) of the chiasm.

Reminding the audience of the "ruler" (ἄρχοντα) of the "authority" (ἐξουσίας) of the air according to which they once walked (2:2) in disunity with God and fellow human beings, that God may now make known to the "rulers" (ἀρχαῖς) and the "authorities" (ἐξουσίαις) in the heavenly places the manifold wisdom of God through the church (3:10) is a gift of God's love for the benefit of believers. It is through the very existence of the church as the visible unity of believing Gentiles with believing Jews that God may make known to the rulers and the authorities in the heavenly places the manifold wisdom of God that includes the mystery of this very unity of Gentiles joined to Jews in the church. As a recipient of this gift of God's love, the audience of believers united together in the church are assured that the rulers and the authorities in the heavenly places may now know that they have been defeated in their attempt to prevent this unity.[29]

But the manifold wisdom of God includes not only the unity of Gentiles with Jews (3:6) in the church but also the unity of all things in the heavens and on earth under one head in Christ (1:10). Reminding the audience that God raised Christ and seated him at his right hand "in the heavenly places" (ἐν τοῖς ἐπουρανίοις), far above every "ruler" (ἀρχῆς) and "authority" (ἐξουσίας) included in all things that he subjected under the feet of

---

28. O'Brien, *Ephesians*, 244: "God has not changed; nor is he abandoning his first creation by forming a new creation in Christ. Salvation and the unity of Jew and Gentile in Christ have always been his purpose . . . And he who created all things in the beginning with this goal in mind will consummate his work of re-creation on the final day when he brings all things together in unity in his Son, the Lord Jesus (1:10)."

29. Gombis, "Ephesians 3:2–13," 322: "[T]he manner in which God has made known his multi-faceted and many-splendored wisdom to the evil powers is by confounding them and their rule over this age in his creation of the church. The powers have ordered the present evil age in such a way as to exacerbate the divisions within humanity created by the Law (2:11–12). God confounds the powers, however, by creating in Christ one unified, multi-racial body consisting of formerly divided groups of people. And it is the existence of the church as such a body set within the hostile environment of the present evil age that proclaims to them the wisdom of God." Arnold, *Ephesians*, 64: "[T]he readers would find great encouragement in knowing that the 'powers' can see that they have been devastatingly foiled by the emergence of the body of Christ, the church."

Christ whom he gave as head over all things to the church (1:20–22), that God may now make known to the "rulers" (ἀρχαῖς) and the "authorities" (ἐξουσίαις) "in the heavenly places" (ἐν τοῖς ἐπουρανίοις) the manifold wisdom of God through the church (3:10), seated with Christ "in the heavenly places" (ἐν τοῖς ἐπουρανίοις) (2:6), is a further gift of God's love for the benefit of believers. It assures the audience of believers that the menacing rulers and authorities in the heavenly places may now know that they themselves are destined to be part of the cosmic unity that includes the unity of the church—the unity of all things under one head in Christ (1:10).[30]

That the manifold wisdom of God may now be made known, as a gift of God's love, to the rulers and the authorities in the heavenly places (3:10) through the love God gave to Paul to preach and enlighten all on the plan of the mystery (3:7–9) is "according to the purpose (cf. 1:11) of the ages which he accomplished in Christ Jesus (ἐν τῷ Χριστῷ Ἰησοῦ)[31] our Lord" (3:11) reinforces for the audience that the unity of believing Gentiles with believing Jews is granted to them as a gift of God's love through their union "in Christ Jesus" (ἐν Χριστῷ Ἰησοῦ) (3:6). The reference to Christ Jesus as "our" (ἡμῶν) Lord continues Paul's assimilation of his audience of Gentile "you" (ὑμῶν, 3:1; ὑμᾶς, 3:2) believers with himself and all of "us" believers.

In 2:18 Paul declared that through Christ we both (believing Jews and believing Gentiles) "have" (ἔχομεν), as a gift of God's love, the "access" (προσαγωγήν) in one Spirit before the Father. Now, in 3:12 he declares that in Christ we "have" (ἔχομεν), as a gift of God's love, the boldness and "access" (προσαγωγήν) in confidence through faith in him.[32] The audience thus realize that the hostile rulers and the authorities in the heavenly places (3:10) cannot prevent the bold and confident access before God that Gen-

---

30. O'Brien, *Ephesians*, 247: "Ephesians 3:9, 10 bears a significant relation to the consummation of the mystery, the bringing together of 'all things' into unity in Christ (1:9, 10). . . . There Christ's summing up of all things involved 'the things in heaven' (the chief representatives of which are the powers) and 'the things on earth' (especially the church) coming under Christ's lordship so that these divine purposes might be fulfilled." See also Schwindt, *Weltbild*, 368. Hoehner, *Ephesians*, 462: "The formation of the church is tangible evidence that the evil angelic leaders' power has been broken, demonstrating that even the most diverse elements of creation are subject to Christ. . . . the union of Jews and Gentiles in one body must be acknowledged by the 'powers' to be a display of the multifaceted wisdom of God. This union is an evidence of the grace of God."

31. On the use of the definite article before "Christ" here, Best (*Ephesians*, 328–29) suggests: "This could be a deliberate messianic reference, for the divine intention included the history of the people from whom the Messiah came. It is through the Messiah that Jew and Gentile are united in one body and that wisdom is proclaimed even to the powers."

32. As indicated especially from 1:13, 15, διὰ τῆς πίστεως αὐτοῦ in 3:12 should be understood as "through faith in him (Christ)" rather than as "through his (Christ's) faith," contra Paul Foster, "The First Contribution to the πίστις Χριστοῦ Debate: A Study of Ephesians 3.12," *JSNT* 85 (2002): 75–96. Lincoln, *Ephesians*, 190: "[T]he readers' faith has already been mentioned earlier in this letter in 1:13, 15, 19; and 2:8."

tiles united with Jews through their faith in Christ, as well as Paul himself as a "prisoner of Christ Jesus" (3:1),[33] now have as a gift of God's love granted them in their union with Christ Jesus.[34]

With regard to the love theme in 3:7–12, the audience are to realize that Paul "became a minister" of the gospel as a gift of God's love (3:7) according to the power that God worked in raising us up with and seating us with Christ in the heavenly places (2:6) as a manifestation of the great love with which God loved us (2:4). To the humiliated Paul "has been given," as a gift of God's love, the grace to preach not only to the "you" Gentiles but to "the" Gentiles in general (cf. 3:6) the gospel of the unfathomable wealth of the Christ (3:8) that includes the unity of believing Gentiles with believing Jews (3:6). As a recipient of the gift of God's love in making known to the rulers and the authorities in the heavenly places the unity of Gentiles and Jews in the church, the audience are assured that the rulers and the authorities may now know not only that they have been defeated in their attempt to prevent this unity (3:9–10) but that they cannot prevent the bold and confident access to God that all of "us" believers have as a gift of God's love granted to us in our union with Christ Jesus our Lord (3:11–12).

5. Eph 3:13 (A'): Paul's Tribulations on Behalf of You is Your Glory

Paul's personal love for his audience of "you" believers as expressed in his declaration that "I, Paul, am *the* prisoner of Christ Jesus on behalf of you (ὑπὲρ ὑμῶν) Gentiles" in the A element (3:1) progresses, by way of the chiastic parallelism, to Paul's love for his audience as expressed in his exhortation, "Therefore I ask you not to lose heart in my tribulations on behalf of you (ὑπὲρ ὑμῶν), which is your (ὑμῶν) glory," in the A' element of the chiasm in 3:1–13.

---

33. Gombis, "Ephesians 3:2–13," 322: "This paradoxical situation magnifying the triumph of God in Christ is still in view in v. 12, where Paul teases out the irony. He mentions the blessings of 'boldness' or 'freedom of speech' and 'access in confidence'—while he is in prison, a position in which he most likely enjoys little or no freedom or confident access to anything or anyone of consequence."

34. H. Richard Lemmer, "ἡ οἰκονομία τοῦ μυστηρίου τοῦ ἀποκεκρυμμένου ἐν τῷ θεῷ— Understanding 'Body of Christ' in the Letter to the Ephesians," *Neot* 32 (1998): 490: "It is in their union with Christ that the *ekklesia* have both παρρησίαν καὶ προσαγωγήν; and not by any other rituals or quests." Lincoln, *Ephesians*, 191: "While in 2:18 the access was the common access of two previously divided groups, here in 3:12 the access can be seen as one no longer impeded by the menace of hostile principalities and authorities." See also O'Brien, *Ephesians*, 249. Jeal, *Ephesians*, 172–73: "This language elicits a sense of security among the recipients. They may also experience a strong sense of identification, realizing that they are part of the 'we' (ἔχομεν) to whom the author refers, and knowing, too, that they have faith in Christ. The whole effect is strengthened by the words παρρησία ('boldness') and προσαγωγή ('access') which together form a hendiadys, evident by the single article (τήν) used for both words, and by the alliterative sound of παρρησίαν, προσαγωγήν and πεποιθήσει."

Paul asks his audience not to become discouraged by his tribulations as a prisoner because they are the consequence of his mediation to them of the love he received from God to preach the good news of the gospel that makes known to all (3:7–11) the mystery that believing Gentiles are united to believing Jews as a gift of God's love in their union with Christ Jesus (3:6). The prisoner Paul's tribulations on behalf of "you" is "your" *glory*—a "glory" that comes from God (1:6, 12, 14, 17, 18), because Paul's audience of Gentile "you" believers have received God's love not only in being united with Jewish believers (3:6) but also in having bold and confident access with them to God (3:12), and in being destined ultimately to be united along with all things, including the presently menacing rulers and authorities in the heavenly places (3:10), under one head, as a gift of God's love, in their union with Christ (1:10).[35]

B. Summary on Ephesians 3:1–13

1. Paul accepts his imprisonment as "the" prisoner of the Christ Jesus for the sake of the unity of Gentile and Jewish believers as part of his love for them as Gentile "you" believers (3:1).

2. The audience realize that listening to the Letter Paul wrote to them as a gift of his personal love empowers them to perceive Paul's insight into the mystery (3:3–4) of the unity of believing Jews and Gentiles that God made known as a special gift of God's love not only to Paul (3:2), the preeminent apostle and prisoner of Christ Jesus, but also to the holy apostles and prophets, the foundation of all the believing holy ones who are united in the Spirit (3:5). Listening to the Letter thus empowers the audience to likewise receive the love God gave especially to Paul and the holy apostles and prophets to know the mystery. Not only the mystery of Gentiles being united with Jews but also knowledge of that mystery is a gift of God's love.

---

35. Cassidy, *Paul in Chains*, 97: "Paul's facility in repeating the truth that his suffering is for his readers' benefit deserves to be highlighted. In 3:1 he averred that his imprisonment was 'on behalf of you Gentiles.' Now in 3:13 he states that his suffering is 'for you.' Further, Paul implies that his suffering advances his readers' progress to 'glory' (δόξα). According to the mystery of God's plan in Christ, Paul's own sufferings help his readers on their way to the heavenly glory to which they are called." Gombis, "Ephesians 3:2–13," 323: "Paul's readers have no reason to despair at his sufferings and his present situation, since it is his paradoxical ministry to the Gentiles—the workings of which he has outlined in full—that facilitates their eschatological glory." Jeal, *Ephesians*, 174: "The rhetorical force of 3:13 is such that it emphasizes the value for the audience of Paul's sufferings while simultaneously de-emphasizing possible dismay over those sufferings, focusing the attention of the audience members instead on the extension of the gospel to Gentiles generally, to cosmic powers, and, indeed, to themselves."

3. The unity of Gentile believers with Jewish believers as fellow heirs and fellow members of the body and fellow sharers of the promise as well as the unity of all believers with and in Christ Jesus (2:6) are gifts of the great love with which God loved us (2:4) and which is the mystery of Christ made known through listening to the reading of the Letter (3:3–4) and through the preaching of the "gospel" (3:6), the "gospel" of salvation in Christ Jesus (1:13).

4. The audience are to realize that Paul "became a minister" of the gospel as a gift of God's love (3:7) according to the power that God worked in raising us up with and seating us with Christ in the heavenly places (2:6) as a manifestation of the great love with which God loved us (2:4). To the humiliated Paul "has been given," as a gift of God's love, the grace to preach to the Gentiles the gospel of the unfathomable wealth of the Christ (3:8) that includes the unity of believing Gentiles with believing Jews (3:6). As a recipient of the gift of God's love in making known to the rulers and the authorities in the heavenly places the unity of Gentiles and Jews in the church, the audience are assured that the cosmic powers may now know not only that they have been defeated in their attempt to prevent this unity (3:9–10), but that they cannot prevent the bold and confident access to God that all of "us" believers have as a gift of God's love granted to us in our union with Christ Jesus our Lord (3:11–12).

5. The prisoner Paul's tribulations on behalf of his audience are for their "glory" (3:13) because they have received God's love not only in being united with Jewish believers (3:6) but also in having bold and confident access with them to God (3:12), and in being destined ultimately to be united along with all things, including the presently menacing cosmic powers (3:10), under one head, as a gift of God's love, in their union with Christ (1:10).

CHAPTER 9

Ephesians 3:14–21: The Love of Christ That Surpasses Knowledge (G)

A: ¹⁴ Because of this I bow my knees before the Father ¹⁵ from whom *every* family in heaven and on earth is named,

    B: ¹⁶ that he may give you according to the wealth of his glory to be strengthened with *power* through his Spirit in the inner person,

        C: ¹⁷ that the *Christ* may dwell through faith in your hearts, *in love* rooted and grounded,

            D: ¹⁸ that *you might have the strength to comprehend* with all the holy ones *what is the breadth and length and height and depth,*

        C´:   ¹⁹ and so to know the *love* of the *Christ* that surpasses knowledge, that you might be filled to all the fullness of God.

    B´:   ²⁰ Now to him who has the *power* to do far more beyond all that we ask or imagine according to the *power* that is working in us,

A´:   ²¹ to him be glory in the church and in Christ Jesus to *all* the generations, for ever and ever. Amen.[1]

A. Audience Response to Ephesians 3:14–21

1. Eph 3:14–15 (A): Paul Kneels before God the Father of Every Family

"Because of this" (τούτου χάριν, 3:14) refers back to all that Paul has been stating in the Letter to this point, especially, recalling the same phrase,

---

1. For the establishment of Eph 3:14–21 as a chiasm, see ch. 2.

149

"because of this" (τούτου χάριν), in 3:1a, that Paul is *the* prisoner of Christ Jesus (3:1) and minister of the gospel (3:6–8) "on behalf of you" (ὑπὲρ ὑμῶν, 3:1, 13)—his Gentile audience of "you" believers. Because Paul is *the* prisoner and minister on behalf of his audience, he thus bows his knees before the Father in prayer, continuing the personal love he expressed for them when he reported that he "does not cease giving thanks for you (ὑπὲρ ὑμῶν), making mention of you in my prayers" (1:16).

Exemplifying for his audience the bold and confident "access" that we believers have "before the Father" (πρὸς τὸν πατέρα) as a gift of God's love in and through our union with Christ (2:18; 3:12), Paul declares: "I bow my knees before the Father (πρὸς τὸν πατέρα)" (3:14).[2] That Paul dramatically "bows his knees" before the Father prepares the audience for a particularly reverential and awe-inspiring prayer on their behalf.[3] Recalling God's plan to unite under one head all things (πάντα) in the Christ, the things in the heavens (οὐρανοῖς) and the things on earth (γῆς) in him" (1:10), Paul's description of God the Father as the sovereign origin for the existence, power, and authority of every grouping of related entities in the cosmos—"from whom every (πᾶσα) family in heaven (οὐρανοῖς) and on earth (γῆς) is named" (3:15; cf. 3:9)[4]—pre-

---

2. That the phrase "before the Father" (πρὸς τὸν πατέρα) occurs only in 2:18 and 3:14 in Ephesians enhances this connection.

3. Jeal, *Ephesians*, 113: "While hearing the words of 3:14 is not the same as seeing the actual physical act of bowing the knees, the effect of the vivid imagery is impressive.... standing was the usual Jewish posture of prayer. Yet surely the function of . . . 3:14 is . . . to persuasively affect the audience members with the emotional image of the author physically bowing in an attitude of worship and entreating God on their behalf. This sort of imagery and entreaty could hardly fail to gain the goodwill and respect of the audience for the author and the message of Ephesians. Since κάμπτω [bow] is the principal verb for the whole sentence, the attitude of respect toward God and its concomitant emotions prevail throughout the prayer and following doxology."

4. That the phrase "in heaven (οὐρανοῖς) and on earth (γῆς)" occurs only in 1:10 and 3:15 in Ephesians enhances this connection. On the phrase in 3:15 Hoehner (*Ephesians*, 475) comments: "This concept of heaven and earth is similar to Eph 1:10 where it states that Christ will head up all things in heaven and on earth. In the present context the heavenly families are linked to the earthly families in their common dependence on the Father." According to Ulrich Hutter ("πατρία," *EDNT* 3.57), πατρία (family) "is derived from πατήρ [father] as a designation of origin from the same father or ancestor." On the translation of πᾶσα πατριά as "every family" rather than "whole family," see Johnston, *Use of Πᾶς*, 173–74. O'Brien, *Ephesians*, 256: "Every family in heaven points to family groupings and classes of angels, good and rebellious alike, which owe their origin to God, while every family on earth speaks of family groupings and so of the basic structure of human relationships which owe their existence to him." On the significance of every family being "named" (ὀνομάζεται) by God, Arnold (*Ephesians*, 96) states: "The act of granting a name signifies much more than the granting of a verbal symbol as a means of identification: it amounts to the exertion of power and the conveyance of an authority." O'Brien, *Ephesians*, 256: "So for God to give creatures a name was not simply to provide them with a label, but signifies his bringing them

pares the audience for a prayer on their behalf involving the cosmic creative and unifying power of God as the Father of all.[5]

2. Eph 3:16 (B): Paul's Prayer for God's Gift of Power in the Inner Person

Developing his previous prayer "that" (ἵνα) God, the Father of "glory" (δόξης), "may give you" (δώῃ ὑμῖν), as a gift of God's love, the "Spirit" (πνεῦμα) so that you may know what is the "wealth of the glory" (πλοῦτος τῆς δόξης) of "his" (αὐτοῦ) inheritance and what is the surpassing greatness of his "power" (δυνάμεως) for us who believe according to the working of the "might" (κράτους) of his strength (1:17–19), Paul now prays "that" (ἵνα) God the Father "may give you" (δῷ ὑμῖν) according to the "wealth of his glory" (πλοῦτος τῆς δόξης αὐτοῦ) "to be strengthened" (κραταιωθῆναι) with "power" (δυνάμει) through his "Spirit" (πνεύματος) in the inner person (3:16).

Recalling not only the "wealth of the glory" (πλοῦτος τῆς δόξης) of his inheritance (1:18) but "according to the wealth of his grace" (κατὰ τὸ πλοῦτος τῆς χάριτος αὐτοῦ, 1:7; cf. 2:7), that is, the grace with which God graced us in our union with the Beloved as a manifestation of God's glory— "to the praise of the glory of his grace (δόξης τῆς χάριτος αὐτοῦ)" (1:6), that Paul now prays that God may give to you "according to the wealth of his glory" (κατὰ τὸ πλοῦτος τῆς δόξης αὐτοῦ, 3:16) indicates to the audience that Paul is praying for a gift from God that accords with the lavish wealth of the glory God manifested in gracing believers with an abundant wealth of grace as a gift of the great love with which God loved us (2:4) in our union with Christ.[6]

---

into existence, exercising dominion over them (cf. Ps. 147:4; Isa. 40:26), and giving each their appropriate role."

5. Jeal, *Ephesians*, 113–15: "The obvious word-play between the like-sounding words of common root, πατήρ [father] (3:14) and πατριά [family] (3:15), is recognized by many commentators. . . . The effect is to enhance the language, to maintain attention and impress the notion of God as Father on the mind. . . . The cosmic scope of fatherhood enhances the sense of respect and homage being paid to the Father by denoting the extent of his power. The tone and action are those of worship, drawing the audience members into an emotional collaboration with the author so that they identify with and share in the devotion and worship of the Father to whom they look for the blessings sought in 3:16–19."

6. Usami, *Somatic Comprehension*, 169 n. 90: "The κατά-phrase ('according to the riches of His glory') in Eph 3,16 resumes the significations of κατά-phrases in the previous passages of Ephesians, which relate to the Divine power and to the Divine decision and will or benevolent grace of His will." O'Brien, *Ephesians*, 257: "Here this preposition [κατά], which Paul often uses in petitions and thanksgivings, draws attention not simply to the idea of source, thereby signifying 'out of the wealth of his glory', but also indicates that his giving corresponds to the inexhaustible riches of that glory. It is on a scale commensurate with his glory; he gives as lavishly as only he can. . . . κατά ('according to') with the accusative is found in both the Old Testament and Pauline prayers, where it points to God's power, grace, or glory as the source of blessing to the recipient" (n. 143).

Recalling that he became a minister of the gospel according to the "working" of God's "power" (δυνάμεως, 3:7), that is, the great "power" (δυνάμεως) that God "worked" according to the "working" of the might of his strength for us who believe in raising Christ from the dead and seating him at his right hand in the heavenly places (1:19–20), Paul now prays that God grant his audience to be strengthened with that same divine "power" (δυνάμει) through God's Spirit in the inner person (3:16). Paul is thus praying that each individual member of his audience interiorly—in the "inner person" (ἔσω ἄνθρωπον, singular)—be strengthened (divine passive) with God's power as a gift of God's love given through the agency of God's Spirit.[7]

3. Eph 3:17 (C): In Love Rooted and Grounded

Paul continues his prayer that each member of his audience be individually strengthened with God's power through God's Spirit in the "inner person" (3:16) by praying that the Christ may dwell through faith in "your" (ὑμῶν, plural) "hearts," that is, in your "inner persons," collectively as a community (3:17a).[8] Whereas Paul previously prayed that the "eyes" of "your" (ὑμῶν) collective "heart" (καρδίας, singular) may be enlightened through the Spirit as a gift of God's love, so that you may know the surpassing greatness of the power God worked for us who believe in raising Christ from the dead and seating him at God's right hand in the heavenly places (1:17–19), he now prays that Christ may dwell through faith in "your hearts" (καρδίαις

---

7. On "inner person" (ἔσω ἄνθρωπον) Fee (*God's Empowering Presence*, 695–96) states: "This is a uniquely Pauline phrase in the NT, used to refer to the interior of our being. This is not only the seat of personal consciousness, but the seat of our moral being." Nikolaus Walter, "ἔσω," *EDNT* 2.65: "[T]he center of the person is intended." Hoehner, *Ephesians*, 479: "In the present context it is the innermost being of the believer which is to be strengthened with God's power. That innermost being corresponds with the heart of the believer in the following verse." On "be strengthened" (κραταιωθῆναι) Hoehner (*Ephesians*, 478) notes: "The passive voice reinforces the idea that it is God who gives the strength; it is not self-endowed." See also O'Brien, *Ephesians*, 257 n. 144. On "through his Spirit" Hoehner (*Ephesians*, 478) remarks: "While in 1:17 the Holy Spirit bestows insight and disclosure into the knowledge of God, here the Spirit acts as agent. In this capacity God enables believers to be strengthened with his power. This is not new or unusual, for already in the first prayer (1:15–23) Paul prayed that believers might know God's power that he directs toward them. Hence, it is through God's Spirit that the believer is to be strengthened with God's ability to act." O'Brien, *Ephesians*, 257: "The agency of the Spirit in dispensing divine power is in line with other New Testament teaching where the Spirit and power are intimately linked (Acts 1:8; Rom. 1:4; 15:19; 1 Cor. 2:4; 1 Thess. 1:5)."

8. Jeal, *Ephesians*, 118–19: "The κατοικῆσαι ['dwell'] statement, because of the asyndeton, gives the sense of being an enhancement of the κραταιωθῆναι ['be strengthened'] statement rather than being a separate and supplementary thought." O'Brien, *Ephesians*, 258: "Christ's indwelling defines more precisely the strengthening role of the Spirit in v. 16. His indwelling is not something additional to the strengthening. To be empowered by the Spirit in the inner person means that Christ himself dwells in their hearts."

ὑμῶν, plural) collectively (3:17a), strengthened with power interiorly as individuals through God's Spirit (3:16) as a gift of God's love.

Whereas it is "through faith" (διὰ πίστεως) that the "you" believers have been saved as a gift of God's love (2:8) and "through faith in him" (διὰ τῆς πίστεως αὐτοῦ) that all of us believers have as a gift of God's love confident and bold access (3:12) in one Spirit before God the Father (2:18), Paul now prays that the Christ may dwell "through faith" (διὰ τῆς πίστεως) in your hearts (3:17a), strengthened with power interiorly through God's Spirit (3:16) as a gift of God's love.

Paul's prayer that the Christ may "dwell" (κατοικῆσαι) in the hearts of his audience of Gentile "you" believers (3:17a) complements their being built together with believing Jews as a gift of God's love (divine passive) within their union of being "in Christ" into a "dwelling place" (κατοικητήριον) of God in the Spirit (2:22). This "dwelling place" stands in parallel apposition to the whole "building" that, being fitted together by God, grows into a temple holy in the Lord (2:21), whose "foundation" is the apostles and prophets and whose "capstone" or "head stone" is Christ Jesus himself (2:20). Paul is thus praying that the Christ who is united with believers not only as the "capstone" or "head stone" of the metaphorical "building" and "dwelling place" that is the church, but as the "head" over all things that God has given as a gift of God's love to the church which is his "body" (1:22–23), may now dwell interiorly within the hearts of his audience as a further gift of God's love.

Rather than expressing a further request of the prayer, the clause, "in love rooted and grounded" (3:17b), describes what the audience have already become and continues to be in terms of the mixture of agricultural and architectural metaphors for the church. Recalling that God chose us believers in Christ before the foundation of the world that we might be holy and blameless before him within the dynamic realm of being "in love" (ἐν ἀγάπῃ) (1:4), that Paul's audience already have been and still are "rooted and grounded" (perfect passives) "in love" (ἐν ἀγάπῃ) means not only that they have love (ἀγάπην) for all the holy ones (1:15) and have received love from Paul (3:1–13), but that they have received the great love (ἀγάπην) with which God loved (ἠγάπησεν) us (2:4) in our union with the Beloved (ἠγαπημένῳ) (1:6).[9]

As part of the architectural metaphor for the church, that Paul's audi-

---

9. Hoehner, *Ephesians*, 484: "This root and foundation of love refers to God having chosen them, predestined them, bestowed them in the beloved, redeemed them, made them a heritage, sealed them with the Holy Spirit, made them alive, raised and seated them in the heavenlies, and placed them equally in one new person in the body of Christ. Therefore, for the believer, the origin of this love is God's love." Lincoln, *Ephesians*, 207: "[L]ove is to be seen as God's love embodied in Christ and mediated by the Spirit, but also as the power that moves believers to love others with no expectation of reward."

ence have been "grounded" or "founded" (τεθεμελιωμένοι) in love reminds them that they have been built as a gift of God's love (divine passive) upon the "foundation" (θεμελίῳ) of the apostles and prophets, Christ Jesus himself being the "capstone" or "head stone" (2:20). And, as part of the agricultural metaphor for the church, that they have been firmly "planted" or "rooted" (ἐρριζωμένοι) in love reminds them that they, who have been built together with believing Jews as a gift of God's love (divine passive) into a "dwelling place" (2:22) which is a "building" fitted together as a gift of God's love (divine passive), have been empowered by that love to "grow" (αὔξει) into a temple holy in the Lord (2:21).[10]

4. Eph 3:18 (D): To Comprehend with All the Holy Ones the Cosmic Totality

Continuing his prayer that his audience of Gentile "you" believers, already rooted and grounded in love, may be strengthened with power interiorly through the indwelling of Christ (3:16–17), Paul prays "that you might have the strength to comprehend with all the holy ones what is the breadth and length and height and depth" (3:18).

Here Paul is praying that his audience of Gentile "you" believers may have the strength to comprehend together "with all the holy ones" (σὺν πᾶσιν τοῖς ἁγίοις), that is, "all the holy ones" (πάντας τοὺς ἁγίους) for whom they have love (1:15) and with whom they have been united as "fellow citizens of the holy ones" (συμπολῖται τῶν ἁγίων) (2:19) to form in their union with Christ the whole building that is fitted together and that is growing into a temple "holy" (ἅγιον) in the Lord (2:21). It is as they are "growing" in union with all the holy ones, having already been "rooted and grounded" in love (3:17b) with them, into a temple of those who are holy ones in the Lord, then, that Paul prays that his audience may have interior strength through the indwelling of Christ to comprehend "what is the breadth and length and height and depth" (3:18).

The expression, "what is the breadth and length and height and depth" (3:18b), functions as the single object that is to be comprehended, comprised of four words that form a pair of rhetorical merisms, that is, opposites to express totality.[11] The first merism, absolute "breadth and length," refers to the opposite dimensions of horizontal space; taken together as a merism,

---

10. Jeal, *Ephesians*, 120–21: "The mixed imagery of horticulture and construction is rhetorically powerful in that it carries on the notion of 'depth' evident in the terms 'inner person' and 'in your hearts,' and accents the notions of stability, security, and strength that are fundamental to the author's desire for the audience in the passage. The metaphors serve to clarify the author's prayer wishes for the audience members, showing his continuing concern for their welfare and growth."

11. Hoehner, *Ephesians*, 486: "The indirect question introduced with τί expresses the object of what is to be comprehended. The one article (τό) with the four words indicates that,

they refer to the totality or fullness of horizontal space in the cosmos. The second merism, absolute "height and depth," refers to the opposite dimensions of vertical space; taken together as a merism, they refer to the totality or fullness of vertical space in the cosmos. As a coordinated pair, these merisms together express the immense vastness of the cosmos in all of its totality and fullness that embraces and thus unifies all things within its expansive dimensions of absolute horizontal and vertical space.[12]

As an expression of the absolute cosmic fullness that embraces all things in the universe, "what is the breadth and length and height and depth" (3:18b), reminds the audience of Paul's previous description of the church as the "body" (σῶμα) of Christ, to whom God gave Christ as "head" over "all things" (πάντα), the "body" which is the "fullness" of the Christ who is filling "all things" (πάντα) in all ways (1:22–23), so that "all things" (πάντα)—the things in the heavens and the things on earth—will ultimately be united under one head in Christ (1:10). This church is the one "body" (σώματι) in which Christ has reconciled and thus united believing Gentiles with believing Jews (2:16) to form the whole "building" of which Christ is the "head" or "capstone," the building and body of the church that is in the process of growing into a temple holy in the Lord (2:20–21). "What is the breadth and length and height and depth," the cosmic fullness that embraces and thus unifies all things, then, expresses the ultimate destiny of the growth of the church as the "body" and "building" of which Christ is the "head."

The cosmic horizontal dimensions of "breadth and length" embrace the spatially separated "far" and "near," the believing Gentiles and believing Jews that Christ has united in the one body of the church (2:13–17). And the cosmic vertical dimensions of "height and depth" embrace the spatially separated things in heaven ("height"), including the cosmic powers (1:21; 3:10), and things on earth ("depth"), including believing Gentiles and believing Jews, that will ultimately be united together under Christ (1:10) as "head" over all things (1:22). Paul is thus praying that his audience of Gentile "you" believers, rooted and grounded in love in their union with all the

---

although they are distinct, they are to be treated as one. . . . Some prefer to view these words as a merism where the parts (especially when opposites are expressed) signify the whole."

12. Abbott, *Ephesians*, 99: "The four words seem intended to indicate, not so much the thoroughness of the comprehension as the vastness of the thing to be comprehended." Many take these four words as a description of the vast dimensions of the love of Christ that surpasses knowledge as expressed in 3:19. But these four words are absolute expressions without further specification or qualification (cf. Usami, *Somatic Comprehension*, 176–77) and although the conjunction τέ in 3:19 closely links the love of Christ with "what is the breadth and length and height and depth" in 3:18, it is a coordinate not a synonymous connection. On the four words as a reference to the dimensions of the cosmos, see also van Kooten, *Cosmic Christology*, 179–82. For other proposed interpretations of these four words and the problems involved with them, see Lincoln, *Ephesians*, 208–13; Hoehner, *Ephesians*, 486–88; O'Brien, *Ephesians*, 261–63.

holy ones with whom they form the "body" and "building" of the church, may be given as a gift of God's love the interior strength to comprehend already the immense and absolute vastness of the ultimate destiny of cosmic fullness and unity toward which they are now growing—"what is the breadth and length and height and depth" (3:18).[13]

5. Eph 3:19 (C´): To Know the Love of Christ

In the C element Paul prayed that Christ (Χριστόν) may dwell interiorly in the hearts of his Gentile audience of "you" believers, who are rooted and grounded within the realm of being "in love" (ἐν ἀγάπῃ) (3:17), that is in the realm of both receiving love from God (2:4) and extending love to all the holy ones (1:15). Now, in the C´ element, by way of a progressive chiastic parallelism, Paul's prayer focuses more specifically on the profound love of Christ for his audience: "and so to know the love (ἀγάπην) of Christ (Χριστοῦ) that surpasses knowledge" (3:19a).

Closely coordinated by the conjunction "and so" (τε) to Paul's prayer that his audience have the strength interiorly to comprehend the cosmic fullness and unity of all things—"what is the breadth and length and height and depth" (3:18)—is the result of that comprehension—to know the love of Christ (3:19a), that is, to experience interiorly through the indwelling of Christ (3:17) the love that empowers the audience, already rooted and grounded in love as part of the church that is the "body" and "building" of Christ, to grow toward the cosmic fullness and unity of all things that they are destined to become.[14] This love of Christ that empowers the church as Christ's body to grow to the fullness of cosmic unity recalls for the audience not only the love that Christ gave to the church in unifying Gentiles with Jews in one body (2:14–17), but to the love that Christ, as "head" over all things whom God gave to the church as a gift of love (1:22), is still giving

---

13. According to Usami (*Somatic Comprehension*, 177–78), "The comprehending subject is the community itself: self-comprehension of the Body. . . . The inner self-comprehension is totally different from a normal comprehension of being as if it stood outside the man who comprehends. This comprehension of the four dimensions is internally related to our self-awareness and to its self-realization (somatization) of the mystery of God in Christ in the community and in all the communities which belong to Christ. . . . The 'you,' for whom the apostle intercedes, are seen standing at the vital 'centre' of the Body. They see it absorbing other groups, new groups of men in the city of Ephesus and in the whole world, elevating them to unity with Christ, the Head who is in heaven. The Body grows and extends in the four dimensions as if it were extending into the whole cosmos and reaching to the infinite fullness of God."

14. Hoehner, *Ephesians*, 488: "The postpositive conjunction τέ introduces this clause. Although it is nearly impossible to state explicitly the difference of meaning between it and other coordinating conjunctions, it can generally be claimed to express an internal logical relationship (whereas καί is an external relationship) and probably can be translated in this context as 'and so.'"

to his body the church as the one who "is filling" (πληρουμένου) all things in all ways so that his body the church can grow into his "fullness" (πλήρωμα) (1:23). That Paul's audience are paradoxically to "know" the love of Christ that "surpasses knowledge" (3:19a) underlines how the knowledge and experience of this love transcends human knowledge and experience so that it can only be given as a gift of God's love. As the audience recall, it was as a gift of God's love that God "*made known* to us the mystery of his will" (1:9) and "may give to you the Spirit of wisdom and revelation in *knowledge* of him" (1:17) that "you may *know* what is the hope of his calling, what is the wealth of the glory of his inheritance in the holy ones" (1:18). And it is as a gift of God's love that the mystery of Christ was *made known* to Paul (3:3) and to the holy apostles and prophets (3:5), and may now be *made known* to the rulers and to the authorities in the heavenly places (3:10). Paul now prays that his audience's comprehension, by the interior strength that God may give them as a gift of love, of the cosmic fullness and unity toward which they are growing (3:18) may result in a further gift of God's love that they may *know* the love of Christ that surpasses *knowledge*.

The audience then hear the climactic purpose of Paul's prayer for them: "that you might be filled to all the fullness of God" (3:19b). Paul is thus praying that his audience might be filled with and by the love of Christ that surpasses knowledge but that they may know (3:19a) when God gives them the interior strength to comprehend together with all the holy ones the cosmic fullness and unity toward which they are growing (3:18). That "you might be filled" (πληρωθῆτε) with and by the love of Christ means being filled by the Christ who "is filling" (πληρουμένου) all things in all ways (1:23). The final goal of the audience, as part of the church which is the body and the "fullness" (πλήρωμα) of the Christ who is filling *all* things in *all* ways (1:23), being filled by and with the love of Christ is to attain to (εἰς) *all* the "fullness" (πλήρωμα) of God, that is, to the complete cosmic fullness and unity to which God has destined the church and which the audience may comprehend interiorly as the absolute "breadth and length and height and depth" (3:18).[15]

With regard to the love theme in 3:14–19, then, Paul is praying that God as the cosmic Father (3:14–15) may give to his audience of Gentile "you"

---

15. Lincoln, *Ephesians*, 214: "In 1:23 the Church was said to be the fullness of Christ who fills the cosmos in every respect. Here, however, it is the fullness of God himself which is in view, and the prayer is that believers should attain to the fullness. εἰς does not so much signify that with which one is filled, as it conveys movement toward a goal, a being filled up to the measure of God's fullness. . . . It is this eschatological perspective that explains how the Church, which is already the fullness, is still to be filled and to attain to the fullness." For a view that being filled to all the fullness of God means being filled with the glory of God, see Robert L. Foster, "'A Temple in the Lord Filled to the Fullness of God': Context and Intertextuality (Eph. 3:19)," *NovT* 49 (2007): 85–96.

believers as a gift of God's love the interior strength (3:16) of the indwelling of Christ, so that the audience, already rooted and grounded within the dynamic realm of being "in love" (3:17), may know and experience the profound love of the Christ who is filling them with all things in all ways (1:23), so that they, as part of the church which is the "body" (1:22–23) and "building" (2:20–22) of which Christ is the "head," may grow until they reach the complete cosmic fullness and unity to which God has destined them (3:19) and which they, together with all the holy ones, may already comprehend interiorly as the cosmic and absolute "breadth and length and height and depth" (3:18).[16]

6. Eph 3:20 (B´): The One Who Has the Power To Work in Us

In the B element Paul prayed that God may give to his audience of "you" believers as a gift of God's love according to the wealth of his glory that they be strengthened with "power" (δυνάμει) through his Spirit in the inner person (3:16). And now in the B´ element, by way of a progressive chiastic parallelism, Paul addresses, as the beginning of his concluding doxology, God as the one who "has the power" (δυναμένῳ) to do far more beyond all that we ask or imagine according to the "power" (δύναμιν) that is working in us (3:20).[17] In accord with Paul's assimilation of the "you" believers with all of "us" believers, the focus on "power" as a gift of God's love to "you" (ὑμῖν) in the B element progresses to the divine "power" that is working in "us" (ἡμῖν) in the B´ element of the chiasm.

Paul's description of God as the one who has the power to do "far more" (ὑπερεκπερισσοῦ) "beyond" (ὑπέρ) all that we ask or imagine (3:20a) assures his audience that God can empower them as a gift of God's love to know the love of Christ that "surpasses" (ὑπερβάλλουσαν) knowledge (3:18).[18]

---

16. According to J. Armitage Robinson, *St. Paul's Epistle to the Ephesians: A Revised Text and Translation with Exposition and Notes* (London: Macmillan, 1904), 89: "No prayer that has ever been framed has uttered a bolder request. It is a noble example of παρρησία, of freedom of speech, of that 'boldness and access in confidence' of which he has spoken above [3:12]."

17. O'Brien, *Ephesians*, 267: "The doxology not only follows Paul's petitionary prayer; it is also integrally connected with it: the ascription of power to God in the designation 'to him who is able', the mention of his power at work within the readers (cf. v. 16), and the fact that he can achieve more than they can ask (in prayer), all show plainly that this ascription of praise is closely linked with the preceding intercession." Lincoln, *Ephesians*, 216: "Whereas the prayer-report is expressed in the first-person singular (cf. v 14), the doxology employs the first-person plural in this clause. In this way, the readers are drawn further into sharing the writer's prayer concerns—'we ask'—and his praise. They are also drawn further into the breadth of his vision of God's power."

18. Lincoln, *Ephesians*, 216: "Something of the force of the writer's rhetoric can be captured by showing the build-up of the thought reflected by his language. God is said to be able to do what believers ask in prayer; he is able to do what they might fail to ask but what they can think; he is able to do all (πάντα) they ask or think; he is able to do above all (ὑπέρ

That God has the power to do this according to the power (δύναμιν) that is working (ἐνεργουμένην) in "us" (3:20b) reminds the audience of Paul's previous prayer that they know "what is the surpassing greatness of his power (δυνάμεως) for 'us' who believe according to the working (ἐνέργειαν) of the might of his strength, which he worked (ἐνήργησεν) in the Christ, raising him from the dead and seating him at his right hand in the heavenly places" (1:19–20). The power by which God raised Christ is the power now working in us through the indwelling of Christ that empowers us to know the love of Christ with a knowledge that far surpasses anything we can ask or imagine.[19]

With regard to the love theme, the audience realize that the power by which God raised Christ from the dead (1:19–20) and raised us up with him (2:5–6) is the power that empowers love. Paul became a minister of the gospel as a gift of God's love "according to the gift of the grace of God that was given to me according to the working of his power" (3:7). To know the love of Christ that surpasses knowledge (3:19a) is a gift of God's love empowered by that same power now working in us believers (3:16, 20). And the love of Christ with and by which believers may be filled to all the fullness of God (3:19b) by the Christ who is filling all things in all ways as the risen and exalted "head" over all things whom God gave as a gift of God's love to the church (1:22–23) is empowered by that same power.

7. Eph 3:21 (A´): Glory to God in the Church and in Christ to All Generations

In the A element Paul began his prayer for his audience in humble reverence to God as the cosmic Father from whom "every" (πᾶσα) family in heaven and on earth is named (3:14–15). And now in the A´ element, by way of a progressive chiastic parallelism, Paul exclaims the climax of the doxology to God that concludes his prayer: "To him be glory in the church and

---

πάντα) they ask or think; he is able to do abundantly above all (περισσοῦ ὑπὲρ πάντα) they ask or think; he is able to do more abundantly above all (ἐκπερισσοῦ ὑπὲρ πάντα) they ask or think; he is able to do infinitely more abundantly above all (ὑπερεκπερισσοῦ ὑπὲρ πάντα) they ask or think. And what is more, says the writer, this inexpressable power is at work within us!"

19. Fee, God's *Empowering Presence*, 697: "'The power that is at work in us' is precisely what was said above in vv. 16–17: 'to be strengthened by his power through the Spirit in the inner person,' which takes the form of 'Christ [and thereby his love] dwelling in our hearts by faith.'" O'Brien, *Ephesians*, 267: "In the earlier petition of chapter 1, God's effective power towards believers (1:19) was said to be nothing less than 'the operation of his mighty strength' exerted in the resurrection of Christ (1:20). Now that same power which raised Christ from the dead, enthroned him in the heavenlies, and then raised and enthroned us with him, is at work within us to achieve infinitely more than we can ask or imagine."

in Christ Jesus to all (πάσας) generations, for ever and ever. Amen" (3:21).[20] The address to God as the source of power for "every" family in the cosmic spatial dimensions expressed by "in heaven and on earth" thus progresses and climaxes to the address to God as the recipient of glory to "all" generations in the cosmic temporal dimensions expressed by "for ever and ever."[21]

Paul invites his audience to join him in rendering the "glory" (δόξα) (3:21),[22] that is, the praise and honor, that is reciprocally due to God as the one who gives them power in their inner person as a gift of God's love according to the wealth of his "glory" (δόξης) (3:16) and who gives them as a gift of God's love the Spirit of wisdom and revelation to know what is the wealth of his "glory" (δόξης) as the Father of "glory" (δόξης) (1:17–18). They may now appropriately praise God by attributing to God the "glory" in response to the "glory" God gave them as recipients of God's love in their union with Christ as indicated in the rhythmic refrain—"to the praise of the glory (δόξης) of his grace with which he graced us in the Beloved" (1:6, 12, 14; cf. 3:13).

The giving of glory to God by the audience as those who are "in the church (ἐκκλησίᾳ)" (3:21) is most appropriate for the following reasons: It is "through the church (ἐκκλησίας)" that the manifold wisdom of God may be made known now as a gift of God's love to the rulers and to the authorities in the heavenly places (3:10) for the benefit of those in the church. And it is "to the church (ἐκκλησίᾳ)" that God gave as a gift of God's love Christ as "head" over all things, the Christ who is filling as a gift of the love of Christ

---

20. On the concluding "amen" Jeal (*Ephesians*, 128) states: "The final ἀμήν acts as a closing liturgical and rhetorical feature. It adds a final note of solemnity and confirmation, possibly uttered as suggestive of a congregational response, thereby encouraging acquiescence and participation in the language of worship that precedes." O'Brien, *Ephesians*, 269: "The 'Amen' makes it clear that the ascription of praise is not simply a matter of the lips, but is the spontaneous response of the whole congregation."

21. With regard to the phrase "to all generations for ever and ever," Hoehner (*Ephesians*, 495) points out: "This is a unique ending to a prayer or doxology. Both the terms 'generation' and 'age' are used. It is an apparent mixture of both time and eternity. . . . the generations (τὰς γενεάς) refer to periods of human life which ultimately are terminated and engulfed into the ages (αἰῶνος), periods of the divine economy where generations no longer exist. . . . The repetition of αἰών in both the singular and plural forms may be intended to emphasize longevity or, as in this case, eternity. The preposition εἰς gives the direction of the praise: 'to' or 'throughout' all generations. Therefore, God is to be glorified 'forever and ever' beginning in this age and continuing into eternity." Jeal, *Ephesians*, 128: "[T]he word play between the αἰών forms accentuates the impression of extended time. The precise definition of 'the age of the ages' is immaterial to rhetorical analysis, and may have been of little immediate concern to the speaker/writer and audience. Rather, its relevance is in the impression of the extent of the glory and praise that is offered to God."

22. This is the final and climactic occurrence of the word "glory" (δόξα) in Ephesians.

all things in all ways, so that this church which is his "body" and "fullness" (1:22–23) might be filled to all the "fullness" of God (3:19).[23]

The giving of glory to God by the audience as those who are "in Christ Jesus" (3:21) is most appropriate in light of the following reverberations:[24] It is "in Christ Jesus" that believing Gentiles are fellow heirs and fellow members of the body and fellow sharers of the promise with believing Jews as a gift of God's love (3:6). It is "in Christ Jesus" that "you" Gentiles who were far off have become near as a gift of God's love in the blood of Christ (2:13). It is "in Christ Jesus" that we believers were created as a gift of God's love for good works which God prepared beforehand, that we might walk in them (2:10). As a gift of the great love with which God loved us (2:4), God raised us up with Christ and seated us with him in the heavenly places "in Christ Jesus" (2:6), that he might show in the ages to come the surpassing wealth of his grace in kindness upon us "in Christ Jesus" (2:7). And it is "in Christ Jesus" that Paul's audience are faithful ones, the holy ones in Ephesus (1:1), those among all of us believers whom God chose as a gift of God's love to be holy and blameless before him "in love" (1:4).[25]

With regard to the theme of love, Paul's prayer and concluding doxology in 3:14–21 places the love of God in a cosmic, universal framework. The love that Paul prays that God may give (3:16) to his audience, already rooted and grounded within the dynamic realm of being "in love" (3:17), according to the divine power working in all of us believers (3:20), to interiorly comprehend along with "all" the holy ones what is the cosmic fullness and unity to which they are growing (3:18) and to know the love of Christ by and with which they may be filled to "all" the fullness of God (3:19) comes from God as the cosmic Father of "every" family in heaven and on earth (3:14–15) to whom is due glory in the church and in Christ Jesus to "all" generations for ever and ever (3:21).

---

23. Lincoln, *Ephesians*, 217: "In line with the writer's earlier emphasis on the Church as the sphere of God's presence and rule (e.g., 1:22b, 23; 2:22; 3:10), his doxology sees the Church as the sphere in which God's glory is acknowledged. Glory is ascribed to God in the worship and praise of the redeemed community, but this will be not only in its cultic activity but also in the whole of its existence (cf. 1:6, 12, 14). There is an eschatological aspect to this, for God will only be perfectly glorified in the Church when it fully shares in his glory (cf. 3:13; 5:27)."

24. This is the final and climactic occurrence of the phrase "in Christ Jesus" (ἐν Χριστῷ Ἰησοῦ) in Ephesians.

25. Lincoln, *Ephesians*, 217: "Because believers have been incorporated into Christ, he can be seen as the sphere in which their glorification of God takes place. This is the writer's way of stressing that the Church's ascription of glory to God is dependent on Christ, both as the mediator of God's activity to humanity in the first place and as the mediator of humanity's response of praise to God (cf. also 5:20)."

B. Summary on Ephesians 3:14–21

1. Recalling that God chose us believers in Christ before the foundation of the world that we might be holy and blameless before him within the dynamic realm of being "in love" (1:4), that Paul's audience already have been and still are "rooted and grounded" (perfect passives) "in love" (3:17b) means not only that they have love for all the holy ones (1:15) and have received love from Paul (3:1–13), but that they have received the great love with which God loved us (2:4) in our union with the Beloved (1:6).

2. Paul prays that his audience of Gentile "you" believers, rooted and grounded in love in their union with all the holy ones with whom they form the "body" and "building" of the church, may be given as a gift of God's love the interior strength to comprehend already the immense and absolute vastness of the ultimate destiny of cosmic fullness and unity toward which they are now growing—"what is the breadth and length and height and depth" (3:18).

3. The "love of Christ" (3:19a) that empowers the church as Christ's body to grow to the fullness of cosmic unity recalls for the audience not only the love that Christ gave to the church in unifying Gentiles with Jews in one body (2:14–17), but to the love that Christ, as "head" over all things whom God gave to the church as a gift of love (1:22), is still giving to his body the church as the one who "is filling" all things in all ways so that his body the church can grow into his "fullness" (1:23).

4. That Paul's audience are paradoxically to "know" the love of Christ that "surpasses knowledge" (3:19a) underlines how the knowledge and experience of this love transcends human knowledge and experience so that it can only be given as a gift of God's love.

5. The climactic purpose of Paul's prayer for his audience, as part of the church which is the body and the "fullness" of the Christ who is filling *all* things in *all* ways (1:23), is that they might be filled by and with the love of Christ so as to attain to *all* the "fullness" of God (3:19b), that is, to the complete cosmic fullness and unity to which God has destined the church and which the audience may comprehend interiorly as the absolute "breadth and length and height and depth" (3:18).

6. The love of Christ with and by which believers may be filled to all the fullness of God (3:19b) by the Christ who is filling all things in all ways as "head" over all things whom God gave as a gift of God's love to the church (1:22–23) is empowered by the power that God worked in raising Christ from the dead (1:19–20) and raising us up with him (2:5–6).

7. Paul's prayer and concluding doxology in 3:14–21 places the love of God in a cosmic, universal framework. The love that Paul prays that God may give (3:16) to his audience, already rooted and grounded within the dynamic realm of being "in love" (3:17), to know the love of Christ by and with which they may be filled to "all" the fullness of God (3:19) comes from God as the cosmic Father of "every" family in heaven and on earth (3:14–15) to whom is due glory in the church and in Christ Jesus to "all" generations for ever and ever (3:21).

CHAPTER 10

Ephesians 4:1–16:
To Walk toward the Unity of All in Love (H)

A: ¹ I, then, exhort you, I, the prisoner in the Lord, to walk worthy of the calling with which you were called, ² with all humility and gentleness, with patience, forbearing one another *in love*,

> B: ³ striving to preserve the *unity* of the Spirit in the bond of peace: ⁴ one body and one Spirit, as also you were called in one hope of your calling; ⁵ one Lord, one *faith*, one baptism, ⁶ one God and Father of all, who is over all and through all and in all. ⁷ But to each one of us grace was given according to the *measure* of the gift of the Christ.

>> C: ⁸ Therefore it says, "Having *ascended* on high he captured the captives, he gave gifts to people." ⁹ Now this "he *ascended*," what is it, if not that also he *descended* to the lower parts of the earth?

>> C´: ¹⁰ The one who *descended* is also the one who *ascended* far above all the heavens, that he might fill all things.

> B´: ¹¹ And he gave some as apostles, others as prophets, others as evangelists, others as pastors and teachers, ¹² for the equipping of the holy ones for the work of ministry for building up the body of the Christ, ¹³ until we all attain to the *unity* of the *faith* and of the knowledge of the Son of God, to a mature person, to the *measure* of the stature of the fullness of the Christ, ¹⁴ that we might no longer be infants, tossed by waves and carried about by every wind of teaching in the craftiness of people in deceitfulness toward the scheming of error,

A´: ¹⁵ but rather being truthful *in love*, we might cause all things to grow to him, who is the head, the Christ, ¹⁶ from whom the whole body, fitted together and held together through every supporting connection according to the working in measure of each individual part, brings about the growth of the body for the building up of itself *in love*.[1]

A. Audience Response to Ephesians 4:1–16

1. Eph 4:1–2 (A): Walk Worthy of Your Calling in Love

With an emphatic "I" (ἐγώ) Paul proclaimed to his audience that "I, Paul, am *the* prisoner (ὁ δέσμιος) of the Christ Jesus on behalf of you (ὑμῶν) Gentiles" (3:1b) to express his personal love in enduring prison for the sake of them as Gentile "you" believers. And now, as a consequence of all that he has said in the Letter to this point ("then," οὖν),[2] Paul, again with an emphatic "I," develops the personal love of his being a prisoner on behalf of his audience by exhorting and/or encouraging them: "I, then, exhort you (ὑμᾶς),[3] I (ἐγώ), *the* prisoner (ὁ δέσμιος) in the Lord" (4:1a).[4]

Paul's exhortation "to walk (περιπατῆσαι) worthy of the calling with which you were called" (4:1b) reminds the audience that our "walking" (περιπατήσωμεν) in the good works which God has prepared beforehand for us, who have been created in Christ Jesus (2:10), is a way that we, whom God chose and thus called before the foundation of the world, might be holy

---

1. For the establishment of Eph 4:1–16 as a chiasm, see ch. 2.

2. Hoehner, *Ephesians*, 502: "[T]his conjunction ["then," οὖν in 4:1a] is drawing an inference from all the preceding chapters of Ephesians."

3. On "I exhort" (παρακαλῶ) here Hoehner (*Ephesians*, 503) remarks: "[A]lthough the verb can have more than one English meaning, it seems the context demands the primary idea of exhortation. This conclusion is viable even though Paul is addressing fellow believers because friendship does not exclude authoritative exhortation. In fact, his close relationship to the readers makes the exhortation all the more effective."

4. The translation reflects the fact that the first-person singular pronoun is already given in the ending of the verb, παρακαλῶ, "I exhort," so that the addition of the separate pronoun ἐγώ is emphatic. According to Cassidy (*Paul in Chains*, 98), "Paul is, in effect, holding high 'prisonership' as a startling dimension of his Christian identity." And, according to Cassidy (ibid.), the audience here is "encouraged to embrace Paul's pastoral and ethical instructions out of regard for him as one who renders faithful and self-sacrificing service to Christ as a prisoner." On the phrase "in the Lord" (ἐν κυρίῳ) Hoehner (*Ephesians*, 504) states: "It denotes the sphere or locale, indicating Paul's connection or union with Christ. Hence, the reference to him as a prisoner in 3:1 focuses on both the possessive and causal ideas, for it was the cause of Christ that made him a prisoner, whereas in the present context [4:1], he stresses his union with Christ. This union with Christ resulted in his obedience to the will of God. Consequently, he became a missionary among the Gentiles, including the Ephesians, and was imprisoned for their sake. He now exhorts them likewise to obey their Lord with whom they too have union."

and blameless before God "in love" (1:4)—a way to respond to the great love with which God loved us (2:4).[5]

The use of the divine passive in the expression, the "calling (κλήσεως) with which you were called (ἐκλήθητε)" (4:1b), underlines that this calling is a gift of God's love to the audience.[6] The use of cognate noun and verb in the expression, "calling with which you were called," echoes previous uses of this stylistic device to rhetorically intensify descriptions of God's love for the audience—God's "great love with which he loved us" (2:4) and God's "grace with which he graced us in the Beloved" (1:6). This "calling" reminds the audience of Paul's prayer that they know the hope of God's "calling" (κλήσεως, 1:18), that is, that they may experience the hope that they, living before God in the dynamic realm characterized as "in love" (1:4), will play a role in the plan of God to unite under one head all things in the Christ (1:10). Paul is exhorting his audience to "walk," that is, live lives, "worthy" and thus in accord with this calling.

Paul further describes what it means for his audience to walk worthy of the calling with which they have been called by God's love: "with all humility and gentleness, with patience, forbearing one another in love (ἐν ἀγάπῃ)" (4:2). Reminding his audience that they, already rooted and grounded "in love" (ἐν ἀγάπῃ, 3:17), have been called by God to be holy and blameless before God "in love" (ἐν ἀγάπῃ, 1:4), Paul now develops what it means to live in the dynamic realm of being "in love," that is, in the realm of not only receiving God's love but extending love to others.

Within the realm of being recipients of God's love Paul's audience are to extend love to one another by mutually "forbearing" one another, that is, enduring and tolerating differences among themselves.[7] "With all humility and gentleness, with patience" functions as a rhetorical triplet to intensify the kind of attitudes that are to accompany this forbearing within the realm of being "in love."[8] It is a forbearing in love accompanied by all "humility,"

---

5. O'Brien, *Ephesians*, 275: "Within Ephesians the apostle has already used the language of 'walking' to describe the readers' former lifestyle in sin and death (2:1–2; cf. v. 3) and then, by contrast, in relation to the good works God has prepared for them to walk in (v. 10). Now, at the beginning of the exhortatory material in chapters 4–6, this significant motif appears again, as the readers are admonished to lead a life that is in conformity with the calling they have received, and it continues like a scarlet thread through the next two chapters (4:17; 5:2, 8, 15)."

6. Hoehner, *Ephesians*, 505: "The cognate verb ἐκλήθητε, 'to call,' is passive, indicating that it was God who called them to salvation and to their position in the body of Christ and their union with Christ."

7. Hoehner, *Ephesians*, 509: "Paul asks them to bear with those in the assembly. Thus, to translate this word 'forbear' is appropriate. . . . In other words, differences between believers are to be tolerated."

8. On "with" (μετά) as expressing attendant circumstances here, see BDAG, 637. Walter Radl, "μετά," *EDNT* 2.413: "Μετά can also designate the accompanying circumstances

that is, "in selflessness and renunciation of any will to rule, or (positively) in goodness and with understanding."[9] It is a forbearing in love accompanied by all "gentleness," implying "the conscious exercise of self-control, exhibiting a conscious choice of gentleness as opposed to the use of power for the purpose of retaliation."[10] And it is a forbearing in love accompanied by "patience" (literally, "long temper" as opposed to a short temper), that is, "the ability to make allowances for others' shortcomings" and the "tolerance of others' exasperating behavior."[11]

2. Eph 4:3–7 (B): To Each of Us Grace Was Given as a Gift of God's Love

The audience are to walk worthy of the calling with which they have been called as a gift of God's love not only by forbearing one another with all humility and gentleness and with patience "in love" (4:1–2), but by "striving to preserve the unity (ἑνότητα) of the Spirit (πνεύματος) in the bond of peace (εἰρήνης)" (4:3).[12] This reminds the audience of the unity and peace that are gifts of Christ's love. Indeed, Christ himself is our "peace" (εἰρήνη), who made the both—believing Jews and Gentiles—"one" (ἕν), that the two he might create in himself into "one" (ἕνα) new person making "peace" (εἰρήνην), and that he might reconcile the both in "one" (ἑνί) body. He preached "peace" (εἰρήνην) to you who are far away and "peace" (εἰρήνην) to those who are near, so that through Christ, as a gift of his love,

---

within which something takes place. Here belong esp. spiritual and bodily conditions." Hoehner, *Ephesians*, 507: "The adjective πάσης, 'all,' modifies both humility and gentleness. When this adjective is used with anarthrous singular nouns it can denote the highest degree, 'full, greatest, all.'"

9. According to Heinz Giesen ("ταπεινοφροσύνη," *EDNT* 3.334) in reference to the same expression used by Paul in Acts 20:19.

10. Hoehner, *Ephesians*, 507; see also Hubert Frankemölle, "πραΰτης," *EDNT* 3.146–47. BDAG, 861: It refers to "the quality of not being overly impressed by a sense of one's self-importance."

11. Lincoln, *Ephesians*, 236; see also Harm W. Hollander, "μακροθυμία," *EDNT* 2.380–81. BDAG, 612: It refers to the "state of being able to bear up under provocation." Hoehner, *Ephesians*, 508: "A walk worthy of their call demands humility, gentleness, and patience. In other words, these words do not describe an automatic response but one that demands conscious effort on the part of the believer who relies on the Spirit."

12. On 4:3 Lincoln (*Ephesians*, 237) points out: "This clause is parallel to the previous one in that it too begins with a participle and ends with a prepositional phrase with ἐν." See also Hoehner, *Ephesians*, 510; O'Brien, *Ephesians*, 279 n. 26. On the participle "striving" (σπουδάζοντες) here, O'Brien (*Ephesians*, 279) remarks: "Paul's appeal is urgent and cannot be easily translated into English. The verb he uses has an element of haste, urgency, or even a sense of crisis to it." On the word play between Paul as the prisoner or the one who is "bound" (ὁ δέσμιος, 4:1; 3:1) and the bond or "binding together" (συνδέσμῳ) of peace (4:3), Hoehner (*Ephesians*, 512) comments: "Paul chained as a prisoner of the Lord (3:1; 4:1) speaks of the binding or chaining together of peace. . . . It is better to consider ἐν as denoting the place or sphere in which the unity of the Spirit is to be preserved and manifested, namely, in the bond of peace."

we both have the access in "one" (ἑνί) "Spirit" (πνεύματι) before the Father (2:14–18).

With regard to the love theme, forbearing one another within the dynamic realm of being "in love" (4:2) is the way Paul's audience can preserve, maintain, and protect the unity and peace they have already been given as a gift of Christ's love within the dynamic realm of being "in love" (4:3).[13]

A sevenfold use of "one" elaborates the elements that effectively emphasize this unity as a gift of Christ's and/or God's love for the audience. The list begins with "one body" (ἓν σῶμα, 4:4a), recalling for the audience that as Gentile believers they are united with Jewish believers as "fellow members of the body" (σύσσωμα, 3:6), the "one body" (ἑνὶ σώματι) in which Christ reconciled Gentile and Jewish believers to God (2:16), the "body" (σῶμα) of Christ which is the church, the fullness of the Christ who is filling all things in all ways through his love (1:22–23).

Reinforcing the "unity of the Spirit" (ἑνότητα τοῦ πνεύματος, 4:3), the list continues with "one Spirit" (ἓν πνεῦμα, 4:4b), reminding the audience that through Christ we believers—both Jewish and Gentile—have received, as a gift of love, the access in "one Spirit" (ἑνὶ πνεύματι) before the Father (2:18). Paul's audience are thus to realize that the Holy "Spirit" (πνεύματι) with which they were sealed when they became believers (1:13) is a gift of God's love shared by all other believers—there is only "one" Spirit (cf. 1:17; 2:22; 3:5, 16).

Reinforcing and developing Paul's exhortation for his audience to walk worthy of "the calling (κλήσεως) with which you were called (ἐκλήθητε)" (4:1), the list continues with another reference to "one"—"as also you were called (ἐκλήθητε) in one hope of your calling (κλήσεως)" (4:4c). With its emphasis on "one hope" (μιᾷ ἐλπίδι) this clause again, but now even more pointedly than in 4:1, reminds the audience, who from the Jewish perspective were once considered to be without "hope" (ἐλπίδα, 2:12), of Paul's prayer that they know what is the "hope" (ἐλπίς) of his (God's) "calling" (κλήσεως) (1:18),[14] that is, that God before the foundation of the world has chosen and thus called them together with all other believers for the hope of being holy and blameless before God within the dynamic realm of being "in love" (1:4),[15] the hope that they together with all other things in the cosmos

---

13. Fee, *God's Empowering Presence*, 701 n. 142: "Peace is not the 'means' to unity, but its primary evidence. . . . love is the means, and peace is the end result." Dawes, *Body*, 176: "This is the first hint in Ephesians that Christians may have a role to play in the maintenance of that unity which has been (already) achieved by Christ (cf. 2:14–18)."

14. Lincoln, *Ephesians*, 238: "The hope of his calling earlier in the letter in 1:18 is a reference to the same reality as the hope of your calling here. It is simply that the former describes it in terms of the one who calls; the latter, in terms of those who are called."

15. O'Brien, *Ephesians*, 282: "God's calling finds its origin in the choice of his people in Christ before the world's foundation (Eph. 1:4)."

will be united under one head in Christ (1:10). Paul's audience are to realize that they share this "one hope" in which they were called as a gift of God's love (divine passive) with all other believers.[16]

Continuing the list of references to "one" as an elaboration of the unity the audience have as a gift of the love of Christ and/or God, "one Lord" (εἷς κύριος, 4:5a)—in reference to the one Lord Jesus Christ (1:2, 3, 15, 17; 3:11)—reminds the audience that with all other believers they share in the love the "one" Lord extended to them in making both Jewish and Gentile believers "one" (ἕν) (2:14) that the two he might create in himself into "one" (ἕνα) new person (2:15), the "building" that, with Christ Jesus (the Lord) himself as the "head stone," is growing into a temple holy in the Lord (κυρίῳ) (2:20–21). The audience are to realize that with all other believers they are under the lordship of the one Lord Jesus Christ, the "head" over all things that God gave as a gift of God's love to the church (1:22), his "body" and the "fullness" that is being filled in all ways (1:23) to the "fullness" of God through the love of Christ (3:19).[17]

Next in the list of references to "one"—"one faith" (μία πίστις, 4:5b)—reminds the audience, who have "faith" (πίστιν) in the Lord Jesus (1:15), that it is through this one "faith" (πίστεως) that they have been saved as a gift of God's love (2:8), that it is through this one "faith" (πίστεως) that they, along with believing Jews, have, as a gift of God's love, access before the Father (2:18; 3:12), and that it is through this one "faith" (πίστεως) that Christ may dwell in their hearts as a gift of God's love so that they may know the love of Christ that surpasses knowledge (3:16–19). The next reference to "one"—"one baptism" (ἓν βάπτισμα, 4:5c)—complements "one Lord" and "one faith" as a triad:[18] It is in the one baptism that the audience share with all other believers the confession of their one faith in the one Lord.[19]

---

16. Hoehner, *Ephesians*, 515: "Hope for believers is not the world's 'hope so' but the absolute certainty that God will deliver what he has promised. In this context the emphasis is on objective hope."

17. O'Brien, *Ephesians*, 283: "Already in Ephesians, where there are some twenty references to Jesus as Lord, the apostle has spoken of the Lord Jesus Christ as the one in whom every spiritual blessing comes (1:3; cf. v. 2), as the sphere in which faith is exercised (1:15), and as the one in whom God's new creation, the holy temple, is growing (2:21). God's eternal purpose has been accomplished in Christ Jesus, our Lord, while Paul exhorts the readers as one who is a 'prisoner in the Lord' (4:1). Jesus is the Lord who fills the universe with his sovereign rule (1:23; cf. 4:10), and who as head has been given to the church (1:23; cf. 4:15, 16)." Hoehner, *Ephesians*, 516: "Christ is the 'one Lord' who provided redemption (1:7), hope (1:12), and headship over the church (1:22–23). Indeed, it was Christ who brought the Jews and Gentiles into one body, both now having access to God (2:13–18; 3:6, 12)."

18. Lincoln, *Ephesians*, 239: "In the Greek there is a striking change from the masculine to the feminine to the neuter of the numeral one, which gives the whole triad a ringing quality."

19. Hoehner, *Ephesians*, 518: "[T]he 'one baptism' most likely refers to the internal reality of having been baptized into (identified with) the 'one Lord' by means of the 'one faith'

The audience then hear the seventh and climactic reference to "one" as an elaboration of the unity of the Spirit (4:3)—"one God and Father of all, who is over all and through all and in all" (4:6). Recalling Paul's prayer to God as the "Father" (πατέρα) from whom "every" (πᾶσα) family in heaven and on earth is named (3:14–15; cf. 1:2, 3, 17: 2:18), this reference to the one God and "Father" (πατήρ) of "all" (πάντων) things in the cosmos makes the audience aware that the "one" God is the ultimate origin of the unity they share with all other believers as a gift of God's love.[20] That this one God and Father of "all" (πάντων) is sovereignly *over* "all" (πάντων) and dynamically at work *through* "all" (πάντων) and immanently *in* "all" (πάντων) recalls that God is the One at work in "all things" (τὰ πάντα, 1:11) to unite under one head "all things" (τὰ πάντα) in the Christ, the things in the heavens and the things on earth (1:10). The audience are to realize, then, that this cosmic unity is the ultimate destiny of the unity of the Spirit that they share with all other believers as a gift of God's love.[21]

After the sevenfold reference to "one" (4:4–6) as an elaboration of the unity of the Spirit (4:3) the audience hear yet another "one" in reference to each individual that is part of this unity: "But (δέ) to each one (ἑνί) of us grace was given according to the measure of the gift of the Christ" (4:7). With emphasis upon the "one," Paul focuses upon each individual believer as part of "us" (ἡμῶν) believers, thus furthering his assimilation of his audience of "you" (ὑμᾶς, 4:1; ὑμῶν, 4:4) believers with Paul himself as well as with all of us believers.[22]

---

mentioned in this verse." Lincoln, *Ephesians*, 240: "The 'one baptism' is water baptism, the public rite of confession of the one faith in the one Lord. This baptism is one, not because it has a single form or is administered on only one occasion, but because it is the initiation into Christ, into the one body, which all have undergone and as such is a unifying factor."

20. We take πάντων in 4:6 as neuter with reference to "all things" rather than as masculine with reference to "all people" in accord with O'Brien, *Ephesians*, 285: "[A] cosmic understanding of 'all' makes good sense in this context. First, at significant points in Ephesians where the sovereignty of God and Christ are in view, 'all' denotes the whole universe (1:10, 11, 22, 23; 3:9; cf. 4:10). Secondly, in similar (confessional?) formulae within Paul's letters (1 Cor. 8:6; Rom. 11:36; Col. 1:16) where different prepositions (e.g., 'from', 'into', 'in', 'through') are skilfully linked together in order to qualify God's or Christ's relationship to 'all', the word regularly signifies 'everything', not just persons or even believers." See also Lincoln, *Ephesians*, 240.

21. O'Brien, *Ephesians*, 285: "Paul is affirming that God is supremely transcendent 'over everything' and that his immanence is all-pervasive: he works 'through all and in all'. . . . God's universal sovereignty and presence are set forth as the climactic ground for the unity of the Spirit that believers are to maintain. His universal rule is being exercised to fulfil his ultimate purpose of unifying all things in Christ."

22. Best, *Ephesians*, 376: "δέ signals a change of subject and ἑνί picks up the use of 'one' in vv. 4–6, perhaps making the appeal to individual believers a little more emphatic, since ἑκάστῳ by itself would have conveyed what is needed." Lincoln, *Ephesians*, 241: "Whereas 'one' had been used in vv 4–6 to signify unity, now it is employed to refer to the individuals

That to each one of us grace was given according to the measure, that is, according to the full measure or in proportion with,[23] the "gift of the Christ" (δωρεᾶς τοῦ Χριστοῦ, 4:7) makes each member of Paul's audience aware that they have individually been recipients of the "love of the Christ" (ἀγάπην τοῦ Χριστοῦ) that surpasses knowledge and by which they may be "filled" to all the "fullness" of God (3:19) by the Christ who is "filling" the church, his body and "fullness," with all things in all ways (1:22–23).

The audience realize that just as Paul became a minister of the gospel according to the "gift" (δωρεάν) of the "grace" (χάριτος) of God that was "given" (δοθείσης) to him, this "grace" (χάρις) that was "given" (ἐδόθη) to him as the least of all the holy ones (3:7–8), so also to each one of them as individuals "grace" (χάρις) was "given" (ἐδόθη) according to the measure of the "gift" (δωρεᾶς) of the Christ (4:7). Just as to Paul the "grace" (χάριτος) of God was "given" (δοθείσης) as a gift of God's love to be shared with his audience ("for you") (3:2), so it is implied that each individual believer to whom grace has been given as a gift of Christ's love is to share that love with others as a way to preserve the unity of the Spirit (4:3) which they have received as a gift of God's love.[24]

3. Eph 4:8–9 (C): The Ascended Christ Gave Gifts of Love to People

Introducing an adaptation of Ps 68:18 with "therefore it says" (διὸ λέγει), Paul reinforces and develops for his audience what he has just said about grace being given to each one of us believers according to the measure of the gift of love of the Christ (4:7), as he endows it with divine scriptural authority: "Having ascended on high he captured the captives, he gave gifts to people" (4:8).[25] In 1:19–22a Christ was the recipient of God's powerful

---

who make up that unity." Hoehner, *Ephesians*, 522: "Every single believer (changed from 'you' in vv. 1 and 4 to 'us') is included, no one is excluded, it is not only for the leaders of the assembly." See also Christfried Böttrich, "Gemeinde und Gemeindeleitung nach Epheser 4," *TBei* 30 (1999): 138–40; Peter W. Gosnell, "Networks and Exchanges: Ephesians 4:7–16 and the Community Function of Teachers," *BTB* 30 (2000): 135–43.

23. According to Best (*Ephesians*, 377) "measure" (μέτρον) here "has probably the sense of 'full measure'. The giving is not random but in accordance with Christ's plan; he apportions gifts to believers."

24. O'Brien, *Ephesians*, 288: "So grace was given to the apostle Paul for his ministry to Gentiles (cf. 3:2, 7, 8); now it is said to be given to each individual Christian for the benefit of the whole body."

25. O'Brien, *Ephesians*, 288: "This bestowal of gifts by the ascended Christ is now confirmed by the application of an important Old Testament text—Psalm 68:18. The quotation is introduced by the formula, 'therefore it says' (cf. Eph. 5:14), which probably implies 'Scripture says', although for the apostle 'Scripture says', 'God says', and 'David says' are simply different ways of expressing the same thing: the words quoted are God's and come with his authority." For discussions and various interpretations of this adaptation of Ps 68:18, see Richard A. Taylor, "The Use of Psalm 68:18 in Ephesians 4:8 in Light of the Ancient Versions," *BSac* 148 (1991): 319–36; W. Hall Harris, *The Descent of Christ:*

love as God raised him from the dead and seated him at his right hand in the heavenly places "far above every ruler and authority and power and dominion and every name that is named, not only in this age but also in the one to come, and all things he subjected under his feet." But now the quotation expresses that same cosmic domination but with Christ, God's agent, as the acting subject—"having ascended on high he captured the captives."[26] Whereas God "gave" (ἔδωκεν) Christ as head over all things to the church as a gift of God's love (1:22b), now that exalted Christ himself "gave" (ἔδωκεν) gifts of love to people.[27]

Paul's rhetorical question to explain the quotation (4:8), "Now this 'he ascended,' what is it, if not that also he descended to the lower parts of the earth?" (4:9),[28] reinforces for the audience that it was only after Christ descended in death and burial to the "lower" (κατώτερα) parts of the earth that he ascended on "high" (ὕψος) via God's raising him from the dead. The Christ who received God's love in being raised from the dead (1:20) after descending to the lower parts of the earth in death and burial is the Christ who ascended on high so that he is in an exalted position of extending the divine love he received to others, as he "gave gifts to people."[29]

Ephesians 4:7–11 and Traditional Hebrew Imagery (AGJU 32; Leiden: Brill, 1996); Richard Dormandy, "The Ascended Christ and His Gifts," *ExpTim* 109 (1998): 206–7; J. F. Brug, "Psalm 68:19—He Received Gifts among Men," *Wisconsin Lutheran Quarterly* 96 (1999): 122–26; Timothy G. Gombis, "Cosmic Lordship and Divine Gift-Giving: Psalm 68 in Ephesians 4:8," *NovT* 47 (2005): 367–80; Moritz, *Profound Mystery*, 56–86; Schwindt, *Weltbild*, 399–430; O'Brien, *Ephesians*, 288–93; Hoehner, *Ephesians*, 524–30. As Hoehner (*Ephesians*, 528) concludes: "Regardless of the interpretation one prefers, it must be acknowledged that Ps 68:18 has been changed by Paul to make it applicable to the present Ephesian context. He declares that the gifts to which he refers are of a spiritual nature and are given to the believers in the Ephesian assembly and by application, to the believers down through the ages."

26. Arnold, *Ephesians*, 56–58: "In light of the reference to Christ subjugating the 'powers,' his enemies, in 1:20ff., it would be natural to assume that these are the captives the author has in mind when he cites Eph 4:8.... He has successfully triumphed over the demonic forces and they are his prisoners.... Eph 4:8–10 should therefore be seen as providing supplementary evidence to Eph 1:19ff. to establish Christ's supremacy over all the 'powers' of evil in addition to its function of introducing Christ's gifts to the church."

27. That 4:8 employs the next occurrence of the third-person singular indicative aorist of the verb "gave" (ἔδωκεν) after its only other prior occurrence in Ephesians at 1:22 enhances the significance of this development (cf. 4:11).

28. For the inclusion of "parts" (μέρη) as the original reading, see Hoehner, *Ephesians*, 533 n. 3.

29. For the suggestion that Christ's descent in 4:9 is a veiled reference to the Plutonium of Hierapolis (near Ephesus) as a passageway to the underworld, see Larry Joseph Kreitzer, "The Plutonium of Hierapolis and the Descent of Christ Into the 'Lowermost Parts of the Earth' (Ephesians 4,9)," *Bib* 79 (1998): 381–93. And for a critique of this suggestion as unconvincing, see Hoehner, *Ephesians*, 533–34 n. 7. For the interpretation of Christ's descent in 4:9–10 as the Pentecostal descent of the Spirit after Christ's ascension, see especially

4. Eph 4:10 (C′): Christ Ascended Above All the Heavens To Fill All Things

With the C and C′ elements the audience hear the center of the chiasm in 4:1–16, which pivots around the terms "ascend" and "descend." In the C element the Christ who "ascended" (ἀναβάς) on high captured the captives and gave gifts to people after he "descended" (κατέβη) to the lower parts of the earth (4:8–9). The C′ element emphasizes that the Christ "who descended (καταβάς) is the same one who ascended (ἀναβάς) far above all the heavens, that he might fill all things" (4:10).[30] At this pivotal center of the chiasm the audience experience a progression from the Christ who ascended "on high" in the C element (4:8) to the Christ who ascended "far above (ὑπεράνω) all the heavens" in the C′ element (4:10), recalling that God seated the risen Christ at his right hand in the heavenly places "far above" (ὑπεράνω) every ruler and authority and power and dominion and every name that is named, not only in this age but also in the one to come (1:20–21).[31]

And the ascended Christ who "gave gifts to people" (4:8) progresses to the ascension of Christ "that he might fill all things" (4:10). That Christ "might fill" (πληρώσῃ) "all things" (τὰ πάντα) recalls Paul's prayer that his audience "might be filled" (πληρωθῆτε) to all the fullness of God by the love of the Christ (3:19) who "is filling" (πληρουμένου) "all things" (τὰ πάντα) in all ways (1:23). The audience are thus to realize that the gifts of love that the ascended Christ gave to people (4:8), to each one of us believers (4:7), are part of the love of the Christ who is filling "all things" (τὰ πάντα) in all ways as part of God's plan to unite "all things" (τὰ πάντα) under one head in the Christ as the ultimate gift of God's love (1:10).

W. Hall Harris, "The Ascent and Descent of Christ in Ephesians 4:9–10," *BSac* 151 (1994): 198–214; idem, *Descent of Christ*. For the refutation of this view, see Hoehner, *Ephesians*, 531–33. In preference for the view that Christ's descent in 4:9 refers to his death and burial rather than to his incarnation or descent into Hades, Hoehner (*Ephesians*, 536–36) points out: "[T]here is a parallel between this verse and 1:20 in that the death of Christ (1:20; 2:16; 5:2, 25) is connected with his resurrection (1:20–23; 2:5) and not with his incarnation or to a descent into Hades." And note that "to the lower parts of the earth" (εἰς τὰ κατώτερα μέρη τῆς γῆς) in Eph 4:9 resembles "to the depths of the earth" (εἰς τὰ κατώτατα τῆς γῆς) in LXX Ps 62:10 as a reference to the grave.

30. Hoehner, *Ephesians*, 536: "The use of the participle ὁ καταβάς, 'he who descended,' is emphatic by its position and it relates back to the finite verb κατέβη, 'he descended,' in the previous verse. The personal pronoun with the verb 'to be' and the conjunction (αὐτός ἐστιν καί) that is used adjunctively further stresses the emphasis and can be translated 'he precisely is also' or 'is himself also.' . . . With this emphasis, Paul stresses that the very person who descended is the one who ascended. The order is first descent and then ascent."

31. That the preposition "far above" (ὑπεράνω) occurs only in 1:21 and 4:10 within Ephesians enhances this connection. According to O'Brien (*Ephesians*, 296) "all the heavens" in 4:10 "is best understood as a metaphorical reference to the powers of 1:21 who have been subjugated to him."

5. Eph 4:11–14 (B´): The Unity of the Faith and the Maturity of Christ

With the B´ element (4:11–14) the audience hear a progression, via the chiastic parallelism, of the B element (4:3–7) regarding the terms "unity," "faith," and "measure." The "unity" (ἑνότητα) of the Spirit (4:3), further elaborated as one "faith" (πίστις), that Paul exhorts his audience to preserve as a gift of God's love in the B element by loving one another (4:2) progresses to the "unity" (ἑνότητα) of the "faith" (πίστεως) that all of us believers are still to attain (4:13) by the gifts of love that the ascended Christ gave for the building up of the body of the Christ (4:11–12) in the B´ element. And the "measure" (μέτρον) of the gift of the Christ according to which each one of us believers has been given grace (4:7) as a gift of Christ's love in the B element progresses to the "measure" (μέτρον) of the stature of the fullness of the Christ that all of us believers are still to attain (4:13) by the gifts of love that the ascended Christ gave for the building up of the body of the Christ (4:11–12) in the B´ element.

That "he" (αὐτός, 4:11), that is, "he himself" (αὐτός, 4:10), the Christ who not only descended but ascended far above all the heavens, that he might fill all things (4:10),[32] "gave (ἔδωκεν) some as apostles, others as prophets, others as evangelists, others as pastors and teachers" (4:11) develops for the audience the gifts that the ascended Christ "gave" (ἔδωκεν) to people (4:8), as the scriptural basis for the grace that was "given" (ἐδόθη) to each one of us believers according to the measure of the gift of the Christ (4:7). The ascended Christ not only gave gifts of love to people, but gave gifted people as gifts of love to people, that is, to each and all of us believers in the church.[33]

Reminding the audience that the mystery of the Christ has now been revealed as a gift of God's love (divine passive) to the holy "apostles" (ἀπόστολοι) and "prophets" (προφῆται) in the Spirit (3:4–5), that the ascended Christ gave some as "apostles" (ἀποστόλους) and others as "prophets" (προφήτας) (4:11) further develops the love theme in Ephesians. It implies that the gift of God's love that the apostles and prophets have received they are in turn to share with their fellow believers, since not only the gift they

---

32. On Eph 4:11 Hoehner (*Ephesians*, 541) states: "The personal pronoun αὐτός, 'he,' is emphatic, linking it with the αὐτός of the previous verse and showing that 'he' who descended and ascended is also 'he' who gave gifts."

33. Hoehner, *Ephesians*, 541: "In verse 7 he [Paul] mentions that a gift is given to each, but in verse 11 he refers to the giving of a gifted person. There is no contradiction here because the person who receives a gift is a gifted person." Lincoln, *Ephesians*, 249: "In relation to vv 7, 8b, he [Christ] gives not just grace to people, but he gives specific people to people." O'Brien, *Ephesians*, 297: "[H]ere the gifts are the persons themselves, 'given' by the ascended Christ to his people to enable them to function and develop as they should. Christ supplies the church with gifted ministers."

have received but they themselves have been given as gifts of love from the ascended Christ for the benefit of each and every one of us believers (4:7).

That the ascended Christ gave some as "apostles" (ἀποστόλους) and others as "prophets" (προφήτας) as gifts of his love (4:11) to believers reinforces for the audience that, as part of the "building" which is the body of Christ, they have been "built" (divine passive) upon the foundation of the "apostles" (ἀποστόλων) and "prophets" (προφητῶν) as a gift of divine love (2:20). And that the ascended Christ gave not only apostles and prophets but also evangelists, pastors and teachers broadens and strengthens this "foundation" of divine love for believers.[34] Indeed, that these gifted leaders, as the "foundation" of the "building," are to share their gifts and themselves, as gifts of divine love, with their fellow believers is confirmed as the audience hear that the ascended Christ gave them "for the equipping of the holy ones for the work of ministry for building up the body of the Christ" (4:12).[35]

In 1:15 Paul affirmed his audience's love for all the "holy ones" (ἁγίους). Now Paul makes his audience aware that, as "holy ones" (ἁγίοις) themselves (1:1), they, along with all of us believers (4:7), who are "holy ones" (1:18; 2:19; 3:8, 18), are recipients of love from the gifted "holy ones" (cf.

---

34. For discussions of the differing but somewhat overlapping roles of these gifted individuals who are given by the ascended Christ as foundational leaders for the church, see Fee, *God's Empowering Presence*, 705–8; Lincoln, *Ephesians*, 249–53; O'Brien, *Ephesians*, 297–301; Hoehner, *Ephesians*, 541–47.

35. Some scholars have suggested a different interpretation and translation of Eph 4:12, which views the three prepositional phrases as coordinate and thus expressing three different purposes for the giving of the gifted persons in 4:11: "for the completion/maturity of the holy ones, for the work of ministry, for building up the body of the Christ." For the various aspects and discussions of this view, see T. David Gordon, " 'Equipping' Ministry in Ephesians 4?" *JETS* 37 (1994): 69–78; John Jefferson Davis, "Ephesians 4:12 Once More: Equipping the Saints for the Work of Ministry?" *Evangelical Review of Theology* 24 (2000): 167–76; John C. O'Neill, " 'The Work of the Ministry' in Ephesians 4:12 and the New Testament," *ExpTim* 112 (2001): 336–40; Sydney H. T. Page, "Whose Ministry? A Re-appraisal of Ephesians 4:12," *NovT* 47 (2005): 26–46. For arguments refuting this interpretation in favor of the interpretation that we are adopting, which views the three prepositional phrases not as coordinate but as consequential to one another, see Markus Barth, *Ephesians: Translation and Commentary on Chapters 4–6* (AB 34A; New York: Doubleday, 1974), 478–81; O'Brien, *Ephesians*, 301–5; Hoehner, *Ephesians*, 548–49: "[T]he first preposition (πρός) gives the purpose to the main verb ἔδωκεν (v. 11), the second preposition (εἰς) depends on the first preposition, and the third preposition (εἰς) depends on the second preposition. It is suggested that the commas between the prepositional phrases be omitted. . . . it seems that the first preposition (πρός) expresses the immediate purpose while the other two prepositions (εἰς) denote direction or goal. The progression indicates, therefore, that he gave gifted people for the immediate purpose of preparing all the saints with the goal of preparing them for the work of the ministry, which in turn has the final goal of building up the body of Christ."

"holy [ἁγίοις] apostles and prophets in 3:5) whom the ascended Christ gave "for the equipping of the holy ones (ἁγίων)" (4:12a).[36]

This equipping of the holy ones is "for the work (ἔργον) of ministry" (4:12b), one of the good "works" (ἔργοις) which God has prepared beforehand for us believers, who have been saved by grace (2:8) as a gift of the great love with which God loved us (2:4), that we should walk in them (2:10). That the holy ones are equipped for the work of "ministry" (διακονίας) as a gift of Christ's love reminds the audience that Paul became (divine passive) a "minister" (διάκονος) of the gospel as a gift of God's love (3:7). Just as Paul shared the gift of divine love he received to be a minister or servant with the Gentiles (3:8), and just as the gifted persons (4:11) are given by Christ to share with the holy ones the gifts of love Christ has given them (4:12a), so, it is implied, the audience are to share with fellow believers, fellow holy ones, the gifts of love the ascended Christ has given to each of them (4:7) for the work of ministry.

The equipping of the holy ones for the work of ministry has as a further goal "the building (οἰκοδομήν) up of the body of the Christ" (4:12c). Whereas in union with Christ the whole "building" (οἰκοδομή) of believers that is growing into a temple holy in the Lord is doing so by being fitted together (divine passive) as a gift of God's love (2:21), now the audience are to realize that it is by the gift of Christ's love given to each believer (4:7-8, 11) and which they are to share with fellow believers in the work of ministry for which they have been equipped as a gift of Christ's love (4:11-12) that they have a role to play in the growth of the temple holy in the Lord, in the building up of the body of the Christ. The audience are to realize, then, that the equipping of the holy ones for the work of ministry for the building up of the "body" (σώματος) of Christ, the *one* "body" (2:16; 4:4) that unites all believers, is a result of the love that the church, the "body" (σῶμα) of Christ, is receiving from the ascended Christ who is filling all things in all ways (1:22-23).

This building up of the body of Christ by the gifts of love given to it by the ascended Christ (4:11-12) is to continue "until we all attain to the unity of the faith and of the knowledge of the Son of God" (4:13a).[37] Although all of us believers have been given the "unity" of the Spirit as a gift of God's love to be maintained (4:3) by loving one another (4:2), there is still a further "unity" of the faith and of the knowledge of the Son of God that all believers together are to attain by loving one another through sharing with

---

36. On the meaning of καταρτισμόν as the "equipping" or "preparation" of the holy ones here, see *EDNT* 2.268; BDAG, 526.

37. Lincoln, *Ephesians*, 255: "μέχρι, 'until,' has both a prospective and a final force. The ministers are to carry out their task both until the whole Church reaches this goal and in order that it might reach this goal."

them the gifts of love given us by the ascended Christ. Extending to one another the gifts of love we have received from the ascended Christ unites us
in the experiential knowledge of the Son of God as the Beloved (1:6) of the
Father, the one who extends to us the love he received from the Father as the
love of the Christ that surpasses knowledge (3:19).[38]

Until we all attain to the unity of the faith and the knowledge of the
Son of God is further explained as attaining "to a mature person" (4:13b).
We believers whom Christ has created into "one new person (ἄνθρωπον)"
out of believing Jews and Gentiles (2:15) and brought into one body (2:16)
are thus to become one corporate "mature person (ἄνδρα)" by loving one
another with the gifts of love we have received from the ascended Christ
(4:7, 11–12).[39]

And attaining to a mature person is further explained as attaining "to
the measure of the stature of the fullness of the Christ" (4:13c). We believers
are thus to use the "measure" of the gift of the Christ according to which
each of us has been given grace (4:7) by loving one another with those gifts
of grace in order that we may attain to the "measure" of the bodily stature
of the fullness of the Christ. We believers, the church which is the body of
Christ, the "fullness" (πλήρωμα) of the Christ who is filling all things in all
ways (1:22–23), are to love one another (4:2) with the gifts of love given us
by the ascended Christ to build up the body of the Christ (4:11–12) until
we attain to the ultimate goal of that "fullness" that we already are, that
is, the full measure of the bodily stature of the "fullness" (πληρώματος) of
the Christ (4:13c).[40] Then will be answered Paul's prayer that his audience

---

38. As Hoehner (*Ephesians*, 554) points out, this "is the only place in Ephesians where
Christ is called Son of God. In 1:17 the emphasis was on knowing God and here it is on
knowing his Son, Jesus Christ. The emphasis has changed because of the subject of the context, that is, Christ's bestowal of gifts (v. 7) and gifted persons (v. 11) to the church so that
it may be built up not only in the unity of the faith but also in the unity of the knowledge
of him."

39. Lincoln, *Ephesians*, 256: "τέλειος has the nuance of mature rather than perfect,
while ἀνήρ denotes here an adult male, a full-grown man. The emphasis is on the mature
adulthood of this person in contrast with the children to be mentioned in the next verse. The
Church, which has already been depicted as one new person (ἄνθρωπος) in Christ (2:15), is
to attain to what in principle it already has in him—maturity and completeness." Hoehner,
Ephesians, 555–56: "The singular form 'mature person' points to a body of believers, not to
individual believers in the body since the context refers to all believers in the body of Christ."
See also Lilly Nortjé, "The Meaning of ἄνδρα τέλειον in Ephesians 4:13: A Full-Grown Person, as Perfect and Mature as Christ," *Ekklesiastikos Pharos* 77 (1995): 57–63.

40. On the word translated as bodily "stature" (ἡλικίας), Lincoln (*Ephesians*, 257)
notes: "There is some debate about whether to take ἡλικία as a reference to age or to bodily
size, as it can denote either aspect of matured growth. Since the context contains the contrast between children and adults, some interpret it in terms of age as a further part of this
contrast and as an explanation of what was meant by the 'mature person.' It seems prefer-
able, however, to treat this third depiction as introducing a new image of completion and to

be filled to all the "fullness" (πλήρωμα) of God by the love of the Christ (3:19).

We believers are to attain to the full measure of the bodily stature of the fullness of the Christ as one mature, adult person (4:13), "that we might no longer be infants, tossed by waves and carried about by every wind of teaching in the craftiness of people in deceitfulness toward the scheming of error" (4:14).[41] We are to be *one* unified mature person (singular) rather than individuals disunited as immature infants (plural).[42] By forbearing one another within the dynamic realm of being "in love" (4:2), that is, within the realm in which we have received gifts of love from the ascended Christ to share as gifts of love to one another (4:7–12), we will remain "rooted and grounded in love" (3:17b) on our way to the unity of the faith (4:13) rather than "tossed by waves and carried about" in disunity, immaturity, and instability by various erroneous teachings.[43]

To sum up, in 4:11–14 Paul informs his audience that the ascended Christ has given gifts of gifted believers as gifts of love (4:11) to equip their fellow believers in turn to share their gifts of love (4:7) with one another to build up the body of Christ (4:12), until all of us believers together attain to the unified, mature, and complete bodily stature of the fullness of the body of the Christ (4:13), so that we are no longer disunited, immature, and unstable infants tossed and carried about by erroneous teachings (4:14) but

---

recognize that πλήρωμα, 'fullness,' more naturally has spatial connotations, so that 'stature' is probably the more appropriate interpretation. The standard for believers' attainment is the mature proportions that befit the Church as the fullness of Christ. Again, we should recall that this is a continuation of the discussion of Christ's gifts and that it is through his gifts of ministers that Christ enables the Church to attain to the complete realization of what it already is." See also O'Brien, *Ephesians*, 307–8. Although Eph 1:10 refers to the "fullness" (πληρώματος) of the times," so that "fullness" has a temporal aspect in that context, in the context of 4:13 in which "fullness" refers to the body of Christ (4:12; 1:23), it has a bodily aspect.

41. Hoehner, *Ephesians*, 562, 564: "As in verse 12, here we have three prepositional phrases with one of the prepositions different from the other two (ἐν . . . ἐν . . . πρός). Most likely, each depends on the immediately preceding prepositional phrase, building up to a climax in thought. Therefore, it is better to leave out the comma after this first prepositional phrase. . . . [T]he passage conveys the idea that childish understanding is easily confused by all sorts of doctrines which are devised by the trickery of people. These people use deceitfulness for their own ends (plan) which are characterized by error."

42. Lincoln, *Ephesians*, 257: "νήπιοι, 'children,' contains a double contrast to 'the mature person.' Not only do silly infants contrast with the mature adult, but the plural of 'children' also contrasts with the singular of 'the mature person,' individualism being a sign of childishness, unity a sign of maturity. . . . [I]mmaturity is evidenced in instability, rootlessness, lack of direction, and susceptibility to manipulation and error."

43. The pairing of the plural passive participles enhances this contrast between "tossed by waves and carried about" (κλυδωνιζόμενοι καὶ περιφερόμενοι in the present tense) in 4:14 and "rooted and grounded" (ἐρριζωμένοι καὶ τεθεμελιωμένοι in the perfect tense) in 3:17.

one unified, mature, and stable adult person rooted and grounded within the dynamic realm of being "in love" (3:17b; 4:2).

6. Eph 4:15–16 (A´): Being Truthful in Love the Body Builds Itself Up in Love

With the final, climactic A´ element (4:15–16) of the chiasm in 4:1–16 the audience hear a progression, via the chiastic parallelism, of the A element (4:1–2) regarding the prepositional phrase "in love." Paul's audience forbearing one another "in love" (ἐν ἀγάπῃ, 4:2) in the A element progresses to all of us believers being truthful "in love" (ἐν ἀγάπῃ, 4:15) and to the whole body of Christ building itself up "in love" (ἐν ἀγάπῃ, 4:16) in the A´ element.

In contrast to our being tossed and carried about by every wind of teaching "in" (ἐν) the craftiness of people "in" (ἐν) deceitfulness toward the scheming of error (4:14), is rather our "being truthful" (ἀληθεύοντες), living in accord with the word of "truth" (ἀληθείας) which is the gospel of salvation (1:13), "in" (ἐν) love (4:15a).[44] Being truthful "in love" (ἐν ἀγάπῃ), that is, within the dynamic realm of receiving and sharing love, means not only forbearing one another in this realm of being "in love" (ἐν ἀγάπῃ, 4:2), but being genuinely reliable, faithful, and upright in sharing with one another the gifts of love we have received from the ascended Christ (4:7–12), so that thus rooted and grounded in this realm of being "in love" (ἐν ἀγάπῃ, 3:17) we will not be tossed and carried about by false teachings.[45]

It is by being truthful within the realm of being "in love"—receiving and sharing love—that we believers "might cause all things to grow to him, who is the head, the Christ" (4:15b).[46] This marks a significant development

---

44. Although ἀληθεύοντες is often translated as "speaking the truth," Hoehner (*Ephesians*, 565) states that "in Ephesians the concept of 'being truthful' is the best sense of the word. In contrast to the preceding verse [4:14], where there are three prepositional phrases to denote falsehood and deceit, the present word speaks of being real or truthful in both conduct and speech." Spicq (*TLNT* 1.82) suggests the translation "remaining in the truth, in love" and states that "the emphasis is on remaining attached to the truth (of the gospel), holding fast to it . . . conforming one's conduct to it." According to Hans Hübner ("ἀλήθεια," *EDNT* 1.58), "being truthful" has the sense of being "dependable, constant, real, genuine, and faithful. . . . in Eph 4:15 be genuine, upright (in love)."

45. O'Brien, *Ephesians*, 312: "In love describes the sphere of the Christian life and spells out the manner in which the ministry of all is to occur. . . . while a life of love should embody the truth of the gospel." See also Claudio Basevi, "La missione di Cristo e dei cristiani nella Lettera agli Efesini: Una lettura di Ef 4,1–25," *RivB* 38 (1990): 27–55.

46. For the reading that includes the article—"the Christ" rather than "Christ"—as the original, see Hoehner, *Ephesians*, 567 n. 1. Although Eph 4:15b is often construed intransitively as "we might grow to him in all ways, who is the head, the Christ," this makes "all the things" (τὰ πάντα) an adverbial accusative rather than the direct object of a verb as it is in each of its five previous uses in Ephesians (1:10, 11, 23; 3:9; 4:10). A construal of the verb as transitive ("to cause, make, or allow to grow"; cf. BDAG, 151) with "all things" as

in the role we believers are to play in God's plan for the cosmic unity of all things as part of the love theme in Ephesians.

In each of the previous occurrences of the term "all the things" (τὰ πάντα) in reference to the cosmos in Ephesians it has been the direct object of divine activity—either that of God (1:10, 11; 3:9) or of Christ (1:23; 4:10).[47] But now in this final and climactic occurrence of the term "all the things" in Ephesians it is the direct object of the activity of us believers. By being truthful in love—genuinely and reliably loving one another by sharing with one another the gifts of love we have received from the ascended Christ (4:7–12)—we believers, the "building" that is "growing" (αὔξει) into a temple holy in the Lord (2:21), may cause or allow to "grow" (αὐξήσωμεν) "all things" (τὰ πάντα) to him, who is the "head" (κεφαλή), the Christ (4:15), and so play our role in God's plan to unite under one "head" (ἀνακεφαλαιώσασθαι) "all things" (τὰ πάντα) in the Christ (1:10), whom God gave as "head" (κεφαλήν) over "all things" (πάντα) to the church (1:22).

It is from the Christ, as the head over all things (1:22), that "the whole body," the one body (2:16; 4:4) of Christ (4:12) which is the church (1:22–23), is "being fitted together and held together" (4:16a) as a further gift of Christ's love (divine passives).[48] Whereas the whole building "being fitted together" (συναρμολογουμένη) referred to God's uniting, as a gift of God's love, believing Jews and Gentiles into the church (2:21), the whole body "being fitted together (συναρμολογούμενον) and held together" now refers not only to the unity of believing Jews and Gentiles but to Christ's uniting, as a further gift of Christ's love, all of the various members of the church who have been diversely gifted by the ascended Christ (4:7–12), so that all of us believers might attain to the unity of the faith (4:13).[49]

---

its object thus fits the context of Ephesians much better, as Schlier (*Epheser*, 206) cogently argues in relating 4:15b to 1:10. See also Franz-Josef Steinmetz, *Protologische Heils-Zuversicht: Die Sturkturen des soteriologischen und christologischen Denkens im Kolosser- und Epheserbrief* (Frankfurter Theologische Studien 2; Frankfurt: Knecht, 1969), 120.

47. In 1:22 and 4:6 (3x) "all things" (anarthrous) refers to the cosmos but is the object of a preposition rather than of a verb.

48. With regard to the passive voice of the participles, "being fitted together and held together," O'Brien (*Ephesians*, 313 n. 172) notes: "The passive voice has been interpreted to signify that God (through Christ), or Christ himself, is the one effectively at work in the process of joining and knitting together the body."

49. The two participles, "being fitted together and being held together" (συναρμολογούμενον καὶ συμβιβαζόμενον), are "virtually synonymous and indicate that there is an ongoing, unified growth to the body," according to O'Brien, *Ephesians*, 313–14. Hoehner, *Ephesians*, 570: "They show how the body is causing the growth. They are very functional words since the various members of a body do fit precisely and are united integrally with one another. Both of the participles have the prepositional prefix συν-, which is common in Ephesians and only intensifies the concept of fitting and holding together. . . . They

The ascended Christ is fitting and holding together the whole body "through every supporting connection according to the working in measure of each individual part" (4:16b). "Through every supporting connection" refers to the connections that individual members of the body make with one another as they share with them their gifts of love from the ascended Christ.[50] The audience are to realize that the "working" (κατὰ τὴν ἐνέργειαν) of the power according to which God raised Christ from the dead and seated him at his right hand in the heavenly places (1:19–20), so that he became the ascended Christ, the "working" (κατὰ τὴν ἐνέργειαν) of the power according to which God made Paul a minister of the gospel (3:7), is the "working" (κατ᾽ ἐνέργειαν) according to which the ascended Christ is fitting and holding together the whole body as a further gift of his love.[51]

This working of the ascended Christ is "in measure (μέτρῳ) of each (ἑκάστου) individual (ἑνός) part" (4:16b) of the body, that is, according to the "measure" (μέτρον) of the gift of the Christ, the grace he gave as a gift of his love to "each" (ἑκάστῳ) "one" (ἑνί) of us believers (4:7). As we believers share our individual "measure" of these gifts with one another "in love," the ascended Christ works through them to fit and hold together the whole body "in love," until we all attain to the "measure" (μέτρον) of the bodily stature of the fullness of the Christ (4:13).[52]

With the ascended Christ fitting and holding it together by working through the gifts of love given to and by each of its individual members, the whole body "brings about the growth of the body for the building up of itself in love" (4:16c). The audience thus realize that the whole "building" (οἰκοδομή) being fitted together in Christ that is growing into a temple holy in the Lord (2:21) is the whole "body" (σῶμα) that is bringing about

---

grow by being carefully fitted and held together rather than growing individually apart from one another."

50. After a lengthy discussion of the various possibilities for translating ἁφῆς in 4:16b, Hoehner (*Ephesians*, 573) concludes that "it seems apparent that ἁφή is best rendered 'contact' because this is the predominant meaning of the word in classical and LXX usage and makes the best sense in the present context. It can be translated 'contact' or 'connection.' Actually, the latter is preferred here as it denotes a connection between two objects or, in this case, believers when they 'touch' or 'contact' one another." And on the meaning of the phrase, "through every supporting connection," Hoehner (*Ephesians*, 574) states that "it describes the whole body as being fitted and held together by means of each contact that contributes to the growth of the whole. This supports the ongoing concept that each member of the body has been gifted and as each member utilizes the gifts as he or she makes contact or connection with other members of the body, the body will grow.

51. Lincoln (*Ephesians*, 263) points out how "according to the working" in 4:16b recalls the same phrase in 1:19 and 3:7, "where God's power which raised Christ was said to be operative in believers and in the apostle Paul."

52. Hoehner, *Ephesians*, 577–78: "Christ, therefore, is the source of the gifts that enables the individual to build up the body of Christ, and Christ is also the source of the body's unification through the interaction of believers which causes growth of the body."

its own growth of the "body" (σώματος) for the "building" (οἰκοδομήν) up of itself by sharing its gifts with one another "in love," in other words, for the "building" (οἰκοδομήν) up of the "body" (σώματος) of the Christ (4:12), the church (1:22–23), by sharing the gifts of love they have received from the ascended Christ with one another within the dynamic realm of being "in love."[53]

And the audience further realize that the whole building being fitted together in Christ is "growing" (αὔξει) into a temple holy in the Lord (2:21) through the "growth" (αὔξησιν) that the whole body brings about for itself when its individual members share the gifts of love they have received from the ascended Christ with one another "in love" (4:16). By thus being truthful in sharing with one another "in love" we believers may cause to "grow" (αὐξήσωμεν) all things to the Christ, the head over all things (4:15; 1:22). As "head," then, the ascended Christ is not only the final goal or destiny of all things that are growing "to him" (εἰς αὐτόν, 4:15), but also the source or origin "from whom" (ἐξ οὗ, 4:16) the whole body, the church, is being filled with gifts of love in order to cause all things to grow to Christ, the head, so that all things will be summed up under one head in Christ (1:10).

To sum up, with regard to the dynamic realm of being "in love," the audience have heard the following development: God has chosen all of us believers in Christ, the "Beloved" (ἠγαπημένῳ, 1:6), before the foundation of the world to be holy and blameless before him "in love" (ἐν ἀγάπῃ, 1:4), that is, within the dynamic realm of sharing with one another (1:15; 4:12–16) the love we have received from God (2:4) and Christ (3:19; 4:7–16). "In love" (ἐν ἀγάπῃ) rooted and grounded (3:17), we are no longer infants tossed and carried about by false teachings (4:14). By not only forbearing one another "in love" (ἐν ἀγάπῃ, 4:2) but being truthful with one another "in love" (ἐν ἀγάπῃ, 4:15), we bring about the growth of the church as the body of Christ "in love" (ἐν ἀγάπῃ, 4:16), that we may cause to grow all things to the Christ, the head over all things (4:15; 1:22), and thereby play our role in God's cosmic plan to unite under one head all things in the Christ (1:10). The love of God and Christ for us and our love for one another within the realm of being "in love" is thus bringing about the unity of all things in Christ.

---

53. Lincoln, *Ephesians*, 264: "If any corporate growth or building up is to take place, love is the indispensable means. . . . Love is the lifeblood of this body, and, therefore, the ultimate criterion for the assessment of the Church's growth will be how far it is characterized by love." O'Brien, *Ephesians*, 316: "If it is only in love that the body increases, then it is only in love that true Christian ministry will contribute to the building of the body."

B. Summary on Ephesians 4:1–16

1. The use of cognate noun and verb in the expression, "calling with which you were called" (4:1), echoes previous uses of this stylistic device to rhetorically intensify descriptions of God's love for the audience—God's "great love with which he loved us" (2:4) and God's "grace with which he graced us in the Beloved" (1:6).

2. Forbearing one another within the dynamic realm of being "in love" (4:2), that is, enduring and tolerating differences among themselves, is the way Paul's audience can preserve, maintain, and protect the unity and peace they have already been given as a gift of Christ's love within the dynamic realm of being "in love" (4:3).

3. Each individual believer to whom grace has been given as a gift of Christ's love (4:7) is to share that love with others as a way to preserve the unity of the Spirit (4:3–6) which they have received as a gift of God's love.

4. Whereas God "gave" Christ as head over all things to the church as a gift of God's love (1:22b), the ascended Christ himself "gave" gifts of love to people (4:8).

5. The Christ who received God's love in being raised from the dead (1:20) after descending to the lower parts of the earth in death and burial is the Christ who ascended on high so that he is in an exalted position of extending the divine love he received to others, as he "gave gifts to people" (4:8–9).

6. That Christ "might fill all things" (4:10) recalls Paul's prayer that his audience "might be filled" to all the fullness of God by the love of the Christ (3:19) who "is filling all things" in all ways (1:23). The audience are thus to realize that the gifts of love that the ascended Christ gave to people (4:8), to each one of us believers (4:7), are part of the love of the Christ who is filling "all things" in all ways as part of God's plan to unite "all things" under one head in the Christ as the ultimate gift of God's love (1:10).

7. In 4:11–14 Paul informs his audience that the ascended Christ has given gifts of gifted believers as gifts of love (4:11) to equip their fellow believers in turn to share their gifts of love (4:7) with one another to build up the body of Christ (4:12), until all of us believers together attain to the unified, mature, and complete bodily stature of the fullness of the body of the Christ (4:13), so that we are no longer disunited, immature, and unstable infants tossed and carried about by erroneous teachings (4:14) but

one unified, mature, and stable adult person rooted and grounded within the dynamic realm of being "in love" (3:17b; 4:2).

8. God has chosen all of us believers in Christ, the "Beloved" (1:6), before the foundation of the world to be holy and blameless before him "in love" (1:4), that is, within the dynamic realm of sharing with one another (1:15; 4:12–16) the love we have received from God (2:4) and Christ (3:19; 4:7–16). "In love" rooted and grounded (3:17), we are no longer infants tossed and carried about by false teachings (4:14). By not only forbearing one another "in love" (4:2) but being truthful with one another "in love" (4:15), we bring about the growth of the church as the body of Christ "in love" (4:16), that we may cause to grow all things to the Christ, the head over all things (4:15; 1:22), and thereby play our role in God's cosmic plan to unite under one head all things in the Christ (1:10). The love of God and Christ for us and our love for one another within the realm of being "in love" is thus bringing about the cosmic unity of all things in Christ.

CHAPTER 11

Ephesians 4:17–32:
Walk in the Truth of Christ's Love (G´)

A: [17] This then I say and testify in the Lord, that you no longer walk, just as also the Gentiles walk in the futility of their mind, [18] being darkened in understanding, alienated from the life of *God* because of the ignorance that is in them because of the hardness of their heart, [19] who, having become callous, have given themselves over to indecency for the practice of *every* kind of impurity in greediness.

   B: [20] But you have not so learned the Christ, [21] inasmuch as about him you *heard* and in him you were taught, as there is *truth* in Jesus,

      C: [22] that you have *put off according to* the former lifestyle the *old person* who is being corrupted *according to* the desires of deceit,

      C´: [23] but you are being renewed in the spirit of your mind [24] and have *put on* the *new person* created *according to* God in righteousness and holiness of truth.

   B´: [25] Therefore having put off falsehood, speak *truth*, each one with his neighbor, for we are members of one another. [26] Be angry but do not sin; let not the sun set on your anger, [27] and do not give room to the devil. [28] Let the stealer no longer steal, but rather let him labor working with his own hands that which is good, that he might have something to share with one who has need. [29] Let no harmful word come out of your mouth, but only such as is good for the building up of what is needed, that it might give grace to *those who hear*.

A´:   ³⁰ And do not grieve the Holy Spirit of *God*, in whom you were sealed for the day of redemption. ³¹ Let *all* bitterness and fury and wrath and shouting and reviling be put away from you along with *all* malice. ³² But become kind to one another, compassionate, being gracious to each other, just as also *God* in Christ was gracious to us.[1]

A. Chiastic Development from Ephesians 3:14–21 (G) to 4:17–32 (G´)

With Eph 4:17–32, the G´ unit within the macro-chiastic structure embracing the entire Letter, the audience hear resonances of 3:14–21, the corresponding G unit in the overall chiasm. That "you have not so learned the Christ (Χριστόν)" (4:20) in the G´ unit recalls Paul's prayer that "the Christ (Χριστόν) may dwell through faith in your hearts" (3:17), so that you may "know the love of the Christ (Χριστοῦ) that surpasses knowledge" (3:19) in the G unit. That you have put off the "old person" (παλαιὸν ἄνθρωπον, 4:22) and put on the "new person" (καινὸν ἄνθρωπον, 4:24) in the G´ unit recalls Paul's prayer that you may be strengthened in the "inner person" (ἔσω ἄνθρωπον, 3:16) in the G unit. Not to grieve the Holy "Spirit" (πνεῦμα, 4:30) of God in the G´ unit recalls Paul's prayer that you may be strengthened with power through God's "Spirit" (πνεύματος, 3:16) in the G unit. And that God "in Christ" (ἐν Χριστῷ) was gracious to us in the G´ unit (4:32) recalls Paul's declaration of glory to God "in Christ" (ἐν Χριστῷ) to all generations (3:21) in the G unit.

With regard to the love theme, then, Paul's assertion that his audience "have not so learned the Christ" (4:20) as the motivation for his exhortation that they not behave like the Gentiles (4:17–19) in the G´ unit follows upon his prayer that his audience may "know the love of the Christ that surpasses knowledge" (3:19) in the G unit. That the audience have put off the "old person" (4:22) and put on the "new person" (4:24) as a gift of Christ's love in the G´ unit is a consequence of their being strengthened in the "inner person" (3:16) as gift of God's love in the G unit. The exhortation for the audience not to grieve the Holy "Spirit" of God (4:30) with their behavior in the G´ unit is motivated by Paul's prayer that they be strengthened with power through God's "Spirit" (3:16) as a gift of God's love in the G unit. And that God was gracious in giving us gifts of love within the realm of our being "in Christ" (4:32) in the G´ unit provides a further reason for Paul's declaration of glory to God for the gifts of love we have received within the realm of our being "in Christ" (3:21) in the G unit.

---

1. For the establishment of Eph 4:17–32 as a chiasm, see ch. 2.

B. Audience Response to Ephesians 4:17–32

1. Eph 4:17–19 (A): Do Not Walk as Gentiles Alienated from God

The audience heard Paul begin his exhortation in 4:1 with the words, "I, then (οὖν), exhort you (ὑμᾶς), I, the prisoner in the Lord (ἐν κυρίῳ), to walk (περιπατῆσαι) worthy of the calling with which you were called." And now the audience hear Paul resume and develop that exhortation with similar words but with a negative example, "This then (οὖν) I say and testify in the Lord (ἐν κυρίῳ), that you (ὑμᾶς) no longer walk (περιπατεῖν), just as also the Gentiles walk (περιπατεῖ) in the futility of their mind" (4:17).[2]

Paul's exhortation to his audience that "you" no longer "walk" as the "Gentiles" (τὰ ἔθνη) "walk," namely, "in the futility of their mind" (4:17), reminds them that when "you" were "Gentiles" (τὰ ἔθνη) in the flesh (2:11) "you" once "walked" (περιεπατήσατε) "according to the age of this world, according to the ruler of the authority of the air, of the spirit that is now working in the sons of disobedience" (2:2). But Paul's audience of "you" believers along with all of us believers have been "created in Christ Jesus for good works which God prepared beforehand, that we might walk (περιπατήσωμεν) in them" (2:10). And so for the audience to no longer "walk" (περιπατεῖν) as the Gentiles "walk" (περιπατεῖ) means for them to "walk" (περιπατῆσαι) worthy of the calling with which they were called (4:1), which includes forbearing one another "in love" (4:2), being truthful "in love" (4:15), and building up the body of Christ "in love" (4:16).

The extended elaboration of the interior mentality involved in the way that the Gentiles "walk"—"in the futility of their *mind*, being darkened in *understanding*, alienated from the life of God because of the ignorance (ἄγνοιαν) that is *in them* because of the hardness of their *heart* (καρδίας)" (4:17b-18)[3]—stands in stark contrast to Paul's prayer that his audience "be strengthened with power through his Spirit *in the inner person*, that the

---

2. Hoehner, *Ephesians*, 582: "The οὖν, 'therefore,' does not serve as an inferential conjunction but has a resumptive force resuming the thought of verses 1–3 that had been interrupted at verse 4. . . . The demonstrative pronoun τοῦτο, 'this,' refers to the exhortation that follows. In effect Paul is saying, 'In resuming my exhortation I say this.' . . . The verb μαρτύρομαι, 'I testify,' is not an oath with the Lord as a witness, as though ἐν κυρίῳ meant 'by the Lord.' Instead, Paul is solemnly declaring his exhortation in the sphere of or in connection with the Lord. . . . Consistently throughout this letter (2:21; 4:1; 5:8; 6:1, 10, 21) the prepositional phrase ἐν κυρίῳ, 'in the Lord,' refers not to God but to Christ."

3. Hoehner, *Ephesians*, 588–89: "The scenario could be reconstructed by reversing the direction of the statements. The hardness of their hearts toward God cause their ignorance. Their ignorance concerning God and his will caused them to be alienated from the life of God. Their alienation caused their minds to be darkened, and their darkened minds caused them to walk in the futility of mind."

Christ may dwell through faith in your *hearts* (καρδίαις) . . . to know (γνῶναί) the love of the Christ that surpasses knowledge (γνώσεως)" (3:16–19).[4]

Reminding the audience that even the "we" believers once were "doing the wishes of the flesh and of the thoughts (διανοιῶν)" (2:3), that the Gentiles were "darkened" in "understanding" (διανοία) because of the hardness of their "heart" (καρδίας) (4:18) contradicts Paul's prayer for his audience that with the eyes of their "hearts" (καρδίας) having been "enlightened" they may "know" what is the hope of their calling (1:18). And recalling that the audience of "you" believers were once "alienated" (ἀπηλλοτριωμένοι) from the community of Israel and "Godless" (ἄθεοι) in the world (2:12), that the Gentiles are "alienated" (ἀπηλλοτριωμένοι) from the "life" (ζωῆς) of "God" (θεοῦ) (4:18) contradicts the situation of the audience, whom God has now "made alive with" (συνεζωοποίησεν) the Christ, after they were "dead" in their sins (2:1, 5), because of the great love with which God (θεός) loved us (2:4–5).[5]

The audience are not to "walk" as the Gentiles "walk," as those "who, having become callous, have given themselves over to indecency for the practice (ἐργασίαν) of every kind of impurity in greediness" (4:19) because we believers have been created in Christ Jesus for good "works" (ἔργοις) which God prepared beforehand, that we might "walk" in them (2:10). And among the good "works" we are to practice instead of what the Gentiles practice is the "work" (ἔργον) of ministry for building up the body of the Christ (4:12), that is, for the body's building up of itself "in love" (4:16) by sharing as gifts of love for one another the gifts of love they have received from the ascended Christ (4:7–12). Rather than giving themselves over to indecency for the practice of every kind of impurity "in greediness" (ἐν πλεονεξία, 4:19) the audience are to give of themselves and their gifts to build up the body of Christ "in love" (ἐν ἀγάπη, 4:16).[6]

To sum up, in 4:17–19 for the audience not to "walk" as the Gentiles "walk" (4:17) means for them to "walk" in accord with their calling (4:1), forbearing one another "in love" (4:2), being truthful "in love" (4:15), and building up the body of Christ "in love" (4:16). Instead of "walking" in the ignorance that is within the hearts of the Gentiles (4:18), the audience are

---

4. O'Brien, *Ephesians*, 321: "Knowledge has to do with an obedient and grateful response of the whole person, not simply intellectual assent. Likewise 'ignorance' is a failure to be grateful and obedient. It describes someone's total stance, and this includes emotions, will, and action, not just one's mental response."

5. That "alienated" (ἀπηλλοτριωμένοι) occurs in Ephesians only in 2:12 and 4:18 and words for "life" (συνεζωοποίησεν-ζωῆς) only in 2:5 and 4:18 enhances this recall.

6. Hoehner, *Ephesians*, 592–93: "The three words of ἀσέλγεια (indecency), ἀκαθαρσία (impurity), and πλεονεξία (greediness) are a powerful combination used to describe unregenerate people as those who are totally consumed with themselves. . . . It is love of self in contrast to love of others and of God."

to "walk" in the knowledge of the love of the Christ (3:19) that is in their hearts (3:17). Instead of "walking" in alienation of the life of God like the Gentiles, the audience are to "walk" as those whom God has now made alive with the Christ, after they were dead in their sins (2:1, 5), because of the great love with which God loved us (2:4–5). And instead of "walking" like the Gentiles who practice every kind of impurity in greediness (4:19), the audience are to "walk" by practicing the work of ministry (4:12)—sharing as gifts of love for one another the gifts of love they have received from the ascended Christ (4:7–12)—within the dynamic realm of being "in love" (4:2, 15–16).

2. Eph 4:20–21 (B): You Heard about and Learned Christ as Truth Is in Jesus

The audience hear the B element (4:20–21) as a mini-chiasm in itself:

> a: But you have not so learned the *Christ* (Χριστόν) (4:20)
> b: inasmuch as about *him* (αὐτόν) you heard (4:21a)
> b´:   and *in him* (ἐν αὐτῷ) you were taught (4:21b)
> a´: as there is truth *in Jesus* (ἐν Ἰησοῦ) (4:21c)

In the "a" sub-element (4:20) the audience hear that the "Christ" in the accusative case is the object they learned. In the "b" sub-element (4:21a) the Christ is referred to with the accusative pronoun "him" in the emphatic position as the object about whom the audience heard. In the "b´" sub-element (4:21b) occurs the pivot from the accusatives to refer to Christ (Χριστόν, αὐτόν) as object to a prepositional phrase "in him" (ἐν αὐτῷ) in the emphatic position to refer to Christ as the one in union with or in the realm in which the audience were taught.[7] And in the "a´" sub-element (4:21c) the audience hear the climactic prepositional phrase "in Jesus" (ἐν Ἰησοῦ), complementing the reference to "Christ" in the "a" sub-element, as the one in union with or in the realm in which there is truth for the audience who learned the Christ. The proper nouns "Christ" and "in Jesus" (4:20; 4:21c) to complete the Christ-Jesus sequence which has reverberated in the ears of the audience (2:6, 7, 10, 13, 20; 3:1, 6, 11, 21) thus frame the pronouns "him" and "in him" (4:21ab).[8]

With emphasis upon "you" (ὑμεῖς) in contrast to "the Gentiles" (τὰ

---

7. O'Brien, *Ephesians*, 325 n. 220: "In both clauses [4:21ab] the reference to 'him' receives the emphasis since it precedes the finite verb: 'about him you heard, and in him you were taught.'" On the meaning of the prepositional phrase "in him" Hoehner (*Ephesians*, 595) comments that "it is the sphere or locale of the teaching, 'in connection with him' or 'in communion with him.' Hence, Christ is the object and the sphere of a believer's learning.

8. After Eph 1:1 which contains two references to "Christ Jesus," the sequence becomes "Jesus Christ" in 1:2, 3, 5, 17. But with 2:6 the sequence returns to "Christ Jesus" until it climaxes with the sequence of "Christ" and "in Jesus" (separated by the two pronouns in

ἔθνη, 4:17), that Paul's audience of "you" believers "have not so learned the Christ" (4:20) intensifies the contrast between their present "walking" or conduct as believers with their past conduct as Gentiles (cf. 2:11).[9] That they have already "learned" the Christ in this G′ unit of the chiasm follows upon Paul's previous prayer that they may now "know" the love of the Christ that surpasses knowledge (3:19) in the G unit. Their initial learning of Christ is thus to progress more specifically to their personal, experiential knowledge of the love they received from the ascended Christ (4:7–12) with whom they have been raised and seated in the heavenly places (2:6).[10]

That it was indeed about "him," the Christ, that Paul's audience have "heard" (ἠκούσατε) (4:21a) reminds them that it was because "you heard" (ἠκούσατε) of the love that Paul received from God and shared with them in terms of "the plan of the grace of God that was given to me for you" (3:2) that they may perceive Paul's insight into the mystery of the Christ (3:4). It also recalls that it was by "hearing" (ἀκούσαντες) the word of truth that they became believers who were sealed with the Holy Spirit of the promise (1:13) as a gift of God's love.

That it was "in him," that is, within the realm of being "in Christ," that "you were taught" (ἐδιδάχθητε) (4:21b) reminds the audience that they were taught as recipients of the gifts of love from the gifted people, among whom were "teachers" (διδασκάλους), that the ascended Christ gave to us believers (4:11). That the audience have already been taught in Christ, then, reinforces Paul's exhortation "that we might no longer be infants, tossed by waves and carried about by every wind of teaching (διδασκαλίας) in the craftiness of people in deceitfulness toward the scheming of error" (4:14).

"As there is truth (ἀλήθεια) in Jesus" (4:21c) means that the audience who have been taught in him (4:21b) and heard about him (4:21a)—which includes their having heard the word of "truth" (ἀληθείας, 1:13)—have learned that there is "truth" within the realm of being in union with Jesus, the Christ (4:20). Indeed, in their union with Christ Jesus, the audience have experienced "truth," that is, the genuine faithfulness and reliability of the ascended Christ in giving them gifts of love (4:11–12), which empowers

---

reference to Christ Jesus) in 4:20–21. The remaining occurrences in Ephesians of "Jesus" together with "Christ" return to the sequence "Jesus Christ" (5:20; 6:23–24).

9. Hoehner, *Ephesians*, 593: "The emphatic contrast with the previous verses is noted by: (1) the adversative δέ; (2) the change from τὰ ἔθνη το ὑμεῖς, which is emphatically placed; and (3) the adverbial conjunction οὕτως, which applies what had been stated before, namely, that the conduct of Gentiles is not what believers learned regarding Christ."

10. Hoehner, *Ephesians*, 594: "The implication is that factual learning is insufficient, the goal is to know Christ personally. . . . Believers continually 'learn' Christ who is alive and seated at the right hand of God in the heavenlies (1:20; 2:6)." O'Brien, *Ephesians*, 324: "Learning Christ means welcoming him as a living person and being shaped by his teaching."

them in turn to "being truthful" (ἀληθεύοντες) by dependably sharing their gifts of love with one another within the realm of being "in love" (4:15a). This is the kind of "truth"—the "truth" involved in believers loving one another—that empowers the audience to counter not only the false and erroneous teaching of human beings (4:14) but the Gentiles' wrong way of "walking" (4:17–19). This "truth" that is "in (ἐν) Jesus" thus contradicts the "in (ἐν) greediness" of Gentile conduct (4:19) and complements the "in (ἐν) love" within which the body of Christ is building itself up (4:16).[11]

3. Eph 4:22 (C): You Have Put Off the Old Person Corrupted by Deceit

What more specifically the audience in the realm of being "in Christ Jesus" were taught is then further elaborated.[12] "That you have put off according to the former lifestyle (ἀναστροφήν) the old person who is being corrupted according to the desires (ἐπιθυμίας) of deceit" (4:22) reminds the audience of the pre-Christian lifestyle of us believers:[13] "We all once lived (ἀνεστράφημέν) in the desires (ἐπιθυμίαι) of our flesh doing the wishes of the flesh and of the thoughts" (2:3).[14] But this lifestyle of the "old person" being corrupted unto death was able to be "put off" as a consequence of the great love with which God loved us in making us alive by grace in union with Christ (2:4–5).[15] That you "have put off" (ἀποθέσθαι, aorist middle

---

11. According to Lincoln (*Ephesians*, 283), Paul "asserts that his readers had not been instructed in the Christian tradition falsely according to the Gentile pattern of life he has depicted in vv 17–19 but had been instructed according to the proper content of that tradition, that is, the truth in Jesus." Hoehner, *Ephesians*, 597: "Truth here is to be understood as reality in contrast to that which is false or deceptive as seen in the next verse, a description Paul used to characterize the unregenerate Gentiles in verses 17–18."

12. On the infinitive "put off" (ἀποθέσθαι) in 4:22, as well as the infintives "being renewed" (ἀνανεοῦσθαι) and "put on" (ἐνδύσασθαι) in 4:23–24, as complementary or epexegetical infinitives of "you have been taught" in 4:21, rather than as imperatival infinitives, see Hoehner, *Ephesians*, 598–602.

13. On the background of the clothing imagery of "putting off" and "putting on" in Eph 4:22–24, see Pieter Willem van der Horst, "Observations on a Pauline Expression," *NTS* 19 (1973): 181–87; Jung Hoon Kim, *The Significance of Clothing Imagery in the Pauline Corpus* (JSNTSup 268; London: Clark, 2004), 175–92.

14. Lincoln, *Ephesians*, 286: "The use of ἀναστροφή, 'way of life' [4:22], recalls the use of the cognate verb in the earlier depiction . . . in 2:3."

15. Hoehner, *Ephesians*, 605: "The old person, found in Rom 6:6 and Col 3:9, is the preconversion unregenerate person. Paul then is teaching that, having been taught in him, believers should know that the old person according to the former lifestyle was laid aside." Lincoln, *Ephesians*, 285: "The change of clothing imagery signifies an exchange of identities, and the concepts of the old and the new persons reinforce this. These old and new persons are not simply Adam and Christ as representatives of the old and new orders . . . They are individuals, as those individuals are identified either with the old or with the new order of existence. The old person is the person living under the dominion of the present evil age and its powers, and this previous identity has to be dealt with decisively."

infinitive) the "old person," then, is not ultimately a human accomplishment but a further benefit of God's love.[16]

4. Eph 4:23–24 (C'): You Have Put On the New Person Created by God

With the C' element (4:23–24) of the chiasm the audience hear an antithetical pivot from the C element (4:22)—from their having "put off" (ἀποθέσθαι) the "old person" (παλαιὸν ἄνθρωπον) to their having "put on" (ἐνδύσασθαι) the "new person" (καινὸν ἄνθρωπον). And there is an antithetical pivot from the prepositional phrases, "according to (κατά) the former lifestyle" and "according to (κατά) the desires of deceit" (4:22), in the C element to the prepositional phrase, "created according to (κατά) God in righteousness and holiness of truth" (4:24), in the C' element.

Instead of the former lifestyle of the "old person" that is being corrupted unto death according to the desires of deceit (4:22), the audience "are being renewed in the spirit of your mind" (4:23).[17] The audience's being renewed "in the spirit of your mind (τοῦ νοὸς ὑμῶν)" thus supplants the Gentile "walking" or conduct that is "in the futility of their mind (τοῦ νοος αὐτῶν)" (4:17). In their union with Christ Jesus the audience have been taught (4:21) that they are "being renewed" (ἀνανεοῦσθαι as divine passive) continually by God as a further gift of God's love.[18] And that they are being renewed in the spirit of their mind, that is, in their "inner person," serves as a further basis for Paul's prayer that his audience be strengthened with power through God's Spirit in the inner person (3:16) so that they may know the love of Christ that surpasses knowledge (3:19).[19]

In complementary contrast to the audience having "put off," as a gift

---

16. Hoehner, *Ephesians*, 603: "The middle voice emphasizes that the subject receives the benefits of his or her action. It is not a reflexive idea, for the person could not do it by his or her own strength. Hence, believers were taught that they have put off or have laid aside the old person at conversion." On the figurative use of "putting off," see Gerhard Schneider, "ἀποτίθεμαι," *EDNT* 1.146.

17. On Eph 4:23, Hoehner (*Ephesians*, 607) remarks: "The conjunction δέ marks the contrast with the previous verse, there the negative, here the positive."

18. On "being renewed" in 4:23 O'Brien (*Ephesians*, 329) comments: "The verb is best taken as a passive (meaning 'to be made new') rather than as a middle, and this suggests that God is the one who effects the ongoing work of renewing his people." Hoehner, *Ephesians*, 607: "[I]t is best to view it not as a middle but as a passive where the believer is the recipient of the renewing. The present tense suggests that the renewal of the mind is a repeated process throughout the believer's life, which is in contrast to the inceptive act involved in putting off the old person (v. 22) and putting on the new person (v. 24)."

19. On the "spirit" in 4:23 as referring to the human rather than divine spirit, see Hoehner, *Ephesians*, 608; Fee, *God's Empowering Presence*, 709–12. Lincoln, *Ephesians*, 287: "In Ephesians' characteristic style of pleonastic accumulation of synonyms, both spirit and mind are employed to designate a person's innermost being. In this way, the reference is similar to that of 3:16 to the inner person." See also O'Brien, *Ephesians*, 330; Kim, *Clothing Imagery*, 189.

of God's love, the "old person" (παλαιὸν ἄνθρωπον) (4:22) they have "put on," as a gift of God's love, the "new person" (καινὸν ἄνθρωπον) (4:24), that is, the one "new person" (καινὸν ἄνθρωπον) that Christ created out of the two—believing Jews and Gentiles (2:15).[20] This one "new person" that Christ created the audience have corporately and individually appropriated by "putting on" as the "clothing" of their external conduct in accord with their being internally renewed in the spirit of their mind (4:23), and thus not "walking" or conducting themselves in the futility of their mind like the Gentiles (4:17).[21] This one "new person" that Christ "created" (κτίσῃ) in himself (2:15) is also "created" (κτισθέντα) according to God (4:24), recalling that we believers are God's work "created" (κτισθέντες) in Christ Jesus for good works which God prepared beforehand, that we might "walk," that is, conduct ourselves, in them (2:10).

Whereas the audience have "put off" the "old person" that was "according" (κατά) to the former lifestyle and that is being corrupted "according" (κατά) to the desires of deceit (4:22), they have "put on" the "new person" created (as a divine passive) "according" (κατά) to God (4:24) as a further gift of God's love. That the audience have "put on" the "new person" created according to God "in righteousness (δικαιοσύνη) and holiness (ὁσιότητι) of truth" (4:24) means they have adopted an external conduct with the attributes of God himself, who is known as both "righteous (δίκαιος) and holy (ὅσιος)" (LXX Deut 32:4; Ps 144:17).[22] And these divine attributes come from "the truth" (τῆς ἀληθείας), in contrast to the desires of "the deceit" (τῆς ἀπάτης, 4:22), the "truth" (ἀλήθεια) that there is for believers in the

---

20. On the aorist middle infinitives, "put off" (ἀποθέσθαι) in 4:22 and "put on" (ἐνδύσασθαι) in 4:24, Hoehner (*Ephesians*, 609) points out that they "are middle voice signifying that the subject is receiving the benefit of his or her action." In other words, although the audience themselves have performed the action of "putting off" and "putting on," they were able to accomplish this only as a gift of God's love.

21. On the concept of "newness" and the synonymous words used to express it in the NT, see Roy A. Harrisville, "The Concept of Newness in the New Testament," *JBL* 74 (1955): 69–79.

22. O'Brien, *Ephesians*, 332–33: "God is not only the author of this mighty work; he is also the pattern or model of the new creation. It is made 'in his likeness' (lit. 'in accordance with God'), that is, created 'like him'. It is not surprising, therefore, that the qualities of righteousness and holiness which characterize the new person are predicated of God in both the Old and New Testaments. . . . The paired expression thus explains what it means to be like God." Hoehner, *Ephesians*, 612: "The difference between δικαιοσύνη, 'righteousness,' and ὁσιότης, 'holiness,' is not great. In using both of these words in connection with Abraham, Philo suggested that a person must exhibit both qualities: justice to humans and holiness to God. This expresses it well and may be the nuance Paul intended. Furthermore, the preposition ἐν is probably not an instrumental, which would indicate that the new person was made by means of righteousness and piety, but it more likely indicates sphere, that is, the new person has been created in the sphere or element of righteousness and piety which denotes the quality of the new person."

realm of being in Jesus (4:21), as they are "being truthful" (ἀληθεύοντες) with one another by sharing the gifts of love they have received from Christ with one another within the realm of being "in love" (4:15).

5. Eph 4:25–29 (B'): Speak Truth and Give Grace to Those Who Hear

With the B' element of the chiasm the audience hear a progression from the "truth" (ἀλήθεια) that there is in Jesus (4:21) in the B element to the "truth" (ἀλήθειαν) the audience are to speak to one another (4:25) in the B' element. And the hearing of the audience who have "heard" (ἠκούσατε) about Christ (4:21) in the B element develops to the giving of grace to "those who hear" (ἀκούουσιν) the good word (4:29) in the B' element.

"Therefore having put off (ἀποθέμενοι) falsehood" (4:25a),[23] that is, having "put off" (ἀποθέσθαι) the "old person" being corrupted unto death according to the desires of deceit (4:22),[24] the audience are exhorted by Paul that "you speak truth, each one with his neighbor, for we are members of one another" (4:25b).[25] That the audience are to *speak* "truth" (ἀλήθειαν) with one another, recalling the word of "truth" (ἀληθείας) they have heard, the gospel of their salvation (1:13), exemplifies what it means for them, who have "put on" the "new person" created according to God, to conduct themselves within the realm of the righteousness and holiness that comes from "truth" (ἀληθείας) (4:24), the "truth" (ἀλήθεια) that there is within the realm of being "in Jesus" (4:21). By sharing with one another as a gift of love the truth that is a gift of God's love, then, the audience are "being truthful" (ἀληθεύοντες) within the realm of being "in love" (4:15).

"Each" (ἕκαστος) individual in the audience is to speak truth with his neighbor (4:25) as a way of sharing the grace God gave as a gift of love to

---

23. Lincoln, *Ephesians*, 300: "The opening διό ['therefore'] marks the link with the preceding pericope and a move from the more general to the more specific, as the deeds appropriate to those newly created in God's likeness are outlined."

24. O'Brien, *Ephesians*, 337 n. 270: " 'Falsehood' (τὸ ψεῦδος) brings to mind the deceitful (ἀπάτη) desires in their former manner of life."

25. "Speak truth, each one with his neighbor" (λαλεῖτε ἀλήθειαν ἕκαστος μετὰ τοῦ πλησίον αὐτοῦ) in Eph 4:25 is very similar to LXX Zech 8:16: "Speak truth, each one to his neighbor" (λαλεῖτε ἀλήθειαν ἕκαστος πρὸς τὸν πλησίον αὐτοῦ). The only difference is that Eph 4:25 uses the preposition μετά ("with") while Zech 8:16 uses the preposition πρός ("to"). Paul, however, does not introduce these words as a scriptural quotation. On their significance, see Moritz, *Profound Mystery*, 88–89. For the view that the form of the series of exhortations that begins in Eph 2:25 is patterned on Zech 8:16–17, see J. Paul Sampley, "Scripture and Tradition in the Community as Seen in Ephesians 4:25ff," *ST* 26 (1972): 101–9. And for the view that these exhortations are connected with the Lord's Supper, see Felice Montagnini, "Echi de parenesi cultuale in Ef 4,25–32," *RivB* 37 (1989): 257–82. Both are unconvincing in the view of Hoehner (*Ephesians*, 614 n. 3).

"each" (ἑκάστῳ) one of us believers (4:7).[26] By each one speaking truth as a gift of love to his neighbor, and thus being truthful "in love" (4:15), the whole body of Christ, through the working in measure of "each" (ἑκάστου) individual part, builds itself up within the realm of being "in love" (4:16).[27]

Further assimilating his audience of "you" believers with all of us believers, Paul exhorts each individual "you" believer in his audience to speak truth to his neighbor, "for *we* are (ἐσμέν) members of one another" (4:25). And for us to speak truth with our neighbor because we are members of "one another" (ἀλλήλων) within the body of Christ further exemplifies what it means for us to respectfully forbear "one another" (ἀλλήλων) within the realm of being "in love" (4:2).[28]

Paul then elaborates on what kind of conduct is appropriate within the realm of being "in love" for us who are members of one another (4:25), forbearing one another "in love" (4:2): "Be angry but do not sin; let not the sun set on your anger, and do not give room to the devil" (4:26–27). The command, "be angry but do not sin" (4:26a), a verbatim quotation of LXX Ps 4:5a, foresees becoming angry with one another but places a limitation upon it—do not let it result in sin against a fellow believer.[29] Indeed, the sun should not set on your anger (4:26b; cf. Deut 24:15), implying that it should be resolved as quickly as possible before the day is over.[30] Anger is not to be

---

26. Hoehner, *Ephesians*, 616: "The second person plural along with the substantival adjective ἕκαστος, 'each one, everyone,' reinforces the idea of individual responsibility in this matter."

27. O'Brien, *Ephesians*, 338: "The means by which this body is built, according to 4:15, is speaking the truth of the gospel in love."

28. Commenting on the word "members" (μέλη) in 4:25, Hoehner (*Ephesians*, 618) states: "It is interesting to observe that this word μέλος is never used of members of an organization but always of members of an organism. In other words, members of an organization may not necessarily have a relationship to other members, but members of an organism demand a close-knit relationship to the other members and they are accountable to one another. The concept of a close relationship is enhanced by the use of the reciprocal pronoun ἀλλήλων, 'one another.' "

29. On "be angry" (ὀργίζεσθε) as a command rather than a condition, see Daniel B. Wallace, " 'ΟΡΓΙΖΕΣΘΕ in Ephesians 4:26: Command or Condition?" *CTR* 3 (1989): 353–72. On the quotation of Ps 4:5, see Moritz, *Profound Mystery*, 89–91. According to Hoehner (*Ephesians*, 621), "it is necessary to acknowledge that anger is not intrinsically sinful. . . . God expresses anger. What causes God to become angry? When wrong has been done against a person or against God himself. However, when God is angry, he is always in control of his anger. Unlike God, however, people have a tendency to allow anger to control them. Hence, the second command, 'do not sin' is necessary." O'Brien, *Ephesians*, 339–40: "Since anger is not explicitly called 'sin', it has been suggested that the reference here is to righteous indignation, while the anger of v. 31 which is to be put away is evidently unrighteous anger. There is a proper place for righteous anger . . . If ours is not free from injured pride, malice, or a spirit of revenge, it has degenerated into sin."

30. On the noun "anger" (παροργισμῷ) in Eph 4:26 Hoehner (*Ephesians*, 621–22) comments: "It seems that the prepositional prefix (παρα-) intensifies this word. Whereas

prolonged so as not to "give room to the devil" (4:27), that is, to allow the "devil," the personification of evil, the opportunity to exploit such anger for his own divisive and wicked purposes.[31]

For us who are members of one another (4:25) to forbear one another within the realm of being "in love" (4:2) also means: "Let the stealer no longer steal, but rather let him labor working with his own hands that which is good, that he might have something to share with one who has need" (4:28).[32] For the stealer among the community of believers to no longer steal but instead labor "working" (ἐργαζόμενος) with his own hands that which is "good" (ἀγαθόν) reminds the audience that we believers have been created in Christ Jesus for "good works" (ἔργοις ἀγαθοῖς) which God prepared beforehand, that we might walk in them (2:10). And for the former stealer thus to use his hands to work in order to provide for himself instead of stealing from others and to have something to share with a fellow believer in need further exemplifies for the audience what it means to be genuinely truthful to one another, that is, to share what we have as gifts of love within the realm of being "in love" (4:15).[33]

And for us who are members of one another (4:25) to forbear one another within the realm of being "in love" (4:2) means: "Let no harmful word

---

ὀργή is the disposition of anger, παροργισμός is provocation, exasperation, violent anger or a 'state of being intensely provoked.' A good rendering is 'festering anger, provocation, or irritation.'" O'Brien, *Ephesians*, 340: "Apparently this saying was proverbial. Plutarch [in *Moralia* 488c] mentions that if ever the Pythagoreans were led by anger into recrimination, they were never to let the sun go down before they joined hands, embraced one another, and were reconciled."

31. Otto Böcher, "διάβολος," *EDNT* 1.297: "In the dualistic worldview that the NT shares with ancient Judaism, the heavenly βασιλεία stands in opposition to that of the demons. The devil is the highest sovereign of the demons." Eph 4:27 is translated as "do not give the devil a chance to exert his influence" by BDAG, 1012. Hoehner, *Ephesians*, 623: "[I]n the present context the term διάβολος is fitting because the devil is a slanderer who wants to see divisiveness in the body, which is caused by festering anger." O'Brien, *Ephesians*, 341: "Anger can give the devil an opportunity to cause strife within the life of the individual and the community. Such discord is to be avoided by managing the anger properly and speedily."

32. Eph 4:28 refers not so much to fellow believers stealing from one another as to seasonal workers stealing the things they handled or shopkeepers cheating their customers because they may have felt forced to do so in order to provide for themselves and their families, according to Ernest Best, "Thieves in the Church: Ephesians 4:28," *IBS* 14 (1992): 2–9. On the relation of "let the stealer no longer steal" in Eph 4:28 to Lev 19:11, see Moritz, *Profound Mystery*, 91–92.

33. Lincoln, *Ephesians*, 304: "The motive for work is not individual profit but rather communal well-being. . . . and is perhaps more directly related to the ideal of Christian love." O'Brien, *Ephesians*, 343 n. 306: "The verb μεταδίδωμι ('to give part of, give a share'; cf. Rom. 1:11; 12:8; 1 Thess. 2:8) here indicates that the hard worker will have something to share with others. His industrious effort will obviously result in benefit to himself, but the particular point here is that he is to share the good that he has with others in need."

come out of your mouth,[34] but only such as is good for the building up of what is needed, that it might give grace to those who hear" (4:29). As the "good" (ἀγαθόν) for which one works to share with one having "need" (χρείαν) (4:28), so the "good" (ἀγαθός) rather than harmful word spoken by the audience of believers is for the building up of the "need" (χρείας),[35] in order to give grace to one another (4:29).[36] That the good word is for the "building up" (οἰκοδομήν) of what is needed reminds the audience that they have been given gifts of love from the ascended Christ for the "building up" (οἰκοδομήν) of the body of Christ (4:12), so that by the members of the body sharing these gifts with one another the whole body brings about the growth of the body for the "building up" (οἰκοδομήν) of itself within the realm of being "in love" (4:16).

Whereas the audience have "heard" (ἠκούσατε) about Christ (4:21) in the B element, having "heard" (ἀκούσαντες) the "word" (λόγον) of truth, the gospel of their salvation (1:13), the good "word" (λόγος) that is to come out of their mouth is to give grace to "those who hear" (ἀκούουσιν) it (4:29) in the B′ element of the chiasm. That this good word is to "give" (δῷ) "grace" (χάριν) to those who hear it reminds the audience that each of us "has been given" (ἐδόθη) "grace" (χάρις) as a gift of Christ's love (4:7). Thus, the audience who have been given grace are, by the good word and truth (4:25) that they speak, in turn to give grace to those who hear as a further way of being truthful by sharing their gifts of love with one another within the realm of being "in love" (4:15).

6. Eph 4:30–32 (A′): Be Gracious as God in Christ Was Gracious to Us

The A′ element (4:30–32) of the chiasm introduces a focus on God into the motivation for us who are members of one another (4:25) to forbear one another within the realm of being "in love" (4:2). With a contrastive parallel to the A element (4:17–19), where the Gentiles are said to be alienated from the life of "God" (θεοῦ, 4:18), Paul exhorts his audience not to grieve the Holy Spirit of "God" (θεοῦ, 4:30) but to be gracious to one another just as also "God" (θεός, 4:32) in Christ has been gracious to us in the A′

---

34. O'Brien, *Ephesians*, 344 n. 310: "The singular for mouth (στόμα) is a Semitic distributive singular relating to each member of the group. All are to heed the apostolic command."

35. On the sense of "the building up of the need" here Hoehner (*Ephesians*, 630) concludes that "the purpose of our speech is to supply that which is lacking in other believers' lives by the utterance of beneficial words, thus contributing to the spiritual growth of the body."

36. As Lincoln (*Ephesians*, 306) points out, "the sentence of v 29 has links with that of v 28. ἀγαθός and χρεία function as catchword links: the contrast between evil and good is repeated but now associated with speech rather than action, with the mouth rather than the hands, and in both cases the well-being of others is the goal."

element. Whereas in the A element the Gentiles have given themselves over to indecency for the practice of "every" or "all" (πάσης) kind of impurity in greediness (4:19), Paul exhorts his audience to let "all" (πᾶσα) bitterness and fury and wrath and shouting and reviling be put away from them along with "all" (πάσῃ) malice (4:31) in the A´ element. The audience thus hear a progression from single references to "God" and "all" in the A element to double references in the A´ element.

Paul's audience are not to grieve, by a harmful word out of their mouth (4:29), the "Holy" (ἅγιον) "Spirit" (πνεῦμα) of God,[37] in whom "you were sealed" (ἐσφραγίσθητε)—as a gift of God's love (divine passive)—for the day of "redemption" (ἀπολυτρώσεως) (4:30), because in becoming believers "you were sealed" (ἐσφραγίσθητε)—as a gift of God's love (divine passive)—with the "Holy" (ἁγίῳ) "Spirit" (πνεύματι) of the promise (1:13) for "redemption" (ἀπολύτρωσιν) (1:14; cf. 1:7).[38] The audience are to realize then that grieving the Holy Spirit of God with a harmful word to one another contradicts their forbearing one another within the realm of being "in love" (4:2).[39]

The transition from the active verb, "do not grieve" (λυπεῖτε, 4:30), to the passive verb, "be put away" (ἀρθήτω), in Paul's exhortation to "let all bitterness and fury and wrath and shouting and reviling *be put away* from you along with all malice" (4:31) connotes that the audience can do this only with the help of God's Holy Spirit with which they have been sealed as a further gift of God's love.[40] The concluding and climactic prepositional

---

37. On the expression "the Holy Spirit of God" here Fee (*God's Empowering Presence*, 714) remarks: "Here the full ascription is not just a form of solemn speech, calling special attention to the role of the Spirit in ethical life, but also an emphatic declaration that the Holy Spirit is none other than the Spirit of God."

38. There is a subtle progression then from being sealed with the Holy Spirit (1:13) to being sealed within the realm of being in union with the Holy Spirit (4:30). The Holy Spirit "in whom" (ἐν ᾧ) you were sealed recalls that the audience who have been sealed with the Holy Spirit are now living within the dynamic realm of being "in the Spirit" (cf. "in one Spirit" [ἐν ἑνὶ πνεύματι, 2:18]; "in the Spirit" [ἐν πνεύματι, 2:22; 3:5; 5:18; 6:18]). In other words, you have not only been sealed with the Holy Spirit (1:13), but in your union with the Holy Spirit you have been sealed for the day of redemption (4:30).

39. On the relation of "grieving the Holy Spirit" here to Isa 63:10 and Exod 33:12–14, see Moritz, *Profound Mystery*, 92–93; Fee, *God's Empowering Presence*, 713–15; O'Brien, *Ephesians*, 346–48.

40. On the passive verb "let be put away" here Hoehner (*Ephesians*, 636) remarks: "The passive idea may be used because the believer cannot change his or her behavior but must depend on the power of the Holy Spirit with whom he or she was sealed (v. 30)." According to Barth (*Ephesians 4–6*, 22), "in Eph 4:31 the taking away of all malice from man certainly cannot be effected by man's Herculean effort alone. While God must do it himself, man is called upon not to resist the lifting away of 'malice'." Fee, *God's Empowering Presence*, 716: "Paul understood the Spirit to be the empowering presence of God, enabling the ethical life which has God's glory as its ultimate goal."

phrase, "along with all malice," places this kind of behavior in a malicious framework that intensifies the harmfulness of the word that may come out of the mouth of the audience (4:29) as a contradiction to their forbearing one another and being truthful toward one another within the realm of being "in love" (4:2, 15).[41]

Further developing their forbearing "one another" (ἀλλήλων) "in love" (4:2) because we are members of "one another" (ἀλλήλων) (4:25), the audience are to become "kind" (χρηστοί) and compassionate to "one another" (ἀλλήλους) (4:32a), remembering the "kindness" (χρηστότητι) with which God graced us in Christ Jesus (2:7).[42] The audience's "being gracious to one another just as also God in Christ was gracious to us" (4:32b) further develops not only Paul's continual assimilation of the "you" believers to all of us believers but also the theme of love in Ephesians. The audience's "being gracious" (χαριζόμενοι) to one another by sharing with fellow believers the "grace" (χάριν) of the good word as a gift of love (4:29) is an appropriate response to God's "having been gracious" (ἐχαρίσατο) to us in Christ with the "grace" (χάριτί) by which God saved us in our union with Christ (2:5, 8)—the "grace" (χάριτος) with which he "graced" (ἐχαρίτωσεν) us in the Beloved (1:6)—as a gift of the great love with which God loved us (2:4).[43]

---

41. On the word "malice" (κακία) here Hoehner (*Ephesians*, 637) comments: "This word colors all the other words mentioned earlier in the verse. Certain words like anger and wrath need not have an evil connotation but with this last noun united to them, they denote a malicious anger and wrath. Therefore, Paul urgently exhorts believers to put away all of these qualities which are defined by malice." Lincoln, *Ephesians*, 309: "It may well be, as a number of commentators have suggested, that his indictment had added rhetorical force, because within the comprehensive listing there is also a progression from anger's inner center (πικρία) through its initial eruption (θυμός) and steady festering (ὀργή) to its external expression (κραυγή) and damaging of others (βλασφημία)." O'Brien, *Ephesians*, 349: "Paul's list appears to be climactic, progressing from an inner resentful attitude, through its indignant outburst and seething rage, to public shouting and abusive language or cursing."

42. Lincoln, *Ephesians*, 309: "Kindness has been attributed to God in 2:7, and the consideration of the needs and interests of others that it entails is now required of humans."

43. For the reasons to translate the two uses of χαρίζομαι in 4:32 as "being gracious" rather than as "forgiving," see Hoehner, *Ephesians*, 639–40. Lincoln, *Ephesians*, 310: "What God has done in Christ for believers, which has been the theme of the first half of the letter, now provides both the norm and the grounds for believers' own behavior." Hoehner, *Ephesians*, 641: "The prepositional phrase ἐν Χριστῷ speaks of the sphere or locale in which God has been gracious. This gracious act was directed toward 'us' (ἡμῖν) and was demonstrated by sending his Son to die on the cross for us. It is spoken of in 1:7–12 and 2:4–10. In fact, 2:4 states that it was God's rich mercy expressed in love toward us who had been dead in transgressions that made us alive. All this gracious love and redemption was done in Christ."

C. Summary on Ephesians 4:17–32

1. That "you have not so learned the *Christ*" (4:20) in the G′ unit (4:17–32) of the overall chiastic structure of Ephesians recalls Paul's prayer that "the *Christ* may dwell through faith in your hearts" (3:17), so that you may "know the love of the *Christ* that surpasses knowledge" (3:19) in the G unit (3:14–21).

2. For the audience not to "walk" as the Gentiles "walk" (4:17) means for them to "walk" in accord with their calling (4:1), forbearing one another "in love" (4:2), being truthful "in love" (4:15), and building up the body of Christ "in love" (4:16). Instead of "walking" in the ignorance that is within the hearts of the Gentiles (4:18), the audience are to "walk" in the knowledge of the love of the Christ (3:19) that is in their hearts (3:17). Instead of "walking" in alienation of the life of God like the Gentiles, the audience are to "walk" as those whom God has now made alive with the Christ, after they were dead in their sins (2:1, 5), because of the great love with which God loved us (2:4–5). And instead of "walking" like the Gentiles who practice every kind of impurity in greediness (4:19), the audience are to "walk" by practicing the work of ministry (4:12)—sharing as gifts of love for one another the gifts of love they have received from the ascended Christ (4:7–12)—within the dynamic realm of being "in love" (4:2, 15–16).

3. The "truth" involved in loving one another that believers learned in Christ Jesus (4:20–21) empowers the audience to counter not only the false and erroneous teaching of human beings (4:14) but the Gentiles' wrong way of "walking" (4:17–19). This "truth" that is "*in* Jesus" (4:21) thus contradicts the "*in* greediness" of Gentile conduct (4:19) and complements the "*in* love" within which the body of Christ is building itself up (4:16).

4. That the audience "have put off" the "old person" (4:22) is not ultimately a human accomplishment but a further benefit of God's love.

5. In their union with Christ Jesus the audience have been taught (4:21) that they are "being renewed" continually by God (4:23) as a further gift of God's love.

6. That the audience have "put on" the "new person" created according to God "in righteousness and holiness of truth" (4:24) means they have adopted an external conduct with the attributes of God himself, who is known as both "righteous and holy" (LXX Deut 32:4; Ps 144:17). And these divine attributes come from "the truth," in contrast to the desires of "the deceit" (4:22), the "truth" that there is for believers in the realm of being in Jesus

(4:21), as they are "being truthful" with one another by sharing the gifts of love they have received from Christ with one another within the realm of being "in love" (4:15).

7. By "each" one speaking truth as a gift of love to his neighbor (4:25), and thus being truthful "in love" (4:15), the whole body of Christ, through the working in measure of "each" individual part, builds itself up within the realm of being "in love" (4:16).

8. For us to speak truth with our neighbor because we are members of "one another" (4:25) within the body of Christ further exemplifies what it means for us to respectfully forbear "one another" within the realm of being "in love" (4:2).

9. "Be angry but do not sin; let not the sun set on your anger, and do not give room to the devil" (4:26–27) elaborates on what kind of conduct is appropriate within the realm of being "in love" for us who are members of one another (4:25), forbearing one another "in love" (4:2).

10. For the former stealer to use his hands to work in order to provide for himself instead of stealing from others and to have something to share with a fellow believer in need (4:28) further exemplifies for the audience what it means to be genuinely truthful to one another, that is, to share what we have as gifts of love within the realm of being "in love" (4:15).

11. That the good word the audience speak is for the "building up" of what is needed (4:29) reminds them that they have been given gifts of love from the ascended Christ for the "building up" of the body of Christ (4:12), so that by the members of the body sharing these gifts with one another the whole body brings about the growth of the body for the "building up" of itself within the realm of being "in love" (4:16).

12. The audience are to realize that grieving the Holy Spirit of God (4:30) with a harmful word to one another (4:29) contradicts their forbearing one another within the realm of being "in love" (4:2).

13. The audience's "being gracious" to one another by sharing with fellow believers the "grace" of the good word as a gift of love (4:29) is an appropriate response to God's "having been gracious" to us in Christ with the "grace" by which God saved us in our union with Christ (2:5, 8)—the "grace" with which he "graced" us in the Beloved (1:6)—as a gift of the great love with which God loved us (2:4).

CHAPTER 12

Ephesians 5:1–6:
Walk in Love as Christ Loved Us (F′)

A: ¹ Become then imitators *of God* as *beloved children*² and walk in love just as also the Christ loved us and handed himself over for us as an offering and sacrifice to God for a fragrant aroma.

B: ³ But do not let *sexual immorality* and any *impurity* or *greed* even be named among you, as is fitting for holy ones,

C: ⁴ no *shamefulness* or *foolish talk* or *sarcastic ridicule*, which are inappropriate, but rather *thanksgiving*.

B′:   ⁵ For this know assuredly, that no *sexually immoral* or *impure* or *greedy* one, who is an idolater, has an inheritance in the kingdom of the Christ and God.

A′:   ⁶ Let no one deceive you with empty words; for because of these things the wrath *of God* is coming upon the *sons of disobedience*.¹

A. Chiastic Development from Ephesians 3:1–13 (F) to 5:1–6 (F′)

With Eph 5:1–6, the F′ unit within the macro-chiastic structure embracing the entire Letter, the audience hear resonances of 3:1–13, the corresponding F unit in the overall chiasm. The references to the "Christ" (Χριστός) who loved us (5:2) and the kingdom of "Christ" (Χριστοῦ) and God (5:5) in the F′ unit recall the references to Paul as the prisoner of the "Christ" (Χριστοῦ) Jesus (3:1), to the mystery of "Christ" (Χριστοῦ, 3:4), to the promise in "Christ" (Χριστῷ) Jesus (3:6), to the wealth of the "Christ" (Χριστοῦ, 3:8), and to the purpose of the ages which God accomplished in "Christ" (Χριστῷ) Jesus our Lord (3:11) in the F unit.

---

1. For the establishment of Eph 5:1–6 as a chiasm, see ch. 2.

Paul's command for the audience to become imitators "of God" (τοῦ θεοῦ) as beloved children (5:1), that Christ handed himself over for us as an offering and sacrifice "to God" (τῷ θεῷ, 5:2), the kingdom of Christ and "God" (θεοῦ, 5:5), and the wrath "of God" (τοῦ θεοῦ, 5:6) in the F′ unit recall the grace "of God" (τοῦ θεοῦ) that was given to Paul as a gift of God's love to be shared with the audience (3:2), the grace "of God" (τοῦ θεοῦ) that was given to Paul to become a minister of the gospel (3:7), the plan of the mystery which had been hidden from the ages "in God" (τῷ θεῷ, 3:9), and the manifold wisdom "of God" (τοῦ θεοῦ, 3:10) in the F unit. And not having an "inheritance" (κληρονομίαν) in the kingdom of the Christ and God (5:5) in the F′ unit forms a contrastive parallel to the Gentiles being "fellow heirs" (συγκληρονόμα) as a gift of God's love in Christ Jesus (3:6) in the F unit.

With regard to the love theme, that Christ loved us (5:2) in the F′ unit provides the motivation for Paul's being the prisoner of the Christ Jesus (3:1), develops the content of the mystery of the Christ (3:4) and the wealth of the Christ (3:8), and gives the reason why the Gentiles are fellow heirs and fellow members of the body and fellow sharers of the promise in Christ Jesus (3:6), as well as how God accomplished the purpose of the ages in Christ Jesus our Lord (3:11) in the F unit. Paul's command for the audience to imitate God as children beloved by God and Christ who share that love with one another by "walking" within the realm of being "in love" (5:1–2) in the F′ unit finds further motivation in the example of Paul who shared with the audience the grace of God he received as a gift of God's love to be a minister of the gospel (3:2, 7) in the F unit. And that there is no "inheritance" in the kingdom of Christ and God for one who is sexually immoral, impure, or greedy (5:5) in the F′ unit warns the audience not to forfeit being "fellow heirs" in Christ Jesus (3:6) as a gift of God's love in the F unit.

B. Audience Response to Ephesians 5:1–6

1. Eph 5:1–2 (A): As God's Beloved Children Walk in Love as Christ Loved Us

At the conclusion of the previous unit (4:17–32) Paul exhorted his audience, "But become (γίνεσθε) kind to one another" (4:32a). Now, with a resumptive and inferential "then" (οὖν), Paul further draws out the implications of this exhortation for his audience: "Become (γίνεσθε) then imitators of God as beloved children" (5:1).[2] Now that they are no longer "children"

---

2. Hoehner, *Ephesians*, 643–44: "The conjunction οὖν is a resumptive inferential conjunction that goes back to 4:1 and 17 making another application from the first three chapters. It also builds on the previous section (4:17–32) where Paul told them not to walk as the Gentiles do because they have put off the old person and have put on the new person and

(τέκνα) of wrath (2:3) but "children" (τέκνα) beloved by God, the audience are to become imitators of God with regard to God's love. As God in Christ was gracious to them as a gift of God's love, so they are to imitate God, as children imitate their father (cf. God as "Father" in 1:2, 3, 17; 2:18; 3:14; 4:6), by being gracious to each other (4:32) as a gift of love from children "beloved" (ἀγαπητά) by God, that is, children whom God has graced with his grace in their union with the "Beloved" (ἠγαπημένῳ) (1:6).

Although the audience once "walked" (περιεπατήσατε), that is, "conducted themselves" or "lived," according to the age of this world (2:2), we believers were created in Christ Jesus for the good works which God prepared beforehand, that we might "walk" (περιπατήσωμεν) in them (2:10). Paul then exhorted his audience "to walk" (περιπατῆσαι) worthy of the calling with which they were called (4:1) and not "to walk" (περιπατεῖν) as the Gentiles "walk" (περιπατεῖ), that is, in the futility of their mind (4:17). And now Paul, with an explanatory conjunction "and" or "that is" (καί) further specifying what it means to imitate God (5:1), exhorts his audience, "and walk (περιπατεῖτε) in love" (5:2a).[3]

We believers were chosen before the foundation of the world to be holy and blameless before God "in love" (ἐν ἀγάπῃ) (1:4). Paul prayed that his audience, "in love" (ἐν ἀγάπῃ) rooted and grounded, may have the inner strength (3:17) to know the "love" of Christ that surpasses knowledge (3:19). Paul's exhortation for his audience to "walk" or "live" worthy of their calling (4:1) included their forbearing one another "in love" (ἐν ἀγάπῃ) (4:2). By being truthful "in love" (ἐν ἀγάπῃ) (4:15), we believers bring about the growth of the body of Christ for the building up of itself "in love" (ἐν ἀγάπῃ) (4:16). And so now Paul exhorts his audience to "walk," that is, to conduct themselves and continually live, within this dynamic realm of being "in love" (ἐν ἀγάπῃ) (5:2a), that is, with a lifestyle in which they share with one another the gifts of love they have received from God as "beloved" children of God (5:1).

With regard to the love theme in Ephesians, this is the final, climactic occurrence of the dynamic prepositional phrase, "in love," which encapsulates all of its previous occurrences. We believers are not only to be holy and blameless before God "in love" (1:4), rooted and grounded "in love" (3:17),

---

practices which concluded with reference to God's gracious action in Christ as a motivation for them to be kind, compassionate, and gracious to one another. Paul again uses, as he did in 4:32, the present imperative 'to become' rather than 'to be.' They are to develop continuously into imitators of God."

3. Hoehner, *Ephesians*, 646: "The καί serves as a coordinating or an epexegetical conjunction giving further specification of the injunction in verse 1. These two statements parallel each other, for to be an imitator of God is to walk in love." According to Wallace (*Greek Grammar*, 722), the verb "walk" here is a "customary" present—"continue to walk in love."

forbearing one another "in love" (4:2), being truthful "in love" (4:15), building up the body of Christ "in love" (4:16), but we are also therefore to
"walk"—as a continual way of life—within this realm of being "in love"
(5:2).

Further assimilating the "you" believers to all of us believers, Paul
grounded his exhortation for his audience to become kind to one another,
being gracious to each other, with a comparison to God as the giver of gracious love to us believers—"just as also God in Christ was gracious to *us*"
(4:32). But now Paul, again assimilating the "you" believers to all of us believers, grounds his exhortation for his audience to become imitators of God
as beloved children (5:1) by "walking" in love (5:2a) with a comparison to
Christ as the giver of love to us believers—"just as also the Christ loved *us*"
(5:2b):

4:32: καθὼς καὶ ὁ θεὸς ἐν Χριστῷ ἐχαρίσατο ἡμῖν

5:2b: καθὼς καὶ ὁ Χριστὸς ἠγάπησεν ἡμᾶς

This marks a significant development with regard to the use of the verb
"to love" within the theme of love that pervades Ephesians. In the first occurrence of a verbal form of "love" in Ephesians Christ was the object and
God the implied subject within a broader expression of God's gracious love
for us believers in our union with Christ—the grace with which God graced
us in the "Beloved" (ἠγαπημένῳ, 1:6). The next occurrence developed this
expression of God's gracious love for us in terms of the great love with
which God "loved" (ἠγάπησεν) us (2:4) in making us alive with Christ and
thus saving us by grace (2:4–8). God was again the subject but we believers the direct object. But now for the first time Christ is the subject and we
believers the direct object in the statement that the Christ, the one Beloved
by God (1:6), "loved" (ἠγάπησεν) us (5:2b), the beloved children of God
(5:1) as an example for us to "walk" in love (5:2a). For us to imitate God
as beloved children by "walking" within the realm of being "in love" thus
means imitating Christ as the Beloved one who also loved us.[4]

With an explanatory conjunction "and" or "that is" (καί) Paul further
specifies for his audience how Christ loved us—"and he handed himself over
for us as an offering and sacrifice to God for a fragrant aroma" (5:2c). In
contrast to the Gentiles who selfishly "have given themselves over (ἑαυτοὺς
παρέδωκαν) to indecency for the practice of every kind of impurity in greedi-

---

4. Lincoln, *Ephesians*, 311: "In fact, the imitation of God turns out to be the imitation
of Christ, as in the motivating clause it is the latter's love and self-giving that are the ground
and the norm for the behavior required of believers. The sudden change of focus from God
in 5:1 to Christ in 5:2 should be seen in the light of the dual reference to God's activity in
Christ in the motivating clause of 4:32 . . . The love involved in the events of salvation can be
attributed both to God, as it is in 2:4, and to Christ, as it is here."

ness" (4:19), Christ selflessly "handed himself over" (παρέδωκεν ἑαυτὸν) as a gift of love on our behalf.[5] Whereas Paul previously expressed his love for his audience in terms of giving thanks "for you" (ὑπὲρ ὑμῶν, 1:16), being a prisoner of Christ Jesus "for you" (ὑπὲρ ὑμῶν, 3:1), and suffering "for you" (ὑπὲρ ὑμῶν, 3:13), Christ expressed his love for all of us believers by handing himself over "for us" (ὑπὲρ ἡμῶν, 5:2c) in a sacrificial death offered to God.[6]

That Christ loved us by handing himself over for us "as an offering and sacrifice to God for a fragrant aroma" (5:2c),[7] referring to the offering of his blood and flesh in a sacrificial death on the cross, is the preconditional basis for the previous expressions in Ephesians of Christ's love for us that did not employ the verb "to love." It is by Christ's sacrificial "blood" that we have redemption (1:7) and that the "you" believers have become near (2:13) as gifts of Christ's love. It was by his sacrificial "flesh" (2:14) offered through his death on the cross that Christ reconciled both believing Jews and Gentiles in one body to God (2:16) as a gift of the love of Christ.

---

5. Hoehner, *Ephesians*, 647–48: "The verb παρέδωκεν means 'to hand over, give over' and the reflexive pronoun ἑαυτόν indicates that he took his own initiative in handing himself over (cf. 4:19; 5:25). This shows how much Christ loved us."

6. Hoehner, *Ephesians*, 648: "The prepositional phrase ὑπὲρ ἡμῶν shows the object for which Christ laid down his life. The preposition with a genitive signifies that it was done 'for our sake, in our behalf,' showing interest in the object and has 'been characterized as the particle of love.' He did it 'for us.' "

7. O'Brien, *Ephesians*, 355: "The two terms 'offering and sacrifice', which are probably a hendiadys and appear in Psalm 40:6 (LXX 39:7), include all kinds of sacrifices, both grain and animal. . . . while the final phrase, 'for a fragrant aroma', which was used in the Old Testament of all the main types of sacrifice in the levitical ritual, indicates what is well pleasing to God. Paul is here capturing this Old Testament sense of a sacrifice that is truly acceptable to God. Christ willingly offered himself as a sacrifice to the Father, and this was fully pleasing to him." On "offering," see Wolfgang Schenk, "προσφορά," *EDNT* 3.178. On "sacrifice," see Hartwig Thyen, "θυσία," *EDNT* 2.161–63. For a consideration of the meaning of Christ's death against the OT background of the concepts of sacrifice, see Jürgen Werbick, "Ein Opfer zur Versöhnung der zürnenden Gottheit?: Über die Zwiespältigkeit eines soteriologischen Denkmodells," *BK* 49 (1994): 144–49. Lincoln, *Ephesians*, 312: "The imagery performs a doxological function at the end of the sentence, as through it the writer indicates that Christ's sacrifice of love was supremely pleasing and glorifying to God. But the rhetoric still serves the paraenesis, and the readers are reminded that Christ's sacrificial love should find a response in analogous acts of love toward each other." Gerhard Dautzenberg, "εὐωδία," *EDNT* 2.90: "[T]he phrase [fragrant aroma] is used to interpret the self-giving of Christ with the terms of sacrificial language. One may assume, however, that the appeal for imitation of Christ is not limited to the example of ἀγάπη given by him. If the memory of his self-sacrifice 'for us' is indebted to the traditional christological formula and the saving sacrifice can be imitated only in a limited way, the characterization of this offering as a 'gift and sacrifice . . .' is probably not to be considered just an example of the plerophoric style of Ephesians. Instead it may be parenetically motivated, with Christ placed before the eyes of the addressees as the example and model of the spiritual worship to which they have been called."

It was after he descended to the lower parts of the earth (4:9) through his sacrifical death that the ascended Christ gave gifts of love to each of us believers for the building up of the one body of Christ "in love" (4:7–16). And it was after God raised Christ from his sacrificial death that he gave him as head over all things to the church, which is his body, the fullness of the Christ who is filling all things in all ways (1:20–23), as an expression of the "love" of Christ by which the audience may be filled to all the fullness of God (3:19).

2. Eph 5:3 (B): Behave as Is Fitting for Holy Ones

Paul then further specifies what it means for his audience to "walk" or conduct themselves within the realm of being "in love" (5:2a): "Do not let sexual immorality and any impurity or greed even be named among you, as is fitting for holy ones" (5:3).[8] That the audience is not even to talk about sexual immorality along with "all impurity" (ἀκαθαρσία πᾶσα) and "greed" (πλεονεξία) continues the contrast with the unloving and selfish way that the Gentiles "walk" in their behavior toward one another (4:17)—they have "given themselves over" to indecency for the practice of "every kind of impurity" (ἀκαθαρσίας πάσης) in "greediness" (πλεονεξία) (4:19).[9] In sharp contrast to the Gentiles, then, the audience are to "walk" in a loving and selfless way toward one another within the realm of being "in love" by imitating the love of Christ who selflessly "handed himself over" for us in his sacrificial death (5:2b).[10]

Avoiding such vices is fitting for "holy ones" (ἁγίοις, 5:3b). This reminds the audience that as "holy ones" (ἁγίοις) in Ephesus (1:1), who are joined with (1:18; 2:19; 3:18) and love all the "holy ones" (ἁγίους, 1:15), they have received gifts of love from the ascended Christ for the equipping of the "holy ones" (ἁγίων, 4:12), so that they may not only "walk in love"

---

8. On "sexual immorality" (πορνεία) O'Brien (*Ephesians*, 359 n. 2) notes: "The πορνεία word-group was employed in the LXX to denote unchastity, harlotry, prostitution, and fornication. In later rabbinic literature the noun was understood to include not only prostitution and any kind of extramarital sexual intercourse, but also all marriages between relatives forbidden by rabbinic law. Incest and all kinds of unnatural sexual intercourse were regarded as fornication (πορνεία)."

9. Lincoln, *Ephesians*, 322: "Believers' distancing from such vices must extend to their conversation. Presumably, the assumption behind this prohibition is that thinking and talking about sexual sins creates an atmosphere in which they are tolerated and which can indirectly even promote their practice."

10. Hoehner, *Ephesians*, 654: "Paul gives the negative exhortation against the sins of self-love that are so diametrically opposed to the love seen in Christ's sacrificial death."

(5:2a) but be "holy" (ἁγίους) and blameless before God within the realm of being "in love" (1:4).[11]

3. Eph 5:4 (C): Thanksgiving Rather Than Shamefulness

Paul then continues his elaboration on what it means for his audience to "walk" or conduct themselves within the realm of being "in love" (5:2a): "no shamefulness or foolish talk or sarcastic ridicule, which are inappropriate, but rather thanksgiving" (5:4).[12] That the audience are to speak among themselves "no shamefulness or foolish talk or sarcastic ridicule" (5:4a) develops Paul's previous exhortations regarding their speech: "Let all bitterness and fury and wrath and shouting and reviling be put away from you along with all malice" (4:31) and "Let no harmful word come out of your mouth" (4:29a). And the contrastive clause, "but (ἀλλά) rather thanksgiving" (5:4b) develops the contrastive clause, "but (ἀλλά) only such as is good for the building up of what is needed, that it might give grace to those who hear" (4:29b).

With an alliterative play on words εὐτραπελία ("sarcastic ridicule") is to be replaced by εὐχαριστία ("thanksgiving"). With regard to the love theme in Ephesians, this central element of the chiasm in 5:1–6 adds the notion of "thanksgiving" to what it means for the audience to conduct themselves within the realm of being "in love" (5:2a). As indicated by Paul himself when he declared to his audience whose love for all the holy ones he acknowledged (1:15b), "I do not cease giving thanks (εὐχαριστῶν) for you" (1:16a), thanksgiving includes praise not only for the love that comes from

---

11. Lincoln, *Ephesians*, 322: "The absence of the article with ἁγίοις, 'saints,' places stress on the qualitative dimensions of the term, the holiness of those set apart for God, and serves as a reminder of believers' calling as that is depicted in 1:4."

12. Each of the terms of this triplet—"obscenity" (αἰσχρότης), "foolish talk" (μωρολογία), and "sarcastic ridicule" (εὐτραπελία)—occurs only here in Ephesians (and in the NT). On "sarcastic ridicule" see Pieter Willem van der Horst, "Is Wittiness Unchristian? A Note on εὐτραπελία in Eph. v 4," in *Miscellanea Neotestamentica*, vol. 2 (ed. T. Baarda, et al.; NovTSup 48; Leiden: Brill, 1978), 163–77. Hoehner, *Ephesians*, 656: "In the context it most likely indicates jesting that has gone too far, thus becoming sarcastic ridicule that cuts people down and embarrasses others who are present. It is humor in bad taste. . . . Or, since in the context the preceding words were concerned with sexual sins, εὐτραπελία could even have reference to dirty jokes or humor with suggestive overtones." For the suggestion that Eph 5:4 refers to the obscene language and behavior connected to the mother-goddess Demeter/Cybele in Asia Minor, see Larry Joseph Kreitzer, " 'Crude Language' and 'Shameful Things Done in Secret' (Ephesians 5.4, 12): Allusions to the Cult of Demeter/Cybele in Hierapolis?" *JSNT* 71 (1998): 51–77. But as Hoehner (*Ephesians*, 657) counters, "if Paul were referring specifically to the mother-goddess practices, it seems likely that he would have been more pointed in his remarks. . . . Rather than addressing specific religious practices that were known in Asia Minor, it is more likely then that Paul is referring to inappropriate conduct and speech that was pervasive in all cultures outside the believing community."

God (5:1) and Christ (5:2) but for the love that comes from and for holy
ones (5:3b), fellow believers.[13]

4. Eph 5:5 (B´): No Immoral, Impure, or Greedy One Has an Inheritance

In the B element (5:3) of the chiasm Paul mentioned a triplet of
vices—"sexual immorality" (πορνεία), "impurity" (ἀκαθαρσία), and "greed"
(πλεονεξία)—that should not even be named among his audience. And now
with the B´ element (5:5) the audience hear a progression from these vices
to the individuals who practice them—"sexually immoral one" (πόρνος),
"impure one" (ἀκάθαρτος), and "greedy one" (πλεονέκτης).

After exhorting his audience to avoid the kind of behavior that is not
appropriate for them "to walk in love" (5:2–4), Paul solemnly warns: "For
this know assuredly, that no sexually immoral or impure or greedy one, who
is an idolater, has an inheritance in the kingdom of the Christ and God"
(5:5).[14] That this type of individual has no "inheritance" (κληρονομίαν), either presently or for the future, in the kingdom of the Christ and God stands
in contrast to the glorious "inheritance" (κληρονομίας) of God that the audience share with the holy ones (1:18) as "fellow heirs" (συγκληρονόμα) of the
promise in Christ Jesus (3:6), the "inheritance" (κληρονομίας) that all of us
believers have for final redemption (1:14).[15]

---

13. Hoehner, *Ephesians*, 658: "This exhortation closely parallels the rules of conduct
in the Qumran community that state that a member of the community will not keep Belial
(Satan) in his heart and that there will be no foolishness (= μωρολογία) and malicious lies and
deceit coming from his lips . . . abominations (= αἰσχρότης) will not be found on the tongue
but rather he will sing songs of thanksgiving (= εὐχαριστία) from his mouth (1QS 10:21–23).
When taking into consideration other passages of Scripture, it is clear that 'thanksgiving'
includes praise to God for himself, for his gifts, and for each other. The latter is in contrast
to using speech to destroy each other. Paul models this in his salutation where he gives thanks
to God for other believers (1:15–16)." Lincoln, *Ephesians*, 324: "The writer will elaborate on
the need for thanksgiving in 5:20, but it has already become clear from the opening *berakah*
(1:3–14) and thanksgiving section (1:15–23) that he believes this to be the proper response of
those who have experienced the grace [and thus the love] of God in Christ."

14. We take ἴστε ("know") as an imperative intensified by the participle γινώσκοντες
("knowing" but here translated as "assuredly"). For a construal of ἴστε γινώσκοντες as an
indicative—"you surely know"—based on a chiasm in 5:5, see Stanley E. Porter, "ἴστε
γινώσκοντες in Ephesians 5,5: Does Chiasm Solve a Problem?" *ZNW* 81 (1990): 270–76.
With regard to Porter's proposed chiasm, however, Hoehner (*Ephesians*, 659 n. 5) points out
that "elements of his chiastic structure do not readily fall into place and seem to be forced."
On the "greedy one, who is an idolater" O'Brien (*Ephesians*, 362–63) explains: "The sins
of covetousness and idolatry stood together in Jewish exhortations and were condemned as
part of the horrors of paganism; in particular, fornication and sexual lust were linked with
idolatry. Along with greed for riches and power, sexual lust is an idolatrous obsession; it
places self-gratification or another person at the centre of one's existence, and thus is the
worship of the creature rather than the Creator (Rom. 1:25)."

15. For the idea that in Ephesians "inheritance" is a future rather than present reality, see Paul L. Hammer, "A Comparison of Klēronomia in Paul and Ephesians," *JBL* 79

That a sexually immoral one, or impure one, or idolatrous greedy one has no inheritance "in" (ἐν) the kingdom of the Christ and God, that is, within the domain ruled by the Christ and God (5:5) thus means that such a person, in contrast to what is expected of the audience, is not living "in" (ἐν) love, that is, within the domain ruled by the love of the Christ for us (5:2) and the love of God for us as God's beloved children (5:1).

5. Eph 5:6 (A′): The Wrath of God Is Coming upon the Sons of Disobedience

In the A element (5:1–2) of the chiasm Paul exhorted his audience to become imitators "of God" (τοῦ θεοῦ) as beloved children (5:1), "the God" (τῷ θεῷ) to whom the Christ handed himself over on our behalf (5:2). But now, by way of an antithetical chiastic parallelism, in the A′ element (5:6) Paul warns his audience that the wrath "of God" (τοῦ θεοῦ) is coming upon the sons of disobedience. A positive focus on the love of God in the A element thus becomes a negative focus on the wrath of God in the A′ element.

Whereas Paul has been exhorting his audience about the way they should speak and relate to one another (4:25–5:5), he now warns his audience about the kind of speech they may hear from an unbeliever: "Let no one deceive you with empty words; for because of these things the wrath of God is coming upon the sons of disobedience" (5:6). That the audience are not to let anyone "deceive" (ἀπατάτω) them with empty words warns them not to return to the behavior of the "old person" who is being corrupted according to the desires of the "deceit" (ἀπάτης), in contrast to the truth that they have heard is in Jesus (4:21–22).[16] Whereas, on the one hand, the audience are not to let any harmful "word" (λόγος) come out of their mouth (4:29), on the other hand, they are not to let anyone deceive them with empty "words" (λόγοι), since they are those who have heard the "word" (λόγον) of truth, the gospel of their salvation (1:13).[17]

(1960): 268–69. But, as Hoehner (*Ephesians*, 662 n. 2) points out, "Paul speaks about those characterized in v. 5 as those who do not 'have' the kingdom of God rather than those who 'will' not have the kingdom of God." See also D. R. Denton, "Inheritance in Paul and Ephesians," *EvQ* 54 (1982): 157–58. According to O'Brien (*Ephesians*, 363–64), "The apostle's language here about not sharing in the heavenly inheritance is rather striking: first, unlike the earlier instances in his paraenesis where the verb 'to inherit' appears in the future tense ('will not inherit . . .', 1 Cor. 6:9, 10; Gal. 5:21), Ephesians uses the present: the immoral person 'has no inheritance'. It is possible . . . to regard this as a 'future-referring present', so indicating that evildoers will not have any future lot in the divine kingdom. But it is better to understand the present tense, 'has [no inheritance]', as signifying a process, without reference to past, present, or future: no immoral person has any part in the divine kingdom."

16. Hoehner, *Ephesians*, 663: "The verb ἀπατάω has the same sense as the noun ἀπάτη discussed at 4:22, meaning 'to deceive, mislead.'"

17. With regard to the term "empty words" Hoehner (*Ephesians*, 663) states that "in this context it has the idea of words that are without content or without basis, hence, 'empty

That the "wrath" (ὀργή) of God is coming upon the sons of disobedience (5:6b) warns the audience not to return to the former behavior according to which we were by nature children of "wrath" (ὀργῆς) as also the rest (2:3), but to walk "in love" (5:2a) as beloved children of God (5:1).[18] It likewise reinforces Paul's exhortation for the audience to remove all "anger" (ὀργή) from their midst (4:31), lest they become recipients of the "anger" or "wrath" of God. And that the *wrath* "of God" (τοῦ θεοῦ) is coming upon the sons of disobedience in this F′ unit (5:1–6) within the overall chiastic structure of Ephesians deepens the audience's appreciation not only for the *grace* "of God" (τοῦ θεοῦ) given to Paul to become a minister of the gospel (3:7), the *grace* "of God" (τοῦ θεοῦ) given to Paul as a gift of love for the audience (3:2), but also for the *wisdom* "of God" (τοῦ θεοῦ) that now may be made known to the rulers and to the authorities in the heavenly places through the church (3:10) as a gift of God's love in the F unit (3:1–13).

That the wrath of God is coming upon "the sons of disobedience" (τοὺς υἱοὺς τῆς ἀπειθείας) (5:6b) warns the audience not to return to the way they used to "walk"—according to the age of this world, according to the ruler of the authority of the air, of the spirit that is now working in "the sons of disobedience" (τοῖς υἱοῖς τῆς ἀπειθείας) (2:3).[19] Rather, the audience are to "walk" within the dynamic realm of being "in love," that is, within the realm in which they are to love one another in imitation of the love they have received from the Christ and God as beloved children (5:1–2).

C. Summary on Ephesians 5:1–6

1. Not having an "inheritance" in the kingdom of the Christ and God (5:5) in the F′ unit (5:1–6) in the overall chiastic structure in Ephesians forms a contrastive parallel to the Gentiles being "fellow heirs" as a gift of God's love in Christ Jesus (3:6) in the F unit (3:1–13).

---

words.' This makes good sense here for he had told the believers that unbelievers had minds that were without purpose, being darkened in their reasoning processes and that they were alienated from the life of God (Eph 4:17–18)."

18. On the verb "is coming" Hoehner (*Ephesians*, 664) comments: "The present tense of the verb ἔρχεται signifies 'a solemn present' nature of the wrath of God. But is not the wrath of God in the future? It is both present and future. . . . This present and future notion applies also to the kingdom mentioned in the preceding verse. We are presently in the kingdom (Eph 5:5; Col 1:13) and counted as fellow heirs (Eph 2:11–22), sealed with the Holy Spirit (1:13), and yet we will fully possess the kingdom later when we are finally redeemed from the presence of sin (1:14)." According to O'Brien (*Ephesians*, 365), "the present tense probably depicts the action taking place as a process: those who are disobedient experience the divine wrath (cf. Rom. 1:18–32), whether in this age or in its full manifestation at the end."

19. Hoehner, *Ephesians*, 664: "The word 'sons' conveys distinction, and here the distinctive sons of disobedience."

2. As God in Christ was gracious to the audience as a gift of God's love, so they are to imitate God, as children imitate their father (5:1; cf. God as "Father" in 1:2, 3, 17; 2:18; 3:14; 4:6), by being gracious to each other (4:32) as a gift of love from children "beloved" by God, that is, children whom God has graced with his grace in their union with *the* "Beloved" (1:6).

3. We believers are not only to be holy and blameless before God "in love" (1:4), rooted and grounded "in love" (3:17), forbearing one another "in love" (4:2), being truthful "in love" (4:15), building up the body of Christ "in love" (4:16), but we are also therefore to "walk"—as a continual way of life—within this realm of being "in love" (5:2).

4. For us to imitate God as beloved children by "walking" within the realm of being "in love" means imitating Christ as the Beloved one who also loved us (5:2).

5. That Christ loved us by handing himself over for us "as an offering and sacrifice to God for a fragrant aroma" (5:2c), referring to the offering of his blood and flesh in a sacrificial death on the cross, is the preconditional basis for the previous expressions in Ephesians of Christ's love for us that did not employ the verb "to love" (1:7, 20–23; 2:13–16; 3:19; 4:7–16).

6. Avoiding the vices unfitting for "holy ones" (5:3b) reminds the audience that as "holy ones" in Ephesus (1:1), who are joined with (1:18; 2:19; 3:18) and love all the "holy ones" (1:15), they have received gifts of love from the ascended Christ for the equipping of the "holy ones" (4:12), so that they may not only "walk in love" (5:2a) but be "holy" and blameless before God within the realm of being "in love" (1:4).

7. The central element (5:4) of the chiasm in 5:1–6 adds the notion of "thanksgiving" to what it means for the audience to conduct themselves within the realm of being "in love" (5:2a). Thanksgiving includes praise not only for the love that comes from God (5:1) and Christ (5:2) but for the love that comes from and for holy ones (5:3b), fellow believers.

8. That a sexually immoral one, or impure one, or idolatrous greedy one has no inheritance "in" the kingdom of the Christ and God, that is, within the domain ruled by the Christ and God (5:5) means that such a person, in contrast to what is expected of the audience, is not living "in" love, that is, within the domain ruled by the love of the Christ for us (5:2) and the love of God for us as God's beloved children (5:1).

9. That the *wrath* "of God" is coming upon the sons of disobedience

(5:6) in this F′ unit (5:1–6) within the overall chiastic structure of Ephesians deepens the audience's appreciation not only for the *grace* "of God" given to Paul to become a minister of the gospel (3:7), the *grace* "of God" given to Paul as a gift of love for the audience (3:2), but also for the *wisdom* "of God" that now may be made known to the rulers and to the authorities in the heavenly places through the church (3:10) as a gift of God's love in the F unit (3:1–13).

CHAPTER 13

Ephesians 5:7–14:
Walk as Children of Light in Love (E′)

A: ⁷ Do not then become fellow sharers with them; ⁸ for you were once darkness, but now you are *light* in the Lord; walk as children of *light*—

    B: ⁹ for the *fruit* of *the light* consists in all goodness and righteousness and truth—

        C: ¹⁰ *approving* what is *pleasing* to the Lord,

    B′: ¹¹ and do not be connected with the *unfruitful* works of the darkness, but rather expose them. ¹² For the things done in secret by them are shameful even to mention, ¹³ but all the things exposed by *the light* become visible,

A′: ¹⁴ for everything that becomes visible is *light*. Therefore it says, "Awake, O sleeper, and arise from the dead, and the Christ will shine on you."[1]

A. Chiastic Development from
Ephesians 2:11–22 (E) to 5:7–14 (E′)

With Eph 5:7–14, the E′ unit within the macro-chiastic structure of Ephesians, the audience hear resonances of 2:11–22, the corresponding E unit in the overall chiasm. Paul's command for his audience not to become "fellow sharers" (συμμέτοχοι) with them (5:7), the "sons of disobedience" (5:6), in the E′ unit is motivated by his audience instead being "fellow citizens" (συμπολῖται) with the holy ones (2:19) as a gift of God's love in the E unit. That "you were" (ἦτε) "once" (ποτε) darkness, but "now" (νῦν) are light (5:8) in the E′ unit develops that "once" (ποτέ) "you were" (ἦτε) with-

---

1. For the establishment of Eph 5:7–14 as a chiasm, see ch. 2.

out Christ (2:11–12) but "now" (νυνί) you who were "once" (ποτε) far away have become near in the blood of the Christ (2:13) as a gift of God's love in the E unit. And that you are not to "be connected with" (συγκοινωνεῖτε) the unfruitful works of the darkness (5:11) as you are light "in the Lord" (ἐν κυρίῳ) (5:8) as a gift of God's love in the E′ unit develops that it is "in the Lord" (ἐν κυρίῳ, 2:21) that "you are being built together" (συνοικοδομεῖσθε) into a dwelling place of God in the Spirit (2:22) as a gift of God's love in the E unit.

B. Audience Response to Ephesians 5:7–14

1. Eph 5:7–8 (A): Walk as Children of Light

Continuing his pattern of introducing new sections with the conjunction "then" (οὖν) closely followed by the verb "walk" (περιπατέω) (cf. 4:1, 17; 5:1–2), Paul enjoins his audience anew: "Do not then (οὖν) become fellow sharers with them; for you were once darkness, but now you are light in the Lord; walk (περιπατεῖτε) as children of light" (5:7–8). Whereas you are to "become" (γίνεσθε) kind to one another (4:32) and to "become" (γίνεσθε) imitators of God as beloved children (5:1), you are not to "become" (γίνεσθε) fellow sharers with "them" (5:7), that is, with the "sons of disobedience" upon whom the wrath of God is coming (5:6). Indeed, for the audience to become "fellow sharers" (συμμέτοχοι) with the "sons of disobedience" would contradict their being not only "fellow heirs" (συγκληρονόμα) and "fellow members of the body" (σύσσωμα) and "fellow sharers" (συμμέτοχα) of the promise in Christ Jesus (3:6) but also "fellow citizens" (συμπολῖται) with the holy ones (2:19) as a gift of God's love, and thus contradict what it means for them to "walk" in the realm of being "in love" (5:2).

That "you were" (ἦτε) "once" (ποτε) darkness (5:8a) further characterizes the situation of the audience when "you were" (ἦτε) "once" (ποτέ), as Gentiles in the flesh, "at that time without Christ alienated from the community of Israel and strangers of the covenants of the promise, not having hope and Godless in the world" (2:11–12), when you were "once" (ποτε) far away (2:13), and when you, "being dead in your transgressions and sins" (2:1), "once" (ποτε) "walked according to the age of this world, according to the ruler of the authority of the air, of the spirit that is now working in the sons of disobedience" (2:2). Indeed, all of us "once" (ποτε) "lived in the desires of our flesh doing the wishes of the flesh and of the thoughts, and we were by nature children of wrath as also the rest" (2:3).

And that "you were once darkness (σκότος)" (5:8a) further characterizes the situation of the audience when, like the Gentiles, they were walking "in the futility of their mind, being darkened (ἐσκοτωμένοι) in understanding, alienated from the life of God because of the ignorance that is in them because of the hardness of their hearts, who, having become callous, have given themselves over to indecency for the practice of every kind of impurity in greediness" (4:17–19). The audience thus not only once lived in darkness but could be said once to actually have been "darkness," so darkened were they not only interiorly—in their minds and hearts—but also exteriorly in their sinful conduct and hopeless situation before they knew the love of God in Christ.[2]

That "now" (νῦν) you are light in the Lord (5:8b) further character-izes the audience "now" (νυνί) that "in Christ Jesus you who once were far away have become (divine passive) near in the blood of the Christ" (2:13) as a gift of God's love. The audience *are* "light" (φῶς, 5:8b) in the Lord as a further consequence of the eyes of their heart "having been enlightened" (πεφωτισμένους, 1:18) by God (divine passive). They have been enlightened to the point of being light, then, as a gift of God's love. And they have been so enlightened that they may know what is the surpassing greatness of God's power for us who believe, the power which he worked when he raised Christ from the dead, subjected all things under his feet, and gave him as head over all things to the church (1:18–22) as a gift of God's love.

Whereas the audience were darkness (5:8a) when they were without Christ (2:11), now they are light in their union with Christ within the realm of being "in the Lord" (5:8b). That the audience are now light "in the Lord" (ἐν κυρίῳ) develops what it means for them to walk within the realm of being "in love" (ἐν ἀγάπῃ, 5:2a), because it is within the realm of being "in the Lord" (ἐν κυρίῳ) that they are being built together (divine passive) into a dwelling place of God in the Spirit (2:21–22) as a gift of God's love.[3]

---

2. On the metaphorical sense of "darkness," see Wolfgang Hackenberg, "σκότος," *EDNT* 3.255–56. O'Brien, *Ephesians*, 366–67: "In Ephesians darkness represents igno-rance, error, and evil (cf. 4:18), and in particular comes to signify immorality as the way of life of those who are separated from God." Hoehner, *Ephesians*, 670: "Therefore, darkness signifies sin, both its realm and power. Those who are in darkness must grope through life without the light of God's revelation (4:18). Their future will be a continuation of darkness but to an even greater degree. Interestingly, in this present verse Paul does not say that the believers were in darkness but that they were darkness itself, that is, the embodiment of darkness. As such, they were held in sway by the power of sin."

3. Lincoln, *Ephesians*, 327: "So the readers are not just surrounded by the light but are identified with it. They have become identified with the light because of their identification with Christ." Hoehner, *Ephesians*, 671: "People in darkness are on their own or are there by their own doing, but not so with light. The prepositional phrase ἐν κυρίῳ indicates that the believer is light in the Lord. The source of light is God and Christ. In this context, Christ is identified as the source (vv. 8, 14). 'Lord' in this prepositional phrase refers to Christ as it does elsewhere in this epistle (2:21; 4:1, 17; 6:1, 10, 21)." O'Brien, *Ephesians*, 367: "Those ruled by the dominion of darkness or of light represent that dominion in their own persons. So when they were converted, it was their lives, not their surroundings, that were changed from darkness to light. This radical transformation had taken place in the Lord. He is the

Now that the audience are no longer darkness but light in the Lord they are to "walk as children of light" (5:8c). Paul previously exhorted his audience to "become" (γίνεσθε) imitators of God "as children" (ὡς τέκνα) beloved by God and to "walk" (περιπατεῖτε) or conduct themselves "in love" (5:1–2a), that is, within a realm in which they are to imitate the love they have received not only from God as beloved children but from Christ—"just as also the Christ loved us and handed himself over for us as an offering and sacrifice to God for a fragrant aroma" (5:2b). Paul now further develops this exhortation as he tells his audience not to "become" (γίνεσθε) fellow sharers with the sons of disobedience but to "walk" (περιπατεῖτε) or conduct themselves "as children" (ὡς τέκνα) of "light" (5:8c), that is, as those who are "light" in the Lord (5:8b), having received God's gift of light in their hearts (1:18) enabling them to know not only the great love with which God loved us (2:4) but the love of Christ that surpasses knowledge (3:19).[4]

2. Eph 5:9 (B): The Fruit of the Light Is in All Goodness

Paul then elaborates on what it means for his audience to walk as children of light (5:8c): "For the fruit of the light consists in all goodness and righteousness and truth" (5:9). The progression from the anarthrous uses of "light" in 5:8 (φῶς and φωτός) to the arthrous in 5:9 (τοῦ φωτός) further conceptualizes, identifies, and definitizes the reference to light as *the* light that the audience not only are but of which they are children.[5] For the audience to walk as children of light who are light in themselves they are to produce the fruit of *this* light.[6]

That the fruit of *the* light which the audience are to produce consists in the triplet of "all" (πάσῃ) goodness and righteousness and truth (5:9) stands in contrast to the previous triplets in the immediately preceding context—"any" (πᾶς) sexually immoral or impure or greedy one excluded from the kingdom of the Christ and God (5:5), the obscenity or foolish talk or sarcastic ridicule which are inappropriate (5:4), and the sexual immorality

---

one who has made the decisive difference, and it is through their union with him that they have entered a new dominion and become light."

4. That the audience are "children of light" (τέκνα φωτός, 5:8) thus further elaborates how they are "children beloved" (τέκνα ἀγαπητά, 5:1) by God and Christ. Lincoln, *Ephesians*, 327: "If the readers are light, then they are to walk or live (cf. 2:2, 10; 4:1, 17; 5:2) as children of light, a designation which contrasts with 'the sons of disobedience' in v 6. Their behavior is to conform to their identity."

5. Wallace, *Greek Grammar*, 210: "[A]ll articles that make definite also identify; all articles that identify also conceptualize."

6. Hoehner, *Ephesians*, 673: "[I]n the present context fruit refers to the product of an action. The genitive (φωτός) is a genitive of production, namely, it is the light that produces the fruit." See also Wallace, *Greek Grammar*, 104–5. Lincoln, *Ephesians*, 328: "Light is seen as a fertile power which produces fruit."

and "all" (πᾶσα) impurity and greed which are not even to be named among them (5:3).[7]

That the fruit of *the* light which the audience are to produce in order that "you walk" (περιπατεῖτε; 5:2, 8) as children of light (5:8) and as beloved children "in love" (5:1–2) includes all "goodness" (ἀγαθωσύνη, 5:9) reinforces Paul's previous exhortations regarding the doing of "goodness" within the realm of the audience "walking in love":[8] No harmful word is to come out of the mouths of the audience, but only such as is "good" (ἀγαθός) for the building up of what is needed, that it might give grace, as a gift of love, to those who hear (4:29). The stealer is no longer to steal, but rather to work with his own hands that which is "good" (ἀγαθόν), that he might have something to share, as a gift of love, with one who has need (4:28). And we, who have been created in Christ Jesus for "good" (ἀγαθοῖς) works which God prepared beforehand, are to "walk" (περιπατήσωμεν) in them as part of our "walking in love" (5:2).

That the fruit of *the* light which the audience are to produce in order to "walk" as children of light and as beloved children "in love" (5:1–2, 8) includes every act of "righteousness" (δικαιοσύνη) and "truth" (ἀληθείᾳ) (5:9) recalls that the audience have "put on" the "new person" created according to God in "righteousness" (δικαιοσύνη) and holiness of "truth" (ἀληθείας) (4:24). This means they have adopted an external conduct or "walking" characterized by the righteousness and holiness of God himself, the God they are to imitate as beloved children (5:1). For the audience to "walk in love" as children of light with every act of "righteousness," then, means for them to do right in relation to both God and one another by sharing with one another the love they have received from God and Christ as beloved children (5:1–2).[9]

And that the fruit of *the* light which the audience are to produce in order to "walk" as children of light (5:8) includes every act of "truth" (ἀληθείᾳ) (5:9) reminds the audience that they are to speak "truth" (ἀλήθειαν) with

---

7. Hoehner, *Ephesians*, 673: "The preposition ἐν, 'in,' denotes the sphere in which the fruit of light expresses itself. The adjective πᾶς used with an anarthrous noun means 'every,' and it literally means 'every act of goodness and righteousness and truth' but because it is used in conjunction with these abstract nouns it is best to translate it 'all.' As seen earlier (vv. 3, 5) πᾶς is used in connection with a triad of nouns, here virtues instead of vices."

8. Hoehner, *Ephesians*, 674: "As mentioned earlier ἀγαθός has reference to moral and beneficial good (2:10; 4:28, 29) . . . The same can be said of ἀγαθωσύνη. But, in addition, it can signify generosity in connection with the beneficial good. Therefore, the best translation is 'goodness,' which embraces generosity towards others."

9. Lincoln, *Ephesians*, 328: "Righteousness involves doing right in relation to both God and humanity." O'Brien, *Ephesians*, 368: "The 'new person' of Ephesians has been created to display those ethical qualities that belong to God himself, such as righteousness and holiness, which have their origin in his truth (4:24). As a result, the new person speaks the truth in love (4:15, 25), since he or she has found the truth in Jesus (4:21)."

one another (4:25), recalling the word of "truth" (ἀληθείας) they have heard, the gospel of their salvation (1:13), and to conduct themselves within the realm of the righteousness and holiness that comes from "truth" (ἀληθείας) (4:24), the "truth" (ἀλήθεια) that there is within the realm of being "in Jesus" (4:21). By faithfully and loyally sharing with one another as a gift of love the "truth" given them as a gift of the love of God and Christ, then, the audience are "being truthful" (ἀληθεύοντες) within the realm of "walking in love" as children beloved by both God and Christ (4:15; 5:1–2) and thus producing as children of light the fruit of *the* light in all "truth" (5:9).[10]

3. Eph 5:10 (C): Approving What Is Pleasing to the Lord

Paul then continues to elaborate on what it means for his audience who are now light to "walk" or conduct themselves as children of light (5:8): "Approving what is pleasing to the Lord" (5:10). Examining and discerning their behavior results in the audience "approving" of the kind of conduct that is pleasing to the "Lord" (κυρίῳ), for it is in their union with the "Lord" (κυρίῳ, 5:8b) Jesus Christ that they are now light so that they are to "walk" as children of light.[11]

That the audience are to discern and approve among themselves the kind of behavior that is "pleasing" (εὐάρεστον) to the Lord (5:10) recalls, by way of alliteration of words with a εὐ- prefix, not only the "thanksgiving" (εὐχαριστία) that is to replace "sarcastic ridicule" (εὐτραπελία) (5:4), but also the "fragrant" or "pleasing" (εὐωδίας) aroma that characterizes Christ's love for us, as "he handed himself over for us as an offering and sacrifice to

---

10. On "truth" in Eph 5:9 Lincoln (*Ephesians*, 328) suggests that "in the light of the OT parallels . . . it may well have the force that אמת, *'emet*, frequently has, namely, 'faithfulness' or 'loyality'." Hoehner, *Ephesians*, 674: "It is a quality that comes from God and from which springs the actions of truthfulness." O'Brien, *Ephesians*, 368–69: "Goodness, righteousness and truth, as the fruit of light, are supernatural characteristics, the result of God's creative activity. Yet within the flow of Paul's paraenesis, especially the imperative Live as children of light (v. 8), the readers themselves are expected to demonstrate these Christian graces. Once again in this letter, divine activity and human response are carefully balanced."

11. On the meaning of "approving" (δοκιμάζοντες) in Eph 5:10 Hoehner (*Ephesians*, 675–76) explains: "The word δοκιμάζω has in mind 'to put to the test' as testing witnesses for a trial. Along with this it means 'to approve, sanction' or 'to approve after scrutiny as fit' . . . It obviously means to test or scrutinize something or someone in order to approve that entity rather than testing with failure in mind. . . . Hence, the word in this context carries the hope of a positive outcome, that is, approval." According to Ceslas Spicq, "δοκιμάζω," *TLNT* 1.356: "Δοκιμάζω means 'discern' what it is important to do, the best course to follow, the decision to make, and especially to discern what is pleasing to the Lord (Eph 5:10), which presupposes spiritual renewal and the possession of love, which consequently gives a religious sense, a kind of spiritual instinct that allows a person to recognize true values." And on "Lord" as referring to Christ here Hoehner (*Ephesians*, 676) notes: "In the twenty-six occurrences of 'Lord' in Ephesians, with the possible exception of 6:5 and 9 (referring to human masters), it refers to Christ. Christ is the Lord whom believers are to please."

God for a fragrant aroma" (5:2b). Just as Christ "pleased" God in his love for us, so the audience, who are to imitate the love of God and Christ as beloved children (5:1), are to "please" the Lord (5:10) in their love for one another within the realm of walking "in love" (5:2a) as children of light (5:8c).

4. Eph 5:11–13 (B′): Unfruitful Works Exposed by the Light

The "fruit" (καρπός) of "the light" (τοῦ φωτός) that the audience are to produce in the B element (5:9) of the chiasm in 5:7–14 progresses, by way of the chiastic parallelism, to the "unfruitful" (ἄκαρποι) works of the darkness with which the audience are not to be connected (5:11), the works that are included in all the things exposed and made visible by "the light" (τοῦ φωτός) (5:13), in the B′ element of the chiasm (5:11–13).[12]

In accord with the progression from the anarthrous to the arthrous occurrences of "light" (5:8–9), the audience now hear a progression from the anarthrous to the arthrous use of "darkness." The unfruitful works of "the darkness" (τοῦ σκότους) with which the audience are not to be connected (5:11a) further conceptualizes, identifies, and definitizes the "darkness" (σκότος) that the audience once were before they became "light" in the Lord that they might "walk" as children of "light" (5:8). The unfruitful "works" (ἔργοις) of the darkness in the B′ element contradict not only the fruit of the light that consists in every work of goodness and righteous and truth (5:9) in the B element but also the good "works" (ἔργοις) which God prepared beforehand for us that we might "walk" in them (2:10) as part of what it means for the audience to "walk" within the realm of being "in love" as children beloved by God and Christ (5:1–2).

Instead of connecting themselves with the unfruitful works of the darkness (5:11a), the audience are rather to expose them (5:11b). The reason is that the things done in secret by "them" (αὐτῶν), that is, the sons of disobedience upon whom the wrath of God is coming (5:6), and about whom Paul exhorted his audience not to become fellow sharers with "them" (αὐτῶν) (5:7), are shameful even to mention (5:12).[13] The works done in secret, which are "shameful" (αἰσχρόν) even to speak about much less do, remind

---

12. With reference to Paul's prohibition that introduces Eph 5:11 Hoehner (*Ephesians*, 677) states: "The conjunction καί links this prohibition to the one in v. 7. Hence, believers are not to be fellow participants with sinners (v. 7) and are not to participate in the unfruitful works of darkness (v. 11). The present imperative from συγκοινωνέω means 'to have a joint share in, a connection with.'"

13. With regard to "them" in Eph 5:12 Hoehner (*Ephesians*, 681) comments: "This personal pronoun does not refer back to the works of verse 11 because this would make no sense. Rather, it refers back to the personal pronoun in verse 7 where it reads 'do not become fellow participants with them (αὐτῶν),' that is, those on whom the wrath of God comes." See also Lincoln, *Ephesians*, 330.

the audience of the "shamefulness" (αἰσχρότης) that is inappropriate (5:4) for them as those who are to "walk" within the realm of being "in love" as children beloved by God and Christ (5:1–2).

But all the things exposed by "the light" (τοῦ φωτός, 5:13),[14] that is, by the audience as "the light" (τοῦ φωτός, 5:9; cf. 5:8) that produces the fruit consisting in every work of goodness and righteousness and truth (5:9) in accord with Paul's command that his audience, who are now "light" (5:8b), "walk" as children of "light" (5:8c) within the realm of being "in love" as children beloved by God and Christ (5:1–2), become no longer hidden in the darkness but visible (5:13). In other words, it is by their conduct or life-style of "walking" within the realm of being "in love" as children of "light" beloved by God and Christ (5:1–2) that the audience expose the unfruitful, shameful works hidden in the darkness (5:11–12) so that they become visible (5:13).[15]

5. Eph 5:14 (A′): What Becomes Visible Is Light by the Love of Christ

The anarthrous occurrences of "light" (φῶς) that the audience now are in the Lord so that they are to walk as children of "light" (φωτός) in the A element (5:7–8) of the chiasm in 5:7–14 progresses, by way of the chiastic

---

14. On whether the prepositional phrase, "by the light," should be taken with the preceding participle, "exposed," or the following verb, "become visible," Hoehner (*Ephesians*, 684) concludes that it goes with the participle—"exposed by the light," because "it provides a good progression. In verse 11 believers are told to expose the unfruitful works of darkness and when these works are exposed by the light, they become visible. Also, Paul then continues this concept in the next clause. Further supporting this translation is the fact that Paul normally puts the modifiers after the verbs and participles rather than before them. Thus the prepositional phrase more naturally qualifies the preceding participle and not the following verb." Contra O'Brien, *Ephesians*, 372 n. 55.

15. The root idea of the verb "expose" (ἐλέγχω) in Eph 5:11, 13 is that of "confronting somebody or something with the aim of showing him or it to be, in some determinate respect, at fault," according to Troels Engberg-Pedersen, "Ephesians 5,12–13: ἐλέγχειν and Conversion in the New Testament," *ZNW* 80 (1989): 97. But Lincoln (*Ephesians*, 329) clarifies: "That the object of the verb is the fruitless deeds of darkness also makes it less likely that ἐλέγχειν should be taken as a reference to verbal reproof or rebuke." O'Brien, *Ephesians*, 371 n. 50: "But, in this context, it is the deeds themselves which are to be confronted, and this occurs through their being exposed to a godly lifestyle." Felix Porsch, "ἐλέγχω," *EDNT* 1.428: "Eph 5:11 encourages Christians to expose 'the unfruitful works of darkness,' so that their true (dark) character might come to light (cf. v. 13)." Lincoln, *Ephesians*, 331: "As the children of light expose the deeds of darkness by their living, so what is exposed itself becomes illuminated by the sphere of light." Moritz, *Profound Mystery*, 114: "Strictly speaking the author distinguishes between the act of exposing and the process of illumination. The former is done by the believers themselves (v11), while Christ is the agent of the latter (v14). In fact, the former is only meaningful if supplemented by the latter (v13). This is the main thrust of the phrase ὑπὸ τοῦ φωτός. In other words, in order for something to be exposed properly, this will have to occur in the domain of Christ."

parallelism, to the anarthrous occurrence of "light" (φῶς) that everything that becomes visible is in the A′ element (5:14).

The audience also hear a progression from "all things" (πάντα) in the plural being exposed by the light so that they become visible (5:13) to "everything" (πᾶν) in the singular that becomes visible so that it is light (5:14a). In other words, as a consequence of all the shameful and unfruitful works of the darkness done in secret being exposed by "the light" (5:11–13), that is, by the lifestyle of the audience "walking" as children of "light" who are themselves "light" in the Lord (5:8–10), so that they become visible, every individual shameful and unfruitful work of the darkness that thus becomes visible is itself transformed into "light" (5:14a), as was the audience (5:8b). With every individual shameful and unfruitful work of the darkness that is done in secret by the sons of disobedience becoming visible so that it is "light," the way is open for an appeal for each individual son of disobedience, each unbeliever, to convert and likewise—like both the audience and like the individual works of darkness—become "light."[16]

Such an appeal occurs as Paul continues with an exhortatory quotation aimed not only directly, if rhetorically, at each individual unbeliever but directly at each individual member of his audience as well: "Therefore it says, 'Awake, O sleeper, and arise from the dead, and the Christ will shine on you'" (5:14b).[17] Recalling the introduction to the scriptural quote in 4:8,

---

16. Moritz, *Profound Mystery*, 114–15: "It could be argued that the flow of thought would have been significantly improved if v14a had been omitted. But the writer was interested in highlighting Christ as the centre of the spiral which can be expressed as follows: what is shameful is being exposed by those who are in Christ and at the same time shone upon by Christ, the light and thus revealed. He who is illumined by the true light in this way will continue to be shone upon by Christ, thus being equipped to expose further shameful things. . . . This understanding presupposes to some extent that v14 (πᾶν γάρ) connects with v13 consecutively, not causally. This may seem unusual. However, there are numerous instances in the Pauline letters where γάρ can hardly be taken causally and where a consecutive understanding better fits the syntactical requirement." O'Brien, *Ephesians*, 372–73: "Admittedly, Paul's language is compressed, but the logic appears to be that the light not only exposes; it also transforms. The disclosure of people's sins effected through believers' lives enables men and women to see the nature of their deeds. Some abandon the darkness of sin and respond to the light so that they become light themselves. This understanding is confirmed by v. 8, which speaks of the transformation that had taken place in the readers' experience, and by the confession of v. 14b."

17. Moritz, *Profound Mystery*, 115: "Eph 5.14b preserves an early Christian hymn which in turn is heavily influenced by the wording of Isa 26.19 and 60.1f. While it is highly likely that the hymn alluded to the conversion aspect in a believer's life, there is nothing to suggest that the author of Ephesians was interested in any baptismal overtones it may or may not have had. The writer had a particular interest in the hymn's suitability for bringing out his concept of what could be called the double exposure of what is shameful: believers expose shameful things, Christ provides the light needed to reveal them." On the possible background in Isaiah, see also Paula Qualls and John D. W. Watts, "Isaiah in Ephesians,"

"therefore it says" (διὸ λέγει) alerts the audience to the authoritativeness of the quotation, even though its scriptural origin is not made explicit.[18]

In the quotation itself the imperative second-person singular verb, "awake" (ἔγειρε), exhorts an individual who figuratively "is sleeping" (καθεύδων) (5:14b)—not only an appropriate metaphor for moral indifference, lethargy, or stupor, but, since literal sleep most often occurs in the darkness, an apt characterization of a son of disobedience (cf. 5:6) engaged in the unfruitful works of the darkness done in secret (5:11–12).[19] That the "sleeper" is not only to "awaken" (ἔγειρε) from moral slumber but to arise from the "dead" (νεκρῶν) (5:14b) reminds the audience that, as a consequence of the great love with which God loved us (2:4), the God who "raised" (ἐγείρας) Christ from the "dead" (νεκρῶν) physically or literally (1:20), also "raised with" (συνήγειρεν) him (2:6) not only the "you" believers spiritually or figuratively "dead" (νεκρούς) in transgressions and sins (2:1), but also all of us believers who were likewise "dead" (νεκρούς) in transgressions (2:5).

The result of the "sleeper" awakening and arising from the "dead" is that "the Christ will shine on you" (5:14b). That "the Christ" (ὁ Χριστός), in an emphatically climactic position at the end of the quotation, will shine his light, as a gift of love, on the individual "you" (singular) further develops and individualizes the love of Christ for all of us believers expressed previously in Paul's statement that "the Christ" (ὁ Χριστός) loved us and handed himself over for us as an offering and sacrifice to God for a fragrant aroma" (5:2b).[20] It is as a further gift of Christ's love, then, that the individual be-

---

RevExp 93 (1996): 254–55. According to Hoehner (Ephesians, 687), Eph 5:14b "may well be a hymn of repentance and encouragement sung regularly by earlier believers."

18. O'Brien, Ephesians, 374: "Although this introductory formula suggests that the quotation stems directly from the Old Testament and the substance of the citation is scriptural, the words do not correspond precisely to the biblical text." Lincoln, Ephesians, 331: "The introductory formula διὸ λέγει, 'therefore it is said,' is used with a Scripture citation in Eph 4:8 (cf. also Jas 4:6). Its employment here presumably indicates that for the writer the Christian liturgical material, from which the citation was in all probability taken, was also an authoritative tradition which could provide forceful support for his exhortation."

19. On the figurative sense of "sleep" (καθεύδω) here, see BDAG, 490. O'Brien, Ephesians, 377: "Sleep is also the situation of forgetfulness and drunkenness which is part and parcel of the sinful world of darkness (1 Thess. 5:5–8; Rom. 13:11–14)." Hoehner, Ephesians, 687: "As 'sleepers' they possibly did not even realize their spiritual indifference. This is an interesting metaphor since most sleep is done in darkness. They were sleeping in the unfruitful works of darkness." For more on the figurative use of "sleep" (καθεύδω) in another Pauline letter, see John Paul Heil, "Those Now 'Asleep' (Not Dead) Must Be 'Awakened' for the Day of the Lord in 1 Thess 5.9–10," NTS 46 (2000): 464–71.

20. That these are the first two uses in Ephesians of the term "the Christ" (ὁ Χριστός) in the nominative case enhances this connection. (There are subsequent occurrences in 5:23, 25, 29).

liever not only became "light" but will remain "light" in accord with the authoritative quotation's promise that "the Christ will shine on you."

The quotation in 5:14b thus has a double effect on the audience. First, as rhetorically directed to the individual unbeliever, the authoritative and exhortatory quotation alerts the audience to the potential that their lifestyle of "walking in love" as children of "light" (5:8) beloved by God and Christ (5:1–2) has for converting unbelievers from the unfruitful and shameful works of the darkness done in secret (5:11–12), so that they may be transformed into "light" (5:14a) by the Christ shining on them. And secondly, it urges each individual member of the audience not to fall "asleep" and thus return to the darkness of spiritual and moral "death" but to continue to "walk" as children of light beloved by God and Christ so as to remain "light" as a further gift of the love of the Christ who will shine on each of them within the realm of their being "in love" (5:1–2).[21]

C. Summary on Ephesians 5:7–14

1. That you are not to "be connected with" the unfruitful works of the darkness (5:11) as you are light "in the Lord" (5:8) as a gift of God's love in the E′ unit (5:7–14) recalls that it is "in the Lord" (2:21) that "you are being built together" into a dwelling place of God in the Spirit (2:22) as a gift of God's love in the E unit (2:11–22).

2. For the audience to become "fellow sharers" (5:7) with the "sons of disobedience" (5:6) would contradict their being not only "fellow heirs" and "fellow members of the body" and "fellow sharers" of the promise in Christ Jesus (3:6) but also "fellow citizens" with the holy ones (2:19) as a gift of God's love, and thus contradict what it means for them to "walk" in the realm of being "in love" (5:2).

3. The audience have been "enlightened" (1:18) to the point of being "light" (5:8) as a gift of God's love.

4. That the audience are now light "in the Lord" develops what it means for them to walk within the realm of being "in love" (5:2a), because it is

---

21. On the effect of the quotation in Eph 5:14b Lincoln (*Ephesians*, 333) states that "the lines are meant to have the effect of strengthening the readers' confidence in the power of the light and their determination to live out of that power." O'Brien, *Ephesians*, 377: "Paul reminds the readers of their conversion: they had been summoned by God's call to awaken from their sleep of spiritual death and to turn from the old life. They had responded to this summons, and the mighty light of Christ shone upon them and saved them (cf. 2:5, 8). . . . At the same time, the readers are reminded that Christ's light which had transformed their darkness was able to change the lives of others also."

within the realm of being "in the Lord" that they are being built together into a dwelling place of God in the Spirit (2:21–22) as a gift of God's love.

5. Paul further develops his exhortation for his audience to "walk" as children beloved by God and Christ within the realm of being "in love" (5:1–2) as he tells them το "walk" or conduct themselves "as children" of "light" (5:8c), that is, as those who are "light" in the Lord (5:8b), having received God's gift of light in their hearts (1:18) enabling them to know not only the great love with which God loved us (2:4) but the love of Christ that surpasses knowledge (3:19).

6. The fruit of "*the* light" which the audience as "light" are to produce in order to "walk" as children of "light" (5:8) beloved by God and Christ within the realm of being "in love" (5:1–2) includes all "goodness" and "righteousness" and "truth" (5:9).

7. Just as Christ "pleased" God in his love for us (5:2), so the audience, who are to imitate the love of God and Christ as beloved children (5:1), are to "please" the Lord (5:10) in their love for one another within the realm of walking "in love" (5:2a) as children of light (5:8c).

8. It is by their conduct or lifestyle of "walking" within the realm of being "in love" as children of "light" beloved by God and Christ (5:1–2) that the audience expose the unfruitful, shameful works hidden in the darkness (5:11–12) so that they become visible (5:13).

9. As rhetorically directed to the individual unbeliever, the authoritative and exhortatory quotation in 5:14b alerts the audience to the potential that their lifestyle of "walking in love" as children of "light" (5:8), beloved by God and Christ (5:1–2), has for converting unbelievers from the unfruitful and shameful works of the darkness done in secret (5:11–12), so that they may be transformed into "light" (5:14a) by the Christ shining on them.

10. And the quotation in 5:14b urges each individual member of the audience not to fall "asleep" and thus return to the darkness of spiritual and moral "death" but to continue to "walk" as children of light beloved by God and Christ so as to remain "light" as a further gift of the love of the Christ who will shine on each of them within the realm of their being "in love" (5:1–2).

CHAPTER 14

Ephesians 5:15–6:9:
Walk in Love as Those Who Are Wise (D´)

A. Chiastic Development from
Ephesians 2:1–10 (D) to 5:15–6:9 (D´)

While 5:15–6:9 forms the D´ unit in the overall chiastic structure of Ephesians, it is comprised of four sub-units (5:15–20, 5:21–33, 6:1–4, and 6:5–9) each of which is chiastic in itself.[1] With the D´ unit the audience hear resonances of the corresponding D unit (2:1–10) within the overall chiasm. Paul's warning to watch how carefully you "walk" (περιπατεῖτε) (5:15) in the D´ unit recalls that although the "you" believers once "walked" (περιεπατήσατε) according to the age of this world (2:2), all of us believers may now "walk" (περιπατήσωμεν) in the good works God prepared beforehand (2:10) in the D unit. "Doing the will" (ποιοῦντες τὸ θέλημα) of God (6:6) in the D´ unit recalls and contrasts "doing the wishes" (ποιοῦντες τὰ θελήματα) of the flesh (2:3) in the D unit.

And, with regard to the love theme in Ephesians, Paul's directive for husbands to "love" (ἀγαπᾶτε) their wives as the Christ "loved" (ἠγάπησεν) the church (5:25) and to "love" (ἀγαπᾶν) their own wives as their own bodies, as he who "loves" (ἀγαπῶν) his own wife "loves" (ἀγαπᾷ) himself (5:28) in the D´ unit recalls the great "love" (ἀγάπην) with which God "loved" (ἠγάπησεν) us (2:4) in our union with Christ in the D unit.

---

1. For the establishment of 5:15–6:9 as the D´ unit within the overall chiastic structure of Ephesians and of its four sub-units as chiasms in themselves, see ch. 2. While the entire D´ unit is comprised of chiastic sub-units, other units, as we have seen, also contain chiastic sub-units (see the B, C, E, and G´ units).

B. Always Thanking God in Love (5:15–20)

A: [15] Watch then how carefully you walk, not as unwise but as wise,
       [16] making the most of the time, for the days are evil. [17] Therefore
       do not become foolish, but understand what the will of the *Lord*
       is. [18] And do not get drunk with wine, in which there is dissipa-
       tion, but be filled in the Spirit,

    B: [19] speaking to each other in *psalms* and hymns and Spiritual
       songs,

    B´:   *singing songs* and *singing psalms* in your hearts to the Lord,

A´:   [20] giving thanks always and for all things in the name of our *Lord*
       Jesus Christ to God the Father,

1. Audience Response to Ephesians 5:15–20

a. Eph 5:15–18 (A): Be filled in the Spirit

Paul began this paranetic section of the Letter with a series of exhortatory units concerning how his audience are "to walk" in 4:1, "I, then (οὖν),
exhort you, I, the prisoner in the Lord, to walk (περιπατῆσαι) worthy of
the calling with which you were called." In 4:17, "This then (οὖν) I say and
testify in the Lord, that you no longer walk (περιπατεῖν), just as also the
Gentiles walk (περιπατεῖ) in the futility of their mind." In 5:1–2, "Become
then (οὖν) imitators of God as beloved children and walk (περιπατεῖτε)
in love just as also the Christ loved us." In 5:7–8, "Do not then (οὖν) become fellow sharers with them . . . walk (περιπατεῖτε) as children of light."
And now in 5:15, continuing the "then" (οὖν) and "walk" (περιπατέω) pattern, Paul exhorts his audience, "Watch then (οὖν) how carefully you walk
(περιπατεῖτε), not as unwise but as wise."[2]

Although often understood as being in the indicative mood, "walk" in
the exhortation to "watch then how carefully you walk" (5:15b) seems to
carry an imperative sense not only as a continuation of the previous uses
of "walk" in the imperative mood—"walk as children of light" (5:8) and
"walk in love" (5:2), but also as embedded within a series of imperatives
beginning with "watch" in 5:15a and continuing throughout 5:15–18. Thus,
we might translate, "watch then how carefully you are to walk." Furthermore, that the audience are to walk not "as" (ὡς) unwise but "as" (ὡς) wise
(15:5b) develops the previous imperatives that they walk "as" (ὡς) children
of light (5:8) and "as" (ὡς) beloved children "in love" (5:1–2).

That the audience are to walk not as "unwise" (ἄσοφοι) but as "wise"
(σοφοί) (5:15) recalls that God lavished upon us believers all "wisdom"

---

2. Hoehner, *Ephesians*, 689: "As mentioned previously, in chapters 4–6 the clue for
major breaks is the imperative 'walk' (περιπατέω) used five times in connection with the
inferential conjunction 'therefore' (οὖν)."

(σοφίᾳ) and insight (1:8) as a gift of love, and that Paul prayed that God may give his audience the Spirit of "wisdom" (σοφίας) and revelation in knowledge of him (1:17). That the audience are "wise" from the "wisdom" (σοφία) that comes from God (3:10) as a gift of God's love thus empowers them to walk not as unwise but as wise.[3] That they are able to walk "as wise" thus further develops what it means for them to walk "as children of light" (5:8) and "as children beloved" by God within the realm of being "in love" (5:1–2).[4]

With its noteworthy cadence of alliterations and assonances the opening injunction in 5:15 resonates with a memorable impact in the ears of the audience as the heading for the exhortations to follow. In addition to the "p" and "b" sounds in βλέπετε . . . πῶς ἀκριβῶς περιπατεῖτε there are the "ōs" sounds in πῶς ἀκριβῶς . . . ὡς . . . ὡς, climaxed by a concluding assonance in the contrast between ἄσοφοι ("unwise") and σοφοί ("wise").

For the audience to "walk" not as unwise but as wise (5:15) includes "making the most of the time, for the days are evil" (5:16). Whereas the audience were at that "time" (καιρῷ) in which they were without Christ "alienated from the community of Israel and strangers of the covenants of the promise, not having hope and Godless in the world" (2:12), now that they are in union with Christ and no longer strangers and aliens, but "fellow citizens with the holy ones and members of the household of God" (2:19), they are to make the most of this "time" (καιρόν) in which they are presently living (5:16a). For while the "days" (ἡμέραι) of this time are evil (5:16b), they are nevertheless now living within the realm of being "in the Spirit" in and with whom they have been sealed for the "day" (ἡμέραν) of redemption (4:30; 1:13).[5]

"Therefore,"[6] as Paul continues his exhortation, "do not become foolish,

---

3. On Eph 5:15 BDAG, 935, states: "[W]ise in that the wisdom is divine in nature and origin."

4. O'Brien, *Ephesians*, 382: "By using wisdom language the apostle presents the broad sweep of God's redemptive plan, the mystery, for he wants to expand the readers' horizons and encourage them to live in the light of God's declared intentions for the universe. This will have ramifications for all their relationships, with fellow believers in addition to those outside God's people, as the following verse makes clear."

5. Hoehner, *Ephesians*, 694–95: "The days are evil because they are controlled by the god of this age (2:2) who opposes God and his kingdom and who will try to prevent any opportunities for the declaration of God's program and purposes. Hence, in this present evil age believers are not to waste opportunities because this would be useless and harmful to God's kingdom and to those who are a part of it. . . . It is interesting to notice that he is not recommending that they fear the present evil age or avoid interaction with it. Rather his exhortation is to walk wisely in the evil days by seizing every opportunity."

6. Hoehner, *Ephesians*, 695: "In this text Paul is drawing a conclusion not from the immediately preceding clause, 'because the days are evil,' but from his discussion beginning in verse 15. Paul has summoned the believers to walk wisely, taking advantage of every opportunity because the days are evil. For this reason he warns them not to become foolish."

but understand what the will of the Lord is" (5:17). Paul's commands regarding what his audience are and are not to "become"—"become (γίνεσθε) kind to one another" (4:32), "become (γίνεσθε) imitators of God" (5:1), "do not become (γίνεσθε) fellow sharers" (5:7) with the sons of disobedience (5:6)—continue as he now commands his audience, "do not become (γίνεσθε) foolish (ἄφρονες)" (5:17a), which further develops his command that they "walk" not as "unwise" (ἄσοφοι) (5:15b).

That, instead of becoming foolish, the audience are rather to understand "what" (τί) is the will of the "Lord" (κυρίου) (5:17b) recalls and develops how they are to approve "what" (τί) is pleasing to the "Lord" (κυρίῳ) (5:10), the "Lord" (κυρίῳ) in union with whom they are "light" so that they are to "walk" as children of the "light" beloved by God within the dynamic realm of being "in love" (5:1–2).[7]

And that the audience are to understand what is the "will" (θέλημα) of the Lord (5:17b) recalls that God has made known not only to Paul, called to be an apostle of Christ Jesus through the "will" (θελήματος) of God (1:1; cf. 3:2–12), but also to all of us believers, who have been predestined to sonship through Jesus Christ according to the pleasure of God's "will" (θελήματος) (1:5) and predestined to obtain an inheritance according to the purpose of the God who is working in all things according to the counsel of his "will" (θελήματος) (1:11), the mystery of his "will" (θελήματος) (1:9). The mystery of God's "will" is to unite under one head all the things in the Christ (1:10a). And Christ's "will" is to play his role within God's "will." This he did when he "loved us and handed himself over for us as an offering and sacrifice *to* God for a fragrant aroma" (5:2b).

For the audience to "understand" what the will of the Lord is (5:17b) thus develops what it means for them to "know" this love of the Christ (3:19a) as Christ's will to bring about God's will to unite under one head all the things in the Christ (1:10a).[8] Christ plays his role within God's will

---

7. With regard to "the will of the Lord" as referring to the will of Christ rather than of God, O'Brien (*Ephesians*, 385–86) points out that "there is a christological focus within the preceding paragraph (vv. 8–14), and a flow of thought that begins with the mention of believers now becoming light in the Lord (v. 8) moves to their finding out what pleases the Lord (v. 10) and climaxes with a statement about Christ shining upon them (v. 14). References to the 'Lord' and 'Christ' are bracketed as a rhetorical device to frame the paragraph, which then leads into the final exhortatory section of the letter (5:15–6:9)."

8. Hoehner, *Ephesians*, 698: "This perception or understanding is more than just the understanding of facts; it is an intelligent grasp of knowledge that has resulting consequences." O'Brien, *Ephesians*, 385: "Believers are exhorted to understand the divine will, even though God has already made it known (1:9). The apostle is not suggesting that the readers have no insight into this will. Rather, in a paraenetic context he is admonishing them to appropriate it more fully for themselves. God has revealed to them the mystery of his will in the Lord Jesus Christ. Let them lay hold of it and understand its implications for their day-to-day living. . . . Both the immediate and wider contexts of v. 17 make it plain that the

as the head over all things that God gave to the church, which is the body of the Christ who is filling all things in all ways (1:22–23) with gifts of love. Through their experiential knowledge of this love of the Christ the audience are being filled to all the fullness of God (3:19) by the ascended Christ who gives each member of the body the gift of Christ's love (4:7) as the one who fills all things (4:10). These gifts of love given to each member of the body empower the body to play its role in God's will to unite under one head all the things in the Christ. Being truthful "in love" by sharing with one another the love we have received from Christ, we believers—the body—cause all things to grow to him, who is the head, the Christ, from whom the whole body builds itself up within the realm of being "in love" (4:15–16).

For the audience to understand what the will of the Lord is (5:17b), what is pleasing to the Lord (5:10), means for them to understand that they please the Lord in doing the Lord's will by playing their role within God's will as he did (5:2) and still does (1:23; 3:19). That Christ plays his role within God's will by his ongoing filling of us believers with gifts of love empowers us to play our role within God's will to unite under one head all the things in the Christ (1:10a), causing all things to grow to him, who is the head, the Christ (4:15), by imitating the love of Christ and of God, "walking" as beloved children within the dynamic realm of being "in love" (5:1–2; cf. 1:4; 3:17; 4:2, 15–16).

Paul continues his exhortation, "And do not get drunk with wine, in which there is dissipation, but be filled in the Spirit" (5:18).[9] With this the audience have heard a patterned triplet of antithetical exhortations in which a negative command is followed by an emphatically positive one:[10]

5:15: walk not (μή) as unwise

    but (ἀλλ') as wise

---

apostle does not have in mind simply an intellectual understanding of the Lord's will. . . . in true Hebraic fashion the believers' understanding of God's gracious saving plan is to lead to right conduct."

9. For allusions and background to "do not get drunk" in LXX Prov 23:31; *T.Jud.* 14:1; 16:1; *Hist.Rech.* 1:4, see Moritz, *Profound Mystery*, 94–95; Craig A. Evans, *Ancient Texts for New Testament Studies: A Guide to the Background Literature* (Peabody, MA: Hendrickson, 2005), 390. O'Brien, *Ephesians*, 390 n. 120: "The exhortation in the present tense, μὴ μεθύσκεσθε ('do not get drunk'), does not signify that the Ephesians had been getting drunk and that Paul was urging them to stop. Rather, it has the sense of prohibiting a course of action, viewed as an ongoing process. See Kenneth L. McKay, "Aspect in Imperatival Constructions in New Testament Greek," *NovT* 27 (1985): 201–26; idem, *A New Syntax of the Verb in New Testament Greek: An Aspectual Approach* (Studies in Biblical Greek 5; New York: Lang, 1994), 77–81; Porter, *Verbal Aspect*, 357; Wallace, *Greek Grammar*, 714–17.

10. Fee, *God's Empowering Presence*, 720: "As always in Paul, the emphasis rests altogether on the 'but' clause."

5:17: do not (μή) become foolish,

but (ἀλλά) understand what the will of the Lord is

5:18: do not (μή) get drunk with wine, in which there is dissipation,

but (ἀλλά) be filled in the Spirit

Further developing his antithetical commands to walk *not* as unwise *but* as wise (5:15) and *not* to become foolish, *but* to understand what the will of the Lord is (5:17), Paul exhorts his audience *not* to get drunk with wine, "in" (ἐν) which, that is, within the realm of being drunk or filled with wine, there is dissipation, *but* to be filled "in" (ἐν), that is, within the realm of being in union with the Spirit (5:18).[11] That there is "dissipation" in the realm of being drunk with wine completes a triplet of ἀ–privative terms, with a progression from adjectives to a noun, in the negative commands not to be—"unwise" (ἄσοφοι, 5:15), "foolish" (ἄφρονες, 5:17), or in "dissipation" (ἀσωτία, 5:18).[12] For the audience to be filled "in the Spirit" includes not only their being sealed with the Spirit (1:13) and given the Spirit (1:17) as a gift of God's love, but also their being filled with further gifts of love within the dynamic realm of being in union with the Spirit.

As the audience recall, through Christ we believers have, as a gift of God's love, access to the Father within the realm of our being "in one Spirit" (ἐν ἑνὶ πνεύματι) (2:18). In Christ the audience are being built together, as a gift of God's love (divine passive), into a dwelling place of God within the realm of their being "in the Spirit" (ἐν πνεύματι) (2:22). The mystery of Christ has been revealed, as a gift of God's love (divine passive), to the holy apostles and prophets within the realm of being "in the Spirit" (ἐν πνεύματι) (3:5). It was within the realm of their being "in" (ἐν) the Holy Spirit of God

---

11. Hoehner, *Ephesians*, 702: "The contrast is not between the wine and the Spirit but between the two states expressed by the two verbs."

12. Lincoln, *Ephesians*, 344: "ἀσωτία ['dissipation'] is used elsewhere in the NT only in Titus 1:6 and 1 Pet 4:4, where it is in close association with the mention of drunkenness in the preceding verse, while the cognate adverb is used to describe the way of life of the prodigal son in Luke 15:13. The use of the term here reminds one of the writer's earlier sweeping condemnation of non-Christian Gentile lifestyle in 4:19, where the synonym ἀσέλγεια, 'debauchery,' was employed." Hoehner, *Ephesians*, 701: "Paul instructs believers not to be drunk with wine which causes unrestrained, dissolute living, leading only to ruin. It is difficult to select one precise word that describes this condition but probably 'dissipation' is the closest. It is the opposite of being wise which takes full advantage of every opportunity (vv. 15–16)." For a suggestion that Paul is referring here to the audience's involvement in the cult of Dionysius, the god of wine, see Cleon L. Rogers, "The Dionysian Background of Ephesians 5:18," *BSac* 136 (1979): 249–57. Pointing out that this is unlikely, Hoehner (ibid.) adds: "Drunkenness occurred both inside and outside of the religious practices of the day." See also Peter W. Gosnell, "Ephesians 5:18–20 and Mealtime Propriety," *TynBul* 44 (1993): 363–71.

that the audience were sealed, as a gift of God's love (divine passive), for the day of redemption (4:30). And now, the audience are to be filled by Christ with further gifts of love within the realm of their being "in the Spirit" (ἐν πνεύματι) (5:18).

That "you" are to be continually "filled" (πληροῦσθε, present passive imperative) by Christ within the realm of being in the Spirit (5:18) reminds the audience that Christ ascended that he might "fill" (πληρώσῃ) all things (4:10) with his gifts of love (4:8, 11–16), so that "you" might be "filled" (πληρωθῆτε), as a gift of the love of Christ, to all the "fullness" of God (3:19) by the Christ who is "filling" (πληρουμένου) all things in all ways (1:23) with his gifts of love.[13] By being filled with gifts of love by Christ, we believers may attain to the "fullness" of the Christ (4:13) within the church as the body which is the "fullness" of Christ (1:23).[14] To sum up, then, Paul exhorts his audience to "walk" not as unwise but as wise (5:15) by not becoming foolish but understanding what the will of the Lord is (5:17), and by not being drunk with wine, in which there is dissipation, but being continually filled by Christ with gifts of love within the realm of being in the Spirit

---

13. To interpret, as some do, Eph 5:18 as "being filled by the Spirit," that is, with the Spirit rather than Christ as the agent of the filling ignores the fact that the subject and/or agent of the verb "filling" in Ephesians is best understood as Christ, whether it is active (1:23; 4:10) or passive (3:19). When Paul refers to the agency of the Spirit in Ephesians, he employs the preposition διά (3:16). And note 2:18, where agency is expressed with διά— "through him" (δι᾽ αὐτοῦ)—with reference to Christ, but ἐν expresses being in a dynamic realm—"in one Spirit" (ἐν ἑνὶ πνεύματι). On the other hand, the interpretation of the Spirit as the content of the filling—"being filled with the Spirit"—fails to recognize that the implicit content of "filling" is gifts of Christ's love, both when the direct object of "filling" is "all things" (1:23; 4:10) and when the subject of "being filled" is "you" (the audience; 3:19). As Hoehner (*Ephesians*, 703) points out, "normally verbs of filling take a genitive of content. Moreover, nowhere in the NT does πληρόω followed by ἐν plus the dative indicate content." The filling then includes (cf. 1:13, 17) but is not limited to being filled with the Spirit. Our interpretation accords with the many occurrences in Ephesians of the "in" (ἐν) prepositional phrase to express being in a dynamic realm. For divergent interpretations, see C. Anderson, "Rethinking 'Be Filled with the Spirit': Ephesians 5:18 and the Purpose of Ephesians," *EvJ* 7 (1989): 57–67; Andreas J. Köstenberger, "What Does It Mean to be Filled with the Spirit? A Biblical Investigation," *JETS* 40 (1997): 229–40; Timothy G. Gombis, "Being the Fullness of God in Christ by the Spirit: Ephesians 5:18 in Its Epistolary Setting," *TynBul* 53 (2002): 259–71. For a fuller discussion of our interpretation, see John Paul Heil, "Ephesians 5:18b: 'But Be Filled in the Spirit,'" *CBQ* 69 (2007): 506–16.

14. There is an eschatological tension between the "already" and the "not yet" with regard to the concept of "fullness" in Ephesians. As O'Brien (*Ephesians*, 393) states: "The church as Christ's body already shares his fulness (1:23). Yet Paul's petition for his readers (3:14–19), which is based on God's mighty salvation effected in the Lord Jesus and described in the first three chapters of Ephesians, is that they might be filled to all the fulness of God (v. 19). Paul's intercession presupposes that the readers have not yet been filled: God begins to answer this petition in the here and now, and he will consummate his work on the final day when the readers are filled with all his fulness. Similarly, the body of Christ has not yet reached mature manhood; it is moving towards the fulness of Christ (4:13)."

(5:18), in order that they might "walk" as children of the light (5:8) beloved by God and Christ within the realm of being "in love" (5:1–2).

b. Eph 5:19a (B): Speaking in psalms and hymns and Spiritual songs

Paul then describes for his audience the behavior that results from and responds to their being filled with gifts of love by Christ within the realm of being in the Spirit: "Speaking to each other in psalms and hymns and Spiritual songs" (5:19a).[15] In accord with Paul's previous exhortation for his audience to "speak" (λαλεῖτε) truth, each one with his neighbor, for we are members of one another (4:25), they are "speaking" (λαλοῦντες) to each other in psalms and hymns and Spiritual songs, as a result of being filled with gifts of love by Christ (5:18). And in accord with Paul's exhortation for his audience to become kind to one another, compassionate, being gracious to "each other" (ἑαυτοῖς), just as also God in Christ was gracious to us (4:32), they are speaking to "each other" (ἑαυτοῖς) in psalms and hymns and Spiritual songs, thus responding with love toward each other as a result of being loved by Christ.[16]

As a fitting response to being blessed with every "Spiritual" (πνευματικῇ) blessing in the heavenly places in Christ (1:3), the audience are speaking to each other in psalms and hymns and "Spiritual" (πνευματικαῖς) songs (5:19a).[17] And this is the behavior that appropriately takes place for the audience who are being filled with gifts of love by Christ within the realm of being in the "Spirit" (πνεύματι) (5:18). With regard to the love theme, then, speaking to each other in psalms and hymns and Spiritual songs extends to one another the love the audience members are receiving from Christ, and

---

15. Hoehner, *Ephesians*, 706: "The five participles in verses 19–21 are dependent on the imperative πληροῦσθε, 'be filled,' and thus are considered by some to take on an imperatival force. . . . It is better to see them as participles of result. . . . Furthermore, participles of result are normally in the present tense and follow the main verb as here. The present tense of the participles most likely indicates repetition or progression of the characteristics described by these five participles." See also Lincoln, *Ephesians*, 345; O'Brien, *Ephesians*, 387–88; Wallace, *Greek Grammar*, 639, 644–45; contra Gombis ("Being the Fullness," 268–71), who argues that the participles express means rather than result.

16. Hoehner, *Ephesians*, 707: "As in Eph 4:32 the reflexive pronoun ἑαυτοῖς literally, 'to yourselves,' functions as the reciprocal pronoun ἀλλήλων, 'to one another.' " See also Wallace, *Greek Grammar*, 351.

17. Fee, *God's Empowering Presence*, 653–54: "[E]ven though πνευματικός could well modify all three nouns—the psalms and hymns would also be 'of the Spirit'—it is more likely that it is intended to modify 'songs' only, referring especially to this one kind of Spirit-inspired singing. This word, after all, is the one which the recipients of the letter would least likely associate with worship, since it covers the whole range of 'songs' in the Greek world, whereas the other two are usually sung to a deity." Hence, the three terms—psalms, hymns, and Spiritual songs—function as a rhetorical triplet with a certain emphasis upon the climactic third element as Spiritual songs. See also François S. Malan, "Church Singing According to the Pauline Epistles," *Neot* 32 (1998): 509–24.

further illustrates what it means for the audience to "walk" as beloved children within the dynamic realm of being "in love" (5:1–2).

c. Eph 5:19b (B'): Singing songs and psalms in your heart to the Lord

To the present active participle "speaking" (5:19a) Paul adds two more present active participles, "singing songs and singing psalms in your hearts to the Lord" (5:19b).[18] The audience hear the pivot of the chiasm in 5:15–20 with the progression from the nouns, "psalms" (ψαλμοῖς) and "songs" (ῷδαῖς), in the B element (5:19a) to their corresponding cognate verbs, "singing songs" (ᾄδοντες) and "singing psalms" (ψάλλοντες), in the B' element (5:19b).[19]

Previously Paul prayed that the eyes of the "heart" (καρδίας) of his audience might be enlightened, as a gift of God's love (1:18), so that they may know the great power of God (1:19) and that the Christ may dwell in their "hearts" (καρδίαις) through faith (3:17), so that they may know the love of the Christ that surpasses knowledge (3:19). And now, in contrast to the way that the Gentiles "walk" (4:17), alienated from the life of God because of their ignorance and hardness of "heart" (καρδίας) (4:18), the audience are singing songs and singing psalms in their "hearts" (καρδίαις) to the Lord (5:19b) in response to the gifts of love with which the Lord Christ is filling them (5:18).

That the audience are singing songs and singing psalms in their hearts to the "Lord" (κυρίῳ) (5:19b) results from their understanding that the will of the "Lord" (κυρίου) (5:17) Christ is to please God by loving us (5:2). They are thus demonstrating what is pleasing to the "Lord" (κυρίῳ) (5:10) as those who are "light" in their union with the "Lord" (κυρίῳ), so that they are to "walk" as children of the light (5:8), beloved by God and the Lord Christ within the dynamic realm of being "in love" (5:1–2).

With regard to the love theme, then, the psalms and hymns and Spiritual songs that the audience speak *to each other* as an extension to one another of the love they have received from Christ (5:19a) are the songs and psalms that they sing in their hearts *to the Lord* (5:19b) in response to the gifts of love with which Christ is filling them (5:18) in accord with the will of the Lord Christ (5:17) within the dynamic realm of being "in love" (5:2).[20]

---

18. For the evidence that establishes the reading with the preposition and plural noun—"in your hearts"—rather than the variant reading without the preposition and with the singular noun, see Hoehner, *Ephesians*, 712 n. 4.

19. The pivotal progression is in itself chiastic—(a) psalms and (b) songs to (b') singing songs and (a') singing psalms.

20. O'Brien, *Ephesians*, 396–97: "The two clauses of v. 19 refer not to two separate responses or activities, but to one and the same action, each with a slightly different focus. To start with, the 'audiences' are distinct. According to v. 19a, believers speak in psalms, hymns, and songs to one another, reminding each other of what God has done in the Lord Jesus Christ. A further distinction is the purpose of this singing, namely, to instruct and

d. Eph 5:20 (A´): Giving thanks in the name of our Lord Jesus Christ

Paul then adds a fourth present active participle to the series that began in 5:19a, "Giving thanks always for all things in the name of our Lord Jesus Christ to God the Father" (5:20).²¹ The audience hear a progression from the will of the "Lord" (κυρίου) (5:17) in the A element to the name of the "Lord" (κυρίου) Jesus Christ (5:20) in the A´ element of the chiasm in 5:15–20. And with the progression from "in your (ὑμῶν) hearts" (5:19b) in the B´ element to "in the name of our (ἡμῶν) Lord Jesus Christ" (5:20) in the A´ element, the audience once again experience the thrust of the Letter to assimilate the "you" believers with all of "us" believers.

In imitation of Paul, "giving thanks" (εὐχαριστῶν) to God "for" (ὑπέρ) you, his audience (1:16), and in accord with the "thanksgiving" (εὐχαριστία) that is appropriate (5:4) for those beloved by God and Christ within the realm of being "in love" (5:1–2), the audience are "giving thanks" (εὐχαριστοῦντες) always "for" (ὑπέρ) all things in the name of our Lord Jesus Christ to God the Father (5:20).²² That the audience are giving thanks always for "all things" (πάντων) makes explicit what was implicit in their being filled by the Lord Christ in the Spirit (5:18). They are giving thanks for "all" of the gifts of love with which they are being filled by the Lord Christ who is filling "all things" (πάντα) in "all ways" (πᾶσιν) (1:23; 4:10), so that the audience may be filled to "all" (πᾶν) the fullness of God (3:19).²³

In accord with their understanding that the will of the "Lord" (5:17) is to please "God" (θεῷ) by his love for us (5:2), the audience are giving thanks in the name of our "Lord" Jesus Christ to "God" (θεῷ) the Father (5:20) for the love they have received from God and Christ. The "Father" (πατέρα) to whom believers now have, as a gift of love, access in one Spirit through Christ (2:18), the "Father" (πατέρα) before whom Paul solemnly kneels (3:14) in

---

edify members of the body. In a sense, this singing has a horizontal and corporate focus to it. In v. 19b, the singing and making music are directed to the Lord Jesus. This activity thus has a vertical focus and a personal dimension, for believers praise the Lord Jesus 'with their whole being'."

21. Hoehner, *Ephesians*, 715: "The direction of the thanksgiving is expressed with the personal dative object τῷ θεῷ καὶ πατρί, literally, 'to God and Father.' As in 1:3 the Granville Sharp rule applies, where a singular articular personal noun followed by καί and an anarthrous personal noun in the same case further describes the first noun. Here God is further described as father. . . . The translation 'to God the Father' is accurate." See also Wallace, *Greek Grammar*, 270–74.

22. Snodgrass, *Ephesians*, 291: " 'Name' is a way of referring to what the person stands for and has accomplished. Christians are to give thanks 'on the basis of' who Jesus is and what he has done, or 'in accord' with who he is."

23. Fee, *God's Empowering Presence*, 723: "[I]t is doubtful that the 'all things' for which one gives thanks refers to all the circumstances of one's life, good or ill, but to the richness of God's blessings that have been lavished on us in Christ."

prayer that his audience may know the love of Christ that surpasses knowledge (3:19), and the one God and "Father" (πατήρ) of *all*, who is over *all* and through *all* and in *all* (4:6), is the God and "Father" (πατρί) to whom the audience are appropriately giving thanks always for *all* the things they have received as gifts of love from Christ (5:18) and God the Father (2:4; 5:1).

In sum, by giving thanks to God the Father for all the things they have received as gifts of love (5:20), and by singing songs and psalms not only to the Lord Jesus Christ but to each other (5:19) as a result of and in response to being filled with gifts of love by the Lord Christ in the Spirit (5:18), the audience further demonstrate what it means to "walk" (5:15) as children beloved by God and Christ within the dynamic realm of being "in love" (5:1–2).

2. Summary on Ephesians 5:15–20

1. Paul exhorts his audience to "walk" not as unwise but as wise (5:15) by not becoming foolish but understanding what the will of the Lord is (5:17), and by not being drunk with wine, in which there is dissipation, but being continually filled by Christ with gifts of love within the realm of being in the Spirit (5:18), in order that they might "walk" as children of the light (5:8) beloved by God and Christ within the realm of being "in love" (5:1–2).

2. By giving thanks to God the Father for all the things they have received as gifts of love (5:20), and by singing songs and psalms not only to the Lord Jesus Christ but to each other (5:19) as a result of and in response to being filled with gifts of love by the Lord Christ within the realm of being in the Spirit (5:18), the audience further demonstrate what it means to "walk" (5:15) as children beloved by God and Christ within the dynamic realm of being "in love" (5:1–2).

C. Husbands and Wives Love One Another (5:21–33)

A: ²¹ Submitting to one another in *respect* for Christ, ²² the wives to their own husbands as to the Lord,

   B: ²³ for the *husband* is head of the *wife* as also the *Christ* is head of the *church*,

      C: he himself is savior of the *body*.

         D: ²⁴ But as the *church* submits to the *Christ*, so also the wives to their husbands in everything. ²⁵ Husbands, love your wives, *just as* also the *Christ* loved the *church* and handed himself over for her, ²⁶ that her he might sanctify, cleansing her by the washing of the water in the word, ²⁷ that he might present to himself the *church* glorious, not having a blemish or wrinkle or any of such things, but that she might be holy and blameless.

E: [28] So ought also husbands to *love* their
          own wives as their *own* bodies.
E´:   He who *loves* his *own wife loves himself.*
D´:   [29] For no one ever hates his own flesh but nurtures
          and takes care of it, *just as* also the *Christ* (nurtures
          and takes care of) the *church,*
C´:   [30] for we are members of his *body.*
B´:   [31] "For this reason a *man* shall leave his father and mother
          and shall cleave to his *wife,* and the two shall become one
          flesh." [32] This mystery is great, but I speak with reference to
          Christ and the *church.*
A´:   [33] In any case, also you, each one of you, should so love his own
          wife as himself, and the wife should *respect* her husband.

1. Audience Response to Ephesians 5:21–33

a. Eph 5:21–22 (A): Wives submitting to their husbands

Paul then adds a fifth participle to the series that began in 5:19a, further
describing for his audience the behavior that results from and responds to
their being filled with gifts of love by Christ within the realm of being in
the Spirit (5:18): "Submitting to one another in respect for Christ" (5:21).
The audience who are not only to become kind to "one another" (ἀλλήλους)
(4:32) but to forbear "one another" (ἀλλήλων) within the realm of being
"in love" (4:2), because "we are members of one another (ἀλλήλων)" (4:25),
are now to submit themselves to "one another" (ἀλλήλοι), that is, to submit themselves in obedience to those who have authority over them.[24] The

---

24. "Submitting" (ὑποτασσόμενοι) to one another means not mutual or reciprocal submission to one another in general but submission to appropriate authorities. For the ar-
gumentation, see O'Brien, *Ephesians,* 399–404; Ehrhard Kamlah, "Ὑποτάσσεσθαι in den
neutestamentlichen 'Haustafeln,' " in *Verborum Veritas: Festschrift für Gustav Stählin zum
70. Geburtstag* (ed. Otto Böcher and Klaus Haacker; Wuppertal: Brockhaus, 1970), 238–
40; Stephen B. Clark, *Man and Woman in Christ: An Examination of the Roles of Men and
Women in Light of Scripture and the Social Sciences* (Edinburgh: Clark, 1980), 74–76. See
also BDAG, 1042. The pronoun "one another" (ἀλλήλων) does not always express mutuality
or reciprocity but often simply shows distributive activity within a group, so that Eph 5:21
may be translated, "Out of reverence for Christ, be in subordination among yourselves,"
and paraphrased, "Obey whom you are supposed to," according to W. Walden, "Ephesians
5:21: A Translation Note," *ResQ* 45 (2003): 254. But see S. N. Helton, "Ephesians 5:21: A
Longer Translation Note," *ResQ* 48 (2006): 33–41. On translating ὑποτασσόμενοι in Eph
5:21 Hoehner (*Ephesians,* 717) points out: "The word 'subordinate' may not be the best
word to use since it can imply inferiority. 'Submission' is a better term and its application in
mutual submission to one another would imply that one is willing to submit to those who
have authority, whether it be in the home, church, or in society." According to Gerhard Delling ("ὑποτάσσω," *TDNT* 8.45), this submission "demands readiness to renounce one's own
will for the sake of others, i.e., ἀγάπη, and to give precedence to others."

motivation for their humble and loving submission is the "respect" or "reverence" they have for the Christ in whose name they are giving thanks to God for all the gifts of love (5:20) with which they are being filled by the Lord Christ within the realm of being in the Spirit (5:18).[25] In recognition of the status of Christ under whose feet God has "subjected" (ὑπέταχεν) all things (1:22) believers are "submitting" (ὑποτασσόμενοι) to one another.

This general submission to one another is then further specified:[26] "Wives (submitting) to their own husbands as to the Lord" (5:22).[27] In submitting

---

25. Some (e.g., Lincoln, *Ephesians*, 366; O'Brien, *Ephesians*, 404) insist that φόβος in Eph 5:21 should be translated more strongly as "fear" rather than "respect" or "reverence." But Hoehner (*Ephesians*, 719) comments that "since the word is used in the context of Christ's love that is so amply demonstrated in this letter, it is best to view it as a reverential fear or reverential respect. This quality of 'fear' motivates believers to submit to others within the body." See also Horst Balz, "φόβος," *EDNT* 3.433–34; BDAG, 1062.

26. Craig S. Keener, *Paul, Women, and Wives: Marriage and Women's Ministry in the Letters of Paul* (Peabody, MA: Hendrickson, 1992), 157: "[W]hen Paul calls on wives to submit in Ephesians 5:22, he presents this as a particular example of the submission of all believers to one another in 5:21."

27. For some of the vast literature on the "household code" in this section of Ephesians, see Eric Fuchs, "De la soumission des femmes: Une lecture d'Ephésiens 5, 21–33," *Supplément* 161 (1987): 73–81; P. Wells, "La famille chrétienne à l'image de Christ: Une étude d'Ephésiens 5:22 à 6:4," *RRef* 38 (1987): 11–23; Stephen Francis Miletic, "*One Flesh*": *Eph. 5.22–24, 5.31. Marriage and the New Creation* (AnBib 115; Rome: Biblical Institute, 1988); Robert W. Wall, "Wifely Submission in the Context of Ephesians," *Christian Scholar's Review* 17 (1988): 272–85; James R. Beck, "Is There a Head of the House in the Home? Reflections on Ephesians 5," *Journal of Biblical Equality* 1 (1989): 61–70; G. F. Wessels, "Ephesians 5:21–33: 'Wives, be Subject to Your Husbands . . . Husbands, Love Your Wives . . . ,'" *JTSA* 67 (1989): 67–76; J. E. Toews, "Paul's Radical Vision for the Family," *Direction* 19 (1990): 29–38; A. Augello, "Il rapporto marito e moglie secondo l'antropologia naturale e soprannaturale di Efesini 5, 21–33," *Vivarium* 1 (1993): 437–65; Ernest Best, "The Haustafel in Ephesians (Eph. 5.22–6.9)," *IBS* 16 (1994): 146–60; Karl-Heinz Fleckenstein, *Ordnet euch einander unter in der Furcht Christi: Die Eheperikope in Eph 5, 21–33: Geschichte der Interpretation, Analyse und Aktualisierung des Textes* (FB 73; Würzburg, Germany: Echter, 1994); Jostein Ådna, "Die eheliche Liebesbeziehung als Analogie zu Christi Beziehung zur Kirche: Eine traditionsgeschichtliche Studie zu Epheser 5, 21–33," *ZTK* 92 (1995): 434–65; Russ Dudrey, " 'Submit Yourselves to One Another': A Socio-historical Look at the Household Code of Ephesians 5:15–6:9," *ResQ* 41 (1999): 27–44; Annegret Meyer, "Biblische Metaphorik—gesellschaftlicher Diskurs: Rezeptionsästhetische Betrachtung über die Wirkung von Metaphern am Beispiel Eph 5, 21–33," *TGl* 90 (2000): 645–65; E. R. Campbell-Reed, "Should Wives 'Submit Graciously?' A Feminist Approach to Interpreting Ephesians 5:21–33," *RevExp* 98 (2001): 263–76; Carolyn Osiek, "The Bride of Christ (Ephesians 5:22–33): A Problematic Wedding," *BTB* 32 (2002): 29–39; Gillian Beattie, *Women and Marriage in Paul and His Early Interpreters* (JSNTSup 296; London: Clark, 2005), 76–82; Hoehner, *Ephesians*, 720–29. He notes: "Paul's injunctions reflect a hierarchical structure but still there is no suggestion of misogyny or the sweeping powers of the male head which were practiced in the early Greek household and even to a greater degree in the early Roman household. There is more space given to exhortations for the husband than the wife" (p. 729).

to their own husbands in respect for Christ (5:21) wives are submitting to the "Lord" (κυρίῳ), that is, to our "Lord" (κυρίου) Jesus Christ in whose name the audience are thanking God the Father (5:20) for all of the gifts of love with which they are being filled by Christ in the Spirit (5:18), as they understand what the will of the "Lord" (κυρίου) is (5:17).[28] In submitting to their husbands, then, the wives in the audience are submitting themselves to the reception of further gifts of love that come from the Lord through their husbands.

b. Eph 5:23a (B): The husband is head of the wife

This is confirmed as Paul indicates to his audience the reason for this submission: "For the husband is head of the wife as also the Christ is head of the church" (5:23a). As the audience recalls, God gave, as a gift of love, Christ as "head" (κεφαλήν) over all things to the "church" (ἐκκλησίᾳ), which is the body of the Christ who is filling all things in all ways with gifts of love (1:22–23). And as the "head" (κεφαλή) to which all things are growing, Christ is also the source from whom the body, the church, is building itself up by sharing with one another the gifts of love with which they are being filled by Christ within the realm of being "in love" (4:15–16). Thus, that the husband is "head" (κεφαλή) of the wife as also the Christ is "head" (κεφαλή) of the "church" (ἐκκλησίας) means that as the Christ is not only the authority over but the source of gifts of love for the church, so the husband is not only the authority over but the source of gifts of love for the wife.[29]

---

28. Miletic, *One Flesh*, 38: "Yet in her one act of subordination to her husband she acts as one who is subordinate to the Lord and therefore is related to the Lord in a manner correlative to her married status." Hoehner, *Ephesians*, 738: "[A]s she submits to her husband she also submits to her Lord."

29. The implication that Christ is "head" not only of all things but also of the church as his "body" in Eph 1:22–23 and 4:15–16 thus becomes explicit in 5:23a. Hoehner, *Ephesians*, 739: "In recent times much ink has been spilled over the concept of head. As discussed at 1:22 and 4:15 some think 'head' means 'ruler' or 'authority' while others think it refers to 'source.' However, it is better to view κεφαλή not as inherently denoting either authority or source, but rather 'preeminence' or 'prominence' with the context emphasizing either authority or source. Certainly, the context of 1:22 portrays Christ as the head in the sense of 'ruler' or 'authority over' because it stipulates that everything is subjected under his feet, whereas the context of 4:15–16 emphasizes Christ as the 'source' from which believers grow and from whom the whole body is being fitted together." But, in addition, the context of 4:15–16 indicates that as "head" Christ is not only the "source" or "origin" of gifts of love for the body but also the "goal" or "destiny" to which the body of believers, the church, causes all things to grow: "We might cause all things to grow to him (εἰς αὐτόν)" (4:15). Thus, in Ephesians, that Christ is "head" means that he is the "ruler" over all things God has subjected to him (1:22), the "source" of gifts of love as he is the one who is filling all things in all ways (1:23; 4:10, 16), and the "goal" to which all things are growing (4:15) until they are united under one "head" in Christ (1:10). See also I. Howard Marshall, " 'For the Husband Is Head of the Wife' Paul's Use of Head and Body Language," in *The New Testament in Its First Century*

c. Eph 5:23b (C): Christ is the savior of the body

Paul then emphasizes that as head of the church Christ is "himself savior of the body" (5:23b).[30] As the audience recall, they became believers when they heard the gospel of their "salvation" (σωτηρίας) (1:13), according to which they have been "saved" (σεσῳσμένοι) by grace—the gift of love—from being dead in transgressions so that they are now alive in their union with Christ (2:5), because of the great love with which God loved us (2:4). Indeed, as Paul emphatically insisted, they have been "saved" (σεσῳσμένοι) through faith by the grace which is a gift of God's love (2:8). That Christ himself is the "savior" (σωτήρ) of the body, the one who saved the body of believers, the church, as a gift of God's love, reinforces for the audience that Christ as "head" is the source of gifts of love for the church, and thus that the husband as "head" is similarly a source of love for his wife.[31]

d. Eph 5:24–27 (D): Husbands are to love their wives

Paul then compares the relation of the church to Christ with the relation of wives to their husbands: "But as the church submits to the Christ, so also the wives to their husbands in everything" (5:24).[32] That the "church" (ἐκκλησία) "submits" (ὑποτάσσεται) to the Christ means that it submits not only to the authority of Christ as the "head" under whom God "subjected" (ὑπέταχεν) all things (1:22), but also to the Christ who, as "head" of the "church" (ἐκκλησίας) which is his body (5:23; cf. 1:22–23; 4:12, 16), is the source of gifts of love for the body (4:16), as the one who is filling all things in all ways (1:23; 3:19; 4:10; 5:18). So also the wives in the audience are to submit not only to the authority of their husbands as their "heads," but also to the reception of further gifts of love from their husbands as their "heads" (5:23).[33] As the church submits to Christ in everything, so also wives are to

---

Setting: Essays on Context and Background in Honour of B. W. Winter on His Sixty-fifth Birthday (ed. P. J. Williams et al.; Grand Rapids: Eerdmans, 2004), 165–77.

30. O'Brien, *Ephesians*, 414: "[T]he personal pronoun 'he himself' is emphatic by its presence and position, and clearly refers to Christ. Nowhere in the context is the wife regarded as the husband's body as the church is Christ's body."

31. Lincoln, *Ephesians*, 371: "What it means for Christ to be Savior has been seen in the depiction in 2:1–10 of the divine act of deliverance in which Christ is the agent."

32. On Eph 5:24b, Hoehner (*Ephesians*, 745) points out: "The 'wives' are the subject and the present middle/passive imperative ὑποτασσέσθωσαν ['let them submit'] needs to be supplied." Lincoln, *Ephesians*, 372: "So v 24 restates, and in the process reinforces, the exhortation and its warrant in the analogy of Christ and the Church that has preceded in vv 22, 23."

33. Lincoln, *Ephesians*, 372: "If one asks what the writer thinks is involved in the Church's subordination to Christ, one can look for an answer to the way in which he depicts the Church's relation to Christ in the rest of the letter. The Church receives God's gift of Christ as head over all on its behalf (1:22). In the building imagery of 2:20, 21 the Church looks to Christ as the crowning stone of its structure and the one who holds it all together.

submit to their husbands in "everything" (παντί), echoing "all the things" (πάντων) with which the audience are being filled by Christ (5:18) and for which the audience are "always" (πάντοτε) thanking God (5:20).[34]

With a direct address Paul then exhorts: "Husbands, love your wives, just as also the Christ loved the church and handed himself over for her" (5:25). This command for husbands to "love" (ἀγαπᾶτε) your wives extends and further specifies Paul's previous command that all believers become imitators of God as "beloved" (ἀγαπητά) children and "walk" within the realm of being "in love" (ἐν ἀγάπῃ) (5:1–2a). The model and motivation for both the general command (5:1–2) and the more specific marital command (5:25) is the same self-sacrificial love of Christ for the body of believers, the church:[35]

5:2b: καθὼς καὶ ὁ Χριστὸς ἠγάπησεν ἡμᾶς καὶ παρέδωκεν ἑαυτὸν ὑπὲρ ἡμῶν

It opens itself to his constant presence (3:17) and comes to know his all-encompassing love (3:19). The Church receives his gift of grace (4:7) and his gifts of ministers for its own upbuilding (4:11, 12). It grows toward its head and receives from him all that is necessary for such growth (4:15, 16), including teaching about him (4:20, 21). The Church imitates Christ's love (5:2) and tries to learn what is pleasing to him (5:19) and lives in fear of him (5:21). The Church's subordination, then, means looking to its head for his beneficial rule, living by his norms, experiencing his presence and love, receiving from him gifts that will enable growth to maturity, and responding to him in gratitude and awe. It is such attitudes that the wife is being encouraged to develop in relation to her husband."

34. Hoehner, *Ephesians*, 746: "In essence, the church is to submit to Christ in everything. As the church benefits from submission to Christ so also ought wives benefit from their submission to their husbands." The emphasis is not on the submission of the wives but on the husband's role as "head" of his wife according to Turid Karlsen Seim, "A Superior Minority? The Problem of Men's Headship in Ephesians 5," *ST* 49 (1995): 166, 177–81. The submission of wives to husbands includes the sexual union according to Carolyn Osiek, "Female Slaves, Porneia, and the Limits of Obedience," in *Early Christian Families in Context: An Interdisciplinary Dialogue* (ed. David L. Balch and Carolyn Osiek; Grand Rapids: Eerdmans, 2003), 271: "[T]he reference to Christ as the husband of the church, as metaphoric loving but still dominant husband in marriage, certainly does include sexual union: 'Wives, submit to your husbands as to the Lord . . . in everything' (Eph. 5:22, 24). Much of the rest of the passage about husbands and wives, Christ and the church, is clearly sexual in connotation (vv. 26–31)."

35. Lincoln, *Ephesians*, 374: "Significantly, the call to all to loving sacrifice for one another in 5:1, 2 takes a similar form to that directed to husbands here in 5:25, since in both places the analogy with Christ's own self-sacrificing love provides the warrant for the appeal. The exhortation to sacrifice one's own interests for the welfare of others, which is so necessary for the harmony of the community, now finds a more specific application in the husband's role in contributing to marital harmony. . . . It can now be seen clearly that for this writer the exhortation to wives to submit is not to be separated from this call to husbands to give themselves in love and that any exercise of headship on the part of husbands will not be through self-assertion but through self-sacrifice." O'Brien, *Ephesians*, 419: "Earlier in Ephesians love is seen as a grace that all believers are to show in their relationships with others (1:4; 3:17; 4:2, 15, 16; 5:2). Now it is required of husbands in relation to their wives."

just as also the Christ loved us and handed himself over for us

5:25: καθὼς καὶ ὁ Χριστὸς ἠγάπησεν τὴν ἐκκλησίαν καὶ ἑαυτὸν παρέδωκεν ὑπὲρ αὐτῆς

just as also the Christ loved the church and handed himself over for her[36]

For husbands to "love" their wives as Christ "loved" the church in a self-sacrificial way further illustrates then what it means for the audience of believers, as children "beloved" by God (5:1), to "walk" within the realm of being "in love" (5:2a).[37]

With a triplet of "that" (ἵνα) purpose clauses Paul then indicates the goal of Christ's self-sacrificial love for the church:

1 that (ἵνα) he might sanctify her, cleansing her by the washing of the water in the word (5:26),

2. that (ἵνα) he might present to himself the church glorious, not having a blemish or wrinkle or any of such things (5:27ab),

3. but that (ἵνα) she might be holy and blameless (5:27c).

That by his self-sacrificial love Christ might "sanctify" or "make holy" (ἁγιάσῃ) "her" (αὐτήν)—in emphatic position after the conjunction and before the verb, underlining the importance of the church (5:26a)[38]—provides a further basis empowering the church, as the "building" that is being fitted together in union with Christ as the "head stone," to grow into a temple

---

36. Lincoln, *Ephesians*, 374: "The analogy with Christ's love for the Church is introduced by καθὼς ['just as'], which in addition to its primary comparative force also has causal connotations. Christ's love for the Church not only presents the model but also provides the grounds for the husband's love for his wife." Hoehner, *Ephesians*, 750: "The reflexive pronoun [ἑαυτόν, 'himself'] further enhances his supreme love by indicating that he was not forced to die at the hand of human beings but that he laid down his own life for the church. . . . The preposition [ὑπὲρ] with a genitive signifies that it was done 'for the sake of, in [on] behalf of,' showing interest in the object and has been characterized as the particle of love."

37. Lincoln, *Ephesians*, 373–74: "After the exhortation to wives to submit, with its depiction of husbands as heads, what might well have been expected by contemporary readers would be an exhortation to husbands to rule their wives. Instead the exhortation is for husbands to love their wives. . . . Exhortations to husbands to love their wives are found outside the NT, but they are fairly infrequent." Hoehner, *Ephesians*, 748: "This exhortation to husbands to love their wives is unique. It is not found in the OT, rabbinic literature, or in the household codes of the Greco-Roman era. Although the hierarchical model of the home is maintained, it is ameliorated by this revolutionary exhortation that husbands are to love their wives as Christ loved the church."

38. Hoehner, *Ephesians*, 750: "The personal pronoun αὐτήν, immediately after the ἵνα, suggests the importance Christ places on the church."

"holy" (ἅγιον) in the Lord (2:20–21). In contrast to every kind of "impurity" (ἀκαθαρσίας) practiced by the Gentiles (4:19) and the "impurity" (ἀκαθαρσία) that is not even to be named among the audience (5:3), Christ "cleanses" or "purifies" (καθαρίσας) the church (5:26b).[39]

This cleansing from the impurity of a sinful lifestyle is accomplished "by the washing (λουτρῷ) of the water," a reference to baptism (cf. 4:5),[40] and takes place "in the word" (ἐν ῥήματι) (5:26b), that is, within the dynamic realm established by the proclaimed word of the gospel (cf. 6:17; 1:13) which empowers those who hear it to believe and be baptized[41]—yet another occurrence in Ephesians of an "in" (ἐν) prepositional phrase to express a dynamic realm, sphere, or domain of interaction. This reminds the audience that when they heard the word of truth, the gospel of their salvation, and became believers (1:13) and were baptized, it was by this "one baptism" (4:5) that they were cleansed of the impurity of their sins, reconciled, and united with all other believers in the "one body" of the church as a gift of Christ's self-sacrificial love through his death on the cross (2:16).[42]

Building upon and continuing the first "that" (ἵνα) purpose clause (5:26)

---

39. O'Brien, *Ephesians*, 422: "Because the participle here follows the main verb, it is likely that the cleansing is coincidental with the making holy. . . . It is best, then, to understand the participle as denoting the means by which the action of the main verb was accomplished." See also Porter, *Verbal Aspect*, 383–84.

40. Lincoln, *Ephesians*, 375: "The definite article (lit. 'the washing in [the] water') may well indicate a specific event, and the readers are scarcely likely to have taken this as anything other than a reference to their experience of baptism. In 1 Cor 6:11 washing and sanctifying occur together as metaphors of salvation, with an allusion to baptism highly probable. But here, the explicit mention of water suggests not simply an extended metaphor for salvation but a direct reference to water baptism, not to baptism by the Spirit. . . . the language of 'the washing with water' is likely to have as a secondary connotation the notion of the bridal bath. This would reflect both Jewish marital customs with their prenuptial bath and the marital imagery of Ezek 16:8–14 which stands behind this passage. In Ezek 16:9 Yahweh, in entering his marriage covenant with Jerusalem, is said to have bathed her with water and washed off the blood from her." See also Spicq, "λουτρόν," *TLNT* 2.412–14; Martin Völkel, "λουτρόν," *EDNT* 2.361.

41. Hoehner, *Ephesians*, 756: "The ῥῆμα in the present context is the preached word of Christ's love for the church in that he gave his life for her for the purpose that he might sanctify her by having cleansed her with (instrumental dative) the washing of water. . . . In Jewish customs at the time of betrothal the young man would present his bride-to-be with a gift and say to her, 'Behold, you are consecrated unto me, you are betrothed to me; behold, you are a wife unto me.' With this spoken word they would be betrothed and then married about a year later. Just before the wedding she was bathed, symbolizing the cleansing that would set her apart to her husband."

42. Giuseppe Baldanza, "L'originalità della metafora sponsale in Ef 5, 25–32: Riflessi sull' ecclesiologia," *Salesianum* 63 (2001): 3–21. O'Brien, *Ephesians*, 423–24: "In the light of Christ's complete giving of himself to make the church holy and cleanse her, husbands should be utterly committed to the total well-being, especially the spiritual welfare, of their wives."

is the second: "that (ἵνα) he might present to himself the church glorious, not having a blemish or wrinkle or any of such things" (5:27ab). That the purpose of Christ's self-sacrificial love, twice expressed as his having freely handed "himself" (ἑαυτόν) over (5:2, 25), is that he himself might present to "himself" (ἑαυτῷ) the church glorious underlines for the audience how it is the self-sacrificial love of Christ himself that empowers the "church" (ἐκκλησίαν) to be "glorious" (ἔνδοχον), thus further developing Paul's climactic doxology that to God be "glory" (δόξα) in the "church" (ἐκκλησία) and in Christ Jesus to all generations for ever and ever. Amen" (3:21).[43] The church made glorious by Christ gives glory to God.

What it means for the church to be glorious (5:27a) Paul then elaborates for his audience negatively with a rhetorical triplet of physical terms serving as metaphors for immoral behavior: "not having a blemish or wrinkle or any of such things" (5:27b). The triplet progresses from a single "blemish" (σπίλον) or "wrinkle" (ῥυτίδα) to a climactic and comprehensive plural that includes these and any other possible moral imperfections—"or any of such things (ἤ τι τῶν τοιούτων)."[44]

In an emphatic contrast to the negative triplet (5:27b) is the climactic positive doublet in the third and final "that" (ἵνα) purpose clause: "but that

---

43. Lincoln, *Ephesians*, 377: "The imagery may well again reflect Ezek 16 where in vv 10–14 Yahweh decks out his bride in magnificent clothing and jewelry, so that she displays regal beauty and perfect splendor." O'Brien, *Ephesians*, 424: "[A]ccording to 2 Corinthians 11:2 Paul's role, as the friend of the bridegroom, is to present [παραστῆσαι] the Corinthians as a pure virgin to Christ. Here in Ephesians, however, by adding the personal pronoun '[he] himself', together with the reflexive pronoun 'to himself', Paul goes out of his way to emphasize that it is Christ who will present [παραστήσῃ] the church to himself—not the friend of the bridegroom, nor the bride herself. He has done everything necessary to achieve this goal." Hoehner, *Ephesians*, 758: "The personal pronoun αὐτός, 'he,' following the verb places emphasis on the subject, Christ, who gave himself for the church. This is followed by a reflexive pronoun ἑαυτῷ, 'to himself,' to make it more emphatic that Christ not only sanctified the church in order that he might present her but that he might present her to himself. In the present context Christ presents the universal church to himself. In a human wedding in the first century, the bride prepares herself for the bridegroom and he presents her to his father. Here Christ, the bridegroom, prepares the bride by sanctification and also presents her to himself."

44. Lincoln, *Ephesians*, 377: "Here, the glory with which the Church as the bride is adorned will be elaborated on in terms of her moral perfection. The bride's beauty is to be all-encompassing and is not to be spoiled by anything, by the least spot or wrinkle. σπίλος could mean a stain or defect of any sort, but together with ῥυτίς, which denotes a wrinkle in the skin, may well refer to a spot on the body or a physical defect. . . . The picture is of Christ preparing a bride for himself that has no physical blemish. But it then becomes crystal clear from the final ἵνα clause that this bride's beauty is moral." Hoehner, *Ephesians*, 759–60: "Both σπίλον and ῥυτίδα are singular, possibly to emphasize that not one blemish or one wrinkle marks the church. To be sure nothing is missed, Paul adds the catchall ἤ τι τῶν τοιούτων, 'or any such thing.' Hence, the church has no blemish nor any wrinkle nor anything else that would suggest imperfection in its gloriousness."

(ἵνα) she might be holy and blameless" (5:27c). That the church might be "holy and blameless" (ἁγία καὶ ἄμωμος) reminds the audience that God chose us believers before the foundation of the world that we might be "holy and blameless" (ἁγίους καὶ ἀμώμους) before God in love (1:4). With regard to the love theme, then, the audience now realize that the self-sacrificial love of Christ, which serves as the motive and model not only for believers to love one another (5:1–2), but also for husbands to love their wives (5:25), empowers us believers, the church, to be morally "holy and blameless" not only presently but at that future "fullness of the times" (1:10) within the dynamic realm of living "in love" (1:4; 3:17; 4:2, 15, 16; 5:2)—loving one another in response to and imitation of being loved by the self-sacrificial love of Christ.[45]

e. Eph 5:28a (E): Husbands ought to love their own wives

Paul then continues his presentation to his audience of the self-sacrificial love of Christ as the motive and model for husbands to love their wives: "So ought also husbands to love their own wives as their own bodies" (5:28a). The command that husbands "love" (ἀγαπᾶτε) their wives as also the Christ "loved" (ἠγάπησεν) the church (5:25), which is his "body" (σῶμα) (1:23; cf. 5:23b), now progresses to the obligation that husbands also ought to "love" (ἀγαπᾶν) their own wives as their own "bodies" (σώματα). Just as Christ the "head" (5:23a) loves the church which is his own "body," so also husbands, who are the "heads" of their wives (5:23a), are to love their own wives because they are as their own "bodies."[46]

---

45. Hoehner, *Ephesians*, 761: "The allusion to the church's holiness and blamelessness is important not only in the immediate context but it also serves as a climax to the argument and theology of the whole book. In Eph 1:4 God chose believers in order that they might be holy and blameless before him in love." Lincoln, *Ephesians*, 377: "Here, in line with this writer's more realized eschatology, glory and holiness are seen as present attributes of the Church, and Christ's activity of endowing the Church with these qualities is a present and continuing one. After all, in 1:4 holiness and blamelessness, along with love, are present aspects of Christian existence. His loving and sanctifying have already secured for Christ a completely glorious and pure bride, and his continuing care will maintain her moral beauty. In this way, the perspective on the Church is similar to that of 4:1–16, where the Church is already the fullness of Christ and already one, yet is also to grow into completeness and unity." See also Renzo Infante, "Immagine nuziale e tensione escatologica nel Nuovo Testamento: Note a 2 Cor. 11,2 e Eph. 5,25–27," *RivB* 33 (1985): 45–61.

46. O'Brien, *Ephesians*, 427: "[T]he husband's obligation to love his wife as his own body is not simply a matter of loving someone else just like he loves himself. It is, in fact, to love himself. . . . the idea of husbands loving their wives as their own bodies reflects the model of Christ, whose love for the church can be seen as love for his own body." Hoehner, *Ephesians*, 765: "Certainly, throughout the context the head corresponds to the body, and the head, Christ, loves the body, the church; so also husbands ought to love their wives who, as it were, are their own bodies."

f. Eph 5:28b (E′): He who loves his own wife loves himself

The audience then hear the central pivot that initiates the progressive parallels at work within the chiastic structure of 5:21–33: "He who loves his own wife loves himself" (5:28b). The obligation for husbands in general and in the plural to "love" (ἀγαπᾶν) "their own wives" (ἑαυτῶν γυναῖκας) in general and in the plural as "their own bodies" (ἑαυτῶν σώματα) in general and in the plural in the E element (5:28a) of the chiasm progresses, by way of the chiastic parallelism, to each individual husband in the singular who "loves" (ἀγαπῶν) "his own wife" (ἑαυτοῦ γυναῖκα) in the singular "loving" (ἀγαπᾷ) "himself" (ἑαυτόν) in the singular in the E′ element (5:28b).

That each individual husband in the audience who loves his own wife, who is as his own body (5:28a), loves "himself" (ἑαυτόν) (5:28b) recalls what it meant for Christ himself to love his own body, the church. In his self-sacrificial love Christ handed "himself" (ἑαυτόν) over for us, the body of believers who are the church (5:2, 25). It was by handing his own individual self over on behalf of his own body that Christ was, in effect, loving "himself." Hence, as a further development of the love theme, for each individual husband to love "himself," that is, his own wife who is as his own body (5:28), as Christ loved the church, his own body (5:23b, 25), means for him to hand his own individual self over on behalf of his wife with the same sort of self-sacrificial love.

g. Eph 5:29 (D′): A husband nurtures and cares for his wife

Paul continues his comparison of a husband's love for his wife to Christ's love for the church: "For no one ever hates his own flesh but nurtures and cares for it, just as also the Christ (nurtures and cares for) the church" (5:29). The motive and model for the husbands in the audience to love their wives "just as also the Christ" (καθὼς καὶ ὁ Χριστός) loved "the church" (τὴν ἐκκλησίαν) (5:25) in the D element (5:24–27) of the chiasm progresses, by way of the chiastic parallelism, to the motive and model for each individual husband to nurture and care for his own flesh "just as also the Christ" (καθὼς καὶ ὁ Χριστός) nurtures and cares for "the church" (τὴν ἐκκλησίαν) in the D′ element (5:29). That Christ "nurtures and cares for" the church thus further develops what it means for him to "love" the church:

5:25: just as also the Christ *loves* the church

5:29: just as also the Christ (*nurtures and cares for*) the church

That no one ever hates "his own" (ἑαυτοῦ) flesh (5:29a) means in this context that no husband ever hates "his own" (ἑαυτοῦ) wife, whom in loving he is loving "himself" (ἑαυτὸν), since husbands are to love "their own"

(ἑαυτῶν) wives as "their own" (ἑαυτῶν) bodies/flesh (5:28).[47] That a husband
rather nurtures and cares for his own flesh/body/wife as Christ nurtures and
cares for the church (5:29b) further develops what it means for the audience
to "walk" as beloved children within the realm of being "in love" (5:1–2).
Just as Christ nurtures and cares for the church, his own body, by loving it
and thus empowering it to bring about the growth of the body for the building up of "itself" (ἑαυτοῦ) "in love" (4:16),[48] so a husband is to nurture and
care for his wife, his own flesh/body, by loving her. Then together "in love"
they may do their part not only to bring about the growth and building up
of the body of believers, the church, "in love" but to cause all things to grow
to him, who is the head, the Christ, by being truthful in sharing love within
the dynamic realm of being "in love" (4:15).

h. Eph 5:30 (C′): We are members of his body

Paul then further explains to his audience why each husband nurtures
and cares for his wife, just as Christ nurtures and cares for the church (5:29):
"For we are members of his body" (5:30).[49] The focus on Christ himself
as savior of the "body" (σώματος) in the C element (5:23b) of the chiasm
progresses, by way of the chiastic parallelism, to a focus on us believers as
members of his "body" (σώματος) in the C′ element (5:30). Husbands are
to love their wives, then, to enable both husbands and wives to play their
respective roles as members of the body of Christ, the church.

The statement "for we are members" (ὅτι μέλη ἐσμέν) of his body (5:30)
as an explanation for husbands to love their wives (5:25–29) reminds the
audience of the statement "for we are members (ὅτι ἐσμὲν μέλη) of "one
another" (ἀλλήλων) as an explanation for why the audience are to speak
truth, each one with his neighbor (4:25), as a further way of bearing with

---

47. O'Brien, *Ephesians*, 427 n. 270: "What is referred to as 'bodies' (σώματα) in v. 28a
becomes 'himself' (ἑαυτόν) in v. 28c, and is changed to 'flesh' (σάρξ) in v. 29a. 'Flesh' (σάρξ)
is used interchangeably here with 'body' (σῶμα) and therefore without any negative connotation. Most interpreters agree that the movement to 'flesh' here anticipates the quotation of
Gen. 2:24 in v. 31: 'and the two shall become one flesh' (εἰς σάρκα μίαν)."
48. Lincoln, *Ephesians*, 380: "[T]he imagery as applied to Christ's treatment of
the Church is meant to recall his constant provision for and building up of his body (cf.
4:11–16)."
49. Lincoln, *Ephesians*, 380: "The introduction of the first-person plural into the
discussion in v 30 with ἐσμέν, 'we are,' may well be intended to underline for the letter's
recipients their own participation in the reality of Christ's loving care for his body and to emphasize that what has been said in the preceding argument about the Church applies to them,
because they are, in fact, members of this privileged community, Christ's body." O'Brien,
Ephesians, 428: "[T]he relationship between Christ and his church is presented not simply as
the ideal model for a husband and wife in their marriage. It is also the reality in which they
and other Christians are included."

"one another" (ἀλλήλων) within the realm of being "in love" (4:2).[50] A situation of husbands loving their wives thus further illustrates what it means for members of the body of Christ to bear with one another and be truthful with one another within the dynamic realm of being "in love" (cf. 4:15).

For husbands to love their wives because we are members of his "body" (σώματος) (5:30) confirms and reinforces for the audience how marital love contributes to the building up of the "body" (σώματος) of the Christ, until we all attain to the unity of the faith and of the knowledge of the Son of God, to a mature person, to the measure of the stature of the fullness of the Christ (4:12–13). Marital love between members of the body brings about the growth of the "body" (σώματος) for the building up of itself within the realm of being "in love" (4:16). By being truthful to one another "in love" husbands and wives, as members of his body, play their respective roles in causing all things to grow to him, who is the head, the Christ (4:15), so that ultimately all things might be united under one head in the Christ (1:10).

i. Eph 5:31–32 (B΄): Unity of man and wife and the mystery

With a quotation of Gen 2:24 Paul situates marital unity within God's scriptural plan of creation as part of the great mystery regarding Christ and the church: "'For this reason a man shall leave his father and mother and shall cleave to his wife, and the two shall become one flesh.'[51] This mystery is great, but I speak with reference to Christ and the church" (5:31–32). A "husband" (ἀνήρ) being the head of his "wife" (γυναικός) as also the Christ is head of the "church" (ἐκκλησίας) in the B element (5:23a) of the chiasm progresses, by way of the chiastic parallelism, to a "man" (ἄνθρωπος) becoming a husband by leaving his father and mother and cleaving to his "wife" (γυναῖκα) as part of the great mystery concerning Christ and the "church" (ἐκκλησίαν) in the B΄ element (5:31–32).

That the two—the man and the wife to whom he cleaves—become one "flesh" (σάρκα) (5:31) reinforces for the audience that the wife is not only as the husband's own "body" (5:28a) but also as his own "flesh" (σάρκα) (5:29), so that in loving his own wife the husband is loving himself (5:28b), in response to and in imitation of Christ's love for his body (5:23b, 30), the church (5:25, 29).

---

50. Hoehner, *Ephesians*, 768: "The noun μέλος, 'member' . . . is never used of a member of an organization but always used of a member of an organism. The use of this term demonstrates the close-knit relationship of the members with Christ."

51. The quotation is part of the natural flow of the argument without an introductory formula to indicate to the audience that this is a scriptural quotation (cf. 4:8; 5:14). On the use of Gen 2:24 here and how the wording of Paul's quote differs slightly from that of the LXX, see Lincoln, *Ephesians*, 380; Hoehner, *Ephesians*, 771–72; O'Brien, *Ephesians*, 429 nn. 281–82. Moritz (*Profound Mystery*, 135–36) incorrectly considers the quotation as a "digression" in the train of thought.

That the "two" (δύο)—husband and wife—will become "one" (μίαν) flesh/body (5:31) reminds the audience that a purpose of Christ's self-sacrificial love was that the "two" (δύο)—believing Jews and Gentiles—he might create in himself into "one" (ἕνα) new person, making peace, and that he might reconcile the both in "one" (ἑνί) body, the church, to God through his sacrificial death on the cross (2:15–16). The audience thus realize that the "mystery" (μυστήριον) of the Christ that was hidden from the ages but has now been revealed by Paul includes not only the unity of believing Jews and Gentiles in the one body, the church (3:3–9), but also the marital unity of husbands and wives into one flesh within the one body, the church (5:31).

This is confirmed as Paul follows the scriptural quotation, which places an emphatic stress on the unity of husband and wife (5:31),[52] with the notice: "This mystery (μυστήριον) is great, but I speak with reference to Christ and the church" (5:32). With an emphatic and authoritative clarification—"but I speak" (ἐγὼ δὲ λέγω; cf. 3:1; 4:1, 17)—Paul explains for his audience that this "mystery" he declares to be "great" is that concerning the love of Christ for the church. By his self-sacrificial love for the church (5:2, 25, 29) Christ unites himself as "head" with the church as his "body," a unity analogous to the marital unity by which a husband who loves his wife becomes one flesh/body with her in accord with the scriptural quotation.[53]

This "mystery" of Christ's unifying love for the church is "great," as the audience are to realize, because it embraces not only the love by which Christ united believing Jews and Gentiles into the one body, the church (2:15–3:9), but also the marital love by which a husband unites himself to his wife to become one flesh/body with her within the one body, the church, in imitation of and as an appropriate response to the self-sacrificial love of Christ for the one body of believers, the church (5:2, 25, 29).[54] Both the

---

52. "One" (μίαν) is in an emphatic position as the climactic conclusion of the quotation of Gen 2:24 in Eph 5:31.

53. While it is an analogy, not all of the elements correspond. For example, Paul does not say that Christ as "head" becomes one flesh/body with the church. As "head" both over all things (1:22) and of the body, the church (5:23), Christ is the source and destiny of the unity of the church as his body (1:22–23; 4:15–16). While, on the one hand, Christ as "head" is united to the church as "body," on the other hand, Christ as "head" remains distinct from the body until all things, including the body, grow to the head and are united under the one head in Christ (1:10). On the analogical interpretation of the "mystery" in 5:32, see Andreas J. Köstenberger, "The Mystery of Christ and the Church: Head and Body, 'One Flesh,' " *TJ* 12 (1991): 79–94. O'Brien, *Ephesians*, 433: "Theologically, Paul's argument does not move from human marriage to Christ and his church; rather, Christ and the church in a loving relationship is the paradigm for the Christian husband and wife."

54. "This mystery" in 5:32 refers to "Christ and the church reflected in the dynamic interplay of a truly Christian marriage," according to Raymond C. Ortlund, *Whoredom: God's Unfaithful Wife in Biblical Theology* (New Studies in Biblical Theology 2; Grand Rapids: Eerdmans, 1996), 157. O'Brien, *Ephesians*, 433–34: " '[T]his mystery' does not simply refer to the immediately preceding words of v. 30, but to the line of thought running

unity of believing Jews and Gentiles created by Christ's love for the church and the unity of husbands loving their wives in imitation and because of Christ's love for the church are dimensions of the great cosmic "mystery." The church as the body, growing and being built up within the realm of being "in love"—receiving and sharing the love of Christ—is causing all things to grow to him, who is the "head," the Christ (4:15–16). This accords with the ultimate dimension of the great cosmic "mystery" (μυστήριον, 1:9) of all things being united under one head in the Christ (1:10).[55]

In sum, the unity of husbands loving their wives to become one flesh/body (5:31) is a dimension of the great mystery of the unity of all believers into the one "body" of the church through the self-sacrificial love of its "head," Christ (5:2, 23–30, 32). The love of husbands for their wives adds another element to what it means for believers to "walk" within the dynamic realm of being "in love" (5:1–2). It includes husbands loving their wives in response to and imitation of Christ's love for the church. Marital unity "in love" thus contributes to the great cosmic mystery of unity empowered by love—believers "in love" causing the growth of all things to Christ as the "head" (4:15), so that all things will ultimately be united under one head in the Christ (1:10).

j. Eph 5:33 (A'): The husband should love his wife

With a summarizing exhortation Paul concludes: "In any case, also you, each one of you, should so love his own wife as himself, and the wife should respect her husband" (5:33). The submitting of wives in general to their husbands in "respect" (φόβῳ) for Christ in the A element (5:21–22) of the chiasm progresses, by way of the chiastic parallelism, to the exhortation that each and every individual wife should "respect" (φοβῆται) her husband in the A' element (5:33) of the chiasm.

After turning directly and emphatically to his audience with the words, "In any case, also you," Paul addresses each husband among the "you" of his audience (5:33a).[56] As a response to "each" (ἑκάστῳ) of them being given

---

through the passage. . . . 'Mystery' is thus used consistently with other instances in Ephesians. Elsewhere it points to the once-hidden plan of God which has now been revealed in Jesus Christ. Different aspects of the mystery can be highlighted in any one context; there are not many mysteries but several aspects of the one mystery." Lincoln, *Ephesians*, 381: "Both the OT passage and the marriage relationship of which it speaks are connected with the mystery, but their connection is that they point to the secret that has now been revealed, that of the relationship between Christ and the Church."

55. O'Brien, *Ephesians*, 434: "[W]ithin the wider context of Ephesians as a whole the union between Christian husband and wife which is part of the unity between Christ and the church is thus a pledge of God's purposes of unity for the cosmos."

56. O'Brien, *Ephesians*, 435: "The opening conjunction, which is elsewhere used as an adversative 'however' or 'but', can also conclude a discussion and emphasize what is important. This is its significance here, so it is better to render the word by 'in any case',

grace as a gift of Christ's love (4:7), and in accord with speaking the truth, "each" (ἕκαστος) one to his neighbor (4:25), "each" (ἕκαστος) husband should so love his own wife as himself (5:33b). That each husband in the audience should so "love" (ἀγαπάτω) "his own wife" (τὴν ἑαυτοῦ γυναῖκα) as "himself" (ἑαυτόν), that is, in the self-sacrificial way that Christ loved the church (5:25, 29, 32), emphatically and climactically reinforces what Paul said at the pivot of the chiasm—he who "loves" (ἀγαπῶν) "his own wife" (τὴν ἑαυτοῦ γυναῖκα) "loves" (ἀγαπᾷ) "himself" (ἑαυτόν) (5:28b).[57]

In a reciprocal response to the love of her husband, each wife should respect her husband (5:33c) by submitting to the husband who loves her as she submits to the Lord who loves her (5:22), and as the church submits to the Christ (5:24), who loved the church and handed himself over for her (5:25). For the wife to respect and thus submit to her husband, then, means for her to allow her husband to love her and to graciously accept that love as coming from Christ, the Lord.[58]

To sum up, husbands loving their wives as Christ loved the church and wives submitting to and reciprocally respecting their husbands by accepting their love as coming from Christ (5:21–22, 33) is a result of and response to believers being filled with gifts of love by Christ within the realm of being in the Spirit (5:18). The marital love between husbands and wives thus further demonstrates what it means for the audience to "walk" as children beloved by God and Christ within the dynamic realm of being "in love" (5:1–2).

2. Summary on Ephesians 5:21–33

1. Paul's directive for husbands to "love" their wives as the Christ "loved" the church (5:25) and to "love" their own wives as their own bodies, as he who "loves" his own wife "loves" himself (5:28) in the D′ unit (5:15–6:9) recalls the great "love" with which God "loved" us (2:4) in our union with Christ in the D unit (2:1–10) within the overall chiastic structure of Ephesians.

2. That the husband is "head" of the wife as also the Christ is "head" of

---

or 'now'." Hoehner (*Ephesians*, 781) suggests that the use of the singular address here may be to emphasize individual responsibility. O'Brien, *Ephesians*, 436: "Every husband in the congregations that received this circular letter, not simply the leaders, is addressed directly and personally."

57. Hoehner, *Ephesians*, 782: "The intensity of the love is emphasized by the construction οὕτως ... ὡς, 'so ... as,' a construction already seen in verse 28. As in verse 28 the adverbial conjunction ὡς functions not only as a simple comparison where the husband's love for his own wife should be 'like' his love for himself, but also introduces a characteristic quality of the husband, namely, that he should love his own wife 'as being' himself. Therefore, he loves her because she is united with him, the 'two becoming one.' "

58. The wife's "respect" for her husband "is her appropriate response to her husband's headship exercised in self-sacrificial love," according to Lincoln, *Ephesians*, 385.

the "church" (5:23a) means that as the Christ is not only the authority over but the source of gifts of love for the church, so the husband is not only the authority over but the source of gifts of love for the wife. And that Christ himself is the "savior" of the body (5:23b), the one who saved the body of believers, the church, as a gift of God's love, reinforces this.

3. The self-sacrificial love of Christ, which serves as the motive and model not only for believers to love one another (5:1–2), but also for husbands to love their wives (5:25), empowers us believers, the church, to be morally "holy and blameless" (1:4; 5:27) not only presently but at that future "fullness of the times" (1:10) within the dynamic realm of living "in love" (1:4; 3:17; 4:2, 15, 16; 5:2)—loving one another in response to and imitation of being loved by the self-sacrificial love of Christ.

4. For each individual husband to love "himself," that is, his own wife who is as his own body (5:28), as Christ loved the church, his own body (5:23b, 25), means for him to hand his own individual self over on behalf of his wife with the same sort of self-sacrificial love.

5. Just as Christ nurtures and cares for the church, his own body, by loving it and thus empowering it to bring about the growth of the body for the building up of itself "in love" (4:16), so a husband is to nurture and care for his wife, as his own flesh/body, by loving her (5:29). Then together "in love" they may do their part not only to bring about the growth and building up of the body of believers, the church, "in love" but to cause all things to grow to him, who is the head, the Christ, by being truthful in sharing love within the dynamic realm of being "in love" (4:15).

6. The love of husbands for their wives adds another element to what it means for believers to "walk" within the dynamic realm of being "in love" (5:1–2). It includes husbands loving their wives in response to and imitation of Christ's love for the church. Marital unity "in love" thus contributes to the great cosmic mystery of unity empowered by love—believers "in love" causing the growth of all things to Christ as the "head" (4:15), so that all things will ultimately be united under one head in the Christ (1:10).

7. Husbands loving their wives as Christ loved the church and wives submitting to and reciprocally respecting their husbands by accepting their love as coming from Christ (5:21–22, 33) is a result of and response to believers being filled with gifts of love by Christ within the realm of being in the Spirit (5:18). The marital love between husbands and wives thus further demonstrates what it means for the audience to "walk" as children beloved by God and Christ within the dynamic realm of being "in love" (5:1–2).

D. Children and Parents Respect One Another in Love (6:1–4)

A: ¹ *Children*, obey your parents in the *Lord*, for this is right.
   B: ² "Honor *your* father and mother,"
      C: which is *the first commandment with a promise*,
   B′:   ³ "that it may be well with *you* and you may live long on the earth."
A′:   ⁴ And the fathers, do not anger your *children*, but bring them up in the training and instruction of the *Lord*.

1. Audience Response to Ephesians 6:1–4

a. Eph 6:1 (A): Children are to obey their parents in the Lord

Directly addressing the children in the audience, Paul continues to elaborate on what it means for members of households to submit to one another in respect for Christ (5:21), as a result of and in response to being filled with gifts of love by Christ within the realm of being in the Spirit (5:18): "Children, obey your parents in the Lord, for this is right" (6:1).[59] Previously employing the term "children" metaphorically, Paul referred to all in his audience as formerly "children" (τέκνα) of wrath (2:3), who now are to "walk" not only as "children" (τέκνα) beloved by God and Christ (5:1) but as "children" (τέκνα) of light (5:8). But now he employs the term literally as he enjoins actual "children" (τέκνα) to submit to both the authority and love of their parents by obeying them.[60]

Children are to obey their parents "in the Lord" (ἐν κυρίῳ),[61] that is, within the dynamic realm of being in union with the Lord Jesus Christ (6:1),

---

59. Margaret Y. MacDonald, "Was Celsus Right? The Role of Women in the Expansion of Early Christianity," in *Early Christian Families in Context: An Interdisciplinary Dialogue* (ed. David L. Balch and Carolyn Osiek; Grand Rapids: Eerdmans, 2003), 173: "Most obviously, the direct address to children in the household codes of Colossians and Ephesians (Col. 3:20; Eph. 6:1–2) indicates that the authors expect children to be present when the letters are read aloud in the midst of the assembly."

60. Hoehner, *Ephesians*, 786: "[T]he term τέκνον . . . implies a dependent relationship on the parent. In this context, Paul, no doubt, had in mind children old enough to understand and exercise their free will. . . . the terms ὑπακούω [obey] and ὑποτάσσω, 'be subject,' are basically synonymous" (cf. 1 Pet 3:5–6). O'Brien, *Ephesians*, 440–41: "The term 'children' primarily denotes relationship rather than age, and could on occasion include adult sons and daughters, who were expected to honour their parents, especially fathers, who could maintain authority in the family even until death. Here the text has in view children who are in the process of learning and growing up (cf. v. 4). . . . Children are here addressed as responsible members of the congregations. They are to 'obey' both parents, and this is a further example of the submission within divinely ordered relationships that is expected in God's new society (v. 21)."

61. For the text-critical reasons why the longer reading that includes the phrase "in the Lord" should be taken as original, see Metzger, *Textual Commentary*, 541–42; Hoehner, *Ephesians*, 785–86 n. 1; O'Brien, *Ephesians*, 441 n. 6.

the "Lord" (κυρίῳ) to whom the audience are to sing songs and psalms in their hearts (5:19) as a result of and in thanksgiving for being filled with gifts of love by Christ in the Spirit (5:18).[62] It is "in the Lord" (ἐν κυρίῳ) that the church as a "building" is being held together as a gift of God's love (divine passive) and growing into a holy temple (2:21). It is "in the Lord" (ἐν κυρίῳ) that Paul as a prisoner exhorts his audience to "walk" worthy of the calling with which they have been called (4:1) as a gift of God's love (divine passive). It is "in the Lord" (ἐν κυρίῳ) that Paul testifies for his audience no longer to "walk" in darkness like the Gentiles (4:17–18). Indeed, since they are now "light" as a gift of God's love "in the Lord" (ἐν κυρίῳ), so that they are to "walk" as "children" of light (5:8), the children in the audience are to obey their parents within the realm of being "in the Lord" as a way of appropriately responding to and further receiving gifts of love.

That it is "right" (δίκαιον) for children to obey their parents in the Lord (6:1) accords with their having "put on the new person" created "according to God," and thus as a gift of God's love, in "righteousness" (δικαιοσύνη) and holiness of truth (4:24). The fruit of their "walking" as "children of the light" (5:8) is to consist in all goodness and "righteousness" (δικαιοσύνη) and truth (5:9). Indeed, that it is "right" for children to obey their parents in the Lord accords with the kind of righteous behavior that is not "inappropriate" (5:4) but rather "fitting" (5:3) for holy ones, who, as "children" beloved by God and Christ, are to "walk" within the realm of being "in love" (5:1–2).[63] For children to obey their parents within the realm of being "in the Lord" is thus a way for them to "walk" as "children" beloved by God and Christ within the dynamic realm of being "in love," that is, demonstrating love in grateful response for the love they have received and will further receive.

b. Eph 6:2a (B): "Honor your father and mother"

Moving from an address to children more generally in the plural (6:1), Paul addresses each individual child in the audience in the singular, as he quotes, again without an introductory formula (cf. 5:31), the scriptural commandment: "Honor your (σου) father and mother" (6:2a; cf. LXX Exod 20:12; Deut 5:16).[64] Each and every child within the households of the audi-

---

62. Hoehner, *Ephesians*, 786–87: "[T]he prepositional phrase 'in the Lord' more likely qualifies the verb, thus emphasizing the children's ultimate obedience to the Lord. . . . Hence, the prepositional phrase does not define the limits of obedience, but rather it shows the spirit in which the obedience is to be accomplished."

63. Snodgrass, *Ephesians*, 320; O'Brien, *Ephesians*, 439–40.

64. Hoehner, *Ephesians*, 788: "It is more likely that he [Paul] is quoting from the LXX of Exod 20:12 because his wording is closer to it." For discussions of LXX Exod 20:12 and Deut 5:16, see John William Wevers, *Notes on the Greek Text of Exodus* (SBLSCS 30; Atlanta: Scholars Press, 1990), 313; idem, *Deuteronomy*, 103–4.

ence is not only to submit to (5:21) and obey his or her parents within the realm of being in the Lord (6:1), but to demonstrate a high esteem or honor for both the father and mother (6:2) as a result of and in grateful response to being filled with gifts of love by the Lord Jesus Christ (5:17–20). Each child will then further demonstrate what it means to "walk" as "children" beloved by God and Christ within the dynamic realm of being "in love" (5:1–2).[65]

c. Eph 6:2b (C): The first commandment with a promise

To the scriptural command to honor your father and mother (6:2a) Paul adds a further description: "which is the first commandment with a promise" (6:2b).[66] Although at the time that they were without Christ the audience were alienated from the community of Israel and strangers of the covenants of the "promise" (ἐπαγγελίας) of God, not having hope and God-less in the world (2:12), when they became believers, they were sealed, as a gift of God's love (divine passive), with the Holy Spirit of the "promise" (ἐπαγγελίας) of God (1:13). Indeed, through the gospel they are now fellow sharers, as a gift of God's love, of the "promise" (ἐπαγγελίας) of God within the realm of being "in Christ" (3:6), that is, they are fellow sharers of the "promise" of further gifts of God's love in Christ. That the scriptural com-mandment to honor your father and mother is the first commandment with a "promise" (ἐπαγγελίᾳ), then, implies that demonstrating love for God "in

---

65. According to Lincoln (*Ephesians*, 405), to "honor" both parents "was understood as involving not only a respectful attitude but also care for the parents' physical needs when they became old. So for children still in the father's house it would mean obedience to par-ents, and for those who had left home it would mean continued deference to and care for aging parents." Hoehner, *Ephesians*, 788–89: "It is interesting to note that honor/obedi-ence and dishonor/disobedience include both father and mother and not just the father, the head of the hierarchical family. . . . A child's honor and obedience to the parents is the first important step in learning to honor and obey God." The commandment to honor parents "takes pride of place among the 'horizontal' commandments which regulate social relation-ships. . . . the parents to be honoured stand in the place of God and mediate his will to the entire household," according to Moritz, *Profound Mystery*, 158.

66. With regard to the problem that a prior commandment in Exod 20:4–6 "also ap-pears to include a promise about God showing steadfast love to those who love him and keep his commandments," Lincoln (*Ephesians*, 404) points out: "Strictly speaking, the words 'but showing steadfast love to thousands of those who love me and keep my commandments' in Exod 20:6 are not a promise connected with 'you shall not make for yourself a graven image' in Exod 20:4, but are the positive side of the description of Yahweh as a jealous God which follows in Exod 20:5. It is not surprising, therefore, for Exod 20:12 to be thought of as the first commandment with a promise." After discussing the problem, Hoehner (*Ephesians*, 791) concludes that the commandment here "is more specific, addressed to a specific audi-ence and directly related to the command to 'honor your father and mother.' . . . The whole law comprises many commandments with promises. Thus this would be the first promise in-cluded in the Ten Commandments which are an introductory summary of the whole law."

the Lord" (6:1) by obeying God's commandment to honor one's father and mother carries with it the "promise" of further gifts of God's love.[67]

d. Eph 6:3 (B'): "That it may be well with you"

After his interpretive insertion regarding its promise (6:2b) Paul concludes his quotation of the scriptural commandment to honor your father and mother (6:2a) with the content of its promise: "that it may be well with you and you may live long on the earth" (6:3). The use of the second-person singular pronoun "your" in the scriptural commandment to honor "your" (σου) father and mother in the B element (6:2a) of the chiasm in 6:1–4 progresses, by way of the chiastic parallelism, to the use of the second-person singular pronoun "you" in the promise of the commandment—that it may be well with "you" (σοι)—in the B' element (6:3) of the chiasm. Thus, Paul's interpretive insertion into the middle of the scriptural commandment in the central C element (6:2b) of the chiasm pivots the audience from the commandment for each individual child to honor his or her father and mother in the B element (6:2a) to the promise of well-being and long life for each individual child who fulfills the commandment in the B' element (6:3) of the chiasm.

With regard to the love theme, the well-being and long life (6:3) that God will grant to each child who not only obeys but honors his or her father and mother (6:1–2), because of and in grateful response to being filled with gifts of love by the Lord Jesus Christ within the dynamic realm of being "in the Spirit" (5:17–20), adds two more gifts of God's love for children who "walk" within the dynamic realms of being "in the Lord" (6:1) as well as "in love" (5:1–2).

e. Eph 6:4 (A'): Fathers do not anger children

Directly addressing the fathers of households within the audience, Paul exhorts: "And the fathers, do not anger your children, but bring them up in the training and instruction of the Lord" (6:4).[68] Paul's command for "the children" (τὰ τέκνα) to obey "your" (ὑμῶν) parents in the "Lord" (κυρίῳ) in

---

67. Alexander Sand, "ἐπαγγελία," *EDNT* 2.14: "The promise proceeds from God, who is its guarantor. Thus because of the firmly fixed form and the unmistakeable age, the gen[itive] of θεός [God] does not need to appear. . . . The promise is addressed to people . . . who are chosen by God. . . . The content of the promise is the messianic salvation . . . as it has dawned in Jesus Christ."

68. Hoehner, *Ephesians*, 794: "The coordinating conjunction καί, 'and,' closely ties the fathers' responsibility with the childrens' responsibility." Lincoln, *Ephesians*, 406: "The plural οἱ πατέρες, 'fathers,' can refer to parents in general and not just fathers (cf. Heb 11:23), and some suggest that this may be the meaning here. But the change of wording from γονεῖς, 'parents,' in v 1, the omission of the mention of mothers after this has been explicit in the commandment of v 2, and the fact that in the ancient world in both Greco-Roman and Jewish writings it is fathers in particular who are held responsible for the education of the

the A element (6:1) of the chiasm in 6:1–4 progresses, by way of the chiastic parallelism, to the reciprocal command for the fathers not to anger "your" (ὑμῶν) "children" (τὰ τέκνα) but to bring them up in the training and instruction of the "Lord" (κυρίου) in the A´ element (6:4) of the chiasm.

Previously Paul commanded his audience: "Be angry (ὀργίζεσθε) but do not sin; let not the sun set on your anger (παροργισμῷ)" (4:26) and let all "wrath" or "anger" (ὀργή) be put away from you (4:31), because we believers are members of one another (4:25), who are to bear with one another as part of what it means to "walk" within the dynamic realm of being "in love" (4:2). Paul now applies these exhortations regarding love more specifically to the fathers of households as a way of loving their children in reciprocation for their children obeying and honoring both fathers and mothers (6:1–3): "Do not anger (παροργίζετε) your children" (6:4a).[69]

Previously Paul stated that no husband ever hates his own flesh/body/wife "but rather nurtures" (ἀλλὰ ἐκτρέφει) and cares for it/her, just as also the Christ nurtures and cares for the church (5:29), as a further elaboration for how husbands are to love their wives in imitation and because of Christ's love for the church (5:25). Now similarly, fathers are not to anger their children "but rather nurture or bring them up (ἀλλὰ ἐκτρέφετε) in the training and instruction of the Lord (κυρίου)" (6:4).[70] By so loving their children, then, fathers play their role within the thanksgiving that the audience are to render to God the Father in the name of our "Lord" (κυρίου) Jesus Christ as a result of and response to all of the gifts of love (5:20) with which believers are being filled in the Spirit (5:18) in accord with the will of the "Lord" (κυρίου) (5:17). The love of fathers for their children thus contributes to the

---

children, make it far more likely that Ephesians is in conformity with this way of thinking and is addressing male heads of households in their role as fathers."

69. Lincoln, *Ephesians*, 406: "Fathers are made responsible for ensuring that they do not provoke anger in their children. This involves avoiding attitudes, words, and actions which would drive a child to angry exasperation or resentment and thus rules out excessively severe discipline, unreasonably harsh demands, abuse of authority, arbitrariness, unfairness, constant nagging and condemnation, subjecting a child to humiliation, and all forms of gross insensitivity to a child's needs and sensibilities." O'Brien, *Ephesians*, 446: "Behind this curbing of a father's authority is the clear recognition that children, while they are expected to obey their parents in the Lord, are persons in their own right who are not to be manipulated, exploited, or crushed." Hoehner, *Ephesians*, 796: "The present prohibitory imperative παροργίζετε does not say 'stop doing what has already started' but rather 'make it a practice not to do it,' that is, 'do not provoke' your children." See also Wallace, *Greek Grammar*, 724–25.

70. Hoehner, *Ephesians*, 798: "Several think that παιδεία ['training'] is education emphasizing activity and discipline and νουθεσία ['instruction'] is education, emphasizing the verbal aspect, whether it be encouragement or reproof." Dudrey, "Submit Yourselves," 41: "Fathers are no longer to view their children as their possessions, nor treat them distantly, delegating their nurture to slaves and pedagogues; rather, fathers are to involve themselves personally in training their children in the teachings of Christ."

love involved in "walking" within the dynamic realms of being both "in love" (5:2) and "in the Lord" (ἐν κυρίῳ) (6:1).[71]

To sum up, with regard to the love theme, fathers not angering their children but rather loving them by nurturing or bringing them up in the training and instruction of the Lord (6:4), in reciprocation for their children loving them by obeying and honoring both their fathers and mothers (6:1–3), and just as not only the Christ loved the church but husbands are to love their wives (5:25, 29), further demonstrate what it means for believers to "walk" as children beloved by God and Christ within the dynamic realm of being "in love" (5:1–2).

2. Summary on Ephesians 6:1–4

1. For children to the obey their parents within the realm of being "in the Lord" (6:1) is a way for them to "walk" as "children" beloved by God and Christ within the dynamic realm of being "in love" (5:1–2), that is, demonstrating love in grateful response for the love they have received and will further receive.

2. The well-being and long life (6:3) that God will grant to each child who not only obeys but honors his or her father and mother (6:1–2), because of and in grateful response to being filled with gifts of love by the Lord Jesus Christ within the dynamic realm of being "in the Spirit" (5:17–20), adds two more gifts of God's love for children who "walk" within the dynamic realms of being "in the Lord" (6:1) as well as "in love" (5:1–2).

3. Fathers not angering their children but rather loving them by bringing them up in the training and instruction of the Lord (6:4), in reciprocation for their children loving them by obeying and honoring both their fathers and mothers (6:1–3), and just as not only the Christ loved the church but husbands are to love their wives (5:25, 29), further demonstrate what it means for believers to "walk" as children beloved by God and Christ within the dynamic realm of being "in love" (5:1–2).

E. Slaves and Masters Respect One Another in Love (6:5–9)

A: ⁵ Slaves, obey the earthly *masters* with respect and trembling in the sincerity of *your* heart as to the Christ,

---

71. Lincoln, *Ephesians*, 408: "[T]he genitive [κυρίου] is a genitive of quality, indicating that the training and admonition is that which is in the sphere of the Lord or has the Lord as its reference point. . . . The learning Christ and being taught in him spoken of in 4:20, 21 is to be an activity that takes place not only in the Christian community in general but also specifically in the family, with the fathers as those who teach their children the apostolic tradition about Christ and help to shape their lives in accordance with it."

B: ⁶ not according to eye-service as people-pleasers but as *slaves* of Christ *doing* the will of God wholeheartedly,
C: ⁷ with *good will rendering service* as to the Lord and not to people,
B′:   ⁸ knowing that whatever good each *does*, this he will receive back from the Lord, whether *slave* or free.
A′:   ⁹ And the *masters*, do the same things to them, stopping the threatening, knowing that both their Master and *yours* is in heaven and there is no partiality with him.

1. Audience Response to Ephesians 6:5–9

a. Eph 6:5 (A): You slaves obey masters in the sincerity of your hearts

After addressing the relationships of wives to husbands (5:21–33) and children to parents (6:1–4), Paul turns to slaves and masters, as he continues to elaborate on what it means for members of households to submit to one another in respect for Christ (5:21), as a result of and in response to being filled with gifts of love by Christ within the realm of being in the Spirit (5:18): "Slaves, obey the earthly masters with respect and trembling in the sincerity of your heart as to the Christ" (6:5).[72] For members of the audience to submit themselves to proper authorities (5:21) means not only for children to "obey" (ὑπακούετε) their parents (6:1) but for slaves to "obey" (ὑπακούετε) their earthly masters (6:5). As a wife should "respect" (φοβῆται) her husband (5:33) out of "respect" (φόβῳ) for Christ (5:21), so slaves are to obey their earthly masters with "respect" (φόβου) and trembling as if obeying the Christ (6:5).[73]

It is in the "heart" (καρδίας) of his audience, that is in their intellectual and moral interior, that Paul prays that they may know the surpassing greatness of the power of God in raising Christ from the dead and giving him, as head over all things, to the church as a gift of love to be the source of further gifts of love for the church, his body (1:18–23). It is in your "hearts" (καρδίαις) that Paul prays that his audience, "in love" rooted and grounded, may know the love of Christ that surpasses knowledge (3:17–19). It was

---

72. O'Brien, *Ephesians*, 448–49: "What is remarkable here is that Paul directly exhorts slaves in a manner that is unprecedented, for in traditional discussions of household management the focus of attention was on how a master should rule his slaves." See also Keener, *Paul*, 204–5.

73. Hoehner, *Ephesians*, 806–7: "The term [τρόμος, 'trembling'] specifically denotes the outward manifestation of fear, fear so great that it cannot be concealed. It is not uncommon for this word to be used in connection with φόβος, for the combination of these two words occurs thirteen times in the LXX and four times in the NT [1 Cor 2:3; 2 Cor 7:15; Eph 6:5; Phil 2:12]." Lincoln, *Ephesians*, 421: "[I]n their service to their masters, slaves are to see the opportunity to serve Christ and to perform their work as if they were doing it for Christ."

because of the hardness of their "heart" (καρδίας) that Gentiles were alienated from the life and thus love of God (4:18). And it is in your "hearts" (καρδίαις) that the audience are to sing songs and psalms to the Lord in grateful response for being filled with gifts of love by the Lord Jesus Christ in the Spirit (5:18–19). Appropriately, then, it is in your "hearts" (καρδίαις) as to the Christ that slaves are to obey their earthly masters (6:5) as a moral continuation and complement of their liturgical thanksgiving for being filled with gifts of love by the Christ.[74]

The church submits herself to "the Christ" (τῷ Χριστῷ) in reverential recognition of Christ as not only her authority but her source of love, who, as "head" and savior is filling the church, his body, with gifts of love (5:24; cf. 5:18; 1:22–23). Within the households of the church slaves are to further demonstrate this submission by obeying and thus submitting themselves to their earthly masters as to "the Christ" (τῷ Χριστῷ) in reverential recognition of their earthly masters as not only their more immediate authority but as a further source of Christ's love for them (6:5). Hence, by obeying and submitting themselves to their earthly masters as to the Christ, slaves not only appropriately respond to but submit themselves to receiving further gifts of Christ's love.

b. Eph 6:6 (B): As slaves of Christ, do the will of God wholeheartedly

With an antithesis between negative and positive behavior Paul continues his exhortation for the household slaves in his audience to obey their earthly masters: "not according to eye-service as people-pleasers but as slaves of Christ doing the will of God wholeheartedly" (6:6). That slaves are to obey their earthly masters (6:5a) not according to eye-service, that is, only doing what their masters see in order to please them as mere people-pleasers, but as "slaves of Christ" (δοῦλοι Χριστοῦ) (6:6a) confirms and reinforces for the audience that "slaves" (δοῦλοι) are to obey their earthly masters as if obeying the "Christ" (Χριστῷ) (6:5b).[75] Indeed, in obeying their earthly mas-

---

74. O'Brien, *Ephesians*, 450: "In the contemporary world masters controlled their slaves through fear, since it was believed that fear produced greater loyalty. The perspective of Christian slaves, however, has changed. They have been delivered from the bondage of human intimidation, and now are 'enslaved' to the Lord Jesus Christ. Their service to their masters, then, is to be rendered out of reverence and awe for him. It will also be characterized by integrity and singleness of purpose—what is here called sincerity of heart. As the inner centre which determines attitudes and actions, the heart is marked by sincerity and purity of motive. The Christian slave will not be guided by false, ulterior motives but will serve his or her master conscientiously and with sincerity. This kind of inner commitment can occur only as slaves recognize that in serving their masters they are rendering obedience to their heavenly Lord, Christ."

75. On "eye-service" here Hoehner (*Ephesians*, 808) states: "It could convey the idea that the goal of performance is strictly to impress the master and to leave undone anything

ters slaves are ultimately obeying and thus submitting themselves to Christ as the source of the love they have and will receive as slaves of Christ.

In contrast to "doing" (ποιοῦντες) the "wishes" (θελήματα) of the flesh, which we believers did before being "in Christ" (2:3), slaves of Christ are "doing" (ποιοῦντες) the "will" (θέλημα) of God wholeheartedly (6:6b). In doing the will of God by obeying their masters not as people-pleasers but as pleasing the Lord (5:10), slaves wisely further their understanding of the "will" (θέλημα) of the Lord Jesus Christ (5:17) to please God by handing himself over in love for us as a sacrificial offering pleasing to God (5:2). By thus obeying their masters as slaves of Christ within the dynamic realm of being "in love," the household slaves within the audience do their part in causing all things to grow to him, who is the head, the Christ (4:15), and thus further the plan of the "will" (θελήματος) of God to unite under one head all the things in the Christ (1:9–10; cf. 1:1, 5, 11).[76]

c. Eph 6:7 (C): With good will rendering service as to the Lord

Continuing his exhortation for slaves in the households of the audience to obey their masters as slaves of Christ, Paul adds: "with good will rendering service as to the Lord and not to people" (6:7). As "slaves" (δοῦλοι) of Christ (6:6) the household "slaves" (δοῦλοι) or servants are to obey their masters as the Christ (6:5) by "rendering service" (δουλεύοντες) as to the Lord (6:7). That they are to serve with "good will" (εὐνοίας) continues the theme of obeying in the sincerity of their "heart" (6:5), thus doing the will of God "wholeheartedly" (6:6). That they are to render service as to the Lord and not "people" (ἀνθρώποι) reinforces the exhortation for slaves not to be "people-pleasers" (ἀνθρωπάρεσκοι) (6:6).

For the household slaves in the audience to render service to their earthly masters "as to the Lord" (6:7) completes a chiastic pattern of occurrences of the comparative conjunction "as" (ὡς) in 6:5–7:

a) as (ὡς) to the Christ (6:5)
   b) not . . . as (ὡς) people-pleasers (6:6a)
   b′) but as (ὡς) slaves of Christ (6:6b)
a′) as (ὡς) to the Lord (6:7)

The chiasm begins with a comparison of slaves obeying their earthly

---

which would not be noticed by him. However, more likely it refers to the outward activity of work without the corresponding inward dedication."

76. O'Brien, *Ephesians*, 451: "The divine will has already been understood in terms of God's gracious saving plan in which it is his intention to sum up all things in Christ (1:5, 9, 11). In the latter half of Ephesians the divine will (5:17; 6:6) turns up in exhortatory contexts where the stress falls upon believers' responsibility to work out that will day by day. Here God's will is to be performed by 'slaves of Christ' within the everyday life of the household."

masters "as" they obey the Christ in the "a" sub-element (6:5), progresses to an antithetical comparison of obeying not "as" people-pleasers in the "b" sub-element (6:6a), but, by way of the pivot at the center of the chiasm, "as" slaves of Christ in the "b´" sub-element (6:6b), and reaches its climactic conclusion with a comparison of slaves rendering service "as" to the Lord in the "a´" sub-element (6:7).[77] Hearing the chiasm thus reinforces for the audience that in obeying their earthly "masters" or "lords" (κύριοι) household slaves are obeying Christ as the "Lord" or "Master" (κυρίῳ). By their moral behavior of rendering service with good will as to the "Lord," slaves thus complement the audience's grateful liturgical response of singing songs and psalms in their hearts to the "Lord" (κυρίῳ, 5:19) in thanksgiving for being filled with gifts of love by the Lord Jesus Christ in the Spirit (5:18–20).[78]

d. Eph 6:8 (B´): Each good slave will receive back from the Lord

Paul then not only individualizes his exhortation for slaves to obey their masters, but extends the consequences for doing such good beyond slaves to those who are free: "knowing that whatever good each does, this he will receive back from the Lord, whether slave or free" (6:8).[79] The address to slaves in the plural as "slaves" (δοῦλοι) of Christ "doing" (ποιοῦντες) the will of God wholeheartedly in the B element (6:6) of the chiasm in 6:5–9 progresses, by way of the chiastic parallelism and after the pivotal reference to Christ as the Lord in the central C element (6:7), to an address to each individual in the singular, "slave" (δοῦλος) or free, receiving back from the Lord for whatever good each "does" (ποιήσῃ) in the B´ element (6:8).

Recalling for the audience that "each" (ἕκαστος) should love his own wife (5:33) and "each" (ἕκαστος) should speak truth with his neighbor (4:25), that "each" (ἕκαστος), whether slave or free, does whatever is good (6:8) means that "each" (ἑκάστῳ) to whom grace was given as a gift of Christ's love (4:7) is doing his or her part as a member of the body of Christ, from whom the whole body, fitted together and held together through every supporting connection according to the working in measure of "each"

---

77. Hoehner, *Ephesians*, 810: "There is an ellipsis of a participle (δουλεύοντες) in connection with the comparative conjunction ὡς, which when included would be translated, 'serving with goodwill as if serving the Lord and not people.'"

78. O'Brien, *Ephesians*, 452: "Clearly their enthusiastic service will benefit their masters. But the slaves are reminded of a significant reason or motivation for their conduct: they are serving the Lord and not simply humans. As they engage in wholehearted work for their masters, so in that very action they honour and glorify their heavenly Lord." Hoehner, *Ephesians*, 810: "Although ostensibly slaves are carrying out the orders of earthly masters, the attitude of goodwill that accompanies this service in the end seeks to please the perfect heavenly Lord and not the faulty earthly master."

79. With regard to "receive back" (κομίσεται), it is stated in *EDNT* 2.307: "In the Pauline corpus κομίζομαι is used of receiving the appropriate recompense (2 Cor 5:10; Col 3:25; Eph 6:8)."

(ἑκάστου) individual part, brings about the growth of the body for the building up of itself "in love" (4:16). In other words, each individual who uses the
gift of love given by Christ to do good by sharing that gift of love builds up
the body of Christ within the dynamic realm of being "in love."

For each in the audience to do whatever is "good" (ἀγαθόν) (6:8) demonstrates on an individual level that we believers have been created in Christ
Jesus for "good" (ἀγαθοῖς) works which God prepared beforehand, that we
might "walk" in them (2:10). Just as the stealer is no longer to steal, but
rather to labor, working with his own hands that which is "good" (ἀγαθόν),
that he might have something to share, as a gift of love, with one who has
need (4:28), and just as only such as is "good" (ἀγαθός) for the building up
of what is needed should come out of the mouth of the audience, that it
might give grace, as a gift of love, to those who hear (4:29), so "each" in the
audience who does "good" (6:8) is sharing a gift of love in response to the
gift of Christ's love given to "each" believer (4:7).[80]

That each individual believer, whether slave or free, who does whatever
is good will receive back from the Lord (6:8) adds yet another element to
what it means for the audience to "walk" as children beloved by God and
Christ within the dynamic realm of being "in love" (5:1–2): Whoever shares
the gift of love by doing good in response to receiving Christ's gift of love
(4:7) can expect to receive in return *this* good, this gift of love, back and thus
be further filled with a gift of love from the Lord Jesus Christ (5:17–20).[81]

e. Eph 6:9 (A'): Both masters and slaves have an impartial Master

Complementing his exhortation to slaves, Paul similarly exhorts their
earthly masters, thus establishing a mutual responsibility between them:
"And the masters, do the same things to them, stopping the threatening,
knowing that both their Master and yours is in heaven and there is no
partiality with him" (6:9).[82] The exhortation for slaves to obey their earthly
"masters" (κυρίοι) in the sincerity of "your" (ὑμῶν) heart in the A element of
the chiasm (6:5) in 6:5–9 progresses, by way of the chiastic parallelism, to
a complementary exhortation for "masters" (κύριοι) to act similarly toward

---

80. Hoehner, *Ephesians*, 812: "As seen in 2:10 and 4:28, 29, the term ἀγαθός denotes
that which is morally and beneficially good. In other words, the implication is that while the
slave is doing good that is beneficial to the master, at the same time this good will be mea-
sured by God's standards as morally upright."

81. Hoehner, *Ephesians*, 812: "The demonstrative pronoun τοῦτο, 'this,' refers back to
the ἀγαθόν and is emphatic by its position. In other words, 'this' good and not something else
will not go unnoticed." See also O'Brien, *Ephesians*, 453 n. 56.

82. For the suggestion that in the household codes the Christian master is exhorted as
a vilicus, that is, an elite slave "bailiff" who oversees the estate in the place of an absentee
estate owner, in this case, the Lord Jesus Christ, see J. Albert Harrill, *Slaves in the New Testament: Literary, Social, and Moral Dimensions* (Minneapolis: Fortress, 2006), 4, 85–117.

their slaves, knowing that both their Master and "yours" (ὑμῶν) is in heaven in the A´ element (6:9). Furthermore, the reference to "earthly" (κατὰ σάρκα) masters in the A element progresses, by way of an antithetical chiastic parallelism, to the reference to *the* Lord or Master "in heaven" (ἐν οὐρανοῖς) in the A´ element.

The exhortation for masters to "do" (ποιεῖτε) the same things to them (6:9a), that is, to their slaves, means that they are to do good to them, and thus share Christ's gift of love with them, as it echoes in the ears of the audience whatever good that each slave "does" (ποιήσῃ) to his or her master (6:8).[83] That slaves are to obey their earthly masters not according to eye-service as people-pleasers (6:6) has a corresponding complementary obligation for masters to stop threatening their slaves (6:9b).[84] As slaves are to "know that" (εἰδότες ὅτι) whatever good each does, this he will receive back "from" (παρά) *the* Lord (6:8), so masters are to "know that" (εἰδότες ὅτι) *the* Lord or Master of both slaves and their masters is in heaven and there is no partiality "with" (παρ᾽) him (6:9c).[85] The reference to "*the* Lord" (ὁ κύριός) with whom there is no partiality climaxes the pivot from slaves obeying Christ to serving "*the* Lord" (τῷ κυρίῳ) that was introduced in the central C element of the chiasm (6:7) and continued with the notice that from *the* "Lord" (κυρίου) each receives back good (6:8), as a gift of love.

With regard to the love theme, then, earthly masters are to reciprocate the love they receive from their slaves in terms of the good that each slave does in obeying his or her master by in turn doing good to their slaves as a gift of love (6:8–9). That there is no partiality with *the* Lord and Master in heaven regarding both slaves and their masters (6:9) means that when they, who are both being filled with gifts of love from Christ *the* Lord (5:17–20),

---

83. O'Brien, *Ephesians*, 454: "In what is a shocking exhortation to slave owners in the first-century Graeco-Roman world, the apostle admonishes masters: treat your slaves in the same way. . . . In the immediate context, slaves have already been instructed to show respect, sincerity of heart, and goodwill; now masters are urged to treat them in a similar manner."

84. On the exhortation to "stop threatening them," Hoehner (*Ephesians*, 814) states: "This prohibition is appropriate, for there was a proverbial statement that 'all slaves are enemies' because masters were tyrants and abusive. Abuse was displayed in various ways such as threats of beating, sexual harassment of female slaves, threats to sell the male slaves. . . . Paul urged them not to impose threats in the same way non-Christian masters might do."

85. On the term "partiality" (προσωπολημψία), which is modeled after the Hebrew expression of lifting up, "as a sign of appreciation, the face of one who has prostrated himself in greeting," see Klaus Berger, "προσωπολημψία," *EDNT* 3.179; Jouette M. Bassler, *Divine Impartiality: Paul and a Theological Axiom* (SBLDS 59; Chico, CA: Scholars Press, 1982); R. A. Faber, "The Juridical Nuance in the NT Use of προσωπολημψία," *WTJ* 57 (1995): 299–309. Hoehner, *Ephesians*, 815: "The word προσωπολημψία, 'partiality,' is developed from the two words πρόσωπον λαμβάνω . . . literally translated 'I receive a face,' in reference to judgment on the basis of externals." Lincoln, *Ephesians*, 424: "[T]he assertion of Christ's impartiality functions more to make masters conscious of their present accountability, which they share equally with their slaves, to their heavenly Lord."

do good to one another as a gift of love, they will receive good back from *the* impartial Lord as a further gift of love, further demonstrating what it means for believers to "walk" as children beloved by God and Christ within the dynamic realm of being "in love" (5:1–2).

2. *Summary on Ephesians 6:5–9*

1. By obeying and submitting themselves to their earthly masters as to the Christ (6:5), slaves not only appropriately respond to but submit themselves to receiving further gifts of Christ's love.

2. By obeying their masters as slaves of Christ, doing the will of God wholeheartedly (6:6) within the dynamic realm of being "in love," the household slaves within the audience do their part in causing all things to grow to him, who is the head, the Christ (4:15), and thus further the plan of the will of God to unite under one head all the things in the Christ (1:9–10; cf. 1:1, 5, 11).

3. By their moral behavior of rendering service with good will as to *the* "Lord" (6:7), slaves complement the audience's grateful liturgical response of singing songs and psalms in their hearts to *the* "Lord" (5:19) in thanksgiving for being filled with gifts of love by *the* Lord Jesus Christ in the Spirit (5:18–20).

4. That each individual believer, whether slave or free, who does whatever is good will receive back from the Lord (6:8) adds yet another element to what it means for the audience to "walk" as children beloved by God and Christ within the dynamic realm of being "in love" (5:1–2): Whoever shares the gift of love by doing good in response to receiving Christ's gift of love (4:7) can expect to receive in return *this* good, this gift of love, back and thus be further filled with a gift of love from the Lord Jesus Christ (5:17–20).

5. Earthly masters are to reciprocate the love they receive from their slaves in terms of the good that each slave does in obeying his or her master by in turn doing good to their slaves as a gift of love (6:8–9). That there is no partiality with *the* Lord and Master in heaven regarding both slaves and their masters (6:9) means that when they, who are both being filled with gifts of love from Christ *the* Lord (5:17–20), do good to one another as a gift of love, they will receive good back from *the* impartial Lord as a further gift of love, further demonstrating what it means for believers to "walk" as children beloved by God and Christ within the dynamic realm of being "in love" (5:1–2).

CHAPTER 15

Ephesians 6:10–13: Be Empowered in Love to Withstand Evil (C′)

A: ¹⁰ Finally, be empowered in the Lord, that is, in the might of his strength. ¹¹ Put on the *full armor of God* so that you may *have the power to stand* against the schemes of the devil;

    B: ¹² for our struggle is not *against* blood and flesh but *against* the rulers,

    B′:   *against* authorities, *against* the cosmic powers of this darkness, *against* the spiritual beings of evil in the heavenly places.

A′:   ¹³ Therefore, take up the *full armor of God*, that you may *have the power to withstand* on the evil day and having done everything, *to stand*.[1]

A. Chiastic Development from Ephesians 1:15–23 (C) to 6:10–13 (C′)

With Eph 6:10–13, the C′ unit within the macro-chiastic structure of Ephesians, the audience hear echoes of 1:15–23, the corresponding C unit in the overall chiasm. Paul's command for his audience to be empowered in the Lord, that is, in "the might of his strength" (τῷ κράτει τῆς ἰσχύος αὐτοῦ) (6:10) in the C′ unit recalls his prayer for his audience to know what is the surpassing greatness of God's power for us who believe according to the working of "the might of his strength" (τοῦ κράτους τῆς ἰσχύος αὐτοῦ) (1:19) in the C unit.[2] That our struggle is against "rulers" (ἀρχάς) and "au-

---

1. For the establishment of Eph 6:10–13 as a chiasm, see ch. 2.
2. That these are the only two occurrences in Ephesians of this phrase enhances this chiastic connection.

thorities" (ἐξουσίας) (6:12) in the C′ unit recalls that God seated Christ far above every "ruler" (ἀρχῆς) and "authority" (ἐξουσίας) (1:21) in the C unit. And that the spiritual beings of evil are "in the heavenly places" (ἐν τοῖς ἐπουρανίοις) (6:12) in the C′ unit recalls that God seated Christ at his right hand "in the heavenly places" (ἐν τοῖς ἐπουρανίοις) (1:20) in the C unit.

With regard to the love theme, then, the audience may be empowered "in the might of the strength" of the Lord Jesus Christ (6:10) to stand against the "rulers" and "authorities" who are "in the heavenly places" (6:12) in the C′ unit (6:10–13) because of "the might of the strength" (1:19) that God worked in raising Christ from the dead and seating him "in the heavenly places" (1:20), far above every "ruler" and "authority" (1:21), subjecting all things under his feet and giving him as head over all things to the church as a gift of God's love (1:22) in the C unit (1:15–23).

B. Audience Response to Ephesians 6:10–13

1. Eph 6:10–11 (A): Put On the Full Armor of God to Withstand Evil

Paul complements his exhortations for how his audience are to "walk" (περιπατέω, 4:1, 17; 5:2, 8, 15) with how they are to "stand," as he begins to bring the Letter's exhortations to a close:[3] "Finally,[4] be empowered in the Lord, that is, in the might of his strength.[5] Put on the full armor of God so that you may have the power to stand against the schemes of the devil" (6:10–11). After addressing various relationships within the households of his audience (5:21–6:9), Paul reverts to exhorting his entire audience to be "empowered" (ἐνδυναμοῦσθε), as a gift of God's love (divine passive), "in the Lord" (ἐν κυρίῳ; cf. 2:21; 4:1, 17; 5:8; 6:1), that is, within the dynamic realm of being united with the Lord Jesus Christ (6:10a).[6] This accords with

---

3. On Eph 6:10–20 as not simply the conclusion to the exhortations but also the conclusion to the Letter as a whole, see Andrew T. Lincoln, "'Stand, Therefore . . .': Ephesians 6:10–20 as Peroratio," BibInt 3 (1995): 99–114.

4. "Finally" (τοῦ λοιποῦ) has a synonymous variant reading, τὸ λοιπόν, which Hoehner (Ephesians, 819 n. 1) prefers on the basis of external evidence, but notes: "Internal evidence could go either way." O'Brien, Ephesians, 460 n. 82: "τοῦ λοιποῦ is synonymous with the more frequent accusative τὸ λοιπόν ('finally') and indicates that 6:10–20 is the last in a chain of exhortations." Acceptance of the τοῦ λοιποῦ reading as original enhances the assonance throughout 6:10–11, with τοῦ λοιποῦ ("finally") forming an alliterative inclusion with τοῦ διαβόλου ("the devil"): Τοῦ λοιποῦ . . . ἰσχύος αὐτου . . . τοῦ θεου . . . τοῦ διαβόλου. For an additional argument for its acceptance, see Moritz, Profound Mystery, 181 n. 9.

5. Hoehner, Ephesians, 821: "καί [before 'in the might of his strength'] is probably epexegetical ('that is'), explaining the preceding words 'be strengthened in the Lord.'" See also O'Brien, Ephesians, 461 n. 86.

6. The plural imperative, "be empowered" (ἐνδυναμοῦσθε), "should not be understood, as it usually is, in individualistic terms," according to Thomas R. Yoder Neufeld, "Put On the Armour of God": The Divine Warrior from Isaiah to Ephesians (JSNTSup 140; Shef-

Paul's previous prayer that his audience be strengthened, as a gift of God's love (divine passive), with "power" (δυνάμει) through God's Spirit in the inner person (3:16).

For the audience to be empowered in the Lord, as Paul explains, means for them to be empowered in "the might of his strength" (τῷ κράτει τῆς ἰσχύος αὐτοῦ), with "his" referring to the Lord Jesus Christ (6:10b). This develops Paul's previous prayer that his audience may know what is the surpassing greatness of God's power for us who believe, the power that is according to the working of "the might of his strength" (τοῦ κράτους τῆς ἰσχύος αὐτοῦ), with "his" referring to God (1:19). By the might of his strength God raised Christ from the dead and gave, as a gift of love, the Christ whom God exalted as head over all things to the church, the body of Christ and the fullness of the Christ who is filling all things in all ways with gifts of love (1:20–23). For the audience to be empowered within the realm of being "in the Lord," that is, in the might of his strength, then, means for them to be filled with powerful gifts of love by the exalted Lord Jesus Christ (cf. 3:19; 4:7–10; 5:18).[7]

With an alliterative progression from the passive voice imperative "be empowered" (ἐνδυναμοῦσθε, 6:10a) to the more active middle voice imperative "put on" (ἐνδύσασθε, 6:11a), Paul exhorts his audience to actively "clothe" themselves—a metaphor for behavior—with the powerful gifts of love with which they have been empowered in the might of the Lord's strength. The powerful gifts of love which the audience are to "put on" are metaphorically characterized as "the full armor of God" (6:11a), with "full armor" (πανοπλίαν) referring to the full armor of a heavily equipped foot soldier.[8] The audience who have "put on" (ἐνδύσασθαι) the "new person"

---

field: Sheffield Academic Press, 1997), 111 n. 52. O'Brien (*Ephesians*, 460 n. 84) counters: "But Neufeld has presented a false dichotomy. The plural here (as often elsewhere in Ephesians) signifies common action: believers both individually and corporately are to heed the apostolic injunction." Hoehner, *Ephesians*, 821: "The prepositional phrase ἐν κυρίῳ could be instrumental but more likely denotes the sphere from which the strength comes, namely, in the Lord or in union with the Lord. The sphere encompasses the source, again the Lord." O'Brien, *Ephesians*, 461: "[T]heir strengthening comes from an external source, which the following phrase indicates is the Lord Jesus. He is the person with whom believers have been brought into union, and thus the sphere in whom they now live their Christian lives and from whom they derive their strength. They no longer fall under the tyranny of the prince of the power of the air (2:2), but have come under Christ's loving rule and headship."

7. Hoehner, *Ephesians*, 821–22: "In 1:19 Paul prayed that believers, by knowing God intimately, would understand his mighty power displayed through Christ's resurrection and ascension. He further prayed that they would appropriate this power in their lives. Now Paul exhorts them to continue in that same might in the person of Christ."

8. Horst Balz, "πανοπλία," *EDNT* 3.10: "The model is the armor of the Roman soldiers. In this case, however, God himself is viewed as the one who actually supplies the spiritual weapons in the eschatological battle against the onslaughts of the devil (6:11) and against the evil powers of this world and in the heavenly realms (under God, 6:12). Eph

created according to God in righteousness and holiness of truth (4:24) are now to "put on" (ἐνδύσασθε) the full armor of God (6:11a).[9]

With emphasis on "full" or "all" (παν), the "full armor" (πανοπλίαν) of God that the audience are to "put on" (6:11a) functions as a metaphorical correspondence to "all" (πᾶν) the fullness of God to which the audience are being filled by the love of Christ (3:19; cf. 5:18).[10] In "putting on" the "full armor" of God, then, the audience are actively clothing themselves with all of the powerful gifts of love with which they, as the body which is the fullness of Christ, are being filled by the exalted Christ who is filling "all things in all ways" (τὰ πάντα ἐν πᾶσιν) (1:23), the Christ who ascended far above all the heavens that he migtht fill "all things" (τὰ πάντα) (4:10) with gifts of love (4:7–8) until we all attain to a "mature person," to the measure of the stature of the fullness of the Christ (4:13).

The audience are to "put on" the "full armor" of God (6:11a), that is, all of the powerful gifts of love with which they are being filled, so that they might have the power to "stand" against the schemes of the devil (6:11b).[11] They may have the power to stand against the "schemes" (μεθοδείας) of the devil because all of the powerful gifts of love with which the exalted Christ is filling them (1:23; 3:19; 4:7–10; 5:18) are enabling them to attain to a mature person, to the measure of the stature of the fullness of the Christ (4:13), that they might no longer be infants, tossed by waves and carried about by every wind of teaching in the craftiness of people in deceitfulness toward the "scheming" (μεθοδείαν) of error (4:14).

By "putting on" the "full armor" of God—all the gifts of love with which they are being filled by the exalted Christ, the audience may have the power to stand against the schemes of the "devil" (διαβόλου) (6:11), because by walking "in love" they are empowered not to give room to the "devil" (διαβόλῳ) (4:27). They do not give room to the devil when they resolve their anger (4:26) and speak truth, each one with his neighbor, for we are mem-

---

6:10–20 shows in connection with 1:20–23 that the lordship of Christ over the world has in principle already been secured. In the present age, however, in which the evil one is still active, the cosmos must be recovered for the lordship of the Creator through the deployment of all the gifts of the Spirit. Behind this, therefore, is not the Greek concept of the 'battle' of the ascetic against self, but the apocalyptic hope of the powerful triumph of the kingdom of God, manifest already now, according to Ephesians 6, in the baptized believer's earthly struggle of faith."

9. O'Brien, *Ephesians*, 462: "Essentially, then to 'put on the new self' is the same as donning the armour of God."

10. With regard to the "full armor of God" (πανοπλίαν τοῦ θεοῦ), Abbott (*Ephesians*, 181) notes: "The emphasis is clearly on παν, not on τοῦ θεοῦ. . . . The completeness of the armament is the point insisted on."

11. Hoehner, *Ephesians*, 823: "The one who stands is not pushed around but firmly holds his or her position. In terms of warfare, it does not connote an offensive, but rather a defensive stance, to hold one's ground."

bers of one another (4:25), who are truthful "in love" (4:15), indeed who forbear one another as part of walking "in love" (4:2).[12] Hence, "putting on" the "full armor" of the gifts of God's love, that is, living in accord with the gifts of love with which they are being filled by the exalted Christ within the dynamic realm of being "in love," empowers the audience to stand against the schemes of the devil (6:10–11).

2. Eph 6:12a (B): Our Struggle Is against the Rulers

As Paul further explains, "for our struggle is not against blood and flesh but against the rulers" (6:12a).[13] Furthering his thrust throughout Ephesians to assimilate his audience of "you" believers to all of us believers, Paul's exhortation that "you" (ὑμᾶς) may have the power to stand against the schemes of the devil (6:11) expands its focus to include all believers—for this is "our" (ἡμῖν) struggle.[14] With an antithetical assertion Paul declares that our struggle is not against "blood and flesh," that is, visible, earthly, human beings in their weakness and frailty, but against "the rulers," that is,

---

12. Lincoln, *Ephesians*, 443: "In 4:14 human scheming had been mentioned; here it is the schemes of the devil against which believers have to stand. This language makes clear that the devil does not always attack through obvious head-on assaults but employs cunning and wily stratagems designed to catch believers unawares. The writer has already mentioned one such ploy in 4:27—exploiting anger in order to sow disruption in the community." O'Brien, *Ephesians*, 463–64: "According to 4:27, Satan tries to gain a foothold and exert his influence over the lives of Christians through uncontrolled anger (v. 26) as well as falsehood (4:25), stealing (v. 28), unwholesome talk (v. 29), indeed any conduct that is characteristic of the 'old way of life' (v. 22)."

13. According to Carr (*Angels and Principalities*, 104–10) Eph 6:12 is not part of the original letter, but a second century Gnostic interpolation. There is, however, no textual evidence for such an omission. For convincing critiques of Carr, see Robert A. Wild, "The Warrior and the Prisoner: Some Reflections on Ephesians 6:10–20," *CBQ* 46 (1984): 285; Clinton E. Arnold, "The 'Exorcism' of Ephesians 6.12 in Recent Research," *JSNT* 30 (1987): 71–87.

14. O'Brien, *Ephesians*, 466: "[B]y speaking of the battle as our struggle, Paul identifies with his readers (and, by implication, all Christians) in this spiritual conflict." The term "struggle" (πάλη) is used here to draw on the figure of a fully armed soldier who was also an accomplished wrestler and thus to impress upon the audience "that the battle being described here is one in which close-quarter struggling is involved," according to Michael E. Gudorf, "The Use of πάλη in Ephesians 6:12," *JBL* 117 (1998): 334. O'Brien, *Ephesians*, 465: "The word used to describe this struggle is a term found nowhere else in the Greek Bible, but which was commonly used for the sport of wrestling in the first century. One might have expected the more regular words for a battle or struggle to appear. But the popularity of wrestling in the games of western Asia Minor may account for the use of the word here." See also J. K. McVay, " 'Our Struggle': Ecclesia Militans in Ephesians 6:10–20," *AUSS* 43 (2005): 91–100.

invisible, heavenly, spiritual beings who exercise power and control over the created order.[15]

As the audience recall, the manifold wisdom of God to unite under one head all things in the Christ (1:10) is still to be made known to the "rulers" (ἀρχαῖς) and to the authorities in the heavenly places through the church (3:10). Thus, it is necessary for the audience as members of the church who once "walked" according to the age of this world, according to the "ruler" (ἄρχοντα) of the authority of the air (2:2), to "put on" the "full armor" of God's gifts of love (6:11) in the ongoing struggle of all of us believers against the "rulers" (ἀρχάς) (6:12a). Nevertheless, the audience can be assured that God raised Christ from the dead and seated him at his right hand in the heavenly places (1:20) far above every "ruler" (ἀρχῆς) (1:21) and that the Christ whom, as the head over all things, God gave, as a gift of love, to the church (1:22) is continually filling the church, which is his body and "fullness," with gifts of love, as he is filling all things in all ways (1:23; cf. 3:19; 4:7–10; 5:18).[16]

3. Eph 6:12b (B´): Against Authorities, Cosmic Powers, Spiritual Beings

As the audience hear the chiastic pivot at the center of the chiasm in 6:10–13, the twofold use of the preposition "against"—not "against" (πρός) blood and flesh but "against" (πρός) the rulers—in the B element (6:12a) moves to a threefold use of this same preposition in the progressive rhetorical triplet that emphatically elaborates upon the rulers—"against" (πρός) the authorities, "against" (πρός) the cosmic powers of this darkness, "against" (πρός) the spiritual beings of evil in the heavenly places in the B´ element (6:12b).[17]

---

15. O'Brien, *Ephesians*, 466: "The apostle's antithesis is not absolute, however, since he does not deny that believers may be tempted or deceived by other human beings, perhaps even by fellow Christians. The readers have already been warned about being misled by deceitful persons who seek to manipulate them through evil trickery (4:14). . . . But Paul's cogent point here is that the Christian life as a whole is a profound spiritual warfare of cosmic proportions in which the ultimate opposition to the advance of the gospel and moral integrity springs from evil, supernatural powers under the control of the god of this world."

16. Lincoln, *Ephesians*, 444: "The evil powers, who are opposing believers and who are listed in this verse, appear to be subject to the devil (v 11), to the ruler of the realm of the air (2:2). They include the 'principalities' and 'authorities' already mentioned in 1:21 (cf. also 3:10) as those over whom Christ rules not only in this age but also in the age to come. Because this age continues and believers live in it as well as enjoying the benefits of the age to come, these powers are still able to threaten and menace them."

17. Hoehner, *Ephesians*, 826: "Following the adversative conjunction, there is a series of prepositional phrases without conjunctions, a device which was most likely used to give greater prominence to those against whom the believers are struggling. The prepositional phrases are introduced with the preposition πρός with an accusative object and are best translated 'against.' " See also O'Brien, *Ephesians*, 466 n. 112. The rhetorical triplet in 6:12b progresses from (1) a simple prepositional phrase—"against the authorities," to (2) a prepo-

That our struggle is against not only the rulers (6:12a) but the "authorities" (ἐξουσίας) (6:12b) reinforces the audience's recall that the manifold wisdom of God to unite under one head all things in the Christ (1:10) is still to be made known not only to the rulers but also to the "authorities" (ἐξουσίαις) in the heavenly places through the church (3:10), making it necessary for the members of the church who once "walked" according to the age of this world, according to the ruler of the "authority" (ἐξουσίας) of the air (2:2), to "put on" the "full armor" of God's gifts of love (6:11) in this continual struggle. But it also reinforces the audience's assurance that the Christ whom God raised from the dead and seated at his right hand in the heavenly places (1:20) far above not only every ruler but every "authority" (ἐξουσίας) (1:21) is the Christ whom, as the head over all things, God gave, as a gift of love, to the church (1:22) to continually fill the church, which is his body and "fullness," with gifts of love, since he is filling all things in all ways (1:23; cf. 3:19; 4:7–10; 5:18).

Our struggle is not only against the rulers (6:12a) and the authorities, but against the cosmic powers of this "darkness" (σκότους) (6:12b).[18] Nevertheless, Paul has already assured his audience that although you were once "darkness" (σκότος), now you are light in the Lord, as a gift of the love of God and Christ, so that you are empowered to "walk" as beloved children of light (5:8) within the realm of being "in love" (5:1–2). The audience, then, have already been empowered by the gifts of divine love not to be connected with the unfruitful works of the "darkness" (σκότους) (5:11).[19]

Our struggle is not only against the rulers (6:12a), the authorities, and the cosmic powers of this darkness, but also against the spiritual beings of evil in the heavenly places (6:12b).[20] Although our struggle is against

---

sitional phrase—"against the cosmic powers," modified by a genitival construction—"of this darkness," to (3) a prepositional phrase—"against the spiritual beings," modified by a genitival construction—"of wickedness," and followed by a closing prepositional phrase—"in the heavenly places." On the centrality of Eph 6:12 in this section of the Letter, see Wild, "The Warrior," 286: "The many Christian authors, whether orthodox or heretical, who in the early church singled out Eph 6:12 for special attention in fact showed good exegetical insight in recognizing its importance in the argument of Ephesians."

18. On the term "cosmic powers" (κοσμοκράτορας) Hoehner (*Ephesians*, 826–27) states: "The third foe is called κοσμοκράτωρ. This word has not been used before NT times and it occurs only here in the NT. It may well have been a term used in the first or second century A.D. of magical or astrological traditions. . . . These potentates are not earthly humans but supernatural beings, and thus it is best to translate the word as 'world rulers' or 'cosmic potentates.'"

19. Lincoln, *Ephesians*, 444: "In Ephesians, darkness has already been associated with the past from which believers have been delivered, with the life of outsiders (5:8, 11), with those who are under the sway of this world-age (cf. 2:2). 'This darkness' therefore has reference to this present age, this world."

20. O'Brien, *Ephesians*, 467: "The final description, 'the spiritual hosts of evil', does not point to a separate category of cosmic powers but is a comprehensive term covering all

the "spiritual beings" (πνευματικά) of evil "in the heavenly places" (ἐν τοῖς ἐπουρανίοις),[21] God has already blessed us with every "Spiritual" (πνευ–ματικῇ) blessing "in the heavenly places" (ἐν τοῖς ἐπουρανίοις) within our union with Christ (1:3), so that in gratitude to God we are to speak to one another in "Spiritual" (πνευματικαῖς) songs (5:19). Indeed, the God who raised Christ from the dead and seated him at his right hand "in the heavenly places" (ἐν τοῖς ἐπουρανίοις) (1:20) also raised us up with him and seated us with him "in the heavenly places" (ἐν τοῖς ἐπουρανίοις) (2:6), as a demonstration of the great love with which God loved us (2:4).

Hence, the gifts of God's love, the "full armor" of God, that we are to "put on" (6:11) as members of the church in our struggle against the rulers, authorities, cosmic powers of this darkness, and the spiritual beings of evil "in the heavenly places" (ἐν τοῖς ἐπουρανίοις) (6:12) empower us to make known to the rulers and authorities "in the heavenly places" (ἐν τοῖς ἐπουρανίοις) the manifold wisdom of God (3:10).[22] This manifold wisdom of God is the plan of the mystery of God to unite under one head all things in Christ (1:10) through the gifts of God's love which we members of the church receive and share within the dynamic realm of being "in love," the gifts of God's love that empower us to cause all things to grow to him, who is the head, the Christ (4:15).

4. Eph 6:13 (A′): Take Up the Full Armor of God to Have the Power to Stand

Paul then resumes and reinforces his exhortation regarding our struggle: "Therefore, take up the full armor of God, that you may have the power to withstand on the evil day and having done everything, to stand" (6:13). Paul's command to put on the "full armor of God" (πανοπλίαν τοῦ θεοῦ) so that you may "have the power" (δύνασθαι) "to stand" (στῆναι) against the schemes of the devil (6:11) in the A element of the chiasm in 6:10–13 pro-

---

classes of hostile spirits, while the additional phrase *in the heavenly realms* indicates their locality. These potentates are not earthly figures but supernatural beings whose essential character is wickedness."

21. Fee, *God's Empowering Presence*, 725: "What is striking is the use of the word πνευματικός in this way. . . . this word is an adjective that has been formed from the noun πνεῦμα, which in Paul ordinarily means belonging to, or pertaining to, the Spirit. This usage is best explained in light of his prior use of πνεῦμα in 2:2 to refer to Satan."

22. Hoehner, *Ephesians*, 830–31: "Although believers are blessed with all the spiritual benefits in the heavenly places (1:3) and are seated together with Christ in the heavenlies (2:6), they do live in the present evil age (5:16). Hence, believers are presently both on earth and in the heavenlies. Furthermore, the devil and his followers are also presently both on earth and in the heavenlies. The devil is portrayed as the one who is 'the ruler of the realm of the air' (2:2), the one who controls this evil world . . . The present battle, then, is played out in the heavenlies and on earth between those who align themselves with the devil and his angelic leaders and those who align themselves with Christ and his angels."

gresses, by way of the chiastic parallelism, to his command to take up the "full armor of God" (πανοπλίαν τοῦ θεοῦ) that "you may have the power" (δυνηθῆτε) not only "to withstand" or "to stand against" (ἀντιστῆναι) the devil on the evil day, but having done everything, "to stand" (στῆναι) in the A′ element (6:13).[23]

Paul's command for his audience to actively "take up" (ἀναλάβετε, active imperative) the full armor of God (6:13) completes a rhetorical progression in his exhortation in 6:10–13 from the command for his audience to passively "be empowered" (ἐνδυναμοῦσθε, passive imperative), by receiving the gifts of God's love (6:10), to the command for his audience to more actively "put on" (ἐνδύσασθε, middle imperative) the full armor of God, that is, all the gifts of God's love with which they are being filled by the exalted Christ (1:23; 3:19; 4:7–10; 5:18). Thus, the audience are not only to "put on" or "clothe themselves" so that they "wear" the gifts of divine love as their external behavior, but also to actively "take up" as powerful weaponry against the devil these gifts of love with which they have been empowered.[24]

By actively taking up the full armor of God, the audience will have the power to resist the devil on "the evil day" (τῇ ἡμέρᾳ τῇ πονηρᾷ) (6:13), the apocalyptic and eschatological climax of "the evil days" (αἱ ἡμέραι πονηραί) in which we believers are presently living (5:16).[25] Having thus done everything possible by equipping themselves with the full armor of God, the audience will be able "to withstand" the devil on that climactic evil day, and so ultimately "to stand" (6:13), empowered by the full armor of all the gifts of divine love with which they are being filled by the exalted Christ (1:23; 3:19; 4:7–10; 5:18) as children beloved by God and Christ within the dynamic realm of "walking in love" (5:1–2).[26]

---

23. O'Brien, *Ephesians*, 470: "Here in v. 13, two forms of the verb are repeated for emphasis: 'in order that you may be able to *withstand* and . . . to *stand*.'" Hoehner, *Ephesians*, 836 n. 1: "It is debatable as to whether there is any difference between ἵστημι and ἀνθίστημι for both have the idea of a defensive stand in this context."

24. Hoehner, *Ephesians*, 832: "The active voice indicates that believers are responsible for putting on the full armor."

25. Lincoln, *Ephesians*, 446: "The readers are to realize that they are already in the evil days (cf. 5:16), but that these will culminate in a climactic evil day, when resistance will be especially necessary. Just as redemption is already experienced but there will be a final day of redemption (1:7 and 4:30), so evil is already experienced but there will also be a final day of evil." O'Brien, *Ephesians*, 471: "The exact phrase, 'the evil day', turns up in three prophetic passages of the Old Testament (Jer. 17:17, 18; Obad. 13; cf. Dan. 12:1), and has an apocalyptic ring to it with its end-time connotations. . . . The definiteness given to the day by the article (ἐν τῇ ἡμέρᾳ τῇ πονηρᾷ) marks it out in some sense as a critical day, a time of peculiar trial or peril" (n. 130).

26. Lincoln, *Ephesians*, 445: "All the resources are available for a successful resistance. These resources are divine and are summed up as the 'full armor' of God, which is mentioned for the second time (cf. v 11). All that believers need to do is to 'take up' the armor to appropriate the resources." With regard to "having done everything, stand"

C. Summary on Ephesians 6:10–13

1. By "the might of his strength" (1:19) in the C unit (1:15–23) of the overall chiasm in Ephesians God raised Christ from the dead and gave, as a gift of love, the Christ whom God exalted as head over all things to the Church, the body of Christ and the fullness of the Christ who is filling all things in all ways with gifts of love (1:20–23). For the audience to be empowered within the realm of being "in the Lord," that is, in "the might of his strength" (6:10) in the C′ unit (6:10–13), then, means for them to be filled with powerful gifts of love by the exalted Lord Jesus Christ (cf. 3:19; 4:7–10; 5:18).

2. In "putting on" the "full armor" of God (6:11), the audience are actively clothing themselves with all of the powerful gifts of love with which they, as the body which is the fullness of Christ, are being filled by the exalted Christ who is filling "all things in all ways" (1:23), the Christ who ascended far above all the heavens that he might fill "all things" (4:10) with gifts of love (4:7–8) until we all attain to a "mature person," to the measure of the stature of the fullness of the Christ (4:13).

3. "Putting on" the "full armor" of the gifts of God's love, that is, living in accord with the gifts of love with which they are being filled by the exalted Christ within the dynamic realm of being "in love," empowers the audience to stand against the schemes of the devil (6:10–11).

4. The gifts of God's love, the "full armor" of God, that we are to "put on" (6:11) as members of the church in our struggle against the rulers, authorities, cosmic powers of this darkness, and the spiritual beings of evil "in the heavenly places" (6:12) empower us to make known to the rulers and authorities "in the heavenly places" the manifold wisdom of God (3:10)—the plan of the mystery of God to unite under one head all things in Christ (1:10) through the gifts of God's love which we members of the church receive and share within the dynamic realm of being "in love," the gifts of God's love that empower us to cause all things to grow to him, who is the head, the Christ (4:15).

(ἅπαντα κατεργασάμενοι στῆναι) in 6:13 Hoehner (*Ephesians*, 835) explains: "There are two major views on its rendering in this text. (1) Some render it 'having subdued or overcome all, stand' conveying the idea that victory has been accomplished, thus, believers can stand. (2) Others contend that it should be rendered 'having done all/everything, stand,' suggesting that since all the necessary preparations are complete (i.e., all the armor is put on), believers are to stand or hold their ground against the attacks of the devil and his henchmen. View (2) is preferred."

5. Having done everything possible by equipping themselves with the full armor of God, the audience will be able "to withstand" the devil on that climactic evil day, and so ultimately "to stand" (6:13), empowered by the full armor of all the gifts of divine love with which they are being filled by the exalted Christ (1:23; 3:19; 4:7–10; 5:18) as children beloved by God and Christ within the dynamic realm of "walking in love" (5:1–2).

Chapter 16

Ephesians 6:14–22: Beloved Tychicus Will Encourage Your Hearts (B´)

A: [14] Stand then having girded *your* waists in truth and having put on the breastplate of righteousness,

   B: [15] and having shod the feet in preparedness from the *gospel* of peace, [16] in all things having taken up the shield of faith, in which you have the power to extinguish all the flaming arrows of the evil one;

      C: [17] and *receive* the *helmet* of salvation and the *sword* of the Spirit, which is the *word of God.*

   B´: [18] Through every prayer and petition praying at every opportunity in the Spirit, and for this purpose being alert in all persistence and petition for all the holy ones, [19] especially for me, that speech may be given to me in opening my mouth, in boldness to make known the mystery of the *gospel,* [20] for which I am an ambassador in chain, that in it I might speak boldly as it is necessary for me to speak.

A´: [21] That *you* also may know the things about me, what I am doing, Tychicus, the beloved brother and faithful minister in the Lord, will make everything known to *you,* [22] whom I am sending to *you* for this very purpose, that you may know the things concerning us and that he may encourage *your* hearts.[1]

---

1. For the establishment of Eph 6:14–22 as a chiasm, see ch. 2.

A. Chiastic Development from
Ephesians 1:3–14 (B) to 6:14–22 (B´)

With Eph 6:14–22, the B´ unit within the macro-chiastic structure of Ephesians, the audience hear echoes of 1:3–14, the corresponding B unit in the overall chiasm. In "truth" (ἀληθείᾳ, 6:14) in the B´ unit recalls word of "truth" (ἀληθείας, 1:13) in the B unit. Preparedness from the "gospel" (εὐαγγελίου) of peace (6:15) and the mystery of the "gospel" (εὐαγγελίου, 6:19) in the B´ unit recall the "gospel" (εὐαγγέλιον) of your salvation (1:13) in the B unit. The helmet of "salvation" (σωτηρίου) and the sword of the "Spirit" (πνεύματος, 6:17) as well as in the "Spirit" (πνεύματι, 6:18) in the B´ unit recall the gospel of your "salvation" (σωτηρίας) and every "Spiritual" (πνευματικῇ) gift (1:3) as well as the Holy "Spirit" (πνεύματι) of the promise (1:13) in the B unit. All the "holy ones" (ἁγίων, 6:18) in the B´ unit recalls that we might be "holy" (ἁγίους, 1:4) as well as "Holy" (ἁγίῳ) Spirit (1:13) in the B unit. "To make known the mystery" (γνωρίσαι τὸ μυστήριον, 6:19) in the B´ unit recalls "having made known . . . the mystery" (γνωρίσας . . . τὸ μυστήριον, 1:9) in the B unit.

And finally, with regard to explicit terms for love in Ephesians, Tychicus, the "beloved" (ἀγαπητός) brother (6:21) in the B´ unit recalls "in love (ἀγάπη, 1:4)" and "in the Beloved (ἠγαπημένῳ, 1:6)" in the B unit.

With regard to the love theme, then, the audience may stand in "truth" (6:14) prepared from the "gospel" of peace (6:15) to receive the helmet of "salvation" and the the sword of the "Spirit" (6:17) in the B´ unit (6:14–22) because they have heard the word of the "truth," the "gospel" of their "salvation" and were sealed with the Holy "Spirit" (1:13) as a gift of God's love in the B unit (1:3–14). Paul wants "to make known the mystery" of the gospel (6:19) in the B´ unit as a consequence of God's gift of love in "having made known to us the mystery" of his will (1:9) in the B unit. And encouraged by the "beloved" Tychicus (6:21–22), the audience are to pray for all the "holy ones" (6:18) in the B´ unit, so that all of us believers may be "holy" and blameless before God within the dynamic realms of being "in love" (1:4) and "in the Beloved" (1:6) in the B unit.

B. Audience Response to Ephesians 6:14–22

1. Eph 6:14 (A): Stand Then Having Girded Your Waists in Truth

Immediately after his use of infinitives in his exhortations for his audience to be empowered to "withstand" (ἀντιστῆναι, 6:13) and to "stand" (στῆναι, 6:11, 13) against the schemes of the devil, Paul employs the imperative, as he directly commands his audience: "Stand (στῆτε) then having girded your waists in truth and having put on the breastplate of righteousness" (6:14).[2] That the audience have girded their waists in truth (6:14a) begins a delineation of the "full armor of God" (6:11, 13) that they are to "put on" and "take up" as the gifts of God's love that empower them to stand against the diabolical spiritual powers in the heavenly places (6:10–13).[3]

The audience have "girded their waists" not just *with* truth but "*in* truth" (ἐν ἀληθείᾳ, 6:14a), another of the many uses in Ephesians of the preposition "in" (ἐν) to denote a dynamic realm or sphere. In this case "in truth" refers to the realm established by "truth" as a gift of God's love that empowers its recipients to be "truthful," faithful, and reliable not only in their relationship with God but with one another. The audience received truth as a gift of God's love when they "put on" the new person created by God in righteousness and holiness of "truth" (ἀληθείας, 4:24), the truth they received as a gift of divine love within the realm of being in union with Jesus Christ, as "truth" (ἀλήθεια) is "in" Jesus (4:21), and the truth they received as a gift of God's love when they heard the word of "truth" (ἀληθείας), the gospel of their salvation, and believed in Jesus Christ (1:13).

This truth the audience have received as a gift of God's love empowers them to speak "truth" (ἀλήθειαν) each one with his neighbor, for we are members of one another (4:25). It empowers them, as children of light (5:8), to produce the fruit of light that consists in all goodness and righteousness and "truth" (ἀληθείᾳ, 5:9). Indeed, it empowers them to "be truthful" (ἀληθεύοντες) within the realm of being "in love" (4:15), that is, to be truthful, faithful, and reliable in sharing the gifts of love they have received from God and Christ with one another. That the audience have girded their waists within the realm of being "in truth" (ἐν ἀληθείᾳ, 6:14a) as a gift of God's love, then, equips them with the "truth" of receiving and sharing the divine gifts of love that empower them to stand against not only the false and erroneous teaching of human beings (4:14) and the Gentiles' wrong way of

---

2. The inferential conjunction "then" (οὖν) once again introduces a new unit in the second or paranetic half of Ephesians (cf. 4:1, 17; 5:1, 7, 15; 6:14). Hoehner, *Ephesians*, 837: "The inferential conjunction οὖν 'therefore' indicates that Paul is introducing a result or an inference from that which he had just stated. Simply put, he had exhorted believers to put on the armor of God in order to stand firmly against spiritual wickedness. Now he exhorts them to do just that, to 'stand.'"

3. Hoehner, *Ephesians*, 838–39: "This is the first in the series of participles describing the articles of equipment the soldier needs for the conflict. The term περιζωσάμενοι ['having girded'] is an aorist middle participle denoting a causal relationship to the imperative στῆτε, 'stand,' . . . From the earliest times it signified girding or binding something around the waist, whether a girdle, belt, or apron. . . . The middle voice indicates that believers are responsible to gird themselves. The noun that follows is ὀσφύς, 'waist, loins,' the middle part of the body where a belt or girdle is worn." See also Wallace, *Greek Grammar*, 629 n. 41.

"walking" (4:17–19), but also the diabolical spiritual beings of evil in the heavenly places (6:11–13).[4]

The audience are not only to "put on" (ἐνδύσασθαι) the new person (4:24), but to "put on" (ἐνδύσασθε) the full armor of God (6:11), since they have "put on" (ἐνδυσάμενοι) the breastplate of righteousness (6:14b; cf. Isa 59:17; Wis 5:18). That the audience have put on the breastplate of "righteousness" (δικαιοσύνης) as a gift of God's love empowers them in turn to be righteous in their behavior. The audience received this gift of God's love when they put on the new person created according to God in "righteousness" (δικαιοσύνη) and holiness of truth (4:24). This righteousness they have received as a gift of God's love in turn empowers them, as beloved children of light (5:8) who "walk in love" (5:1–2), to produce the fruit of the light that consists in all goodness and "righteousness" (δικαιοσύνη) and truth (5:9). The donning of the breastplate of righteousness as part of the full armor of God's gifts of love (6:14b), then, empowers the audience to stand against the devil by behaving righteously within the realm of walking "in love" (5:1–2).[5]

---

4. Neufeld, *Armour of God*, 134: "The prominence of ἀλήθεια ... suggests that its presence in 6.14 functions as a recapitulation of a note sounded repeatedly in Ephesians." O'Brien, *Ephesians*, 473–74: "The apostle's language clearly alludes to the LXX of Isaiah 11, which declares of the Messiah: 'With righteousness shall he be girded around his waist, and with truth bound around his sides' (vv. 4–5). . . . The armour which the Messiah wears in battle is now provided for his people as they engage in spiritual warfare. 'Truth', which occupies a prominent place in Ephesians, refers to the truth of God (4:24; 5:9) revealed in the gospel (1:13; 4:15, 21, 24), which has its outworking in the lives of believers who are members of the new humanity (4:25; 5:9). Here in Ephesians 6 both aspects of truth belong together. As believers buckle on this piece of the Messiah's armour, they will be strengthened by God's truth revealed in the gospel, as a consequence of which they will display the characteristics of the Anointed One in their attitudes, language, and behaviour. In this way they resist the devil, giving him no opportunity to gain an advantage over them (4:27)." Hoehner, *Ephesians*, 840: "Believers have girded their waists with God's objective truth, which in turn has become a part of them. This enables them to be reliable and faithful as God is reliable and faithful. This piece of armor is basic to all other pieces because truth and trustworthiness are basic to all the other qualities that believers need in order to withstand diabolical attacks. As believers internalize God's truth they live and move in [my emphasis] it."

5. Lincoln, *Ephesians*, 448: "'The breastplate of righteousness' was part of Yahweh's armor in the depictions found in Isa 59:17 and Wis 5:18 (cf. also Isa 11:5, where righteousness is the Messiah's girdle). The righteousness or justice of Yahweh is an attribute that it is now essential for the believer to display." O'Brien, *Ephesians*, 474–75: "[T]o speak of donning God's own righteousness or appropriating his salvation is in effect to urge the readers once more to put on the 'new man' of 4:24, who is created to be like God in righteousness and holiness. By putting on God's righteousness believers are committed to being imitators of him (5:1) and acting righteously in all their dealings." Hoehner, *Ephesians*, 840–41: "The word δικαιοσύνης, 'righteousness,' describes the breastplate and is probably a genitive of apposition, that is, the breastplate which is righteousness. . . . in this context believers are, by appropriating God's righteousness, to act righteously in their daily dealings with God and humankind." See also Moritz, *Profound Mystery*, 202–3; Neufeld, *Armour of God*,

2. Eph 6:15–16 (B): In Preparedness from the Gospel of Peace

Paul continues to delineate the "full armor" of the gifts of God's love that empowers the audience to stand against the schemes of the devil (6:11–14): "and having shod the feet in preparedness from the gospel of peace" (6:15). That the audience have shod their feet "in preparedness" (ἐν ἑτοιμασίᾳ) exemplifies yet another of the many instances in Ephesians where the preposition ἐν denotes a dynamic realm.[6] The audience have "shod their feet" within the dynamic realm of the preparedness or readiness that comes from the gospel, the proclamation of the good news, concerning peace as a gift of Christ's love.[7]

As the audience recall, the gospel is not only the "gospel" (εὐαγγέλιον) of their salvation (1:13) but it is through the "gospel" (εὐαγγελίου) that believing Gentiles have been united in peace as fellow heirs and fellow members of the body and fellow sharers together with believing Jews of the promise in Christ Jesus (3:6). Indeed, Christ, who is our "peace" (εἰρήνη, 2:14) and who established "peace" (εἰρήνην, 2:15), came and "preached" (εὐηγγελίσατο), that is, proclaimed the good news and thus brought the gospel concerning "peace" (εἰρήνην) to you who are far away (believing Gentiles) and "peace" (εἰρήνην) to those who are near (believing Jews) (2:17).[8]

It is in this bond of "peace" (εἰρήνης, 4:3), the "peace" (εἰρήνη) that is a gift from God our Father and the Lord Jesus Christ (1:2), that the unity of the Spirit is preserved by forbearing one another "in love" (4:2–3). This unity of the church as the one body (4:4) established by the "peace" that is the gift of Christ's love not only makes known "to the rulers and to the authorities in the heavenly places" the manifold wisdom of God (3:10), but prepares the church to stand "against the rulers, against authorities, against the cosmic powers of this darkness, against the spiritual beings of evil in the heavenly places" (6:12). Thus, the "shodding of their feet" in the preparedness that comes from the "gospel" (εὐαγγελίου) of "peace" (εἰρήνης), as a

---

135–36. And for an analysis of the warfare texts from Isaiah (11:5; 49:2; 52:7; 59:17) alluded to in Eph 6:10–17, see G. Janzen, "Divine Warfare and Nonresistance," *Direction* 32 (2003): 21–31.

6. On "having shod" (ὑποδησάμενοι) Hoehner (*Ephesians*, 842) comments: "The verb always means to bind or fasten under, especially with reference to the feet because ancient sandals were bound on with straps. . . . These were not running sandals but ones able to dig in with their hollow-headed hobnails and stand against the enemy."

7. Hoehner, *Ephesians*, 843: "Thus, readiness or preparedness has its source in the gospel, the contents of which is peace."

8. Lincoln, *Ephesians*, 449: "As we have seen from 2:14–18, the gospel of peace is embodied in Christ who 'is our peace,' and this is a peace with both vertical and horizontal axes: peace with God the Father and peace between human beings, Jews and Gentiles, who were formerly at enmity. Since such peace is the pledge of future cosmic harmony (cf. 1:10; 3:10), its realization in the Church not only sounds the death knell for opposing cosmic powers but also, in the meantime, leads to the intensification of their opposition."

gift of love from Christ and God (6:15), empowers the audience to be prepared to stand against the full array of diabolical spiritual beings of evil in the heavenly places (6:11–14).[9]

Further specifying the "full armor" of the gifts of God's love that empowers the audience to stand against the schemes of the devil (6:11–14), Paul continues: "in all things having taken up the shield of faith, in which you have the power to extinguish all the flaming arrows of the evil one" (6:16). Echoing not only that the one God and Father of all is over all and through all and "in all things" (ἐν πᾶσιν, 4:6), but that Christ is filling all things "in all ways" (ἐν πᾶσιν) with gifts of love (1:23), "in all things" (ἐν πᾶσιν) in this context refers to all of the gifts of love that thus far have delineated the full armor of God's gifts of love, namely, truth (6:14a), righteousness (6:14b), and peace (6:15). Along with these gifts of God's love the audience, who are to "take up" (ἀναλάβετε) the full armor of God (6:13), have "taken up" (ἀναλαβόντες) the shield of faith (6:16a).[10]

The shield of "faith" (πίστεως, 6:16a) that the audience have taken up is a fundamental piece of the full armor of God's gifts of love. The one "faith" (πίστις, 4:5), the "faith" (πίστιν, 1:15) that the audience, as the "faithful" (πιστοῖς, 1:1) who "believe" (πιστεύσαντες, 1:13) possess, even as all of us who "believe" (πιστεύοντας, 1:19) are attaining to the unity of the "faith" (πίστεως, 4:13), denotes the disposition or attitude of receiving and accepting God's gifts of love. It expresses the reception of such gifts of God's love as the salvation that is received through "faith" (πίστεως, 2:8), the boldness and access with confidence that we have before God the Father through

---

9. Lincoln, *Ephesians*, 449: "The reference is, therefore, not to readiness to proclaim the gospel but to the readiness or preparedness for combat and for standing in the battle that is bestowed by the gospel of peace." Hoehner, *Ephesians*, 843–44: "Some would argue that in the midst of attacks from evil powers, believers have shod their feet in their readiness to preach the gospel of peace similar to Eph 3:8–10 or Isa 52:7 and Mic 2:1. However, this is unlikely . . . Paul depicts believers as having put on another defensive piece of armor. Therefore, rather than preach the gospel of peace, believers are ready or prepared to stand grounded in the gospel of peace. . . . It is somewhat paradoxical that the gospel of peace is the preparation for warfare against the hosts of evil." Although Paul is not exhorting the audience as a whole to preach the gospel of peace at this point (but cf. 6:17), note that one of the gifts of love from the exalted Christ to the church is that of "evangelists" (εὐαγγελιστάς), preachers of the gospel, in 4:11.

10. O'Brien, *Ephesians*, 479–80: "The shield referred to is not the small round one which left most of the body unprotected, but the large shield carried by Roman soldiers, which covered the whole person. . . . Here the shield which believers are to take up is 'the shield of faith'; the genitive is best understood as one of apposition, meaning that faith itself is the shield. . . . The large shield used by Roman soldiers was specially designed to quench dangerous missiles, particularly arrows that were dipped in pitch and lit before being fired. These flaming missiles often inflicted deadly wounds, or caused havoc among soldiers, unless the shields had been soaked with water and were able to quench them."

"faith" (πίστεως, 3:12; cf. 2:18), and the dwelling of Christ in our hearts that we receive through "faith" (πίστεως, 3:17).[11]

"In which" (ἐν ᾧ, 6:16b) exemplifies another use in Ephesians of the preposition "in" (ἐν) to denote a dynamic realm or sphere. In this case it refers to the dynamic realm of being "in faith"—being in the dynamic realm established by humbly receiving and graciously accepting God's gifts of love. Within the realm of being "in faith" the audience, in a development of the "power they may have" (δύνασθαι) to stand against the schemes of the devil (6:11) and the "power they may have" (δυνηθῆτε) to withstand on the evil day (6:13), "have the power" (δυνήσεσθε) to extinguish all the flaming arrows of the "evil one" (πονηροῦ, 6:16b), that is, of the devil (6:11), the leader of the spiritual beings of "evil" (πονηρίας) in the heavenly places (6:12), and the one the audience are to withstand on the "evil" (πονηρᾷ) day (6:13).[12] As part of the "full armor" of God's gifts of love (6:11, 13), then, the shield of the faith in which the audience receive the gifts of God's love empowers them to effectively stand against all the assaults directed at them by the devil as the preeminent evil one (6:16).[13]

3. Eph 6:17 (C): Helmet of Salvation and Sword of the Spirit, the Word of God

Concluding his elaboration of the metaphorical "full armor" of the gifts of God's love, Paul exhorts his audience: "and receive the helmet of salvation and the sword of the Spirit, which is the word of God" (6:17). For the final pieces of the "full armor" Paul breaks the previous pattern of participles—"having gird" (6:14a), "having put on" (6:14b), "having shod" (6:15), and "having taken up" (6:16)—and with an imperative verb, paral-

---

11. Lincoln, *Ephesians*, 449: "Faith is mentioned throughout the letter, and in this context it is the confident trust in and receptiveness to Christ and his power that protects the whole person. Faith takes hold of God's resources in the midst of the onslaughts of evil and produces the firm resolve which douses anything the enemy throws at the believer."

12. O'Brien, *Ephesians*, 480 n. 173: "The future δυνήσεσθε ('you will be able') is a logical future, indicating the result of taking up the shield, and does not indicate that the conflict itself lies in the future." Contra Neufeld, *Armour of God*, 110.

13. Hoehner, *Ephesians*, 848: "The genitive τοῦ πονηροῦ, 'of the evil one,' could be a possessive genitive, 'the evil one's flaming arrows,' but preferably it is a genitive of source, 'the flaming arrows from the evil one.' This is not referring to an abstract principle but a person who is called the 'devil' in verse 11 and who heads the host of evil powers vividly described in verse 12." Lincoln, *Ephesians*, 450: "Here the burning arrows represent every type of assault devised by the evil one, not just temptation to impure or unloving conduct but also false teaching, persecution, doubt, and despair. Faith is the power which enables believers to resist and triumph over such attacks."

leling the previous imperative to "stand" (6:14a), directly urges his audience to "receive" (δέξασθε) the helmet of salvation (6:17a).[14]

That the audience are to receive, as a gift of God's love, the helmet which is "salvation" (σωτηρίου, 6:17a) enjoins them to appropriate as a defensive and protective piece of armor the salvation they received when they became believers who heard the word of truth, the gospel of your "salvation" (σωτηρίας, 1:13).[15] When we believers were dead in our transgressions, God, as a manifestation of the great love with which God loved us (2:4), brought us to life with Christ, so that, as Paul insists, by grace you have been "saved" (σεσωσμένοι, 2:5). Indeed, by grace you have been "saved" (σεσωσμένοι) through faith, and this is not from you, of God is the gift (2:8). Receiving as a gift of God's love the helmet which is salvation (6:17a), then, empowers the audience whom God saved by raising them up with Christ and seating them with Christ "in the heavenly places" (ἐν τοῖς ἐπουρανίοις, 2:6) to stand against the spiritual beings of evil "in the heavenly places" (ἐν τοῖς ἐπουρανίοις, 6:12).[16]

Paul then enjoins his audience to receive, as the final piece in the full armor of God's gifts of love, "the sword of the Spirit" (6:17b), that is, the sword that is made effective or empowered by the "Spirit," with which the audience have already been sealed as a gift of God's love (1:13).[17] And, in

---

14. Hoehner, *Ephesians*, 848–49: "This imperative is not parallel to the preceding participles in verses 14–16 but parallel to the imperative στῆτε, 'stand,' in verse 14. . . . the word δέξασθε is an aorist imperative middle/deponent of δέχομαι meaning 'to take, receive, take in hand, grasp.'"

15. Lincoln, *Ephesians*, 450: "Believers are to 'receive,' i.e., from God (v 13) who offers them, 'the helmet' and 'the sword.'" O'Brien, *Ephesians*, 481: "This helmet is salvation itself (the genitive is one of apposition; 'the helmet which is salvation'), and believers are urged to lay hold of it as they engage in the spiritual warfare." Hoehner, *Ephesians*, 850: "This helmet of salvation may well be an allusion to Isa 59:17 (as is the breastplate of righteousness in v. 14 above). The use of the neuter adjective σωτήριον (common in the LXX) rather than the feminine noun σωτηρία confirms the allusion to Isa 59:17, for the neuter adjective is never used elsewhere by Paul."

16. O'Brien, *Ephesians*, 481: "Earlier in the letter, salvation language was used to summarize what God has already accomplished for believers: his making them alive with Christ, raising them up, and seating them with him in the heavenly places (2:5, 6) are comprehensively described as his having saved them by grace (vv. 5, 8). The present aspect of salvation is emphatically stressed: God has rescued them from death, wrath, and bondage, and transferred them into a new dominion where Christ rules. . . . As they appropriate this salvation more fully and live in the light of their status in Christ, they have every reason to be confident of the outcome of the battle."

17. Lincoln, *Ephesians*, 451: "The sharp short sword (μάχαιρα as opposed to ῥομφαία, the long sword) was the crucial offensive weapon in close combat. . . . The Spirit is not so much the one who supplies the sword—both the helmet and the sword are to be received from God—but the one who gives it its effectiveness, its cutting edge. Since the writer has already drawn on Isa 11:5 for v 14, he may well have been influenced in this verse by the imagery and language of LXX Isa 11:4, where the Spirit of God rests on the Messiah who 'shall

turn, the sword of the Spirit is "the word of God" (6:17c), that is, the spoken or proclaimed word that comes, as a further gift of love, from God.[18] The "word" (λόγον) of truth, the gospel of their salvation, which the audience have heard (1:13), is also the proclaimed "word" (ῥῆμα) of God (cf. 5:26) giving the audience an effective "sword" to withstand the schemes of the devil (6:11).[19] Receiving as a gift of God's love the sword of the Spirit, which is the word of God (6:17bc), then, empowers the audience who have heard the word of God also to proclaim it as an effective weapon in their stance against the devil and all the spiritual beings of evil (6:11–14).[20]

4. Eph 6:18–20 (B´): To Make Known the Mystery of the Gospel

The preparedness to stand against the devil and all the spiritual beings of evil that the audience receive from the "gospel" (εὐαγγελίου, 6:15) of peace in the B element (6:15–16) of the chiasm in 6:14–22 progresses, by way of the chiastic parallelism, to Paul's request for the audience to pray that he be given the speech to make known the mystery of the "gospel" (εὐαγγελίου, 6:19) in the B´ element (6:18–20). After the central, unparalleled, and pivotal C element (6:17) of the chiasm, then, the audience hear a pivot from the "gospel" as the source of preparedness for believers in the B element to the "gospel" as the mystery to be revealed to non-believers in the B´ element.

Paul next describes the behavior that is to follow for the audience who

---

smite the earth with the word [λόγος] of his mouth, and with the breath [πνεῦμα] through his lips shall he destroy the ungodly.' If this is so, an assertion about the Messiah would again be transferred to the Christian."

18. Hoehner, *Ephesians*, 852: "This relative clause ['which is the word of God'] further describes the sword of the Spirit. The neuter relative pronoun does not refer to the neuter πνεύματος as its antecedent but is attracted to the predicate neuter ῥῆμα (cf. 3:13). Ultimately, it refers back to the whole phrase 'the sword of the Spirit' as an explanatory clause giving a further description." For an investigation of the term "sword" as symbol for the word of God in the biblical tradition, see Aristide M. Serra, "La 'spada': simbolo della 'Parola di Dio,' nell'Antico Testamento biblico-giudaico e nel Nuovo Testamento," *Marianum* 63 (2001): 17–89.

19. These two terms for "word"—λόγος and ῥῆμα—are near synonyms that can often be used interchangeably. Fee, *God's Empowering Presence*, 728–29: "ῥῆμα tends to put the emphasis on that which is spoken at a given point, whereas λόγος frequently emphasizes the content of the 'message.' If the distinction holds here, then Paul is almost certainly referring still to the gospel, just as he does in Rom 10:17, but the emphasis is now on the actual 'speaking forth' of the message, inspired by the Spirit. To put that in more contemporary terms, in urging them to take the sword of the Spirit and then identifying that sword with the 'word of God,' Paul is not identifying the 'sword' with the book, but with the proclamation of Christ."

20. Hoehner, *Ephesians*, 853: "The spoken word of God is the 'instrument' of the Spirit. Again, it must be remembered that although this is the only offensive weapon listed among the pieces of the armor, in the present context it is not used to make advances but rather to enable the believer to stand firmly in the midst of satanic warfare."

receive, as gifts of God's love, the "helmet" of salvation and the "sword" of
the Spirit, which is the word of God (6:17): "Through every prayer and petition praying at every opportunity in the Spirit, and for this purpose being
alert in all persistence and petition for all the holy ones" (6:18).²¹ The Paul
who does not cease giving thanks for his audience, making mention of them
in his "prayers" (προσευχῶν, 1:16), now exhorts his audience in turn to a
practice of "praying" (προσευχόμενοι), through every "prayer" (προσευχῆς)
and petition at every opportunity and in all persistence, for all the holy ones,
their fellow believers.²²

The audience, who receive, as a gift of God's love, the "sword" made
effective by the "Spirit" (πνεύματος, 6:17), are to pray through every prayer
and petition at every opportunity "in the Spirit" (ἐν πνεύματι, 6:18), that
is, within the dynamic realm of being in union with the "Spirit" (πνεύματι)
with which they have been sealed as a gift of God's love (1:13). It is "in the
one Spirit" (ἐν ἑνὶ πνεύματι) that the audience have access through Christ
before the Father (2:18). It is "in the Spirit" (ἐν πνεύματι) that the audience
are being built together, as a gift of God's love (divine passive), into a dwelling place of God (2:22). It is "in the Spirit" (ἐν πνεύματι) that the mystery
of Christ (3:4) has been revealed, as a gift of God's love (divine passive),
to God's holy apostles and prophets (3:5), the foundation upon which the
audience are built (2:20). And it is "in the Spirit" (ἐν πνεύματι) that the audience are continually being filled with gifts of love by the Lord Jesus Christ
(5:18; cf. 1:23; 3:19; 4:7–10).

In sum, then, as those who are receiving gifts of God's love within the
dynamic realm of being "in the Spirit," the audience are thus to extend love
to their fellow believers—all the holy ones—by praying for them through

---

21. Hoehner, *Ephesians*, 855: "Having commanded believers to take up their helmet of
salvation and sword of the Spirit, Paul now describes the attitude that they should continually maintain. He does this by the use of two participles προσευχόμενοι and ἀγρυπνοῦντες,
'praying' and 'keeping alert.' These participles could express the means, but more likely they
show the manner in which believers are to take up their helmet of salvation and sword of the
Spirit. In a certain sense they express exhortations, not parallel to the imperative (δέξασθε)
in verse 17 but subservient to it. Hence, the punctuation at the end of verse 17 should be a
comma rather than a period." Fee, *God's Empowering Presence*, 730: "[T]he metaphor that
follows our phrase ['praying in the Spirit'] is most likely intended to continue the imagery of
the Christian soldier: 'to this end (i.e., for the purpose of praying in the Spirit at all times)
being on the alert with all perseverance and prayer.' . . . there is every good reason to believe
that he [Paul] intended his readers to hear 'praying in the Spirit' as the final expression of
Christian weaponry in the conflict with the 'powers.'"

22. Lincoln, *Ephesians*, 452: "The writer has demonstrated the importance he attaches
to prayer, and particularly prayer for awareness of divine power and strengthening through
that power, in his own prayers for the readers reported in 1:15–23 and 3:14–21. The immediate context of the battle against evil powers only makes all the clearer the constant need for
calling on divine aid."

every prayer and petition at every opportunity and in all persistence "in the Spirit" (6:18).[23]

The prepositional phrase, "for all the holy ones" (περὶ πάντων τῶν ἁγίων, 6:18), brings to a climax the noteworthy alliteration and assonance, involving especially the "p" sound, that unifies Eph 6:18—διὰ πάσης προσευχῆς καὶ δεήσεως προσευχόμενοι ἐν παντὶ καιρῷ ἐν πνεύματι, καὶ εἰς αὐτὸ ἀγρυπνοῦντες ἐν πάσῃ προσκαρτερήσει καὶ δεήσει περὶ πάντων τῶν ἁγίων.[24] It also climaxes not only the four references to prayer and/or petition but the fourfold use of the adjective "all" (πᾶς) in 6:18 to intensify the all-embracing, comprehensive nature of the audience's prayer—through "every" (πάσης) prayer at "every" (παντί) opportunity in "all" (πάσῃ) persistence for "all" (πάντων) the holy ones.[25]

That the audience, as the "holy ones" (ἁγίοις) to whom the Letter is addressed (1:1), and who are in close union with all the other "holy ones" (cf. 1:18; 2:19; 3:18; 5:3), are to pray for all the "holy ones" (ἁγίων, 6:18) with whom they are united in this spiritual warfare against the evil powers (6:11–17) develops what it means for the audience to walk within the dynamic realm of being "in love" (5:1–2). Paul has already acknowledged his audience's "love" (ἀγάπην) for all the "holy ones" (ἁγίους)—all of their fellow believers (1:15). He has also made his audience aware that the exalted Christ has given gifts of love to every believer (4:7) to be shared with fellow believers for the equipping of the "holy ones" (ἁγίων) for the work of ministry for building up the body of the Christ (4:12). By praying for all the holy ones (6:18), the audience not only further their love for and union with their fellow believers but advance the goal of our divine election—that we might be "holy" (ἁγίους) and blameless before God within the dynamic realm of being "in love" (ἐν ἀγάπῃ) (1:4; cf. 5:27).[26]

---

23. For the strategic role of prayer in the spiritual warfare believers face against evil powers in Ephesians, see James E. Rosscup, "The Importance of Prayer in Ephesians," *Master's Seminary Journal* 6 (1995): 57–78.

24. The preposition περί ("for") may have been chosen instead of the synonymous ὑπέρ (see 6:19; cf. Wallace, *Greek Grammar*, 363; Hoehner, *Ephesians*, 859) for the sake of the alliteration.

25. Hoehner, *Ephesians*, 859: "Prayer and petition are mentioned four times. This is not tautology but done for the sake of emphasis. It suggests the thoroughness and intensity in regards to prayer. The adjective πᾶς ('every, all') is also mentioned four times. As believers take up the helmet of salvation and the sword of the Spirit, they should pray at every opportunity, through every prayer and petition, with all persistence and petition for all the saints. In the midst of spiritual warfare Paul emphasized the vital importance of prayer."

26. O'Brien, *Ephesians*, 486: "The spiritual warfare about which the apostle has been speaking is one in which all believers, both individually and corporately, are engaged; they need the intercession of fellow Christians if they are to stand firm in the thick of battle. The fourfold 'all' in this verse, pray at all times, with all prayer and supplication, with all perseverance, and make supplication for all the saints, underscores in a most emphatic way the significance which the apostle gave to such mutual intercession."

The audience are to pray for "all the holy ones" (πάντων τῶν ἁγίων, 6:18), including Paul, the very least of "all holy ones" (πάντων ἁγίων, 3:8): "especially for me, that speech may be given to me in opening my mouth, in boldness to make known the mystery of the gospel, for which I am an ambassador in chain, that in it I might speak boldly as it is necessary for me to speak" (6:19–20).[27] Christ loved the church and handed himself over "for" (ὑπέρ) her (5:25), that is, loved us and handed himself over "for" (ὑπέρ) us (5:2b) so that the audience, as children beloved by God and Christ (5:1) are to imitate God and "walk" within the dynamic realm of being "in love" (5:2a). Hence, in reciprocation for the love Paul demonstrated toward his audience in not ceasing to give thanks "for" (ὑπέρ) you, making mention of you in my prayers (1:16), in being a prisoner of Christ Jesus "for" (ὑπέρ) you Gentiles (3:1), and in his tribulations "for" (ὑπέρ) you (3:13), so the audience are to demonstrate their love by praying "for" (ὑπέρ) "me"—Paul (6:19).

Whereas Paul prayed for his audience "that" (ἵνα) God may "give" (δώη) you, as a gift of God's love, the Spirit of wisdom and revelation in knowledge of him (1:17), and "that" (ἵνα) God the Father may "give" (δῷ) you, as a gift of God's love, according to the wealth of his glory to be strengthened with power through his Spirit in the inner person (3:16), now the audience are to pray for Paul "that" (ἵνα) speech may "be given" (δοθῇ) to me, as a gift of God's love (divine passive), in opening my mouth, in boldness to make known the mystery of the gospel (6:19). As no harmful "word" (λόγος) is to come out of the "mouth" (στόματος) of the audience, but only such as is good for the building up of what is needed, "that" (ἵνα) it might "give" (δῷ) grace, as a gift of love, to those who hear it (4:29), so "speech," that is, "word" (λόγος) is to be given to Paul for the opening of his "mouth" (στόματός) so that he may make known the mystery of the gospel, as a gift of love, to those who have not yet heard it.[28]

The audience are to pray that God may give speech, as a gift of love, to Paul in the opening of his mouth, so that "in boldness" (ἐν παρρησίᾳ), that is, within the dynamic realm of being in the "boldness" (παρρησίαν) that we believers have in our union with Christ (3:12), he may make known the mystery of the gospel (6:19).[29] God has not only "made known" (γνωρίσας) to us believers, as a gift of love, the "mystery" (μυστήριον) of his will (1:9), but

---

27. O'Brien, *Ephesians*, 486 n. 212: "The conjunction καί ('and') makes the ὑπὲρ ἐμοῦ ('for me') coordinate with the immediately preceding prepositional phrase περὶ πάντων τῶν ἁγίων ('for all the saints') and probably has adjunctive force, 'and pray particularly for me'."

28. Lincoln, *Ephesians*, 454: "Opening the mouth is a common biblical expression for proclaiming God's word (cf. Ps 78:2; Ezek 3:27; 33:22; Dan 10:16)."

29. The prepositional phrase "in boldness" is in an emphatic position at the beginning of the infinitival clause in 6:19b; see Hoehner, *Ephesians*, 862.

also the "mystery" (μυστήριον) of Christ was "made known" (ἐγνωρίσθη), as a gift of love (divine passive), to Paul (3:3), as well as to the holy apostles and prophets (3:4–5). In response to this love of God and through the loving prayer of the audience Paul may "make known" (γνωρίσαι), as a gift of his love, the "mystery" (μυστήριον) which is the gospel (6:19).[30] Paul may thereby play his role that the manifold wisdom of God, that is, the plan of the "mystery" (μυστηρίου, 3:9), may be "made known" (γνωρισθῇ), as a gift of God's love (divine passive), to the rulers and to the authorities in the heavenly places through the church (3:10).

Paul became a minister of the "gospel" (εὐαγγελίου, 3:6) as a gift of God's love—"according to the gift of the grace of God that was given to me" (3:7). To Paul, as the very least of all holy ones, was given this grace, this gift of God's love, to "preach" or "bring the gospel" (εὐαγγελίσασθαι) about the unfathomable wealth of the Christ to the Gentiles (3:8). Paul is now asking that through the prayer of his audience as their gift of love to him God may grant to Paul the speech, as a further gift of God's love, that will enable Paul to make known the mystery of the "gospel" (εὐαγγελίου, 6:19).

That Paul is an ambassador in chain "on behalf of" or "for" (ὑπέρ) the gospel (6:20a) further develops his being a prisoner in the Lord (4:1) and of Christ Jesus "on behalf of" or "for" (ὑπέρ) you Gentiles (3:1).[31] As a prisoner of Christ Jesus for the sake of the Gentiles in his audience, Paul has made known to his audience by means of this very Letter he sent for them to read, as a gift of his love for them, the mystery of Christ that God made known, as a gift of God's love, to Paul (3:2–4). Now, through the audience's prayer, as a gift of their love, for Paul, he, as a paradoxical "ambassador in chain,"

---

30. In the phrase, "mystery of the gospel" (6:19), "of the gospel" is an epexegetical genitive—"the mystery, namely, the gospel" or "the mystery which is the gospel." See Hoehner, *Ephesians*, 863; O'Brien, *Ephesians*, 488. Lincoln, *Ephesians*, 453–54: "The gospel can be identified with this mystery. Since at the heart of making known the mystery is the reconciliation of Jews and Gentiles in the one body of the Church, it is natural for the gospel to be called elsewhere in relation to the Gentile readers 'the gospel of your salvation' (1:13) and 'the gospel of peace' (6:15). As has been emphasized earlier, making known the mystery of the gospel is not a purely human effort but relies on God's grace (cf. 3:2, 7, 8). Here this is underlined through the notion of the word being given. The apostle is dependent on God not only for the revelation of the mystery but also for its proclamation."

31. We take "for which" (ὑπέρ οὗ) to refer to "gospel" in the phrase "mystery of the gospel (εὐαγγελίου, 6:19)." But since "of the gospel" is epexegetical—"the mystery which is the gospel"—it ultimately makes no difference if one takes "for which" to refer to "the mystery" or to "the mystery of the gospel." See O'Brien, *Ephesians*, 488 n. 223; Best, *Ephesians*, 608–9.

may make known, as a gift of love, to all those who are not in the audience and who have not yet heard it, the mystery which is the gospel (6:19).[32]

That "in it" (ἐν αὐτῷ), that is, in the gospel—within the dynamic realm in which the mystery which is the gospel is proclaimed, heard, and believed, Paul may "speak boldly" (παρρησιάσωμαι) (6:20b) reinforces the "in boldness" (ἐν παρρησίᾳ, 6:19) in which Paul, though he is "in chain" (ἐν ἁλύσει, 6:20a),[33] may make known the mystery of the gospel through the speech given to him as a gift of God's love through the prayer of the audience for Paul as a gift of their love for him (6:19).[34] Paul made known to his audience

---

32. Cassidy, *Paul in Chains*, 102: "Paul earlier in this letter has previously referred to himself as the prisoner, using ὁ δέσμιος, a term imaging him as confined and chained. Paul's use of ἐν ἁλύσει is a still more vivid way for referencing his chained condition. ἅλυσις literally means 'a (metal) chain' and conveys the image of such a chain around Paul's arms, legs, waist in some fashion. This reference to a chain is memorable in its own right. Once the image of a chain is joined with the image of an ambassador, however, the resultant combination, 'an ambassador in chain,' is synergistically powerful. . . . what a powerful paradox did Paul now articulate (and live!): a paradox of status and mistreatment, a paradox of faithfulness and humiliation, a paradox of grace and dishonor. All of these aspects, and others as well, did Paul successfully encompass by memorably identifying himself to his readers as 'an ambassador in a chain.' " Lincoln, *Ephesians*, 454: "To talk of an ambassador in chains is to employ an oxymoron. Normally an ambassador had diplomatic immunity and could not be imprisoned by those to whom he was sent, but prison chains now become the appropriate insignia for representing the gospel." Hoehner, *Ephesians*, 864: "Paul, an ambassador in chains, is an incongruity for normally the position of ambassador commands respect and as such is immune to incarceration by those to whom he was sent. Instead, commissioned by the mightiest of all sovereigns, Paul has been imprisoned. . . . In other words, since ambassadors had diplomatic immunity, they could speak boldly whatever they wished in behalf of the government they represented; however, prisoners had no such freedom." Anthony Bash, *Ambassadors for Christ: An Exploration of Ambassadorial Language in the New Testament* (WUNT 2/92; Tübingen: Mohr Siebeck, 1997), 132: "The imprisonment of an ambassador would have been regarded as a serious insult both to the Sender and to the ambassador." O'Brien, *Ephesians*, 489: "But Paul's chains refer not only to his imprisonment; they also testify symbolically to his calling. His chains indicate that he is under obligation and are therefore his credentials as an ambassador. . . . His life was wholly under God's control and direction, even to the extent of his imprisonment as Christ's accredited representative."

33. Best, *Ephesians*, 609: "[T]he singular ἁλύσει ['chain'] is used probably to emphasise the condition of restraint rather than its actual physical means; in any case it is impossible to work out what historical situation is in mind other than that of the imprisonment of 3:1; 4:1." Abbott, *Ephesians*, 189: "ἐν ἁλύσει is in distinct opposition to ἐν παρρησίᾳ." Lincoln, *Ephesians*, 455: "Here too the picture is of the ambassador who continues to pass on his message freely and openly even while he is in chains. Since that message is also called the mystery, there is a further connotation of παρρησία. That which was hidden, but is now revealed openly, is also to be proclaimed openly."

34. As Hoehner (*Ephesians*, 865) points out, Paul "expresses the content of their prayers by the two ἵνα clauses in verses 19 and 20. The first request was that he would be given the words to make known the mystery of the gospel (vv. 19–20a) and the second, that he would speak as boldly as he ought about the mystery (v. 20b)." The preposition ἐν in the phrase ἐν αὐτῷ should be translated in conjunction with παρρησιάσωμαι ("speak boldly") in

the necessity that you "speak" (λαλεῖτε) truth, each one with his neighbor, for we are members of one another (4:25), forbearing one another "in love" (4:2), and that they should be "speaking" (λαλοῦντες) to each other in psalms and hymns and Spiritual songs (5:19) in thanksgiving (5:20) for the gifts of love with which they are being filled by the Lord Jesus Christ (5:18). And now it is necessary that Paul similarly "speak" (λαλῆσαι) boldly in making known, as a gift of love, the mystery which is the gospel to all who have not heard it, including his captors, guards, fellow prisoners, and visitors.[35]

In sum, with regard to the love theme, by praying for all the holy ones (6:18), the audience not only further their love for (1:15) and union with (cf. 1:18; 2:19; 3:18; 5:3) their fellow believers but advance the goal of our divine election—that we might be "holy" and blameless before God within the dynamic realm of being "in love" (1:4; cf. 5:27). And by praying for the Paul (6:19–20) who prayed for them (1:15–23; 3:14–21) and, as a prisoner of Christ Jesus for their sake (3:1), made known to them, as a gift of his love, the mystery which is the gospel (3:2–4), the audience not only develop their love for Paul but play their role in the divine empowerment that will enable Paul, as an ambassador in chain, to boldly make known to others, as a gift of his love, the mystery which is the gospel.

5. Eph 6:21–22 (A´): Tychicus the Beloved Brother Will Encourage Your Hearts

The single occurrence of the second-person plural pronoun "you" in the exhortation to stand having girded "your" (ὑμῶν) waists in truth in the A element (6:14) of the chiasm in 6:14–22 progresses, by way of the chiastic parallelism, to a fourfold occurrence—that "you" (ὑμεῖς) also may know the things about me (6:21a) . . . Tychicus will make everything known to "you" (ὑμῖν, 6:21b), whom I am sending to "you" (ὑμᾶς, 6:22a) . . . that he may encourage "your" (ὑμῶν) hearts (6:22b)—in the A´ element (6:21–22). Thus, having spiritually "girded" their "waists" in truth for the warfare with evil powers (6:10–14), the audience will be interiorly encouraged in their "hearts" by what they learn from Tychicus.

6:20b as "in" or "in the sphere of," according to Nigel Turner, "The Preposition ἐν in the New Testament," BT 10 (1959): 118.

35. O'Brien, Ephesians, 489 n. 231: "The compulsion implied by δεῖ ('it is necessary') is that of divine appointment." Cassidy, Paul in Chains, 104: "[T]he Paul of Ephesians solicits prayers for boldness in order to present uncompromised testimony on behalf of Christ for howsoever long his imprisonment endures. In Ephesians Paul anticipates bearing his chains for the foreseeable future. And he asks prayers that the boldness of his witness will not diminish over what ever time Christ decrees for this important ambassadorial representation." A trial before Nero or one of his prefects is a possible historical setting for Paul's public proclamation of the mystery of the gospel according to Gene R. Smillie, "Ephesians 6:19–20: A Mystery for the Sake of Which the Apostle is an Ambassador in Chains," TJ 18 (1997): 218–22.

After a concerted focus on what his audience may do especially for Paul
by praying for him as an ambassador in chain (6:19–20), Paul reciprocates
with a concerted focus on what he is doing for his audience in sending them
a beloved brother: "That you also may know the things about me, what I
am doing, Tychicus, the beloved brother and faithful minister in the Lord,
will make everything known to you, whom I am sending to you for this
very purpose, that you may know the things concerning us and that he may
encourage your hearts" (6:21–22).[36]

In reciprocation for the prayers of his audience "that" (ἵνα) speech may
be given to him (6:19a) and "that" (ἵνα) he may speak boldly (6:20b), Paul
now states: "That (ἵνα) you also may know the things about me, what I
am doing" (6:21a). Whereas Paul previously prayed that his audience may
"know" (εἰδέναι) what is the hope of God's calling, what is the wealth of
the glory of God's inheritance in the holy ones, and what is the surpassing
greatness of God's power for us who believe (1:18b–19a), he now wants
his audience to "know" (εἰδῆτε) the things about him, what he is doing
(6:21a) in making known the mystery of the gospel as an ambassador in
chain (6:19–20). That you also may know the things about "me" (ἐμέ) thus
marks a transition from a focus on Paul as the recipient of the love of the
audience and of God—for "me" (ἐμοῦ), given to "me" (μοι), "my" (μου)
mouth, for "me" (με) to speak (6:19–20)—to Paul as a giver of love to
"you," his audience (6:21a).

Paul then informs his audience that Tychicus "will make known"
(γνωρίσει, 6:21) to them everything that Paul is doing to "make known"
(γνωρίσαι, 6:19) the mystery of the gospel. The extended description of Tychicus as "the beloved brother and faithful minister in the Lord" (6:21b)
enhances the audience's favorable view toward and receptivity of him as an
intermediary and significant representative of Paul. It indicates in several
ways how Tychicus is mutually related both to Paul and to Paul's Ephesian
audience.[37]

First, that Tychicus is the "beloved" (ἀγαπητός, 6:21 brother singles him
out as one of all the holy ones for whom not only the audience have "love"

---

36. O'Brien, *Ephesians*, 491 n. 235: "καὶ ὑμεῖς ['and you'] could mean: so that 'you for
your part' may know of my affairs, as I for my part have heard about you (cf. Eph 1:15)."

37. In addtion to Eph 6:21 "Tychicus" is mentioned in Acts 20:4; Col 4:7; 2 Tim 4:12;
Titus 3:12. See also BDAG, 1021; Wolf-Henning Ollrog, *Paulus und seine Mitarbeiter: Untersuchungen zu Theorie und Praxis der paulinischen Mission* (WMANT 50; Neukirchen-
Vluyn: Neukirchener Verlag, 1979), 49–50. Lincoln, *Ephesians*, 465: "Tychicus features
elsewhere in the NT as one of Paul's co-workers, who is particularly associated with Asia
Minor. In Acts 20:4 he is one of the representatives from the province of Asia who accompanies Paul on his visit to Jerusalem, while in the Pastorals he is said to have been sent on mis-
sions to both Ephesus and Crete (cf. 2 Tim 4:12; Titus 3:12). He is likely to have been known
to the recipients of the letter as one of the leading representatives of the Pauline mission."

(ἀγάπην, 1:15), but who is beloved by the fellow believers who know him, especially Paul. Second, that Tychicus is the beloved "brother" (ἀδελφός) recommends him as a fellow "brotherly" believer of both Paul and his audience.[38] Third, as the audience to whom the Letter is addressed are "faithful" (πιστοῖς) as believers (1:1), so Tychicus is "faithful" (πιστός) as a minister (6:21). Fourth, as Paul is a "minister" (διάκονος) of the gospel (3:7), so Tychicus is a faithful "minister" (διάκονος) in the Lord (6:21).[39] And fifth, as both the audience (2:21; 5:8; 6:10) and Paul (4:1, 17) are "in the Lord" (ἐν κυρίῳ), so Tychicus is the beloved brother and faithful minister "in the Lord" (ἐν κυρίῳ, 6:21), that is, within the dynamic realm of being in union with the Lord Jesus Christ.

Paul exhorted his audience to pray "for this purpose" (εἰς αὐτό) of being alert in all persistence and petition for all the holy ones (6:18). In reciprocation for this gift of love Paul is sending Tychicus as a gift of love to his audience "for this very purpose" (εἰς αὐτὸ τοῦτο), "that you may know the things concerning us and that he may encourage your hearts" (6:22).[40] Paul's intention "that you also may know the things about *me*" (6:21a) progresses to his intention "that you may know the things concerning *us*" (6:22b):

6:21a: ἵνα δὲ εἰδῆτε καὶ ὑμεῖς τὰ κατ᾽ ἐμέ

6:22b: ἵνα γνῶτε τὰ περὶ ἡμῶν

That Paul wants his audience to know the things concerning not only "me" (ἐμέ, 6:21a), Paul, but also "us" (ἡμῶν, 6:22b), Paul and Tychicus (and

---

38. On the meaning of ἀδελφός as "brother" Johannes Beutler ("ἀδελφός," *EDNT* 1.30) states: "The prevailing sense in Paul is that of fellow Christian, the foundational statement being Rom 8:29: the redeemed are conformed to Christ, the 'first-born among many brethren.'" Andrew D. Clarke, "Equality or Mutuality? Paul's Use of 'Brother' Language," in *The New Testament in Its First Century Setting: Essays on Context and Background in Honour of B. W. Winter on His Sixty-fifth Birthday* (ed. P. J. Williams et al.; Grand Rapids: Eerdmans, 2004), 164: "It is brotherly love which holds together the relationship between brothers . . . Brotherly love is concerned with mutuality, rather than equality." See also Reidar Aasgaard, " 'Role Ethics' in Paul: The Significance of the Sibling Role for Paul's Ethical Thinking," *NTS* 48 (2002): 513–30; idem, *"My Beloved Brothers and Sisters!" Christian Siblingship in Paul* (JSNTSup 265; London: Clark, 2004); Alanna Nobbs, " 'Beloved Brothers' in the New Testament and Early Christian World," in Williams et al., *New Testament in Its First Century Setting*, 143–50; Philip A. Harland, "Familial Dimensions of Group Identity: 'Brothers' (Ἀδελφοί) in Associations of the Greek East," *JBL* 124 (2005): 491–513.

39. Alfons Weiser, "διάκονος," *EDNT* 1.304: "If the meaning of διάκονος as 'minister of the gospel' comes to the foreground in the letters of Paul, it is fully developed in Ephesians and Colossians, where the word is found only in connection with proclamation."

40. Hoehner, *Ephesians*, 871: "The verb ἔπεμψα ['I am sending'] is an epistolary aorist, that is, it views the action from the viewpoint of the recipients as they read the letter and thus should not be translated 'sent' but 'am sending.' If translated in the past tense it might be interpreted that Paul had sent Tychicus before he wrote this epistle."

other fellow believers with them?), marks a new step in the continual thrust throughout the Letter to assimilate the audience of "you" believers with all of "us" believers. For the audience of "you" believers to know the things concerning "us"—the apostle and minister Paul and the beloved brother and faithful minister Tychicus as two premier representatives of all of "us" believers—solidifies their union with and assimilation into all of "us" believers, all of the holy ones who are called to be holy and blameless before God "in love" (1:4).

Paul is sending Tychicus that "you may know" (γνῶτε)—from Tychicus who "will make known" (γνωρίσει) everything to you (6:21)—the things concerning us and so that thus Tychicus may "encourage" (παρακαλέσῃ) your hearts (6:22), thus complementing the "exhortation" or "encouragement" they receive from Paul—"I, then, exhort (παρακαλῶ) you" (4:1a)—in the Letter. Paul previously prayed that the eyes of your "heart" (καρδίας) may be enlightened as a gift of God's love (1:18) and that Christ may dwell in your "hearts" (καρδίαις) through faith (3:17). He indicated that the audience are to sing songs and psalms in your "hearts" (καρδίᾳ) to the Lord (5:19) in thanksgiving (5:20) for being filled with gifts of love by the Lord Jesus Christ (5:18). And now he is sending Tychicus, as a gift of love, that he may encourage your "hearts" (καρδίας) (6:22).[41]

That Tychicus may encourage "your" (ὑμῶν) hearts (6:22) brings to a climactic conclusion the concerted focus on Paul's audience of "you" believers as reciprocal recipients of his love in this A′ element (6:21–22) of the chiasm—that "you" (ὑμεῖς) also may know the things about me . . . Tychicus will make known everything to "you" (ὑμῖν) . . . whom I am sending to "you" (ὑμᾶς). In sum, then, in reciprocation for his audience's love in praying for further gifts of God's love for all the holy ones and especially for Paul (6:18–20), Paul, as a gift of his own love for his audience of "you" believers, is sending the beloved Tychicus, along with the Letter, to "you" to make known everything to "you" that "you" may know the things concerning not only "me" (Paul) but "us" (Paul, Tychicus, and other fellow "we" believers?), so that he may encourage "your" hearts (6:21–22).

C. Summary on Ephesians 6:14–22

1. That the audience have girded their waists within the realm of being "in truth" (6:14a) as a gift of God's love equips them with the "truth" of receiving and sharing the divine gifts of love that empower them to stand against not only the false and erroneous teaching of human beings (4:14) and the Gentiles' wrong way of "walking" (4:17–19), but also the diabolical spiritual beings of evil in the heavenly places (6:11–13).

---

41. Hoehner, *Ephesians*, 871: Heart "is the center of a person, the seat of religious and moral conduct, of will or volition, or, as here, of feelings and emotions."

2. The donning of the breastplate of "righteousness" as part of the full armor of God's gifts of love (6:14b) empowers the audience to stand against the devil by behaving righteously within the realm of walking "in love" (5:1–2).

3. The "shodding of their feet" in the preparedness that comes from the "gospel" of "peace," as a gift of love from Christ and God (6:15), empowers the audience to be prepared to stand against the full array of diabolical spiritual beings of evil in the heavenly places (6:11–14).

4. As part of the "full armor" of God's gifts of love (6:11, 13), the shield of the faith in which the audience receive the gifts of God's love empowers them to effectively stand against all the assaults directed at them by the devil as the preeminent evil one (6:16).

5. Receiving as a gift of God's love the helmet which is salvation (6:17a) empowers the audience whom God saved by raising them up with Christ and seating them with Christ "in the heavenly places" (2:6) to stand against the spiritual beings of evil "in the heavenly places" (6:12).

6. Receiving as a gift of God's love the sword of the Spirit, which is the word of God (6:17bc) empowers the audience who have heard the word of God also to proclaim it as an effective weapon in their stance against the devil and all the spiritual beings of evil (6:11–14).

7. By praying for all the holy ones (6:18), the audience not only further their love for (1:15) and union with (cf. 1:18; 2:19; 3:18; 5:3) their fellow believers but advance the goal of our divine election—that we might be "holy" and blameless before God within the dynamic realm of being "in love" (1:4; cf. 5:27). And by praying for the Paul (6:19–20) who prayed for them (1:15–23; 3:14–21) and, as a prisoner of Christ Jesus for their sake (3:1), made known to them, as a gift of his love, the mystery which is the gospel (3:2–4), the audience not only develop their love for Paul but play their role in the divine empowerment that will enable Paul, as an ambassador in chain, to boldly make known to others, as a gift of his love, the mystery which is the gospel.

8. In reciprocation for his audience's love in praying for further gifts of God's love for all the holy ones and especially for Paul (6:18–20), Paul, as a gift of his own love for his audience of "you" believers, is sending the beloved Tychicus, along with the Letter, to "you" to make known everything to "you" that "you" may know the things concerning not only "me" (Paul) but "us" (Paul, Tychicus, and other fellow "we" believers?), so that he may encourage "your" hearts (6:21–22).

CHAPTER 17

Ephesians 6:23–24: Peace, Love, and Grace (A´)

A: ^{23} Peace to the brothers and *love* with faith from God the Father
and the *Lord Jesus Christ.*
  B: ^{24} *Grace* be with *all*
A´: who *love our Lord Jesus Christ* in immortality.[1]

A. Chiastic Development from Ephesians 1:1–2 (A) to 6:23–24 (A´)

With Eph 6:23–24, the A´ unit that climactically concludes the macro-chiastic structure of Ephesians, the audience hear echoes of 1:1–2, the corresponding A unit that begins the overall chiasm. The wish of "peace" (εἰρήνη) to the brothers "from God the Father and the Lord Jesus Christ" (ἀπὸ θεοῦ πατρὸς καὶ κυρίου Ἰησοῦ Χριστοῦ (6:23) in the A´ unit recalls the wish of "peace" (εἰρήνη) to you "from God our Father and the Lord Jesus Christ" (ἀπὸ θεοῦ πατρὸς ἡμῶν καὶ κυρίου Ἰησοῦ Χριστοῦ) (1:2) in the A unit. And the wish that "grace" (χάρις) be with all (6:24) in the A´ unit recalls the wish of "grace" (χάρις) to you (1:2) in the A unit. Whereas the audience heard no word for "love" in the opening A unit, after hearing the concerted theme of love throughout the body of the Letter, they hear both the noun—"love" (ἀγάπη) with faith (6:23)—and the cognate verb—all who "love" (ἀγαπώντων) (6:24)—in the final A´ unit.

The audience thus experience a development, by way of the chiastically parallel A (1:1–2) and A´ (6:23–24) units, of the prominent love theme in Ephesians. In the introductory A unit the apostle Paul proclaims a prayer wish that grace and peace be granted as implicit gifts of love from God our Father and the Lord Jesus Christ to his audience, the holy ones in Ephesus, the believers who are in Christ Jesus. But in the concluding A´ unit Paul pro-

---

1. For the establishment of Eph 6:23–24 as a chiasm, see ch. 2.

claims a prayer wish that not only peace and grace but also an explicit *love* (6:23) be granted from God the Father and the Lord Jesus Christ not just to his audience but to the brothers, all fellow believers who explicitly *love* the Lord Jesus Christ in immortality (6:24).

B. Audience Response to Ephesians 6:23–24

1. Ephesians 6:23 (A): Peace to the Brothers and Love

Paul begins the closing greeting of the Letter with a prayer wish that functions also as an indirect exhortation: "Peace to the brothers and love with faith from God the Father and the Lord Jesus Christ" (6:23).[2] As the audience recall, "peace" (εἰρήνη) is a gift of love from both God our Father and the Lord Jesus Christ (1:2; 2:14–17; 6:15) that connotes believers being reconciled and united not only with God and Christ but with one another, especially believing Jews and Gentiles being united with each other. As a gift of love to the audience from God and Christ within the realm of being "in love," this "peace" empowers the audience to maintain their unity "in love." Indeed, Paul exhorted his audience to strive to preserve the unity of the Spirit in the bond of "peace" (εἰρήνης) by forbearing one another "in love" (4:1–3). "Peace to the brothers," then, is not only a wish for further peace as a gift of love from God and Christ but an exhortation for the audience to extend the peace they have received to "the brothers," their fellow believers, by forbearing them "in love."[3]

Whereas at the beginning of the Letter Paul wished peace to "you" (1:2), that is, to his audience of "you" believers, now at the Letter's close he wishes peace to the "brothers" (ἀδελφοῖς, 6:23), that is, fellow believers (cf. the designation of Tychicus as the beloved "brother" [ἀδελφός] in 6:21). Hence, this continues and develops the Letter's overall thrust to assimilate Paul's audience of "you" believers to all of us believers—"the brothers." Paul no longer addresses his audience as "you," but includes his audience of "you" believers within "the brothers" as a designation for all Christian believers. In

2. On the wish of "peace" at the end of Pauline letters, see Jeffrey A. D. Weima, "The Pauline Letter Closings: Analysis and Hermeneutical Significance," *BBR* 5 (1995): 183–87; idem, Neglected Endings, 87–100.

3. Lincoln, *Ephesians*, 466: "[A]t this stage of this particular letter the notion of peace takes on connotations beyond that of general Christian well-being. It inevitably recalls the earlier emphasis on that peace which is God's gift to a divided humanity of reconciliation with himself and with one another, a gift which is embodied in Christ and is to be appropriated and maintained by believers (cf. 2:14–18; 4:3; 6:15)." Hoehner, *Ephesians*, 873: "In the present context 'peace' refers to the peace that comes from God, but indeed, peace of God within believers should produce peace between believers. . . . Briefly, then, Paul reminds believers of the peace of God, which is theirs and should flow through them to their fellow believers." See also O'Brien, *Ephesians*, 493.

other words, Paul's audience of "you" believers are now "brothers" in union with all other believing "brothers" with whom the audience are to be united in peace within the dynamic realm of being "in love."[4]

In addition to peace Paul wishes for "love" (ἀγάπη) with faith to the brothers from God the Father and the Lord Jesus Christ (6:23). Coming at the end of the Letter, this wish for love functions as a wish for a continuation of the gifts of love the audience have already received from God—"because of his great *love* (ἀγάπην) with which he loved us" (2:4)—and from Christ— "to know the *love* (ἀγάπην) of the Christ that surpasses knowledge, that you might be filled to all the fullness of God" (3:19; cf. 4:7–10; 5:2, 25). But this wish for love also functions as an indirect exhortation for the audience to continue to love one another, as this love from God and Christ serves as the model and motivation that empowers the audience's "love" (ἀγάπην) in general for all the holy ones (1:15) and, more specifically, husbands who are to "love" (ἀγαπᾶτε) their wives (5:25).[5]

Indeed, this wish and exhortation for "love" (ἀγάπη) to the brothers (6:23), as the final occurrence of the noun for "love" in the Letter, appropriately recalls and climaxes the previous references to the audience as those within the dynamic realm of being "in love," that is, within the realm of receiving gifts of love from God and Christ as the model and motivation that empowers them in turn to share gifts of love with one another. Thus, we believers have been chosen to be holy and blameless before God "in love" (ἐν ἀγάπῃ, 1:4), as we "in love" (ἐν ἀγάπῃ) are rooted and grounded (3:17), forbearing one another "in love" (ἐν ἀγάπῃ, 4:2), being truthful "in love" (ἐν ἀγάπῃ, 4:15), building up the church as the body of Christ "in love" (ἐν ἀγάπῃ, 4:16), and "walking" as beloved children "in love" (ἐν ἀγάπῃ) for one another, as Christ loved us (5:2; cf. 5:25).

That this wish and exhortation is for love with "faith" (πίστεως) to the brothers (6:23) recalls and underlines for the audience that the gifts of love from God and Christ are graciously received and appropriated through faith. Love has been closely associated with faith previously, as Paul has heard of the "faith" (πίστιν) regarding you in the Lord Jesus and of the

---

4. O'Brien, *Ephesians*, 493: "Paul desires peace for the 'brothers (and sisters)', using the third person, rather than 'to you', which is his normal style in addressing his readers. In a circular letter this familial term in the third person applies to members of various churches, whether Jewish Christians or Gentile. Earlier in Ephesians Paul and his readers were called 'members of one another' (4:25), and spoken of as belonging to the same household (2:19). But this is the first time 'brothers [and sisters]' appears." See also Lincoln, *Ephesians*, 465; Hoehner, *Ephesians*, 873.

5. On "love" in Eph 6:23 Best (*Ephesians*, 618) states: "The emphasis lies not on the love of believers for one another but on God's love for them which pre-existed their existence and elected them to be believers (1.4f); God's love should lead those who are brothers to love one another."

"love" for all the holy ones (1:15), and as Christ may dwell through "faith" (πίστεως) in your hearts, in "love" rooted and grounded (3:17). It is through "faith" (πίστεως) that the audience have been saved as a gift of God's love (2:8), and it is through "faith" (πίστεως) in Christ that we have, as a gift of love, the boldness and access in confidence before God the Father (3:12; cf. 2:18). By forbearing one another "in love" (4:2), we maintain the one "faith" (πίστις), the unity of the "faith" (πίστεως) we are attaining (4:13) as we receive and share gifts of love from the exalted Christ (4:7–12). And, taking up the shield of the "faith" (πίστεως) by which we are being filled with gifts of love by Christ (5:18) empowers us to withstand the devil (6:16).[6]

In sum, then, Paul's wish for peace to the brothers and love with faith that comes from God the Father and the Lord Jesus Christ (6:23) functions not only as a prayer wish for continuing gifts of peace and love from God and Christ, but also as an indirect exhortation for the audience, who have already received gifts of peace and love through faith in God and Christ, to be thus motivated and empowered to extend gifts of peace and love to their fellow believers, in order to be united with them within the dynamic realm of being "in love."

2. Ephesians 6:24a (B): Grace Be with All

As the audience of Ephesians realize, "grace" is very closely related to "love," indeed, it is part of the love word field. It expresses love with the connotation of a love that is freely, graciously, and generously given as a purely undeserved gift. Like Paul's wish for "peace" and "love with faith" (6:23), his wish that "grace (χάρις) be with all" (6:24a) functions not only as a prayer wish for continued "grace" and thus love from God and Christ (1:2, 6, 7; 2:5, 7, 8; 3:2, 7, 8) but also as an indirect exhortation for the audience to extend "grace" and thus love to all fellow believers. Indeed, to each one of us "grace" (χάρις) was given according to the measure of the gift of the Christ (4:7), so that we are to be "truthful," that is, reliable and dependable in sharing with one another these gifts of "grace" (4:11–13) within the dynamic realm of being "in love" (4:15). More specifically, no harmful word is to come out of the mouth of the audience, but only such as is good for

---

6. On the phrase "love with faith," Hoehner (*Ephesians*, 873–74) explains that "the preposition μετά with the genitive expresses association with, rather than superiority over, and in this context it shows a close connection with the two nouns, with the emphasis on the first noun [see also BDAG, 637]. Second, the usage of these two nouns in this epistle suggests that they are on equal par rather than faith being superior. . . . Faith is joined with love and not with peace and is not to be considered a separate attribute along with peace and love. Thus it is not 'peace, love, and faith' but 'peace and love.' This love not only presupposes faith but is enlightened from the knowledge faith gives in understanding God's love for the believer. . . . the theme of love has dominant place in Ephesians and hence, the purpose of the book is to promote love."

the building up of what is needed, that it might give "grace" (χάριν) to those who hear" (4:29).

Paul's wish is that grace be with "all" (πάντων) (6:24a), that is, with "all" the brothers (6:23), "all" the fellow believers, "all" the holy ones (cf. 1:15; 3:8, 18; 6:18). Hence, Paul's wish that "grace be with all" is not only a prayer wish that continued gifts of gracious love be given from God and Christ to "all" the holy ones, but also an indirect exhortation for the audience to continue their love for "all" the holy ones (1:15; cf. 6:18) by being truthful, dependable, and reliable in sharing with them the gifts of grace (cf. 4:29) they have received from God (1:2, 6, 7; 2:5, 7, 8) and Christ (4:7–12) within the dynamic realm of being "in love" (4:15–16).[7]

3. Ephesians 6:24b (A´): Who Love Our Lord Jesus Christ in Immortality

Paul's wish for "love" (ἀγάπη) with faith to the brothers in the A element (6:23) of the chiasm in 6:23–24 progresses, by way of the chiastic parallelism and after the wish that "grace" be with "all" in the central B element (6:24a), to all who "love" (ἀγαπώντων) our Lord Jesus Christ in the A´ element (6:24b). Whereas the wish is for the love that comes from God the Father and the Lord Jesus Christ in the A element, the wish is that grace be with all who love "our" (ἡμῶν) Lord Jesus Christ in the A´ element. The audience thus hear a progression from the use of the noun for "love" toward the brothers in the A element to the use of the verb for "love" toward *our* Lord Jesus Christ in the A´ element.

Paul's wish is that "grace," that is, gracious love, be with all (6:24a) "who love our Lord Jesus Christ in immortality" (6:24b). Although the audience have heard throughout the Letter not only of the love of God for believers—"the great love with which he loved (ἠγάπησεν) us" (2:4), but of the love of Christ for believers—"as Christ loved (ἠγάπησεν) us" (5:2) and "as Christ loved (ἠγάπησεν) the church" (5:25; cf. 3:19), as well as of the love of believers for one another (1:15; 3:17; 4:2, 15–16; 5:2, 25, 28, 33), the Letter concludes on a climactic note of believers' love for Christ in response to the great love of God (2:4) and the love of the Christ that surpasses knowledge (3:19) for us—"who love (ἀγαπώντων) our Lord Jesus Christ."[8]

That Paul's wish is for grace for all who love "our" (ἡμῶν) Lord Jesus

---

7. O'Brien, *Ephesians*, 493: " 'Grace be with you' is Paul's basic benediction at the end of a letter, although here it would strike the readers as particularly appropriate, given the earlier stress on all that the readers (together with all other Christians) had received through the undeserved favour of God and Christ (cf. 1:6, 7; 2:5, 7, 8; 4:7)." Hoehner, *Ephesians*, 874: "Grace concludes the letter, just as it had introduced it in 1:2."

8. Lincoln, *Ephesians*, 466: "Elsewhere the letter has referred to God's love for believers (cf. 2:4) and Christ's love for them (cf. 3:19; 5:2, 25), to believers' love for one another (cf. 1:15; 4:2), to believing husbands' love for their wives (cf. 5:25, 28, 33), and to believers'

Christ (6:24b) brings to a climactic conclusion the Letter's overall thrust to assimilate Paul's audience of "you" believers with all of "us" believers. Not only are the "you" believers of Paul's audience united with "the brothers," the fellow believers, to whom they are to continually extend peace and love (6:23), and with "all" the holy ones to whom they are to continually extend grace (6:24a), but with all of "us" believers who are continually loving (present active participle) *our* Lord Jesus Christ. All of us believers, then, together "love" (ἀγαπώντων) our Lord Jesus Christ as the one beloved not only by God but by us in our dynamic union with him—"in the Beloved" (ἐν τῷ ἠγαπημένῳ, 1:6), in whom God has graced us with his gracious love that we might be holy and blameless before God "in love" (ἐν ἀγάπῃ, 1:4).

That Paul's wish is for grace for all who love our Lord Jesus Christ "in immortality" (ἐν ἀφθαρσίᾳ) (6:24b) exemplifies yet another use in Ephesians of the preposition "in" (ἐν) to express a dynamic realm or sphere. Indeed, Ephesians climactically concludes with this final rich and complex "in" prepositional phrase—"in immortality."[9]

This phrase recalls and sums up what it means for us, who were "dead" in our sins and transgressions (2:1, 4; 5:14), to now, as a gift of God's gracious love, be "made alive," with Christ, raised up with him and seated with him in the heavenly places (2:5–6), so that we are now in the dynamic realm of being "in immortality."[10] That we are "in immortality" means that we are united with the exalted Christ in the heavenly places (1:20), the Christ who as head of the church, which is his body, is filling us with gifts of love (1:22–23; 3:19; 4:7–10), so that by being "truthful" in sharing these gifts of love within the dynamic realm of being "in love," we might cause all things to grow to him, who is the head, the Christ (4:15–16), and thus play our role in God's plan to unite under one head all the things in the Christ (1:10). "In immortality" thus expresses the dynamic realm in which we believers are now living and will live forever in the heavenly places with the exalted Christ as a result of the love we are continually receiving from God and Christ within the dynamic realm of being "in love."[11]

In sum, then, Paul's prayer wish that peace, *love*, and grace be with all

love in general (cf. 1:4; 3:17; 4:15, 16; 5:2; 6:23), but this is the only place where their love for Christ is made explicit."

9. Lincoln, *Ephesians*, 466: "The final words of the letter, ἐν ἀφθαρσίᾳ, 'in immortality,' provide a closing rhetorical flourish similar to those with which the readers had become acquainted through the style of the first part of the letter."

10. For the use of the term "immortality" (ἀφθαρσία) to refer to immortal or eternal life, especially the life of the risen Christ, in other Pauline letters, see Rom 2:7; 1 Cor 15:42, 50, 53, 54; 1 Tim 1:10.

11. According to BDAG (155) some prefer to take "in immortality" in Eph 6:24 as referring "either to those who love the Lord, and as such are now partakers of the future life, or to the Lord himself, who reigns in immortal glory." But as the expression of a dynamic realm or sphere, "in immortality" refers to the immortal, risen life both of Christ and those

who are *loving* our Lord Jesus Christ in immortality (6:23–24) concludes the Letter with a recapitulation that epitomizes how the Letter empowers its listeners to walk in love for the unity of all in Christ: The peace, love, and grace that we believers are receiving from God and Christ empower us in turn to share that peace, love, and grace with one another not only to unite us with all believers in the one body of the church (4:1–6) but also that we might cause all things to be united under Christ, the head (4:15–16; 1:10), whom, in response to his love for us we are loving as the "Beloved" one (1:6) within the dynamic realm of being "in immortality," that is, living now and forever in union with the exalted Christ within the dynamic realm of being "in love" (1:4; 3:17; 4:2, 15–16; 5:2).

C. Summary on Ephesians 6:23–24

1. Whereas the audience heard no word for "love" in the opening unit of the Letter (1:1–2), after hearing the concerted theme of love throughout the body of the Letter, they hear both the noun—"love" with faith (6:23)—and the cognate verb—all who "love" (6:24)—in the final unit of the Letter (6:23–24).

2. Paul's wish for peace to the brothers and love with faith that comes from God the Father and the Lord Jesus Christ (6:23) functions not only as a prayer wish for continuing gifts of peace and love from God and Christ, but also as an indirect exhortation for the audience, who have already received gifts of peace and love through faith in God and Christ, to be thus motivated and empowered to extend gifts of peace and love to their fellow believers, in order to be united with them within the dynamic realm of being "in love."

3. Paul's wish that "grace be with all" (6:24a) is not only a prayer wish that continued gifts of gracious love be given from God and Christ to "all" the holy ones, but also an indirect exhortation for the audience to continue their love for "all" the holy ones (1:15; cf. 6:18) by being truthful, dependable, and reliable in sharing with them the gifts of grace (cf. 4:29) they have received from God (1:2, 6, 7; 2:5, 7, 8) and Christ (4:7–12) within the dynamic realm of being "in love" (4:15–16).

4. Paul's prayer wish that peace, *love*, and grace be with all who are *loving* our Lord Jesus Christ in immortality (6:23–24) concludes the Letter with a recapitulation that epitomizes how the Letter empowers its listeners to walk in love for the unity of all in Christ: The peace, love, and grace that

---

who love him, the life shared now and forever by believers in their union with the risen and exalted Christ in the heavenly places.

we believers are receiving from God and Christ empower us in turn to share that peace, love, and grace with one another not only to unite us with all believers in the one body of the church (4:1–6) but also that we might cause all things to be united under Christ, the head (4:15–16; 1:10), whom, in response to his love for us we are loving as the "Beloved" one (1:6) within the dynamic realm of being "in immortality," that is, living now and forever in union with the exalted Christ within the dynamic realm of being "in love" (1:4; 3:17; 4:2, 15–16; 5:2).

CHAPTER 18

Summary and Conclusion

Empowerment to Walk in Love for the Unity of All in Christ

Having provided detailed summary conclusions for each of the fifteen chiastic units in the preceding chapters, we offer in this final chapter an overview of how Paul's Letter to the Ephesians, through its intricate and intriguing chiastic structures, empowers its listeners to walk in love for the unity of all in Christ.

The chiastic A unit which introduces the Letter to the Ephesians (1:1–2) first makes the audience aware that Paul has not only received God's love in being established and empowered as an authoritative apostle of Christ Jesus through the gracious will of God, but responds to this empowering love of God by exercising his apostleship in writing this Letter to the Ephesians. The central elements of the chiasm then give the audience the realization that they too have received God's love and the empowerment to respond to it as not only the holy ones who are in Ephesus but also the believers who are in Christ Jesus (1:1). At the climactic conclusion of the chiasm Paul's introductory prayer wish that continued grace as well as peace be granted to his audience from God our Father and the Lord Jesus Christ (1:2) prepares the audience to further experience, by their listening to what Christ Jesus himself is going to communicate to them in this Letter from his authorized apostle, the empowerment that comes from the grace and peace that are gifts of love from God and Christ.

The chiastic B unit (1:3–14) makes the audience aware that God has chosen us believers to be holy and blameless before God "in love" (1:4), that is, within the dynamic realm of being "in the Beloved" (1:6), the realm of our being united with Jesus Christ so that with him we are recipients of the love of God that empowers us in turn to love God and one another. As a gift of love, God has made known to us "in the Beloved" in whom we are "in love" the mystery of God's will which is expressed at the center of the chiasm—"to unite under one head all the things in the Christ, the things in the heavens and the things on earth" (1:10). The conclusion of the chiasm leaves the audience with the lasting impression that the point of we believers—both those who first hoped in the Christ (1:12) and "you," the audience, who arrived at this faith and hope later (1:13)— being extremely blessed with the love of God is that we might respond to this extravagantly gracious divine love by exuberantly praising God's glory—that we might be "to the praise of his glory!" (1:6, 12, 14).

After affirming the audience's love for all the holy ones (1:15), their fellow believers, at the beginning of the chiastic C unit (1:15–23), Paul prays that God may give to the audience, as a gift of love, the Spirit of wisdom and revelation to experience the surpassing greatness of God's power for us who believe, the power—as expressed at the center of the chiasm—which God "worked in the Christ, raising him from the dead and seating him at his right hand in the heavenly places" (1:20). The conclusion of the chiasm then deepens the audience's experience of this divine empowerment by making them aware that God has given, as a gift of love, the Christ that God exalted as "head" over all things to the church, the assembly—including the audience—of all believing holy ones, which is the "body" of the Christ who is continually filling all things in all ways with gifts of love (1:22–23).

The chiastic D unit (2:1–10) begins by reminding Paul's audience of "you" believers of their past sinfulness, a desperate situation of spiritual death which all of us believers shared with them (2:1–3). But the central, pivotal elements of the chiasm remind the audience of God's merciful and loving response to this sinful situation of spiritual death—"But God being rich in mercy, because of his great love with which he loved us" (2:4). The chiasm then concludes by making the audience realize that the powerful love by which God raised Christ Jesus from the dead and seated him in the heavenly places (1:20) is the same powerful and great love by which God made us believers spiritually alive and raised and seated us with Christ in the heavenly places (2:5–6), thus empowering us to "walk" in the good works God prepared for us beforehand (2:10), so that we may be holy and blameless before God within the dynamic realm of being "in love" (1:4) "in the Beloved" (1:6).

After reminding the Gentile "you" believers of their alienation from the community of Israel at the time that they were without Christ (2:11–12), the chiastic E unit (2:11–22) assures the audience of "you" believers that now Christ, who is himself "our" peace, has created both believing Gentiles and believing Jews into one new entity as a gift of love. Indeed, the center of the chiasm emphasizes this unity that Christ by his sacrificial death created as a gift of love—he created in himself "one new person, making peace, and that he might reconcile the both in one body to God through the cross" (2:15cd–16a). The conclusion of the chiasm assures the "you" believers that they are being built together with all other believers, as a gift of God's love, into a dwelling place of God in the Spirit (2:22), so that they are fellow citizens with the holy ones and members of the household of God, with Christ Jesus as the "head" stone, in union with whom the whole building is being fitted together into a unified corporate entity, as a gift of God's love, and growing into a temple holy in the Lord (2:19–21).

In the chiastic F unit (3:1–13) Paul, as the prisoner of Christ on behalf of his Gentile audience (3:1), shares with them in the Letter itself his insight into the mystery of Christ, which he received as a gift of God's love that he now shares as a gift of his personal love for his audience (3:2–5). By listening to the reading of the Letter, then, the audience experience this gift of Paul's love by sharing his insight into the mystery, as it is expressed at the center of the chiasm—"that the Gentiles are fellow heirs and fellow members of the body and fellow sharers of the promise in Christ Jesus through the gospel" (3:6). After Paul informs his audience that he became a minister of this gospel as a gift of God's love that the mystery of the ultimate cosmic unity of all things under one head in Christ may be made known not only to all the Gentiles but to the evil powers in the heavenly places through the church (3:7–12), the chiasm concludes with his request that his audience not lose heart over his tribulations as a prisoner, which, as a manifestation of his love for them, will result in their ultimate glory (3:13).

In the chiastic G unit (3:14–21) Paul prays that God as the cosmic Father of all may give to the audience, as a gift of God's love, interior strength so that, already "rooted and grounded" within the dynamic realm of being "in love" (3:14–17), the audience in union with all the holy ones may be empowered to already grasp the absolute expanse of the cosmic unity toward which all things in the universe are destined, as expressed by the center of the chiasm—"that you might have the strength to comprehend with all the holy ones what is the breadth and length and height and depth" (3:18). A closely coordinated consequence of this cosmic comprehension is that the audience experience the love of Christ that surpasses knowledge and thus be filled by Christ with gifts of love until they attain to all the fullness of God (3:19). The chiasm brings the first part of the Letter to the Ephesians to a climactic conclusion by inviting the audience to join all of us believers in glorifying to all generations and for ever the God who has the power to do far more beyond all that we ask or imagine (3:20–21).

The chiastic H unit (4:1–16), the beginning of the paranetic half of the Letter as well as the pivotal central unit within the macro-chiastic structure, exhorts the audience to forbear one another within the dynamic realm of being "in love" in order to preserve the unity of believers, each of whom has been given, as a gift of love, grace according to the measure of the gift of the Christ (4:1–7). The pivotal center of this chiasm as well as of the entire macro-chiastic structure makes the audience aware that the Christ who descended to the lower parts of the earth in death and burial also ascended in resurrection from the dead far above all the heavens, that he might fill all things with gifts of love (4:8–10). The chiasm concludes by exhorting the audience to be truthful in sharing gifts of love within the realm of being "in love," so that we believers might cause all things to grow to Christ as the "head"—the destiny for the cosmic unity of all things as well as the source of the gifts of love by which the "body," the church, is building itself up within the dynamic realm of being "in love" (4:11–16).

Within the macro-chiastic structure Paul's assertion that his audience "have not so learned the Christ" (4:20) as the motivation for his exhortation that they not behave like the Gentiles (4:17–19) in the G′ unit (4:17–32) undergirds his prayer that his audience may "know the love of the Christ that surpasses knowledge" (3:19) in the G unit (3:13–21). That the audience have put off the "old person" (4:22) and put on the "new person" (4:24) as a gift of Christ's love in the G′ unit is a consequence of their being strengthened in the "inner person" (3:16) as a gift of God's love in the G unit. The exhortation for the audience not to grieve the Holy "Spirit" of God (4:30) with their behavior in the G′ unit is motivated by Paul's prayer that they be strengthened with power through God's "Spirit" (3:16) as a gift of God's love in the G unit. And that God was gracious in giving us gifts of love within the realm of our being "in Christ" (4:32) in the G′ unit provides a further reason for Paul's declaration of glory to God for the gifts of love we have received within the realm of our being "in Christ" (3:21) in the G unit.

In the chiastic G′ unit (4:17–32) Paul exhorts his audience not to "walk" as the Gentiles "walk" in the futility of their mind (4:17–19), since such Godless behavior does not accord with their learning of Christ and the "truth" of their having received gifts of God's love within the realms of being "in Jesus" and "in love" (4:20–21). At the center of the chiasm the audience experience a pivot from the negative to the positive—from the gift of God's love that empowers them to "put off" the "old person" corrupted according to the desires of deceit (4:22) to the gift of God's love that empowers them to "put on" the "new person" created according to God in righteousness and holiness of truth (4:23–24). The chiasm concludes with Paul's exhortation for the audience to speak to one another what is good for their edification that they might give, as a gift of love, grace to those who listen to them, and thus be gracious in sharing love with each other, just as God was gracious to us in giving us gifts of love within the realm of our being "in Christ" (4:25–32).

That Christ loved us (5:2) in the F′ unit (5:1–6) provides the motivation for Paul's being the prisoner of the Christ Jesus (3:1), develops the content of the mystery of the Christ (3:4) and the wealth of the Christ (3:8), and gives the reason why the Gentiles are fellow heirs and fellow members of the body and fellow sharers of the promise in Christ Jesus (3:6), as well as how God accomplished the purpose of the ages in Christ Jesus our Lord (3:11) in the F unit (3:1–13). Paul's command for the audience to imitate God as children beloved by God and Christ who share that love with one another by "walking" within the realm of being "in love" (5:1–2) in the F′ unit finds further motivation in the example of Paul who shared with the audience the grace of God he received as a gift of God's love to be a minister of the gospel (3:2, 7) in the F unit. And that there is no "inheritance" in the kingdom of Christ and God for one who is sexually immoral, impure, or greedy (5:5) in the F′ unit warns the audience not to forfeit being "fellow heirs" in Christ Jesus (3:6) as a gift of God's love in the F unit.

The chiastic F′ unit (5:1–6) begins with Paul's exhortation for the audience to become imitators of the love they have received from God and Christ as beloved children by "walking" within the dynamic realm of being "in love"—loving one another as the Christ loved us (5:1–2). The center of the chiasm adds to the theme of love the dimension of gratitude that is to replace behavior inappropriate for holy ones (5:3) "walking in love"—"no shamefulness or foolish talk or sarcastic ridicule, which are inappropriate, but rather thanksgiving" (5:4). The chiasm concludes with Paul's warning the audience that any sexually immoral or impure or idolatrous greedy one forfeits an inheritance—a gift of God's love—in the kingdom of the Christ and God (5:5) and that if they allow themselves to be deceived with empty words, they will receive the wrath of God that is coming upon the sons of disobedience (5:6), thus losing their status as children beloved by God and Christ and children who love one another within the dynamic realm of "walking in love" (5:1–2).

Paul's command for his audience not to become "fellow sharers" with "them" (5:7), that is, the "sons of disobedience" (5:6), in the E′ unit (5:7–14) of the macro-chiastic structure is bolstered by his audience's recall that instead they are "fellow citizens" with the holy ones (2:19) as a gift of God's love in the E unit (2:11–22). That "you were once" darkness, but "now" are light (5:8) as a gift of God's love in the E′ unit develops that "once you were" without Christ (2:12) but "now" you who were "once" far away have become near in the blood of the Christ (2:13) as a gift of God's love in the E unit. And that you are not to "be connected with" the unfruitful works of the darkness (5:11) as you are light "in the Lord" (5:8) as a gift of God's love in the E′ unit further develops that it is "in the Lord" (2:21) that "you are being built together" into a dwelling place of God in the Spirit (2:22) as a gift of God's love in the E unit.

In the chiastic E′ unit (5:7–14) Paul exhorts his audience to "walk" as children of light, producing the fruit of the light in all goodness and righ-

teousness and truth, since they are now light as a gift of God's love within
the realm of being not only "in the Lord" but "in love" (5:7–9). The center
of the chiasm—"approving what is pleasing to the Lord" (5:10)— impresses
upon the audience that just as Christ "pleased" God in his love for us (5:2),
so they are to "please" the Lord in their love for one another within the
realm of walking "in love" (5:2) as children of light (5:8). The quotation that
concludes the chiasm (5:14b) alerts the audience to the potential that their
lifestyle of "walking in love" has for converting unbelievers from the works
of darkness (5:11–12), so that they may be transformed into "light" (5:14a)
by the Christ shining on them. And it urges each member of the audience not
to fall "asleep" morally and spiritually but to continue to "walk" as children
of light to remain "light" as a further gift of the love of the Christ who will
shine on each of them within the realm of their being "in love" (5:1–2).

Paul's warning to his audience to watch how carefully you "walk"
(5:15) in the D´ unit (5:15–6:9) of the macro-chiastic structure recalls that
although the "you" believers once "walked" according to the age of this
world (2:2), all of us believers may now "walk" in the good works God
prepared beforehand (2:10) as part of what it means to walk within the
dynamic realm of being "in love" in the D unit (2:1–10). "Doing the will"
of God (6:6) as children beloved by God and Christ in the D´ unit recalls
and contrasts "doing the wishes" of the flesh as children of wrath (2:3) in
the D unit. And Paul's directive for husbands to "love" their wives as the
Christ "loved" the church (5:25) and to "love" their own wives as their own
bodies, as he who "loves" his own wife "loves" himself (5:28) in the D´ unit
is inspired and empowered by the great "love" with which God "loved" us
(2:4) in our union with Christ in the D unit.

In the first chiastic sub-unit (5:15–20) within the D´ unit (5:15–6:9)
Paul exhorts his audience to "walk" not as unwise but as wise (5:15) by
not becoming foolish but understanding what the will of the Lord is (5:17),
and by not being drunk with wine, in which there is dissipation, but being
continually filled by Christ with gifts of love within the realm of being in
the Spirit (5:18). At the pivotal center of the chiasm (5:19) the psalms and
hymns and Spiritual songs that the audience speak to each other as an extension to one another of the love they have received from Christ (5:19a) are
the songs and psalms that they sing in their hearts to the Lord (5:19b). The
chiasm concludes with the audience giving thanks to God the Father in the
name of our Lord Jesus Christ for all the things they have received as a result
of and in response to being filled with gifts of love by the Lord Christ within
the realm of being in the Spirit (5:18), further demonstrating what it means
to "walk" (5:15) as children beloved by God and Christ within the dynamic
realm of being "in love" (5:1–2).

In the second chiastic sub-unit (5:21–33) within the D´ unit (5:15–6:9),
for wives to submit to their husbands as to the Lord (5:22) means that as

the Lord Christ is not only the authority over but the source of gifts of love for the church, so the husband is not only the authority over but the source of gifts of love for the wife. The self-sacrificial love of Christ, which serves as the motive and model for husbands to love their wives (5:25), empowers the church to be morally "holy and blameless" (5:27) within the dynamic realm of living "in love" (1:4). At the pivotal center of the chiasm, for each individual husband to love "himself," that is, his own wife who is as his own body (5:28), as Christ loved the church, his own body, means for him to hand his own individual self over on behalf of his wife with the same sort of self-sacrificial love. At the conclusion of the chiasm, husbands are to love their wives as Christ loved the church and wives submit to and reciprocally respect their husbands by accepting their love as coming from Christ (5:21–22, 33).

At the beginning of the third chiastic sub-unit (6:1–4) within the D′ unit (5:15–6:9), for children to obey their parents within the realm of being "in the Lord" (6:1) is a way for them to demonstrate love in grateful response for the love they have received and will further receive. The well-being and long life (6:3), which specify the content of the promise pronounced at the center of the chiasm (6:2b), that God will grant to each child who not only obeys but honors his or her father and mother, because of and in grateful response to being filled with gifts of love by the Lord Jesus Christ within the dynamic realm of being "in the Spirit" (5:17–20), adds two more gifts of God's love for children who "walk" within the dynamic realms of being "in the Lord" (6:1) as well as "in love" (5:1–2). At the conclusion of the chiasm, fathers are not to anger their children but rather love them by bringing them up in the training and instruction of the Lord (6:4) in reciprocation for their children loving them by obeying and honoring both their fathers and mothers (6:1–3).

At the beginning of the fourth and final chiastic sub-unit (6:5–9) within the D′ unit (5:15–6:9), for slaves to submit themselves to their earthly masters as to the Christ (6:5) means for them not only to appropriately respond to but submit themselves to receiving further gifts of Christ's love. By thus doing the will of God wholeheartedly (6:6), slaves do their part in causing all things to grow to him, who is the head, the Christ (4:15), and thus further the plan of the will of God to unite under one head all the things in the Christ (1:9–10). At the center of the chiasm, by rendering service with good will as to the "Lord" (6:7), slaves complement the audience's response of singing songs and psalms in their hearts to the "Lord" (5:19) in thanksgiving for being filled with gifts of love by the Lord Jesus Christ in the Spirit (5:18–20). At the conclusion of the chiasm, earthly masters are to reciprocate the love they receive from their slaves in terms of the good that each slave does in obeying his or her master by in turn doing good to their slaves as a gift of love (6:8–9).

The audience may be empowered "in the might of the strength" of the Lord Jesus Christ (6:10) to stand against the "rulers" and "authorities" who are "in the heavenly places" (6:12) in the C′ unit (6:10–13) within the overall chiastic structure of Ephesians because of "the might of the strength" (1:19) that God worked in raising Christ from the dead and seating him "in the heavenly places" (1:20), far above every "ruler" and "authority" (1:21), subjecting all things under his feet and giving him as head over all things to the church as a gift of God's love (1:22) in the C unit (1:15–23).

In the chiastic C′ unit (6:10–13) "putting on" the "full armor" of the gifts of God's love, that is, living in accord with the gifts of love with which they are being filled by the exalted Christ within the dynamic realm of being "in love," empowers the audience to stand against the schemes of the devil (6:10–11). As members of the church in our struggle against the rulers, authorities, cosmic powers of this darkness, and the spiritual beings of evil "in the heavenly places," as expressed at the center of the chiasm (6:12), we are empowered to make known to the rulers and authorities "in the heavenly places" the manifold wisdom of God (3:10)—the plan of the mystery of God to unite under one head all things in Christ (1:10) through the gifts of God's love. At the conclusion of the chiasm, having done everything possible by equipping themselves with the full armor of God, the audience will be able "to withstand" the devil on that climactic evil day, and so ultimately "to stand" (6:13), empowered by the full armor of all the gifts of divine love.

The audience may stand in "truth" (6:14) prepared from the "gospel" of peace (6:15) to receive the helmet of "salvation" and the sword of the "Spirit" (6:17) in the B′ unit (6:14–22) within the overall chiastic structure because they have heard the word of the "truth," the "gospel" of their "salvation" and were sealed with the Holy "Spirit" (1:13) as a gift of God's love in the B unit (1:3–14). Paul wants "to make known the mystery" of the gospel (6:19) in the B′ unit as a consequence of God's gift of love in "having made known to us the mystery" of his will (1:9) in the B unit. And encouraged by the "beloved" Tychicus (6:21–22), the audience are to pray for all the "holy ones" (6:18) in the B′ unit, so that all of us believers may be "holy" and blameless before God within the dynamic realm of being "in love" (1:4) as well as "in the Beloved" (1:6) in the B unit.

In the chiastic B′ element (6:14–22) the audience having "girded their waists in truth," having "put on the breastplate of righteousness," having "shod the feet" in preparedness from the gospel, and having "taken up the shield of faith" as gifts of God's love empowers them to stand (6:14–16) against the full array of spiritual beings of evil in the heavenly places (6:11–13). At the center of the chiasm, receiving as a gift of God's love the helmet which is salvation and the sword of the Spirit, which is the word of God (6:17), empowers the audience to proclaim the word of God as an effective weapon in their stance against the devil and all the spiritual beings of evil.

At the conclusion of the chiasm, in reciprocation for his audience's love in praying for further gifts of God's love for all the holy ones and especially for Paul (6:18–20), Paul, as a gift of his own love for his audience, is sending the beloved Tychicus, along with the Letter, that they may know the things concerning not only Paul but "us" (Paul, Tychicus, and perhaps fellow believers), so that he may encourage "your" hearts (6:21–22).

In the A unit (1:1–2) that introduces the overall chiastic structure of Ephesians the apostle Paul proclaims a prayer wish that grace and peace be granted as implicit gifts of love from God our Father and the Lord Jesus Christ to his audience, the holy ones in Ephesus, the believers who are in Christ Jesus. But in the concluding A′ unit (6:23–24), after presenting a concerted theme of love throughout the body of the Letter, Paul proclaims a prayer wish that not only peace and grace but also an explicit love (6:23) be granted from God the Father and the Lord Jesus Christ not just to his audience but to the brothers, all fellow believers who explicitly love the Lord Jesus Christ in immortality (6:24).

At the beginning of the chiastic A′ unit (6:23–24) Paul's wish for peace to the brothers and love with faith that comes from God the Father and the Lord Jesus Christ (6:23) functions not only as a prayer wish but also as an indirect exhortation for the audience to be motivated and empowered to extend gifts of peace and love to their fellow believers (6:23). At the center of the chiasm Paul's wish that "grace be with all" (6:24a) is not only a prayer wish that continued gifts of gracious love be given from God and Christ to "all" the holy ones, but also an indirect exhortation for the audience to continue their love for "all" the holy ones by being truthful, dependable, and reliable in sharing with them the gifts of grace they have received from God and Christ. At the conclusion of the chiasm and of the entire Letter all of us believers are loving our Lord Jesus Christ, the Beloved (1:6), in response to his love for us within the dynamic realm of being "in immortality," that is, living now and forever in union with the exalted Christ within the dynamic realm of being "in love" (1:4; 3:17; 4:2, 15–16; 5:2).

In sum, the chiastic structure of Ephesians begins by assuring its audience that they have been blessed by God with every Spiritual blessing so that they may be holy and blameless before God within the dynamic realm of being "in love" (1:4) as well as "in the Beloved" (1:6). At the center of the central chiastic unit (4:1–16) the audience hear that Christ ascended far above all the heavens, that he might fill all things (4:10) with gifts of love (cf. 4:7), so that, at the climactic conclusion of the central unit, we believers, being truthful "in love," might cause all things to grow to him, who is the head, the Christ (cf. 1:10), from whom the whole body, the church (cf. 1:22–23), brings about the growth of the body for the building up of itself within the dynamic realm of being "in love" (4:15–16). Chiastically developing its opening prayer wish (1:1–2), the Letter concludes on a climactic note of love with Paul's prayer wish for continued love from God the Father and the Lord Jesus Christ as well as grace upon all who are loving the Lord Jesus Christ within the dynamic realm of being "in immortality" (6:23–24).

In conclusion, listening to the intricate and intriguing chiastic patterns of Paul's Letter to the Ephesians empowers its audience to "walk," that is, behave and conduct themselves, "in love," that is, within the dynamic realm of being not only loved by God and Christ but loving God, Christ, and one another, in order to bring about the cosmic unity of all things in the heavens and on earth—including believing Jews and Gentiles as well as all evil powers—within the dynamic realm of being "in Christ." In short, Ephesians functions as the empowerment to walk in love for the unity of all in Christ.

Bibliography

Aasgaard, Reidar. " 'Role Ethics' in Paul: The Significance of the Sibling Role for Paul's Ethical Thinking." *NTS* 48 (2002): 513–30.

———. *"My Beloved Brothers and Sisters!" Christian Siblingship in Paul.* JSNTSup 265. London: Clark, 2004.

Abbott, Thomas Kingsmill. *A Critical and Exegetical Commentary on the Epistles to the Ephesians and to the Colossians.* ICC. Edinburgh: Clark, 1897.

Ådna, Jostein. "Die eheliche Liebesbeziehung als Analogie zu Christi Beziehung zur Kriche: Eine traditionsgeschichtliche Studie zu Epheser 5, 21–33." *ZTK* 92 (1995): 434–65.

Agnew, Francis H. "The Origin of the NT Apostle-Concept: A Review of Research." *JBL* 105 (1986): 75–96.

Aletti, Jean-Noël. "Les difficultés ecclésiologiques de la lettre aux Éphésiens: De quelques suggestions." *Bib* 85 (2004): 457–74.

———. *Saint Paul: Épître aux Éphésiens: Introduction, traduction et commentaire.* EBib 42. Paris: Gabalda, 2001.

Allan, John A. "The 'In Christ' Formula in Ephesians." *NTS* 5 (1958–59): 54–62.

Allen, Leslie C. "The Old Testament Background of (προ)ὁρίζειν in the New Testament." *NTS* 17 (1970–71): 104–8.

Allen, Thomas G. "Exaltation and Solidarity with Christ: Ephesians 1.20 and 2.6." *JSNT* 28 (1986): 103–20.

———. "God the Namer: A Note on Ephesians 1.21b." *NTS* 32 (1986): 470–75.

Anderson, C. "Rethinking 'Be Filled with the Spirit': Ephesians 5:18 and the Purpose of Ephesians." *EvJ* 7 (1989): 57–67.

Arnold, Clinton E. "Ephesians, Letter to The." *DPL*, 238–46.

———. *Ephesians: Power and Magic. The Concept of Power in Ephesians in Light of Its Historical Setting.* SNTSMS 63. Cambridge: Cambridge University, 1989.

————. "The 'Exorcism' of Ephesians 6.12 in Recent Research." *JSNT* 30 (1987): 71–87.

————. "Jesus Christ: 'Head' of the Church (Colossians and Ephesians)." Pp. 346–66 in *Jesus of Nazareth: Lord and Christ. Essays on the Historical Jesus and New Testament Christology.* Edited by Joel B. Green and Max Turner. Grand Rapids: Eerdmans, 1994.

Augello, A. "Il rapporto marito e moglie secondo l'antropologia naturale e soprannaturale di Efesini 5, 21–33." *Vivarium* 1 (1993): 437–65.

Aune, David E. "Archai." *DDD*, 77–80.

Bailey, Kenneth E. *Poet and Peasant: A Literary-Cultural Approach to the Parables in Luke.* Grand Rapids: Eerdmans, 1976.

Baldanza, Giuseppe. "L'originalità della metafora sponsale in *Ef* 5, 25–32: Riflessi sull' ecclesiologia." *Salesianum* 63 (2001): 3–21.

Balla, Peter. *The Child-Parent Relationship in the New Testament and Its Environment.* WUNT 155. Tübingen: Mohr Siebeck, 2003.

Balz, Horst. "πανοπλία." *EDNT* 3.10.

————. "φόβος." *EDNT* 3.432–34.

Barkhuizen, Jan Harm. "The Strophic Structure of the Eulogy of Ephesians 1:3–14." *HvTSt* 46 (1990): 390–413.

Barnett, Paul W. "Apostle." *DPL*, 45–51.

Barr, George K. *Scalometry and the Pauline Epistles.* JSNTSup 261. London: Clark, 2004.

Barth, Gerhard. "πίστις." *EDNT* 3.91–97.

————. "πιστός." *EDNT* 3.97–98.

Barth, Markus. *Ephesians: Introduction, Translation, and Commentary on Chapters 1–3.* AB 34. New York: Doubleday, 1974.

————. *Ephesians: Translation and Commentary on Chapters 4–6.* AB 34A. New York: Doubleday, 1974.

————. "Traditions in Ephesians." *NTS* 30 (1984): 3–25.

Basevi, Claudio. "La Benedizione de Ef 1, 3–14: Il disegno di salvezza di Dio Padre." *AT* 14 (2000): 305–42.

————. "La missione di Cristo e dei cristiani nella Lettera agli Efesini: Una lettura di Ef 4,1–25." *RivB* 38 (1990): 27–55.

Bash, Anthony. *Ambassadors for Christ: An Exploration of Ambassadorial Language in the New Testament.* WUNT 2/92. Tübingen: Mohr Siebeck, 1997.

Bassler, Jouette M. *Divine Impartiality: Paul and a Theological Axiom.* SBLDS 59. Chico, CA: Scholars Press, 1982.

Beattie, Gillian. *Women and Marriage in Paul and His Early Interpreters.* JSNTSup 296. London: Clark, 2005.

Beck, James R. "Is There a Head of the House in the Home? Reflections on Ephesians 5." *Journal of Biblical Equality* 1 (1989): 61–70.

Beisser, F. "Wann und von wem könnte der Epheserbrief verfasst worden sein?" *KD* 52 (2006): 151–64.

Bell, Richard H. *The Irrevocable Call of God: An Inquiry into Paul's Theology of Israel.* WUNT 184. Tübingen: Mohr Siebeck, 2005.

Berger, Klaus. "προσωπολημψία." *EDNT* 3.179–80.

―――. "χάρις." *EDNT* 3.457–60.

Bergmeier, Roland. "περιπατέω." *EDNT* 3.75–76.

Best, Ernest. *Ephesians.* ICC. London: Clark, 1998.

―――. *Essays on Ephesians.* Edinburgh: Clark, 1997.

―――. "The Haustafel in Ephesians (Eph. 5.22–6.9)." *IBS* 16 (1994): 146–60.

―――. "Thieves in the Church: Ephesians 4:28." *IBS* 14 (1992): 2–9.

Beutler, Johannes. "ἀδελφός." *EDNT* 1.28–30.

Bläser, Peter. "ἀπειθέω." *EDNT* 1.118–19.

Blomberg, Craig L. "The Structure of 2 Corinthians 1–7." *CTR* 4 (1989): 3–20.

Boers, Hendrikus. "'Αγάπη and Χάρις in Paul's Thought." *CBQ* 59 (1997): 693–713.

Borse, Udo. "προσαγωγή." *EDNT* 3.161.

Botha, Pieter J. J. "The Verbal Art of the Pauline Letters: Rhetoric, Performance and Presence." Pp. 409–28 in *Rhetoric and the New Testament: Essays from the 1992 Heidelberg Conference.* Edited by Stanley E. Porter and Thomas H. Olbricht. JSNTSup 90. Sheffield: JSOT, 1993.

Bouttier, Michel. *En Christ: Étude d'exégèse et de théologie pauliniennes.* Paris: Presses Universitaires, 1962.

―――. *L'Épître de Saint Paul aux Éphésiens.* CNT IXb. Geneva: Labor et Fides, 1991.

Böcher, Otto. "διάβολος." *EDNT* 1.297–98.

Böttrich, Christfried. "Gemeinde und Gemeindeleitung nach Epheser 4." *TBei* 30 (1999): 137–50.

Breck, John. "Biblical Chiasmus: Exploring Structure for Meaning." *BTB* 17 (1987): 70–74.

Breeze, Mary. "Hortatory Discourse in Ephesians." *JOTT* 5 (1992): 313–47.

Brouwer, Wayne. *The Literary Development of John 13–17: A Chiastic Reading.* SBLDS 182. Atlanta: Society of Biblical Literature, 2000.

Brug, J. F. "Psalm 68:19—He Received Gifts among Men." *Wisconsin Lutheran Quarterly* 96 (1999): 122–26.

Büchsel, Friedrich. " 'In Christus' bei Paulus." *ZNW* 42 (1949): 141–58.

Bühner, Jan-Adolf. "ἀπόστολος." *EDNT* 1.142–46.

Cameron, Peter Scott. "The Structure of Ephesians." *Filologia Neotestamentaria* 3 (1990): 3–17.

Campbell-Reed, E. R. "Should Wives 'Submit Graciously?' A Feminist

Approach to Interpreting Ephesians 5:21–33." *RevExp* 98 (2001): 263–76.

Caragounis, Chrys C. *The Ephesian Mysterion: Meaning and Content.* ConBNT 8. Lund, Sweden: Gleerup, 1977.

Cargal, Timothy B. "Seated in the Heavenlies: Cosmic Mediators in the Mysteries of Mithras and the Letter to the Ephesians." *SBLSP* 33 (1994): 804–21.

Carr, Wesley A. *Angels and Principalities: The Background, Meaning, and Development of the Pauline Phrase Hai Archai Kai Hai Exousiai.* SNTMS 42. Cambridge: Cambridge University Press, 1981.

Carter, Warren, and John Paul Heil. *Matthew's Parables: Audience-Oriented Perspectives.* CBQMS 30. Washington: Catholic Biblical Association, 1998.

Cassidy, Richard J. *Paul in Chains: Roman Imprisonment and the Letters of St. Paul.* New York: Crossroad, 2001.

Clark, Stephen B. *Man and Woman in Christ: An Examination of the Roles of Men and Women in Light of Scripture and the Social Sciences.* Edinburgh: Clark, 1980.

Clarke, Andrew D. "Equality or Mutuality?: Paul's Use of 'Brother' Language." Pp. 151–64 in *The New Testament in Its First Century Setting: Essays on Context and Background in Honour of B. W. Winter on His Sixty-fifth Birthday.* Edited by P. J. Williams et al. Grand Rapids: Eerdmans, 2004.

Connolly, A. L. "Standing on Sacred Ground." *New Docs* 4.105–12.

Dahl, Nils Alstrup. *Studies in Ephesians: Introductory Questions, Text- and Edition-Critical Issues, Interpretation of Texts and Themes.* Edited by David Hellholm, Vemund Blomkvist, and Tord Fornberg. WUNT 131. Tübingen: Mohr Siebeck, 2000.

Dautzenberg, Gerhard. "εὐωδία." *EDNT* 2.90–91.

Davis, John Jefferson. "Ephesians 4:12 Once More: Equipping the Saints for the Work of Ministry?" *Evangelical Review of Theology* 24 (2000): 167–76.

Dawes, Gregory W. *The Body in Question: Metaphor and Meaning in the Interpretation of Ephesians 5:21–33.* BIS 30. Leiden: Brill, 1998.

de la Potterie, Ignace. "Le Christ, Plérôme de l'Église (Ep 1,22–23)." *Bib* 58 (1977): 500–24.

Deissmann, G. Adolf. *Bible Studies: Contribution from Papyri and Inscriptions to the History of the Language, the Literature, and the Religion of Hellenistic Judaism and Primitvie Christianity.* 2d ed. Edinburgh: Clark, 1903.

Delling, Gerhard. "ὑποτάσσω." *TDNT* 8.27–48.

Denton, D. R. "Inheritance in Paul and Ephesians." *EvQ* 54 (1982): 157–62.

Dewey, Joanna. "Mark as Aural Narrative: Structures as Clues to Understanding." *Sewanee Theological Review* 36 (1992): 45–56.

Dormandy, Richard. "The Ascended Christ and His Gifts." *ExpTim* 109 (1998): 206–7.

Dudrey, Russ. " 'Submit Yourselves to One Another': A Socio-historical Look at the Household Code of Ephesians 5:15–6:9." *ResQ* 41 (1999): 27–44.

Dunn, James D. G. *The Theology of Paul the Apostle.* Grand Rapids: Eerdmans, 1998.

Dunning, Benjamin H. "Strangers and Aliens No Longer: Negotiating Identity and Difference in Ephesians 2." *HTR* 99 (2006): 1–16.

Elliger, Winfried. "ἐν." *EDNT* 1.447–49.

Ellis, E. Earle. *History and Interpretation in New Testament Perspective.* Biblical Interpretation Series 54. Atlanta: Society of Biblical Literature, 2001.

Elwell, Walter A. "Election and Predestination." *DPL*, 225–29.

Engberg-Pedersen, Troels. "Ephesians 5,12–13: ἐλέγχειν and Conversion in the New Testament." *ZNW* 80 (1989): 89–110.

Ernst, Josef. *Pleroma und Pleroma Christi: Geschichte und Deutung eines Begriffs der paulinischen Antilegomena.* Biblische Untersuchungen 5. Regensburg, Germany: Pustet, 1970.

Evans, Craig A. *Ancient Texts for New Testament Studies: A Guide to the Background Literature.* Peabody, MA: Hendrickson, 2005.

Faber, R. A. "The Juridical Nuance in the NT Use of προσωπολημψία." *WTJ* 57 (1995): 299–309.

Fatehi, Mehrdad. *The Spirit's Relation to the Risen Lord in Paul: An Examination of Its Christological Implications.* WUNT 128. Tübingen: Mohr Siebeck, 2000.

Faust, Eberhard. *Pax Christi et pax Caesaris: Religionsgeschichtliche, traditionsgeschichtliche und sozialgeschichtliche Studien zum Epheserbrief.* NTOA 24. Göttingen: Vandenhoeck & Ruprecht, 1993.

Fay, Greg. "Paul the Empowered Prisoner: Eph 3:1–13 in the Epistolary and Rhetorical Structure of Ephesians." Ph.D. diss. University of Marquette, 1994.

Fee, Gordon D. *God's Empowering Presence: The Holy Spirit in the Letters of Paul.* Peabody, MA: Hendrickson, 1994.

Finlan, Stephen. *The Background and Content of Paul's Cultic Atonement Metaphors.* SBLAbib 19. Atlanta: Society of Biblical Literature, 2004.

Fitzmyer, Joseph A. "κύριος." *EDNT* 2.328–31.

Fleckenstein, Karl-Heinz. *Ordnet euch einander unter in der Furcht Christi: Die Eheperikope in Eph 5, 21–33: Geschichte der Interpretation, Analyse und Aktualisierung des Textes.* FB 73. Würzburg: Echter, 1994.

Forbes, Chris. "Pauline Demonology and/or Cosmology? Principalities,

Powers, and the Elements of the World in their Hellenistic Context." *JSNT* 85 (2002): 51–73.

———. "Paul's Principalities and Powers: Demythologizing Apocalyptic?" *JSNT* 82 (2001): 61–88.

Foster, Paul. "The First Contribution to the πίστῖς Χριστοῦ Debate: A Study of Ephesians 3.12." *JSNT* 85 (2002): 75–96.

Foster, Robert L. " 'A Temple in the Lord Filled to the Fullness of God': Context and Intertextuality (Eph. 3:19)." *NovT* 49 (2007): 85–96.

Frankemölle, Hubert. "πραΰτης." *EDNT* 3.146–47.

Friesen, Steven J. *Twice Neokoros: Ephesus, Asia, and the Cult of the Flavian Imperial Family*. Religions in the Graeco-Roman World 116. Leiden: Brill, 1993.

Fuchs, Eric. "De la soumission des femmes: Une lecture d'Ephésiens 5, 21–33." *Supplément* 161 (1987): 73–81.

Gelardini, Gabriella. *"Verhärtet eure Herzen nicht": Der Hebräer, eine Synagogenhomilie zu Tischa be-Aw*. BIS 83. Leiden: Brill, 2007.

Gese, Michael. *Das Vermächtnis des Apostels: Die Rezeption der paulinischen Theologie im Epheserbrief*. WUNT 99. Tübingen: Mohr Siebeck, 1997.

Giavini, Giovanni. "La structure litteraire d'Eph 2:11–22." *NTS* 16 (1970): 209–11.

Giesen, Heinz. "ταπεινοφροσύνη." *EDNT* 3.333–34.

Gnilka, Joachim. *Der Epheserbrief*. HTKNT 10/2. Freiburg: Herder, 1971.

Gombis, Timothy G. "Being the Fullness of God in Christ by the Spirit: Ephesians 5:18 in Its Epistolary Setting." *TynBul* 53 (2002): 259–71.

———. "Cosmic Lordship and Divine Gift-Giving: Psalm 68 in Ephesians 4:8." *NovT* 47 (2005): 367–80.

———. "Ephesians 2 as a Narrative of Divine Warfare." *JSNT* 26 (2004): 403–18.

———. "Ephesians 3:2–13: Pointless Digression, or Epitome of the Triumph of God in Christ?" *WTJ* 66 (2004): 313–23.

Gordon, T. David. " 'Equipping' Ministry in Ephesians 4?" *JETS* 37 (1994): 69–78.

Gorman, Michael J. *Apostle of the Crucified Lord: A Theological Introduction to Paul and His Letters*. Grand Rapids: Eerdmans, 2004.

Gosnell, Peter W. "Ephesians 5:18–20 and Mealtime Propriety." *TynBul* 44 (1993): 363–71.

———. "Networks and Exchanges: Ephesians 4:7–16 and the Community Function of Teachers." *BTB* 30 (2000): 135–43.

Gräbe, Petrus J. "Salvation in Colossians and Ephesians." Pp. 287–304 in *Salvation in the New Testament: Perspectives on Soteriology*. Edited by Jan G. van der Watt. NovTSup 121. Leiden: Brill, 2005.

Grelot, Pierre. "La structure d'Éphésiens 1,3–14." *RB* 96 (1989): 193–209.

Grindheim, Sigurd. "What the OT Prophets Did Not Know: The Mystery of the Church in Eph 3,2–13." *Bib* 84 (2003): 531–53.

Gudorf, Michael E. "The Use of πάλη in Ephesians 6:12." *JBL* 117 (1998): 331–35.

Hackenberg, Wolfgang. "σκότος." *EDNT* 3.255–56.

Hammer, Paul L. "A Comparison of *Klēronomia* in Paul and Ephesians." *JBL* 79 (1960): 267–72.

Harding, Mark. "Disputed and Undisputed Letters of Paul." Pp. 129–68 in *The Pauline Canon*. Edited by Stanley E. Porter. Pauline Studies 1. Leiden: Brill, 2004.

Harland, Philip A. "Familial Dimensions of Group Identity: 'Brothers' ('Αδελφοί) in Associations of the Greek East." *JBL* 124 (2005): 491–513.

Harrill, J. Albert. *Slaves in the New Testament: Literary, Social, and Moral Dimensions*. Minneapolis: Fortress, 2006.

Harris, Murray J. *The Second Epistle to the Corinthians: A Commentary on the Greek Text*. NIGTC. Grand Rapids: Eerdmans, 2005.

Harris, W. Hall. "The Ascent and Descent of Christ in Ephesians 4:9–10." *BSac* 151 (1994): 198–214.

———. *The Descent of Christ: Ephesians 4:7–11 and Traditional Hebrew Imagery*. AGJU 32. Leiden: Brill, 1996.

———. " 'The Heavenlies' Reconsidered: Οὐρανός and 'Επουράνιος in Ephesians." *BSac* 148 (1991): 72–89.

Harrison, James R. *Paul's Language of Grace in Its Graeco-Roman Context*. WUNT 172. Tübingen: Mohr Siebeck, 2003.

Harrisville, Roy A. "The Concept of Newness in the New Testament." *JBL* 74 (1955): 69–79.

Hartin, Patrick J. "ἀνακεφαλαιώσασθαι τὰ πάντα ἐν τῷ Χριστῷ (Eph 1:10)." Pp. 228–37 in *A South African Perspective on the New Testament: Essays by South African New Testament Scholars Presented to Bruce Manning Metzger during His Visit to South Africa in 1985*. Edited by J. H. Petzer and Patrick J. Hartin. Leiden: Brill, 1986.

Harvey, John D. *Listening to the Text: Oral Patterning in Paul's Letters*. Grand Rapids: Baker, 1998.

Hay, David M. *Glory at the Right Hand: Psalm 110 in Early Christianity*. SBLMS 18. Nashville: Abingdon, 1973.

Hearon, Holly E. "The Implications of Orality for Studies of the Biblical Text." Pp. 3–20 in *Performing the Gospel: Orality, Memory, and Mark. Essays Dedicated to Werner Kelber*. Edited by Richard A. Horsley, Jonathan A. Draper, and John Miles Foley. Minneapolis: Fortress, 2006.

Heckel, Theo K. "Juden und Heiden im Epheserbrief." Pp. 176–94 in *Kirche und Volk Gottes: Festschrift für Jürgen Roloff zum 70. Geburtstag*. Edited by Martin Karrer, Wolfgang Kraus, and Otto Merk. Neukirchen-Vluyn: Neukirchener Verlag, 2000.

Heil, John Paul. "The Chiastic Structure and Meaning of Paul's Letter to Philemon." *Bib* 82 (2001): 178–206.

———. "Ephesians 5:18b: 'But Be Filled in the Spirit.' " *CBQ* 69 (2007): 506–16.

———. *The Meal Scenes in Luke-Acts: An Audience-Oriented Approach.* SBLMS 52. Atlanta: Society of Biblical Literature, 1999.

———. *The Rhetorical Role of Scripture in 1 Corinthians.* Studies in Biblical Literature 15. Atlanta: Society of Biblical Literature, 2005.

———. "Those Now 'Asleep' (Not Dead) Must Be 'Awakened' for the Day of the Lord in 1 Thess 5.9–10." *NTS* 46 (2000): 464–71.

———. *The Transfiguration of Jesus: Narrative Meaning and Function of Mark 9:2–8, Matt 17:1–8 and Luke 9:28–36.* Anbib 144. Rome: Biblical Institute, 2000.

Helton, S. N. "Ephesians 5:21: A Longer Translation Note." *ResQ* 48 (2006): 33–41.

Hendrix, Holland. "On the Form and Ethos of Ephesians." *USQR* 42 (1988): 3–15.

Hoehner, Harold W. *Ephesians: An Exegetical Commentary.* Grand Rapids: Baker, 2002.

Hofius, Otfried. " 'Erwählt vor Grundlegung der Welt' (Eph. 1.4)." *ZNW* 62 (1971): 123–28.

Hollander, Harm W. "μακροθυμία." *EDNT* 2.380–81.

Hoppe, Rudolf. "Theo-logie und Ekklesio-logie im Epheserbrief." *MTZ* 46 (1995): 231–45.

Horrell, David G. "From ἀδελφοί to οἶκος θεοῦ: Social Transformation in Pauline Christianity." *JBL* 120 (2001): 293–311.

Howard, George. "The Head/Body Metaphors of Ephesians." *NTS* 20 (1974): 350–56.

Hübner, Hans. "ἀλήθεια." *EDNT* 1.57–60.

Hutter, Ulrich. "πατρία." *EDNT* 3.57–58.

Infante, Renzo. "Immagine nuziale e tensione escatologica nel Nuovo Testamento: Note a 2 Cor. 11,2 e Eph. 5,25–27." *RivB* 33 (1985): 45–61.

Janzen, G. "Divine Warfare and Nonresistance." *Direction* 32 (2003): 21–31.

Jayne, Donald. " 'We' and 'You' in Ephesians 1,3–14." *ExpTim* 85 (1974): 151–52.

Jeal, Roy R. *Integrating Theology and Ethics in Ephesians: The Ethos of Communication.* Studies in Bible and Early Christianity 43. Lewiston, NY: Mellen, 2000.

———. "A Strange Style of Expression: Ephesians 1:23." *Filología Neotestamentaria* 10 (1997): 129–38.

Johnston, William J. *The Use of* Πᾶς *in the New Testament*. Studies in Biblical Greek 11. New York: Lang, 2004.

Joosten, J. "Christ a-t-il aboli la loi pour réconcilier juifs et païens?" *ETR* 80 (2005): 95–102.

Kamlah, Ehrhard. "Ὑποτάσσεσθαι in den neutestamentlichen 'Haustafeln.' " Pp. 237–43 in *Verborum Veritas: Festschrift für Gustav Stählin zum 70. Geburtstag*. Edited by Otto Böcher and Klaus Haacker. Wuppertal, Germany: Brockhaus, 1970.

Keener, Craig S. *Paul, Women, and Wives: Marriage and Women's Ministry in the Letters of Paul*. Peabody, MA: Hendrickson, 1992.

Kim, Jung Hoon. *The Significance of Clothing Imagery in the Pauline Corpus*. JSNTSup 268. London: Clark, 2004.

Kirby, John C. *Ephesians, Baptism, and Pentecost: An Inquiry into the Structure and Purpose of the Epistle to the Ephesians*. Montreal: McGill University Press, 1968.

Kittredge, Cynthia Briggs. *Community and Authority: The Rhetoric of Obedience in the Pauline Tradition*. HTS 45. Harrisburg, PA: Trinity Press International, 1998.

Koester, Helmut, ed. *Ephesos: Metropolis of Asia. An Interdisciplinary Approach to Its Archaeololgy, Religion, and Culture*. HTS 41. Valley Forge, PA: Trinity Press International, 1995.

Korting, Georg. "Das Partizip in Eph 1,23." *TGl* 87 (1997): 260–65.

Kourie, Celia E. T. "In Christ and Related Expressions in Paul." *Theologia Evangelica* 20 (1987): 33–43.

Köstenberger, Andreas J. "The Mystery of Christ and the Church: Head and Body, 'One Flesh.' " *TJ* 12 (1991): 79–94.

———. "What Does It Mean to Be Filled with the Spirit? A Biblical Investigation." *JETS* 40 (1997): 229–40.

Kreitzer, Larry Joseph. " 'Crude Language' and 'Shameful Things Done in Secret' (Ephesians 5.4, 12): Allusions to the Cult of Demeter/Cybele in Hierapolis?" *JSNT* 71 (1998): 51–77.

———. "The Plutonium of Hierapolis and the Descent of Christ into the 'Lowermost Parts of the Earth' (Ephesians 4,9)." *Bib* 79 (1998): 381–93.

Kuhli, Horst. "οἰκονομία." *EDNT* 2.498–500.

Lang, Friedrich Gustav. "Ebenmass im Epheserbrief: Stichometrische Kompositionsanalyse." *NovT* 46 (2004): 143–63.

Lee, Aquila H. I. *From Messiah to Preexistent Son: Jesus' Self-Consciousness and Early Christian Exegesis of Messianic Psalms*. WUNT 2/192. Tübingen: Mohr Siebeck, 2005.

Lemmer, H. Richard. "Reciprocity between Eschatology and Pneuma in Ephesians 1:3–14." *Neot* 21 (1987): 159–82.

———. "ἡ οἰκονομία τοῦ μυστηρίου τοῦ ἀποκεκρυμμένου ἐν τῷ θεῷ—Understanding 'Body of Christ' in the Letter to the Ephesians." *Neot* 32 (1998): 459–95.

Leyrer, D. P. "Ephesians 1:23—The 'Fullness' of Ascension Comfort." *Wisconsin Lutheran Quarterly* 99 (2002): 135–37.

———. "Exegetical Brief: Ephesians 2:16—To What Does 'One Body' Refer?" *Wisconsin Lutheran Quarterly* 100 (2003): 203–5.

Lieu, Judith M. " 'Grace to You and Peace': The Apostolic Greeting." *BJRL* 68 (1985): 161–78.

Lincoln, Andrew T. "The Church and Israel in Ephesians 2." *CBQ* 49 (1987): 605–24.

———. *Ephesians*. WBC 42. Dallas: Word Books, 1990.

———. "Ephesians 2:8–10: A Summary of Paul's Gospel?" *CBQ* 45 (1983): 617–30.

———. " 'Stand, Therefore . . .': Ephesians 6:10–20 as *Peroratio*." *BibInt* 3 (1995): 99–114.

Loader, W. R. G. "Christ at the Right Hand—Ps. CX.1 in the New Testament." *NTS* 24 (1978): 199–217.

Lona, Horacio E. *Die Eschatologie im Kolosser- und Epheserbrief*. FB 48. Würzburg, Germany: Echter, 1984.

Longenecker, Bruce W. *Rhetoric at the Boundaries: The Art and Theology of the New Testament Chain-Link Transitions*. Waco, TX: Baylor University Press, 2005.

Lortz, Stephen L. "The Literal Interpretation of Ephesians 3:6 and Related Scriptures." *Journal from the Radical Reformation* 8 (1999): 5–12.

Lotz, John Paul. "The *Homonoia* Coins of Asia Minor and Ephesians 1:21." *TynBul* 50 (1999): 173–88.

Louw, Johannes P. "A Discourse Reading of Ephesians 1.3–14." Pp. 308–15 in *Discourse Analysis and the New Testament: Approaches and Results*. Edited by Stanley E. Porter and Jeffrey T. Reed. JSNTSup 170. Sheffield: Sheffield Academic Press, 1999.

Luter, A. Boyd. "Grace." *DPL*, 372–74.

Luter, A. Boyd, and Michelle V. Lee. "Philippians as Chiasmus: Key to the Structure, Unity, and Theme Questions." *NTS* 41 (1995): 89–101.

MacDonald, Margaret Y. *Colossians and Ephesians*. SP 17. Collegeville, MN: Liturgical Press, 2000.

———. "Was Celsus Right? The Role of Women in the Expansion of Early Christianity." Pp. 157–84 in *Early Christian Families in Context: An Interdisciplinary Dialogue*. Edited by David L. Balch and Carolyn Osiek. Grand Rapids: Eerdmans, 2003.

———. "The Politics of Identity in Ephesians." *JSNT* 26 (2004): 419–44.

Mahoney, Robert. "εὐδοκία." *EDNT* 2.75–76.

Malan, François S. "Church Singing according to the Pauline Epistles." *Neot* 32 (1998): 509–24.

————. "Unity of Love in the Body of Christ: Identity, Ethics, and Ethos in Ephesians." Pp. 257–302 in *Identity, Ethics, and Ethos in the New Testament*. Ed. Jan G. van der Watt. BZNW 141. Berlin: De Gruyter, 2006.

Man, Ronald E. "The Value of Chiasm for New Testament Interpretation." *BibSac* 141 (1984): 146–57.

Marshall, I. Howard. " 'For the Husband Is Head of the Wife': Paul's Use of Head and Body Language." Pp. 165–77 in *The New Testament in Its First Century Setting: Essays on Context and Background in Honour of B. W. Winter on His Sixty-fifth Birthday*. Edited by P. J. Williams et al. Grand Rapids: Eerdmans, 2004.

Mayer, Annemarie C. *Sprache der Einheit im Epheserbrief und in der Ökumene*. WUNT 2/150. Tübingen: Mohr Siebeck, 2002.

McKay, Kenneth L. "Aspect in Imperatival Constructions in New Testament Greek." *NovT* 27 (1985): 201–26.

————. *A New Syntax of the Verb in New Testament Greek: An Aspectual Approach*. Studies in Biblical Greek 5. New York: Lang, 1994.

McKelvey, R. J. *The New Temple: The Church in the New Testament*. Oxford: Oxford University Press, 1969.

McVay, J. K. " 'Our Struggle': *Ecclesia Militans* in Ephesians 6:10–20." *AUSS* 43 (2005): 91–100.

Mehlmann, Ioannes. "Ἀνεξιχνίαστος = Investigabilis (Rom 11,33; Eph 3,8)." *Bib* 40 (1959): 902–14.

Melbourne, B. L. "Ephesians 2:13–16: Are the Barriers Still Broken Down?" *JRT* 57 (2005): 107–19.

Merklein, Helmut. "ἀνακεφαλαιόω." *EDNT* 1.82–83.

————. *Das kirchliche Amt nach dem Epheserbrief*. SANT 33. Munich: Kösel, 1973.

Metzger, Bruce Manning. *A Textual Commentary on the Greek New Testament: Second Edition*. Stuttgart: Deutsche Bibelgesellschaft, 1994.

Meyer, Annegret. "Biblische Metaphorik—Gesellschaftlicher Diskurs: Rezeptionsästhetische Betrachtung über die Wirkung von Metaphern am Beispiel Eph 5, 21–33." *TGl* 90 (2000): 645–65.

Michel, Otto. "πατήρ." *EDNT* 3.53–57.

Miletic, Stephen Francis. *"One Flesh": Eph. 5.22–24, 5.31. Marriage and the New Creation*. AnBib 115. Rome: Biblical Institute, 1988.

Montagnini, Felice. "Echi de parenesi cultuale in Ef 4,25–32." *RivB* 37 (1989): 257–82.

Moritz, Thorsten. " 'Summing Up All Things': Religious Pluralism and Universalism in Ephesians." Pp. 88–111 in *One God, One Lord: Christianity in a World of Religious Pluralism*. Edited by Andrew D. Clarke and Bruce W. Winter. Grand Rapids: Baker, 1992.

————. *A Profound Mystery: The Use of the Old Testament in Ephesians*. NovTSup 85. Leiden: Brill, 1996.

————. "Reasons for Ephesians." *Evangel* 14 (1996): 8–14.

Moser, Paul K. "Apostle." Pp. 78–79 in *Eerdmans Dictionary of the Bible*. Edited by David Noel Freedman. Grand Rapids: Eerdmans, 2000.

Mouton, Elna. "The Communicative Power of the Epistle to the Ephesians." Pp. 280–307 in *Rhetoric, Scripture, and Theology: Essays from the 1994 Pretoria Conference*. Edited by Stanley E. Porter and Thomas H. Olbricht. JSNTSup 131. Sheffield: Sheffield Academic Press, 1996.

————. *Reading a New Testament Document Ethically*. SBLAbib 1. Atlanta: Society of Biblical Literature, 2002.

Muddiman, John. *A Commentary on the Epistle to the Ephesians*. BNTC. London: Continuum, 2001.

Muraoka, Takamitsu. *A Greek-English Lexicon of the Septuagint: Chiefly of the Pentateuch and the Twelve Prophets*. Louvain: Peeters, 2002.

Mussies, Gerard. "Artemis." *DDD*, 91–97.

Müller, Markus. *Vom Schluß zum Ganzen: Zur Bedeutung des paulinischen Briefkorpusabschlusses*. FRLANT 172. Göttingen: Vandenhoeck & Ruprecht, 1997.

Neufeld, Thomas R. Yoder. *"Put on the Armour of God": The Divine Warrior from Isaiah to Ephesians*. JSNTSup 140. Sheffield: Sheffield Academic Press, 1997.

Neugebauer, Fritz. "Das Paulinische 'In Christo.' " *NTS* 4 (1957–58): 124–38.

Newman, Carey C. "Election and Predestination in Ephesians 1:4–6a: An Exegetical-Theological Study of the Historical, Christological Realization of God's Purpose." *RevExp* 93 (1996): 237–47.

Nobbs, Alanna. " 'Beloved Brothers' in the New Testament and Early Christian World." Pp. 143–50 in *The New Testament in Its First Century Setting: Essays on Context and Background in Honour of B. W. Winter on His Sixty-fifth Birthday*. Edited by P. J. Williams et al. Grand Rapids: Eerdmans, 2004.

Nolland, John. "Grace as Power." *NovT* 28 (1986): 26–31.

Nortjé, Lilly. "The Meaning of ἄνδρα τέλειον in Ephesians 4:13: A Full-Grown Person, as Perfect and Mature as Christ." *Ekklesiastikos Pharos* 77 (1995): 57–63.

O'Brien, Peter Thomas. "Ephesians 1: An Unusual Introduction to a New Testament Letter." *NTS* 25 (1978): 504–16.

————. *The Letter to the Ephesians*. Grand Rapids: Eerdmans, 1999.

————. "Principalities and Powers: Opponents of the Church." Pp. 110–50 in *Biblical Interpretation and the Church: Text and Context*. Edited by Donald A. Carson. Exeter, England: Paternoster, 1984.

————. "The Summing Up of All Things (Ephesians 1:10)." Pp. 206–19 in *The New Testament in Its First Century Setting: Essays on Context and Background in Honour of B. W. Winter on His Sixty-fifth Birthday*. Edited by P. J. Williams et al. Grand Rapids: Eerdmans, 2004.

O'Neill, John C. " 'The Work of the Ministry' in Ephesians 4:12 and the New Testament." *ExpTim* 112 (2001): 336–40.

Ollrog, Wolf-Henning. *Paulus und seine Mitarbeiter: Untersuchungen zu Theorie und Praxis der paulinischen Mission.* WMANT 50. Neukirchen-Vluyn: Neukirchener Verlag, 1979.

Ortlund, Raymond C. *Whoredom: God's Unfaithful Wife in Biblical Theology.* New Studies in Biblical Theology 2. Grand Rapids: Eerdmans, 1996.

Osiek, Carolyn. "The Bride of Christ (Ephesians 5:22–33): A Problematic Wedding." *BTB* 32 (2002): 29–39.

———. "Female Slaves, *Porneia*, and the Limits of Obedience." Pp. 255–74 in *Early Christian Families in Context: An Interdisciplinary Dialogue.* Edited by David L. Balch and Carolyn Osiek. Grand Rapids: Eerdmans, 2003.

Oster, Richard E. "Holy Days in Honour of Artemis." *New Docs* 4.74–82.

Page, Sydney H. T. "Whose Ministry? A Re-appraisal of Ephesians 4:12." *NovT* 47 (2005): 26–46.

Patsch, Hermann. "εὐχαριστέω." *EDNT* 1.87–88.

Pelser, Gert M. M. "Once More the Body of Christ in Paul." *Neot* 32 (1998): 525–45.

Perkins, Pheme. *Ephesians.* ANTC. Nashville: Abingdon, 1997.

Perriman, Andrew C. " 'His Body, Which Is the Church . . .': Coming to Terms with Metaphor." *EvQ* 62 (1990): 123–42.

Porsch, Felix. "ἐλέγχω," *EDNT* 1.427–28.

Porter, Stanley E. "ἴστε γινώσκοντες in Ephesians 5,5: Does Chiasm Solve a Problem?" *ZNW* 81 (1990): 270–76.

———. "Holiness, Sanctification." *DPL*, 397–402.

———. *Verbal Aspect in the Greek of the New Testament, with Reference to Tense and Mood.* Studies in Biblical Greek 1. New York: Lang, 1993.

Porter, Stanley E., and Jeffrey T. Reed. "Philippians as a Macro-Chiasm and Its Exegetical Significance." *NTS* 44 (1998): 213–31.

Qualls, Paula, and John D. W. Watts. "Isaiah in Ephesians." *RevExp* 93 (1996): 249–59.

Radl, Walter. "μετά." *EDNT* 2.413–14.

Reicke, Bo. *Re-examining Paul's Letters: The History of the Pauline Correspondence.* Harrisburg, PA: Trinity Press International, 2001.

Reynier, Chantal. "La bénédiction en Éphésiens 1,3–14: Élection, filiation, rédemption." *NRTh* 118 (1996): 182–99.

Richards, E. Randolph. *Paul and First-Century Letter Writing: Secretaries, Composition, and Collection.* Downers Grove, IL: InterVarsity, 2004.

———. *The Secretary in the Letters of Paul.* WUNT 42. Tübingen: Mohr Siebeck, 1991.

Ritz, Hans-Joachim. "βουλή." *EDNT* 1.224–25.

Robbins, Charles J. "The Composition of Eph 1:3–14." *JBL* 105 (1986): 677–87.

Robinson, J. Armitage. *St. Paul's Epistle to the Ephesians: A Revised Text and Translation with Exposition and Notes.* London: Macmillan, 1904.

Rodgers, Peter R. "The Allusion to Genesis 2:23 at Ephesians 5:30." *JTS* 41 (1990): 92–94.

Rogers, Cleon L. "The Dionysian Background of Ephesians 5:18." *BSac* 136 (1979): 249–57.

Romanello, Stefano. "Ef 1,3–14: Una pericope discussa." *RivB* 50 (2002): 31–62.

Roose, Hanna. "Die Hierarchisierung der Leib-Metapher im Kolosser- und Epheserbrief als 'Paulinisierung': Ein Beitrag zur Rezeption paulinischer Tradition in Pseudo-Paulinischen Briefen." *NovT* 47 (2005): 117–41.

Rosscup, James E. "The Importance of Prayer in Ephesians." *Master's Seminary Journal* 6 (1995): 57–78.

Sampley, J. Paul. "Scripture and Tradition in the Community as Seen in Ephesians 4:25ff." *ST* 26 (1972): 101–9.

Sand, Alexander. "ἀρραβών." *EDNT* 1.57–58.

———. "ἐπαγγελία." *EDNT* 2.13–16.

———. "καρδία." *EDNT* 2.249–51.

Saunders, Ross. "Paul and the Imperial Cult." Pp. 227–38 in *Paul and His Opponents.* Edited by Stanley E. Porter. Pauline Studies 2. Leiden: Brill, 2005.

Schenk, Wolfgang. "προσφορά." *EDNT* 3.178.

Schlier, Heinrich. *Der Brief an die Epheser: Ein Kommentar.* Düsseldorf: Patmos, 1968.

Schnabel, Eckhard J. "Die ersten Christen in Ephesus: Neuerscheinungen zur frühchristlichen Missionsgeschichte." *NovT* 41 (1999): 349–82.

Schnackenburg, Rudolf. *Ephesians: A Commentary.* Edinburgh: Clark, 1991.

Schneider, Gerhard. "ἀποτίθεμαι." *EDNT* 1.146.

———. "δῶρον." *EDNT* 1.365.

Schwindt, Rainer. "Die Bitte um Gottes Gaben als Mitte christlicher Existenz: Zur Theologie des Epheserbriefes." *TTZ* 111 (2002): 42–61.

———. *Das Weltbild des Epheserbriefes: Eine religionsgeschichtlich-exegetische Studie.* WUNT 148. Tübingen: Mohr Siebeck, 2002.

Scott, James M. *Adoption as Sons of God: An Exegetical Investigation Into the Background of ΥΙΟΘΕΣΙΑ in the Pauline Corpus.* WUNT 48. Tübingen: Mohr, 1992.

Seifrid, Mark A. "In Christ." *DPL*, 433–36.

Seim, Turid Karlsen. "A Superior Minority? The Problem of Men's Headship in Ephesians 5." *ST* 49 (1995): 167–81.

Sellin, Gerhard. "Adresse und Intention des Epheserbriefes." Pp. 171–86 in *Paulus, Apostel Jesu Christi: Festschrift für Günter Klein zum 70 Geburtstag*. Edited by Michael Trowitzsch. Tübingen: Mohr Siebeck, 1998.

———. "Über einige ungewöhnliche Genitive im Epheserbrief." *ZNW* 83 (1992): 85–107.

Serra, Aristide M. "La 'spada': Simbolo della 'Parola di Dio,' nell'Antico Testamento biblico-giudaico e nel Nuovo Testamento." *Marianum* 63 (2001): 17–89.

Shiell, William David. *Reading Acts: The Lector and the Early Christian Audience*. BIS 70. Boston: Brill, 2004.

Shiner, Whitney Taylor. "Memory Technology and the Composition of Mark." Pp. 147–65 in *Performing the Gospel: Orality, Memory, and Mark. Essays Dedicated to Werner Kelber*. Edited by Richard A. Horsley, Johathan A. Draper, and John Miles Foley. Minneapolis: Fortress, 2006.

———. *Proclaiming the Gospel: First Century Performance of Mark*. Harrisburg, PA: Trinity Press International, 2003.

Slater, Thomas B. "Translating ἅγιος in Col 1,2 and Eph 1,1." *Bib* 87 (2006): 52–54.

Smillie, Gene R. "Ephesians 6:19–20: A Mystery for the Sake of Which the Apostle is an Ambassador in Chains." *TJ* 18 (1997): 199–222.

Smith, Derwood C. "Cultic Language in Ephesians 2:19–22: A Test Case." *ResQ* 31 (1989): 207–17.

Snodgrass, Klyne R. *Ephesians: The NIV Application Commentary*. Grand Rapids: Zondervan, 1996.

Spicq, Ceslas. *Theological Lexicon of the New Testament*. Translated and edited by James D. Ernest. 3 vols. Peabody, MA: Hendrickson, 1994.

Steinmetz, Franz-Josef. *Protologische Heils-Zuversicht: Die Sturkturen des soteriologischen und christologischen Denkens im Kolosser- und Epheserbrief*. Frankfurter Theologische Studien 2. Frankfurt: Knecht, 1969.

Stirewalt, Luther M. *Paul: The Letter Writer*. Grand Rapids: Eerdmans, 2003.

Stock, Augustine. "Chiastic Awareness and Education in Antiquity." *BTB* 14 (1984): 23–27.

Stott, John R. W. *The Message of Ephesians: God's New Society*. Leicester, England: Inter-Varsity, 1979.

Strelan, Rick. *Paul, Artemis, and the Jews in Ephesus*. BZNW 80. Berlin: De Gruyter, 1996.

Stuhlmacher, Peter. " 'He Is Our Peace' (Eph. 2:14): On the Exegesis and Significance of Eph. 2:14–18." Pp. 182–200 in *Reconciliation, Law, and Righteousness*. Philadelphia: Fortress, 1986.

Taylor, Richard A. "The Use of Psalm 68:18 in Ephesians 4:8 in Light of the Ancient Versions." *BSac* 148 (1991): 319–36.

Thomson, Ian H. *Chiasmus in the Pauline Letters.* JSNTSup 111. Sheffield: Sheffield Academic Press, 1995.

Thyen, Hartwig. "θυσία." *EDNT* 2.161–63.

Toews, J. E. "Paul's Radical Vision for the Family." *Direction* 19 (1990): 29–38.

Tolmie, D. Francois. *Persuading the Galatians: A Text-Centered Rhetorical Analysis of a Pauline Letter.* WUNT 190. Tübingen: Mohr Siebeck, 2005.

Turner, Nigel. *A Grammar of New Testament Greek.* Edinburgh: Clark, 1976.

———. "The Preposition ἐν in the New Testament." *BT* 10 (1959): 113–20.

Ubieta, Carmen Bernabé. "Neither *Xenoi* nor *Paroikoi, Sympolitai,* and *Oikeioi Tou Theou* (Eph 2:19) Pauline Christian Communities: Defining a New Territoriality." Pp. 260–80 in *Social Scientific Models for Interpreting the Bible: Essays by the Context Group in Honor of Bruce J. Malina.* Edited by John J. Pilch. BIS 53. Leiden: Brill, 2001.

Usami, Kôshi. *Somatic Comprehension of Unity: The Church in Ephesus.* Anbib 101. Rome: Biblical Institute, 1983.

van der Horst, Pieter Willem. "Is Wittiness Unchristian? A Note on εὐτραπελία in Eph. v 4." Pp. 163–77 in *Miscellanea Neotestamentica,* vol. 2. Edited by T. Baarda, A. F. J. Klijn, and W. C. van Unnik. NovTSup 48. Leiden: Brill, 1978.

———. "Observations on a Pauline Expression." *NTS* 19 (1973): 181–87.

van Kooten, George H. *Cosmic Christology in Paul and the Pauline School: Colossians and Ephesians in the Context of Graeco-Roman Cosmology, with a New Synopsis of the Greek Texts.* WUNT 2/171. Tübingen: Mohr Siebeck, 2003.

Völkel, Martin. "λουτρόν." *EDNT* 2.361.

Walden, W. "Ephesians 5:21: A Translation Note." *ResQ* 45 (2003): 254.

———. "Translating Ephesians 5:21." *ResQ* 47 (2005): 179–82.

Wall, Robert W. "Wifely Submission in the Context of Ephesians." *Christian Scholar's Review* 17 (1988): 272–85.

Wallace, Daniel B. "ΟΡΓΙΖΕΣΘΕ in Ephesians 4:26: Command or Condition?" *CTR* 3 (1989): 353–72.

———. *Greek Grammar beyond the Basics: An Exegetical Syntax of the New Testament.* Grand Rapids: Zondervan, 1996.

Walter, Nikolaus. "ἔσω." *EDNT* 2. 64–65.

Watson, Francis. *Paul and the Hermeneutics of Faith.* London: Clark, 2004.

Weber, Beat. " 'Setzen'-'Wandeln'-'Stehen' im Epheserbrief." *NTS* 41 (1995): 478–80.

Wedderburn, A. J. M. "Some Observations on Paul's Use of the Phrases 'in Christ' and 'with Christ.' " *JSNT* 25 (1985): 83–97.

Weima, Jeffrey A. D. *Neglected Endings: The Significance of the Pauline Letter Closings.* JSNTSup 101. Sheffield: JSOT, 1994.

———. "The Pauline Letter Closings: Analysis and Hermeneutical Significance." *BBR* 5 (1995): 177–98.

Weiser, Alfons. "διάκονος." *EDNT* 1.302–4.

Welch, John W. "Chiasmus in the New Testament." Pp. 211–49 in *Chiasmus in Antiquity: Structures, Analyses, Exegesis.* Edited by John W. Welch. Hildesheim, Germany: Gerstenberg, 1981.

———. "Criteria for Identifying and Evaluating the Presence of Chiasmus." Pp. 157–74 in *Chiasmus Bibliography.* Edited by John W. Welch and Daniel B. McKinlay. Provo, UT: Research, 1999.

Wells, P. "La famille chrétienne à l'image de Christ: Une étude d'Ephésiens 5:22 à 6:4." *RRef* 38 (1987): 11–23.

Wendland, Ernst R. "Contextualising the Potentates, Principalities, and Powers in the Epistle to the Ephesians." *Neot* 33 (1999): 199–223.

Werbick, Jürgen. "Ein Opfer zur Versöhnung der zürnenden Gottheit? Über die Zwiespältigkeit eines soteriologischen Denkmodells." *BK* 49 (1994): 144–49.

Wessels, G. F. "Ephesians 5:21–33: 'Wives, Be Subject to Your Husbands . . . Husbands, Love Your Wives . . .'" *JTSA* 67 (1989): 67–76.

Westerholm, Stephen. *Perspectives Old and New on Paul: The "Lutheran" Paul and His Critics.* Grand Rapids: Eerdmans, 2004.

Wevers, John William. *Notes on the Greek Text of Exodus.* SBLSCS 30. Atlanta: Scholars Press, 1990.

———. *Notes on the Greek Text of Deuteronomy.* SBLSCS 39. Atlanta: Scholars Press, 1995.

Whitlark, Jason. "Enabling Χάρις: Transformation of the Convention of Reciprocity by Philo and in Ephesians." *PRSt* 30 (2003): 325–57.

Wild, Robert A. "The Warrior and the Prisoner: Some Reflections on Ephesians 6:10–20." *CBQ* 46 (1984): 284–98.

Wilder, Terry L. *Pseudonymity, the New Testament, and Deception: An Inquiry into Intention and Reception.* Lanham, MD: University Press of America, 2004.

Williams, David J. *Paul's Metaphors: Their Context and Character.* Peabody, MA: Hendrickson, 1999.

Wilson, R. A. " 'We' and 'You' in the Epistle to the Ephesians." Pp. 676–80 in *Papers Presented to the Second International Congress on New Testament Studies Held at Christ Church Oxford, 1961.* Edited by Frank Leslie Cross. TU 87. Berlin: Akademie, 1964.

Wink, Walter. *Naming the Powers: The Language of Power in the New Testament.* Philadelphia: Fortress, 1984.

Witherington, Ben. *Letters and Homilies for Hellenized Christians.* Vol. 1:

A Socio-Rhetorical Commentary on Titus, 1–2 Timothy, and 1–3 John.
Downers Grove, IL: InterVarsity, 2006.

Witulski, Thomas. "Gegenwart und Zukunft in den eschatologischen Konzeptionen des Kolosser- und Epheserbriefes." *ZNW* 96 (2005): 211–42.

Yates, Roy. "A Re-examination of Ephesians 1:23." *ExpTim* 83 (1972): 146–51.

Yee, Tet-Lim N. *Jews, Gentiles, and Ethnic Reconciliation: Paul's Jewish Identity and Ephesians.* SNTSMS 130. Cambridge: Cambridge University Press, 2005.

Zerwick, Maximilian. *Biblical Greek.* Rome: Biblical Institute, 1963.

Zmijewski, Josef. "καυχάομαι." *EDNT* 2.276–79.

———. "χρηστότης." *EDNT* 3.475–77.

Scripture Index

Old Testament

Genesis
2:24   250 n. 47, 251, 251 n. 51, 252 n. 52
15:7–21   113 n. 10
17:1–21   113 n. 10
17:5   86 n. 23
17:9–14   111 n. 6
26:2–5   113 n. 10
28:13–15   113 n. 10
32:28   86 n. 23

Exodus
19:6   49 n. 9
20:4–6   258 n. 66
20:4   258 n. 66
20:5–6   98 n. 14
20:5   258 n. 66
20:6   258 n. 66
20:12 (LXX)   257, 257 n. 64, 258 n. 66
24:1–8   113 n. 10
29:37–38   60 n. 14
33:12–14   200 n. 39
34:6–7   98 n. 14

Leviticus
11:44   49 n. 9
12:3   111 n. 6
19:2   49 n. 9
19:11   198 n. 32
21:16–24   60 n. 14

Numbers
14:18–19   98 n. 14

Deuteronomy
4:27 (LXX)   61 n. 17
4:37   61 n. 17
5:16 (LXX)   257, 257 n. 64
7:9–10   98 n. 14
7:7–8 (LXX)   61 n. 17
10:15   61 n. 17
24:15   197
28:49   115 n. 19
29:22   115 n. 19
32:4 (LXX)   195, 202

2 Samuel
7   113 n. 10

1 Kings
8:41   115 n. 19

Psalms
2   62 n. 19
4:5   197 n. 29
4:5a (LXX)   197
8:7   87, 87 n. 25, 87 n. 26
15:2   60 n. 14
18:23   60 n. 14
40:6 (LXX 39:7)   209 n. 7
46:5 (LXX)   61 n. 17
62:10 (LXX)   174 n. 29
68:18   172, 172 n. 25, 173 n. 25
77:68 (LXX)   61 n. 17
78:2   292 n. 28
110   86 n. 24
110:1   85, 85 n. 22, 87, 87 n. 25
118:22   128 n. 60
144:17 (LXX)   195, 202
147:4   86 n. 23, 151 n. 4

337

PSALMS (cont'd)
148:14   115 n. 19

PROVERBS
23:31 (LXX)   233 n. 9

ISAIAH
5:26   115 n. 19
8:14   128 n. 60
11:4–5 (LXX)   284 n. 4
11:4 (LXX)   288 n. 17
11:5   284 n. 5, 285 n. 5, 288 n. 17
26:19   225 n. 17
28:16 (LXX)   128 n. 60
40:26   151 n. 4
43:21   72 n. 50
49:2   285 n. 5
52:7   124 n. 51, 285 n. 5, 286 n. 9
57:19   115 n. 19, 124 n. 51
59:17   284, 284 n. 5, 285 n. 5, 288
      n. 15
60:1   225 n. 17
63:10   200 n. 39

JEREMIAH
5:15   115 n. 19
17:17   277 n. 25
17:18   277 n. 25

EZEKIEL
3:27   292 n. 28
16:8–14   246 n. 40
16:9   246 n. 40
16:10–14   247 n. 43
33:22   292 n. 28

DANIEL
10:16   292 n. 28
12:1   277 n. 25

OBADIAH
13   277 n. 25

MICAH
2:1   286 n. 9

ZECHARIAH
8:16 (LXX)   196 n. 25
8:16–17   196 n. 25

MALACHI
3:17   72, 72 n. 50

WISDOM OF SOLOMON
5:18   284, 284 n. 5

New Testament

MARK
12:10   128 n. 60

LUKE
15:13   234 n. 12
17:16   80 n. 9
20:17   128 n. 60
20:18   128 n. 60

ACTS
1:8   152 n. 7
4:11   128 n. 60
16:1–3   9
20:4   296 n. 37
20:19   168 n. 9

ROMANS
1:4   152 n. 7
1:11   198 n. 33
1:18–32   214 n. 18
1:25   212 n. 14
2:7   306 n. 10
5:2   125 n. 51
6:6   193 n. 15
8:8   97 n. 11
8:24   82 n. 15
8:29   62 n. 19, 297 n. 38
8:30   62 n. 19
9:32   128 n. 60
9:33   128 n. 60
10:17   289 n. 19
11:33   143 n. 25
11:36   171 n. 20
12:8   198 n. 33
13:11–14   226 n. 19
14:20   106 n. 35
15:19   152 n. 7
16:4   89 n. 9

I CORINTHIANS
2:3   262 n. 73

Other Literature

Author Index

Johnston, William J., 128 n. 61, 150 n. 4
Joosten J., 119 n. 35

Kamlah, Ehrhard, 240 n. 24
Keener, Craig S., 241 n. 26, 262 n. 72
Kim, Jung Hoon, 193 n. 13, 194 n. 19
Kirby, John C., 23 n. 15
Kittredge, Cynthia Briggs, 39 n. 24
Koester, Helmut, 8 n. 19
Korting, Georg, 88 n. 32
Köstenberger, Andreas J., 235 n. 13, 252 n. 53
Kourie, Celia E. T., 50 n. 12
Kreitzer, Larry Joseph, 173 n. 29, 211 n. 12
Kuhli, Horst, 66 n. 31, 136 n.7

Lang, Friedrich Gustav, 39 n. 24
Lee, Aquila H. I., 87 n. 25
Lee, Michelle V., 16 n. 4
Lemmer, H. Richard, 19 n. 10, 146 n. 34
Leyrer, D. P., 88 n. 31, 122 n. 43
Lieu, Judith M., 52 n. 18
Lincoln, Andrew T., 50 n. 12, 51 n. 14, 52 n. 20, 58 n. 9, 59 n. 11, 59 n. 12, 60 n. 13, 60 n. 15, 62 n. 20, 64 n. 24, 65 n. 26, 65 n. 27, 65 n. 28, 66 n. 33, 67 n. 34, 68 n. 37, 69 n. 39, 70 n. 40, 70 n. 41, 70 n. 42, 71 n. 45, 72 n. 47, 79 n. 7, 80 n. 9, 82 n. 16, 85 n. 22, 86 n. 24, 87 n. 26, 87 n. 27, 88 n. 33, 94 n. 2, 94 n. 3, 94 n. 4, 95 n. 5, 95 n. 6, 96 n. 7, 96 n. 9, 97 n. 10, 97 n. 11, 97 n. 12, 98 n. 13, 98 n. 14, 100 n. 16, 101 n. 20, 102 n. 21, 103 n. 22, 103 n. 23, 104 n. 27, 104 n. 28, 105 n. 29, 106 n. 34, 106 n. 35, 106 n. 36, 107 n. 37, 107 n. 39, 114 n. 14, 115 n. 19, 116 n. 24, 118 n. 29, 118 n. 32, 119 n. 35, 120 n. 38, 123 n. 45, 124 n. 50, 125 n. 51, 126 n. 55, 126 n. 56, 127 n. 57, 128 n. 60, 129 n. 62, 135 n. 4, 135 n. 6, 136 n. 10, 137 n. 11, 137 n. 12, 138 n. 13, 139 n. 15,

143 n. 26, 143 n. 27, 145 n. 32, 146 n. 34, 153 n. 9, 155 n. 12, 157 n. 15, 158 n. 17, 158 n. 18, 161 n. 23, 161 n. 25, 168 n. 11, 168 n. 12, 169 n. 14, 170 n. 18, 171 n. 19, 171 n. 20, 171 n. 22, 175 n. 33, 176 n. 34, 177 n. 37, 178 n. 39, 178 n. 40, 179 n. 42, 182 n. 51, 183 n. 53, 193 n. 11, 193 n. 14, 193 n. 15, 194 n. 19, 196 n. 23, 198 n. 33, 199 n. 36, 201 n. 41, 201 n. 42, 201 n. 43, 208 n. 4, 209 n. 7, 210 n. 9, 211 n. 11, 212 n. 13, 219 n. 3, 220 n. 3, 220 n. 6, 221 n. 9, 222 n. 10, 223 n. 13, 224 n. 15, 226 n. 18, 227 n. 21, 234 n. 12, 236 n. 15, 241 n. 25, 243 n. 31, 243 n. 32, 243 n. 33, 244 n. 35, 245 n. 36, 245 n. 37, 246 n. 40, 247 n. 43, 247 n. 44, 248 n. 45, 250 n. 48, 250 n. 49, 251 n. 51, 253 n. 54, 254 n. 58, 258 n. 65, 258 n. 66, 259 n. 68, 260 n. 69, 261 n. 71, 262 n. 73, 267 n. 85, 270 n. 3, 273 n. 12, 274 n. 16, 275 n. 19, 277 n. 25, 278 n. 26, 284 n. 5, 285 n. 8, 286 n. 9, 287 n. 11, 287 n. 13, 288 n. 15, 288 n. 17, 290 n. 22, 292 n. 28, 293 n. 30, 294 n. 32, 294 n. 33, 296 n. 37, 302 n. 3, 303 n. 4, 305 n. 8, 306 n. 9
Loader, W. R. G., 85 n. 22
Lona, Horacio E., 111 n. 6
Longenecker, Bruce W., 16 n. 4
Lortz, Stephen L., 140 n. 18
Lotz, John Paul, 86 n. 24
Louw, Johannes P., 19 n. 10
Luter, A. Boyd, 16 n. 4, 51 n. 14

MacDonald, Margaret Y., 9 n. 22, 48 n. 6, 256 n. 59
Mahoney, Robert, 63 n. 22
Malan, François S., 3 n. 6, 236 n. 17
Man, Ronald E., 16 n. 4
Marshall, I Howard, 242 n. 29
Mayer, Annemarie C., 88 n. 30
McKay, Kenneth L., 233 n. 9
McKelvey, R. J., 128 n. 61

Printed in the United States
83688LV00004B/109/A